X Window System™ Programming

Second Edition

Nabajyoti Barkakati

SAMS
PUBLISHING

201 West 103rd Street
Indianapolis, Indiana 46290

To my wife Leha, and daughters Ivy, Emily, and Ashley

Trademarks

Publisher
Richard K. Swadley

Associate Publisher
Jordan Gold

Acquisitions Manager
Stacy Hiquet

Managing Editor
Cindy Morrow

Acquisitions Editor
Gregory S. Croy

Development Editors
Phillip W. Paxton
Sunthar Visuvalingam

Software Development Specialist
Wayne Blankenbeckler

Production Editor
Nancy Albright

Editorial Coordinator
Bill Whitmer

Editorial Assistants
Carol Ackerman
Sharon Cox
Lynette Quinn

Technical Reviewer
Mike Patnode

Marketing Manager
Gregg Bushyeager

Cover Designer
Dan Armstrong

Book Designer
Michele Laseau

Director of Production and Manufacturing
Jeff Valler

Imprint Manager
Juli Cook

Manufacturing Coordinator
Paul Gilchrist

Production Analysts
Dennis Clay Hager
Mary Beth Wakefield

Graphics Image Specialists
Tim Montgomery
Dennis Sheehan
Susan VandeWalle

Production
Carol Bowers
Mona Brown
Ayrika Bryant
Mike Dietsch
Rob Falco
Angela P. Judy
Bob LaRoche
Stephanie J. McComb
Jamie Milazzo
Wendy Ott
Linda Quigley
Kim Scott
Scott Tullis
Dennis Q. Wesner

Indexer
Greg Eldred

Overview

Contents

Preface to Second Edition

A lot has happened in the four years since the first edition of *X Window System Programming* was published. X is now the standard windowing system for all UNIX workstations. Of the two graphical user interfaces—Motif and OPEN LOOK—Motif appears to have won the "battle of the desktop." X11R6 has just been released and X appears to be entrenched as the underlying graphical windowing system for workstations. Even though some new capabilities have been added to X, Xlib—the X Application Programming Interface (API)—has remained remarkably stable. The X Toolkit Intrinsics (Xt Intrinsics) and Motif toolkit have changed some; there are new recommended ways to initialize the toolkit, and tear-off menus and drag-and-drop capability have been added to Motif. With each release of X, conventions for interclient communications have become more well-defined.

The continued popularity of X and Motif is good news for UNIX, but UNIX programmers are now expected to write X and Motif applications. Because Motif provides only the user interface components, such as menus, pushbuttons, and dialogs, the programmer must also learn Xlib for displaying application-specific graphics or text in various windows.

X Window System Programming, Second Edition, builds on the successful first edition of the book and continues to serve as a tutorial and reference guide for programmers learning to use Xlib and the Motif toolkit. The second edition brings the coverage of Xlib, Xt Intrinsics, and Motif toolkit up to date. In addition to the tutorials and reference guides of the first edition, the second edition also features the following:

- ✦ Sample programs showing use of individual Motif widgets
- ✦ A description of Motif drag-and-drop programming with a complete example program
- ✦ A step-by-step summary of how to use the 3-D display capabilities of PEX in a Motif application
- ✦ An example program illustrating how to handle protocol messages from an ICCCM-compliant window manager
- ✦ Quick Reference Guides to the Motif Window Manager (mwm), Motif widgets, Xt Intrinsics, and X Events
- ✦ A diskette with source code for all example programs appearing in the book

Even if you have seen X and Motif in action, this book can give you the background that you need to understand how X works and see how X provides the foundation for the Motif graphical user interface. This book is not a complete reference manual to X and Motif. The idea behind the book is to get you familiar with the concepts underlying X, show you how to display text, graphics, and bitmap images using X, and get you started with some programming exercises using the Motif widget set. After going through the information presented in *X Window System Programming, Second Edition,* you will be well on your way to developing complete Motif applications.

Preface to First Edition

Not too long ago, using a computer meant standing in line to submit your batch job on a deck of punch cards and waiting for your results—a printout. Video display terminals, minicomputers, and interactive operating systems such as UNIX and VAX/VMS made things much easier by enabling us to run programs and fix errors without wasting time in the batch queue. Now we are at yet another turning point—the emergence of graphical user interfaces for PCs and their more powerful cousins, the graphics workstations. Rather than interacting with the computer through commands (which many feel are cryptic), you can accomplish most tasks by using a *mouse* to point and click on icons representing files. The Macintosh User Interface and Microsoft Windows are two interfaces that you may have already used.

Applications with graphical user interfaces display output by calling routines from an underlying *window system*, software that manages distinct (usually rectangular) screen regions called windows. The problem with existing interfaces such as the one in Macintosh or in Microsoft Windows is that the basic designs of the window systems are different. The same problem persisted in the graphical interfaces available in the early versions of many powerful workstations, such as the ones from Apollo and Sun. The windowing software, in the form of C-callable routines, were easy to use in programs; however, the routines and the functionality they provided varied from one system to another. This meant application developers had to learn a new window system for every new workstation they wanted to support.

The situation improved greatly in January 1987, when a dozen computer vendors announced a joint effort to support and standardize a windowing system named X. Since then, almost all workstation vendors have decided to accept the X Window System as the basis of the graphical user interface to their hardware. At the same time as X started gaining support, a new breed of affordable workstations based on 32-bit microprocessors (such as the Intel 80386, Motorola 68030, SPARC, and MIPS) became available. Most of these workstations run the UNIX operating system and use X as the windowing system. The net result is that the number of UNIX systems capable of using X is growing steadily.

As a result of this growth in the number of UNIX workstations and the widespread acceptance of X, many C programmers are now expected to implement user interfaces for new applications using the X Window System facilities. X is a powerful windowing system: its Xlib programming interface provides over 350 library routines for a variety of tasks, such as creating a window, tracking the mouse pointer, reading keystrokes, and producing graphics and text output. Additionally, the programmer has to understand how the X Window System works and how the *client-server* approach enables a program running on a system to display output in windows on a workstation across a network. The programmers need all the help they can get to understand and assimilate the X programming model so that they can make effective use of X library routines in their programs.

X Window System Programming is designed to answer the needs of C programmers beginning to use and program in X. This book serves as a tutorial and as a reference guide for programming in X. It provides in-depth tutorials that gently introduce you to the X Window System and show you how to build interactive applications using X. The book features the following:

+ Extensive tutorials on the basic concepts behind the X Window System, including the cilent-server model and the network transparency of X

+ A step-by-step introduction to the X Window System, with short, instructive examples

+ Complete coverage of the latest release of the X Window System, Version 11

+ Discussion of how to handle mouse and keyboard events in X

+ Chapters on drawing graphics, images, and text in X

+ Description of currently available graphical user interface (GUI) toolkits, such as OSF/Motif and OPEN LOOK

+ Coverage of the Xt Intrinsics and the OSF/Motif widget set—complete with examples

+ Reference entries on X Library routines, fonts, cursors, and colors

Although there are several competing graphical user interfaces (GUI) in the UNIX world, all are built upon the X Window System. Therefore, programming in any of the GUIs, be it OSF's Motif or Sun and AT&T's OPEN LOOK, involves learning the X Window System and requires using the facilities of Xlib. Because of Xlib's importance, *X Window System Programming* focuses primarily on Xlib programming. Short example programs illustrate how to use specific Xlib routines. Study the program listings to learn how to use a function in a program. Diagrams and screen snapshots explain concepts and illustrate screen output.

Of course, to build real-world applications, you will need the help of a higher-level toolkit to manage the details of Xlib programming. With this in mind, *X Window System Programming* devotes several chapters to introducing the Xt Intrinsics and shows how to write programs using the OSF/Motif toolkit, one of the leading commercially-available GUIs.

Although *X Window System Programming* is primarily a tutorial, it also includes features that make it a handy reference guide. The appendixes contain reference entries on the X library routines and other handy information, such as X fonts, cursors, and color names. The index helps you locate material quickly and Appendix I provides easy reference to the Xlib functions.

The details of programming the X Window System can overwhelm you at first. However, with a grasp of the fundamental design of X and with the help of a toolkit such as OSF/Motif, you will be pleasantly surprised by how easy it is to create a graphical user interface for your applications. I sincerely hope *X Window System Programming* will get you started on your way to harnessing the full capabilities of X.

Acknowledgments to First Edition

I am grateful to Jim Rounds for having faith in the idea of a tutorial-reference book on the X Window System and for getting me started on this project. Thanks to Linda Sanning for subsequently taking care of the project and seeing it through successful completion.

Thanks to Brigid Fuller and Mark Coleman, formerly of Santa Cruz Operations for providing the copies of SCO UNIX System V/386 Release 3.2 and SCO Xsight 2.0 that were used in developing all the examples in this book. Thanks also to Dave Wood and others at SCO Support who guided me through the initial stages of getting UNIX and X running on my 80386 VGA workstation.

Thanks to Mike Patnode, of SCO, for his technical review of the manuscript, and thanks to Barbara LoFranco and Allen Ginzburg, also of SCO, for furnishing me with copies of SCO Open Desktop Personal System and Open Desktop Development System for further testing of the examples.

Production of a book like this always involves many dedicated professionals doing their part behind the scenes. I would like to give my heartfelt thanks to each and every one involved in turning my raw manuscript into this well-edited, beautifully packaged book. Thanks to Kathy Grider-Carlyle for skilfully managing the copyediting and production, to Midge Stocker for the thorough copyediting, and to Joe Ramon for making sure that the screen snapshots came out just right.

Of course, there would be no reason for this book if it were not for the X Window System. For this, we have Robert W. Scheifler and Jim Gettys, the principal authors of X, to thank.

Finally, my greatest thanks go to my wife Leha for her patience and understanding and to my daughters, Ivy and Emily, for keeping track of my progress and counting the days to the deadline. I could not have finished this book without my family.

Acknowledgments to Second Edition

I am grateful to Greg Croy and Stacy Hiquet for getting me started on the second edition of *X Window System Programming*. I appreciate the guidance and support they gave me during this project.

I would like to thank Mike Patnode for graciously agreeing to review the manuscript for technical accuracy. Karl Nyberg of Grebyn Corporation deserves special thanks for helping me out by downloading X11R6, building everything on a Sun workstation, and providing me with the software on a tape—all ready to go.

Over the past four years, many readers have written to me, expressing their positive opinion of *X Window System Programming, First Edition* and occasionally pointing out errors in the book. I am grateful to all of you for your kind words and comments, which are helpful in correcting the errors that seem to creep into a book, no matter how hard we try.

Even after more than a dozen books to my credit, I am still amazed by the transformation of the raw manuscript into a book—it's nothing short of magic to me. For this magic, I have all the designers, illustrators, editors, and production staff at Sams to thank. In particular, thanks to Cindy Morrow for managing the editorial process, Nancy Albright for the thorough copy and production editing, and Wayne Blankenbeckler for taking care of the companion disk.

Finally, and as always, I am most thankful to my wife Leha and my daughters, Ivy, Emily, and Ashley, for their love and support during these seemingly endless book projects.

Introduction

What This Book Is About

X Window System Programming, Second Edition, is an intermediate level book about the X Window System and the Motif widgets. Its purpose is to get you started as an X user and show you how to write programs using Xlib (the C routines that give you access to X). This book assumes that you already know the C programming language. The goal is to get you, the C programmer, started on X programming so that you can make productive use of an X toolkit, such as OSF/Motif, in your programs. To this end, *X Window System Programming, Second Edition,* focuses on the basic concepts of X, using X applications and Xlib functions in programs. It also covers programming with the Xt Intrinsics and shows how to use the OSF/Motif widget set. Examples and screen snapshots are used extensively to show the result of using a function or a widget. The idea is to get you to say, "Oh, I see! That's what this function does." Once you know this, it is a simple matter to use that function or widget as and when you need it.

Although *X Window System Programming, Second Edition,* includes reference pages on the Xlib functions and Motif widgets, it is *not* a complete reference for Xlib or for the OSF/Motif widgets. This book's goal is to show you how to use these tools, not simply to duplicate the reference manuals that come with the X Window System.

What You Need

To make the best use of this book, you should have access to a graphics workstation with the X Window System or an X terminal connected to a host that runs X. That way, you can test the example programs as you progress through the book.

For those wishing to explore X on their own, a reasonable "workstation" would be the following:

- ✦ An Intel 80486-based PC with a Super VGA display adapter and monitor
- ✦ At least 8M of memory
- ✦ A 300M hard disk running a freely available UNIX system such as Linux

All examples in this book were tested on a Sun SPARCstation IPC running SunOS 4.1.3, X11R6, and Motif 1.2. The examples should compile and link on most UNIX systems without any change.

How to Use This Book

If you are a newcomer to X, you should read the book from front to back. The example programs appearing from Chapter 7 on build upon modules introduced earlier. For example, a program in Chapter 9 needs files that are presented in Chapters 7 and 8. If you read the chapters in order, you will understand the examples easily.

The first four parts of this book are tutorials with four chapters per part:

+ Part One is a user's guide to X.
+ Part Two teaches the basic of X programming.
+ Part Three describes drawing text and graphics in X.
+ Part Four introduces Xt Intrinsics programming and shows how to use the OSF/Motif widget set.

Part Five is a collection of appendixes with reference entries on the Xlib functions, X Events, Xt Intrinsics, and Motif widgets.

From this quick overview, you can decide whether you want to skip any of the parts. For example, if you are already using X, you can go straight to Part Two. On the other hand, if you know Xlib and want to start using a toolkit, you can skip Parts One through Three and start with Chapter 13. To help you decide how to best use the book, the following sections describe the chapters in greater detail.

Part One: Using the X Window System

This part of the book introduces you, the prospective X programmer, to the X Window System and provides an overview of its capabilities. It shows how to set up and use X on a workstation, how to run X applications, and how X applications differ from traditional terminal-based applications. The terminology used to describe the X Window System is presented. You are walked through a number of common X applications to give you a feel for the windowing system before you learn how to create similar applications. The final chapter in Part One describes Open Software Foundation's Motif and AT&T's OPEN LOOK—two graphical user interfaces built on top of X. Part One includes the following:

+ Chapter 1: Your Workstation and X
+ Chapter 2: Clients, Servers, and Window Managers
+ Chapter 3: Exploring X Applications
+ Chapter 4: Graphical User Interfaces and X

Part Two: Programming the X Window System

Part Two introduces you to programming the X Window System. Chapter 5 explains the structure and the parts of an X Window program, using the code for a simple application. The steps involved in compiling and linking an X application are explained, as are the benefits of using the make utility for these tasks. Chapter 6 follows up with a discussion of the programming model used by every X application. Chapters 7 and 8 elaborate on how to create windows and handle keypresses and mouse clicking. The chapters in Part Two include the following:

✦ Chapter 5: A Simple X Application

✦ Chapter 6: The Xlib Programming Model

✦ Chapter 7: Creating and Managing Windows

✦ Chapter 8: Handling Events

Part Three: Drawing in an X Window

In Part Three, you learn how to draw text and graphics in a window. This part describes the graphics context (GC), which is used by all X drawing commands. Chapter 11 explains how color is modeled in the X Window System. Chapter 12 covers drawing images and handling bitmaps. Example programs illustrate the techniques. Part Three includes the following chapters:

✦ Chapter 9: Drawing Graphics

✦ Chapter 10: Drawing Text

✦ Chapter 11: Using Color in X

✦ Chapter 12: Pixmaps, Bitmaps, and Images

Part Four: Developing X Applications

This part covers the topic of developing complete X applications. X toolkits are presented with an explanation of why they are a must for serious software developers. The X Toolkit Intrinsics (Xt Intrinsics) are described. You learn how Xt Intrinsics provides an object-oriented framework for building widgets. The OSF/Motif widget set is covered. Examples show how to develop complete applications by combining widgets with Xlib functions. Chapter 16 covers a number of advanced topics, such as cut-and-paste operations between X applications (interclient communication), drag-and-drop support in Motif, and drawing 3-D graphics using PEX. Part Four includes the following chapters:

✦ Chapter 13: X Toolkits

♦ Chapter 14: OSF/Motif Widgets

✦ Chapter 15: Toolkit-Based Applications

✦ Chapter 16: Advanced Topics in X

Part Five: Appendixes

Part Five contains twelve appendixes, which serve as a programmer's reference manual for X and Motif. They include reference entries for the Xlib and Xt functions, X events, Motif Window Manager (mwm), and the Motif widgets. Also included is information on other important topics, such as names of colors, fonts, and cursors.

Conventions Used in This Book

The following typographic conventions are used in this book:

✦ Code lines, commands, functions, statements, variables, and text you see on the screen appears in a `computer` typeface.

✦ Placeholders in syntax descriptions appear in an *`italic computer`* typeface. Replace the placeholder with the actual filename, parameter, or whatever element it represents.

✦ *Italics* highlight technical terms when they first appear in the text, and are sometimes used to emphasize important points.

How to Contact the Author

If you have any questions or suggestions, or if you want to report any errors, please feel free to contact me either by mail or through electronic mail. Here is how:

✦ Write to: LNB Software, Inc., 7 Welland Court, North Potomac, MD 20878-4847

✦ If you have access to Internet, send e-mail to me at the following address
`naba@access.digex.net`

✦ If you use CompuServe, specify the following as **SEND TO:** address:
`>INTERNET:naba@access.digex.net`

✦ From MCIMAIL, specify the following when sending mail:
EMS: INTERNET
MBX: `naba@access.digex.net`

Please do not phone, even if you happen to come across my telephone number. Instead, drop me a letter or send an e-mail message.

## Part One

Using the
X Window System

Chapter 1

Your Workstation and X

From Apple Macintoshes and 80x86 PCs at the low end to Sun, Hewlett-Packard, IBM, and DEC workstations at the high end, graphics workstations have changed the way people interact with computers. Built-in graphics capabilities have made graphical user interfaces such as the Macintosh User Interface and Microsoft Windows possible. With these interfaces, instead of entering commands from the keyboard, you can use the mouse pointing device to run programs and to edit, copy, and delete files. Additionally, graphical interfaces divide the physical display screen into regions (usually rectangular) called *windows,* where the output of different applications appears.

If you have used a graphical interface, you know the convenience it offers. On the other hand, if you have tried to develop an application for Microsoft Windows or for the Apple Macintosh, you know the difficulty of that task. Application developers know the difference between the two *window systems*—the underlying software that manages the graphics output to the screen. Each of the systems is inextricably tied to the hardware and to the operating system. This makes it difficult to develop applications that will work in both systems.

The difficulty of creating readily transferable applications also plagued high-end graphics workstations, many of which used to come with built-in proprietary windowing systems that are invariably different. Although each window system can be programmed by calling routines from a library, the capabilities of the libraries differ. Even when the same capability exists on all systems, the routine names usually differ. This situation has proven troublesome for those who want to write applications that work on many different workstations. The X Window System, or X, for short, evolved because of the need for a windowing system that can work on a variety of workstations.

To see how X gets around the problem, consider the two ways of supporting several dissimilar window systems. One solution is to put another layer of routines between your application and the existing window systems. For example, to create a new window, you might write a routine called `create_window`, that in turn would call `NewWindow` in the Macintosh or `CreateWindow` when compiled for Microsoft Windows. This solution is difficult to implement if two window systems differ in how they manage the windows. For example, although Microsoft Windows allows a parent-child relationship among windows, the Macintosh assumes no hierarchy among the windows. Because of that difference, you cannot use the full potential of either window system in an application that will run under both systems.

The more sensible solution is to design a new window system with a standard set of library routines and then implement that window system on all graphics workstations. Robert Scheifler, Jim Gettys, and their team members took this approach when they developed the X Window System at Massachusetts Institute of Technology (MIT). They assumed certain basic capabilities in the workstation: a bitmapped graphics display, a keyboard, and a mouse. They settled on a large number of primitive operations to create windows, draw in them, and handle input from the mouse and the keyboard. They added a C-callable library of routines, called Xlib, that enabled programmers to access the basic capabilities of the window system. They even made provisions in X to handle input and output operations from multiple applications.

NOTE:

Graphics displays have two distinct components:

✦ *Video monitor,* the terminal where the output appears

✦ *Video controller,* the circuitry that causes the output to appear by sending the appropriate signals to the monitor

In a bitmapped graphics display, the monitor displays an array of dots (known as *pixels*), and the appearance of each pixel corresponds to the contents of a memory location in the video controller. For a black-and-white display in which each pixel is either bright or dim, a single bit of memory can store the state of a pixel. The term *bitmapped* refers to this correspondence of each bit in memory to a pixel on the screen.

Raster graphics is another common name for bitmapped graphics because the graphics display appearing on the monitor is constructed from a large number of horizontal lines known as *raster lines.* Raster lines are generated in the monitor by an electron beam sweeping back and forth on a phosphor-coated screen. Because each dot of phosphor, corresponding to a pixel, glows in proportion to the intensity of the beam, each line of the image can be generated by controlling the intensity of the beam as it scans across the screen. By drawing the raster lines repeatedly, the illusion of a steady image is created.

To make a good idea even better, the designers of X also decided that the X Window System will perform various actions based on data (which are commands to X) received through a communication path between the application calling the library routines and the windowing software on the workstation. As a result of this decision, the X Window System is capable of displaying, at your workstation's screen, output from an application running on a remote computer that is connected to the workstation through a communication link such as Ethernet, AppleTalk, or even a serial RS-232C connection.

To implement this idea, X follows a well-defined protocol, called the *X protocol,* to interpret the data stream sent by the application. It uses a programming model known as the *client-server* model in which the windowing software running in the graphics workstation is the *server* performing tasks requested by *client* applications. The X protocol, the display server, and the Xlib library routines are collectively referred to as the *X Window System.*

If this summary description of X is too terse for you, don't despair—there is much more to come. This book is designed to help you become familiar with X, see how typical X applications work, and learn how to write your own X applications using the C routines in Xlib and other libraries such as Xt and Motif. This chapter introduces you, the prospective X programmer, to the X Window System and gives an overview of its capabilities and benefits. Chapter 2, "Clients, Servers, and Window Managers," shows how to set up and use X on a workstation and how to run X applications; it also explains the terminology used to describe the X Window System. Chapter 3, "Exploring X Applications," walks you through a number of common X applications to give you a feel for the windowing system and prepare you to learn how to create similar applications. The final chapter in Part One, Chapter 4, "Graphical User Interfaces and X," describes Motif and OPEN LOOK— two graphical user interfaces built on top of Xlib, the C-callable library of routines that represent the basic capabilites of X.

What Is X?

X is a combination of several things: the X protocol, X display server, X clients, and Xlib routines. X clients are applications that use the workstation's display. Let's start by taking a look at the overall picture.

In a typical scenario, your workstation is connected to several other workstations and minicomputers through a *local area network (LAN).* With X running at your workstation, you can interact with several processes, each displaying in its own window on the screen (see Figure 1.1). Some of the processes may run locally at the workstation—provided your workstation's operating system is capable of handling multiple processes—and some may be executing at another system. For example, in Figure 1.1, window 1 is where you are interacting with your workstation. This window appears as a terminal to the workstation. Window 2 shows the output of an X application that also is running in the workstation. Window 3 is another terminal window where you may be interacting with computer A, and the output of another X application executing on computer B appears in the fourth window.

Figure 1.1.
A workstation with the X Window System.

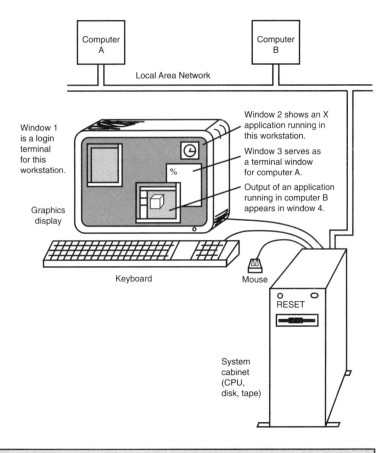

Window 1 is a login terminal for this workstation.

Graphics display

Window 2 shows an X application running in this workstation.

Window 3 serves as a terminal window for computer A.

Output of an application running in computer B appears in window 4.

Keyboard

Mouse

System cabinet (CPU, disk, tape)

NOTE:

In most operating systems, the word *process* refers to an executing program in memory and its associated environment. The environment usually includes the input and output files belonging to the program and a collection of variables known as *environment variables.* You create a process when you run a program. The command interpreter of the operating system (called the *shell* in UNIX) is also a process—one that creates processes at your command.

Clients and Servers

Behind the scene in the scenario shown in Figure 1.1 is the *X display server* (or *X Server* for short), running in your workstation, listening to the network connection at a specific port, and acting on commands sent by the *X clients* (applications that use the workstation's display).

This arrangement, shown in Figure 1.2, is known as the client-server model. The server provides a service that the clients request. Usually, the clients communicate with the server through a network, and server and client processes exchange data using a protocol understood by both processes. You may have seen the client-server model in action. For example, a *file server* stores files and enables clients to access and manipulate the files. Another common application, the *database server,* provides a centralized database from which clients can retrieve data by sending queries. Similarly, as illustrated in Figure 1.2, the *X display server* offers graphics display services to clients that send X protocol requests to the server.

Figure 1.2.
The client-server model.

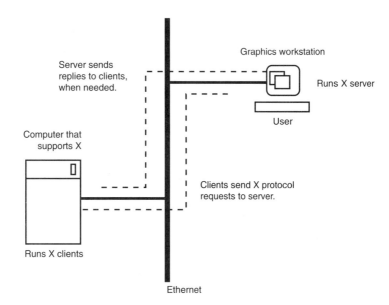

In contrast with file and database servers—which usually are processes executing in remote machines—the X display server is a process executing in your workstation with clients that may be running in remote computers.

The X Server

The functionality of the X Window System is in the X display server—the process executing in your workstation and managing the graphics output and the inputs from the keyboard and mouse. Figure 1.3 shows a basic view of an X display server. It shows modules that read X protocol requests from clients over a network connection and process requests from each client. If a request is for graphics output, a device-dependent graphics module takes care of generating the output on your workstation's display.

Hierarchy of Windows

Creating a window is one of the basic X protocol requests that the X server handles. An X application often appears to have a single output window; in reality, however, most X applications use many windows to construct the user interface.

Figure 1.3.

A simplified view of the X server.

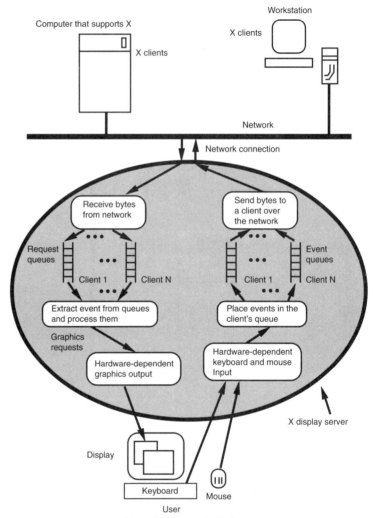

Consider the sample X application shown in Figure 1.4. This text editor has a text entry area and two scrollbars for examining text that may not be visible in the window. Even at this basic level, there are two windows on the screen: the *root window*, which occupies the whole display screen, and the *editor window*, which is inside the root window. On closer examination, the editor window turns out to be a frame that holds three other windows: the *document window* where the text appears and the two *scrollbar windows*. Further, as shown in Figure 1.5, each scrollbar window contains three smaller windows: the thumbwheel in the middle and two arrows at the ends.

Arrangement of windows in a parent-child hierarchy is the norm in X. Figure 1.4 shows the editor window as a child of the root. The editor window has three children: the document window and two scrollbar windows. Each scrollbar window, in turn, has three children: two arrow windows and a thumbwheel window. This results in a tree-like hierarchy of windows for the text editor (Figure 1.6).

Figure 1.4.

The text editor window and its components.

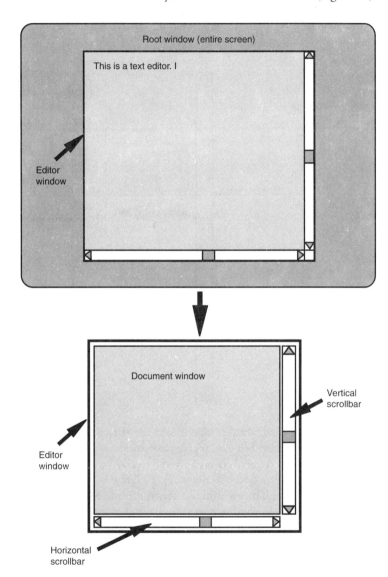

Event Delivery

The X server considers anything you do with the keyboard and the mouse as events to be reported to the clients. Typically, you move the mouse around the screen and a small graphics shape (the *mouse pointer*) follows the motion. When you are running X applications, everything on the screen appears in windows and each window is associated with a specific client. When you press and release a mouse button, the X server sends these *input events* to the client that created the window containing the mouse pointer. For *keyboard events*, the keypress always belongs to a designated window—one that has the *input focus*. (Methods of giving a window the input focus are covered in Chapter 8, "Handling Events.")

Figure 1.5.

Components of the scrollbar window.

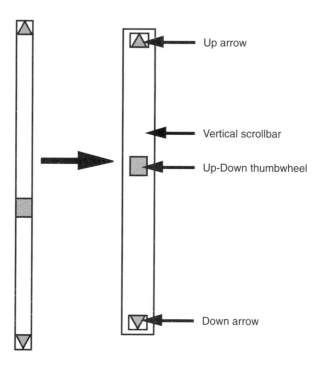

The X server also sends another kind of event to clients. These events inform a client if anything happens to its window. For example, because windows overlay each other, when they are moved around, previously obscured parts of a window may become visible again. In this case, the server will send an *Expose event* to the client application, which must take care of drawing into the exposed area of the window. As with the Macintosh and Microsoft Windows, the burden of maintaining appearance of a window rests with the application that owns it, not with the X server. This is one aspect of the X server that usually surprises newcomers; if your application's code does not handle Expose events, nothing will be drawn in the window.

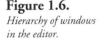

Figure 1.6.
Hierarchy of windows in the editor.

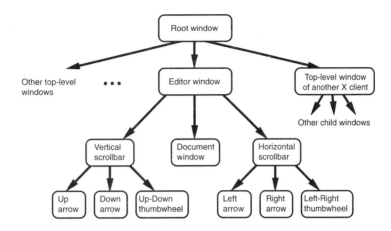

X Protocol: The Machine Language of X

Because X clients communicate with X servers using the X protocol, the X protocol defines exactly what can be achieved with the X Window System. A *protocol* is nothing more than an agreement between the server and the client about how they will exchange information and how that information will be interpreted. In the X protocol, data is exchanged in an asynchronous manner over a two-way communication path that enables transmission of a stream of eight-bit bytes. The X protocol also defines the meaning of the byte stream. By drawing an analogy with microprocessors, you might say that the X protocol is the *machine language* of the X Window System. Just as the logic circuitry in a microprocessor interprets the bit patterns in instruction bytes and performs some simple task, the X display server interprets the X protocol byte stream and generates graphics output. Thus, the X protocol completely defines the capabilities of the X Window System.

Xlib: The Assembly Language of X

You can write an application that uses the X display server by directly sending bytes conforming to the X protocol, but doing so is very tedious—like programming a microprocessor using only machine language. Moreover, you do not have to do it. The X Window System comes with a library of C routines commonly referred to as Xlib. Xlib gives you access to the X protocol through more than 300 utility routines. If the X protocol is the machine language of X, Xlib is its *assembly language*. Programming in assembly language is not easy, but it is much easier than using machine language.

X Toolkits: The High-Level Languages of X

Although the Xlib is very convenient, its capabilities are basic. For example, Xlib does not have a function that displays a menu with a selected list of entries. You can create a menu by calling a number of Xlib routines, but that takes some work. To solve this problem , you need another set of routines to implement objects such as *pushbuttons*, *lists*, and *menus* that can be used to build a graphical user interface. This idea has been pursued by several groups. The X Window System comes with the *X Toolkit Intrinsics* (also known as *Xt Intrinsics*) that uses an object-oriented approach to implement basic building blocks called *widgets*. Other toolkits, such as the Motif toolkit from the Open Software Foundation (OSF), use a higher level of abstraction. The Motif toolkit is built upon the X Toolkit Intrinsics. Continuing with the analogy of microprocessor programming, these are the high-level languages of the X Window System.

X Protocol, Xlib, or Toolkit?

You might wonder when, if ever, anyone uses the X protocol directly. The answer is this: you need to worry about the X protocol only when implementing an X display server or when writing a library of routines to be used in X applications as a programming interface to the X protocol. Of course, just as all C programs are ultimately translated to machine code, all calls to Xlib or X toolkit routines eventually are converted to X protocol requests.

If you are a novice X programmer, Xlib is a good place to start. It enables you to learn what X can do and how to perform basic tasks, such as opening a window, handling a keypress or buttonpress, and drawing text and graphics in a window. When developing complete applications, you will find it more productive to use a toolkit. The penalty for using a toolkit is that toolkit-based applications generally require more memory than those based on bare-bones Xlib. However, the use of shared libraries greatly reduces the memory needs of toolkit-based X applications.

Most meaningful X applications cannot be written using routines from a toolkit alone. Toolkit developers try to build a repertoire of widgets that are most likely to be used in a user interface, but they cannot anticipate the exact purpose of an application. For example, many of the application-dependent tasks involve drawing in a window. The same user interface may be used in a text editor and a drawing program, but each program behaves differently when you press a mouse button inside the display area of the application. The text editor may move a cursor, and the drawing program may draw a line in reponse to the buttonpress. To handle these tasks, the application has to call Xlib routines. Thus, knowledge of Xlib is essential for X application developers.

Figure 1.7 shows the general structure of an X application. The application primarily calls routines from a toolkit. The toolkit may call routines from the Xt Intrinsics, which, in turn, call Xlib. The application may also make direct calls to some Xlib routines for generating text and graphics output in a window.

Learning about Xlib is important for an X programmer. Therefore, this book focuses on teaching you how to write X applications using the Xlib. In later chapters, you revisit the features of X summarized in this chapter and learn more detail about working with Xlib.

Dependence on Operating System

The basic design of X does not depend on any operating system. All X needs is a reliable data path between the clients and the X server. So far, X implementations have used TCP/IP, DECNET, and STREAMS networking protocols for transferring data between the server and clients. However, the operating system sometimes becomes a factor because of its close ties to the networking software being used by a client application to transmit the X protocol requests to the display server.

For example, in Berkeley UNIX (also known as BSD UNIX) systems, X communicates using TCP/IP. In Digital Equipment Corporation's VAX/VMS machines, the X protocol bytes are sent using the DECNET networking protocol.

Figure 1.7.

The general structure of an X application.

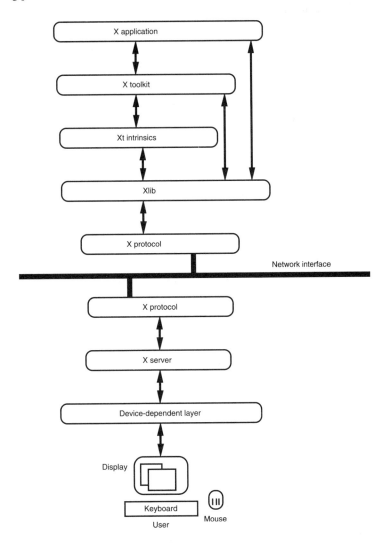

AT&T's implementation of X uses the STREAMS mechanism that is native to UNIX System V. Nevertheless, as long as there is a common networking protocol available for data transfer, the X server can display output from any client without regard to the operating system under which the client executes.

> **NOTE:**
>
> The X Window System does not depend on any specific operating system, but the operating system is important when describing how X is used and programmed. Because most of the graphics workstations that use X run the UNIX operating system, this book presents X from the perspective of a C programmer working in a UNIX environment.

Where X Fits In

X is intended to handle a user's interaction with a computer through a bitmapped graphics display. The basic mission of the X Window System is similar to that of a graphics terminal.

Graphics Output

Until workstations came along, graphics terminals were the only way to get graphics output from a computer program. For the sake of concreteness, consider how a terminal such as the Tektronix 4107 is used and programmed. Typically, this terminal is connected to a minicomputer through a serial RS-232 connection. Application programs that support the 4107 send a stream of bytes to the terminal, which interprets these bytes and produces graphics output. The programmer's guide for the 4107 describes its coordinate system, the basic graphics capabilities of the terminal, and the sequence of bytes that activates each capability. For example, an Escape character (ASCII code 33 octal) followed by a form feed (ASCII code 14 octal) clears the graphics display. Thus, in C, the following line of code does the job:

```
printf("\033\014");   /* Write 2 bytes to clear screen */
```

The X protocol is similar to the byte sequences necessary to program the 4107. Just as bytes sent from the application control the Tektronix 4107 terminal, the X protocol byte stream is used to control the X display server. In the same vein, Xlib is analogous to creating a library for displaying graphics on the 4107. Such a library may include routines such as `ClearGraphics`, for instance, that uses the `printf` function to send the appropriate bytes to clear the display screen.

The crucial difference between X and terminals such as the 4107 is that the Tektronix 4107 is sold as a terminal that works over a serial connection; the X protocol works over any eight-bit network connection. The X protocol also defines a more powerful set of capabilities than that available in the 4107—for example, a hierarchy of windows and conceptual models of hardware display devices to achieve device independence.

User Interaction

X is more than a graphics system. It is a windowing system capable of organizing graphics output in a hierarchy of windows on the screen. This and the capability of accepting inputs from keyboard and mouse make X ideal for handling user interaction.

Graphics terminals are fine for displaying static information such as plots and three-dimensional views of a solid object, but the biggest drawback of these terminals is their slow-speed connection (RS-232 at 9600 baud) to the computer. This limits their handling of rapid changes to the display, such as those necessary for a graphical user interface in which there should be immediate visual feedback when a window is moved or a mouse button is pressed.

Workstations solve this problem by integrating the CPU and display in a single unit with a high-speed data path between the two, but each workstation manufacturer uses a different approach to displaying graphics. X solves both of these problems:

✦ It works over any communication channel. The speed limitations of a serial connection can easily be overcome by using the much faster Ethernet as the channel—10 million bits per second, a thousand times faster than a 9600-baud connection.

✦ It defines a standard model for creating, manipulating, and displaying in windows. Thus, X is well-suited for implementing applications that need graphical user interfaces.

X Terminals: A New Breed of Terminals

The similarity between traditional graphics terminals and the X Window System has prompted the emergence of a new breed of terminals that are based on X. Think of these terminals as stripped-down versions of a workstation with a network connection and running the X server only. These *X terminals* are useful in facilities with minicomputers and mainframes that have to provide standard graphics capabilities to many users. X terminals are much cheaper than full-fledged graphics workstations. Because they do not have any operating system (the CPU in an X terminal runs only one program—the X server), they do not need the attention and care that go with installing and maintaining an operating system.

Demand for X terminals is growing steadily. In anticipation of increased sales, almost every computer and workstation vendor has introduced them. In some ways, X terminals are bringing back the era of computer timesharing—with the added twist of a single X terminal providing access to many computers. For X programmers, the popularity of X terminals is good news; there will be more demand for X applications and, consequently, more demand for programmers proficient in X.

Working with MS-DOS PCs and Macintoshes

Just as a stripped-down workstation can be configured as an X terminal, an MS-DOS PC or a Macintosh can also display output from an X application. Knowing the client-server model of X, you can guess that the main requirement is an X server at the PC or the Macintosh. Together with the server, you also need some form of networking software that will communicate with the machine where the X application is running. Several vendors have developed X servers for PCs and Macintoshes. On the Macintosh, the X server can run under Multifinder, enabling you to run Macintosh applications and X applications side by side. Similar capability exists on MS-DOS PCs, with the X server implemented under Microsoft Windows.

Benefits of X

If you have programmed a window system, you do not need to be convinced that a standard window system is a good idea. You know that with a standard such as X you do not have to learn a new window system for every new machine. With the widespread support X enjoys, once you learn X, you can write applications for a wide variety of workstations. There are several other benefits as well; these are described in the following sections.

Network Transparency

The capability of displaying graphics across the network makes X versatile as a windowing system. To an X client it makes no difference whether the X display server is local or across the network. This is why X is described as a *network transparent* windowing system.

Network transparency leads to what David Rosenthal, an expert on X, calls the *interoperability* of X clients and servers: *if written properly*, an X client can work with any X server. Interoperability is, by no means, guaranteed; the client application must be written properly. The existence of an X protocol request for a particular task does not guarantee that the server will perform the task successfully—it may fail and return an error. Treatment of color, for example, requires careful consideration because workstations have varying color capabilities. To be able to interoperate with any server, your X application must handle all contingencies.

Separation of Computing and Graphics

In the X Window System, there is a clear separation of graphics and computing—the output from an X application is handled by sending X protocol requests to an X server. The rest of the application can perform its computations on a system that best suits its needs. For example, a computation-intensive simulation model can use a Cray for its work and provide a visual representation of the results on a workstation or an X terminal.

Diverse Systems under X

A consequence of the client-server model used by X and its network transparency is that you can mix and match computers and workstations from many different vendors, as long as they support X and they can be networked. This is an important benefit for people who have to select computer hardware and software. Picking a specific system does not have to mean that all future software and hardware upgrades must come from the same vendor. If the hardware and software supports X, additions to the facility can be from any one of the many vendors that also support X. Such heterogeneous computing environments already exist in universities and laboratories, and the trend toward mix-and-match computing is beginning to appear in commercial environments as well.

Mechanism, Not Policy

"X provides mechanism, not policy." This quote from the architects of X states the underlying philosophy of X. The X protocol sets forth the basic tasks that an X server performs. There is no mention of menus, buttons, or labels in the X protocol. The application constructs its own user interface, using the primitive facilities of the X server. You can use X to build any type of user interface you want. For example, the popular Motif toolkit is capable of producing the *look and feel* of Microsoft Windows. It also is possible to develop an X application that mimics the layout and behavior of Macintosh applications.

Room for Future Extensions

The architects of the X Window System realized that they could not envision all the needs that an X server may have to fulfill. To allow for unforeseen tasks, they left room for *extensions* in the X protocol. Already, there is much work done in adding a three-dimensional graphics extension to the X server. This extension to the X protocol makes use of another standard, known as PHIGS, the Programmer's Hierarchical Interactive Graphics Standard, that supports three-dimensional graphics. The new extension to X is being called *PHIGS Extended X*, or *PEX*.

Versions of X

Development of the X Window System started in 1984 at MIT under the auspices of the MIT Laboratory for Computer Science and MIT/Project Athena. From the beginning, X had industry support because of DEC's and IBM's involvement in Project Athena. By early 1986, DEC introduced the first commercial implementation of X running on the VAXstation-II/GPX under the Ultrix operating system. This was X Version 10 Release 3 (X10R3). Soon X attracted the attention of other prominent workstation vendors, such as Hewlett-Packard, Apollo Computer, Sun Microsystems, and Tektronix. (Apollo has since merged with Hewlett-Packard.)

Feedback received from the users of X10 urged project members to start a major redesign of the X protocol. While the design of what would become X Version 11 (X11) was proceeding, X10R4 was released in December of 1986. This was the last release of X Version 10.

In January 1987, during the first X technical conference, eleven major computer vendors announced a joint effort to support and standardize on X11. The first release of X11, X11R1, became available in September of 1987. To ensure continued evolution of X under the control of an open organization, the MIT X Consortium was formed in January 1988. Under the leadership of Robert W. Scheifler, one of the principal architects of X, the consortium has been a major reason for the success of X.

In March 1988, Release 2 of X11, X11R2, became available. X11 Release 3, X11R3, appeared in late October 1988. In January 1990, the MIT X Consortium released X11R4 and followed it with X11R5 in August 1991. As X takes root in the workstation world, the X Consortium continues to improve X in several areas, including support for X programming using the C++ programming language and the addition of an object-based toolkit named Fresco, which was part of X11R6, released in April 1994. Throughout these releases, the X11 protocol has remained unchanged. The enhancements have been through the X11 protocol's capability of supporting extensions. When this book was being written, the most prevalent version of X was X11R5, but X11R6 was already available and this book covers all salient features of X11R6.

> **NOTE:**
>
> This book is based on X11R6.

Other Window Systems

Although X is the most popular window system, another contender, Sun Microsystem's Network Extensible Window System (NeWS), has been vying for its share of this market. As with X, NeWS also uses the client-server model. The protocol between a client and the server is based on the PostScript page description language. PostScript was designed to lay out a page to be printed and therefore does not include any facilities to handle inputs. Sun Microsystems designed the NeWS protocol by adding input handling capabilities to PostScript. Thus, the NeWS server is a PostScript interpreter with the added capability of handling inputs.

You program the NeWS server by sending it PostScript commands. You can extend the capabilities of PostScript by defining procedures. This is why the *e* in NeWS stands for *extensible*. A NeWS application can extend the capabilities of the NeWS server on the fly by downloading a procedure designed to perform a complex task. For example, an application might define a procedure DrawXYGrid to draw a grid on the screen by drawing a number of horizontal and vertical lines that intersect. Once the definition is done, the application can generate the grid by sending the string DrawXYGrid to the NeWS server. This feature of NeWS is very powerful, and X currently provides no equivalent.

NeWS has another advantage over X. In X, coordinates are specified in terms of pixels, which makes X dependent on the resolution (pixels per inch) of the display screen. NeWS, on the other hand, works in physical units such as points and inches. Because of these advantages, many argue that NeWS is technically superior to X. However, X has a much greater following in the market place, with almost all workstation vendors supporting it. The demand for X is so great that even Sun Microsystems, the company that started NeWS, supports both X and NeWS in its workstations.

Summary

X Window System is a network-transparent windowing system based on the client-server model. The X server process, running on a workstation with a bitmapped graphics display, manages regions of the screen known as windows, where the output from X client applications appears. The X clients, whether running locally or on a remote computer, send requests to the server using a communication channel. The bytes exchanged between a client and the server conform to the X protocol. X version 11, X11, consists of the X server, X protocol, and Xlib—the library of C routines that programmers use to access the server. The designers of X sought to provide only the primitive building capabilities necessary to support user interaction. They have refrained from dictating how a user interface should look and feel. Thus, X can be used to build a variety of user interfaces.

By offering a standard window system, X enables clients and servers to interoperate; an X client on a system can display its output on any X server without regard to the display hardware or the operating system. A workstation can become an integral part of an environment as long as it supports X and can be networked with the rest of the systems. X servers are available even for MS-DOS PCs and Macintoshes.

The concept of X is very much like that of a graphics terminal except for the network connection and the better input and output capabilities of X. This similarity is exploited in a new type of terminal—the X terminal—which is a stripped-down workstation running an X server and having a network connection.

Application developers do not work directly with the X protocol. They use the Xlib routines or one of the many X toolkits that provide higher-level objects—widgets—for building a user interface. Even when you are using a toolkit, basic drawing operations usually require you to use Xlib routines. The goal of this book is to introduce you to X and teach you programming with Xlib, because learning Xlib is a basic necessity of X programmers.

Further Reading

Because of the popularity of the X Window System, there are many books and other sources of information on X. The following short list may help you find additional resources if you want more information.

You need a copy of *X Window System*, by Scheifler, Gettys, and Newman for the same reason C programmers need Kernighan and Ritchie—to get the official word on X from the architects of X. It is also a good reference guide for Xlib and the X protocol.

The article by Scheifler and Gettys, "The X Window System," gives a good overview of the basic design philosophy of X. This article, the first to describe X in a journal, is based on version 10 of X, but much of the overview applies to X11.

Oliver Jones' book provides a good introduction to Xlib programming. It has many tips and techniques that you may not find in the standard manuals on X.

Of all X books, the ones from O'Reilly & Associates were the first to appear and are the most widely used by programmers. Many workstation vendors have used these books as their manuals for X.

On the subject of programming with X toolkits, the books by Young were the first available resources. His first book, *X Window Systems Programming and Applications with Xt*, covers the X toolkit intrinsics, and the second one, *Introduction to the X Window System: Programming and Applications with Xt, OSF/Motif Edition*, is based on Motif, which is the most widely used commercial X toolkit.

Magazine articles remain another source of information on X, especially on issues that are important to X programmers. Magazines such as *UNIX Review* and *UNIX World's Open Computing* are good sources of such articles. David Rosenthal's article on interoperability of X clients and servers is a good example of one that covers a topic relevant to X programmers. Another notable article is the one by Ed Lee; it gives a good overview of X.

To keep up with recent developments on how others are using X and how work on any new version of X is progressing, you should consult journals such as *The X Journal*, published by SIGS

Publications, New York, NY. Additionally, O'Reilly & Associates publishes a journal, *The X Resource*, four times a year. This journal provides in-depth articles on X programming, and the January issue serves as the official publication of the X Consortium's X Technical Conference.

There is a book on NeWS, but for an interesting comparison of NeWS and X, read Samuel Leffler's article.

Jones, Oliver. *Introduction to the X Window System.* Englewood Cliffs, NJ: Prentice Hall, 1989.

Lee, Ed. "Window of Opportunity." *UNIX Review* 6 (June 1988): 47-61.

Leffler, Samuel J. "A Window On The Future?" *UNIX Review* 6 (June 1988): 62-9.

O'Reilly & Associates. *Volume 0: X Protocol Reference Manual.* Sebastopol, CA: O'Reilly & Associates, 1992.

———. *Volume 1: Xlib Programming Manual.* Sebastopol, CA: O'Reilly & Associates, 1992.

———. *Volume 2: Xlib Reference Manual.* Sebastopol, CA: O'Reilly & Associates, 1992.

———. *Volume 3: X Window System User's Guide OSF/Motif Edition.* Sebastopol, CA: O'Reilly & Associates, 1993.

———. *Volume 8: X Window System Administrator's Guide.* Sebastopol, CA: O'Reilly & Associates, 1992.

Rosenthal, David S. "Window Exchange." *UNIX Review* 7 (December 1989): 59-64.

Scheifler, Robert W., and James Gettys. "The X Window System." *ACM Transactions on Graphics* 5 (April 1986): 79-109.

Scheifler, Robert W., James Gettys, and Ron Newman. *X Window System.* Burlington, MA: Digital Press, 1992.

Young, Douglas A. *X Window Systems Programming and Applications with Xt.* Englewood Cliffs, NJ: Prentice Hall, 1989.

———. *Introduction to the X Window System: Programming and Applications with Xt, OSF/Motif Edition.* Englewood Cliffs, NJ: Prentice Hall, 1990.

## Chapter 2

Clients, Servers, and Window Managers

Chapter 1, "Your Workstation and X," gave you an overview of the X Window System. Now you have an opportunity to get acquainted with X as a user. Suppose that you have been given a UNIX workstation with X and your assignment is to become familiar with X so that you can implement an X-based user interface for an existing application. To do this, you first want to find out how to run X on your workstation (assuming it is already installed). You also want to see how typical X applications behave. This chapter and Chapter 3, "Exploring X Applications," help you meet these objectives. The first section of this chapter shows you how to install and run X.

Installing X

Depending on your situation, you may or may not have to install X. Several scenarios are possible. Let's consider them one by one.

Because you plan to write programs that need the X Window System, you need the standard UNIX development tools, regardless of your hardware setup:

- ◆ Editor
- ◆ C compiler
- ◆ Linker
- ◆ Libraries, including Xlib and any toolkits such as Xt and Motif that you plan to use

You cannot get by with an X terminal or a Macintosh or an MS-DOS PC that runs only an X server. You need a workstation with UNIX and X, or an X terminal connected to a host computer that has the X development tools.

X on a Workstation

With a full-fledged UNIX workstation, you can have a stand-alone X application development environment. Many workstation vendors include the X Window System with UNIX. With those workstations, the process of installing UNIX also installs X.

The options are different for the lower-priced Intel 80386-based UNIX systems (often referred to as 386 UNIX systems). Typically, the 386 UNIX vendors sell everything piecemeal. UNIX itself may come as a run-time system good only for running applications. To develop applications, you need a *development system.* X may come in two varieties as well: a run-time version and the development system. If you plan to develop X applications, you need the development systems for both UNIX and X.

If you have the necessary software from your 386 UNIX vendor, installation is straightforward (as long as you make sure that your video adapter and mouse work with the vendor's UNIX and X software). An 80486-based PC running UNIX is an affordable choice for small companies and individuals. This is particularly true because of the availability of high-quality freely available UNIX and X development environments such as Linux.

X Terminal and a Host Computer

If you do not have an X workstation, you can manage with an X terminal (or a Macintosh or a PC with the X server software). If you have only an X terminal, you need a host computer with Xlib and the X toolkits that you need to build applications. For situations in which a large minicomputer or mainframe computer is available, this is a good way to develop X applications.

To work effectively with X terminals and a host computer, get the X libraries and toolkits on the central computer, then connect it to as many X terminals as you need and do all programming on the central machine, accessing it through the X terminals. If you are in this situation, you probably do not need to worry about installing X because it is the system manager's job to install Xlib and toolkits on the central system.

Starting X

From the overview of X in Chapter 1, you know that your workstation must be running an X server before you can display output from X applications. Starting X involves running the X server, followed by the X applications you want. If you also want to run applications on remote machines, additional steps are required for logging into the remote system, starting the application, and making sure the application knows where to send the output. The exact steps for doing this differ from one workstation vendor to another. Workstations that also have their own windowing systems may require you to start the X server manually, then follow with the applications. Before you do any of this, you have to learn how to name displays in X.

Naming X Displays and Screens

The X Window System considers a display to consist of one or more screens, a keyboard, and a mouse. There may be several displays in a system and each display may, in turn, have more than one physical screen. Each display has exactly one server process controlling all its input and output. Therefore, the terms *display* and *server* are used synonymously in X.

When an X client runs, it must open a connection to a display. To make this happen, you have to identify the display by a name and cause the output to appear in a specific screen; you can choose to specify the screen as well. Because the display can be anywhere in the network, you have to provide the network name of the system to which the display is connected in order to identify a display. Moreover, because there can be more than one display in a system, you also must give the display number.

In X, the displays in a system are numbered starting with 0 and the name of a display is constructed by appending the display number to the system name, with a colon (:) as the separator. Thus, as shown in Figure 2.1, the first display in the system `lnbsys` is named `lnbsys:0`, the second one, `lnbsys:1`.

Figure 2.1.

Naming X displays and screens.

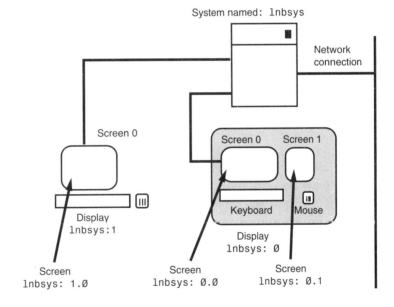

In X, the screens within a display also are numbered starting with 0. A screen is specified by appending the screen number to a display's name, with a period (.) as the separator. The first screen in Figure 2.1, display `lnbsys:0`, is `lnbsys:0.0`. Because display 0 has two screens, refer to the second one as `lnbsys:0.1`. When the screen is not specified, the server assumes that you want screen 0, the default screen.

> **NOTE:**
>
> In UNIX System V, use the command `uname -n` to find the network name of your system. In BSD UNIX (Berkeley UNIX), the equivalent command is `hostname`.

Environment Variables

In UNIX, the environment of a process consists of an array of strings, each string defining an environment variable of the form `VARIABLE=value`. The value of an environment variable is also a string. An environment variable is nothing more than a way to attach a standard name to an arbitrary string.

Environment variables provide a convenient way to pass information to processes. For example, when you type the name of a program to be executed, the UNIX shell searches the list of directories given by the `PATH` environment variable, which is always set to a string containing a list of directory names separated by colons (:). You can examine the current setting of `PATH` with the shell command `echo $PATH`. A typical setting might appear as follows:

```
/bin:/usr/bin:/etc:/usr/bin/X11:
```

With this `PATH` setting, when you enter the name of a program, the shell searches the directories `/bin`, `/usr/bin`, `/etc`, `/usr/bin/X11`, and the current directory, in that order. When using X, be sure the `PATH` environment variable includes the directory that contains most X utility programs, usually `/usr/bin/X11`.

Environment variables are used not only by the shell, but also by many application programs, including X applications, that use the `DISPLAY` environment variable to determine which server receives the output of a client. Accordingly, on the machine where you start an X client, you have to set `DISPLAY` to the name of the server where you want that client's output to appear. If you are going to run X applications locally on your workstation, you have to set the `DISPLAY` variable on that system also. For example, if the system's name is `lnbsys`, to get the output on the first screen of the first display, set `DISPLAY` to `lnbsys:0.0`.

> **NOTE:**
>
> In the Bourne shell, use the command `DISPLAY=sysname:0.0; export DISPLAY` to set up the `DISPLAY` variable for output on a workstation named sysname. In C shell, use `setenv DISPLAY sysname:0.0`.

Other important environment variables are: `HOME`, which specifies your login directory; `SHELL`, which indicates the UNIX shell you are using (`/bin/sh` for Bourne shell, `/bin/csh`, for C shell); and `TERM`, which names your terminal type. X also uses an environment variable called `XENVIRONMENT` to locate a file through which the user can specify parameters (such as colors, fonts, and window sizes) to be used by various applications (see Chapter 3).

> **NOTE:**
>
> Use the env command to see a list of your current environment variables.

X Server Startup with *xinit*

Now that you know how to name an X display and set the DISPLAY variable, you are ready to start the X server and run some X applications. After making sure that the PATH environment variable contains the /usr/bin/X11 directory, you can start the X server by typing this command:

```
xinit
```

This executes the xinit program that comes with the standard X software distribution. You can use xinit to start the X server and a client program. Once this client exits, the server also exits.

If you type xinit without any arguments at the shell prompt, it looks in the user's login directory for a shell script named .xinitrc. If there is no such script file, xinit starts the server and an application named xterm, which behaves like a terminal. By default, xinit assumes that the server is an executable file named X residing in one of the directories listed in the PATH variable.

> **NOTE:**
>
> A *shell script* is a file containing commands for the UNIX shell.

The shell script .xinitrc starts the applications you want to run under X. In the script, each program *except* the last one is started in the background. Because the X server exits when the script ends, this keeps X going until the last application. The trick is to make the last application something permanent. Window managers (to be discussed later in the chapter) fit the bill. For example, if you want to run the Motif Window Manager (mwm) and several other X applications, you should start mwm last because it tends to be very long-lived. In this case, the .xinitrc script might read as follows.

```
#  Clients started by xinit
#  Last client should not be in background

xlogo 2> /dev/null &
xbiff 2> /dev/null &
xterm -sb 2> /dev/null &

mwm 2> /dev/null
```

This starts xlogo, xbiff, xterm (with the -sb option enabling the scrollbar), and the Motif Window Manager (mwm), with all error messages discarded (because of the redirection to the null device).

In summary, this is how you start the X server and X applications:

1. Make sure PATH contains /usr/bin/X11 so that the shell can find the X server program. If your vendor provides the server in a file with a name different from X, make a copy of that file to /usr/bin/X11/X (or make a symbolic link).

2. Set DISPLAY to your workstation's screen and prepare an .xinitrc file.

3. Start X by typing xinit at the shell prompt.

After some rearrangement of the windows, the screen shown in Figure 2.2 was produced on a UNIX workstation with X. The digital clock shown in the lower-right corner of the screen is started by the first command shown in the xterm window. The other command in that window shows the xwd utility program being used to capture the screen to a file. (That file was later converted to PC PaintBrush format and used in this book.)

Figure 2.2.

A typical screen layout in an X workstation.

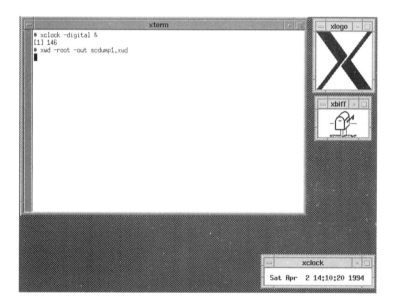

The *startx* Shell Script

Using xinit is better than starting the server and the applications manually; however, it still is rather complicated for newcomers to X. For this reason, most system administrators and vendors of workstations provide a shell script, appropriately named startx, to do everything necessary to get the server and other applications started. In its simplest form, the startx script typically starts off by setting the environment variables—the DISPLAY variable to identify the X server to X clients and PATH to include the directory where the X server program resides—and then uses xinit to get the X server and applications going.

Most sites, however, have many more requirements. For example, a site may have a mix of X workstations and X terminals. Workstations may run local X clients, but the X terminals will run only remote clients. The site administrator may want to have X terminal users log into a specific remote system automatically. Site administrators can meet these requirements by writing a site-specific `startx` script file. If your site uses `startx` to start an X session, consult its documentation or ask the system's staff for information on the site-specific features.

X Display Manager (*xdm*)

A third way to start and manage an X session involves `xdm`, the X display manager. The `xdm` utility is designed primarily for use with X terminals.

The functionality of `xdm` is similar to that provided by the processes `init`, `getty`, and `login` in UNIX for logging into an alphanumeric terminal. You log into the system by typing your name at the `login:` prompt and your password at the `Password:` prompt.

When first run, `xdm` reads in various configuration parameters from a file named `xdm-config`, which is usually in the directory `/usr/lib/X11/xdm`. One of the parameters is the name of a file specifying the displays on which `xdm` will manage login sessions. Usually, this list is in the file `/usr/lib/X11/xdm/Xservers`. The name of a display also indicates whether it is local or remote. Suppose you want to use `xdm` to access your workstation from the local display as well as through two remote X terminals (named `xremote1` and `xremote2`). In this case, the `Xservers` file may contain the following:

```
:0 local /usr/bin/X11/X :0
xremote1:0 foreign
xremote2:0 foreign
```

In X, the terms *server* and *display* are used interchangeably. Local displays are indicated by the `local` keyword following the display number (and the name of the X server executable must be given). For remote displays, the name followed by the keyword `foreign` suffices.

After reading the list of displays, `xdm` spawns a subprocess for each display. Each subprocess takes care of managing the login session, in the following order:

1. For a local X display, the subprocess starts the X server; for connections to a remote display (for example, when connecting to X terminals), it establishes the network connection.

2. Once connected to a display, the subprocess displays a dialog window containing fields for entering a name and a password.

3. When a user enters a name and password, `xdm` verifies them and executes a startup script `Xstartup` (usually in `/usr/lib/X11/xdm`).

4. The subprocess in charge of the session looks for a script file named `.xsession` in the user's home directory. This file is similar to the `.xinitrc` file used by `xinit`. It should list the commands for starting selected X clients. Typically, this includes `xterm`. If there is no `.xsession` file, `xdm`'s startup script `Xstartup` usually runs `xterm`.

5. From this point on, the user can interact with the system through the `xterm` window.

6. When the user logs off the system, `xdm` runs a clean-up script named `Xreset` (also in the `/usr/lib/X11/xdm` directory). At the end of this, `xdm` returns the dialog window display and waits for another user to log in.

This brief description of `xdm` shows that for a site with a central host computer connected to several X terminals, `xdm` is ideal for enabling users to log into the system from the X terminals. In this scenario, illustrated in Figure 2.3, each X terminal runs its own X server and `xdm` executes in the central host.

Figure 2.3.

Using `xdm` to manage login sessions on X terminals.

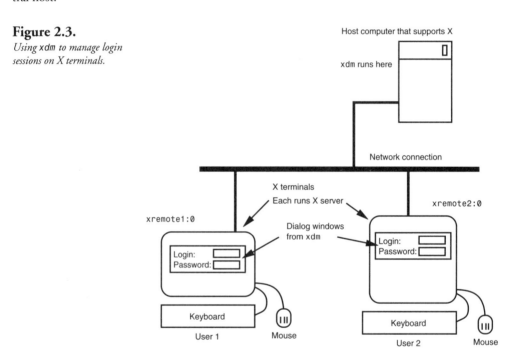

The `Xservers` file in the host lists the X terminals being managed by `xdm`. Assuming that the two X terminals are named `xremote1` and `xremote2`, the `Xservers` file should contain the following:

```
xremote1:0 foreign
xremote2:0 foreign
```

More recently, the use of the `Xservers` file has been superseded by the advent of the X Display Manager Control Protocol (XDMCP), which is meant for requesting login service over the network. Now, X terminals use XDMCP to request login service from an `xdm` process running on a remote host.

Like most X utilities, xdm is highly configurable. The names of the script files listed above are typical ones, but you can specify other names through the file named xdm-config, which, by default, also resides in the directory /usr/lib/X11/xdm.

Running Remote X Clients

You have learned how to start the X server and local clients by using xinit or the startx script file. How do you run remote X clients and have their output appear at your workstation's screen? To run a remote X client, you must follow this basic process:

1. Log into the remote system.
2. Set the DISPLAY environment variable on that system.
3. Execute the client application.

For an X terminal displaying the login window from a remote xdm process, enter your name and password to get to the remote host. Otherwise, you have to log into the remote system from an xterm window on your workstation.

Logging Into Remote Systems from *xterm*

To access a remote system from xterm, a network connection must exist between your workstation and that system. If there is a TCP/IP connection, you can log into the remote system with the rlogin *rname* command, where *rname* is the name of the remote system. If you have an account on that system with the user name under which you have logged into the workstation, you may get the shell prompt from the remote system immediately. Otherwise, you are prompted for user name and password. Once you are on the remote system, you can set the DISPLAY variable to your workstation and run the X clients of your choice.

Controlling Access to Your Workstation

When running a remote X client, a typical problem is that your workstation may refuse connection to the client; the remote client fails with an error message. If this happens, examine the contents of the file /etc/X0.hosts (assuming that your workstation has only one display). This file is used as an *access list* for display 0 and should contain the names of remote systems that are allowed to establish connection with your workstation's X server. If you want clients running in two remote systems named remote1 and remote2 to display on your workstation, your workstation's /etc /X0.hosts file should contain the following:

```
# List of authorized foreign hosts
#
remote1
remote2
```

Alternatively, while logged into your workstation you can give the command xhost +remote1 to add this system to the access list of your display.

Understanding Window Managers

A *window manager* is a special X client that takes care of interactions among windows from various clients on the display's screen. To see why a window manager is necessary, consider the case of two clients, A and B, displaying on the same screen. Neither client has any idea of the other's needs. Suppose you run client B after A, and B takes over the entire screen (the root window) as its output window. At this point, A's window is obscured underneath B's and there is no way for you to reach A's window.

A window manager can provide a means to switch from B to A, even when B is ill-behaved. For example, the Motif Window Manager, mwm, adds a decorative frame to the top-level window of each application. This frame enables you to move and resize the windows. You can shrink B's window by pressing the mouse button while the pointer is in one of the corners of the frame and moving the mouse while the button is pressed. The Motif Window Manager shows an outline of the window that changes size with movement of the mouse. This enables you to make the top window smaller to expose other windows underneath. Additionally, with mwm you can get a pull-down menu by clicking at the upper-left corner of the frame (see Figure 2.4). This menu can be configured to have options that enable you to move and resize windows.

You need a window manager in order to control the placement and size of each client's window. If no window manager is running, there is no way to change a window's location or alter its size.

Figure 2.4.

Frame and menu added to a client's window by the Motif Window Manager.

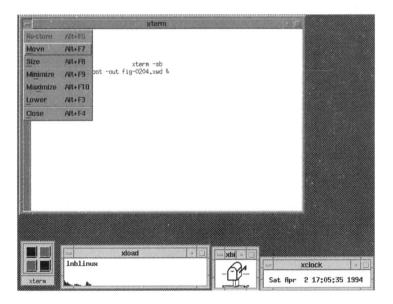

NOTE:

OSF/Motif, or Motif for short, is the common user interface style selected by the Open Software Foundation (OSF). The OSF was formed in 1988 by a group of major hardware vendors that includes IBM, DEC, and Hewlett-Packard. OSF/Motif is a combination of several things: an X toolkit for developing applications, the Motif Window Manager (mwm), and a style guide for developers. The Motif Window Manager has a three-dimensional look and was derived from work done by Hewlett-Packard and Microsoft. The look and feel of Motif comes from Microsoft's Presentation Manager, which, in turn, is derived from Microsoft Windows. This heritage of OSF/Motif has eased its acceptance among the large number of PC users who are familiar with Microsoft Windows and Presentation Manager.

Window Layout Management

As the name implies, a window manager manages the layout and appearance of windows on the display's screen. Despite their task of overseeing clients, window managers are also ordinary X clients. The Xlib library includes routines that enable any client to find out information about other windows and to intercept certain events that indicate when a window is about to be drawn and when it moves or changes size. Window managers are X clients that make use of these special Xlib routines.

The manner in which a window manager handles placement and sizing of windows differs from one window manager to another. Usually, the window manager adds a title bar to the window when the window first appears on the screen. Simpler window managers may pop up a menu when you press a particular mouse button in the title bar. Advanced managers such as mwm also add a frame to the main window of each client, enabling you to resize a client's window by pressing the mouse button while the pointer is in the border and dragging it in the desired direction.

Window managers provide two types of layout for the main windows of client applications (see Figure 2.5). Most window managers allow windows to overlap and provide some mechanisms to bring obscured windows to view. A few rearrange and resize the windows to ensure that no windows overlap on the screen. The overlapped layout is the most general one, and the preferred style for small screens. The tiled layout is a special case of the overlapped style. The Motif Window Manager allows overlapped windows.

Figure 2.5.

Overlapped versus tiled layout of windows.

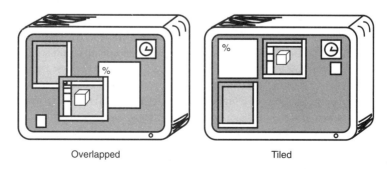

Overlapped   Tiled

Focus Window

A window manager usually controls another important aspect of an X application—which window has the input focus. This refers to the window that receives the keyboard events. Mouse input is easy to control; the window that gets the mouse events is the window with *mouse pointer* in it. The keyboard, however, has no on-screen pointer to indicate which window should receive the actions generated by keypresses. X Window System solves this problem by specifying that all keystrokes go to the window with keyboard focus. The window manager helps determine which window gets the focus. There are two ways a window manager can do this:

◆ Some window managers give the focus to the window with the mouse pointer in it.

◆ Other window managers, including mwm, use the concept of a *listener window*—the window with the focus. The user selects the listener window by moving the pointer into it and clicking the mouse button. Once selected, that window remains the focus window no matter where the mouse pointer moves.

In one case, the window with the mouse pointer gets the keyboard events. In the other, you have to move the pointer into a window and click to indicate that all subsequent keyboard events should go to that window.

Users familiar with Microsoft Windows or Macintosh applications tend to prefer the similar convention adopted by mwm. You can, however, configure mwm to enable the keyboard focus to follow the mouse pointer.

Look and Feel

In the process of controlling the layout of windows and deciding how windows get the focus, a window manager ends up imparting certain common characteristics to the clients. Under a specific window manager, the way you move or resize a client's window becomes standard. Moreover, the frame and menus provided by the window manager also add to the appearance and behavior (the look and feel) of the clients. Nevertheless, the window manager alone cannot make all X applications behave identically. To achieve a common look and feel, the applications must follow a common style guide and use a standard toolkit. Chapter 4, "Graphical User Interfaces and X," discusses this issue further.

Interclient Communications

An important responsibility of a window manager is to act as an intermediary between clients. Interaction among clients is important so that many different X applications can coexist in a display screen and be used productively. Suppose, for example, that you are using two applications: a text editor to write programs and an on-line reference guide to browse through the Xlib functions. Both are useful stand-alone tools, but imagine how useful they can be if the two applications can exchange information. Suppose, in your program, you want to call the Xlib routine XDrawArc to draw an arc, but you cannot recall its exact syntax. You could go to the Xlib browser, find more information on XDrawArc, select the sample call shown there, switch to the editor, and paste the function call into your program—all with a few mouse buttonpresses.

To some extent, this type of interclient communication is possible among existing X clients. To ensure that this happens flawlessly in the future, David Rosenthal of Sun Microsystems has prepared the *Inter-Client Communications Conventions Manual* (ICCCM), which puts forth the conventions that clients and window managers should follow to interact properly with each other. (See Chapter 16, "Advanced Topics in X," for further discussion of interclient communications and the ICCCM.)

Using the Motif Window Manager

Window managers play an important role by enabling you to—at a bare minimum—move and resize windows. For a closer look at a full-fledged window manager, consider the Motif Window Manager.

Recall that the executable file for the Motif Window Manager is named mwm; it usually resides in /usr/bin/X11 with the other X clients. Typically, you start it from a shell script that is input to xinit or a site-specific X startup script named startx. For example, you can run mwm by making the following command the last line in the script:

```
mwm 2> /dev/null
```

Once started, mwm adds a frame to all on-screen client windows. It enables users to move windows, resize them, change a window to an icon, and change the input focus. It also adds a menu to each window that enables you to kill that application by closing the window. Additionally, mwm provides a menu for the root window. This root menu enables you to launch new applications.

The following discussion assumes the default settings of mwm. Like most X applications, mwm is highly configurable. Therefore, do not be surprised if you find that mwm in your system does not behave exactly as described here.

NOTE:

X provides for a mouse with up to five buttons (although in practice most workstations have mice with one, two, or three buttons). By default, the buttons on a three button mouse are numbered one through three from left to right, but this can be changed through configuration files. The mouse pointer indicates the current location as you move the mouse around. Note that you can interact with most X clients using the left mouse button (button one).

The terms *click* and *drag* are used to describe the user interactions with the mouse. To click, the user presses and releases a mouse button while the pointer is in a particular area of the screen. To drag, the user presses a mouse button and moves the mouse while keeping that button pressed.

Window Frame

Under mwm, users can perform a variety of window management functions via the components built into the window frame that mwm adds to a client's window. As shown in Figure 2.6, the OSF/Motif window frame includes the following distinct components:

◆ *Title area.* This area displays the title of the window and also enables you to move the window. Press the left mouse button while the pointer is in the title area. Keep the button pressed and move the mouse. You will see an outline that follows the mouse movements. Select the new location and release the mouse button to indicate the new position.

◆ *Minimize button.* The button to the right of the title area enables you to reduce the window to an icon, a small rectangle with the window's title in it. To activate this button, click the left button of the mouse while the pointer is in the button.

◆ *Maximize button.* The button next to the Minimize button is used to enlarge the window to the full screen (or to the largest size allowed by the application). Activate it by clicking it once.

◆ *Window menu button.* This button appears to the left of the title area. When you press the left button with the pointer in this area, mwm displays a menu that enables you to perform window resizing and placement functions (see Figure 2.4). The Close option in the menu can be used to kill a client.

◆ *Outer border.* By dragging at a corner, you can enlarge the window in that direction. Additionally, you can resize the window by dragging on any of the four straight line segments of the frame. The window manager changes the cursor when you are in the border and draws an outline of the window as feedback while you drag the mouse.

Figure 2.6.

Components of the window frame in OSF/Motif.

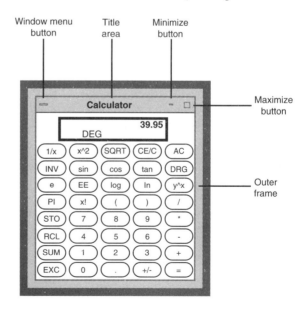

Root Menu

Under mwm, when you press the left mouse button (some configurations use the right button) anywhere in the root window, you will get a menu (often called the *root menu*). This menu is configurable by the user. Typically, it lists items that start an application when selected. The menu may also include choices for rearranging windows. You can configure the root menu so that a selected item pops up yet another menu pane with further selections. For example, in the root menu shown in Figure 2.7, pressing the mouse button with the pointer in the Clients item brings up a list of clients. To start any of these clients, move the pointer to the client's name and release the mouse button.

Figure 2.7.

*A typical root menu
in mwm.*

Customizing a Window Manager

All well-designed X clients, including window managers, enable users to customize the appearance and behavior of the application by specifying *resources* in a text file. Chapter 3 describes the standard resource naming conventions of X. Here, you focus on another form of customization that most window managers support.

The window manager reads a special configuration file at startup. (This is in addition to the standard resource description file that most X applications read.) In this file, the user specifies the contents of any menus displayed by the window manager. Each user also can indicate how keys and mouse buttons are tied to specific actions (known as *key bindings* and *button bindings*). This section describes how the Motif Window Manager is customized using such a configuration file.

> **NOTE:**
>
> In X, the meaning of the word *resource* depends on the context in which it is used. When describing X's client-server architecture and in Xlib routines, resources are data items, such as windows, fonts, colormaps, and bitmaps, that are created and maintained in the X server. These resources are accessed by clients through a resource ID (identification).
>
> In the user's manual for X clients, a resource is any feature of the application that can be specified by the user. This includes the size of a window, its placement, the foreground and background colors, the font used to display text, and so on. (For further discussion of resources, see Chapter 3.)

Configuration File

If you start mwm without any command-line options, it reads resource settings from a file named /usr/lib/X11/app-defaults/Mwm. In this file, a resource named configFile gives the name for the configuration file that specifies menus and bindings for mouse buttons and keys. If this resource is not found, mwm looks for a file named .mwmrc in the user's home directory. If there is no .mwmrc file in that directory, mwm uses the contents of the file /usr/lib/X11/system.mwmrc to configure its menus and bind the keys and mouse buttons to specific actions.

> **NOTE:**
>
> The HOME environment variable indicates your home or login directory.

Input Focus

You can control the style of input focus through a Motif Window Manager resource named keyboardFocusPolicy. For example, to get a Microsoft Windows-style behavior in which you explicitly indicate which window has the focus, place the following line in your .mwmrc file:

```
Mwm*keyboardFocusPolicy:      explicit
```

On the other hand, if you want the focus to follow the mouse pointer, set this resource as follows:

```
Mwm*keyboardFocusPolicy:      pointer
```

This is the format for specifying resources. Chapter 3 further explains this syntax. The mwm window manager has a large number of configurable resources, including background and foreground colors.

Defining Menus

The configuration file is a text file whose format is best understood by looking at a sample. Take the configuration file that generates the menu shown in Figure 2.7, for example. The lines in the .mwmrc file defining this menu are as follows:

```
#   This is a comment. Comments and blank lines are ignored.
#   Define the root menu for mwm

Menu RootMenu
{
    "Root Menu"                 f.title
    "Clients"           _C      f.menu  ClientsSubMenu
    "xterm"             _x      f.exec "xterm -sb  &"
    "Shuffle Up"        _U      f.circle_up
    "Shuffle Down"      _D      f.circle_down
    "Refresh"           _R      f.refresh
    no-label                    f.separator
    "Restart"                   f.restart
}
```

```
# Now the menu of clients...

Menu ClientsSubMenu
{
    "xclock"            f.exec "xclock &"
    "xload"             f.exec "xload &"
    "xcalc"             f.exec "xcalc &"
    "xbiff"             f.exec "xbiff &"
    "xmag"              f.exec "xmag &"
    "bitmap"            f.exec "bitmap $HOME/TEMP.bitmap &"
    "xeyes"             f.exec "xeyes &"
    "ico"               f.exec "ico &"
}
```

As you can see from this section of the configuration file, definition of each menu has the following form:

```
Menu <MenuName>
{
  <Label1>     [Mnemonic1]    [Accelerator1]   <function1>
  <Label2>     [Mnemonic2]    [Accelerator2]   <function2>
                    .
                    .
                    .
  <LabelN>     [MnemonicN]    [AcceleratorN]   <functionN>
}
```

where the fields enclosed in angle brackets (<>) are required, but those in square brackets ([]) are optional. Each line specifies an item in the menu. The label is normally a string without any double quotation marks. However, if the label has blank spaces embedded in it, you have to use double quotation marks around the string. You can even display a bitmap as a label by providing the filename with an at-sign (@) as its prefix.

The mnemonic field is optional. There, you can specify a single character (which must appear in the label) that will be a shortcut. Press the key to select that menu item. To specify the mnemonic, precede the character with an underscore. The mnemonics in the root menu example do not make sense because that menu does not stay popped (and the shortcut key does not work while the mouse button is pressed). The shortcuts in the window menu are more useful because, once you click on the button that pops the menu, it stays visible (see Figure 2.4). While visible, you can press the shortcut key to select that menu item. For example, you can reduce the window to an icon by typing n.

The optional accelerator specifies another way of accessing a menu item. The accelerator is the combination of a regular key pressed together with a special key (Alt or Meta key, or Ctrl, the Control key). Unlike the mnemonic key, it does not require you to make the menu visible. Thus, you can perform an action solely with the accelerator keystrokes.

> **NOTE:**
>
> *Meta key* is the generic name of a special key in X. On most keyboards, the key labeled Alt serves as the Meta key.

The last required field, the function, specifies what happens when you release the mouse button while the pointer is in that item. The definition that results in the menu of Figure 2.7 shows a large number of functions. The function names start with f (see Table 2.1). Because a large number of functions exist, you can customize almost everything in mwm. In the table, *selected window* means the window at the top of the stacking order, the one with which you are interacting.

Table 2.1. X Window Function Actions

Function Name	*Action*
f.beep	Causes a beeping sound.
f.circle_down	Moves the top window to the bottom of the stack of windows.
f.circle_up	Moves the window at the bottom to the top, thus making it visible (the opposite of f.circle_down).
f.exec	Executes a command using the shell (you can specify a shell by setting the SHELL environment variable; otherwise, /bin/sh is used by default). A single exclamation mark (!) can be substituted for f.exec.
f.focus_color	Installs the color map belonging to the current window.
f.focus_key	Changes the keyboard input focus to the current window.
f.kill	Kills the currently selected client.
f.lower	Sends the selected window to the bottom of the stack of windows being displayed on the screen.
f.maximize	Displays the window using the entire screen or the maximum size allowed by the client that owns the window.
f.menu	Pops up the menu specified by the argument. For example, f.menu ClientsSubMenu creates a pop-up window and displays the menu defined by ClientsSubMenu in it.
f.minimize	Reduces the selected window into an icon. The icon appears in the icon box, if there is one. Otherwise, the icon appears at the bottom of the screen.

Function Name	Action
f.move	Changes the cursor to a cross with arrows at each end and enables you to move the selected window interactively. You can place the window at the selected position by clicking the mouse button.
f.next_cmap	Installs the next colormap from the list of colormaps associated with the window with the current colormap focus.
f.next_key	Sets the keyboard input focus to the next window in the stacking order.
f.nop	Displays a menu item that acts like a label—you click on it but nothing happens.
f.normalize	Changes the size of the selected window to its default normal size.
f.normalize_and_raise	Changes the size of the selected window to its default normal size and raises it to the top of the stacking order.
f.pack_icons	Rearranges the icons in the icon box in a packed grid.
f.pass_keys	Works as a toggle to enable or disable the key bindings for the window manager. For example, suppose you assign Alt+4 to kill the window (press **4** while holding down the Alt key). If an application happens to need Alt+4, you can use f.pass_keys to disable its assigned binding.
f.post_wmenu	Posts the window menu, the menu that appears when you press the Window Menu button to the left of the title area in a window.
f.prev_cmap	Installs the previous colormap in the list of colormaps for the selected window. The opposite of f.next_cmap.
f.prev_key	Switches the input focus to the previous window in the stacking order. The opposite of f.next_key.
f.quit_mwm	Kills the OSF/Motif Window Manager mwm. This function does not always stop the X server. However, if you start the X server with xinit

continues

Table 2.1. continued

Function Name	Action
	using a script that has mwm as the last foreground process, the X server also exits.
f.raise	Brings the selected window to the top of the stack so that it is no longer obscured.
f.raise_lower	Raises the selected window to the top if it is obscured; otherwise, sends the window to the bottom of the stacking order.
f.refresh	Redraws all windows currently on the screen.
f.refresh_win	Redraws the selected window.
f.resize	Changes the cursor and waits for the user to resize the selected window.
f.restart	Stops and immediately restarts mwm.
f.send_msg	Sends a message (indicated by a message number) to a client. This works only with clients that follow certain rules (specifically, the message number has to appear in a property of type _MOTIF_WM_MESSAGES in the client's window).
f.separator	Draws a separator between menu items. The menu label is irrelevant for this function.
f.set_behavior	Restarts mwm with its default behavior.
f.title	Inserts the label as a title at this place in the menu.

Customizing a Menu

From what you have learned so far, you should be able to customize the Motif Window Manager's menus. If you have not already done so, make a local copy of the systemwide configuration file in your home directory with the following commands:

```
cd
cp /usr/lib/X11/system.mwmrc .mwmrc
chmod +w .mwmrc
```

Because system.mwmrc is usually read-only, its copy, .mwmrc, is the same. Because you plan to alter it, first use the chmod command to enable overwriting the file. Then use your favorite text editor and change the ClientsSubMenu to the following:

```
Menu ClientsSubMenu
```

```
{
        "CLIENTS"                               f.title
        "xclock"                                f.exec "xclock &"
        "xload"                                 f.exec "xload &"
        "xcalc"                                 f.exec "xcalc &"
        @/usr/include/X11/bitmaps/flagdown      f.exec "xbiff &"
        "xmag"                                  f.exec "xmag &"
        "bitmap"                    f.exec "bitmap $HOME/TEMP.bitmap &"
        "xeyes"                                 f.exec "xeyes &"
        "ico"                                   f.exec "ico &"
}
```

You are adding a title to this menu and replacing the old entry xbiff with the mailbox icon (whose bitmap is in the file named /usr/include/X11/bitmaps/flagdown). After saving the changes to .mwmrc, select Restart from the root menu of mwm (see Figure 2.7). This restarts the Motif Window Manager, forcing it to read the altered configuration file. Press the left mouse button with the pointer anywhere in the root window. When the root menu appears, select the Clients item. The resulting clients menu is shown in Figure 2.8. It has a title and the mailbox icon appears in place of xbiff.

Figure 2.8.
The new customized root menu in mwm.

Key Bindings and Button Bindings

Another aspect of a window manager that you can specify is what happens when certain keys or mouse buttons are pressed. This is referred to as *key bindings* and *button bindings*. The mwm manager enables you to specify these bindings, and you can do so in the configuration file where the menus are defined (either .mwmrc in your home directory or system.mwmrc in /usr/lib/X11).

Key Bindings

The syntax of defining key bindings is similar to that of the menu definition. For example, you specify the default key bindings by a table named DefaultKeyBindings. A typical definition of the default key bindings may look like the following:

```
! A short list of default key bindings

Keys DefaultKeyBindings
```

```
{
    Shift<Key>Escape            icon¦window         f.post_wmenu
    Meta<Key>space              icon¦window         f.post_wmenu
    Meta<Key>Tab                root¦icon¦window    f.next_key
    Meta Shift<Key>Tab          root¦icon¦window    f.prev_key
}
```

The first line of the list specifies the following: if the user presses the Shift and Escape keys together while in an icon or a window, execute the function f.post_wmenu. From the list of functions, you know that this causes the window menu to pop up. Similarly, the second line performs the same action when the user presses the Meta key (Alt or Extend on most keyboards) and the spacebar.

The general syntax of each line is the following:

```
<key>   <context>   <function>
```

where *key* specifies the key combinations, *function* describes what action is taken and *context* indicates when that action is taken. As shown in the example, the key combination starts with one or more modifiers (Shift, Meta, Ctrl). Then comes the exact string <Key> followed by the name of a key to be pressed together with the modifiers. The valid names of keys are listed in Appendix E, "X Keyboard Symbols." Use the name from the appendix without the XK_ prefix.

The context is one of the following keywords:

```
root icon window title frame border app
```

where each word indicates an area of the screen. In other words, the action of the key takes place when the current active area is the one specified by the context keyword.

Button Bindings

Button bindings indicate what happens when a mouse button is pressed, particularly when done in combination with modifier keys such as Alt, Ctrl, or Shift. The syntax for specifying button bindings is identical to that for key bindings. Here is a short list of default button bindings:

```
! A few default button bindings for mwm

Buttons DefaultButtonBindings
{
    <Btn1Down>          root        f.menu   RootMenu
    <Btn1Down>          frame¦icon  f.raise
    <Btn2Down>          frame¦icon  f.post_wmenu
    <Btn3Down>          frame¦icon  f.post_wmenu
    Meta<Btn1Down>      icon¦window f.move
}
```

The first line explains why the root menu pops up every time you press the left button (one) in the root window. That line says that when button one is down—<Btn1Down> translates to this—with the mouse pointer in the root window (the context keyword root), mwm should execute the f.menu function with the menu named RootMenu (described earlier).

The second line specifies that if button one is pressed in any frame or icon, that window should be brought to the top of the stacking order. Because of the next line, if buttons two and three are pressed in these areas, the window menu pops up. The last line uses a modifier key. It specifies the following: if button one is pressed while the pointer is in a window or an icon and if the Meta (Alt) key is down, allow the user to move the window interactively.

Window Manager Customization

Now that you have some idea how configuration files work, you can tap the full potential of your window manager. (Techniques similar to those used with mwm are used by almost all window managers.) The trick is to start with a working configuration file. Usually you can start with the systemwide file called system.mwmrc in the directory /usr/lib/X11. Copy this file to your home directory under the name .mwmrc. Change its read/write protection if you have to, and edit it to alter one or two features at a time. You can do this from your xterm window while running X. Once you make some changes, use the restart option from the default root menu. When mwm restarts, it will accept your changes and you can verify whether everything worked properly. Following this approach, you can incrementally arrive at a configuration file that suits your needs.

If you are a system administrator, you can follow the same steps to build a customized root menu that enables users to log into specific systems in your local network. When the .mwmrc file is in its final version, you can replace the system.mwmrc file with the .mwmrc from your home directory.

Summary

Before you develop X applications, you should be familiar with X as a user. If you are the sole user of a workstation, you may have to install X in your system. This chapter describes how to install X and use it.

Because X can work across a network connection, an X application has to open a connection to the display where its output appears. In X, the display is synonymous with the X server and is identified by a name of the form *sysname*:*m*.*n* where *m* and *n* are integers identifying the display and the screen within a display. Because most workstations have only one display with a single screen, the typical name for an X display is *sysname*:0.0, where *sysname* is the network name of the workstation.

Once you know how to name an X display, you can start X by using the xinit utility. Many sites also have a custom shell script, usually called startx, to start X and some selected clients. A utility named xdm is also available to manage sessions on X terminals.

Of all X clients, the xterm terminal emulator and the window manager are special. The xterm application enables you to maintain a shell process so that you can interact with your system, start other clients, and log into remote systems. The window manager manages the layout of several clients' windows on the screen. The window manager also imparts a certain amount of look and feel to X applications. There are several window managers, with the Motif Window Manager (mwm) and the Open Look Window Manager (olwm) garnering the most support from users.

Window managers control some look and feel, but the developers of window managers cannot guess what each user wants. The problem is solved by making window managers easy to customize, using configuration files that are read and interpreted by the window manager at startup. A configuration file is a text file in which, following a specific format, the user can define menus and indicate what should happen when certain keys and mouse buttons are pressed.

Further Reading

To learn more about various aspects of UNIX systems, consult the books by Harley Hahn and Daniel Gilly. Kochan and Wood's book on UNIX networking has a chapter devoted to explaining how the X protocol works over a network. Another book by Kochan and Wood, *UNIX Shell Programming*, can help you understand (and write) the shell scripts used to start the X server and clients.

The paper by Brad Myers compares several window managers, including Microsoft Windows, Macintosh, and X under uwm, and classifies them according to common characteristics.

Gilly, Daniel, and the staff of O'Reilly & Associates. *UNIX in a Nutshell (System V).* Sebastopol, CA: O'Reilly & Associates, 1992.
Hahn, Harley. *A Student's Guide to UNIX.* New York: McGraw-Hill, 1993.
Kochan, Stephen G., and Patrick H. Wood, eds. *UNIX Networking.* Indianapolis: Hayden Books, 1989.
————. *UNIX Shell Programming.* 2d ed. Indianapolis: Hayden Books, 1989.
Myers, Brad A. "A Taxonomy of Window Manager User Interfaces." *IEEE Computer Graphics and Applications* (September 1988): 65-84.

Chapter 3

Exploring X Applications

Before diving into X programming, you should examine some representative X applications to see how they work. Because of the popularity of the X Window System, there are quite a few X-based commercial products in widespread use. However, the standard X software distribution includes a number of utilities, which also can serve as adequate examples. Your vendor may include them with X, or you can get the source code for these utilities from MIT. After observing how an X application behaves, you can examine its source code to see how that behavior was achieved.

This chapter provides a guided tour of several of these applications. The latter part of the chapter explains how you can customize X applications using resource files and command-line options.

Terminal Emulator (*xterm*)

If you were asked to name one truly indispensable X application, it would have to be the xterm terminal emulator. The window manager and xterm are the two applications most users run when starting X on a workstation. When first run, xterm emulates a VT102 terminal (24 lines by 80 columns). You interact with the UNIX shell in this window as you would in any alphanumeric terminal. Character-oriented applications can be run directly in this window, and you can start more xterm processes, thus creating several terminals on the same screen.

The VT102 terminal window in xterm is also useful for starting X applications on remote machines. For a networked machine, you can use the remote login command, rlogin or telnet, to log into the remote machine. On the remote system, you first should set the DISPLAY environment variable so that X clients executing there can send their output to your workstation. After that, you can start the X applications you want.

In addition to the VT102 terminal, xterm can also emulate the Tektronix 4014 graphics terminal. If you start xterm with the command xterm -t, it comes up in the Tektronix 4014 mode. As you will see soon, there are ways to switch back and forth between the VT102 and Tektronix 4014 modes while xterm is running.

Main Menu

The main menu in xterm is labeled the Main Options menu. To activate it, press the Ctrl key and the left mouse button simultaneously. This menu is available in both VT102 and Tektronix modes. The primary purpose of this menu is to stop xterm (see Figure 3.1). Selecting any of the last four options in the menu terminates xterm, and its window disappears from the screen. Each option works by sending a specific signal.

> **NOTE:**
>
> UNIX uses *signals* to notify a process that a specific event has occurred. The SIGKILL and SIGHUP signals terminate a process.

The entries labeled Send STOP Signal and Send CONT Signal are grayed out if your system does not have *job control*. On 4.3BSD systems, for example, you can suspend the current process by pressing Ctrl+Z, and resume it with Ctrl+Y. The Send STOP Signal and Send CONT Signal menu items provide an alternate way of doing this.

> **NOTE:**
>
> *Job control* enables you to start multiple programs from your terminal and have some control over their execution. It is available in 4.3BSD UNIX.

Figure 3.1.
The Main Options menu
in xterm.

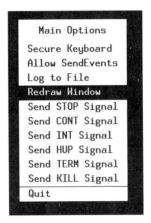

```
        Main Options
     Secure Keyboard
     Allow SendEvents
     Log to File
     Redraw Window
     Send STOP Signal
     Send CONT Signal
     Send INT Signal
     Send HUP Signal
     Send TERM Signal
     Send KILL Signal
     Quit
```

The Log to File option offers another convenient feature. When enabled, xterm saves all output in a log file (with a default name XtermLog.xxxxx, where xxxxx varies from one session to another). You can use this feature to capture output appearing in xterm.

VT102 Mode

In addition to providing a way to interact with the UNIX shell, emulating an alphanumeric terminal in a window has an added benefit: you can scroll back and look at old output, something you cannot do on a real VT102 terminal. For example, if a directory listing displayed in response to the ls command is too long, you can scroll the window's contents to view the lines that have scrolled off the VT102 window.

Another convenient feature of the VT102 window is that you can cut and paste text. For example, if you type a long command that you need to repeat later, you can select the line and paste it as the new command.

Scroll Function

Scrolling is not enabled by default. To enable scrolling, you have to start xterm with the command xterm -sb &. The option -sb causes xterm to display a scrollbar attached to the left edge of the VT102 window.

You can scroll the VT102 window because xterm allocates a 64-line buffer to hold lines being sent to the terminal. Of these, only 24 lines are visible in the window. The scrollbar indicates the amount of text in this buffer by changing the size of the *thumb*, the highlighted area in the scrollbar. When the buffer is empty, the thumb fills the scrollbar. As text fills the buffer, the thumb gradually becomes smaller. The 64-line size of the buffer can be enlarged by specifying a new value through the command-line option -sl or through the resource mechanism (explained later in this chapter).

To scroll back and forth and view the rest of the buffer, you have to bring the mouse pointer inside the scrollbar and then click a button. If you have a three-button mouse, pressing the left button in the scrollbar causes xterm to scroll the contents of the window up; clicking the right button scrolls the contents down. If you press the middle button, the window scrolls to a position that corresponds to the location of the pointer in the scrollbar. In other words, if you press the middle button at the top of the scrollbar, the window shows the oldest 24 lines in the buffer. If you move the mouse while the middle button remains pressed, the window's contents scroll in keeping with the mouse movement.

Cut-and-Paste

In xterm's VT102 window, unlike with a real VT102 terminal, you can cut and paste text. There is no explicit cut operation in X. Instead, the convention is to use selections (to be described further in Chapter 16, "Advanced Topics in X"). When you select text in xterm, it becomes the current selection. You then can paste the text into any application that can accept selections.

In xterm, you can select text in several ways. One way is by pressing the left button and dragging it up to the character to be selected. As the mouse is dragged, the selected text is highlighted. Another way is to double-click on a word to select it. A third way is to use the right button to select everything between the current location of the pointer and the point where the left button was last clicked. You can paste a selection into xterm by pressing the middle button.

Cut-and-paste is commonly used to avoid typing long repetitive commands. Simply select the command and paste it at the command prompt by pressing the middle mouse button. Another use of cut-and-paste is to start two xterm processes, each running an editor, (for example, vi). Suppose you are editing two files in the two editor sessions. You can select from the window of one editor and paste into the other using the paste mechanism of xterm. For this to work, the editor receiving the pasted text has to be in insert mode.

VT102 Menus

If you press the Ctrl key together with the middle button while in the VT102 window, a pop-up menu labeled VT Options appears (see Figure 3.2). This menu enables you to set a number of features of the VT102 emulation. For example, if you had not started xterm with the scrollbar enabled, you can do so by selecting Enable Scrollbar from this menu.

The last section of the menu has another important item. You can switch to the Tektronix emulation mode by bringing the pointer into the Switch to Tek Mode item and releasing the mouse button. To get back to the VT102 window, you have to select the Hide Tek Window option from the Tek Options menu that is available in the Tektronix emulation mode.

There is another menu in the VT102 mode that enables you to change the font used in the VT102 window. Press the Ctrl key along with the right mouse button while the mouse pointer is in the VT102 window. You will see the menu shown in Figure 3.3. Usually, the VT102 window uses the Default font. Select another font, for instance, Large. The VT102 window will resize, and its contents will appear in a larger font. This is helpful on large-screen displays in which the Default font may be too small for practical use.

Figure 3.2.

*The VT Options menu in
the VT102 mode of* xterm.

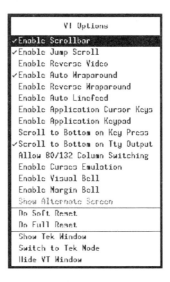

Figure 3.3.

*The VT Fonts menu in the
VT102 mode of* xterm.

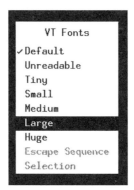

A *termcap* Entry for *xterm*

All alphanumeric terminals support programming that you can use to move the cursor, erase portions of the screen, and occasionally display characters in bold or reverse video. To perform these actions, you have to send the terminal special sequences of characters (*escape sequences*), which usually start by pressing the Esc key.

UNIX uses a clever approach to programming the alphanumeric terminals. The capabilities of the terminals are stored in a file (called `termcap` in 4.3BSD and `terminfo` in System V and located in the `/etc` directory). Each `termcap` entry identifies the terminal by name (for example, `vt100`, `ansi`, or `tek4014`) and specifies the escape sequence necessary to activate each feature of the terminal. With this approach, support for a new terminal can be added by including an entry for that terminal in the `termcap` file. The `termcap` entry for `xterm`'s VT102 emulation usually appears under the name `xterm`. MIT provides the necessary termcap entry in a file named `termcap` together with the source code for `xterm`.

Most UNIX processes that need to program the terminal extract the `termcap` entry for the terminal specified by the `TERM` environment variable. Thus, when using `xterm`, you should set `TERM` to `xterm`.

Tektronix 4014 Mode

The Tektronix 4014 emulation in `xterm` is useful for displaying output from older graphics programs that require the older Tektronix graphics terminal. If you are developing X applications, you are not likely to use this emulation mode, because X gives you much greater control over the display than the Tektronix 4014 does.

If you do get to the Tektronix 4014 mode, you can interact with `xterm` using the Tek Options menu, which is popped up when you press the Ctrl key together with the middle button of the mouse (see Figure 3.4). The most important item in this menu is the one labeled Switch to VT Mode. By selecting this item, you can get rid of the Tektronix window and revert back to the VT102 emulation.

Figure 3.4.
The Tek Options menu in the Tektronix 4014 mode of `xterm`.

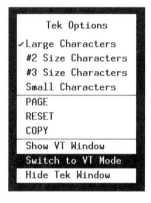

Desk Accessories

X comes with several popular utilities that fall in the category of *desk accessories*, a term that became popular with the Apple Macintosh. On the Macintosh, each desk accessory is a small application devoted to a single task and available to the user at any time—much like real-life accessories (such as a clock or a calculator) on one's desk. In X, the clock (`xclock`), the calculator (`xcalc`), and the mail notifier (`xbiff`) are the most popular desk accessory programs. (Most UNIX system suppliers include these utilities or some equivalent, but they are not required to do so.) You can start these programs from the `xterm` window. For example, you can start the three accessories and put them in the background with these commands:

```
xclock &
xcalc &
xbiff &
```

This starts each program with their default settings. Typically, users arrange the `xclock`, `xcalc`, and `xbiff` windows along the edge of the screen, and continue their main task in another window (either the xterm window or in another application). The xclock window always shows the current time. While working, if you suddenly need the calculator, you can move the mouse pointer to the calculator and start using it.

xclock

The clock is one of the most common items on any X workstation or X terminal. By default, xclock displays an analog clock (as shown in Figure 3.5). You can, however, get a digital clock by starting xclock with the command xclock -digital &. Figure 3.6 shows the 24-hour format used by the digital clock.

Figure 3.5.

xclock in analog mode.

Figure 3.6.

xclock in digital mode.

X11R4 added a new twist to the clock—a new analog clock, named oclock, that displays the clock's face as an oval. The oclock application uses an extension to the X protocol, called SHAPE, that is supported by X servers starting with the X11R4 server provided by MIT. Figure 3.7 shows the result of running oclock with an oclock& command. Figure 3.7 shows oclock's window without the frame placed by the window manager. You can clearly see that oclock's window has an oval shape.

Figure 3.7.

Analog clock with oval face displayed by oclock.

xcalc

The xcalc calculator, by default, displays a calculator styled after the Texas Instrument's TI-30 model (Figure 3.8). You can use the calculator by clicking on the buttons or by pressing the numbers on the keyboard. For the keypresses to work, you have to make xcalc's window the current focus window. The window manager defines how this is done—usually by clicking on it once or by bringing the mouse pointer into the window.

If you prefer the Reverse Polish Notation (RPN) of the Hewlett-Packard calculators, you can get a calculator modeled after the HP-10C with the command xcalc -rpn &. Figure 3.9 shows the HP-10C look-alike.

In RPN calculators, the operands precede the operation. For example, on an HP-10C, to add 2.25 to 9.95, you press the keys in the following order:

```
2.25 ENTER 9.95 +
```

Figure 3.8.

The TI-30 style calculator.

Figure 3.9.

The HP-10C style calculator.

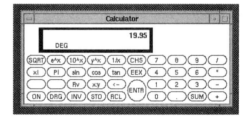

xbiff

The xbiff mail notifier utility alerts you when you have new mail. It is named after the UNIX biff utility which serves the same purpose in alphanumeric terminals. The program displays a mailbox icon in a window. As shown in Figure 3.10, when there is no mail, the flag on the mailbox is down. When mail arrives, xbiff raises the flag on the mailbox and displays its window in reverse video (see Figure 3.11). You can revert the window back to the "no mail" condition by clicking in it.

Figure 3.10.

The xbiff window when there is no mail.

Figure 3.11.
The xbiff *window announcing new mail.*

Window Capture and Viewing Utilities

The category of X utilities that enables you to capture and view the image of a window is an important one because you often need to print images of the screen for inclusion in the documentation of your programs. The pair xwd and xwud are for capturing and viewing images. The xpr utility prints images captured by xwd.

Capturing a Window Image with *xwd*

The xwd utility is written in the style of many other UNIX utilities: it sends the image of a selected window to the standard output. To get the image into a file, you have to redirect standard output to a file. For example, here is how you can capture the image of a selected window and save it in a file named windump1:

1. Type the following command:

   ```
   xwd > windump1
   ```

2. The cursor changes to a small crosshair. Move the cursor to the selected window and press the left button of the mouse.

3. A single beep warns you that the image is being captured and you should not change the appearance of the window. Two beeps tell you that the image capture is complete.

Another way to capture the image to a file is with the -out option:

```
xwd -out windump1
```

What can you do with the captured image? You can preview the image using the companion utility xwud. For example, the command xwud < windump1 displays the captured image in another window. Click once in this window to exit xwud.

Capturing Pop-Up Menus with *xwd*

Capturing the image of a pop-up menu is one problem that often baffles a beginner. If you do not mind an image of the entire screen, you can do this easily from your xterm window with the following procedure:

1. Type this command:

   ```
   sleep 10; xwd -root > scdump1 &
   ```

2. Promptly press the appropriate mouse button to get the menu popped up.

3. Wait until you hear the beeps from xwd indicating that the image capture has been completed.

The sleep 10; in the command-line before xwd gives you 10 seconds to pop the menu or bring a specific window to the top of the stack of windows on the screen.

The -root option is interpreted by xwd as a request to capture the root window. Therefore, it does not prompt for a window to be captured—it saves the entire screen.

Formatting Window Images for a Printer with *xpr*

The xpr utility enables you to format the image captured by xwd for printing. Unfortunately, xpr is geared toward printing on a few specific printers. You specify the printer by the -device option. You can specify a generic PostScript printer by using the option -device ps.

Suppose you want to generate a PostScript file for the image windump1, generated in the earlier example. To do this, type this command:

```
xpr -device ps windump1 > windump1.ps
```

This generates a PostScript file named windump1.ps, which you can print by sending it to a PostScript printer.

By default, xpr prints images in black and white—it converts color or grayscale images to black and white by assuming that any nonwhite color is black. To print an image in grayscale, use the -gray option; xpr supports only a limited number of gray levels.

Processing *xwd*-Generated Image Files

If xpr does not handle color or grayscale images adequately, how do you print them? One way is to use a utility program to convert the image into a format that can be displayed and handled by desktop publishing programs. Another approach is to process the image yourself. The format of the image saved by xwd is straightforward. Once you know this format, with a little knowledge of PostScript, you can generate grayscale images on a PostScript printer such as the Apple LaserWriter or Hewlett-Packard Laserjet 4M. The following sections describe how to convert xwd-generated screen images into PostScript.

Format of *xwd*-Generated Files

To understand the format of image files saved by xwd, you need some rudimentary knowledge of bitmapped displays. Consider, for example, a 256-color display with a resolution of 640x480 (480 raster lines with 640 dots per line). Because 8 bits are needed to represent 256 distinct colors, you can think of each pixel as an 8-bit value. The content of each pixel is often called the *pixel value*. The colormap determines how each pixel value is translated to a specific color. When xwd saves the image of a window to a file, it saves the contents of all the pixels that lie inside the window. To be able to interpret the image later, it must save, at a minimum, the following information:

✦ The width and height of the rectangle whose pixel values are being saved
✦ The colormap (for a 256-color display, this has 256 entries)
✦ The pixel values for the selected rectangle

An xwd-generated image file starts with a header containing the information about the image size and many other details, followed by the name of the image, the colormap, and finally the image itself. The header is defined in a header file XWDFile.h (in /usr/include/X11) as the following:

```
typedef unsigned long xwdval;

#define XWD_FILE_VERSION 7

typedef struct _xwd_file_header
{
    xwdval header_size;          /* Total size of header (bytes) */
    xwdval file_version;         /* XWD_FILE_VERSION             */
    xwdval pixmap_format;        /* Pixmap format               */
    xwdval pixmap_depth;         /* Pixmap depth                */
    xwdval pixmap_width;         /* Pixmap width                */
    xwdval pixmap_height;        /* Pixmap height               */
    xwdval xoffset;              /* Bitmap x offset             */
    xwdval byte_order;           /* MSBFirst, LSBFirst          */
    xwdval bitmap_unit;          /* Bitmap unit                 */
    xwdval bitmap_bit_order;     /* MSBFirst, LSBFirst          */
    xwdval bitmap_pad;           /* Bitmap scanline pad         */
    xwdval bits_per_pixel;       /* Bits per pixel              */
    xwdval bytes_per_line;       /* Bytes per scanline          */
    xwdval visual_class;         /* Class of colormap           */
    xwdval red_mask;             /* Z red mask                  */
    xwdval green_mask;           /* Z green mask                */
    xwdval blue_mask;            /* Z blue mask                 */
    xwdval bits_per_rgb;         /* Bits to represent each color */
    xwdval colormap_entries;     /* Number of entries in colormap*/
    xwdval ncolors;              /* Number of XColor structures  */
    xwdval window_width;         /* Window width                */
    xwdval window_height;        /* Window height               */
    long window_x;               /* Window top left X coordinate */
    long window_y;               /* Window top left Y coordinate */
    xwdval window_bdrwidth;      /* Window border width         */
} XWDFileHeader;
```

> **NOTE:**
>
> Many terms in the header are explained later in the book. Ignore them for now.

Because a long integer takes 4 bytes of storage, the XWDFileHeader structure is 100 bytes long. The field header_size includes the size of the window name, which follows the header. By default, xwd uses the null-terminated string xwdump as the window name. This adds 7 more bytes to the header size (the string size plus the null character). Thus, the header_size field is typically 107 bytes.

Immediately following the header comes the colormap. This part contains as many XColor structures as there are colors specified by the field colormap_entries (for example, 256 for a 256-color display). The XColor structure is defined in Xlib.h (you need it here primarily to determine the size of the structure):

```
typedef struct
{
    unsigned long   pixel;   /* 4-byte pixel value     */
    unsigned short  r, g, b; /* 6 bytes of R G B values */
    unsigned char   flag;    /* 1-byte flag (total 11)  */
    unsigned char   pad;     /* Padded to 12 bytes      */
} XColor;
```

Thus, for a 256-color display, a 3,072-byte colormap (256 times the 12 bytes of storage needed for each XColor structure) follows the header.

Next comes the actual image data. For a selected rectangle, by default, xwd saves the pixel values in the ZPixmap format. This is indicated by the field pixmap_format; a 1 indicates the XYPixmap format and a 2 means the ZPixmap format.

In the ZPixmap format, xwd saves the contents of the pixels one after another, starting at the upper-left corner and traversing the rectangle one raster line at a time, from left to right. The pixel values are packed into bytes, and the packing order is indicated by the byte_order flag in the header. A byte_order of MSBFirst (defined to be 1) means the pixel values are packed from most-significant to least-significant bit. Figure 3.12 illustrates a 4-bit ZPixmap image data stored in the MSBFirst byte_order.

Figure 3.12.

A ZPixmap *image stored in the* MSBFirst *byte order.*

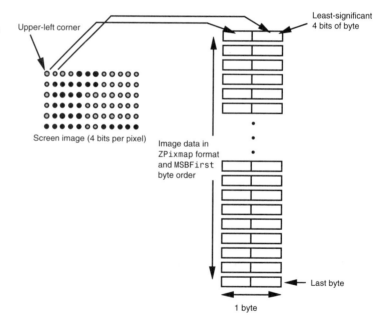

Header Interpretation

There is an important point to remember when interpreting the values in the header of the image file saved by xwd. For an image file with the MSBFirst byte order, all long integers are saved in the *big-endian* order. In other words, of the 4 bytes in a long integer, the first one you retrieve from the file will be its most-significant byte. If your system's CPU is *little-endian* (that is, it expects the least-significant byte of a long integer to be at the starting address), you first have to reverse the order of the bytes. Examples of some little-endian CPUs are Intel 80x86 and DEC VAX. Motorola 680xx CPUs and most RISC systems are big-endian.

Once you know that conversion is necessary, reversing the order of the bytes is straightforward. Here is a sample C function `bel2lel` (big-endian long to little-endian long) that does the job:

```
/*-------------------------------------------------*/
/* b e l 2 l e l
 *
 * Reverse bytes to convert a big-endian long
 * to little-endian
 */
unsigned long bel2lel(unsigned long be)
{
    union
    {
        unsigned long x;
        unsigned char y[4];
    } beb4;

    register unsigned char t;

    beb4.x = be;
/* Exchange bytes 0 and 3 */
    t = beb4.y[3];
    beb4.y[3] = beb4.y[0];
    beb4.y[0] = t;
/* Exchange bytes 1 and 2 */
    t = beb4.y[2];
    beb4.y[2] = beb4.y[1];
    beb4.y[1] = t;
    return (beb4.x);
}
```

Similarly, the short integers in the colormap are stored in big-endian order. Remember to swap the bytes in a little-endian system.

Format Conversion to PostScript

To convert the `ZPixmap` image to PostScript format, you need some knowledge of PostScript. Specifically, the PostScript operator `image` is used to print the image. The PostScript output should have a prolog that defines your image printing operator, followed by the image data in hexadecimal format, and finally an epilog that actually prints the page with the `showpage` command. You store a standard prolog and epilog in an array of strings. Assuming an 8-bit image, you can use the following as the prolog:

```
char *prolog[] =
{
"%%Pages: 1\n",
"%%EndProlog\n",
"%%Page: 1 1\n",
"/draw_image % stack should have: width, height\n",
```

```
"% Draw image (lower-left corner at current origin)\n",
"{\n",
"% arguments...\n",
"    /height exch def\n",
"    /width exch def\n",
"/oneline\n",
"    width\n",
"    string\n",
"    def\n",
"% Read and draw image. Assume 8-bit image...\n",
"    width height 8 [width 0 0 height 0 0]\n",
"    {currentfile oneline readhexstring pop }\n",
"    image\n",
"} def\n",
NULL
};
```

The following short epilog is sufficient for your purposes:

```
char *epilog[] =
{
    "\n",
    "showpage\n",
    "%%Trailer\n",
    NULL
};
```

When converting the image to PostScript, first write the prolog to the output file. Next write the image data in hexadecimal format. A typical 640x480 image fits better in the landscape mode, so write the image data in a format that conforms to what PostScript expects for a landscape image.

Assuming that `infile` and `outfile` are the input and output streams, and that you have already read the header, the window name, and the colormap, the following code shows how to generate the PostScript image file:

```
#include <stdio.h>
#include <time.h>

void *malloc(size_t);

XWDFileHeader xwdhdr;
time_t        bintime;
int           i, j, w, h, looph, file_ended = 0;
unsigned char **image;
unsigned char *rowi;
double        graylevel;
unsigned int  tc;
size_t        rowsize, numread;
char          *psname; /* Initialize to name of image file */

/* Open input and output files */
    .
    .
    .

/* Read header, window name, and color map */
    .
    .
    .
```

```
/* Get width and height of image.
 * See above for function be2lel
 */
    w = bel2lel(xwdhdr.pixmap_width);
    h = be2llel(xwdhdr.pixmap_height);

/* Write PostScript prolog */
    fprintf(outfile, "%%!PS-Adobe-2.0 EPSF-1.2\n");
    fprintf(outfile, "%%%%Creator:Naba Barkakati\n");
    fprintf(outfile, "%%%%For:X Window System Programming, 2E\n");
    fprintf(outfile, "%%%%Title:%s\n", psname);
    time(&bintime);
    fprintf(outfile, "%%%%CreationDate: %s", ctime(&bintime));

    lmargin = 50+left;
    bmargin = 50+bottom;

/* Ignore header and trailer... for now. */
    if(h%2)h++;
    hact = (int)(((long)scale * (long)h)/ 100L);
    wact = (int)(((long)scale * (long)w)/ 100L);
    fprintf(outfile, "%%%%BoundingBox: %d %d %d %d\n", lmargin,
            bmargin, lmargin+wact, bmargin+hact);
    fprintf(outfile, "%%%%EndComments\n");

    for(i = 0; prolog[i] != NULL; i++)
        fprintf(outfile, "%s", prolog[i]);

/* Change these for different margin */
    lmargin = 50;
    bmargin = 50;

/* Always write out even number of columns */
    looph = h;
    if(h%2) looph += 1;
    fprintf(outfile,"%d %d translate\n", lmargin,
            bmargin);
    fprintf(outfile, "%d %d scale\n", hact, wact);
    fprintf(outfile,"%d %d draw_image\n", h, w);

/* Read entire image into memory and process it */
    rowsize = be12lel(xwdhdr.bytes_por_linc);

/* Allocate space for entire image */
    if((image = (unsigned char **)
        malloc(looph * sizeof(unsigned char *))) == NULL)
    {
        fprintf(stderr, "Error allocating memory...");
        fprintf(stderr,"%d bytes for image row addresses\n", h);
        exit(1);
    }

/* Read in entire image...*/
    for(i = 0; i < h && !file_ended; i++)
    {
        if((image[i] = (unsigned char *)malloc(rowsize))
            == NULL)
        {
            fprintf(stderr, "Error allocating memory...");
```

```
                fprintf(stderr,"%d bytes for %d-th row\n",
                        i+1, rowsize);
                exit(1);
            }
/* Read in a row */
        if((numread = fread(image[i], 1, rowsize,
                            infile)) < rowsize)
        {
            if(ferror(infile) != 0)
            {
                puts("Error during read. Exiting...");
                fclose(infile);
                fclose(outfile);
                exit(1);
            }
            if(feof(infile) != 0)
            {
                puts("File ended");
                fclose(infile);
                file_ended = 1;
            }
        }
    }

/* If h is odd, add one more row to image in memory.
 * Otherwise, images with odd h will not produce working
 * PostScript files
 */
    if(looph > h)
    {
        if((image[looph] = (unsigned char *)
                        malloc(rowsize)) == NULL)
        {
            fprintf(stderr, "Error allocating memory...");
            fprintf(stderr,"%d bytes for %d-th row\n",
                    looph+1, rowsize);
            exit(1);
        }
/* Initialize the extra row to all 0xff */
        for(j=0; j<rowsize; j++)
            image[looph][j] = 0xff;
    }

/*************** MAIN PROCESSING LOOP ****************/
/* Write out image in landscape mode as required
 * by PostScript
 */
    for(j=0; j<rowsize; j++)
    {
/* Process a row at a time */
        for(i=0; i<looph; i++)
        {
            rowi = image[i];
            tc = rowi[j] & 0xff;
/* Convert RGB to grayscale. Use the NTSC formula for
 * luminosity (0.299 * Red + 0.587 * Green + 0.114 * Blue)
 */
                graylevel = (double)(colormap[tc].r * 0.299 +
                        colormap[tc].g * 0.587 +
```

```
                    colormap[tc].b * 0.114) / 256.0;
            tc = graylevel;
/* Write it out as 2 hexadecimal digits */
            fprintf(outfile, "%2.2x", tc);
        }
    }
/************* END OF MAIN PROCESSING LOOP ************/

/* Write PostScript epilog */
    for(i = 0; epilog[i] != NULL; i++)
        fprintf(outfile, "%s", epilog[i]);

/* Close input and output files */
    fclose(outfile);
    fclose(infile);
```

Once the PostScript image is in a file, you can print it by sending the file to any PostScript printer.

Utilities to Display Information about X

A few other utilities included with X provide information on windows. The xwininfo utility prints information about a selected window, and xlswins displays the entire hierarchy of windows.

Displaying Information Using *xwininfo*

When invoked without any arguments, xwininfo changes the cursor to a crosshair and prints the following message asking you to identify the window about which you want information:

```
xwininfo ==> Please select the window about which you
         ==> would like information by clicking the
         ==> mouse in that window.
```

Once you click on the window, xwininfo displays a host of useful information about the window. For example, clicking on the xterm window might generate the following list:

```
xwininfo ==> Window id: 0x10000d (xterm)

         ==> Absolute upper-left X:  8
         ==> Absolute upper-left Y:  24
         ==> Relative upper-left X:  0
         ==> Relative upper-left Y:  0
         ==> Width: 499
         ==> Height: 316
         ==> Depth: 8
         ==> Border width: 0
         ==> Window class: InputOutput
         ==> Colormap: 0x80065 (installed)
         ==> Window Bit Gravity State: NorthWestGravity
         ==> Window Window Gravity State: NorthWestGravity
         ==> Window Backing Store State: NotUseful
         ==> Window Save Under State: no
         ==> Window Map State: IsViewable
         ==> Window Override Redirect State: no
         ==> Corners:  +8+24  -517+24  -517-401  +8-401
```

The window location and size are displayed by the first four items in the list. This information is often useful in deciding the default settings for the placement and size of an application's window.

In the later chapters of this book, you learn more about the rest of the information displayed by xwininfo. At that time, you can use xwininfo to verify that the settings for your applications window match what you did in the code.

Window Hierarchy Listing with *xlswins*

If you invoke xlswins without any argument, it displays the entire tree of windows, starting with the root window and identifying each window with its own ID, a hexadecimal number. It is instructive to see the list because it gives you a feeling for the way windows are used in X applications. What will amaze you is that most X applications use a large number of windows—scrollbars, menus, and message boxes are all built out of a hierarchy of windows. Additionally, the frame added by a window manager around an application's main window is also composed of many smaller windows.

Take, for example, the case of xterm running under the Motif Window Manage (mwm). The following is an annotated printout showing the tree of windows displayed by xlswins for this simple scenario:

```
0x8006a  ()                    <- The root window
  0x300001  ()
  0x200006  (mwm)              <- Motif Window Manager
  0x20001f  ()
  0x20002c  ()
  0x20002d  ()
    0x20002f  ()
  0x200034  ()
    0x200035  ()
  0x200039  (mwm)
  0x20003c  ()
    0x20003d  ()
  0x200049  ()
  0x20003e  ()                 <- xterm's frame
    0x20003f  ()               <- These are the
    0x200040  ()               <- "gadgets" added
    0x200041  ()               <- added by mwm
    0x200042  ()
    0x200043  ()
    0x200044  ()
    0x200045  ()
    0x200046  ()
    0x200047  ()
    0x200048  ()
      0x10000d  (xterm)        <- Main window of xterm
        0x100012  ()           <- VT102 window
          0x100013  ()         <- scrollbar
  0x100020  ()
```

The notes next to the arrows explain the major components in the tree of windows that exists for this scenario. The child windows are indicated by an indentation. As expected, a root window and windows exist for each of the following: mwm and xterm. There are many more windows in the hierarchy than most people expect. The additional windows are created by mwm when it provides a frame around the main window of each application. For example, the `xterm` application has a main window labeled `xterm` (ID = 0x10000d). Inside that window, `xterm` has the VT102 window (0x100012) and the scrollbar window (0x100013).

If you have trouble identifying windows in the tree, you can find the size and placement of each window by using `xlswins -l`. By knowing the size and location of a window, you may be able to identify it on the screen.

Appearance and Behavior of X Applications

You have seen a number of X applications in action, with mention of what they do by default. This may prompt you to conclude that there must be ways to alter the behavior of X applications. If so, you are correct.

Most X applications, especially those based on any Xt-based toolkit, are highly configurable. You can alter the appearance—and, to some extent, even the behavior of an application—in two ways:

+ By using options specified in the command line that starts the application
+ By accepting values for options from a text file called a *resource file* (after the terminology used by X programmers to refer to any user-configurable options in an application)

Resources

Specifying options on the command line works fine for small UNIX utilities, but X applications tend to have a large number of variables that can be (and should be) set by the user. For example, an X application may contain a large number of windows, each of which may have a border, a background color, and a foreground color. There is no reason to force a user to live with the colors selected by a programmer. Instead, the application should provide default values that can be overridden by the user.

Similarly, if a window contains several child windows, you may want the user to be able to specify the location and size of each child. There also are fonts for any text to be displayed. There are too many variables in an X application to set through the command-line mechanism alone. The authors of X recognized this problem and, starting with X11R2, included utility routines in the Xlib library to manage a database of resources.

The term *resource* has two meanings in the X Window System. In the context of programming with Xlib, windows, colors, bitmaps, and fonts are resources that are maintained by the X server and accessed by the X client applications through X protocol requests. For an X application, however, a resource is any parameter that affects its behavior or appearance. Thus, foreground and background colors, fonts, size and placement of windows are typical resources.

A resource does not have to be a parameter related to X. It can be anything that controls the behavior of an application and should be specified by the user. For example, an application might have a variable named `debug`, which, when set, enables printing of detailed information as it runs. In addition to the application's window size and location, `debug` also qualifies as a resource of this application.

Resource File and Resource Manager

The resources for an X application are specified in the resource file or a *resource database.* A set of utility routines (with names having the Xrm prefix), collectively known as the *resource manager,* can read and interpret the resource files. This does not happen automatically. The X application has to call the resource manager to retrieve the user's selections for various parameters. For applications built with a toolkit, higher-level resource management routines do the job.

The resource database in X is a simple text file in which the user can specify the value of various parameters, using a well-defined format. X resource files are not as complicated and sophisticated as a traditional database. The X resource database contains specifications of the form "all foreground colors are white," "xterm's background is light cyan," and so on.

The X resource manager is designed to extract the value of precisely identified individual parameters from this rather imprecise database. For example, a query might be "what is the foreground color of the xclock application?" If the user has specified the foreground color of xclock in the resource file, the resource manager returns this value. If, however, the only specification for foreground color in the database is the general statement "all foreground colors are white," the value returned for xclock's foreground color is white.

Resource Naming Convention

How do you specify that xterm's foreground color should be light cyan, for instance? To do this, you must learn how to name a resource and how to specify the value for a resource.

The name of a resource depends on the name of the application and the names of its components, which are usually the major child windows. For X toolkit-based applications, the components are the names of widgets used to build the application. The names of the application and its components can be of two types: *class name* and *instance name.* The class name indicates the general category to which the application or the component belongs, and each individual copy can have its own instance name.

Consider a concrete example—the xterm application. This application is of the class XTerm, and the instance goes by the name xterm. The xterm application uses a component named vt100 of class VT100 (yes, it emulates a VT102, but the internal name is VT100), which further contains a component named scrollbar of the class Scrollbar. Now consider the following resources: the foreground color of the VT100 window and the visibility of the scrollbar in that window. In xterm, as in most X applications, the foreground color resource has the class name Foreground and instance name foreground. The scrollbar's visibility is controlled by a Boolean variable named on.

Most X applications follow this convention of naming the class of a resource by capitalizing the first letter of its instance name. Class names of applications also start with a capital letter; instance names start with a lowercase letter. This is a good convention because it promotes some consistency among applications, but the naming of the application, its components, and the resources is an issue entirely under the control of the application. (Only toolkit applications are somewhat constrained by the built-in names of predefined widgets.)

Now you are in a position to name these resources uniquely in xterm and specify values for them. The foreground color of the VT100 window and the on variable of its scrollbar can be assigned values in the following manner:

```
xterm.vt100.foreground:      light cyan
xterm.vt100.scrollbar.on:    true
```

This illustrates the syntax of naming resources and giving their values. The name of a resource is constructed by the name of the application, followed by names of the components, each separated from the next by a period. The resource name comes last, and the value of the resource follows a colon (:). The value is given as text string. It is up to the application to interpret it internally. The resource manager has utility routines to help the programmer with this task.

The names illustrated so far are full instance names showing the application and all its components. You also can have full class names, which for xterm.vt100.foreground is XTerm.VT100.Foreground, obtained by replacing the instance name of each component with the corresponding class name. When querying the value of a resource, X applications must use either its full instance or full class name.

Partial Names for Resources

You have seen how to specify a resource by its full name, but recall that the specification can be imprecise. What sort of imprecise entries can you specify? For example, you might indicate that all components of class VT100 should have a yellow foreground color. This can be done by the following entry in the resource database:

```
*VT100.Foreground:   yellow
```

Because no application name is specified, this foreground color applies to the VT100 component used in any application. Similarly, to specify that the background of every component in the xterm application should be navy, include the following line in the resource file:

```
xterm*background:navy
```

To understand the resource naming scheme, you have to know something about the inner workings of the X resource manager. By now, you probably guessed that the X resource manager locates a resource's value by matching a precisely specified resource name against the imprecise entries in the resource database. The search algorithm used by the resource manager follows certain rules when matching a full resource name with the partial names in the resource database. Knowing these rules can help you understand what kind of specification for a resource is precise enought to suit your needs. The rules are as follows:

1. An asterisk (*) matches zero or more components in the name. Thus, the query for xterm.vt100.foreground matches this entry:

   ```
   xterm*foreground:   yellow
   ```

2. After accounting for the asterisk, the application name, component names, and resource name (class or instance) must match the items present in the entry. Thus, a query for XTerm.VT100.Scrollbar.Background matches this entry:

```
xterm.vt100.scrollbar.background: navy
```

but not this one:

```
xterm.vt100.scrollbar.on: true
```

This is, of course, common sense.

3. More specific resource specifications take precedence over less specific settings. For example, entries with a period (.) take precedence over ones that have an asterisk (*). Thus, if you specify the following:

```
xterm*background: navy
xterm.vt100.scrollbar.background:   white
```

everything in `xterm` will have the navy background, but the scrollbar will have a white background.

4. Instance names take precedence over class names. Thus, the specific entry `xterm*background` overrides the one that uses class names: `XTerm*Background`.

5. An entry with a class name or an instance name takes precedence over one that uses neither. For example, in `xterm`, the value given in the entry `XTerm*Foreground` overrides that under the more general entry `*Foreground`.

6. Match names from left to right because the hierarchy of components in the name of a resource goes from left to right. In other words, when looking for the resource named `xterm.vt100.scrollbar.background`, the resource manager will match this entry:

```
xterm.vt100*background: white
```

rather than this one:

```
xterm*scrollbar.background: navy
```

because `vt100` appears to the left of `scrollbar`.

Resource Placement

Now you know how to specify resources for an X application, but how do you ensure that your resource specifications take effect? An X application must include explicit code to read and interpret a resource file. Most toolkit-based applications do this, but an X application does not have to accept resource specifications from a database. It is, however, not advisable to ignore resources because such applications without resources tend to be unpopular with users. Users may never set any resources, but they take comfort in knowing that the facility is there should they ever decide to change any aspect of the application.

Most X applications (especially toolkit-based ones) load resource settings from several sources in a specific order. First, they look for a file named `/usr/lib/X11/app-defaults/`*app_class*, where *app_class* is the class name of the application. Thus, `xterm` looks for its resources in `/usr/lib/X11/app-defaults/XTerm`.

Next, the application looks for a string named `RESOURCE_MANAGER` attached to the root window of the display where the application is sending its output. This is known as a *property* of the root window. (Properties are further explained in Chapter 16.) You can use the utility routine `xprop` to see if this property exists on your display's root window. Type `xprop -root` and look for an entry labeled `RESOURCE_MANAGER(STRING)` in the output. The `xrdb` utility also can read a resource file and load the contents into this property (as a long string).

If the `RESOURCE_MANAGER` property does not exist, the application reads the resource specifications from the file `.Xdefaults` in your home directory. Then the application loads the resources specified by the file indicated by the environment variable `XENVIRONMENT`, if any. If this variable is not set, the next source for resources is a file named `.Xdefaults-hostname` in your home directory. Here, `hostname` is the system where the application is running.

Of course, the user still can override any of the resource specifications through command-line options.

If you want to see the effect of the resources, here is an example of how you might do it. From your current `xterm` window, use an editor to create the file `testrm` containing the following lines:

```
xterm.vt100.scrollBar.on:       true
*VT100.Foreground:              yellow
xterm*background:               navy
xterm.vt100.scrollbar.background: white
```

Then use the `xrdb` utility program to load these settings into the `RESOURCE_MANAGER` property under the root window with this command:

```
xrdb -load testrm
```

You can use `xprop -root` to verify that the resources are loaded. You will notice how the contents of the resource file are stored internally in the property `RESOURCE_MANAGER` as a very long string. Start another `xterm` session using the command `xterm &`. You will see that the new `xterm` window has yellow characters on a navy background, except for the scrollbar, which has a white background.

Common Resources

Some resource names are, by convention, standard in X applications. These include parameters such as foreground and background colors, window size and location (collectively known as *geometry*), and font. Table 3.1 lists some of the common resources. The last field in each line shows the command-line option used to specify the resource.

Table 3.1. Standard X Resources

Instance Name	Class Name	Command-Line Option	Specifies
background	Background	-bg -background	Background color
borderColor	BorderColor	-bd -border	Border color

continues

Table 3.1. continued

Instance Name	Class Name	Command-Line Option	Specifies
borderWidth	BorderWidth	-bw -borderwidth	Border width in pixels
display	Display	-display -d	Name of display
foreground	Foreground	-fg -foreground	Foreground color
font	Font	-fn -font	Font name
geometry	Geometry	-geometry	Size and location
reverseVideo	ReverseVideo	-rv	Reverse video
title	Title	-title	Title string

Command-Line Options

Recall that, in addition to resource databases, X applications accept command-line arguments as most conventional UNIX applications do. As Table 3.1 shows, most common features of an X application can be specified on the command line.

Display Specification

An important command-line option for X applications is -display, which enables you to specify the display where the application's output should appear. You can use this as an alternative to setting the DISPLAY environment variable before starting an application. For example, if you are logged into a remote host and want to run the client xclock on that system, you can start it with this command:

```
xclock -display mysys:0 &
```

where *mysys* is the node name of your workstation.

Window Size and Location

Another common option is -geometry, used to specify the size and location of the application's main window. The geometry is specified in a standard format:

```
widthxheight[+-]xoffset[+-]yoffset
```

where you pick one of the two signs shown in the square brackets. The `width` and `height` usually specify the size of the window in pixels (in `xterm` they are given in number of columns and rows of text). The `xoffset` and `yoffset` quantities are also in pixels. The meaning of these two numbers depend on the application. In `xterm`, for instance, a positive `xoffset` indicates the number of pixels that the left side of the window is offset from the left side of the screen. A negative `xoffset`, on the other hand, specifies the number of pixels that the right edge of the window is offset from the right edge of the screen. Similarly, positive and negative `yoffset` respectively indicate offsets of the top and bottom edges of the window from the corresponding edge of the screen.

For example, the following command places a 120-pixel by 120-pixel clock in the upper-right corner of your screen, with a 16-pixel gap between the clock's frame and the screen's top and right edges:

```
xclock -geometry 120x120-16+16 &
```

Window Appearance

Most of the other command-line options determine the appearance of an application's window. They specify the foreground color (`-fg`), the background color (`-bg`), the border color (`-bd`), and the border width (`-bw`) in pixels. The colors are given by names (see Appendix D, "X Colors," for a list of acceptable names). For example, to start an `xterm` session with yellow characters on a navy background, use this command:

```
xterm -bg navy -fg yellow &
```

If a color name includes embedded space, you have to give the name in quotes. For example, to specify *light blue* as the background for `xterm`, use the following:

```
xterm -bg "light blue" &
```

Alternative Color Naming in Resource Files

In addition to the descriptive name for a color, you can specify it as a hexadecimal number, usually with six hexadecimal digits, which works out to two digits for each of the three components in a color—red (R), green (G), and blue (B). The digits in a six-digit hexadecimal RGB value of a color are interpreted from left to right, with the most-significant pair of digits assumed to be for R, the middle pair for G, and the least-significant pair for B. The character # precedes the hexadecimal digits to signify that this is a color specification in hexadecimal format. Here are some of the common colors expressed in this format:

```
black    #000000
red      #ff0000
green    #00ff00
blue     #0000ff
yellow   #ffff00
cyan     #00ffff
magenta  #ff00ff
white    #ffffff
```

After noticing how the standard colors are specified, you can start experimenting with new colors you want to see as background or foreground of a window. For example, you can try out a strange color for `xterm`'s background with the following line in your resource file:

```
XTerm*Background: #ccb0b0
```

Note that although RGB values of colors in hexadecimal format are often specified with six digits, the X server correctly interprets colors specified by as many as nine (three digits per component) or twelve (four digits per component) hexadecimal digits. Internally, each of the R, G, and B components are 16-bit quantities.

Font Specification

The font resource of an application usually controls how the text output looks. Like colors, fonts are specified by a name. Starting with X11R3, the font names became very descriptive. Here is an example:

```
-adobe-courier-medium-r-normal--12-120-75-75-m-60-iso8859-1
```

For this font, `adobe` is the maker, `courier` is the family, and the font is of `medium` weight (it can be `bold`, for example). The `r` indicates that the font is roman. An `i` at this position indicates italic, and `o`, oblique. The `normal` is a parameter for character width and spacing between characters; it also can be `condensed`, `narrow`, or `double`.

The numbers following the double dash (`--`) indicate the font's size. The `12` indicates the pixel size of the font, and `120` gives the size in one-tenth of a printer's point. The next two numbers (`75-75`) give the horizontal and vertical resolution for which the font is designed. The letter following the resolution (`m`) is the spacing—this can be `m` for monospace, `p` for proportional. The next number (`60`) is the average width of all characters in this font, measured in tenths of a pixel (in this case it is six pixels). The string `iso8859-1` identifies the character set of the font as specified by the International Standards Organization (ISO). In this case, the character set is the ISO Latin 1, a superset of the ASCII character set.

Luckily, you do not have to give the entire name when specifying a font in a resource file. You can use asterisks (*) for fields that can be arbitrary. For example, suppose you want the VT100 window in `xterm` to use a medium weight 12-point `courier` font. With a judicious sprinkling of asterisks, you can specify this as follows:

```
*VT100*Font: -*-courier-medium-r-normal--*-120-*-*-*-*-iso8859-1
```

This is the recommended way to specify a font name—with 14 hyphens in the pattern, one of which is the first character. You can substitute an asterisk (*) for any field in the pattern. When you specify a well-formed font name in this format, the X server is able to provide a matching font by deriving one from a scalable font. (A *scalable font* is one from which fonts of arbitrary size can be derived.)

Resource Specification on Command Line

In addition to the command-line options described so far, there is an additional option, `-xrm`, accepted by most X applications (in particular those based on the X toolkits), that enables the user to pass a string to the resource manager. For example, when starting `xterm`, you could turn the background to light cyan with this command:

```
xterm -xrm "XTerm*Background: light cyan" &
```

Summary

This chapter provides a guided tour of some interesting X applications so that you can get a feel for the appearance and behavior of them before writing one on your own. The `xterm` terminal emulator is an indispensable application in the suite of programs that accompanies the X software distribution. You use this DEC VT-102-compatible terminal emulator to interact with the local as well as the remote system and to start X clients. Other commonly distributed X applications include the clock (`xclock`) and calculator (`xcalc`) desk accessories, utilities to save (`xwd`) and view (`xwud`) the image of a window, and `xwininfo` and `xlswins` to get information about the windows on the screen. By experimenting with these applications, you will learn that most X applications are built from a large number of windows, organized in a multilevel hierarchy.

The latter part of this chapter explains how you can customize the appearance and behavior of most X applications by specifying options on the command line or by providing values for parameters in a text file. User-configurable parameters in an X application are commonly referred to as *resources* and the text file containing the values for parameters is known as the *resource database*. The Xlib library includes a set of utility routines, collectively known as the X resource manager, that enables you to retrieve the value of a parameter from the resource database. You must follow a specific syntax when specifying the resources, but once you know the syntax, it is a straightforward process to customize an X application.

An X application is customizable only if it includes appropriate code to call the resource manager routines to read and interpret a resource file. When you develop your own applications, you should exploit the resource mechanism so that users have the option of modifying such parameters as colors and fonts used by your application. Toolkit-based applications need not worry about these details because the toolkit hides them from the application programmer.

Further Reading

Your UNIX system should have on-line manual pages for the commonly available X applications. You should consult these for complete information on the command-line options and resources available in each application. For example, by typing `man xterm`, you can get detailed information on the `xterm` application (provided your vendor has included the manual pages and your system administrator has installed them).

Resources are used extensively by X toolkit-based applications. Accordingly, Douglas Young's book on the OSF/Motif toolkit includes a good description of the X resource manager.

> Young, Douglas A. *The X Window System: Programming and Applications with Xt, OSF/Motif Edition.* Englewood-Cliffs, NJ: Prentice-Hall, 1990.

## Chapter 4

Graphical User Interfaces and X

If you are familiar with window systems such as the Macintosh Operating System and Microsoft Windows, you may be surprised to learn that the X Window System does not really offer any specific on-screen appearance. This is because the designers of the X Window System wisely refrained from imposing any requirements on how the windows are laid out. X is policy-free about how user interface objects (widgets), buttons, scrollbars, and other icons appear. All X provides is a way to create a hierarchy of windows, draw in them, and determine whether any key is struck or mouse button pressed. With X, you are free to create any appearance and behavior you like. This chapter explains what a graphical user interface is and briefly describes OSF/Motif and OPEN LOOK, two prominent graphical user interfaces based on the X Window System.

X is not a graphical user interface. It is a network windowing system, an enabling technology for heterogeneous organization-wide networks. You need examine only a handful of X applications to realize that all X applications do not interact with the user in the same way.

The Macintosh Operating System and Microsoft Windows are graphical interfaces. For example, most Macintosh applications have a menubar with a list of items, the first two of which are usually File and Edit. When you press the mouse button with the pointer in any of the items in the menubar, a pull-down menu appears. You can select an item from the pull-down menu by moving the pointer to the item and releasing it. The application's output appears in a window. Messages to the user appear in pop-up windows known as *dialog boxes*. These standard methods of interacting with a Macintosh application gives it a distinct appearance (the look) and behavior (the feel). This standard look and feel is possible because all Macintosh applications use calls to a toolbox of routines that reside in the system's read-only memory (ROM). This ROM-resident toolkit in the Apple Macintosh systems provides the capability of creating items such as menus, dialog boxes, and windows.

The X programming interface, Xlib, enables you to create windows and handle basic input and output. To create menus and dialog boxes, however, you have to write your own higher-level toolbox. This is why X is not a graphical user interface. In fact, you can use Xlib to build any graphical user interface you want.

Graphical User Interface Definition

An application's user interface determines its look and feel. When the user interface makes use of graphical objects such as windows and menus, it is called a *graphical user interface (GUI)*. You might call it a point-and-click user interface, because users generally interact with a GUI by moving the mouse pointer on the screen and clicking it. (For example, to indicate consent to the closing of a file, the user may click the mouse button with the pointer inside a box labeled OK.)

Graphical user interfaces were pioneered at the Xerox Palo Alto Research Center (PARC). Subsequently, such interfaces were made popular by Apple Computer in their Lisa and Macintosh systems. By now, graphical interfaces are available on most systems. Microsoft Windows is available for MS-DOS PCs, Presentation Manager is available for OS/2, and several interfaces built on X are available for UNIX.

Components

A GUI has four components:

◆ Window system
◆ Window manager
◆ Toolkit
◆ Style guide

The graphical *window system* organizes output on the display screen and performs the basic text and graphics drawing functions.

The *window manager* provides the mechanism by which, when several windows are on the screen, users can indicate the window with which they intend to interact. This is referred to as giving the focus to a window. To maximize the use of the limited size of the screen, the user has to be able to move windows around and resize them, and the window manager manages that. A window manager is also partly responsible for the look and feel of an application, because it usually adds a decorative frame to a window and controls how the user manipulates the windows (see Chapter 2, "Clients, Servers, and Window Managers").

The third component, the *toolkit*, is a library of routines with a well-defined programming interface. This is often called the *application programming interface (API)*, and it enables programmers to write applications that make use of the facilities of the window system and that have a consistent look and feel.

At first glance, these three components—the window system, the window manager, and the toolkit API—seem to be enough for a GUI. They are not. Unless programmers follow a common set of guidelines, the look and feel of applications built using a GUI may not be consistent. You may have seen examples of this in the Macintosh world; certain applications break the norm and do not behave at all like typical Macintosh programs. Thus, a GUI has a crucial fourth component—the *style guide*, which specifies the appearance and behavior of the user interface of an application.

You may feel that the requirement of following a style guide robs programmers of their creativity, but the style guide applies only to the common elements of the user interface of applications. It establishes basic conventions such as the relative location of File, Edit, and Help pull-down menus and the meaning of mouse button bindings. The GUI does not impose any restrictions on the specific functions that an application performs. Programmers have ample opportunity to be creative in designing these application-specific parts.

A GUI may, optionally, include a fifth component—a high-level *language* to describe the layout of a user interface. For example, the OSF/Motif GUI includes the User Interface Language (UIL) that can be used by developers to describe the user interface of an application in a plain text file. A compiler for UIL converts the text file to a binary one that is read by the application's main program during start-up. If you define an interface in UIL, you can change its look by editing and recompiling the UIL file alone.

GUI Construction with X

The window system is a basic component of any GUI. Because X is a window system, it is only natural that you can build a GUI using the facilities of X.

The basic capabilities of X are rather primitive. As mentioned previously, you can define a hierarchy of windows, draw in them, and determine when a key or a mouse button is pressed. An application with a graphical interface, on the other hand, typically enables users to interact by selecting items from menus and clicking on buttons. The toolkit for a GUI must provide routines that enable programmers to create items such as menus and buttons, display them, and handle mouse clicks in them—all with ease. Although the primitive operations in X do not include these capabilities, you can build the toolkit for a GUI by writing higher-level routines that call Xlib functions to do their job. For example, you may want to use an object-oriented approach and create a hypothetical `StaticButton` object that displays some text or a bitmap image in a window. You can then create a `CommandButton` out of this `StaticButton` by assigning a function that is called whenever the user clicks a mouse button inside the `StaticButton`'s window. Finally, a more complex `Menu` object can be constructed out of a number of `CommandButtons`.

Saying that a GUI is built from X means that the GUI's toolkit is based on Xlib, the low-level C language interface to the X protocol. Many GUI toolkits are based on another set of routines called the Xt Intrinsics which can be thought of as a library of utility functions for building other toolkits. The Xt Intrinsics is not an exclusive standard, but it is distributed with the X software from MIT and therefore used by several GUI toolkits.

X Toolkits

The standard C language interface to X, Xlib, does not include routines to create—menus and buttons, for instance. You can use a number of Xlib routines to create an application with menus and buttons, but it is much more productive to develop a well-designed library of routines that can be used to create user interfaces for any application. The Xt Intrinsics routines included in the X software have done this. These routines are collectively called the Intrinsics because they can serve as the basis of other toolkits, such as the one for the OSF/Motif GUI.

The Intrinsics do not dictate any specific look and feel, which is why they can be used as the basis for any GUI. Rather, the Xt Intrinsics are a set of utility routines that programmers can use to build user-interface components, such as labels, menus, dialog boxes, forms, and scrollbars. Think of each user-interface component, or widget, as a hierarchy of X windows with functions that operate in the window. The toolkit of a GUI is a collection of such widgets. Thus, toolkits are sometimes called *widget sets*. Chapter 13, "X Toolkits," explores the Xt Intrinsics, a few common widget sets, and shows you how to write application programs using these widgets.

Mechanism, Not Policy

You need GUI toolkits or widget sets because the architects of the X Window System wanted it to provide mechanism but not impose any policy. X includes the basic graphics functions necessary to build a user interface, but does not actually dictate any particular style of interface. This turned out to be a wise choice. Instead of fighting over the look and feel, X has ended up as the basis of almost all popular GUIs available for UNIX workstations. Among the prominent ones are OSF/Motif from the OSF and OPEN LOOK from Sun Microsystems and AT&T.

Exploring Some GUIs

OSF/Motif and OPEN LOOK are two prominent GUIs for UNIX systems, both based on the X Window System. Each of these GUIs provides a unique look and feel and includes a toolkit and a style guide for programmers. The programming interface is defined by the toolkit and, unfortunately, it is different from one GUI to another. If you plan to develop applications, one approach is to pick one of these GUIs—or develop and use your own toolkit that, for instance, conforms to the style stipulated by one of the popular GUIs.

The choice of one GUI over the other is a matter of personal preference. However, a choice may already be made for you by your workstation vendor because of the vendor's decision to include a specific GUI with that workstation. Sun Microsystems and AT&T used to be the major backers of OPEN LOOK, but now all UNIX workstation manufacturers support the OSF/Motif GUI with their hardware.

OSF/Motif

Rather than building a GUI from scratch, the OSF solicited submissions from various organizations for existing X-based user interfaces. After reviewing over 30 submissions, the OSF decided on a hybrid GUI built from parts of other user interface systems. OSF/Motif uses X as the underlying window system, includes Digital Equipment Corporation's toolkit API (a window manager with a three-dimensional look from Hewlett-Packard), and provides the look and feel of the Presentation Manager (which provides a look and feel similar to that of Microsoft Windows).

Motif Window Manager

Recall from the discussion of the Motif Window Manager in Chapter 2 that mwm enables you to move and resize windows and designate which window gets the keyboard input; it also provides a configurable menu through which you can start X client applications. As shown in Figure 4.1, mwm adds a frame around the top-level window of an application. This frame, with an optional three-dimensional look, has room for a title and gives you the capability of moving and resizing the window by pressing mouse buttons in regions of the frame known as handles. The mwm window manager also adds a System Menu that can be activated by clicking on the button to the left of the title area (see Figure 4.1). The title area and the other boxes (collectively known as *gadgets*) added to the frame have been taken from Presentation Manager and Microsoft Windows.

Figure 4.1.
Frame and menu added by the Motif Window Manager.

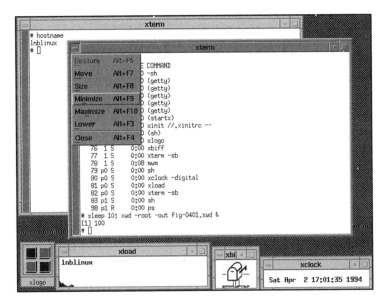

Motif Toolkit

The OSF/Motif toolkit (widget set and convenience routines) is based on the Xt Intrinsics. There are a large number of widgets in the toolkit. Shell widgets are used as the top level window of an application and cause the display of Menus and Dialog Boxes through which to get user's selections. The Text widget is available for editing text, and a variety of Labels, ArrowButtons, ScrollBars, and Lists are useful for constructing other customized components of an application's user interface.

Motif widgets have the three-dimensional appearance of a raised button, achieved by shading the boundary of the button's rectangle. The magnified version of the upper-right corner of a Motif window frame illustrates the type of shading used to achieve this effect (see Figure 4.2). Reversing the shading of the top and bottom areas creates the illusion of a button being pressed down.

Another interesting feature of the Motif widgets is that you can specify the size of objects in several different units. By default, the Motif toolkit assumes that all sizes are specified in pixels, but you can set the unit type to a device-independent one, such as 1/100 of a millimeter, 1/1000 of an inch, 1/100 of a point, or 1/100 of a font size.

Figure 4.2.
Magnified version of Motif window frame showing three-dimensional shading.

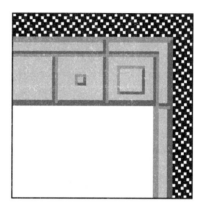

OSF/Motif Style Guide

The OSF/Motif style guide specifies the way an application should interact with the user. The style guide states how to indicate that a particular window is to receive all future keystrokes, how to move around in the screen, and how to perform common tasks, such as selecting one or more objects for an operation.

The primary goal of these specifications is to promote consistency. All applications with similar menus and dialog boxes should act in a similar manner. The menu selections for an application should be presented to the user in an orderly manner.

The secondary goal is to enable the user to perform tasks by manipulating graphical representations of objects displayed on the screen. Such direct manipulations include pushing a button to start some action and dragging a slider to scroll the display.

Flexibility is another key concern of the style guide. Users should be able to perform a task in many different ways. There should be ways of performing actions through a menu selection or by pressing a special combination of keys. (This requirement comes from Motif's Microsoft Windows and Presentation Manager heritage.) Users should also be able to specify parameters, such as colors, fonts, and key bindings, through resource files. This means that applications should make use of the X resource manager to access these user-specified resources. (See Chapter 3, "Exploring X Applications," for a description of the X resource manager.)

The Motif style guide also requires applications to provide as much help information as possible. This information should depend on context. For example, if the user asks for help while attempting to print a document, the information displayed should pertain to printing and not something else. Applications are also expected to request confirmation from the user whenever an action may irreversibly destroy anything. For example, if the user selects the Quit option from the menu while working on a drawing, the application must ask for confirmation through a dialog box that asks the question `Do you want to save this drawing?`.

Because the window manager determines part of the look and feel of a GUI, the style guide also specifies the requirements to be met by any window manager meant for the OSF/Motif environment. The guidelines for window managers should not concern you unless you plan to write a new window manager.

Next to the Motif toolkit, the style guide is the most important document for application developers. You can learn most of the stylistic requirements by using existing Motif applications. For detailed information, consult the Motif Style Guide from the OSF (see the Further Reading section at the end of this chapter).

OPEN LOOK

OPEN LOOK from Sun Microsystems and AT&T is another commercially available GUI. OPEN LOOK is also based on the X Window System and includes the OPEN LOOK Window Manager (`olwm`), a toolkit API, and a user interface standard. The OPEN LOOK GUI started out as a set of specifications that describes the standard elements of the OPEN LOOK user interface and the way the user works with the interface. AT&T and Sun Microsystems jointly developed the OPEN LOOK GUI specifications and released the information in two books published by Addison-Wesley in 1990 (see the Further Reading section at the end of this chapter). Anyone interested in developing an OPEN LOOK GUI can do so by following the specifications; the actual choice of the hardware and windowing system is irrelevant. However, anyone wishing to sell a GUI based on the OPEN LOOK specifications has to license the rights to these specifications from AT&T, the owner of the OPEN LOOK GUI specifications.

The *OPEN LOOK GUI Application Style Guidelines* emphasizes that there is no single product named OPEN LOOK; rather, there are products that conform to the OPEN LOOK GUI specifications. One such product is Sun Microsystems' *OpenWindows*, a windowing environment based on the X11/NeWS Window System that combines the X Window System and Sun's Network Extensible Window System (NeWS). The `OpenWindows` environment conforms to the OPEN LOOK GUI specifications and includes the OPEN LOOK Window Manager (`olwm`). As if to underscore the point that the OPEN LOOK interface is independent of the toolkit, Sun and AT&T provide three distinct OPEN LOOK toolkits:

✦ OLIT—the OPEN LOOK Intrinsics Toolkit (also known as AT&T's OPEN LOOK X Toolkit, Xt+, and Xol), which is built on the MIT Xt Intrinsics and provides widgets with a three-dimensional appearance.

✦ XView—a toolkit patterned after Sun Microsystems' SunView programming interface and layered atop Xlib.

✦ tNt—a toolkit for creating OPEN LOOK applications with Sun's NeWS Development Environment. OLIT and XView use X as the window system; NDE is based on Sun's NeWS, which, in turn, relies on an extension of the PostScript page description language.

To support these two window systems, Sun has merged X and NeWS into a combined X11/NeWS window system. The OPEN LOOK window manager and the XView toolkit are included in the X Window System (X11R4) from the MIT X Consortium.

Look and Feel

When designing the OPEN LOOK GUI, Sun Microsystems started with the pioneering work on GUIs at Xerox PARC. The goal of the project was to design a user interface that is simple, consistent, and efficient. In keeping with these design goals, OPEN LOOK sports an uncluttered and consistent layout. The design team paid particular attention to certain problems with point-and-click interfaces on large display screens. For example, if the up and down arrows of a vertical scrollbar are located at its extremities, the user has to move the mouse a lot when scrolling back and forth. In OPEN LOOK, the up and down arrows of the scrollbar are placed at either end of the thumbwheel, placing all the controls of the scrollbar together and making it convenient to switch from scrolling one way to another.

OPEN LOOK provides all the amenities users take for granted in a GUI. Windows are resized by moving the mouse pointer to one of the four corners, pressing the left button, and dragging it to enlarge or reduce the window. At the top of each window is a header where the window manager displays the window title. Each window has a menu that can be activated by pressing the window menu button (the rectangle with a down arrow) that appears in the left edge of the header. The window menu enables the user to close the window, quit the application, and alter some other characteristics of the window. Windows also have a footer area. Applications can display status and error messages in this area.

Pushpins and Menu Buttons

Pushpins and menu buttons (called *button stacks* prior to OPEN LOOK Release 2.0) are two unique features of the OPEN LOOK GUI. The OPEN LOOK pushpin, which looks like a real-life pushpin, appears in many menus and pop-up windows. At first, the pushpin appears lying next to a hole. By clicking on the pin, you can insert the pin into the hole. Once this is done, that window stays visible (*pinned*) on the screen. To get rid of the window, you have to click on the pinned pushpin. This pops the pushpin out of the hole and the pinned window disappears.

> **NOTE:**
>
> Motif (Version 1.2 and later) also enables the user to pin menus on the screen—in Motif, this feature is called *tear-off menus.*

In OPEN LOOK, a menu button is shown as a button with a downward arrow (called the *menu mark*) next to the label. A menu button behaves the same way that an entry in the menubar found in the Microsoft Windows or Macintosh environments does. When the user presses the left mouse button on the menu button, a menu appears underneath the button. The user then selects a menu item by dragging the mouse to the desired item and releasing the button.

Summary

A graphical user interface (GUI) is a user interface that makes use of windows, menus, and other graphical objects and that, to a large extent, enables users to interact with the application by pointing and clicking mouse buttons. From an application developer's point of view, a GUI is a combination of a window manager, a style guide, and a library of routines (toolkit) that can be used to build the user interface.

By design, the X Window System provides the basic functions that can be used to build a graphical user interface (GUI), but does not require the programmer to follow any specific style. Because of this, X itself is not a GUI, but many GUIs are built upon X. OSF/Motif and OPEN LOOK are examples of such GUIs. Each GUI has its unique style and terminology, but neither offers enough benefits over the other to be the clear winner. Both OSF/Motif and OPEN LOOK provide adequate facilities for building user interfaces for applications. The choice of one over another is dictated primarily by personal taste. However, often a choice is made for the user because of the workstation vendor's decision to pick one GUI over another. Because most workstation vendors provide the Motif GUI with their workstations, Motif has emerged as the winner in the marketplace.

Further Reading

The article by Brad Myers provides a description number of window managers, which he classifies according to common elements in their look and feel. Myers uses the term *window manager* to mean a GUI.

For the official word on all aspects of OSF/Motif, you may want to get the OSF's five-volume set on Motif published by Prentice Hall. If you use OPEN LOOK, your choice will be the two volumes from Sun Microsystems.

Myers, Brad A. "A Taxonomy of Window Manager User Interfaces." *IEEE Computer Graphics & Applications* (September 1988): 65-84.

Open Software Foundation. *Application Environment Specification (AES) User Environment Volume.* Englewood-Cliffs, NJ: Prentice Hall, 1993.

———. *OSF/Motif Programmer's Guide.* Englewood Cliffs, NJ: Prentice Hall, 1993.

———. *OSF/Motif Programmer's Reference.* Englewood Cliffs, NJ: Prentice Hall, 1993.

———. *OSF/Motif Style Guide.* Englewood Cliffs, NJ: Prentice Hall, 1993.

———. *OSF/Motif User's Guide.* Englewood Cliffs, NJ: Prentice Hall, 1993.

Sun Microsystems, Inc. *OPEN LOOK Graphical User Interface Application Style Guide.* Reading, MA: Addison-Wesley, 1990.

———. *OPEN LOOK Graphical User Interface Functional Specification.* Reading, MA: Addison-Wesley, 1990.

## Part Two

Programming the
X Window System

## Chapter 5

A Simple X Application

In the first part of this book, you became familiar with the X Window System as a user. You saw how to start X on a workstation, run X applications, and customize them through resource files. Now you are ready to develop your first X program. This chapter starts you with an X version of the classic C program that prints `Hello, World` on your screen. The example shows the structure and the parts of a simple X application from this example. This chapter demonstrates the steps involved in compiling and linking an X application as well as the benefits of using the `make` utility to automate these tasks.

X Version of the Classic Example: *xhello*

You probably remember, from when you learned the C programming language, the following snippet of code that prints `Hello, World`:

```
#include <stdio.h>

main()
{
    printf("Hello, World\n");
}
```

Your first program for the X Window System does the same thing, except that `Hello, World` appears in an X window. You develop it as a fairly complete X application that you can use as a model for your own programs. The program accepts common command-line options and enables users to set resources such as the font and the foreground and background colors. This chapter describes the steps that the program must follow to do this, then identifies the Xlib functions required to do the job, explains how to draw in an X window, and finally, shows a complete listing of `xhello.c`, the source code for the executable program `xhello`.

Specifying *xhello*

First specify what you expect from `xhello`. The program should do the following things:

♦ Create two X windows—one to display the message and the other to act as an Exit button

♦ Display the `Hello, World` message using a specified foreground color and font

♦ Assume default values for the font and the background and foreground colors, but, if a resource file is present (usually the `.Xdefaults` file in the home directory of the user), accept values for these resources from that file

♦ Enable users to specify as command-line options the display where output should appear and the size and location (geometry) of the window

♦ Provide a convenient way to exit from the program

♦ Enable users to customize the text that appears in the main window and the Exit button, using command-line options as well as resources

Designing *xhello*

The first step in designing an X program is to determine the hierarchy of windows. Based on the specification of what you want `xhello` to do, you need one X window—the main window—to display the string `Hello, World`. The Exit button can be another X window and should appear inside the main window; therefore, you can make it a child of the main window. This gives you a window hierarchy such as the one shown in Figure 5.1. The figure also shows the layout of the windows on the screen.

Figure 5.1.

Hierarchy and layout of windows for `xhello`.

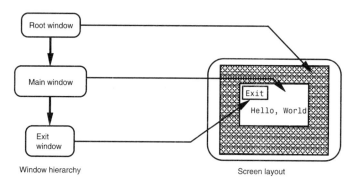

User-Customizable Resources

Having decided on the number of windows and their hierarchy, you can go on to the task of deciding which of xhello's resources should be customizable by the user. Table 5.1 provides a list of those resources. The first column shows the exact name of the resource. This is the name that is used when xhello queries the value of the resource. Users can specify resources with wildcards. For example, you can use the following resource specification to indicate that a 12-point Courier font should be used to display all text in xhello:

```
xhello*font: -*-courier-*-r-*--*-120-*-*-*-*-iso8859-1
```

Table 5.1. xhello's Resources

Name	Description
xhello.background	Background color of the main window
xhello.foreground	Foreground color of the main window
xhello.font	Name of font to be used for text displayed in the main window
xhello.geometry	Size and location of the main window
xhello.text	Text to appear in main window (default is Hello, World)
xhello.exit.background	Background color for the Exit button
xhello.exit.foreground	Foreground color for the Exit button
xhello.exit.font	Name of font to be used for text displayed in the Exit button
xhello.exit.text	Text to appear in the Exit button

This example will include a resource named text that specifies what appears in each of the windows. The resource xhello.text is the text to be displayed in the main window, and xhello.exit.text indicates what appears inside the Exit button. There also will be command-line options to handle these two settings.

Command-Line Options

The xhello program accepts four command line options: -display, -geometry, -msgtext, and -extext. This example enables the user to abbreviate the options to -d, -g, -m, and -e, respectively.

The -display option specifies the X display where xhello's output should appear. If the option is not specified, xhello uses the display specified by the environment variable DISPLAY. An example of this option might be the following:

```
xhello -display sysname:0 &
```

where *sysname* is the name of the workstation where output is sent.

The -geometry option specifies a preferred size and location for xhello's main window. You can display Hello, World in a 100-pixel-by-100-pixel window at the upper-right corner of the screen with the following command:

```
xhello -geometry 100x100+0+0 &
```

The -msgtext and -extext options enable users to specify the text that appears in the main window and in the Exit button. For example, to display the message All Done in the main window and OK in the Exit button, you invoke xhello:

```
xhello -mtext "All Done" -etext OK
```

Implementing *xhello*

To implement xhello, you have to know the standard steps that an X application must follow. This chapter summarizes the steps and shows you how xhello implements them. Chapter 6, "The Xlib Programming Model," reviews them in further detail. The goal here is to give you an overall view of a complete Xlib-based X application. If some details are not explained fully, do not despair. Subsequent chapters cover them.

At a minimum, an X application should do the following:

1. Get any command-line options that the user may have specified.

2. Open a connection to the display. Use the XOpenDisplay function. If the user has specified a name with the -display command option, use that name.

3. Load resources using the resource manager routines (the routines whose names start with the Xrm prefix) in Xlib.

4. Set up fonts and colors based on the values specified in the resource file. If there is no resource file, use reasonable default values. You use the Xlib routines XLoadQueryFont, XParseColor, and XAllocColor in this step.

5. Decide the initial position and size of the top window. Allocate an XSizeHints structure (by calling the XAllocSizeHints routine) and fill out the appropriate fields. The XSizeHints structure is used in step 7 to inform the window manager. Use the XGeometry function to process the geometry specification here.

6. Create the top-level window of the application, using position, size, and colors set up in the previous steps. Use the Xlib routine XCreateSimpleWindow for this. Save the window identification (ID) number returned by XCreateSimpleWindow for future use.

7. Set window manager properties to inform the window manager of the desired size and location of the top-level window. Also set the minimum width and height of the window, the name of the window (displayed in the title area), and the name of the icon (displayed when the window is reduced to an icon). Use the Xlib routines XStringListToTextProperty and XSetWMProperties.

8. Create a graphics context (GC) for the top-level window, using the XCreateGC function. The graphics context is a structure containing information about the font and foreground and background colors.

9. Set any necessary window attributes. For example, set the colormap for the main window so that the window manager knows which colormap to use for this application. You also can set an attribute known as the Bit Gravity to reduce the need to repaint the window when it is exposed.

10. Select which of the events occurring in the top window should be processed by the application. Typically, Expose events are the ones selected. Use the XSelectInput routine for this step.

11. Make the top-level window visible using the XMapWindow function. This is known as *mapping* the window.

12. Create the rest of the windows in the hierarchy. Save the window ID for each window so that you can identify the windows later. Select the events to be reported for each of the child windows. Make each window visible. Create more graphics contexts, if needed.

13. Read, interpret, and process events in a loop. Use XNextEvent to get event reports from the server. To interpret an event, look at the window ID and the type of event. Decide what to do based on this information. For example, in xhello, a mouse buttonpress inside the Exit window should break the event handling loop. All application-specific work is done in this step.

14. When done, destroy the top window (using XDestroyWindow), close the connection to the server by calling XCloseDisplay, and exit the program with a call to the C run-time library function exit.

The following sections examine how you can implement these steps.

Command-Line Options and Resources

A common mechanism handles both command-line options and resource specifications. As you might already know, in a C program, the command-line options are received in an array of character pointers. For example, if your main function is the following:

```
main(int argc, char **argv)
{
/* command-line arguments are in argv */
    .
    .
    .
}
```

then argc is the number of arguments and argv is the array of strings representing the arguments. The first argument, argv[0] is the program name. If xhello is invoked with this command line:

```
xhello -msgtext "Goodbye, World!" -extext Bye
```

then argc is 5 and the arguments are the following:

```
argv[0] = xhello
argv[1] = -msgtext
argv[2] = Goodbye, World!
argv[3] = -extext
argv[4] = Bye
```

All options have a name (-msgtext) and a corresponding value (Goodbye, World!). The situation is similar with resources. There is a resource name, and when you call XGetDefault with this name, a character pointer to the value is returned.

You can handle both command-line options and resources conveniently through a single mechanism:

1. Define char * variables that point to character representations of user-customizable parameters. For example, the char * variable display_name points to the name of the display, and the variables mbgcolor and mfgcolor respectively contain the names of foreground and background colors for the main window.

2. Define an XHELLO_PARAMS structure with a name and a pointer to a character string representing a value:

```
typedef struct XHELLO_PARAMS
{
    char *name;
    char *cname;
    char **p_value_string;
} XHELLO_PARAMS;
```

The value of an option whose name is in the name field is stored in the string whose address is in the p_value_string field. Suppose you define an array of XHELLO_PARAMS structures describing the acceptable command-line options:

```
/* List of command-line options */

XHELLO_PARAMS options[] =
{
    "-display",   "-d", &display_name,
    "-geometry",  "-g", &mgeom_cline,
    "-msgtext",   "-m", &msgtext_cline,
    "-extext",    "-e", &extext_cline
};

int num_options = sizeof(options) / sizeof(XHELLO_PARAMS);
```

where the name field of each XHELLO_PARAMS structure is initialized to the name of an option, and the p_value_string field is set to the address of an appropriate char * variable. The cname field is used to store a shorter name for the option. For example, display_name is the string where the value of options -display and -d are to be stored.

Some of these char * variables end with the _cline suffix, which indicates that this value is set through the command line. Users can also set these parameters through a resource file. By storing the two values separately, you can decide which one to use in the program.

With this table in hand, you can process all command-line options with a simple loop:

```
int i, j;
.
.
for (i = 1; i < argc; i += 2)
{
    for(j = 0; j < num_options; j++)
    {
        if(strcmp(options[j].name, argv[i]) == 0 ||
           strcmp(options[j].cname, argv[i]) == 0)
        {
            *options[j].p_value_string = argv[i+1];
            break;
        }
    }
    if(j >= num_options)
        usage();
}
```

The loop starts at index 1 because argv[0] always refers to the program's name. Also, each option in xhello is expected to have a value, which is why all arguments are processed in pairs. If an unknown argument is encountered, the usage function is called. This function exits after printing a message showing how xhello should be called.

In case of resources, the situation is handled similarly. First, define a resource table:

```
/* List of user-customizable resources */

XHELLO_PARAMS resources[] =
{
    "xhello.background"     , "XHello.Background", &mbgcolor,
    "xhello.foreground"     , "XHello.Foreground", &mfgcolor,
    "xhello.font"           , "XHello.Font",        &mfont,
    "xhello.geometry"       , "XHello.Geometry",   &mgeom_rsrc,
    "xhello.text"           , "XHello.Text",       &msgtext_rsrc,
    "xhello.exit.background", "XHello.Exit.Background", &ebgcolor,
    "xhello.exit.foreground", "XHello.Exit.Foreground", &efgcolor,
    "xhello.exit.font"      , "XHello.Exit.Font", &efont,
    "xhello.exit.text"      , "XHello.Exit.Text", &extext_rsrc
};

int num_resources = sizeof(resources) / sizeof(XHELLO_PARAMS);
```

As in the options table, the first entry in each line is the name of a resource and the second entry is the address of a string where the value of that resource will be stored. The variables with the _rsrc suffix denote values obtained through the resource database mechanism.

To process resources, you have to open a connection to the display. Assuming this is done, and p_disp is a pointer to the display, you can read in all the resources by calling X resource manager functions in a loop:

```
    char                rfilename[80];
    char                *type;
    XrmValue            value;
    XrmDatabase         rdb;
    .
    .
    XrmInitialize();
```

```
/* Read resources from .Xdefaults file in user's home directory */
    strcpy(rfilename, getenv("HOME"));
    strcat(rfilename, "/.Xdefaults");
    rdb = XrmGetFileDatabase(rfilename);

    if(rdb != NULL)
    {
        for (i = 0; i < num_resources; i++)
        {
            if(XrmGetResource(rdb, resources[i].name,
                              resources[i].cname,
                              &type, &value))
            {
                *resources[i].p_value_string = value.addr;
            }
        }
    }
```

Connection to the X Display

Every X program must open a connection to display before it can use the facilities of the X server. You use the routine XOpenDisplay for this purpose. Call this function with the name of the display as an argument. It returns a pointer to a Display data structure. You must save this pointer because it is needed in all operations with the X server. You should treat the returned pointer in the same way you treat the pointer to FILE returned by the C library routine fopen.

In xhello, the name of the display is the string display_name. It is initialized to a null string, but it can be overridden by a -display or -d command-line option. Thus, in xhello, XOpenDisplay is called as follows:

```
char        *display_name = NULL /* Name of X display       */
Display     *p_disp;             /* Connection to X display */
    .
    .
    if ((p_disp = XOpenDisplay(display_name)) == NULL)
    {
        fprintf(stderr, "%s: can't open display named %s\n",
                argv[0], XDisplayName(display_name));
        exit(1);
    }
```

If display_name is NULL, the XOpenDisplay function gets the name of the display from the environment variable DISPLAY. When printing the error message, the macro XDisplayName is used to get the name of the X display so that the name is correct even when display_name is NULL.

Fonts and Colors

In X, fonts and colors are resources (the kind that denote objects maintained in the X server, not the user-customizable parameters), and they have to be created at the server before using them. You use an Xlib routine, XLoadQueryFont, to locate a font in the server by its name and, if found, load it for use. What you get back is a pointer to an XFontStruct structure that holds information about the font (width and height of characters, for instance). As with the Display pointer, you have to save this pointer so that you can use the font in the future.

Handling colors is complicated in X, but in xhello, you dodge the issues by using the default colormap and by asking for white and black colors only. Almost all servers should be able to satisfy the request for these colors. As with the font, you use XParseColor to parse the name of a color into its RGB components in an XColor structure. Then you call XAllocColor with the colormap and the XColor structure to get back a pixel value that you can use in the future.

Window Size

In xhello, pick the size of the main window by computing the sizes of the Exit button and the size of the string to be displayed in the main window (Hello, World, by default). Use the XTextWidth function to determine the width of a text string (in pixels) in a specific font. For example, to pick the size of the Exit button, you use the following:

```
if(extext_cline != NULL) extext = extext_cline;
else
    if(extext_rsrc != NULL) extext = extext_rsrc;

if(msgtext_cline != NULL) msgtext = msgtext_cline;
else
    if(msgtext_rsrc != NULL) msgtext = msgtext_rsrc;

extxt = efontstruct->max_bounds.width / 2;
eytxt = efontstruct->max_bounds.ascent +
        efontstruct->max_bounds.descent;
ewidth = extxt + XTextWidth(efontstruct, extext,
                            strlen(extext)) + 4;
eheight = eytxt + 4;
```

Here, extext_cline and extext_rsrc are the character strings for the Exit button specified by the command line and resource file, respectively. The string actually used is named extext. The first if...else block selects the string to be used. The command-line option gets precedence over the resource file. If none are specified, extext defaults to the string Exit.

NOTE:

X expects dimensions and positions of windows in pixels.

The variables extxt and eytxt are integers representing the *x* and *y* position of the string in the Exit button. Note that efontstruct is the pointer to the XFontStruct structure containing information on the font to be used for the Exit button.

The width and height of the Exit window, ewidth and eheight, are based on the width of the string and the height of the characters. A padding of four pixels is added to each.

Once you know the size of the Exit button, you can decide on the size of the main window by getting the width and height of the text string that will appear in it. The initial size and position of this top-level window should be set in an XSizeHints structure so that the information can later be passed to the window manager. The initial location of the window can be in the center of the screen. The following code achieves this:

```
XSizeHints    *p_xsh;       /* Size hints for window manager */
    .
    .

if((p_xsh = XAllocSizeHints()) == NULL)
{
    fprintf(stderr, "Error allocating size hints!\n");
    exit(1);
}
    .
    .

p_xsh->flags = (PPosition | PSize | PMinSize);
p_xsh->height = mfontstruct->max_bounds.ascent +
                mfontstruct->max_bounds.descent + eheight + 10;
p_xsh->min_height = p_xsh->height;
p_xsh->width = XTextWidth(mfontstruct, msgtext, strlen(msgtext)) + 2;
p_xsh->width = max(p_xsh->width,ewidth);

p_xsh->min_width = p_xsh->width;
p_xsh->x = (DisplayWidth(p_disp, DefaultScreen(p_disp)) -
            p_xsh->width) / 2;
p_xsh->y = (DisplayHeight(p_disp, DefaultScreen(p_disp)) -
            p_xsh->height) / 2;
```

Here, msgtext is the string for the main window and mfontstruct is the pointer to XFontStruct for the font to be used in the main window. Notice how the macros DisplayWidth and DisplayHeight are used to get the width and height of a screen in a display. The screen itself is identified by the DefaultScreen macro, meaning that you want the size of the default screen of that display (usually screen 0). (See Chapter 2, "Clients, Servers, and Window Managers," for a description of X displays.)

The flags field in the XSizeHints structure says that you are setting the preferred position, size, and minimum size of the window. Once the size and position of the top-level window is known, you should prepare a default geometry string. (Chapter 3, "Exploring X Applications," shows how to specify the geometry in X applications.) In xhello, this is done with the following code:

```
char *mgeom;               /* Actual geometry string  */
char default_geometry[80];  /* Default geometry string */
    .
    .

/* Construct a default geometry string */
    sprintf(default_geometry, "%dx%d+%d+%d", xsh.width,
            xsh.height, xsh.x, xsh.y);
    mgeom = default_geometry;

/* Override the geometry, if necessary */
    if(mgeom_cline != NULL) mgeom = mgeom_cline;
    else
        if(mgeom_rsrc != NULL) mgeom = mgeom_rsrc;
```

This default geometry is used with the user-specified geometry (through the `-geometry` option or the `geometry` resource) in a call to the function `XGeometry`. This function returns an integer with specific bits set to indicate whether the user-specified geometry overrides any of the fields (width, height, and x, y positions) in the default geometry. All necessary changes are recorded in the `flags` field of the `XSizeHints` structure. This structure is later sent to the window manager.

```
/* Process the geometry specification */
    bitmask = XGeometry(p_disp, DefaultScreen(p_disp), mgeom,
                 default_geometry, DEFAULT_BDWIDTH,
                 mfontstruct->max_bounds.width,
                 mfontstruct->max_bounds.ascent +
                 mfontstruct->max_bounds.descent,
                 1, 1, &(xsh.x), &(xsh.y),
                 &(xsh.width), &(xsh.height));

/* Check bitmask and set flags in XSizeHints structure */
    if (bitmask & (XValue | YValue)) xsh.flags |= USPosition;
    if (bitmask & (WidthValue | HeightValue))
                              xsh.flags |= USSize;
```

Window Creation

Once the position and size of the top window is known, you can create the window by calling `XCreateSimpleWindow`:

```
Window Main;   /* Window ID of main window */
    .

    .
    Main = XCreateSimpleWindow(p_disp, DefaultRootWindow(p_disp),
                 xsh.x, xsh.y, xsh.width, xsh.height,
                 DEFAULT_BDWIDTH, mfgpix, mbgpix);
```

The first argument to `XCreateSimpleWindow` identifies the X display. The second argument is the parent of this window. In this case, the parent is the root window, identified by the macro `DefaultRootWindow(p_disp)`. You have to save the window identification number, `Main`, for future use.

After the window is created, inform the window manager of the name of the window, the command-line arguments used to start the application, and the size hints. You use the following call to do this:

```
/* Set up a class hint structure */
    if((p_ch = XAllocClassHint()) == NULL)
    {
        fprintf(stderr, "Error allocating class hint!\n");
        exit(1);
    }
    p_ch->res_name = app_name;
    p_ch->res_class = "XHello";

/* Set up XTextProperty for window name and icon name */
    if(XStringListToTextProperty(&window_title, 1, &wname) == 0)
    {
```

```
            fprintf(stderr, "Error creating XTextProperty!\n");
            exit(1);
    }
    if(XStringListToTextProperty(&window_title, 1, &iname) == 0)
    {
            fprintf(stderr, "Error creating XTextProperty!\n");
            exit(1);
    }

/* Set up window manager hints */
    if((p_xwmh = XAllocWMHints()) == NULL)
    {
            fprintf(stderr, "Error allocating Window Manager hints!\n");
            exit(1);
    }
    p_xwmh->flags = (InputHint|StateHint);
    p_xwmh->input = False;
    p_xwmh->initial_state = NormalState;
    XSetWMProperties(p_disp, Main, &wname, &iname, argv, argc,
                     p_xsh, p_xwmh, p_ch);
```

The window manager saves all supplied information as data items attached to the main window in the server. These are known as *properties* and can be retrieved by calling specific Xlib routines. The window manager also uses the size hints to decide where to place the window and how far the window can be shrunk by the user.

The hints tell the window manager about certain aspects of the application's behavior. For xhello, the hints specify that the window should appear normally (not as an icon) and that xhello does not accept input focus.

Graphics Context Creation

In X, the *graphics context* (GC) is a structure that holds all relevant information for drawing text and graphics in a window. This information includes the foreground and background colors and the font. You use the XCreateGC to create a GC. For example, a GC with specific background, foreground, and font is created with the following:

```
GC            theGC,  /* The graphics context for main     */
XGCValues     gcv;    /* Structure used to set fields in GC */

unsigned long mfgpix, mbgpix;    /* Pixel values */
    .
    .
    .
    gcv.font = mfontstruct->fid;
    gcv.foreground = mfgpix;
    gcv.background = mbgpix;
    theGC = XCreateGC(p_disp, Main,
              (GCFont | GCForeground | GCBackground), &gcv);
```

Event Solicitation

The application has to inform the X server what events it wants reported. You can select a specific set of events for each individual window. For example, in xhello, you want to know if the main window is exposed (whether it needs to be redrawn). You can select this event with the following function call:

```
XSelectInput(p_disp, Main, ExposureMask);
```

Window Mapping

In the X Window System, as in most other window systems, creating a window is not enough to make it visible. You have to explicitly *map*, or make the window visible, by calling XMapWindow. The following call maps the main window in xhello:

```
XMapWindow(p_disp, main);
```

Child Windows

The main window is more difficult to create than its children because when creating the main window, your application is taking over a part of the screen that requires it to be courteous and give the window manager and the user every opportunity to decide where the window appears. Child windows, on the other hand, are confined to their parent. What your application does with its child windows does not affect any other windows on the screen. Thus, creating child windows requires the following:

◆ Calls to XCreateSimpleWindow with the proper arguments

◆ Creation of separate graphics contexts where necessary

◆ Mapping of the child windows

The following function calls perform this task for the sole child window in xhello:

```
/* Create the child window */
    ex = 1;
    ey = 1;
    Exit = XCreateSimpleWindow(p_disp, Main, ex, ey,
                ewidth, eheight, DEFAULT_BDWIDTH,
                efgpix, ebgpix);

/* Select events to be reported */
    XSelectInput(p_disp, Exit, ExposureMask |
                                ButtonPressMask);
/* Map it */
    XMapWindow(p_disp, Exit);

/* Create a separate GC */
    gcv.font = efontstruct->fid;
    gcv.foreground = efgpix;
    gcv.background = ebgpix;
    exitGC = XCreateGC(p_disp, Exit, (GCFont | GCForeground |
                    GCBackground), &gcv);
```

The Event Loop

An application's event loop is where all the action takes place. Up to now, you have been setting up windows for X. In the event loop, you retrieve events and process them. Each event comes tagged with the window where it occurred and its type. In xhello, the handling loop looks like the following:

```
{
    int Done = 0;
    .
    .
    .
    while (!Done)
    {
        XNextEvent(p_disp, &theEvent);
        if(theEvent.xany.window == Main)
        {
/* Handle events for the main window */
            .
            .
            .
        }
        if(theEvent.xany.window == Exit)
        {
/* Handle events occurring in the Exit window */
            switch(theEvent.type)
            {
                case Expose:
                    if (theEvent.xexpose.count == 0)
                    {
                        XClearWindow(p_disp, Exit);
                        XDrawString(p_disp, Exit, exitGC, extxt,
                            eytxt, extext, strlen(extext));
                    }
                    break;

                case ButtonPress:
                    Done = 1;
            }
        }
    }
/* Clean up and exit */

    XFreeGC(p_disp, theGC);
    XFreeGC(p_disp, exitGC);
    XUnloadFont(p_disp, mfontstruct->fid);
    XUnloadFont(p_disp, efontstruct->fid);
    XDestroyWindow(p_disp, Main);
    XCloseDisplay(p_disp);
    exit(0);
}
```

The only event that should be reported for the main window is the Expose event. The Exit window gets the Expose as well as mouse buttonpresses. The standard response to the Expose event is to redraw the contents of the window. You can see how this is done for the Exit window. The window is first cleared by calling XClearWindow. Then the string is repainted by XDrawString.

The buttonpress in the Exit button should terminate xhello. This is handled by setting the flag Done to 1, which causes the while loop to exit. The GCs are released by calling XFreeGC and the top window is destroyed by calling XDestroyWindow. Finally, the XCloseDisplay breaks the connection to the display. The program then exits by calling the C library routine exit with a status code of 0 to indicate no error.

Putting It All Together

This chapter has shown the steps necessary to set up the windows in an X application and a good way to handle command-line options and resources. Now it is time to put it all together so that you can see how a complete X application is constructed. Listing 5.1 shows xhello.c. This is the source code of xhello, the program that displays Hello, World (and a lot more) in X.

Listing 5.1. xhello.c—Saying "Hello, World" in X.

```
/*----------------------------------------------------------*/
/*  File: xhello.c
 *
 *  Display "Hello, World" in an X window. User can exit by
 *  pressing a mouse button in the "Exit" button.
 *
 */
#include <stdio.h>
#include <string.h>
#include <stdlib.h>

#include <X11/Xlib.h>
#include <X11/Xutil.h>
#include <X11/Xresource.h>

#define max(x,y)      (((x) > (y)) ? (x) : (y))

#define DEFAULT_MAIN_TEXT      "Hello, World"
#define DEFAULT_EXIT_TEXT      "Exit"

#define DEFAULT_BGCOLOR        "white"
#define DEFAULT_FGCOLOR        "black"
#define DEFAULT_BDWIDTH        1
#define DEFAULT_FONT           "fixed"

typedef struct XHELLO_PARAMS
{
    char *name;
    char *cname;
    char **p_value_string;
} XHELLO_PARAMS;

/* Default parameter values (as strings) */
char *mbgcolor      = DEFAULT_BGCOLOR,
     *mfgcolor      = DEFAULT_FGCOLOR,
     *mfont         = DEFAULT_FONT,
     *ebgcolor      = DEFAULT_BGCOLOR,
```

continues

Listing 5.1. continued

```
    *efgcolor     = DEFAULT_FGCOLOR,
    *efont        = DEFAULT_FONT,
    *mgeom_rsrc   = NULL,
    *msgtext_rsrc = NULL,
    *extext_rsrc  = NULL,
    *display_name = NULL,
    *msgtext_cline= NULL,
    *extext_cline = NULL,
    *mgeom_cline  = NULL,
    *msgtext      = DEFAULT_MAIN_TEXT,
    *extext       = DEFAULT_EXIT_TEXT,
    *mgeom        = NULL;

/* List of user-customizable resources */

XHELLO_PARAMS resources[] =
{
    "xhello.background"    , "XHello.Background", &mbgcolor,
    "xhello.foreground"    , "XHello.Foreground", &mfgcolor,
    "xhello.font"          , "XHello.Font",        &mfont,
    "xhello.geometry"      , "XHello.Geometry",   &mgeom_rsrc,
    "xhello.text"          , "XHello.Text",        &msgtext_rsrc,
    "xhello.exit.background", "XHello.Exit.Background", &ebgcolor,
    "xhello.exit.foreground", "XHello.Exit.Foreground", &efgcolor,
    "xhello.exit.font"     , "XHello.Exit.Font", &efont,
    "xhello.exit.text"     , "XHello.Exit.Text", &extext_rsrc
};

int num_resources = sizeof(resources) / sizeof(XHELLO_PARAMS);

/* List of command-line options */

XHELLO_PARAMS options[] =
{
    "-display",  "-d", &display_name,
    "-geometry", "-g", &mgeom_cline,
    "-msgtext",  "-m", &msgtext_cline,
    "-extext",   "-e", &extext_cline
};

int num_options = sizeof(options) / sizeof(XHELLO_PARAMS);

char *app_name = "xhello";

/* Non-string parameters of xhello */
XFontStruct     *mfontstruct, *efontstruct;
unsigned long  mbgpix, mfgpix, ebgpix, efgpix;

/* Size and location of the Exit button */
unsigned int ewidth, eheight;
int          ex, ey, extxt, eytxt;

/* Other global variables */

XWMHints       *p_xwmh;    /* Hints for the window manager  */
```

```
XSizeHints      *p_xsh;       /* Size hints for window manager */
XClassHint      *p_ch;        /* Class hint for window manager */
XTextProperty   wname;        /* Window name for title bar    */
XTextProperty   iname;        /* Icon name for icon label      */
Display         *p_disp;      /* Connection to X display       */
Window          Main, Exit;   /* Window ID of the two windows  */
GC              theGC,        /* The graphics context for main */
                exitGC;       /* GC for Exit button            */
XEvent          theEvent;     /* Structure for current event   */
int             Done = 0;     /* Flag to indicate when done    */
char            default_geometry[80];

char *window_title = "Hello";
void usage();

/*-------------------------------------------------------------*/
main(argc, argv)
int argc;
char **argv;
{
    int                 i, j;
    char                *tmpstr;
    Colormap            default_cmap;
    XColor              color;
    int                 bitmask;
    XGCValues           gcv;
    XSetWindowAttributes xswa;
    char                rfilename[80];
    char                *type;
    XrmValue            value;
    XrmDatabase         rdb;
/*-------------------------------------------------------------*/
/* STEP 1:  Parse command line. Each of xhello's options
 *          require a value. So we process the command-line
 *          arguments in pairs.
 */
    for (i = 1; i < argc; i += 2)
    {
        for(j = 0; j < num_options; j++)
        {
            if(strcmp(options[j].name, argv[i]) == 0 ||
               strcmp(options[j].cname, argv[i]) == 0)
            {
                *options[j].p_value_string = argv[i+1];
                break;
            }
        }
        if(j >= num_options)
            usage();
    }
/*-------------------------------------------------------------*/
/* STEP 2:  Open connection to display */

    if ((p_disp = XOpenDisplay(display_name)) == NULL)
    {
        fprintf(stderr, "%s: can't open display named %s\n",
                argv[0], XDisplayName(display_name));
        exit(1);
```

continues

Listing 5.1. continued

```c
    }
/*--------------------------------------------------------------*/
/* STEP 3: Get resources from the resource file */
    XrmInitialize();
    strcpy(rfilename, getenv("HOME"));
    strcat(rfilename, "/.Xdefaults");
    rdb = XrmGetFileDatabase(rfilename);
    if(rdb != NULL)
    {
        for (i = 0; i < num_resources; i++)
        {
            if(XrmGetResource(rdb, resources[i].name,
                              resources[i].cname,
                              &type, &value))
            {
                *resources[i].p_value_string = value.addr;
            }
        }
    }
/*--------------------------------------------------------------*/
/* STEP 4: Set up colors and fonts */
/*        First the fonts...      */

    if ((mfontstruct = XLoadQueryFont(p_disp, mfont)) == NULL)
    {
        fprintf(stderr, "%s: display %s cannot load font %s\n",
                app_name, DisplayString(p_disp), mfont);
        exit(1);
    }
    if ((efontstruct = XLoadQueryFont(p_disp, efont)) == NULL)
    {
        fprintf(stderr, "%s: display %s cannot load font %s\n",
                app_name, DisplayString(p_disp), efont);
        exit(1);
    }

/* Now select the colors using the default colormap */
    default_cmap = DefaultColormap(p_disp,
                                   DefaultScreen(p_disp));

/* Main window's background color */
/* Use white background in case of failure */
    if (XParseColor(p_disp, default_cmap, mbgcolor,
                    &color) == 0 ||
        XAllocColor(p_disp, default_cmap, &color) == 0)
        mbgpix = WhitePixel(p_disp, DefaultScreen(p_disp));
    else
        mbgpix = color.pixel;

/* Main window's foreground color */
/* Use black foreground in case of failure */
    if (XParseColor(p_disp, default_cmap, mfgcolor,
                    &color) == 0 ||
        XAllocColor(p_disp, default_cmap, &color) == 0)
        mfgpix = BlackPixel(p_disp, DefaultScreen(p_disp));
```

```
        else
            mfgpix = color.pixel;

/* Exit window's background color */
/* Use white background in case of failure */
        if (XParseColor(p_disp, default_cmap, ebgcolor,
                        &color) == 0 ¦¦
            XAllocColor(p_disp, default_cmap, &color) == 0)
            ebgpix = WhitePixel(p_disp, DefaultScreen(p_disp));
        else
            ebgpix = color.pixel;

/* Exit window's foreground color */
/* Use black foreground in case of failure */
        if (XParseColor(p_disp, default_cmap, efgcolor,
                        &color) == 0 ¦¦
            XAllocColor(p_disp, default_cmap, &color) == 0)
            efgpix = BlackPixel(p_disp, DefaultScreen(p_disp));
        else
            efgpix = color.pixel;
/*------------------------------------------------------------*/
/* STEP 5: Select initial position and size of top window */
/* Allocate and fill out an XsizeHints structure to inform the
 * window manager. Here we pick a default size large enough to
 * fit the text and the Exit button.
 */
        if((p_xsh = XAllocSizeHints()) == NULL)
        {
            fprintf(stderr, "Error allocating size hints!\n");
            exit(1);
        }
        if(extext_cline != NULL) extext = extext_cline;
        else
            if(extext_rsrc != NULL) extext = extext_rsrc;

        if(msgtext_cline != NULL) msgtext = msgtext_cline;
        else
            if(msgtext_rsrc != NULL) msgtext = msgtext_rsrc;

        extxt = efontstruct->max_bounds.width / 2;
        eytxt = efontstruct->max_bounds.ascent +
                efontstruct->max_bounds.descent;
        ewidth = extxt + XTextWidth(efontstruct, extext,
                                    strlen(extext)) + 4;
        eheight = eytxt + 4;

        p_xsh->flags = (PPosition ¦ PSize ¦ PMinSize);
        p_xsh->height = mfontstruct->max_bounds.ascent +
                    mfontstruct->max_bounds.descent + eheight + 10;
        p_xsh->min_height = p_xsh->height;
        p_xsh->width = XTextWidth(mfontstruct, msgtext, strlen(msgtext)) + 2;
        p_xsh->width = max(p_xsh->width,ewidth);

        p_xsh->min_width = p_xsh->width;
        p_xsh->x = (DisplayWidth(p_disp, DefaultScreen(p_disp)) -
                p_xsh->width) / 2;
        p_xsh->y = (DisplayHeight(p_disp, DefaultScreen(p_disp)) -
```

continues

Listing 5.1. continued

```
                 p_xsh->height) / 2;

/* Construct a default geometry string */
    sprintf(default_geometry, "%dx%d+%d+%d", p_xsh->width,
            p_xsh->height, p_xsh->x, p_xsh->y);
    mgeom = default_geometry;

/* Override the geometry, if necessary */
    if(mgeom_cline != NULL) mgeom = mgeom_cline;
    else
        if(mgeom_rsrc != NULL) mgeom = mgeom_rsrc;

/* Process the geometry specification */
    bitmask = XGeometry(p_disp, DefaultScreen(p_disp), mgeom,
                        default_geometry, DEFAULT_BDWIDTH,
                        mfontstruct->max_bounds.width,
                        mfontstruct->max_bounds.ascent +
                        mfontstruct->max_bounds.descent,
                        1, 1, &(p_xsh->x), &(p_xsh->y),
                        &(p_xsh->width), &(p_xsh->height));

/* Check bitmask and set flags in XSizeHints structure */
    if (bitmask & (XValue | YValue)) p_xsh->flags |= USPosition;
    if (bitmask & (WidthValue | HeightValue))
                                     p_xsh->flags |= USSize;
/*------------------------------------------------------------*/
/* STEP 6: Create top-level window                    */
/* Use position and size information derived above.
 * For border color, use the foreground color.
 */
    Main = XCreateSimpleWindow(p_disp, DefaultRootWindow(p_disp),
                p_xsh->x, p_xsh->y, p_xsh->width, p_xsh->height,
                DEFAULT_BDWIDTH, mfgpix, mbgpix);
/*------------------------------------------------------------*/
/* STEP 7: Set Window Manager properties (window name, icon
 * name, command-line, and size hints)
 */
    if((p_ch = XAllocClassHint()) == NULL)
    {
        fprintf(stderr, "Error allocating class hint!\n");
        exit(1);
    }
    p_ch->res_name = app_name;
    p_ch->res_class = "XHello";

/* Set up XTextProperty for window name and icon name */
    if(XStringListToTextProperty(&window_title, 1, &wname) == 0)
    {
        fprintf(stderr, "Error creating XTextProperty!\n");
        exit(1);
    }
    if(XStringListToTextProperty(&window_title, 1, &iname) == 0)
    {
        fprintf(stderr, "Error creating XTextProperty!\n");
```

```
        exit(1);
    }

    if((p_xwmh = XAllocWMHints()) == NULL)
    {
        fprintf(stderr, "Error allocating Window Manager hints!\n");
        exit(1);
    }
    p_xwmh->flags = (InputHint¦StateHint);
    p_xwmh->input = False;
    p_xwmh->initial_state = NormalState;
    XSetWMProperties(p_disp, Main, &wname, &iname, argv, argc,
                     p_xsh, p_xwmh, p_ch);
/*----------------------------------------------------------*/
/* STEP 8: Create a graphics context for the main window */

    gcv.font = mfontstruct->fid;
    gcv.foreground = mfgpix;
    gcv.background = mbgpix;
    theGC = XCreateGC(p_disp, Main,
                (GCFont ¦ GCForeground ¦ GCBackground), &gcv);
/*----------------------------------------------------------*/
/* STEP 9: Set window attributes (colormap, bit_gravity) */

    xswa.colormap = DefaultColormap(p_disp,
                                    DefaultScreen(p_disp));
    xswa.bit_gravity = CenterGravity;
    XChangeWindowAttributes(p_disp, Main, (CWColormap ¦
                            CWBitGravity), &xswa);
/*----------------------------------------------------------*/
/* STEP 10: Select input events for the main window */

    XSelectInput(p_disp, Main, ExposureMask);
/*----------------------------------------------------------*/
/* STEP 11: Map the main window--to make it visible */

    XMapWindow(p_disp, Main);
/*----------------------------------------------------------*/
/* STEP 12: Create any child windows, if any.
 * Also, select input events, create graphics contexts
 * and map the child windows.
 */

    ex = 1;
    ey = 1;
    Exit = XCreateSimpleWindow(p_disp, Main, ex, ey,
                ewidth, eheight, DEFAULT_BDWIDTH,
                efgpix, ebgpix);

    XSelectInput(p_disp, Exit, ExposureMask ¦
                              ButtonPressMask);

    XMapWindow(p_disp, Exit);

    gcv.font = efontstruct->fid;
    gcv.foreground = efgpix;
    gcv.background = ebgpix;
```

continues

Listing 5.1. continued

```
    exitGC = XCreateGC(p_disp, Exit, (GCFont | GCForeground |
                    GCBackground), &gcv);
/*------------------------------------------------------------*/
/* STEP 13: Retrieve and process events until done */

    while (!Done)
    {
        XNextEvent(p_disp, &theEvent);
        if(theEvent.xany.window == Main)
        {
            if(theEvent.type == Expose &&
                theEvent.xexpose.count == 0)
            {
                int x, y, itemp;
                unsigned int width, height, utemp;
                Window wtemp;
/* Determine the current size of the main window */
                if(XGetGeometry(p_disp, Main, &wtemp,
                        &itemp, &itemp, &width, &height,
                        &utemp, &utemp) == 0) break;
/* Compute new position for string */
                x = (width - XTextWidth(mfontstruct, msgtext,
                        strlen(msgtext))) / 2;
                y = eheight + (height - eheight +
                    mfontstruct->max_bounds.ascent -
                    mfontstruct->max_bounds.descent) / 2;
                XClearWindow(p_disp, Main);
                XDrawString(p_disp, Main, theGC, x, y,
                        msgtext, strlen(msgtext));
            }
        }
        if(theEvent.xany.window == Exit)
        {
            switch(theEvent.type)
            {
            case Expose:
                if (theEvent.xexpose.count == 0)
                {
                    XClearWindow(p_disp, Exit);
                    XDrawString(p_disp, Exit, exitGC, extxt,
                        eytxt, extext, strlen(extext));
                }
                break;

            case ButtonPress:
                Done = 1;
            }
        }

        }
    }
/*------------------------------------------------------------*/
/* STEP 14:  Close connection to display and exit. */

    XFreeGC(p_disp, theGC);
    XFreeGC(p_disp, exitGC);
```

```
        XUnloadFont(p_disp, mfontstruct->fid);
        XUnloadFont(p_disp, efontstruct->fid);
        XDestroyWindow(p_disp, Main);
        XCloseDisplay(p_disp);
        exit(0);
}
/*------------------------------------------------------------*/
void usage ()
{
        fprintf (stderr, "usage:  %s [-display host:display] \
[-geometry geom] [-msgtext text] [-extext text]\n", app_name);
        exit (1);
}
```

The X version of the Hello, World program is much more complex than the plain vanilla C version. This is unavoidable because of the large number of steps involved in setting up the windows, fonts, and colors in X before you can draw the string in a window. You want xhello.c to be complete enough to serve as a model for other small applications that you may wish to build.

Some of the complexity of xhello can be hidden by a set of utility routines, or you may decide to use a toolkit that also hides the complexity. There is no substitute, however, for seeing the details once to clarify the underlying principles of X programming.

Building and Testing *xhello*

You have seen the source file for xhello, but not how to build the executable file. You know that xhello.c has to be compiled and linked—the question is "With which libraries?" This section summarizes the procedure for building and testing xhello.

Compiling and Linking *xhello*

You can compile and link xhello with a single command, cc. The only problem is that libraries necessary to complete the linking may differ from one system to another. On most UNIX systems, the following UNIX shell command does the job:

```
cc -o xhello xhello.c -lX11
```

Xlib-based X applications need only the libX11.a library (indicated by the option -lX11) in order to use the Xlib routines.

After building xhello, you can run it from a UNIX shell in an X terminal emulator (for example, xterm) with the following command:

```
xhello
```

This produces the window shown in Figure 5.2. The frame around the window comes from the Motif Window Manager. You can close the window and exit the application by pressing any mouse button with the pointer inside the Exit button.

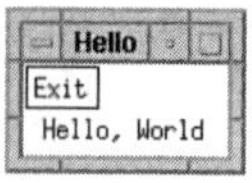

Figure 5.2.
Hello, World
from xhello.

Making Things Easy with *make*

A better way to build xhello is to prepare a *makefile* and use the UNIX make utility. The makefile describes the names of files that make up a program and how they are interrelated. It also includes information about how to create the program. The make utility reads the makefile and, based on the time of last modification, decides which files need compiling and follows any other specified steps to create an updated version of the program. With make you can avoid retyping long commands and, more importantly, avoid unnecessary recompilations (and avoid getting errors because you forgot to compile a file that was affected by your most recent changes).

The makefile for xhello is simple because it has only one source file. Listing 5.2 shows this file. This sample makefile shows how you can use xhello as a general-purpose notifier under X—it is somewhat like the dialog boxes in Macintosh or MessageBox in Microsoft Windows. Figure 5.3 shows the result of running make with the makefile of Listing 5.2.

Listing 5.2. Makefile for xhello.

```
###########################################################
#  Make file for "xhello" -- X version of "Hello, World" #
#                                                         #
###########################################################
# Some common definitions...

RM = rm -f
CC = cc


# Compiler flags, paths for include files and libraries

CFLAGS =
DEFINES =
INCLUDES = -I. -I/usr/include -I/usr/include/X11
LIBS = -lX11

# Rule to create .o files from .c files
.c.o:
    $(RM) $@
    $(CC) -c $(CFLAGS) $(INCLUDES) $*.c

# Targets...

all::   xhello

# Notice how "xhello" is used to display a message at
# completion
```

```
xhello: xhello.o
    $(RM) $@
    $(CC) -o $@ $(CFLAGS) xhello.o $(LIBS)
    xhello -m "$@ Successfully Made!" -e " OK " &
```

Specifying Command-Line Options and Resources

By design, xhello accepts input from a resource file as well as from the command line. In Listing 5.2, you see how to use the command-line options -msgtext and -extext to alter the text strings displayed in xhello. Using resources is equally easy. For example, add the following lines in the .Xdefaults file in your login directory (if you do not have such a file, create a new one):

```
xhello*font: -*-courier-*-r-*--*-140-*-*-*-*-iso8859-1
xhello.exit.font: -*-helvetica-bold-r-*--*-180-*-*-*-*-iso8859-1
xhello.geometry:  100x100+10+10
xhello.exit.text: Bye
```

Figure 5.3.
xhello announces that it was successfully made.

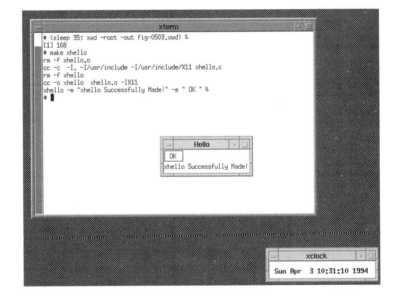

Next, invoke xhello again from the xterm window. Figure 5.4 shows the resulting window. Notice how the window size, the text string in the Exit button, and the fonts have changed. This happens because the call to XrmGetResource, in xhello, reads the settings for these parameters from the .Xdefaults file and uses them.

In xhello, command-line options can override resource specifications. You can verify this by invoking xhello with the following command:

```
xhello -mtext "Step 1 Complete" -etext " OK "&
```

Figure 5.4.

The xhello *window after setting resources.*

Figure 5.5 shows the resulting output. Notice how the text in each window matches what you specified on the command-line.

Figure 5.5.

Command-line override resources in xhello.

Summary

This chapter introduces you to Xlib programming by showing a complete application—the X version of the classic Hello, World program. Each X program has to follow certain steps to set up everything before it can draw anything in a window. The size and position of the top-level window requires giving hints to any existing window manager so that the application can coexist peacefully with others. All action in an X application takes place in the event processing loop where you retrieve events from the X server and take necessary action.

The resulting X version of the xhello program appears complicated compared to its sparsely elegant C counterpart, but it also provides additional capabilities. An innovative use of the xhello application is in shell scripts and makefiles to provide informative messages.

Using a toolkit is one way to reduce the complexity of X programs. However, even with a toolkit, you have to take care of many basic drawing functions by calling routines in Xlib. Thus it is necessary to understand the steps you go through before drawing in a window.

Further Reading

David Rosenthal's article gives an excellent description of how to write the Hello, World program using Xlib and the Xt toolkit. In that article, he also compares the performance of the two versions of the program—one using Xlib and the other based on Xt toolkit—and comes to the conclusion that it is wise to use a toolkit to develop X applications, a conclusion you probably share after seeing xhello.c in Listing 5.1.

Rosenthal, David S. "Going for Baroque." *UNIX Review* 6 (June 1988): 71-9.

Chapter 6

The Xlib
Programming Model

Chapter 5, "A Simple X Application," presents a complete X application, outlines the steps that a typical X program follows, and shows how to compile and link an X application. This chapter begins by summarizing the event-driven programming model used by X applications. Then it goes on to describe how the facilities of Xlib are used in X applications. This chapter provides an overview of Xlib programming—how to open and close the connection to the X display, how resources such as windows, fonts, and graphics contexts are created and manipulated, and how events and errors are handled. Later chapters provide detailed descriptions of individual Xlib programming topics.

Event-Driven Applications

Applications designed for window systems such as Macintosh and Microsoft Windows differ from traditional applications. For example, a traditional word processor might have several modes in which it operates to perform various functions:

✦ Editing text

✦ Opening and closing files

✦ Printing a document

In each mode, users are constrained to a specific set of operations. To make matters worse, a command that does one thing in one mode may do something else in another mode. This style of user interface tends to confuse the users, but it is still prevalent because such applications are easier to write.

Word processors based on window systems, on the other hand, do not constrain users with unnecessary modes. Users can copy, cut, and paste text by selecting items from a menu. Printing or saving a document to a file involves selecting another item from a menu. Users are constrained by modes only when absolutely necessary; for example, the application is in a file selection mode when you want to open a file. Even then, users indicate the choice by selecting an item from a list, and they have the option of clicking on a Cancel button. This style of interaction gives the user total control over the application. To achieve this flexibility, the application's developer must follow a programming model in which the application continually checks what the user wants and performs the appropriate tasks to fulfill those requests. This programming model is referred to as the *event-driven model* because task requests come from the mouse pointing device and from the keyboard and are reported to the application as events.

Structure

If you have written programs for the Macintosh or Microsoft Windows, you know event-driven programming. As shown in Figure 6.1, a typical event-driven program has three major sections:

✦ Initialization

✦ Event loop

✦ Clean-up

The initialization section sets up the window system for user interaction. After initialization, the program enters a loop in which it repeatedly solicits events from the window system and processes them. Finally, before exiting, the program performs any necessary clean-ups.

Initialization

Listing 5.1 in Chapter 5 shows xhello, an event-driven program that displays a message in a window. Most of the code in that program handles the steps involved in setting up X before any output can be sent to the windows. You can think of this as the initialization of the X Window System. What this initialization does is create a number of resources in the X server that the application will use for displaying output and receiving inputs from the user. These resources include windows, fonts, colormaps, and GCs, all of which are used in xhello to display the message and handle user input. In general, the initialization of an X application involves the following steps:

1. Open a connection to the display.
2. Set up fonts and colors based on user's choices.
3. Create the top-level window of the application.
4. Inform the window manager of the window's title, its size, its position, and its minimum width and height.
5. Create a GC for the window.
6. Select which of the input events occurring in the window will be processed by the application.
7. Make the top-level window visible (map it).
8. Create other windows in the hierarchy and map them. Create more GCs, if needed.

Figure 6.1.
General structure of an event-driven program.

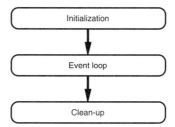

Event Loop

Once initialization has been done, the application is ready to handle events. In an event-driven programming model, the application does all its work in the event loop. As you saw in Listing 5.1, the event loop is often implemented as a while loop in which the program reads, interprets, and processes events. The program uses the Xlib routine, XNextEvent, to get event reports from the server. To interpret an event, the code must check the window identification and the type of event and decide what to do based on this information.

Usually, the while loop is broken when a variable (for example, Done in Listing 5.1) changes its value from zero to something nonzero. One of the events (perhaps when the user selects the Quit option in a menu) should set this variable to indicate that the application has to terminate. For example, in xhello, when a mouse buttonpress occurring inside the Exit window is detected, the code sets Done to 1, which ends the event loop.

The event loop is a crucial part of every X application. All application-specific work is done in the event loop. Even the initial drawing in a window must occur only in response to a special event known as the `Expose` event. In fact, events control everything an X application does. The X server maintains queues of events, one for each client, and it sends the events to the clients as they occur. At the client, Xlib buffers the events in a queue. Xlib doles out the events, one at a time, as the client asks for an event using one of the Xlib functions, such as `XNextEvent`.

Clean-Up

Before exiting, an X application should destroy the resources it created at the server. The resources consume memory in the server and the final clean-up should free this memory by destroying the resources. In the simplest case, closing the connection to the server is enough to free the resources. However, an application may set parameters in the X server so that this does not happen automatically. In these cases, the application must explicitly destroy windows and free `GC`s before closing the connection.

Xlib Overview

The X Window System uses a client-server model to provide its services. The X server takes care of input and output at the display. X applications are the clients that use the capabilities of the server by sending X protocol requests. The X protocol requests are delivered over a communication link between the clients and the X server. For clients and server running on different machines, this link is a network connection. If both client and server are on the same machine, the communication may be through a shared block of memory or some other interprocess communication (IPC) mechanism supported by the operating system.

Although it is conceivable that you can write an X application that performs all input and output by sending X protocol requests to the server, doing so would be like programming a microprocessor directly in its machine language. To ease the programmer's job, the X Window System includes Xlib, a set of C language functions and macros that can be used by X client applications to access the facilities of the X server.

X Programming Made Easy

The primary purpose of Xlib is to provide an easy way for C programmers to send X protocol requests to the server. However, Xlib is much more than a set of functions with one-to-one correspondence to all possible X protocol requests. It includes many convenience functions to ease the burden of handling common tasks while hiding how the X protocol is utilized to get the job done. For example, only one X protocol request exists to create a window, but Xlib has two routines for creating windows, `XCreateSimpleWindow` and `XCreateWindow`, one simpler than the other. Similarly, the foreground and background colors for a window are specified in a `GC`. To set these colors, you call the Xlib routines `XSetForeground` and `XSetBackground`. Xlib takes care of setting up the proper protocol requests to change only these colors in the specified `GC`.

Buffering X Protocol Requests

Each X protocol request involves sending a packet of data to the X server. When an X program calls an Xlib function that generates a protocol request, the function places the protocol requests in a buffer and returns (see Figure 6.2). This improves performance by enabling the program to continue execution at full tilt and by minimizing the number of data packets sent to the server. Xlib sends the accumulated requests to the X server when one of the following happens:

✦ The buffer becomes full.

✦ The application calls an Xlib routine to flush the buffer.

✦ The application calls a routine to get an event and that routine has to wait until an event is received from the server.

✦ The application calls a routine that needs a reply from the X server.

Figure 6.2.

Xlib buffers protocol requests and event reports.

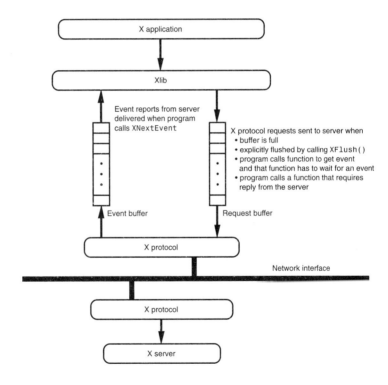

A side effect of this buffering is that a protocol request that results in an error will result in an error report that does not correlate with the current Xlib function being called by the application. This makes it harder to pinpoint the function that caused the error.

Xlib also buffers event reports that arrive from the X server (Figure 6.2). These events are sent to the application when it calls an event retrieval function, such as XNextEvent.

Utility Functions

In addition to the convenience functions that relieve the programmer of having to worry about the details of X protocol requests, Xlib includes many utility functions. These functions help programmers with chores that have to be done in an X application. For example, the XParseGeometry function enables you to extract the size and position information from a geometry specified as a string. For instance, if the geometry string is 200x100+10-10, XParseGeometry identifies 200 and 100 as the width and height, and 10 and -10 as the x and y offsets.

The utility functions available in Xlib help you get the user's choices from a resource file, manipulate screen images and bitmaps, translate names of colors to pixel values, and use the resource manager. Routines that are collectively called *context manager functions* enable you to attach your own data to each window. Such data is maintained locally and can serve as a database for your application. (These utility functions are discussed in later chapters.)

Xlib Capabilities

Broadly speaking, Xlib functions enable an application to connect to an X display, create windows and draw in them, retrieve events, and close the connection. Most of the time, you can get by with a few Xlib functions. Table 6.1 summarizes commonly used Xlib functions, grouped according to task. This list is by no means complete, yet it is rather long. Do not be overwhelmed by the list; it is here simply to give you an overall view of Xlib's capabilities. Subsequent chapters provide detailed coverage of these and other Xlib functions.

Table 6.1. Common Xlib Functions

Task	*Function*
Opening and closing connection to an X display	XOpenDisplay, XCloseDisplay
Getting user's choices from resource file or command line	XGetDefault, XrmInitialize, XrmGetResource, XrmParseCommand
Creating and managing windows	XCreateSimpleWindow, XCreateWindow, XDestroyWindow, XMapRaised, XMapWindow, XUnmapWindow, XGetWindowAttributes, XChangeWindowAttributes
Controlling window's size, position, and stacking order	XGeometry, XGetGeometry, XMoveWindow, XResizeWindow, XMoveResizeWindow, XLowerWindow,

Task	Function
	XRaiseWindow, XCirculateSubWindows
Interacting with window manager	XSetStandardProperties, XGetWMHints, XSetWMHints
Soliciting and handling events	XSelectInput, XEventsQueued, XNextEvent, XPeekEvent
Synchronizing with server	XFlush, XSync, XSynchronize
Error handling	XGetErrorText, XSetErrorHandler, XSetIOErrorHandler
Manipulating graphics contexts	XCreateGC, XChangeGC, XCopyGC, XFreeGC, XSetForeground, XSetState, XSetBackground, XSetFunction
Drawing graphics	XDrawArc, XDrawArcs, XDrawLine, XDrawLines, XSetDashes, XSetArcMode, XDrawPoints, XDrawPoint, XDrawRectangle, XDrawRectangles, XFillArc, XFillArcs, XSetFillRule, XFillRectangle, XFillRectangles, XFillPolygon, XSetLineAttributes
Clearing and copying areas	XClearWindow, XClearArea, XCopyArea, XCopyPlane
Drawing text	XLoadFont, XLoadQueryFont, XSetFont, XUnloadFont, XDrawString, XDrawImageString, XDrawText, XTextWidth, XListFonts
Using color	XDefaultColorMap, XDefaultVisual, XGetVisualInfo, XParseColor, XAllocColor, XGetStandardColorMap, XSetWindowColorMap, XFreeColors
Manipulating bitmaps, pixmaps, and images	XCreatePixmap, XFreePixmap, XCreatePixmapFromBitmapData, XReadBitmapFile,

continues

Table 6.1. continued

Task	*Function*
	XWriteBitmapFile, XCreateImage, XDestroyImage, XGetImage, XPutImage, XGetPixel, XPutPixel
Processing keystrokes and mouse events	XQueryPointer, XTranslateCoordinates, XCreateFontCursor, XDefineCursor, XFreeCursor, XUndefineCursor, XGetMotionEvents, XLookupString, XRefreshKeyboardMapping, XRebindKeysym
Communicating between applications	XInternAtom, XChangeProperty, XGetWindowProperty, XDeleteProperty, XSendEvent, XGetSelectionOwner, XSetSelectionOwner, XConvertSelection

Common Features of Xlib

Among the large number of routines available in Xlib are some common features, and knowing them can help you use Xlib effectively. This section summarizes these features, starting with header files and proceeding to naming conventions and the order of arguments.

Header Files

All Xlib-based programs need to include the following header files:

```
#include <X11/Xlib.h>
#include <X11/Xutil.h>
```

The first header file defines the basic data structures needed by Xlib. The second header file is used by the utility functions of Xlib. Additionally, you may need to include <X11/Xresource.h> if you use the resource manager functions (their names start with the prefix Xrm). These header files also include declaration of all functions that return noninteger values.

Now that an ANSI standard exists for the C programming language (ANSI X3.159 1989), header files are expected to include *prototypes* (complete declarations of a function including its arguments) for all functions. Starting with X11R4, the Xlib header files include prototypes.

Naming Conventions

Xlib follows a consistent naming convention for all functions, macros, and data structures. Being knowledgeable about this naming scheme helps you guess function names and avoid common typing errors. The following summarizes the major conventions:

◆ *Functions and Macros.* Names of Xlib functions and macros are built by concatenating one or more words, with the first letter of each word capitalized (see Table 6.1 for examples). Names of functions begin with a capital *X*, but macros never start with *X*. In fact, if a function and a macro work identically, the function's name is derived by adding an *X* prefix to the macro's name. For example, the macro that returns the name of the current X display is `DisplayString`, and the equivalent function is named `XDisplayString`.

◆ *Data Structures.* User-accessible data structures are named the same way functions are: their names begin with a capital *X*. The names of members in a data structure are in lowercase, with underscores (_) separating multiple words. For example, the `XImage` data structure has an integer field named `bits_per_pixel`. This rule does not apply to data structures whose members are not to be accessed by user. An example is the `Display` data structure whose name does not begin with *X* because the user is not supposed to access the internals of this structure directly.

Knowing these conventions also helps you select names for your own data structures and functions. You can use lowercase names for your variables and all uppercase for your macros. To be safe, you may decide to add a unique prefix (perhaps your organization's initials) to all your external functions and variables.

Order of Arguments for Functions

In addition to the naming convention, Xlib also orders the arguments for functions and macros in a consistent manner. The rules for this ordering are the following:

◆ *Display.* When display is an argument to a function or a macro, it is the first argument.

◆ *Windows, Fonts, and Other Resources.* Other resources, such as window, font, and pixmap, appear immediately after the display argument. When there are several resources, windows and pixmaps precede all others. The `GC` also appears last among the resources.

◆ *Source and Destination.* Many functions perform tasks that involve taking something from one or more arguments (the source) and storing the result in other arguments (the destination). In these cases, the source arguments always precede the destination arguments.

◆ *x, y, width, height.* Many functions take the position (x, y) and size (width, height) of windows or pixmaps as arguments. Among x and y, the x argument always precedes y, and width always comes before height. When all four arguments are present, the order is x, y, width, height.

✦ *Bit Mask.* Xlib has some functions that selectively change one or more members in a structure. Indicate the members being changed by setting bits in a *bit mask* (an integer variable where each bit position corresponds to a member of the structure). When a function takes a bit mask as argument, the mask always precedes the pointer to the structure.

Knowing the convention for argument order is even more helpful than knowing how functions are named. Once you get accustomed to programming in Xlib, you often can guess the argument list for a function simply because you know these rules.

Xlib Usage

The rest of the chapter discusses how Xlib functions are used to accomplish the major tasks in an X application:

✦ Connecting to an X display

✦ Using resources in the server

✦ Managing events

✦ Handling errors

What follows is a summary of how Xlib functions are used for these tasks. These topics are discussed in more detail later in the book.

Connecting to an X Display

Because of the client-server architecture, each X application needs the services of an X server to work properly. Thus, your program's first job is to establish communications with the server (or the X display).

Opening the Connection

Thanks to the Xlib function XOpenDisplay, opening a connection to an X display is a matter of naming the display. XOpenDisplay takes as its sole argument the name of the display, in the form of a null-terminated C string. It returns a pointer to a Display data structure. Save this pointer because this is the display argument that most other Xlib functions require. (See Chapter 2, "Clients, Servers, and Window Managers," for information on how to name X displays, and Chapter 5 for an example of XOpenDisplay.)

Closing the Connection

Before an X application exits, it should disconnect the link to the X server by calling the XCloseDisplay function:

```
XCloseDisplay(p_disp);     /* p_disp is the pointer to Display */
```

where `p_disp` is the pointer to the `Display` structure that identifies this connection.

Even when running on the same system, the X application and the X server are two distinct processes. When the application creates resources such as windows and fonts, the server uses memory for them. If the application exits without closing the connection, the server eventually will detect this by observing the lack of any protocol requests within some reasonable period of time; then it will dispose of that application's resources automatically. It is better to call `XCloseDisplay` explicitly, however, because on its own the server may take a while to conclude that the application has quit.

When an application closes the connection, the server, by default, destroys all windows and other resources, such as fonts, colormaps, and graphics contexts, created by that application, thus freeing the memory allocated for these resources.

Using the Resources of the X Server

Once you have established connection to a display, you can begin to use the resources of that server. In Chapter 3, "Exploring X Applications," the word resource means user-customizable parameters in an application. In the X server, however, *resource* signifies anything created at the request of an application. Thus, X resources include windows, graphics contexts, fonts, cursors, colormaps, and pixmaps (see Figure 6.3). A large part of this book deals with creating and using these resources because that is how you generate output in windows and accept input from the mouse and keyboard.

Applications create resources by calling Xlib functions. When your program creates any of these resources, the Xlib function returns a resource ID, a 32-bit identifier (of type `unsigned long` in the C programming language). For your convenience, the header file `X.h` uses the C `typedef` statement to define a number of synonyms, such as `Window`, `Font`, `Pixmap`, `Cursor`, and `Colormap`, for the resource identifiers. When you create a window, you can refer to the returned resource ID as a `Window`.

You might think that the creation of a resource such as a window must involve a protocol request to the X server (the request to create the window), followed by a reply from the server (returning the ID of the newly created window). Luckily, a clever decision during the design of X11 manages to avoid this round-trip communication. When Xlib opens a connection to a display, the X server returns a block of resource identifiers. Xlib assigns resource identifiers to newly created resources from this block. Thus, a single one-way protocol request is enough to create a resource. Xlib gets an unused resource ID from the block, adds that ID to the protocol request for creating the resource, and returns the same ID to the application, without having to wait for a reply from the server.

Figure 6.3.
Resources of the X server.

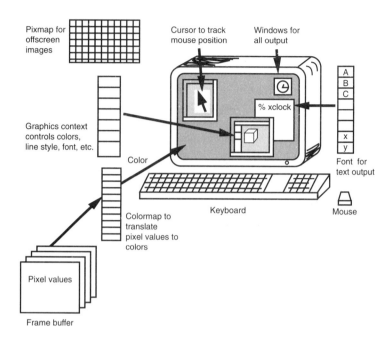

Windows

Among the resources of the X server, windows are the most important. The X Window System exists to enable applications to use windows. In X, a window is an area of the display screen for displaying output and accepting input. X enables windows to be nested in a parent-child hierarchy, with all child windows clipped at the boundary of the parent. When an X application draws text or graphics, it must specify a window, and all inputs from the mouse and the keyboard are associated with a window. Xlib includes many functions to control the size, color, and hierarchy of windows. Chapter 7, "Creating and Managing Windows," discusses the topic of creating, using, and managing the windows in X.

Graphics Contexts

Prior to X11, X was *stateless*. In other words, it had no provision for setting the font and colors, for instance, and used them repeatedly for drawing text and graphics. Every call to a drawing function required a complete list of arguments specifying the colors, fonts, and other details. For example, to display text in a window, you had to provide as arguments to the now defunct XText function, the window ID, the x and y location of the text, the string and its length, the font, and the foreground and background colors. This approach was flexible, but expensive, because the protocol requests had to include too many parameters.

To avoid repeatedly sending graphics attributes to the server, X11 introduced the concept of a *state*, the GC, that holds all graphics attributes such as colors and font necessary to draw in a window. These graphics attributes control the appearance of the output. The advantage of this approach is that an application can create one or more GCs at the server, initialize them, and later on, use them for drawing into a window. Because a GC is identified by a resource identifier, the server can be asked to use a specific set of attributes by including a single graphics context identifier in the drawing request instead of a variable number of attributes.

Returning to the previous example of text output, with the introduction of GCs, the X11 text output routine, XDrawString, needs the arguments, the display, the window, the GC, x and y coordinates of the output, and the string and its length. The font and the foreground and background colors come from the GC. This means that you have to create the GC and set up the font and colors prior to calling XDrawString. Chapter 9, "Drawing Graphics," further describes GCs and shows how to use Xlib routines such as XCreateGC and XChangeGC that are used to create and manipulate GCs.

Fonts

Font refers to a collection of bitmaps (a pattern of 1s and 0s) that represents the size and shape of characters from a set. The X server uses a font when displaying text in a window. When you call an Xlib function such as XDrawString to draw one or more characters, the server retrieves and draws the image corresponding to each character from the current font. X provides a large number of fonts with a standard naming convention. You have to load one of these fonts before drawing text in a window (otherwise, the server uses a default font). To specify a font, use a resource indentifier of type Font. Chapter 10, "Drawing Text," provides more information on using fonts for text output in windows. The font naming convention of X is summarized in Chapter 3.

Cursors

The cursor represents the shape of the on-screen pointer that indicates the current position of the mouse pointing device. As you move the mouse, the cursor tracks the movement on the screen. A cursor is similar to a single character from a font. In fact, you can use the XCreateFontCursor function to create a new cursor by selecting one of the characters from a special cursor font. When you create a cursor, you get back a resource identifier of type Cursor. After creating a cursor, you can assign it to a window using the function XDefineCursor. If you do not define any cursor for a window, the X server uses the cursor of its parent.

Changing cursors is a useful way to inform users about the special purpose of a particular window. For example, if a window manager enables you to resize a window by dragging the corners of a window's frame, the window manager changes the cursor when the user has the mouse at the corners. You will find more information on cursors in Chapter 8, "Handling Events."

Colormaps

An X display screen has a block of memory, known as the *frame buffer* (or *video memory*), that is capable of storing a fixed number of bits (usually 1 or 8) for each pixel on the screen. This is the so-called *pixel value*. The color displayed at each pixel, on the other hand, is the result of varying the intensities of three closely located dots of the basic colors: red (R), green (G), and blue (B). The intensity of these three components is often referred to as the *RGB value* or the *RGB triplet*.

The *colormap* is the key to generating an RGB triplet from a pixel value—it maps a pixel value to a color. For example, if the frame buffer stores 8-bit pixel values, a pixel can take one of 2^8, or 256, possible values. Thus, the colormap must have 256 entries and each entry must show the intensities of the R, G, and B components.

When an X application uses colors, it works with pixel values. To ensure that a pixel value appears as the correct color, the application has to identify the colormap used to translate that pixel value to a color. This is done through the colormap resource.

The video hardware in most X displays can use only one colormap at a time, which creates the notion of installing a colormap. If multiple applications sharing a display start to install colormaps independently, the result will be chaos. The convention is that X applications should never install their own colormaps; rather, they should inform the window manager of the colormaps they need. The window manager will take care of installing the right colormap for each application. Chapter 11, "Using Color in X," discusses the complex topic of colormaps more fully.

Pixmaps

Recall that a pixmap is a block of memory in the X server, in which you can draw as you would in a window. In fact, window and pixmap resources are collectively known as *drawables* in X. All drawing functions accept drawables as arguments. What you draw in a pixmap does not appear on the display. To make the contents of a pixmap visible, you have to copy from the pixmap to a window. You can think of a pixmap as an off-screen window, a two-dimensional array of pixel values that can be used to hold graphics images and fill patterns. If each pixel value in a pixmap is represented by a single bit, the pixmap is known as a bitmap. Chapter 12, "Pixmaps, Bitmaps, and Images," discusses how to create, use, and manipulate pixmaps and bitmaps in X.

Managing Events

Events move X. Everything in an X application happens in response to events received from the X server. For instance, when an application creates a window and makes it visible by mapping it, the application cannot tell whether the server has actually finished preparing the window for output. To draw in that window, the application must wait for a specific event, an Expose event, from the server. All inputs from the user also arrive at the X application in the form of events.

Because the basic design of X does not impose any particular style of user interface, X events contain an extraordinary amount of detail. For example, you can get an event when a mouse button is pressed and another when it is released. For each event, you can find out—among other things—which button was involved, the window containing the cursor, the time of the event, and the x and y coordinates of the cursor location. This level of detailed event reporting is one reason why X is the basis of popular graphical user interfaces such as OSF/Motif and OPEN LOOK. The detailed events enable programmers to implement any type of user interface using X.

Summary of X Events

X provides for a large number of events to handle everything from mouse and keyboard to messages from other X clients (see Table 6.2). The types of events, shown in the first column of the table, are defined in the include file X11/X.h. Note that you do not have to include this file explicitly because X11/Xlib.h already includes it.

Table 6.2. X Events

Event Type	When Generated
Mouse Events	
ButtonPress	Mouse button pressed with pointer in window
ButtonRelease	Mouse button released with pointer in window
EnterNotify	Mouse pointer enters window
LeaveNotify	Mouse pointer leaves window
MotionNotify	Mouse is moved after stopping
Keyboard Events	
FocusIn	Window receives input focus (all subsequent keyboard events come to window)
FocusOut	Window loses input focus
KeyMapNotify	Used after EnterNotify or FocusIn event occurs (to inform application of the state of the keys after these events)
KeyPress	Key pressed (when window has focus)
KeyRelease	Key released (when window has focus)
MappingNotify	Keyboard reconfigured (the mapping of a key to a string is changed)
Expose Events	
Expose	Previously obscured window or part of window becomes visible
GraphicsExpose	During graphics copy operations, parts of source image are obscured (copied image not complete)
NoExpose	Graphics copy successfully completed
Colormap Notification Event	
ColormapNotify	Window's colormap changed
Interclient Communication Events	
ClientMessage	Another client sends message using XSendEvent function
PropertyNotify	Property associated with window changed (see Chapter 16, "Advanced Topics in X")

continues

Table 6.2. continued

Event Type	When Generated
Interclient Communication Events	
SelectionClear	Window loses ownership of selection (see Chapter 16)
SelectionNotify	Selection successfully converted (see Chapter 16)
SelectionRequest	Selection needs conversion (see Chapter 16)
Window State Notification Events	
CirculateNotify	Window raised or lowered in stacking order
ConfigureNotify	Window moved or resized, or its position in stacking order changed
CreateNotify	Window created
DestroyNotify	Window destroyed
GravityNotify	Window moved because its parent's size changed
MapNotify	Window mapped
ReparentNotify	Window's parent changed
UnmapNotify	Window unmapped
VisibilityNotify	Window's visibility changed (became visible or invisible)
Window Structure Control Events	
CirculateRequest	Request received to raise or lower window in stacking order (used by window managers)
ConfigureRequest	Request received to move, resize, or restack window (used by window managers)
MapRequest	Window about to be mapped (used by window managers)
ResizeRequest	Request received to resize window (used by window managers)

The X server never sends unsolicited events to an application. Table 6.2 shows 33 events, but X applications are not required to process all of them and incur the overhead of unnecessary event handling code. The application usually calls the Xlib function XSelectInput to indicate the events that it wants to receive. It can, in fact, request events on a per-window basis. This approach of selective reporting of events is good for the server also, because it relieves the server of the necessity of keeping track of all events for all clients.

One exception to the rule of selective reporting exists: the MappingNotify event, generated when the meaning of keys are changed, is sent to all X clients automatically.

The 33 X events shown in Table 6.2 can be broadly grouped into seven categories:

✦ *Mouse Events.* The server generates these events when the user presses a mouse button or moves the mouse. X applications trying to provide a point-and-click graphical interface usually accept and handle these events.

✦ *Keyboard Events.* Keyboard events are generated when the user presses or releases any key on the keyboard. They are delivered to an application only if a window owned by the application has the input focus. Usually, the window manager decides how the focus is transferred from one window to another. There are two common models: clicking on a window to type in it (used by the Macintosh and Microsoft Windows), and giving the focus to the window containing the mouse pointer.

✦ *Expose Events.* Of all X events, the `Expose` event is the most crucial—applications draw in their windows in response to this event. Almost all X applications request and process this event. The `GraphicsExpose` and `NoExpose` events copy from one part of a window or a pixmap to another. They enable applications to handle the case where the source of the copy operation is obscured by another window and the contents of the obscured area are unavailable for copying. Chapter 9 describes these events further.

✦ *Colormap Notification Event.* The server generates the `ColorMapNotify` event when an application changes the colormap associated with a window or installs a new colormap. Chapter 11 explains how colormaps are handled by well-behaved X applications.

✦ *Interclient Communication Events.* These events send information from one X application to another. The concept of property and selection are used for this purpose. Chapter 16 discusses these topics.

✦ *Window State Notification Events.* The server generates these events when a window is moved or resized, or its place in the stacking order is altered. These events are useful for keeping track of changes in the layout of windows on the screen. Typically, window managers use these events for this purpose. Your application can use them if you want to alter the size and position of the subwindows when the user resizes the top window.

✦ *Window Structure Control Events.* These events are used almost exclusively by window managers to intercept an application's attempt to change the layout of its windows. For example, by monitoring the `MapRequest` event, the window manager can tell when an application maps its top window. When this happens, the window manager can add its own frame to the window and place it at an appropriate location on the screen.

Selecting Events

When you write an X application, you have to select the events that you want to receive from the server. You can select events for each window in the application. The selection is usually done by calling the `XSelectInput` function:

```
Display      *p_disp;     /* Connection to X server       */
Window       w_id;        /* Window ID                    */
unsigned long event_mask; /* Bit pattern to select events */
.
.
XSelectInput(p_disp, w_id, event_mask);
```

where `w_id` identifies the window for which events are being selected. The `event_mask` parameter is an `unsigned long` integer whose bit patterns indicate the events being selected. You can construct the `event_mask` by the bitwise-OR of selected masks defined in the `<X11/X.h>` header file.

For example, you may decide that you want to receive Expose and ButtonPress events for a window. In this case, the event_mask is the following:

```
event_mask = ExposureMask | ButtonPressMask;
```

Table 6.3 shows the name of the event mask corresponding to each of the 33 X events of Table 6.2. Notice that there are fewer event masks than events. This is because several events, such as ClientMessage and MappingNotify, cannot be controlled by masks. A single mask often enables the delivery of multiple events. For example, both FocusIn and FocusOut events are enabled by the mask FocusChangeMask. On the other hand, sometimes several masks enable only one event (for example, the MotionNotify event).

Table 6.3. Event Masks Corresponding to X Events

Event Type	Name of Event Mask in X11/X.h
ButtonPress	ButtonPressMask
ButtonRelease	ButtonReleaseMask
CirculateNotify	StructureNotifyMask, SubstructureNotifyMask
CirculateRequest	SubstructureRedirectMask
ClientMessage*	—
ColormapNotify	ColormapChangeMask
ConfigureNotify	StructureNotifyMask, SubstructureNotifyMask
ConfigureRequest	SubstructureRedirectMask
CreateNotify	SubstructureNotifyMask
DestroyNotify	StructureNotifyMask, SubstructureNotifyMask
EnterNotify	EnterWindowMask
Expose	ExposureMask
FocusIn	FocusChangeMask
FocusOut	FocusChangeMask
GraphicsExpose	ExposureMask
GravityNotify	StructureNotifyMask, SubstructureNotifyMask
KeyMapNotify	KeymapStateMask
KeyPress	KeyPressMask
KeyRelease	KeyReleaseMask
LeaveNotify	LeaveWindowMask
MapNotify	StructureNotifyMask, SubstructureNotifyMask
MappingNotify*	—
MapRequest	SubstructureRedirectMask

Event Type	*Name of Event Mask in X11/X.h*
MotionNotify	ButtonMotionMask, Button1MotionMask, Button2MotionMask, Button3MotionMask, Button4MotionMask, Button5MotionMask, PointerMotionMask, PointerMotionHintMask
NoExpose	ExposureMask
PropertyNotify	PropertyChangeMask
ReparentNotify	StructureNotifyMask, SubstructureNotifyMask
ResizeRequest	ResizeRedirectMask
SelectionClear*	—
SelectionNotify*	—
SelectionRequest*	—
UnmapNotify	StructureNotifyMask, SubstructureNotifyMask
VisibilityNotify	VisibilityChangeMask

*No event mask is available to control selection of this event.

Receiving Events

Xlib maintains a queue of events received from the X server and an output buffer to hold the protocol requests to be sent to the X server. When an application is ready to process an event, it can call the Xlib function XNextEvent to get an event. The XNextEvent function first sends any protocol requests in the output buffer to the X server.

When Xlib sends waiting protocol requests to the server, it "flushes" the output buffer. After flushing the output buffer, XNextEvent returns the oldest event waiting in the queue. If there are no events available, XNextEvent waits until an event arrives from the server. XNextEvent "blocks" until an event arrives from the server. Functions that return without waiting are called *nonblocking*.

When using XNextEvent to receive an event, you have to define storage for the data structure to hold the information about the event. The call takes the following form:

```
Display   *p_disp;    /* Connection to X server      */
XEvent    theEvent;   /* Structure to hold event info */
.
.
XNextEvent(p_disp, &theEvent);
```

What you do with the information returned in the XEvent data structure depends on the type of event. The example program, xhello in Chapter 4, "Graphical User Interfaces and X," shows how Expose and ButtonPress events are handled. Chapter 8 describes event handling in detail.

Synchronizing the Client and the Server

Recall that the client-server architecture of X means that the operation of your program and the X server is asynchronous. While your program is making its fifth call to a window creation routine, the server may be processing only the third request. Additionally, to improve performance, Xlib avoids sending protocol requests to the server one at a time. Instead, it saves them in an output buffer and sends them to the server in blocks. Thus, even if an application makes a number of calls to drawing functions, the output will not appear on the screen until the buffer has been flushed.

Luckily, simple applications that rely on XNextEvent for event retrieval are not affected by the buffering because XNextEvent always flushes the buffer before getting the next event. If, however, you start a long computation before calling XNextEvent, you may notice that the screen does not reflect the result of the last few graphics functions. In such cases, you should explicitly flush the buffer before starting any operation that takes too long. To do this, use XFlush:

```
Display  *p_disp;
.
.
XFlush(p_disp);
```

XFlush ensures that all requests in Xlib's buffer are sent to the server; it does not guarantee that all requested operations are indeed complete. To wait until all protocol requests have been processed, use XSync:

```
Display *p_disp;            /* Connection to X server      */
int     discard_events = 0; /* 1 = discard events, 0 = don't */
.
.
XSync(p_disp, discard_events);
```

By setting the integer flag discard_events to 1, you can optionally discard all accumulated events in the event queue. Use XSync sparingly because it degrades the performance of your program.

On those rare occasions when you do not want Xlib to buffer any protocol requests, you can use the XSynchronize function to stop the buffering:

```
int disable_buffering = 1; /* 1 = stop buffering, 0 = reenable */
.
.
XSynchronize(p_disp, disable_buffering);
```

When buffering is disabled, the application is running synchronously. In this mode, the application's performance is bound to be very slow because Xlib sends every protocol request to the X server separately and waits for it to be completed before sending the next. Therefore, it is unlikely that you would ever use this mode in final versions of your programs. Use it only for tracking down errors.

Handling Errors

When you program using Xlib, there can be two types of errors:

✦ Errors in parameters sent to the X server

✦ *Fatal I/O errors,* errors locally detected by Xlib (for example, when the connection to the server fails)

The X server detects the first type and reports it by a special event: the X error event. When Xlib receives an error event, it calls a function, the error handler. For the second type of errors, Xlib uses another error handler. You have the opportunity to provide your own function to handle both types of errors.

Default Error Handler

If you haven't already, you will see the default error handler in action soon after you begin writing programs using Xlib. Take, for example, Listing 5.1 for the xhello program. That listing has two calls to XCreateSimpleWindow. In the second call, suppose you set the parent window ID to 0 instead of the variable Main as shown in the listing. When you compile and link the program, there is no way to know that the parameter is invalid. However, when you execute the resulting program, the server detects an error and the program exits with the following message:

```
X Error of failed request:  BadWindow (invalid Window parameter)
  Major opcode of failed request:  1 (X_CreateWindow)
  Resource ID in failed request:  0x0
  Serial number of failed request:  29
  Current serial number in output stream:  33
```

This message is printed by the default error handler in Xlib. The error occurred in a protocol request to create a new window as indicated by the string X_CreateWindow within the parentheses on the second line.

The error message seems cryptic at first, but once you realize that the failed protocol request is one for creating a window, you make progress toward locating the error. After all, Listing 5.1 has two calls to create a window, so the error must be in one of them. After noting which protocol request failed, you should pay attention to the first line of the message—the error itself. In this case, the error is BadWindow, which is due to a bad window identifier (see Appendix B, "X Errors"). Because the parent window identifier is the only Window parameter in the call to XCreateSimpleWindow, you can guess that this ID must be at fault. In fact, the Resource ID line in the message shows that the bad ID is 0 (it shows the value in hexadecimal).

The last two lines in the error message show the serial number of the protocol request that caused the error and the next unprocessed request. (This number is reported by Xlib, not the error event.) The serial number is the number of protocol requests sent to the server since the connection opened, starting at one for the first request. In this example, the error occurred in the 29th request to the server. The 33rd protocol request has already been made but not yet serviced.

Tracking a real error is not as easy as explaining the error message using a simulated error. If you know what to notice, however, you can pinpoint the location of the offending Xlib function.

Programmed Error Handler

The default error handler in Xlib always exits after printing a message. If you do not like this behavior, or if you want to close some files before exiting the program, you can install your own error handling function. The error handler is called with two arguments: a display argument and a pointer to an XErrorEvent data structure, which is defined in <X11/Xlib.h>:

```
typedef unsigned long XID;

typedef struct
{
  int            type;        /* Type of event                    */
  Display        *display;    /* Server that reports the error    */
  XID            resourceid;  /* Resource id                      */
  unsigned long serial;       /* Serial number of failed request  */
  unsigned char error_code;   /* Error code of failed request     */
  unsigned char request_code; /* Major opcode of failed request   */
  unsigned char minor_code;   /* Minor opcode of failed request   */
} XErrorEvent;
```

Using this information, you can write a simple error handler:

```
int myErrorHandler(Display *p_disp, XErrorEvent *p_error)
{
    char err_msg[80];
    XGetErrorText(p_disp, p_error->error_code, err_msg, 80);
    fprintf(stderr, "Error detected.\n  %s\n", err_msg);
    fprintf(stderr, "  Protocol request: %d\n",
                                    p_error->request_code);
    fprintf(stderr, "  Resource ID:     0x%x\n",
                                    p_error->resourceid);

/* Perform necessary clean-ups (close files etc.) and exit */
    fprintf(stderr, "\nCleaning up and exiting...\n");
    exit(1);
}
```

The handler calls the function `XGetErrorText` to get a descriptive message for the `error_code`. The rest of the function prints the message. Although this function simply exits, in a full-fledged application, you include calls to C library functions to close files and perhaps perform other necessary clean-ups before exiting.

If you want, you can return from the error handler to continue executing the program. Of course, the error must be such that you can recover from it. If you return from the handler, you should return a `0`.

The error handler is installed by calling `XSetErrorHandler`:

```
int myErrorHandler();
.
.
.
XSetErrorHandler(myErrorHandler);
```

If you install this handler prior to the second call to `XCreateSimpleWindow` in Listing 5.1, the error due to a wrong parent window ID generates the following error message:

```
Error detected.
  BadWindow, invalid Window parameter
  Protocol request: 1
  Resource ID:     0x0

Cleaning up and exiting...
```

You can change the error handler as often as you want. If you want to revert back to the default handler, call `XSetErrorHandler` with a NULL pointer as the argument.

Fatal I/O Errors

Fatal I/O errors refer to errors that occur when Xlib tries and fails to send protocol requests to or read replies from a server. These usually are system errors such as failure of the TCP/IP or Streams connection. The default handler for fatal I/O errors prints an error message and exits, and you can install your own handler for these errors. The handler is called with a single argument, the pointer to the display. For fatal I/O errors, the handler should always print a message and exit. Of course, you can perform tasks such as closing files to leave your application's files in a stable state. To install your own handler for fatal I/O errors, use the XSetIOErrorHandler function in Xlib:

```
int myFatalIOErrorHandler(Display *p_disp);
.
.
.
XSetIOErrorHandler(myFatalIOErrorHandler);
```

The first argument to XSetIOErrorHandler is not a pointer to the display. Afterward, if you want to revert back to the default handler, call XSetIOErrorHandler with a NULL argument.

Functions Returning Error Status

Xlib automatically calls an error handler when an error occurs. This is not true of all Xlib functions. There are two dozen or so that behave like normal C library routines. They return an integer value indicating success or failure. It is your responsibility to handle error returns from these functions. How do you identify these functions? The Xlib manual shows that these functions return Status, an integer error indicator. When one of these functions fails, it returns a 0. The following is a list of the Xlib functions that return Status:

```
XAllocColor,          XAllocColorCells,      XAllocColorPlanes,
XAllocNamedColor, XCloseIM,
XFetchName, XGetCommand, XGetGCValues, XGetGeometry, XGetIconName,      XGetIconSizes,
XGetNormalHints,      XGetSizeHints,        XGetStandardColormap,
XGetTransientForHint, XGetWindowAttributes, XGetWMColormapWindows, XGetWMProtocols,
XGetZoomHints,
XIconifyWindow , XLookUpColor,          XMatchVisualInfo, XmbTextPerCharExtents,
XParseColor,
XQueryBestCursor,     XQueryBestSize,       XQueryBestStipple,
XQueryBestTile,       XQueryTree, XReconfigureWMWindow, XSendEvent,
XSetWMColormapWindows, XSetWMProtocols,
XwcTextPerCharExtents, XWithdrawWindow
```

Summary

This chapter describes the X programming model. All X programs are responsible for the contents of their windows, and they must perform their tasks in response to events. Events are the X server's way of notifying the application of anything that needs attention. For instance, an event is generated when the user does anything with the keyboard (pressing or releasing a key) or the mouse (moving, pressing, or releasing a button). An event is also generated if parts of a window need repainting. Thus, X applications spend their time in a loop, retrieving events and processing them. This style of programming, frequently referred to as event-driven, is common in window systems such as the Macintosh and Microsoft Windows.

In the context of X programming, the word *resource* means objects (basically data structures in the server), such as windows, fonts, colormaps, and bitmaps, that are created and maintained by the server. The basic steps in an X application are opening a connection to the display (or, equivalently, the server), creating the necessary resources, and handling events until the user quits the application.

In an X program, you access the facilities of the X server through Xlib—the C-callable library of functions that make up the basic application programming interface (API) of the X Window System. The result of calling most Xlib functions is to send X protocol requests to the server. Because your application and the server are two distinct processes, there is no synchronism between the two. By the time the action of a particular Xlib call takes place, your program is usually calling some other Xlib function. This asynchronous nature of X makes errors difficult to correct; you cannot easily tell the exact line of code that caused the error. However, you can force the X server to work synchronously with your program, but you should limit this to the times when you are tracking errors in your program.

## Chapter 7

Creating and Managing Windows

The preceding chapters provide an overview of X: how to use it, how an X application is structured, how Xlib is used to create and manage X resources, and how to handle events. This chapter begins an examination of individual aspects of X programming, beginning with a description of the basic concepts of windows in X and then delving into the details of creating, destroying, and otherwise manipulating windows in X.

Basic Window Concepts

Windows are the reason programmers use the X Window System. Windows are the mechanism that enables several applications to share the limited space in a physical display screen. Each application confines its output to its own window—an area of the screen—and accepts input from the mouse and the keyboard when the pointer focus is in that window. By enabling windows to overlap one another, the X Window System can give each application a reasonable amount of space on screen without one getting in another's way. The user can interact with a specific application by adjusting the view of that application's window so that the entire window is visible. You can think of each window as a small virtual display screen (virtual because it is not real). Each application can use this virtual screen without regard to the other applications that also are displaying in the same physical screen. The windowing system ensures that output meant for a specific window does not affect the contents of any other windows.

The idea of using windows to organize output is not new. It is widely used for graphics as well as character-oriented displays. For example, many applications for MS-DOS systems use character-oriented windows, or text windows, for their user interface. The Macintosh user interface, Microsoft Windows, and X use bitmapped graphics windows. Despite the common goal of organizing output in a logical manner, the window systems have varying terminologies, coordinate systems, and ways of organizing the windows. For example, each window has a parent in X and Microsoft Windows, but the Macintosh does not have that concept. To make effective use of windows, you must learn the terms and concepts that are unique to the window system you are using.

In X, windows are usually rectangular areas of the screen where applications display their output. Windows can overlap one another on the screen. Typically, each X application has at least one window on the screen. A special X application, the window manager, enables users to arrange the windows and shuffle them around as if they were pieces of paper on a desktop. One important aspect of X's model of windows is that they are organized in a strict parent-child hierarchy.

Window Hierarchy

All windows in X are organized in a hierarchy:

✦ At the top of the hierarchy is the root window, which occupies the entire screen.

✦ Every window, except the root, must have a parent.

✦ Each window is the child of some other window.

The main window of an application is a child of the root window. Many more windows usually exist within an application's main window. A window can be of arbitrary size, but the server does not draw any part of a child window that falls outside the boundaries of its parent.

Think of the hierarchy of windows as a family tree, with the root window at the top. A window may have one or more children and each child may have more children. Figure 7.1 shows a hypothetical layout of windows together with their tree structure. Notice how there are several levels in the tree, and there are one or more windows at each level. You can think of the number of levels as the depth of the tree, and the windows at the same level as its breadth. X enables you to have as deep a hierarchy with as much width at each level as you want. Applications routinely use a large number of windows to build a user interface.

You are already familiar with the terms *parent* and *child*. Additionally, the following terms apply to the window hierarchy:

✦ *Sibling.* All children of a parent are called siblings. In Figure 7.1, the windows B.1, B.2, and B.3 are siblings. They are also called the *subwindows* of B.

✦ *Descendant.* The descendants of a window are all windows below it in that branch of the hierarchy. Thus, in Figure 7.1, B has nine descendants—the windows B.1, B.2, B.3, B.2.1, B.2.2, B.2.3, B.3.1, B.3.2, and B.3.3. None of these windows is a descendant of A. Descendants are also referred to as *inferiors*.

✦ *Ancestor.* The ancestors of a window are all windows above it in that branch of the family tree. Thus, the root window is the ancestor of all windows. In Figure 7.1, B is the ancestor of B.1, but A is not, because A is not in the same branch as B.1.

Figure 7.1.

A hierarchy of windows in X.

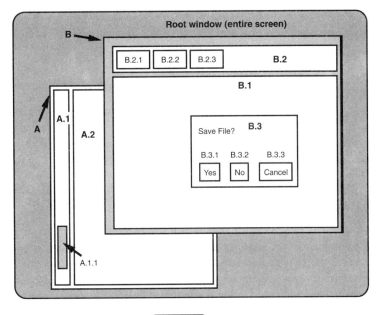

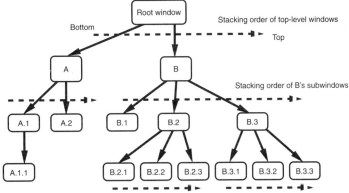

Stacking Order

X clips all children against the boundary of their parent. In case of overlap among siblings, however, the order determines which windows will be fully visible. This order of displaying the siblings is known as the *stacking order*. If the siblings do not overlap, the order in which they are displayed does not matter.

The stacking order of the root window's children is very important, because these are the top-level windows of applications. For example, in Figure 7.1, windows A and B are siblings of the root, with A at the bottom and B at the top of the stacking order. That is why all of B is visible but portions of A are obscured by B. By changing the stacking order of the root window's children, the user can decide which application's window is fully visible on the screen. The user manipulates the stacking order through the window manager, which does the job by calling Xlib functions, such as `XCirculateSubWindows`, `XRaiseWindow`, `XLowerWindow`, and `XRestackWindow`.

Coordinate System and Geometry

In X, a window has a width, a height, and a border width. The height and width do not include the border. Each window also has a coordinate system with the origin at the upper-left corner just inside the border (see Figure 7.2). Additionally, the position of the window is specified by the coordinates of its upper-left corner (outside the border) in its parent's coordinate frame. Collectively, the position and size of a window is known as its *geometry*. Applications usually enable the user to specify the geometry of the main window. (See Chapter 3, "Exploring X Applications," for an example of how to specify the geometry.)

The dimensions of windows and the units of the coordinate systems are specified in pixels, but Xlib has functions that enable you to get the width and height of the screen in millimeters (`XWidthMMOfScreen` and `XHeightMMOfScreen`) as well as in pixels (`XWidthOfScreen` and `XHeightOfScreen`). Using the information provided by these functions, you can convert back and forth between pixels and millimeters.

Figure 7.2.

Coordinate system and geometry of a window in X.

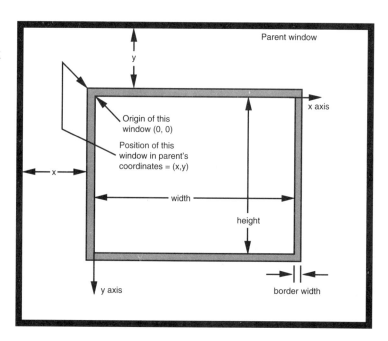

X assumes that the coordinates are discrete and each coordinate lies at the center of a pixel. Thus, the origin (0,0) is at the center of the pixel at the upper-left corner, inside the border (see Figure 7.3).

Figure 7.3.
Coordinates lie on pixel centers.

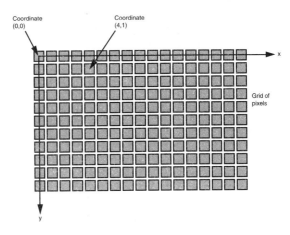

Window Usage

Make liberal use of windows in the user interface of your X application. Take for example, the application `xedit`, a simple text editor that comes with the X software. Figure 7.4 shows the layout of `xedit`'s interface when editing a file named `xhello.c`. Excluding the frame added by the Motif window manager, `xedit`'s main window is divided into three areas:

- ✦ A command menu at the top
- ✦ A message area under the command menu
- ✦ An edit window occupying the rest of the main window (`xedit` displays the contents of the file being edited)

Each area is represented by a window. Both the edit window and the message area have scrollbars to the left. These scrollbars are windows. The command menu at the top shows each command inside its own window. As you can see, the entire interface uses windows liberally.

Most applications have a single main window. All other windows used to build the user interface are descendants of this top-level window. Menus can be constructed by grouping a number of small child windows inside a larger parent window, which can be thought of as a shell to hold the menu items. Each child window in the shell represents a menu item. You can map or unmap the shell window to achieve the effect of pull-down or pop-up menus that must appear in response to a certain event (for example, when the mouse button is pressed in a specific location).

If you want to have a dialog window to get confirmation from the user (for example, the window B.3 in Figure 7.1), you can create the window with the necessary subwindows for messages such as `Yes`, `No`, and `Cancel`. Then, anytime you need the dialog window, map it. After accepting the user's input, you can unmap the window to hide it.

It is somewhat tedious to create and work with a large hierarchy of windows. One solution to this problem is to use a toolkit. Chapters 13, "X Toolkits," 14, "OSF/Motif Wedges," and 15, "Toolkit-Based Applications," show how to develop X applications using toolkits.

Figure 7.4.
The user interface of
xedit.

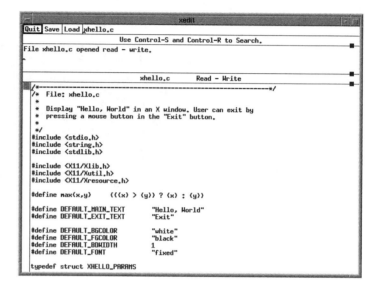

Main Window

After establishing a connection to an X server, the first task of an X application is to create the necessary windows. Windows are not displayed automatically; you have to map them to show them on the screen. All input and output is organized through windows. Therefore, in addition to creating the windows, you have to specify the events to be reported for each window.

Setting Up the Main Window with *initapp.c*

Most applications have a main window that is the top window in the hierarchy of windows used by that application. Setting up the main window requires extra work because this window is a child of the root window and it shares the screen with the top-level windows of all other applications using that X server.

To illustrate how to set up the main window of an application, you will develop a utility function, `initapp.c`. You write this function so that it establishes the connection to the X display and sets default colors and fonts. Additionally, you want this function to accept some common command-line arguments and resources (as shown in the `xhello` program of Chapter 5, "A Simple X Application"). Once you have such a function, you can use it in the subsequent examples for the routine steps of connecting to a display and getting the main window set up.

Arguments

You want the `initapp.c` function to require as few arguments as possible. Because it will accept command-line arguments, you have to pass to `initapp.c` the command-line arguments received by the application's `main` function. To set up the main window, all you should need are the preferred location and size of the window. Thus, the ANSI prototype of the function is the following:

```
void initapp(int argc,          /* No. of command-line args */
             char **argv,       /* Command-line arguments   */
             int x, int y,      /* Position of window       */
             unsigned width,    /* Width and height of      */
             unsigned height);  /* the main window          */
```

Some Global Variables

Because `initapp.c` sets up the connection to the display and sets up colors and fonts for the main window, you need some global variables to return the result of these operations. Accordingly, Listing 7.1 shows the necessary global variables. The filename is `app_glob.c`—with a `.c` extension instead of an `.h` because it actually declares variables. Header files with an `.h` extension customarily are used for defining structures and function prototypes, not for anything that actually allocates storage space.

Listing 7.1. `app_glob.c`—Global variables for X applications.

```
/* File: app_glob.c
 *
 * Declare the common global variables for X applications.
 *
 */

#ifndef APP_GLOB_C   /* To ensure that it is included once */
#define APP_GLOB_C

#ifdef DEF_APP_GLOB      /* Defined in the initapp.c file */

XWMHints       *p_XWMH;      /* Hints for the window manager  */
XSizeHints     *p_XSH;       /* Size hints for window manager */
XClassHint     *p_CH;        /* Class hint for window manager */
XTextProperty WName;         /* Window name for title bar     */
XTextProperty IName;         /* Icon name for icon label       */
Display        *theDisplay;  /* Connection to X display       */
GC             theGC;        /* The graphics context for main */
int            AppDone = 0;  /* Flag to indicate when done    */
XEvent         theEvent;     /* Structure for current event   */
XFontStruct    *theFontStruct; /* Info on the default font    */
unsigned long theBGpix,      /* Background and foreground     */
              theFGpix;      /* pixel values of main window   */
char           *theAppName = " "; /* Application's name       */
Window         theMain;      /* Application's main window      */
XWindowAttributes
               MainXWA;      /* Attributes of main window     */
#else

extern XWMHints       *p_XWMH;
extern XSizeHints     *p_XSH;
extern XClassHint     *p_CH;
extern XTextProperty  WName;
```

continues

Listing 7.1. continued

```
extern XTextProperty  IName;
extern  Display        *theDisplay;
extern  GC             theGC;
extern  int            AppDone;
extern  XEvent         theEvent;
extern  XFontStruct    *theFontStruct;
extern  unsigned long theBGpix,
                       theFGpix;
extern  char           *theAppName;
extern  Window         theMain;
extern  XWindowAttributes
                       MainXWA;

#endif   /* #ifdef DEF_APP_GLOB */
#endif   /* #ifndef APP_GLOB_C  */
```

The variable theDisplay identifies the connection to the X display. Other functions will use this in their Xlib calls. The window ID of the main window is saved in the theMain variable. The graphics context, font structure, and pixel values of colors are used for drawing in the main window. The AppDone variable is used as a flag to indicate when the application should exit its event handling loop. (Listing 7.4, later in this chapter, clarifies its use.)

The *initapp.c* File

Listing 7.2 shows the file initapp.c containing the function initapp. The first few tasks handled in initapp are routine command-line processing and resource handling. The approach used to perform these chores has been adapted from the technique used in the xhello program of Chapter 5.

Once the display is identified from the optional -display command-line option (if this is unspecified, a NULL string is used as the name), initapp calls XOpenDisplay to open the connection. The display identifier is saved in the global variable theDisplay.

Next comes the job of setting up the colors and fonts to draw in the window. These steps are necessary and therefore included here; Chapters 9, "Drawing Graphics," 10, "Drawing Text," and 11, "Using Color in X," explain them further.

The steps of interest for this chapter follow next:

✦ Informing the window manager

✦ Creating the window

✦ Setting window attributes

✦ Selecting events

✦ Mapping the window

Let's examine each of these in detail, referring, when necessary, to the code shown in Listing 7.2.

Listing 7.2. `initapp.c`—Setting up the main window in X.

```
/*------------------------------------------------------------*/
/*  File: initapp.c
 *
 *  Function to process command-line arguments, connect to the
 *  X display, and set up the main window of a generic
 *  X application.
 *
 */
#include <stdio.h>
#include <string.h>
#include <stdlib.h>

#include <X11/Xlib.h>
#include <X11/Xutil.h>
#include <X11/Xresource.h>

#define  DEF_APP_GLOB     /* so that globals get defined */
#include "app_glob.c"

#define max(x,y)      (((x) > (y)) ? (x) : (y))

#define DEFAULT_BGCOLOR          "white"
#define DEFAULT_FGCOLOR          "black"
#define DEFAULT_BDWIDTH          1
#define DEFAULT_FONT             "fixed"

typedef struct APP_PARAMS
{
    char *name;
    char *cname;
    char **p_value_string;
} APP_PARAMS;

/* Default parameter values (as strings) */
char *theBGcolor     = DEFAULT_BGCOLOR,
     *theFGcolor     = DEFAULT_FGCOLOR,
     *theFont        = DEFAULT_FONT,
     *theGeom_rsrc   = NULL,
     *display_name   = NULL,
     *theGeom_cline  = NULL,
     *theGeom        = NULL;

/* List of user-customizable resources */

APP_PARAMS app_resources[] =
{
    "background", "Background",   &theBGcolor,
    "foreground", "Foreground",   &theFGcolor,
    "font",       "Font",         &theFont,
    "geometry",   "Geometry",     &theGeom_rsrc,
};

int num_resources = sizeof(app_resources) / sizeof(APP_PARAMS);

/* List of command-line options */
```

continues

Listing 7.2. continued

```
APP_PARAMS app_options[] =
{
    "-display",  "-d", &display_name,
    "-geometry", "-g", &theGeom_cline
};

int num_options = sizeof(app_options) / sizeof(APP_PARAMS);

void usage();
static char rname[80];
/*-----------------------------------------------------------*/
void initapp(argc, argv, x, y, width, height)
int argc, x, y;
char **argv;
unsigned width,  height;
{
    int                 i, j;
    char                *tmpstr;
    Colormap            default_cmap;
    XColor              color;
    int                 bitmask;
    XGCValues           gcv;
    XSetWindowAttributes xswa;
    char                default_geometry[80];
    char                rfilename[80];
    char                *type;
    XrmValue            value;
    XrmDatabase         rdb;

    theAppName = argv[0];
    AppDone = 0;

/* Parse command-line options. Since each option has a value,
 * they are processed in pairs.
 */
    for (i = 1; i < argc; i += 2)
    {
        for(j = 0; j < num_options; j++)
        {
            if(strcmp(app_options[j].name, argv[i]) == 0 ||
               strcmp(app_options[j].cname, argv[i]) == 0)
            {
                *app_options[j].p_value_string = argv[i+1];
                break;
            }
        }
        if(j >= num_options)
            usage();
    }

/*  Open connection to display selected by user */

    if ((theDisplay = XOpenDisplay(display_name)) == NULL)
    {
        fprintf(stderr, "%s: can't open display named %s\n",
```

```
                    argv[0], XDisplayName(display_name));
        exit(1);
    }

/* Get resources from the resource file */
    XrmInitialize();
    strcpy(rfilename, getenv("HOME"));
    strcat(rfilename, "/.Xdefaults");
    rdb = XrmGetFileDatabase(rfilename);
    if(rdb != NULL)
    {
        for (i = 0; i < num_resources; i++)
        {
/* Construct a complete resource name by appending the
 * resource name to the application's name.
 */
            strcpy(rname, theAppName);
            strcat(rname, "*");
            strcat(rname, app_resources[i].name);

            if(XrmGetResource(rdb, rname, rname,
                        &type, &value))
            {
                *app_resources[i].p_value_string = value.addr;
        }
        }
    }

/* Set up colors and fonts */

    if ((theFontStruct = XLoadQueryFont(theDisplay,
                                    theFont)) == NULL)
    {
        fprintf(stderr, "%s: display %s cannot load font %s\n",
                theAppName, DisplayString(theDisplay), theFont);
        exit(1);
    }

/* Now select the colors using the default colormap */

    default_cmap = DefaultColormap(theDisplay,
                            DefaultScreen(theDisplay));
/* Main window's background color */
    if (XParseColor(theDisplay, default_cmap, theBGcolor,
                &color) == 0 ||
        XAllocColor(theDisplay, default_cmap, &color) == 0)

/* Use white background in case of failure */
        theBGpix = WhitePixel(theDisplay,
                            DefaultScreen(theDisplay));
    else
        theBGpix = color.pixel;

/* Main window's foreground color */
```

continues

Listing 7.2. continued

```
    if (XParseColor(theDisplay, default_cmap, theFGcolor,
                    &color) == 0 ¦¦
        XAllocColor(theDisplay, default_cmap, &color) == 0)
/* Use black foreground in case of failure */
        theFGpix = BlackPixel(theDisplay,
                                DefaultScreen(theDisplay));
    else
        theFGpix = color.pixel;

/* Fill out an XsizeHints structure to inform the window manager
 * of desired size and location of main window.
 */
    if((p_XSH = XAllocSizeHints()) == NULL)
    {
        fprintf(stderr, "Error allocating size hints!\n");
        exit(1);
    }
    p_XSH->flags = (PPosition ¦ PSize ¦ PMinSize);
    p_XSH->height = height;
    p_XSH->min_height = p_XSH->height;
    p_XSH->width = width;
    p_XSH->min_width = p_XSH->width;
    p_XSH->x = x;
    p_XSH->y = y;

/* Construct a default geometry string */
    sprintf(default_geometry, "%dx%d+%d+%d", p_XSH->width,
            p_XSH->height, p_XSH->x, p_XSH->y);
    theGeom = default_geometry;

/* Override the geometry, if necessary */
    if(theGeom_cline != NULL) theGeom = theGeom_cline;
    else
        if(theGeom_rsrc != NULL) theGeom = theGeom_rsrc;

/* Process the geometry specification */
    bitmask =  XGeometry(theDisplay, DefaultScreen(theDisplay),
                    theGeom, default_geometry, DEFAULT_BDWIDTH,
                    1, 1, 0, 0, &(p_XSH->x), &(p_XSH->y),
                    &(p_XSH->width), &(p_XSH->height));

/* Check bitmask and set flags in XSizeHints structure */
    if (bitmask & (XValue ¦ YValue)) p_XSH->flags ¦= USPosition;
    if (bitmask & (WidthValue ¦ HeightValue))
                                p_XSH->flags ¦= USSize;

/* Create the main window using the position and size
 * information derived above. For border color, use the
 * foreground color.
 */
    theMain = XCreateSimpleWindow(theDisplay,
                    DefaultRootWindow(theDisplay),
                    p_XSH->x, p_XSH->y, p_XSH->width, p_XSH->height,
                    DEFAULT_BDWIDTH, theFGpix, theBGpix);
```

```
/* Set up class hint */
    if((p_CH = XAllocClassHint()) == NULL)
    {
        fprintf(stderr, "Error allocating class hint!\n");
        exit(1);
    }
    p_CH->res_name = theAppName;
    p_CH->res_class = theAppName;

/* Set up XTextProperty for window name and icon name */
    if(XStringListToTextProperty(&theAppName, 1, &WName) == 0)
    {
        fprintf(stderr, "Error creating XTextProperty!\n");
        exit(1);
    }
    if(XStringListToTextProperty(&theAppName, 1, &IName) == 0)
    {
        fprintf(stderr, "Error creating XTextProperty!\n");
        exit(1);
    }

    if((p_XWMH = XAllocWMHints()) == NULL)
    {
        fprintf(stderr, "Error allocating Window Manager hints!\n");
        exit(1);
    }
    p_XWMH->flags = (InputHint¦StateHint);
    p_XWMH->input = False;
    p_XWMH->initial_state = NormalState;
    XSetWMProperties(theDisplay, theMain, &WName, &IName, argv, argc,
                     p_XSH, p_XWMH, p_CH);

/* Finally, create a graphics context for the main window */

    gcv.font = theFontStruct->fid;
    gcv.foreground = theFGpix;
    gcv.background = theBGpix;
    theGC = XCreateGC(theDisplay, theMain,
                (GCFont ¦ GCForeground ¦ GCBackground), &gcv);

/* Set main window's attributes (colormap, bit_gravity) */

    xswa.colormap = DefaultColormap(theDisplay,
                                    DefaultScreen(theDisplay));
    xswa.bit_gravity = NorthWestGravity;
    XChangeWindowAttributes(theDisplay, theMain, (CWColormap ¦
                            CWBitGravity), &xswa);

/* Select Exposure events for the main window */

    XSelectInput(theDisplay, theMain, ExposureMask);

/* Map the main window */
```

continues

Listing 7.2. continued

```
    XMapWindow(theDisplay, theMain);
    XFlush(theDisplay);
    if(XGetWindowAttributes(theDisplay, theMain, &MainXWA) == 0)
    {
        fprintf(stderr, "Error getting attributes of Main.\n");
        exit(2);
    }
}
/*----------------------------------------------------------*/
void usage ()
{
    fprintf (stderr, "%s [-display name] [-geometry geom]\n",
            theAppName);
}
```

Window Manager Interaction

The extra steps in setting up the top-level window of an application involve cooperating with the window manager. In addition to maintaining the layout of all top-level windows of the application, it takes care of other important tasks, such as deciding which window gets the keystrokes and when to install a new colormap so that applications can display colors properly. For all this to work, the applications must cooperate with the window manager; by design, the window manager is a peer of the other applications, not a superior.

Cooperation with the window manager takes the form of giving hints to it. You call certain Xlib functions to notify the window manager of the main window's recommended position and size. The window manager does its best to accommodate the request, but the application should be prepared to handle the contingency of having a window smaller than it requests.

Program-Specified Position and Size

You can use the convenience function XSetWMProperties to give the window manager several useful hints and to inform it of the main window's preferred position and size. You specify the position and size, or geometry, in an XSizeHints structure, which is defined in <X11/Xutil.h> as the following:

```
typedef struct
{
    long flags;      /* Indicates which fields are defined */
    int x, y;          /* Suggested position and size        */
    int width, height;  /* for old window managers            */
    int min_width, min_height; /* Minimum width and height */
    int max_width, max_height; /* Minimum width and height */
    int width_inc, height_inc; /* Width, height increments */
    struct
    {
        int x;            /* Numerator of aspect ratio    */
        int y;            /* Denominator of aspect ratio */
```

```
    } min_aspect, max_aspect;
    int base_width, base_height; /* Window size and gravity */
    int win_gravity;            /* (see later in this chapter) */
} XSizeHints;
```

When setting up an XSizeHints structure, you need not specify all fields of the structure. The x, y, width, height, min_width, and min_height are the most commonly specified fields. You set bits in flags to indicate the fields being specified. You can do this by setting flags to the bitwise-OR of named constants defined in the header file <X11/Xutil.h>. For example, to set the fields mentioned above, flags is set to the bitwise-OR of the constants PPosition, PSize, and PMinSize. Here is how these fields are set in initapp:

```
XSizeHints     *p_XSH;        /* Size hints for window manager */
   .
   .
   .
/* Fill out an XsizeHints structure to inform the window manager
 * of desired size and location of main window.
 */
    if((p_XSH = XAllocSizeHints()) == NULL)
    {
        fprintf(stderr, "Error allocating size hints!\n");
        exit(1);
    }
    p_XSH->flags = (PPosition | PSize | PMinSize);
    p_XSH->height = height;
    p_XSH->min_height = p_XSH->height;
    p_XSH->width = width;
    p_XSH->min_width = p_XSH->width;
    p_XSH->x = x;
    p_XSH->y = y;
```

The position and size come from the arguments passed to the initapp function. The minimum size is assumed to be the same as the specified size. The window manager will not enable the user to reduce the window below this minimum size.

The P prefix in the names for the constants used to define the flags means that these are program-specified values.

NOTE:

Xlib has many structures with several data fields for which not all fields need to be specified for a function. In such cases, the structure includes a flags field whose bits are used to indicate which of the other fields are set. You can set the flags field by bitwise-OR of constants that have been defined in the header file <X11/Xutil.h>. Each of these constants indicate that certain fields in the structure have been specified. For example, in setting the XSizeHints structure, setting flags to (PPosition | PSize) indicates that values are provided for the location (x, y) and size (width, height) fields.

User-Specified Position and Size

The user's choice of a window's position and size can come through the -geometry command-line option or the geometry resource. If neither of these is specified, the program provides a default geometry. The geometry is specified by a string of the form width x height + x + y, where width and height are integers specifying size of window in pixels, and x and y indicate the position in the parent's coordinate frame. (For more information about geometry, see Chapter 3.)

The user's specification of the geometry need not be complete; the string can have either the size or the position alone. The programmer's problem is to have the application figure out what the user specifies and reconcile it with the default geometry. Xlib's XGeometry utility function is designed to do the job; however, it requires the program's default geometry in a string. Handling user-specified geometry requires the following steps:

1. Construct a string containing the default geometry:

   ```
   char default_geometry[80];

       .

       .

   /* Construct a default geometry string */
       sprintf(default_geometry, "%dx%d+%d+%d", p_XSH->width,
               p_XSH->height, p_XSH->x, p_XSH->y);
   ```

2. Set the user-specified geometry string, stored in the string theGeom in initapp.

3. Check whether the command-line or the resource file (.Xdefaults in the user's home directory) provides a geometry string. If so, set the string theGeom to the user's definition of the geometry, giving precedence to the command-line option over the contents of the resource file. This enables the user to override specifications in the resource file with command-line options. The following example shows how initapp sets the user-defined geometry:

   ```
       theGeom = default_geometry;

   /* Override the geometry, if necessary */
       if(theGeom_cline != NULL) theGeom = theGeom_cline;
       else
           if(theGeom_rsrc != NULL) theGeom = theGeom_rsrc;
   ```

4. Call XGeometry to get the position and size. The values come from the user-specified geometry, except where items are missing in the user's specification. XGeometry takes the display and screen as the first two arguments. For the screen argument, you can use the DefaultScreen macro. The default screen for the display theDisplay is DefaultScreen(theDisplay). Next come two string arguments: the user-specified geometry followed by the default geometry. The fifth argument is the border width in pixels. The next four arguments are the following:

   ◆ unsigned int width_factor, height_factor;
     The user-specified width and height are multiplied by these two factors. If you are displaying text, these arguments can be the width and height of characters for the

selected font. If you want the user's specifications to remain as is, use 1 for both arguments.

✦ `int xadd, yadd;`

These are values to be added to the width and height, respectively. If you do not want any padding, provide 0s for these arguments.

The last four arguments are the addresses of the integers where `XGeometry` returns the selected x, y, `width`, and `height`. In `initapp`, you accept the values directly in the appropriate fields of the `XSizeHints` structure:

```
    int bitmask;

    .

    .
/* Process the geometry specification */
    bitmask = XGeometry(theDisplay, DefaultScreen(theDisplay),
                  theGeom, default_geometry, DEFAULT_BDWIDTH,
                  1, 1, 0, 0, &(p_XSH->x), &(p_XSH->y),
                  &(p_XSH->width), &(p_XSH->height));

/* Check bitmask and set flags in XSizeHints structure */
    if (bitmask & (XValue ¦ YValue)) p_XSH->flags ¦= USPosition;
    if (bitmask & (WidthValue ¦ HeightValue))
                            p_XSH->flags ¦= USSize;
```

The `XGeometry` function returns an integer value that should be viewed as a pattern of bits (a `bitmask`). The set bits in the returned `bitmask` indicate which of the x, y, `width`, and `height` variables were altered by `XGeometry`. As the previous code shows, if the position or size was altered because of a user-specified geometry, the `flags` field of the `XSizeHints` structure is modified to indicate it. The constants named `USPosition` and `USSize` are bit patterns that tell the window manager that these are user-specified options. Ideally, the window manager should use any user-specified options as is, without any change. The exact behavior depends on the window manager.

Standard Properties

After you settle on a size for the main window, you can create it using `XCreateSimpleWindow`. This simple function requires the following arguments:

✦ Display.
✦ Parent window's ID
✦ Window's location
✦ Window's size
✦ Border width
✦ Border color
✦ Background color

In the case of the main window, the parent is the root window, which is identified by the macro `DefaultRootWindow(theDisplay)`.

Creating the window does not show anything on the screen. The window appears only when you map it—and before you map it, you have to inform the window manager about it. This enables the window manager to intervene and place the window correctly when it is mapped.

The convenience function, `XSetWMProperties`, is useful for this. As the name implies, you are setting the properties of a window (the one you just created). In X, a *property* is some data stored at the server and tagged by a window ID. You can store a property in a window and restore it. The interpretation of the data represented by a property depends on the applications that use it. Properties are used for exchanging information among X applications—an example being the communication between your application and the window manager.

The arguments to `XSetWMProperties` are the following:

+ Display in which your application's windows are located
+ Window for which you are setting the properties
+ `XTextProperty`, representing the window's name (use `XStringListToTextProperty` function to convert a string to `XTextProperty`)
+ `XTextProperty`, representing the name to be displayed in the window's icon
+ Command-line arguments used in starting the application
+ Number of command-line arguments
+ Pointer to the `XSizeHints` structure that holds the preferred geometry of the window
+ Pointer to the `XWMHints` structure holding additional hints for the window manager (explained in the next section)
+ Pointer to the `XClassHint` structure specifying the application's name and its class name

In `initapp`, the following code accomplishes the creation of the main window and the setting of the window manager properties:

```
/* Create the main window using the position and size
 * information derived above. For border color, use the
 * foreground color.
 */
    theMain = XCreateSimpleWindow(theDisplay,
                    DefaultRootWindow(theDisplay),
                    p_XSH->x, p_XSH->y, p_XSH->width, p_XSH->height,
                    DEFAULT_BDWIDTH, theFGpix, theBGpix);

/* Set up class hint */
    if((p_CH = XAllocClassHint()) == NULL)
    {
        fprintf(stderr, "Error allocating class hint!\n");
        exit(1);
    }
    p_CH->res_name = theAppName;
    p_CH->res_class = theAppName;

/* Set up XTextProperty for window name and icon name */
```

```
    if(XStringListToTextProperty(&theAppName, 1, &WName) == 0)
    {
        fprintf(stderr, "Error creating XTextProperty!\n");
        exit(1);
    }
    if(XStringListToTextProperty(&theAppName, 1, &IName) == 0)
    {
        fprintf(stderr, "Error creating XTextProperty!\n");
        exit(1);
    }
/* Allocate and set up an XWMHints structure (see next section) */
    .
    .
    .

XSetWMProperties(theDisplay, theMain, &WName, &IName, argv, argc,
                    p_XSH, p_XWMH, p_CH);
```

XSetWMProperties combines the functionality of several Xlib functions. You can set the window's name and its icon's name using the functions XSetWMName and XSetWMIconName, respectively. Xlib provides XSetCommand for storing the command-line parameters as a property of a window. You can use XSetWMNormalHints to provide the size hints to the window manager. Finally, you could use XSetWMHints and XSetClassHint to transmit the information in XWMHints and XClassHint structures to the X server. If you use these functions instead of XSetWMProperties, this is the equivalent sequence of calls:

```
    XClassHint      *p_CH;
    XWMHints        *p_XWMH;
    XSizeHints      *p_XSH;
    XTextProperty WName;
    XTextProperty IName;
/* Allocate and initialize the hint structures */
    .
    .
    .
    XSetWMName(theDisplay, theMain, &WName);
    XSetIconName(theDisplay, theMain, &IName);
    XSetCommand(theDisplay, theMain, argv, argc);
    XSetWMNormalHints(theDisplay, theMain, p_XSH);
    XSetWMHints(theDisplay, theMain, p_XWMH);
    XSetClassHint(theDisplay, theMain, p_CH);
```

NOTE:

Xlib provides several ways to perform certain tasks. For example, you can inform the window manager of a window's preferred size by calling one of two functions: XSetWMNormalHints or XSetWMProperties. Similarly, you can specify a window's background and border colors when creating it with XCreateSimpleWindow or by calling XSetWindowBackground and XSetWindowBorder later. To avoid swamping you with too many details, this book usually shows the most convenient function and then lists the alternate functions. You can look up the description of these functions in Appendix A, "Xlib Functions."

Additional Hints

The window manager needs a few more hints from your application. These hints tell the window manager if you want the main window to appear in a normal form or as an icon. Also, the window manager needs information on your program's model of keyboard input. These hints are provided in an XWMHints structure, defined in <X11/Xutil.h> as the following:

```
#define Bool int

typedef unsigned long XID;

typedef struct
{
    long   flags;        /* Indicates which fields are defined */
    Bool   input;        /* True if window manager's help is
                            needed in getting keyboard input    */
    int    initial_state; /* Normal size or icon?              */
    Pixmap icon_pixmap;   /* Pixmap to be used as window's icon */
    Window icon_window;   /* Window to be used to show icon     */
    int    icon_x, icon_y;/* Initial position of icon window    */
    Pixmap icon_mask;     /* Bitmap used as mask for icon       */
    XID    window_group;  /* ID of window group leader          */
} XWMHints;
```

Specifying hints in this structure is similar to the way fields are set in the XSizeHints structure. You can provide values for the fields you want and indicate your choices by setting bits in the flags field. In setting up the main window of a simple application, you are most likely to set the initial_state of the window and the input parameter. If your window will accept keyboard input, set input to True. The initial_state determines whether the window appears as a full-sized window or as an icon. You usually set this to NormalState. The following code shows how to set up the XWMHints structure for a typical X application's main window:

```
    XWMHints  *p_XWMH;

/* Allocate XWMHints structure by calling XAllocWMHints() */
    .
    .
/* Give other hints to window manager by filling out an
 * XWMHints structure and calling XSetWMProperties()
 */

    if((p_XWMH = XAllocWMHints()) == NULL)
    {
        fprintf(stderr, "Error allocating Window Manager hints!\n");
        exit(1);
    }
    p_XWMH->flags = (InputHint¦StateHint);
    p_XWMH->input = False;
    p_XWMH->initial_state = NormalState;

/* Call XSetWMHints or XSetWMProperties. */
    .
    .
```

Window Attributes

A window in X has a number of attributes that control many aspects of its appearance and behavior, and how it is is used in an application. You can set the attributes by calling XChangeWindowAttributes. The values for the attributes are passed to this function via an XSetWindowAttributes structure, which is defined in <X11/Xlib.h> as the following:

```
#define Bool int

typedef struct
{
    Pixmap          background_pixmap;    /* Background pixmap   */
    unsigned long   background_pixel;     /* Background pixel    */
    Pixmap          border_pixmap;        /* Pixmap for border   */
    unsigned long   border_pixel;         /* Border pixel value  */
    int             bit_gravity;          /* See description     */
    int             win_gravity;          /* See description     */
    int             backing_store;        /* Use backing store?  */
    unsigned long   backing_planes;       /* If yes, which planes*/
    unsigned long   backing_pixel;        /* For restoring planes*/
    Bool            save_under;           /* Save bits in window?*/
    long            event_mask;           /* Events accepted     */
    long            do_not_propagate_mask;/* Events not forwarded*/
    Bool            override_redirect;    /* See description     */
    Colormap        colormap;             /* Colormap for window*/
    Cursor          cursor;               /* Cursor for window   */
} XSetWindowAttributes;
```

The XSetWindowAttributes structure provides for a large number of attributes. Specifically, the following aspects of a window are controlled by the attributes:

+ *Background.* The appearance of the window's background is controlled by the attributes background_pixmap and background_pixel. If you set the background_pixel to a pixel value, you get a solid color (corresponding to that pixel) as the background. On the other hand, by setting background_pixmap to an 8x8 or 16x16 pixmap, you can have a repeating pattern as the window's background. If you set background_pixmap to the symbolic constant None, the window will have a transparent background. Set background_pixmap to ParentRelative to use the parent's background pixmap in a window. Note that when you set the background pixmap, the X server makes a copy of the pixmap. Thus, you can destroy your copy of the pixmap after setting the background. Also, the last setting of background_pixmap or background_pixel overrides the previous background setting.

+ *Border.* Like the background, the border can be a solid color (border_pixel) or a pattern (border_pixmap).

+ *Colormap.* The color_map attribute controls how the pixel values in that window get translated to actual colors. To set this to the parent window's colormap, use CopyFromParent as the value.

✦ *Cursor.* The cursor attribute determines the shape of the mouse cursor. For a new cursor, you have to set this attribute to the resource ID returned by a function, such as the XCreateFontCursor function, which creates a cursor out of a character from a special font. XCreateGlyphCursor is another function for creating a new cursor.

✦ *Off-Screen Memory.* The fields backing_store, save_under, backing_planes, and backing_pixel are for informing the X server whether your window will benefit from using off-screen memory (or, "backing store") for saving obscured parts. Note, however, that this is only a hint to the server; not all servers have off-screen memory. Even when backing_store is present, the server may not have enough for your window (perhaps it already used all memory to service another client). Thus, your application is still responsible for the contents of all its windows. If your application maps and unmaps a window without changing the contents (for example, to display a pop-up menu), you should set backing_store to the constant Always. Other values are NotUseful and WhenMapped, each indicating when backing store is useful. Set the save_under attribute to True for a pop-up window. The server will save anything under such a window and restore the area when the window goes away. The backing_planes attribute indicates which bit planes are to be saved and backing_pixel provides the pixel value used when reconstructing a saved window (useful when all planes are not saved).

✦ *Bit gravity.* The bit_gravity attribute determines what happens to the contents of a window after it is resized. It essentially tells the X server where to place the old contents of a window after the window is shrunk or enlarged. It is as if the old bits move by gravitational attraction to a specific side or corner of the window. The default setting for bit_gravity is the defined constant ForgetGravity which means that the old contents of the window are discarded after any resize. Table 7.1 summarizes the disposition of the old contents of the window when it is resized. When a window is resized by the user, the server generates Expose events to inform your application of the areas that need redrawing. The bit_gravity setting determines the areas that need refreshing.

✦ *Window gravity.* Analogous to bit gravity, the window gravity attribute, win_gravity, determines where the window is positioned when its parent's size changes. The settings of this attribute are similar to that of bit_gravity. For example, the default win_gravity setting of NorthWestGravity states that when its parent is resized, the window moves to the upper-left corner of the parent. Because this corner corresponds to the parent's origin, the window appears fixed to its parent.

Table 7.1. Bit Gravity Constants

Defined Constant	*Disposition of Old Contents*
ForgetGravity	Old contents discarded
NorthWestGravity	Placed in upper-left corner of resized window
NorthGravity	Placed in top center of resized window
NorthEastGravity	Placed in upper-right corner of resized window
EastGravity	Placed in right center of resized window

Defined Constant	*Disposition of Old Contents*
SouthEastGravity	Placed in lower-right corner of resized window
SouthGravity	Placed in bottom center of resized window
SouthWestGravity	Placed in lower-left corner of resized window
WestGravity	Placed in left center of resized window
CenterGravity	Placed in center of resized window
StaticGravity	Resized window retains old contents

The rest of the attributes in the XSetWindowAttributes structure—event_mask, do_not_propagate_mask, and override_redirect—are for setting up event handling. When you call the function XSelectInput, you are, in effect, altering the event_mask attribute. (Event handling mechanisms are further described in Chapter 8, "Handling Events.")

Attribute Setting

As with the XSizeHints and XWMHints structures, in the XSetWindowAttributes structure, you can set only a select few attributes. You have to use a bit flag to indicate which of the fields you are specifying. Unlike XSizeHints and XWMHints structures, however, the bit flag is not a member of the XSetWindowAttributes structure. Instead, the bit flag is the third argument for the XChangeWindowAttributes function, which takes four arguments:

+ Display
+ Window
+ Bit flag
+ Pointer to the XSetWindowAttributes structure

For example, in initapp, you want to set the colormap and the bit_gravity fields. The flag, in this case, is (CWColormap | CWBitGravity):

```
XSetWindowAttributes xswa;
   .
   .
   .
/* Set main window's attributes (colormap, bit_gravity) */

   xswa.colormap = DefaultColormap(theDisplay,
                                DefaultScreen(theDisplay));
   xswa.bit_gravity = NorthWestGravity;
   XChangeWindowAttributes(theDisplay, theMain, (CWColormap |
                        CWBitGravity), &xswa);
```

To set the colormap, use DefaultColormap macro to get the default colormap.

Attribute Retrieving

At the end of the `initapp` function in Listing 7.2, you read back the attributes of the newly created main window. The attributes are returned in an `XWindowAttributes` structure, which has the following definition in `<X11/Xlib.h>`:

```
typedef struct
{
    int           x, y;             /* Position of window       */
    int           width, height;    /* Window's width and height*/
    int           border_width;     /* Border width of window   */
    int           depth;            /* Bits per pixel in window */
    Visual        *visual;          /* Color handling model     */
    Window        root;             /* Root window's ID         */
    int           class;            /* InputOutput or InputOnly */
    int           bit_gravity;      /* The bit gravity          */
    int           win_gravity;      /* The window gravity       */
    int           backing_store;    /* Use off-screen memory?   */
    unsigned long backing_planes;   /* Which bit planes to save?*/
    unsigned long backing_pixel;    /* Pixel value for restoring*/
    Bool          save_under;       /* Save bits under window?  */
    Colormap      colormap;         /* Colormap of window       */
    Bool          map_installed;    /* Colormap installed?      */
    int           map_state;        /* Is window mapped and if  */
                                    /* yes, is it viewable?     */
    long          all_event_masks;  /* Events selected by all   */
    long          your_event_mask;  /* Your application's events*/
    long          do_not_propagate_mask; /* See Chapter 8       */
    Bool          override_redirect;     /* See Chapter 8       */
    Screen        *screen;               /* Pointer to screen   */
} XWindowAttributes;
```

As you can see from its definition, `XWindowAttributes` has several more fields than `XSetWindowAttributes` does. The extra fields are other attributes that contain useful information about the window. For example, you can determine the position and size of the window from this structure. The size is especially important because the top-level window may not always have the size requested in the program. You can get the window's attributes using the `XGetWindowAttributes` function:

```
XWindowAttributes MainXWA;
    .
    .
    .
/* Get the window's attributes and save them for future */

    if(XGetWindowAttributes(theDisplay, theMain, &MainXWA) == 0)
    {
        fprintf(stderr, "Error getting attributes of Main.\n");
        exit(2);
    }
```

Among the fields you see in the `XWindowAttributes` structure, `class`, `visual`, and `depth` are three items that are set for the lifetime of a window:

✦ The `class` field can be one of the defined constants: `InputOut` or `InputOnly`. As the name implies, `InputOutput` windows can be used for displaying output as well as for accepting event inputs. `InputOnly` windows are invisible windows that can receive input events but cannot display any output. If you try to draw into an `InputOnly` window, the server will generate an error. You can use `InputOnly` windows, for example, to change the cursor shape as you move from one area of the screen to another, because these windows can have cursor shapes associated with them.

✦ The `visual` attribute indicates the color model used by the physical display screen where the window appears.

✦ The `depth` is the number of bits per pixel of the window. The `depth` of an `InputOnly` window must be `0`. Chapter 11 discusses `visual`, `depth`, and other concepts of color.

Event Selection

Among the attributes that you can set in the `XSetWindowAttributes` structure, there is a long integer field named `event_mask`. The value of this mask determines which types of events occurring in the window are reported to your application. Recall from Chapter 6, "The Xlib Programming Model," that you can use the `XSelectInput` function to select the events to be reported for a window. For the main window, `initapp` selects the `Expose` event:

```
/* Select Exposure events for the main window */

    XSelectInput(theDisplay, theMain, ExposureMask);
```

You can select multiple events by using as the last argument of `XSelectInput` the bitwise-OR of defined event masks from the header file `<X11/X.h>`. For example, to enable buttonpresses as well as `Expose` events, you can use the following call:

```
XSelectInput(theDisplay, theMain,
             ExposureMask | ButtonPressMask);
```

Instead of calling `XSelectInput`, you can set the `event_mask` field in an `XSetWindowAttributes` structure and select the events with a call to the `XChangeWindowAttributes` function. For example, to select the `Expose` and `ButtonPress` events for the main window, you can use the following code:

```
XSetWindowAttributes xswa;
    .
    .
    xswa.colormap = DefaultColormap(theDisplay,
                                    DefaultScreen(theDisplay));
    xswa.bit_gravity = NorthWestGravity;
    xswa.event_mask = ExposureMask | ButtonPressMask;
    XChangeWindowAttributes(theDisplay, theMain,
            (CWColormap | CWBitGravity | CWEventMask), &xswa);
```

Sometimes you may want to select a new event or drop an event without disturbing the other input selections. If you have to change the event selections, use the following procedure:

1. Get the window attributes using `XGetWindowAttributes`.

2. Copy the `your_event_mask` field of the `XWindowAttributes` structure into the `event_mask` field of an `XSetWindowAttributes` structure.

3. Alter the mask as needed, and set the new mask using the XSetWindowAttributes function.

A good approach is to develop two utility functions, AddNewEvent and IgnoreEvent, that respectively enable or disable an event specified by an event mask. Listing 7.3 shows such a pair of functions. These functions can be very handy. For example, if you want to stop receiving ButtonPress events in a section of your code, you can use these functions to achieve your objective:

```
    IgnoreEvent(theMain, ButtonPressMask);
/* No more buttonpresses reported... */
    .
    .
/* Reenable buttonpresses... */
    AddNewEvent(theMain, ButtonPress);
```

Listing 7.3. Utility routines AddNewEvent and IgnoreEvent.

```
/*------------------------------------------------------------*/
/*  A d d N e w E v e n t
 *
 *  Add a new event to a window's event mask.
 *
 */
void AddNewEvent(Window xid, long event_mask)
{
    XWindowAttributes    xwa;
    XSetWindowAttributes xswa;

    if (XGetWindowAttributes(theDisplay, xid, &xwa) != 0)
    {
        xswa.event_mask = xwa.your_event_mask ¦ event_mask;

        XChangeWindowAttributes(theDisplay, xid,
                            CWEventMask, &xswa);

    }
}
/*------------------------------------------------------------*/
/*  I g n o r e E v e n t
 *
 *  Stop handling an event (by altering the window's mask)
 *
 */
void IgnoreEvent(Window xid, long event_mask)
{
    XWindowAttributes    xwa;
    XSetWindowAttributes xswa;

    if (XGetWindowAttributes(theDisplay, xid, &xwa) != 0)
    {
        xswa.event_mask = xwa.your_event_mask & (~event_mask);

        XChangeWindowAttributes(theDisplay, xid,
```

```
                    CWEventMask, &xswa);

    }
}
```

Using the *initapp* Function

Now that you have the initapp function to set up the main window, it is time for an example that uses it. As a first example, you will write a program that is similar to the xhello program of Chapter 5. This example program, wintest.c shown in Listing 7.4, displays a message in the main window and has one child window. You can quit the program by pressing the mouse button labeled Quit inside this child window. The following is the UNIX makefile for building the program:

```
# Common definitions...

RM = rm -f
CC = cc

# Compiler flags, paths for include files and libraries

CFLAGS =
INCLUDES = -I. -I/usr/include -I/usr/include/X11
LIBS = -lX11

# Rule to create .o files from .c files
.c.o:
    $(RM) $@
    $(CC) -c $(CFLAGS) $(INCLUDES) $*.c

# Targets and dependencies

all::    wintest

wintest.o: wintest.c app_glob.c

initapp.o: initapp.c app_glob.c

wintest: wintest.o initapp.o
    $(RM) $@
    $(CC) -o $@ $(CFLAGS) wintest.o initapp.o $(LIBS)
```

> **NOTE:**
>
> The compiler flags and linker options for building X applications may vary from one system to another. To properly build an X application, please follow the instructions provided by your system's manufacturer. In general, on most UNIX systems you need the linker option -lX11. Additional compiler options and libraries may be needed depending on the interprocess communication mechanism used by the X clients.

Figure 7.5 shows the output of the program without any command-line options or resource specifications.

Figure 7.5.

Output of the wintest *program with default settings.*

The initapp function includes the capability of accepting resource settings from the .Xdefaults file in your login directory. For example, place the following lines in the .Xdefaults file (create a new file, if necessary):

```
wintest*font:   -*-courier-*-r-*—*-140-*-*-*-*-iso8859-1
wintest.geometry:  300x100+10+10
```

Now execute the wintest program again. This time the output appears as shown in Figure 7.6.

Figure 7.6.

Output of the wintest *program with user-defined font and geometry.*

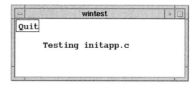

Listing 7.4. A program to test initapp.c.

```
/*-------------------------------------------------------------*/
/* File: wintest.c
 *
 * Test initapp.c
 */
#include <stdio.h>

#include <X11/Xlib.h>
#include <X11/Xutil.h>

#include "app_glob.c"

char *quit_text = "Quit";
char *message = "Testing initapp.c";

void initapp();

/*-------------------------------------------------------------*/
main(argc, argv)
int argc;
char **argv;
{
    Window QuitButton;
    unsigned quit_width, quit_height;
```

```
    initapp(argc, argv, 20, 20, 200, 100);

    printf("Assigned window geometry: %dx%d+%d+%d\n",
            MainXWA.width, MainXWA.height, MainXWA.x, MainXWA.y);

/* Create a quit button */
    quit_width = XTextWidth(theFontStruct, quit_text,
                            strlen(quit_text)) + 4;
    quit_height = theFontStruct->max_bounds.ascent +
                  theFontStruct->max_bounds.descent + 4;

    QuitButton = XCreateSimpleWindow(theDisplay, theMain, 1, 1,
                quit_width, quit_height, 1, theFGpix, theBGpix);

    XSelectInput(theDisplay, QuitButton, ExposureMask |
                            ButtonPressMask);

    XMapWindow(theDisplay, QuitButton);

    while (!AppDone)
    {
        XNextEvent(theDisplay, &theEvent);
        if(theEvent.xany.window == theMain)
        {
            if(theEvent.type == Expose &&
               theEvent.xexpose.count == 0)
            {
                XClearWindow(theDisplay, theMain);
                XDrawString(theDisplay, theMain, theGC,
                        50, 50, message, strlen(message));
            }
        }
        if(theEvent.xany.window == QuitButton)
        {
            switch(theEvent.type)
            {
                case Expose:
                    if (theEvent.xexpose.count == 0)
                    {
                        XClearWindow(theDisplay, QuitButton);
                        XDrawString(theDisplay, QuitButton,
                            theGC,
                            theFontStruct->max_bounds.width / 2,
                            theFontStruct->max_bounds.ascent +
                            theFontStruct->max_bounds.descent,
                            quit_text, strlen(quit_text));
                    }
                    break;

                case ButtonPress:
                    AppDone = 1;
            }
        }
    }
}
```

continues

Listing 7.4. continued

```
/* Close connection to display and exit */

    XCloseDisplay(theDisplay);
    exit(0);
}
```

Other Window Operations

In the course of setting up the main window, you have to go through many basic operations on windows. For example, you have to create the window, map it, select events for it, and inform the window manager of its location and size. If you study the example shown in Listing 7.4, you will realize that these basic operations are enough for a small program. Let's reexamine these basic window operations and consider a few others that can be useful in certain applications.

Window Creation and Destruction

XCreateSimpleWindow provides the simplest way to create a window. This function creates an InputOutput window that can be used for both drawing output and for accepting events. The calling syntax of the XCreateSimpleWindow function takes the following form:

```
Display        *display;              /* X display     */
Window         parent, new_window;    /* Window IDs    */
int            x, y;                  /* Position      */
unsigned int   width, height, border_width;/* Size     */
unsigned long  border, background;    /* Pixel values */

new_window = XCreateSimpleWindow(display, parent, x, y, width,
            height, border_width, border, background);
```

The arguments to XCreateSimpleWindow specify the size, position, background, and border colors. Because windows are organized in a hierarchy, you also have to specify the parent window's ID. This function returns a window resource identifier that you have to save for later use.

XCreateWindow is another, more general, function for creating windows. You have to use this function if you want to create an InputOnly window for receiving events only. Whereas XCreateSimpleWindow sets the attributes of the newly created window from the parent, XCreateWindow requires you to specify the attribute values explicitly. Unless you need InputOnly windows, you can get by without any problems with XCreateSimpleWindow only.

Usually, you do not have to destroy windows explicitly. When you close the connection to a display (with XCloseDisplay), the X server automatically destroys all resources associated with your application. However, if you have an occasion in which you want to destroy a window and all its subwindows, you can use XDestroyWindow to do the job:

```
Display  *display;
Window   this_window;

XDestroyWindow(display, this_window);
```

If you want to destroy only the subwindows of a window, but not the window itself, you can use the function XDestroySubwindows, which is called in the same manner as XDestroyWindow.

Window Mapping and Unmapping

When a window is created, it does not appear on the screen automatically. First you have to map it—using, for example, the XMapWindow function. In fact, even after mapping a window, it may not appear on the display. In X terminology, the window must be *viewable*, which means that all ancestors of the window must be mapped. Even then, the window may not be visible because other windows, higher up in the hierarchy, may be obscuring it.

As a window is created, it is placed on top of the stack of siblings. The commonly used XMapWindow function maps a window without changing its position in the stacking order. The XMapSubwindows function maps all the subwindows of a window. You can create a hierarchy of windows and map all windows by calling XMapSubwindows followed by XMapWindow, with the top window as the argument. This is more efficient than calling XMapWindow for each window in the hierarchy. These functions are called as follows:

```
Display  *display;
Window   main_window;
.
.
.
XMapSubwindows(display, main_window);
XMapWindow(display, main_window);
```

When a window is mapped, the X server generates a MapNotify event. If the window becomes viewable (because all its ancestors are mapped), the server also generates Expose events for all visible parts of the window. Because window managers usually intervene when you map the main window, it is safer to draw in the windows only in response to the Expose events.

Another mapping function is useful for pop-up windows. XMapRaised, with a syntax similar to that of XMapWindow, raises the window to the top of its siblings and maps it. A pop-up menu or a dialog box should be fully visible; you can use XMapRaised to achieve this.

When you use pop-up windows, you have to hide them once their job is done (for example, after the user has selected an item from a pop-up menu). You can use the XUnmapWindow to hide a window. All descendants of the window become invisible when you unmap a window. You can unmap the window with the ID DialogBox, from the display connection p_disp, by calling XUnmapWindow:

```
Display  *p_disp;
Window   DialogBox;
.
.
.
XUnmapWindow(p_disp, DialogBox);
```

Use XUnmapSubwindows to unmap only the subwindows of a window.

Window Positioning and Sizing

Having created your windows, you are by no means stuck with your original choice of position and size. You can resize and reposition windows by calling certain Xlib functions. Typically, an application should not move or resize the top-level window. The user does this through the window manager.

The programmer can, however, move and reposition the child windows in an application as and when necessary. You can arrange it so that the application receives a `ConfigureNotify` event when the window manager moves or resizes the main window. In certain applications, you may want to rearrange the child windows in response to the `ConfigureNotify` event on the main window.

An example that requires moving a window is a scrollbar. If you implement the thumbwheel of a scrollbar as a window, you have to move this window to indicate the current thumbwheel position. You can achieve this effect by calling the `XMoveWindow` function to reposition the thumbwheel window with respect to its parent's origin:

```
Display *p_disp;        /* Identifies the X display */
Window  this_window;    /* The window being moved   */
int     new_x, new_y;   /* New origin of window     */
    .
    .

XMoveWindow(p_disp, this_window, new_x, new_y);
```

Here, new_x and new_y are the new coordinates of the window's origin in its parent's coordinate frame.

You can resize a window using the function `XResizeWindow`. The call is similar to that for `XMoveWindow` except that you specify the new width and height in place of the new position. To move and resize a window at the same time, use `XMoveResizeWindow`. Here is an example call to this function:

```
XMoveResizeWindow(p_disp, this_window, new_x, new_y,
                  new_width, new_height);
```

Stacking Order Alteration

Suppose you have implemented a word processing program in which each document is displayed in a subwindow of the main window. When there are several open documents, these windows overlap one another as reflected by the stacking order among these sibling windows. Now suppose you have a menu item that enables the user to bring a document to the top. To implement this in X, you have to change the stacking order of the windows. For this example, you can use `XRaiseWindow` to bring the selected document's window to the top. For example, the following call brings the window w on display p_disp to the top of the stack:

```
XRaiseWindow(p_disp, w);
```

Other functions for manipulating the stacking order include the following:

- ✦ `XLowerWindow` brings a window to the bottom of the stack.
- ✦ `XMapRaised` maps and brings a window to the top at the same time.
- ✦ `XCirculateSubwindowsUp` brings the current bottom window to the top.
- ✦ `XCirculateSubwindowsDown` sends the top window to the bottom of the stack.
- ✦ `XCirculateSubwindows` can circulate up or down, depending on the value of its last argument.

The circulating window's function is used mostly by window managers. Applications typically use `XMapRaised` and `XRaiseWindow`.

Summary

In the X Window System, a window is an area of screen in which the input and output operations of an application take place. Although windows generally are rectangular in shape, X provides an experimental extension that enables arbitrarily shaped windows. In X, windows are organized in a hierarchy. The root window (usually the entire screen) is at the top of the hierarchy. The root window's next level of children is the top-level windows of all applications currently displaying in that screen. Applications usually confine their output to a single top-level window, which is the parent of all other windows used by the application.

All children at a particular level in the hierarchy are clipped at the borders of their parent, and the order in which they overlap each other is determined by their stacking order. The stacking order of the top-level windows determines which application's window is at the top and ready for interaction with the user.

The user manipulates the top-level windows of applications through the window manager, a special type of X application. The window manager enables the user to move and resize the topmost windows of applications and alter their stacking order. Because of this, the top-level window of an application requires special treatment. When creating it for the first time, you should inform the window manager of its placement and size.

When a window is created, it does not automatically appear on the screen. You have to map it to make it visible. Of course, you can unmap it to hide it. There are a number of Xlib routines to help you create and manage windows. In X, the following are the basic operations on windows:

- ✦ Creating and destroying
- ✦ Mapping and unmapping
- ✦ Positioning and sizing
- ✦ Enabling and disabling event reports
- ✦ Setting attributes
- ✦ Altering stacking order

Windows are the reason programmers use the X Window System, the mechanism that enables several applications to share the limited space in a physical display screen.

## Chapter 8

Handling Events

The event-driven X programming model (described in Chapter 6, "The Xlib Programming Model") relies on events for everything from maintaining the contents of a window to receiving mouse and keyboard input from the user. X applications rely on events to pace the program and do the user's bidding. The programs of Chapters 5, "A Simple X Application," and 7, "Creating and Managing Windows," provide examples of event handling. This chapter further describes events and how they are handled. Rather than giving an encyclopedic description of each type of event, additional examples illustrate event handling. The chapter begins by describing a smart way to manage the event loop when there are too many windows in a program. Later in the chapter, you learn the details of several types of X events, including mouse events, keyboard events, and Expose events.

Smart Event Handling

When building a small application with three or four windows, you can get by with the structure used by the examples shown in Listing 5.1 in Chapter 5 and Listing 7.4 in Chapter 7. In those programs, you create the main window and then the child windows. The event handling loop gets events from Xlib by calling XNextEvent. The exact action in response to an event depends on the window where the event occurred. Thus, the event handling loop uses a number of if statements to compare the window ID reported by the event, with the identifier of each window in the program. This results in an event processing loop:

```
int     AppDone = 0;          /* Exit event loop when 1  */
XEvent  theEvent;             /* Structure to hold event */
Window  theMain, QuitButton;  /* Window identifiers       */

while (!AppDone)
{
    XNextEvent(theDisplay, &theEvent);
    if(theEvent.xany.window == theMain)
    {
/* Process events occurring in the main window */
        .
        .
        .
    }
    if(theEvent.xany.window == QuitButton)
    {
/* Process events occurring in the QuitButton window */
        .
/* On ButtonPress, set the flag AppDone to 1.        */
        .
        .
        .
    }
/* Check for other windows ... and process events */
    .
    .
    .
}
```

The problem with this processing loop is that as the number of windows grows, the event handling loop gets out of hand. There are too many if statements testing for the window ID and processing the events. Because there are many windows in any reasonable user interface, you need to organize the program in a way that helps you manage the complexity of event handling. This is where the *context management* routines of Xlib can help you. A side benefit of using these routines is that you can begin to develop a structure that enables you to create and manage multiple copies of a single type of window (for example, several buttons for menus).

Xlib Context Manager

One way to manage the complexity of event handling is to have an event handling function for each window and somehow store that information so that it can be retrieved by using the window ID as a key. Xlib provides this capability through its context manager utility routines. The routine XSaveContext enables you to save any data (actually, you store a pointer to a data structure) indexed by the window ID and a *context*, which is an integer identifier (defined as a data type named XContext in the header file <X11/Xresource.h>). For example, suppose you decide that you want to store in window w a pointer p_data to a data structure. This is what you do:

1. Call XUniqueContext to get a unique context identifier for this type of data:

    ```
    #include <X11/Xresource.h>

    XContext  context1;
        .
        .
        .
    context1 = XUniqueContext();
    ```

2. Once you have decided on a context, save the data:

```
if(XSaveContext(theDisplay, w, context1,
                (caddr_t) new_p_data) != 0)
{
    fprintf(stderr, "Error saving context data");
    exit(1);
}
```

Even though the display pointer appears as an argument to XSaveContext, storing data this way has nothing to with the X server, and everything is handled locally by Xlib. (An arbitrary collection of data stored in a window at the server is known as that window's *property*; properties are described in Chapter 16, "Advanced Topics in X.")

Context is used to identify the type of data. You can use the same context to store the same type of data in many different windows. You do not have to have a separate context for each window. The context helps you distinguish between different data types stored at a window.

Finally, the last argument to XSaveContext is of type caddr_t, which denotes the address of any type of data or function in C (caddr_t is usually defined in the header file <sys/types.h>). The exact meaning of the data is irrelevant to the context management routines. How you interpret this data is up to you.

You can retrieve the stored data using XFindContext:

```
caddr_t data;

if(XFindContext(theDisplay, w, context1,
                    (caddr_t *) &data) == 0)
{
/* Data retrieved without error. Use data in this block */
    .
    .
    .
}
```

Window-Specific Data Management

Now you know the mechanics of saving and retrieving data for a window using the context manager. How can you use that knowledge to help you manage the complexity of the event handling loop? The following example illustrates the use of the context manager to set up multiple button windows and handle the events in a convenient manner.

First, you set up the following data structure named XWIN to store information needed by each window:

```
typedef struct XWIN
{
    Window   xid;                /* The ID of the window     */
    Window   parent;            /* The ID of parent window  */
    void     *data;             /* Pointer to data          */
    int      (*event_handler)(); /* Pointer to event handler */
} XWIN;
```

The data field is a catch-all pointer to any private data needed by a window. For example, in a labeled button window, the data field points to a structure containing the text of the label as well as the address of a routine that defines the action of a mouse buttonpress in that window. The xid and parent fields are the resource identifiers of the window and its parent, respectively. The event_handler is a pointer to the routine that processes events for that window.

The idea is to associate a single context with the data structure of type XWIN. The name of the context will be a global variable because several files may have to share it. For this reason, you place the definitions in a header file, xwins.h, shown in Listing 8.1.

Listing 8.1. xwins.h—Header file for context-managed reusable windows.

```
/*   File: xwins.h
 *
 *   Defines data structures for windows
 *
 */
#ifndef XWINS_H
#define XWINS_H

#include <stdlib.h>
#include <X11/Xlib.h>
#include <X11/Xutil.h>
#include <X11/Xresource.h>

typedef struct XWIN
{
    Window   xid;
    Window   parent;
    void     *data;
    int      (*event_handler)();
} XWIN;

/* Function prototypes */
void xwin_init(/* void */);
XWIN *MakeXButton(/* int x, int y,
      unsigned width, unsigned height, unsigned bdwidth,
      unsigned long bdcolor, unsigned long bgcolor,
      Window parent, char *text, int (*button_action)(),
      caddr_t action_data */);

XWIN *MakeXMenu(/*int x, int y, unsigned bdwidth,
      unsigned long bdcolor, unsigned long bgcolor,
      Window parent, int style,...*/);

/* Global variable */
#ifdef XWIN_UTIL

XContext      xwin_context;

#else
```

```
extern XContext      xwin_context;

#endif /* #ifdef XWIN_UTIL */

#endif /* #ifndef XWINS_H */
```

The symbol XWIN_UTIL restricts the definition of the global variable to one file only. You do this in a file named xwinutil.c where you have the function xwin_init; this calls XUniqueContext and sets the context xwin_context. Listing 8.2 shows the file xwinutil.c. As the name suggests, this file is meant for utility routines used in the application. For now, it has the xwin_init function only.

Listing 8.2. xwinutil.c—Utility routine for context-managed reusable windows.

```
/*  File:  xwinutil.c
 *
 *  Utility functions for Xlib programming.
 */

#define XWIN_UTIL

#include "xwins.h"
#include "app_glob.c"

/*------------------------------------------------------------*/
void xwin_init()
{
/* Create a unique context to reference data associated
 * with the windows
 */
    xwin_context = XUniqueContext();

}
```

Button Window

To continue this example, let's create a type of window that can be used as buttons in a user interface. Recall that a button is a window with a label and for which some action takes place when the user presses a mouse button inside the window. The following data structure with the type name D_BUTTON is used to store the data used by the button windows:

```
typedef struct D_BUTTON
{
    char    *text;                  /* Label in the button   */
    int     (*action)(/*caddr_t*/);/* Called on ButtonPress */
    caddr_t action_args;            /* Argument for action   */
} D_BUTTON;
```

To create a button, you allocate an XWIN data structure and a D_BUTTON structure, initialize both, and return a pointer to the XWIN structure. The data field of the XWIN structure is set to point to the newly created D_BUTTON structure. You also create the window itself, saving the resource identifier in the xid field of the XWIN structure. Before returning, you save the pointer to the XWIN structure as a context-managed data item for that window. Here is the calling syntax for the routine MakeXButton that does this job:

```
XWIN *MakeXButton(int x, int y,
        unsigned width, unsigned height, unsigned bdwidth,
        unsigned long bdcolor, unsigned long bgcolor,
        Window parent, char *label, int (*button_action)(),
        caddr_t action_data)
```

The arguments x, y, width, and height specify the dimensions of the button. The border width, border color, and the background color are given by bdwidth, bdcolor, and bgcolor, respectively. The parent argument should be the resource identifier of the parent of the button. The last three arguments specify the label, the routine to be called when the button is pressed, and the data passed to that action routine.

The MakeXButton function appears in the file xbutton.c shown in Listing 8.3. The other function in this file, button_handler, takes care of handling events occurring in this window. The routine is not called from this file; rather, MakeXButton saves its address in the event_handler field of the XWIN structure corresponding to this window. The event handling loop in button_handler is similar to that for the Quit button in Chapter 7, Listing 7.4.

Listing 8.3. xbutton.c—A reusable button window.

```
/*-----------------------------------------------------------*/
/*  File: xbutton.c
 *
 *  Implement a "button window"—a window that displays
 *  a message and calls an "action" routine when the
 *  user presses any mouse button inside the window.
 *  (Uses Xlib's context management routines)
 *
 */
/*-----------------------------------------------------------*/
#include <stdio.h>
#include "xwins.h"
#include "app_glob.c"

typedef struct D_BUTTON
{
    char    *text;
    int     (*action)(/* caddr_t */);
    caddr_t action_args;
} D_BUTTON;

static int button_handler(/* XWIN * */);
/*-----------------------------------------------------------*/
/*  M a k e X B u t t o n
```

```
 *
 *   A labeled "button" that you can press to perform an "action"
 *
 */
XWIN *MakeXButton(x, y, width, height, bdwidth, bdcolor,
                  bgcolor, parent, text, button_action,
                  action_data)
int             x, y;
unsigned        width, height, bdwidth;
unsigned long   bdcolor, bgcolor;
Window          parent;
char            *text;
int             (*button_action)();
caddr_t         action_data;
{
    XWIN    *new_button;
    D_BUTTON *p_data;

/* Allocate button-specific data */
    if((p_data = (D_BUTTON *)calloc(1, sizeof(D_BUTTON)))
        == NULL)
    {
        fprintf(stderr, "No memory for button's data");
        exit(1);
    }

/* Allocate an XWIN structure */
    if((new_button = (XWIN *)calloc(1, sizeof(XWIN))) == NULL)
    {
        fprintf(stderr, "No memory for button");
        exit(1);
    }

/* Initialize button's data and save pointer in new_button */
    p_data->action = button_action;
    p_data->action_args = action_data;
    p_data->text = text;
    new_button->data = p_data;
    new_button->event_handler = button_handler;
    new_button->parent = parent;
    new_button->xid = XCreateSimpleWindow(theDisplay, parent,
                      x, y, width, height, bdwidth, bdcolor,
                      bgcolor);

/* Save new_button as data associated with this window ID
 * and the context "xwin_context"
 */
    if(XSaveContext(theDisplay, new_button->xid, xwin_context,
                (caddr_t) new_button) != 0)
    {
        fprintf(stderr, "Error saving xwin_context data");
        exit(1);
    }
```

continues

Listing 8.3. continued

```
    XSelectInput(theDisplay, new_button->xid,
        OwnerGrabButtonMask | ExposureMask | ButtonPressMask);

    XMapWindow(theDisplay, new_button->xid);
    return (new_button);
}
/*----------------------------------------------------------*/
/* b u t t o n _ h a n d l e r
 *
 *  Event handler for the "button"
 */
static int button_handler(p_xwin)
XWIN *p_xwin;
{
    D_BUTTON *p_data = (D_BUTTON *) p_xwin->data;

/* Handle events occurring in this window */
    if(theEvent.xany.window == p_xwin->xid)
    {
        switch(theEvent.type)
        {
            case Expose:
                if (theEvent.xexpose.count == 0)
                {
                    XClearWindow(theDisplay, p_xwin->xid);
                    XDrawString(theDisplay, p_xwin->xid,
                        theGC,
                        theFontStruct->max_bounds.width / 2,
                        theFontStruct->max_bounds.ascent +
                        theFontStruct->max_bounds.descent,
                        p_data->text, strlen(p_data->text));
                }
                break;
            case ButtonPress:
/* Call the action routine, PROVIDED it is valid */
                if(p_data->action != NULL)
                    (*p_data->action)(p_data->action_args);
                break;
        }
    }
    return 0;
}
```

Multiple Buttons

MakeXButton is a function that you can call repeatedly to create as many buttons as you want. You have to provide the functions to be called when each button is pressed. The event handling for this turns out to be very simple. When an event is received, you look up its associated data by calling XFindContext. The retrieved data will be a pointer to the XWIN structure for that window. To handle the event, call the function whose address is stored in the event_handler field of this structure.

Thus, the event handling can be achieved with the following simple loop:

```
        XWIN  *which_xwin;
        int   AppDone = 0;

/* Event handling loop */

        while (!AppDone)
        {
            XNextEvent(theDisplay, &theEvent);

/* Look up the XWIN structure for the event window */

            if(XFindContext(theDisplay, theEvent.xany.window,
                    xwin_context, (caddr_t *) &which_xwin) == 0)
            {
/* Call the event handler of this XWIN structure */
                if (*(which_xwin->event_handler) != NULL)
                    (*(which_xwin->event_handler))(which_xwin);
            }
        }
```

Listing 8.4 shows the file `xctest.c`, which implements a sample program to test the buttons. The makefile for building the program is in Listing 8.5. Figure 8.1 shows how `xctest` uses two buttons, both created by calling `MakeXButton`. You provide individual action routines for each button. One button is used for quitting the program. Its action routine sets the `AppDone` flag, which causes the event loop to terminate. Pressing the other mouse button changes the text displayed in the main window.

Figure 8.1.

An example showing
multiple buttons.

Listing 8.4. `xctest.c`—Testing the buttons.

```
/*--------------------------------------------------------*/
/* File: xctest.c
 *
 *  Use Xlib Context management routines to save data
 *  associated with each window.
 *
 */
 /*--------------------------------------------------------*/
#include <stdio.h>

#include <X11/Xlib.h>
#include <X11/Xutil.h>

#include "xwins.h"
#include "app_glob.c"
```

continues

Listing 8.4. continued

```
char *quit_label = "Quit";
char *flip_label = "Next Message";

char *messages[] =
{
    "Testing Xlib Context Manager",
    "You can create multiple buttons easily",
    "All buttons share the same code",
    "Each button has its own data"
};
int max_messages = sizeof(messages) / sizeof(char *);
int msgnum = 0;


/* Function prototypes */

void initapp(/* int, char **, int, int, unsigned, unsigned */);
int  quit_action(/* caddr_t */);
int  flip_action(/* caddr_t */);
/*-------------------------------------------------------------*/
main(argc, argv)
int argc;
char **argv;
{
    XWIN     *QuitButton, *FlipButton, *which_xwin;
    unsigned quit_width, quit_height, flip_width;

    xwin_init();

    initapp(argc, argv, 20, 20, 300, 100);

    printf("Assigned window geometry: %dx%d+%d+%d\n",
            MainXWA.width, MainXWA.height, MainXWA.x, MainXWA.y);

/* Create the two buttons */
    quit_width = XTextWidth(theFontStruct, quit_label,
                        strlen(quit_label)) + 4;
    quit_height = theFontStruct->max_bounds.ascent +
                theFontStruct->max_bounds.descent + 4;

    QuitButton = MakeXButton(1, 1, quit_width, quit_height,
                        1, theFGpix, theBGpix, theMain,
                        quit_label, quit_action, NULL);

    flip_width = XTextWidth(theFontStruct, flip_label,
                        strlen(flip_label)) + 4;
    FlipButton = MakeXButton(quit_width+4, 1, flip_width,
                    quit_height, 1, theFGpix, theBGpix,
                    theMain, flip_label, flip_action, NULL);

/* Event handling loop */

    while (!AppDone)
    {
        XNextEvent(theDisplay, &theEvent);
```

```
/* Main window is handled here */
        if(theEvent.xany.window == theMain)
        {
            if(theEvent.type == Expose &&
               theEvent.xexpose.count == 0)
            {
                XClearWindow(theDisplay, theMain);
                XDrawString(theDisplay, theMain, theGC,
                            50, 50, messages[msgnum],
                            strlen(messages[msgnum]));
            }
        }
/* For all other windows, retrieve the XWIN data from
 * Xlib using the context manager routine XFindContext
 */
        if(XFindContext(theDisplay, theEvent.xany.window,
               xwin_context, (caddr_t *) &which_xwin) == 0)
        {
/* Call the event handler of this XWIN structure */
            if(*(which_xwin->event_handler) != NULL)
                (*(which_xwin->event_handler))(which_xwin);
        }
    }

/* Close connection to display and exit */

    XCloseDisplay(theDisplay);
    exit(0);
}
/*-----------------------------------------------------------*/
/* q u i t _ a c t i o n
 *
 * This routine is called when a ButtonPress event occurs in
 * the quit window.
 */
int quit_action(data)
caddr_t data;
{
/* Set the done flag */
    AppDone = 1;
    return 1;
}
/*-----------------------------------------------------------*/
/* f l i p _ a c t i o n
 *
 * This routine is called when a ButtonPress event occurs in
 * the quit window.
 */
int flip_action(data)
caddr_t data;
{
/* Change the message to be displayed */
    msgnum = (msgnum + 1) % max_messages;
```

continues

Listing 8.4. continued

```
/* Clear the main window, so that new message is displayed */
    XClearArea(theDisplay, theMain, 0, 0, 0, 0, True);
    return 1;
}
```

Listing 8.5. Makefile for `xctest`.

```
###############################################################
# Some common definitions...

RM = rm -f
CC = cc

# Compiler flags, paths for include files and libraries

CFLAGS =
INCLUDES = -I. -I/usr/include -I/usr/include/X11
LIBS = -lX11

# Rule to create .o files from .c files
.c.o:
    $(RM) $@
    $(CC) -c $(CFLAGS) $(INCLUDES) $*.c

# Targets...

all::    xctest

xctest.o: xctest.c app_glob.c xwins.h

initapp.o: initapp.c app_glob.c

xwinutil.o: xwinutil.c app_glob.c xwins.h

xbutton.o: xbutton.c app_glob.c xwins.h

xctest: xctest.o initapp.o xwinutil.o xbutton.o
    $(RM) $@
    $(CC) -o $@ $(CFLAGS) xctest.o initapp.o \
        xwinutil.o xbutton.o \
        $(LIBS)
```

This design enables easy event handling for a large number of windows. In developing this, you also have been able to create a button window that can be reused. By calling `MakeXButton`, you can create as many buttons as you want. When you create multiple copies of buttons, each has its unique data, but all share the same event handling code. This is, of course, one of the ideas behind the object-oriented approach to organizing programs. In this design, there is no way to inherit from another module, but, with a little forethought, you can write objects such as the button in `xbutton.c` that actually inherit data and code from others.

Modal Dialog

Listing 8.4 shows the easy way to handle events using the Xlib context manager. That program shows only one event processing loop, but in other situations—for example, when you want to conduct a dialog with the user—you need more than one loop. Suppose that, in the midst of editing a file, the user presses the Quit button. A well-designed program displays a message asking the user if the current file should be saved before exiting. The user will be required to answer Yes, No, or Cancel (meaning "I changed my mind"). Such dialogs are known as *modal dialogs* because the user is forced into a mode where there are only a few well-defined choices offered to the user.

Modal dialogs are not always visible on the display. A dialog must appear to get the user's response; after the task is complete, it must disappear.

It is easy to use the button shown in xbutton.c and create a modal dialog (see Listing 8.3). Modal dialogs are an important part of any user interface, and your rudimentary button window can satisfy the need. Listing 8.6 shows the program xdialog.c that displays a modal dialog when the user presses the mouse button with the pointer inside the button labeled Quit. The makefile for this example is the same as that of Listing 8.5 except that you have to change all occurrences of xctest to xdialog. Figure 8.2 shows the resulting display after you press the mouse button in the button labeled Quit.

Figure 8.2.

A modal dialog.

Listing 8.6. `xdialog.c`—A modal dialog.

```
/*------------------------------------------------------------*/
/*  File: xdialog.c
 *
 *  Demonstrates a modal dialog box.
 */
 /*------------------------------------------------------------*/
#include <stdio.h>

#include <X11/Xlib.h>
#include <X11/Xutil.h>

#include "xwins.h"
#include "app_glob.c"

char *quit_label = "Quit";
char *dialog_label = "Save File?",
     *yes_label = "Yes",
     *no_label = "No",
     *cancel_label = "Cancel";
```

continues

Listing 8.6. continued

```
char *message = "Press Quit for pop-up dialog box";

int   DialogDone = 0;  /* Indicates when dialog is over */

/* Function prototypes */

void initapp(/* int, char **, int, int, unsigned, unsigned */);
int  quit_action(/* caddr_t */);
int  yes_action(/* caddr_t */);
int  no_action(/* caddr_t */);
int  cancel_action(/* caddr_t */);

/* Windows in the application */
XWIN  *QuitButton, *DialogButton, *YesButton, *NoButton,
      *CancelButton;
/*-------------------------------------------------------------*/
main(argc, argv)
int argc;
char **argv;
{
    XWIN      *which_xwin;
    Window    parent;
    int       yloc, x_dialog, y_dialog;
    unsigned quit_width, quit_height, dialog_width,
             dialog_height, yes_width, no_width, cancel_width;

    xwin_init();

/* Create the main window */
    initapp(argc, argv, 20, 20, 300, 100);

    printf("Assigned window geometry: %dx%d+%d+%d\n",
           MainXWA.width, MainXWA.height, MainXWA.x, MainXWA.y);

/* Compute sizes of windows */
    quit_width = XTextWidth(theFontStruct, quit_label,
                           strlen(quit_label)) + 4;
    quit_height = theFontStruct->max_bounds.ascent +
                 theFontStruct->max_bounds.descent + 4;
    yes_width = XTextWidth(theFontStruct, yes_label,
                          strlen(yes_label)) + 4;
    no_width =  XTextWidth(theFontStruct, no_label,
                          strlen(no_label)) + 4;
    cancel_width = XTextWidth(theFontStruct, cancel_label,
                             strlen(cancel_label)) + 4;
    dialog_width = yes_width + no_width + cancel_width + 16;
    dialog_height = 2 * quit_height + 12;
    x_dialog = (MainXWA.width - dialog_width) / 2;
    y_dialog = (MainXWA.height - dialog_height) / 2;

/* Create the quit button */
    QuitButton = MakeXButton(4, 4, quit_width, quit_height,
                            1, theFGpix, theBGpix, theMain,
                            quit_label, quit_action, NULL);
```

```
/* Create dialog box outer shell */
    DialogButton = MakeXButton(x_dialog, y_dialog,
                    dialog_width, dialog_height, 1, theFGpix,
                    theBGpix, theMain, dialog_label, NULL, NULL);

/* Create the three internal buttons */
    yloc = dialog_height - quit_height - 4;
    parent = DialogButton->xid;
    YesButton = MakeXButton(4, yloc, yes_width, quit_height,
                    1, theFGpix, theBGpix, parent, yes_label,
                    yes_action, NULL);
    NoButton = MakeXButton(yes_width+8, yloc, no_width,
                    quit_height, 1, theFGpix, theBGpix, parent,
                    no_label, no_action, NULL);
    CancelButton = MakeXButton(yes_width + no_width + 12, yloc,
                    cancel_width, quit_height, 1, theFGpix,
                    theBGpix, parent, cancel_label,
                    cancel_action, NULL);

/* Hide the dialog box */
    XUnmapWindow(theDisplay, parent);

/* Event handling loop */

    while (!AppDone)
    {
        XNextEvent(theDisplay, &theEvent);

/* Main window is handled here */
        if(theEvent.xany.window == theMain)
        {
            if(theEvent.type == Expose &&
               theEvent.xexpose.count == 0)
            {
                XClearWindow(theDisplay, theMain);
                XDrawString(theDisplay, theMain, theGC,
                    50, 50, message, strlen(message));
            }
        }
/* For all other windows, retrieve the XWIN data from
 * Xlib using the context manager routine XFindContext
 */
        if(XFindContext(theDisplay, theEvent.xany.window,
            xwin_context, (caddr_t *) &which_xwin) == 0)
        {
/* Call the event handler of this XWIN structure */
            if ((which_xwin->event_handler) != NULL)
                (*(which_xwin->event_handler))(which_xwin);
        }
    }

/* Close connection to display and exit */
```

continues

Listing 8.6. continued

```
    XCloseDisplay(theDisplay);
    exit(0);
}
/*--------------------------------------------------------------*/
int yes_action(data)
caddr_t data;
{
/* Save file (not done here) and set the done flag */
    AppDone = 1;
    DialogDone = 1;
    return 1;
}
/*--------------------------------------------------------------*/
int no_action(data)
caddr_t data;
{
/* Don't save file. Just set done flag */
    AppDone = 1;
    DialogDone = 1;
    return 1;
}
/*--------------------------------------------------------------*/
int cancel_action(data)
caddr_t data;
{
/* Do nothing, set flag to indicate end of dialog */
    DialogDone = 1;
    return 1;
}
/*--------------------------------------------------------------*/
int quit_action(data)
caddr_t data;
{
    XWIN *which_xwin;

/* Pop up dialog box */
    XMapRaised(theDisplay, DialogButton->xid);
    DialogDone = 0;
    while (!DialogDone)
    {
        XNextEvent(theDisplay, &theEvent);
        if(XFindContext(theDisplay, theEvent.xany.window,
            xwin_context, (caddr_t *) &which_xwin) == 0)
        {
/* Process only those events where the parent of window is
 * the dialog box.
 */
            if(which_xwin->parent == DialogButton->xid ||
                    which_xwin->xid== DialogButton->xid)
            {
                if ((which_xwin->event_handler) != NULL)
                    (*(which_xwin->event_handler))(which_xwin);
            }
        }
    }
```

```
/* Now unmap the dialog window */
    XUnmapWindow(theDisplay, DialogButton->xid);

    return 1;
}
```

The dialog window is created from four button windows—three child buttons inside a button that acts as an outer shell. Creating the hierarchy of buttons for the dialog window is straightforward. Determining the position and size of the outer window takes some effort. This is a chore you have to handle in any program—sizing windows to fit text strings. When you establish the sizes and positions, you can create the button windows by calling MakeXButton with the appropriate arguments. After the window has been created, you can hide it by unmapping the outer button with a call to XUnmapWindow.

The rest of the interesting action takes place in the quit_action function, which is called when a mouse buttonpress occurs inside the window labeled Quit. The first task in quit_action is to pop up the dialog. Use XMapRaised to do this. This brings the dialog to the top of the stacking order and makes it visible.

The modal nature of the dialog is achieved by a separate event loop inside the quit_action function. Before entering the loop, the variable DialogDone is set to 0. The loop looks similar to the one in the main function with one important difference. After retrieving an event, the event handler is called only if the parent of the event window is the same as the outer window of the dialog box. This ensures that only events from the Yes, No and Cancel buttons are processed. The action routines of these buttons set the DialogDone flag to terminate this event loop when appropriate.

Common Features of X Events

By now you have seen several examples of event handling. Before getting into the details of the various types of events, let's review the common features of events and how they should be handled.

As illustrated in the example programs, there are three steps to handling events:

1. For each window, select the events to be reported by the X server.
2. Call an Xlib function (usually XNextEvent) to get the event.
3. Process the event.

Repeat steps two and three until the program terminates. When you write X applications, a large part of your effort is spent in interpreting what an event means and deciding how to process it. To do this, you need to know when each type of event is reported and what information is reported in the event data structure. Data structures are discussed next, and specific events in detail later in the chapter.

The *XEvent* Union

When an event is reported by the X server, the program must be able to determine the type of the event and, depending on the type, other relevant information describing the event. For example, if the event reports a mouse buttonpress, you may want to know which button and the location of the mouse pointer at the time of the buttonpress. Because of the diversity of events in X, the information necessary to describe one class of events (mouse events, for example) differs significantly from that needed by another (keyboard events). Thus, a number of different data structures are used to describe the events. Because a common format is needed to report all events, a C union of these data structures is used to hold the information. The header file <X11/Xlib.h> defines this union, named XEvent:

```
typedef union _XEvent
{
    int                     type;   /* Event's type comes first */
    XAnyEvent               xany;
    XKeyEvent               xkey;
    XButtonEvent            xbutton;
    XMotionEvent            xmotion;
    XCrossingEvent          xcrossing;
    XFocusChangeEvent       xfocus;
    XExposeEvent            xexpose;
    XGraphicsExposeEvent    xgraphicsexpose;
    XNoExposeEvent          xnoexpose;
    XVisibilityEvent        xvisibility;
    XCreateWindowEvent      xcreatewindow;
    XDestroyWindowEvent     xdestroywindow;
    XUnmapEvent             xunmap;
    XMapEvent               xmap;
    XMapRequestEvent        xmaprequest;
    XReparentEvent          xreparent;
    XConfigureEvent         xconfigure;
    XGravityEvent           xgravity;
    XResizeRequestEvent     xresizerequest;
    XConfigureRequestEvent  xconfigurerequest;
    XCirculateEvent         xcirculate;
    XCirculateRequestEvent  xcirculaterequest;
    XPropertyEvent          xproperty;
    XSelectionClearEvent    xselectionclear;
    XSelectionRequestEvent  xselectionrequest;
    XSelectionEvent         xselection;
    XColormapEvent          xcolormap;
    XClientMessageEvent     xclient;
    XMappingEvent           xmapping;
    XErrorEvent             xerror;
    XKeymapEvent            xkeymap;
    long                    pad[24];
} XEvent;
```

The data type XEvent is defined as the union of a large number of different data structures. You encounter some of these structures later in this chapter. Appendix J, "X Event Reference," includes detailed information on each of these structures.

The *XAnyEvent* Structure

The simplest of the event data structures is XAnyEvent:

```
typedef struct
{
    int           type;       /* The event type               */
    unsigned long serial;     /* Number of last processed event */
    Bool          send_event;/* True = event is from SendEvent */
    Display       *display;   /* Identifies the reporting server*/
    Window        window;     /* Window requesting this event   */
} XAnyEvent;
```

The fields appearing in the XAnyEvent structure happen to be the first five entries in every event's data structure. The type field tells you the kind of event being reported. The X server keeps track of the sequence of protocol requests it has processed so far and reports the sequence number of the last processed request in the serial field.

The next field, send_event, describes how the event originated. In X, you can send a simulated event to a window. For example, even when there is no keypress, you can prepare an event structure for a keypress event and send it to a window using the XSendEvent function. The server indicates such events by setting the send_event flag in the event structure to True. If the event was generated by the server, send_event will be 0 (False).

TIP:

If you do not want your application to be spoofed by fake keyboard and mouse events sent by other X clients, process these events only if the xany.send_event field in the XEvent union is False.

The display field identifies the server from which the event arrives. The next field is the window that requested this type of event. The window hierarchy determines which window receives an event.

Fields in an Event

Suppose you get event reports in the XEvent union theEvent. You can test the event's type by comparing the type field with the names of events defined in <X11/Xlib.h>. If your program has a single window, you can process the events with a few if statements:

```
if(theEvent.type == Expose)
{
/* Process Expose event ... Redraw contents of window */
    XClearWindow(theEvent.xny.display, theEvent.xany.window);
    .
    .
}

if(theEvent.type == EnterNotify || theEvent.type == LeaveNotify)
{
```

```
/* Pointer entered or left window. */
        .
        .
}
```

For more complicated window hierarchies, you should use a more organized approach (such as the method illustrated in Listings 8.4 and 8.6). In that scheme, each window has its own event handling routine. In such a routine, you can use a `switch` statement to handle the different events that may have been selected by that window:

```
switch(theEvent.type)
{
    case Expose:
        if (theEvent.xexpose.count == 0)
        {
/* Redraw contents of window */
        .
        .
        }
        break;

    case ButtonPress:
/* Do whatever is appropriate for a buttonpress */
        if(theEvent.xbutton.button == Button1)
        {
/* Button 1 (usually the leftmost button) was pressed */
        .
        .
        }
        .
        .
        break;
}
```

When processing an event, you can use the members of the XAnyEvent data structure—theEvent.xany.display and theEvent.xany.window—to refer to the display and the window, respectively. For event-specific information, you have to use names of members appearing in that event's data structure. For example, in the preceding code, theEvent.xbutton.button identifies the button that was pressed in a ButtonPress event.

Destination Window for Events

The X server does not send unsolicited events to any X client (with the two exceptions described later in this chapter). For each window in your application, you must explicitly request what events you want reported. The event selections for each window are indicated by the individual bits of its event_mask attribute. You can set the event_mask attribute by calling the convenience function XSelectInput or by explicitly changing this attribute with a call to XChangeWindowAttributes.

Some of the events are easy to report—when parts of a window that were previously obscured become visible again, the Expose event should indicate the window and the area that needs redrawing. To provide maximum flexibility in handling mouse and keyboard events, the X server uses a more complicated reporting scheme.

Keyboard and Mouse Event Propagation

When reporting `ButtonPress`, `ButtonRelease`, `KeyPress`, `KeyRelease`, and `MotionNotify` events, the X server first determines which window should receive the event. For keyboard events, this is the window with the input focus. For mouse events, this is a visible window, lowest in the hierarchy of windows that enclose the mouse pointer. The server checks the `event_mask` of this window to determine if the window accepts this event. If it does, the server reports the event for this window. In this case, this window is the *event window*—the window to which the event is reported.

If this window does not request the event, the server does not discard the event. Instead, it propagates the event up the hierarchy. The first step in the propagation is to send the event to the parent. If the parent window accepts the event, the server reports the event to it. The event data structure for these keyboard and mouse events includes a `subwindow` field, in which the server reports the child window where the event actually occurred. If the immediate parent does not accept the event, it is sent to the next higher level, until the server encounters a window that has selected the event or one that stops the propagation of the event. The server discards the event only if it cannot find any window that has requested the event.

The programmer can control the propagation of keyboard and mouse events. By default, keyboard and mouse events propagate up the window hierarchy, but a field named `do_not_propagate_mask` in the window attribute controls this feature (see the `XWindowAttributes` structure in Chapter 7). If you do not want an event to propagate to the ancestors of a window, set the `do_not_propagate_mask` of that window to that event's mask. Use the same names you use when selecting events with `XSelectInput` (see Table 6.3 in Chapter 6). For example, if you want `ButtonPress` and `ButtonRelease` events to stop at the window win, you can use the following code to set it up:

```
Display              theDisplay;
Window               win1;
XWindowAttributes    xwa;
XSetWindowAttributes xswa;
.
.
.
/* Stop propagation of Button events at window win1 */

if (XGetWindowAttributes(theDisplay, win1, &xwa) != 0)
{
    xswa.do_not_propagate_mask = xwa.do_not_propagate_mask |
                    ButtonPressMask | ButtonReleaseMask;

    XChangeWindowAttributes(theDisplay, win1,
                    CWDontPropagate, &xswa);
}
```

This code fragment gets the current attributes of the window and changes the `do_not_propagate_mask` without disturbing anything else. You can use a similar approach when altering any attribute of a window.

Event propagation can be handy for centralized event handling. For example, you may decide to implement a menu with several small child windows (the menu items) inside a larger parent window that serves as an outer shell. You can handle mouse clicks on the menu items by enabling

ButtonPress and ButtonRelease events in the outer window only. When the user presses on one of the menu items, the events are reported to the outer window, but the event's information indicates the subwindow where it actually occurred. You then can use this information to process the menu selection.

Unsolicited Events: *MappingNotify* and *ClientMessage*

Recall that the X server never reports events that were not explicitly solicited. There are, however, two types of events that are always sent to applications. The first one is the MappingNotify event. This event is generated when any application rearranges the keyboard keycodes or changes the numbering of the mouse buttons. It makes sense because all applications using a display share the keyboard and the mouse. It is easy to handle this event. Put the following case statement in the switch statement of the main event handling loop:

```
XEvent theEvent;    /* Event is received in theEvent */
   .
   .
switch (theEvent.type)
{
    case MappingNotify:
        XRefreshKeyboardMapping(&theEvent);
        break;
   .
   .
}
```

The examples shown thus far lack this code, but *you should include this in all your X applications.*

Another type of unsolicited event delivered to your application is a ClientMessage event sent by another X client using the XSendEvent function. The interpretation of the information passed by these events is up to the sender and the receiver. Window managers often use ClientMessage events to communicate with applications. The exact message type and the recommended handling of the event depends on the window manager. Of course, even when ClientMessage events reach your application, your application is not required to do anything with these events.

Event Retrieval from Xlib

When the X server sends events to the application, Xlib automatically saves the events in a queue. Your programs have to call certain routines to get the events from the queue. So far, the example programs in this book have used the XNextEvent function to get events from Xlib's event queue:

```
Display *theDisplay;
XEvent  theEvent;
   .
   .
XNextEvent(theDisplay, &theEvent);
```

This code performs two tasks:

✦ It sends to the server any X protocol requests waiting in Xlib's buffer. This feature is handy because, unless this buffer is flushed, the effect of drawing functions does not appear on the screen. You can call XFlush to perform the operation, but inclusion of this task in XNextEvent makes the flushing almost automatic, because most applications rely on XNextEvent to get events from Xlib.

✦ XNextEvent looks for any events waiting in Xlib's event queue. If there is an event, XNextEvent returns after copying the information about the event into the XEvent union whose address you provide as an argument to XNextEvent. If no events are available yet, XNextEvent waits until an event arrives from the server. XNextEvent "blocks" until it receives an event.

Some applications have a problem with the fact that XNextEvent does not return until an event becomes available. For example, suppose your application is performing some lengthy computations and displaying the results as work progresses. If you want to do the computation and still respond to the user's input (perhaps a click on a Cancel button), you cannot use XNextEvent.

To achieve your goal, you must break the computation into smaller chunks. After you organize the work into smaller portions, you need ways to check whether any events are waiting and to process the waiting events. If no events are available, you can perform a small chunk of computation. You can use the XEventsQueued function together with XNextEvent to do the job:

```
    XEvent  theEvent;
    Display *theDisplay;
    int     AppDone, events_pending;
     .
     .
    AppDone = 0;
    while (!AppDone)
    {
/* Process all current events in the queue */
        if((events_pending = XEventsQueued(theDisplay,
                            QueuedAfterReading)) == 0)
        {
/* Perform a small part of your computations including
 * any drawing operations
 */
            .
            .
            XFlush(theDisplay);
        }
/* Process all waiting events */
        while(events_pending—)
        {
            XNextEvent(theDisplay, &theEvent);
            switch(theEvent.type)
            {
                case MappingNotify:
                    XRefreshKeyboardMapping(&theEvent);
                    break;
/* Handle other events... */
                case ButtonPress:
                    .
                    .
```

```
                    }
               }
          }
```

XEventsQueued returns the number of events currently waiting to be processed. The last argument to this function is a flag that indicates how XEventsQueued determines whether there are waiting events. If this argument is QueuedAfterReading, as in the example, XEventsQueued calls a system routine to read from the network connection to the X display and returns the number of events found after the read operation. If you do not want to read from the network connection, use QueuedAlready for this argument. A third choice, QueuedAfterFlush works as QueuedAfterReading does except that Xlib's request buffer is flushed before XEventsQueued returns.

If XEventsQueued returns a nonzero number of waiting events, you can process them one by one. Use XNextEvent to get the events this time. Note that if you use the QueuedAfterFlush mode with XEventsQueued, the buffer will always be flushed. Because XNextEvent also flushes Xlib's protocol buffer, it is more efficient to use the QueuedAfterReading mode with XEventsQueued and then make an extra call to XFlush if no events are found.

Minimal Events

Recall that many X events are available. Chapter 6 tabulates the 33 types of events that can be reported by the X server. The variety comes from the fact that X reports events in excruciating detail. For example, pressing a key on the keyboard generates a KeyPress as well as a KeyRelease event. Such detailed event reporting gives you the flexibility of designing the user interface to match any style of interaction. For example, using X, you can easily implement the "menubar with pull-down menus" type of interface popularized by Apple Macintosh and Microsoft Windows.

Although 33 types of events are available, you do not have to worry about handling all of them. Most applications can get by with just a few. Let's take a quick look at some of the important ones.

If you draw anything in your application's windows, you need to handle Expose events. The X Window System does not require the server to maintain the contents of a window. Each application is responsible for the contents of its windows. When a previously obscured window becomes visible again (for example, when the user moves around windows), the server draws the border and fills the window with the background color (or the background pixmap, if you select pixmap). If you draw anything else in the window and you want that drawing to show again, you must request Expose events for the window. For a window with the identifier this_window on the display theDisplay, you can enable Expose events:

```
XSelectInput(theDisplay, this_window, ExposureMask);
```

The X server generates an Expose event for each rectangular region of the window that has become visible again. To help you manage these events efficiently, the server includes a count field in the event's data structure. This field indicates the number of Expose events still to come from the server. Once the count is zero, you know that all Expose events for that window have arrived. Thus, the simplest way to handle the Expose events efficiently is to draw everything appearing in the window when you get the Expose event with count equal to zero. The case statement handling the event may be as follows:

```
/* Handle events occurring in this window */
if(theEvent.xany.window == this_window)
{
    switch(theEvent.type)
    {
        case Expose:
            if (theEvent.xexpose.count == 0)
            {
                XClearWindow(theDisplay, this_window);

/* Draw contents of window—depends on application */

            }
            break;
        .
        .
    }
}
```

As you can see, the field `theEvent.xexpose.count` represents the count of `Expose` events. When the count is zero, you can clear the window and draw the graphics and text that should appear in the window. This part of the operation depends on the application. Chapter 9, "Drawing Graphics," provides more details on `Expose` events.

Recall also that some X displays may have off-screen memory known as "backing store" that enables them to save the contents of a window when it gets obscured. With backing store, the server can refresh the window automatically when it becomes visible again. In these cases, the server does not send any `Expose` events, which, in turn, spares the application the computational burden of redrawing its windows. Because not all displays have backing store, you should always include code to handle `Expose` events so that your application can run on all X displays. Additionally, backing store is usually in limited supply; once the server runs out of memory for backing store, it has to use `Expose` events for maintaining the contents of windows.

Mouse Events

X applications always handle events from mouse input, keyboard input, or both. For a graphical user interface, handling mouse events—including buttonpress, button-release, and, occasionally, mouse movement—is essential. Applications such as word processors and editors also handle events from the keyboard. Because these input devices are so important, most of the rest of this chapter is devoted to the discussion of the events generated by the mouse and the keyboard.

Pointing devices are crucial in graphical point-and-click user interfaces. Thus, workstations that support the X Window System include some sort of pointing device, usually a mouse. Recall that the mouse controls a small graphical shape known as the cursor or pointer that appears on the screen; as you move the mouse, the pointer tracks the motion on the screen. In a graphical interface, you interact with the application by bringing the mouse pointer to well-defined areas of the screen and pressing the mouse button. You essentially can press a button to get a job done. In a drawing application, for example, you draw a line by dragging the mouse, which involves moving the mouse while keeping a mouse button pressed. You can quickly press and release a mouse button to achieve the effect of clicking on a window. On the Macintosh and on Microsoft Windows, you start applications by double-clicking on their icons. This requires two clicks in quick succession with the pointer at the same location.

In the X Window System, there are no events equivalent to button clicks or double-clicks. Instead, the X server reports a few basic mouse events: when a button is pressed and released, when the mouse is moved, and when the mouse pointer enters or leaves a window. If you understand when these basic events are generated and how they are reported, you can write your own event handling code to give the appearance of a button click or double-click.

Buttons, Pointer, and Cursor

The number of mouse buttons varies from one workstation to another. The mouse in the Apple Macintosh has only one button; the Microsoft mouse, prevalent in the MS-DOS and Microsoft Windows world, uses two buttons. Most UNIX workstations and some MS-DOS systems use a three-button mouse. X allows for mice with up to five buttons, named `Button1` through `Button5`. Usually, the mouse buttons are numbered from left to right, but a programmer can call the `XSetPointerMapping` function to change the ordering.

The *pointer* refers to the graphical indication of the mouse's position in the display screen. The *cursor* is the actual graphical object that determines the appearance of the pointer in the screen.

Pointer Control

Although the X server automatically moves the pointer to track the movements of the mouse, you have control over several aspects of the pointer. You can, for example, call the `XWarpPointer` function to move the pointer forcibly to a specified location on the screen. This can be disconcerting to the user; therefore, you probably should not warp the pointer unless absolutely necessary for some task in your application.

Two other parameters of the pointer, *acceleration* and *threshold*, can also be set by programmers. Acceleration refers to how fast the pointer moves as you move the mouse. The acceleration is applied only when the mouse movement exceeds the threshold. You can use `XGetPointerControl` and `XChangePointerControl` to change these parameters, but you rarely need to do so. Many users run the utility program named `xset` to set the acceleration and threshold. On most UNIX workstations, you should be able to get further information on `xset` by typing the command `man xset` at the shell prompt.

Pointer Position

Sometimes your application may have to determine the current position of the mouse pointer. Xlib includes the function `XQueryPointer` for this purpose:

```
Display        *theDisplay;    /* Identifies the X server */
Window         w,              /* Window of interest      */
               root, child;    /* For return values       */
int            root_x, root_y, /* Position in root         */
```

```
                win_x, win_y;   /* Position in w's frame   */
unsigned int    keys_buttons;   /* Info on mouse buttons   */


if(!XQueryPointer(theDisplay, w, &root, &child, &root_x, &root_y,
           &win_x, &win_y, &keys_buttons))
{
/* Pointer is not on the screen where window w is */
}
```

Here, w is the window in whose coordinate frame you want to find the pointer's position.
XQueryPointer returns a zero if the pointer is not on the screen where window w is displayed. In
this case, in the root variable, it returns the ID of the root window on the screen where the pointer
appears.

If successful, XQueryPointer provides the information in a set of variables. You have to declare
these variables and pass their addresses as arguments to the function. In root and child, you get
back the window ID of the root window and any visible subwindow of w that contains the pointer.
If the pointer is in w and not in any of its child windows, child will be set to None. The coordinates
of the pointer with respect to the root window are returned in root_x and root_y, and win_x,
win_y are the coordinates in w's frame.

The keys_buttons variable is a bit mask that indicates which mouse button and which modifier
key (Shift, Ctrl, Meta, or Alt) is pressed at that moment. To decipher this information, you have to
perform bitwise-AND of keys_buttons with bitmask names defined in the header file <X11/X.h>.
For example, to see if Button1 is pressed, you might write the following:

```
if(keys_buttons & Button1Mask)
{
/* Yes, button 1 is pressed */
    .
    .
    .
}
```

> **TIP:**
>
> Because XQueryPointer has to get its information from the X server, each call to this
> function requires a costly round trip over the network connection to the server. Thus,
> excessive use of XQueryPointer can hurt the performance of your application. To keep
> track of mouse positions in a window, use the MotionNotify event instead.

After you find the coordinates of the pointer in one window's coordinate frame, you can convert it
to another window's frame by calling XTranslateCoordinates. Unfortunately, this conversion is
also performed by sending a protocol request to the server and getting a reply back. Thus,
XTranslateCoordinates is as costly as using XQueryPointer.

One interesting use of XTranslateCoordinates is to determine the window where a point lies.
For example, if you know the coordinates x and y of a point, relative to the root window, you can
determine the ID of the top-level window containing the point:

```
Window   toplevel;  /* Window that contains the point (x,y) */
int      x, y;      /* Coordinates of the point of interest */
int      xx, yy;    /* Storage for value being discarded    */

XTranslateCoordinates(theDisplay, DefaultRootWindow(theDisplay),
    DefaultRootWindow(theDisplay), x, y, &xx, &yy, &toplevel);
```

On return from XTranslateCoordinates, the variable toplevel contains the ID of the window where the point (x, y) lies. If the point lies in the root window, but not in any top-level subwindow, the returned ID will be the constant None.

Cursor Selection

The cursor determines the on-screen appearance of the pointer. In X, a cursor is defined by a source bitmap, a mask bitmap, foreground and background colors specified as RGB values, and a hotspot. You can think of the bitmaps as a small rectangular array of 1s and 0s (usually 16x16 or 32x32). When drawing the cursor, the server paints the pixels corresponding to 1s using the foreground color; pixels at locations with 0s appear in the background color. The mask bitmap determines the outline within which the cursor shape is drawn. The *hotspot* is a point that defines the location of the pointer in the screen. For many cursor shapes, the hotspot is at the center of the cursor's bitmap. For an arrow cursor, the hotspot is the point of the arrow.

You can assign a cursor to any window in your application. Typically, you create a new cursor from a standard cursor font and assign it to a window:

```
#include <X11/cursorfont.h>
Cursor   arrow_cursor;
   .
   .
   .
arrow_cursor = XCreateFontCursor(theDisplay, XC_arrow);

XDefineCursor(theDisplay, my_window, arrow_cursor);
```

Once this is done, the cursor shape changes to the arrow cursor when the pointer enters the window my_window. This selection remains in effect until you undefine the cursor for that window by calling XUndefineCursor. When you remove the cursor from a window, the server displays the cursor of its parent when the pointer is in this window.

Note that the second argument to XCreateFontCursor specifies the cursor shape with a symbolic name. These names are defined in the header file <X11/cursorfont.h>.

After assigning a cursor to a window, if you do not intend to refer to it any more, you can free the cursor by calling XFreeCursor. Any window that displays this cursor will continue to do so. The server will get rid of the cursor only after that cursor is not defined for any window. Once you undefine a cursor, you must not refer to that cursor's ID again.

Cursor Color

When a cursor is created, it has, by default, a black foreground and a white background color. To change the color of a cursor, use the XRecolorCursor function:

```
XColor  fgcolor, bgcolor;  /* Colors in XColor structure */
Cursor  arrow_cursor;      /* Cursor whose color is set  */

XRecolorCursor(theDisplay, arrow_cursor, &fgcolor, &bgcolor);
```

To specify the color, you have to use RGB values. For more information on color, see Chapter 11, "Using Color in X."

Other Cursor Creation Methods

You can use your own source and mask bitmaps to define a cursor. After you have the two pixmaps—bitmaps are pixmaps of depth one—you can use `XCreatePixmapCursor` to create a new cursor. This function needs the two pixmaps, the foreground and background colors, and the coordinates of the hotspot:

```
Display      *theDisplay;
Cursor       my_cursor;
Pixmap       source, mask;
XColor       fgcolor, bgcolor;
unsigned int x_hot, y_hot;

my_cursor = XCreatePixmapCursor(theDisplay, source, mask,
                    &fgcolor, &bgcolor, x_hot, y_hot);
```

Another way to get a cursor is to select a specific character from a font and use the bitmap of that character as a cursor. Before using the font, you have to load the font by calling `XLoadFont` (see Chapter 10, "Drawing Text"). Then you can create the cursor using the function `XCreateGlyphCursor` (see its reference page in Appendix A for information on calling this function).

> **NOTE:**
>
> In the text of this book, some Xlib functions are described in detail; many others are mentioned briefly. If you need more information on the calling syntax of any function, please consult the reference pages in Appendix A, "Xlib Functions." For quick access to the Xlib functions, check Appendix I, "Xlib Reference."

ButtonPress and *ButtonRelease* Events

After you know how to create and control the cursor, you are ready to use the mouse in a user interface. For a simple case, in which you want something done when the user presses the mouse button in a specific window, you can handle the `ButtonPress` event only and ignore the `ButtonRelease` events. If you want to support mouse button clicks and double-clicks, you have to process both button events.

The file `xbutton.c` shown in Listing 8.3 shows an example of handling mouse buttonpress events. To handle the event, you have to look for the event type `ButtonPress`. Once you get the event, you can perform the action associated with the buttonpress.

Multiple Buttons

What should you do about all the buttons on a mouse? It is up to you, the software developer, to decide. If you handle the buttonpress and button-release events by looking at the event's type only, you assume that pressing any button will perform the same task. This is the safest approach because all mouses have at least one button.

If you decide to assign different functions to each button, you can handle the event for each button:

```
XEvent  theEvent;

while (!AppDone)
{
    XNextEvent(theDisplay, &theEvent);

    switch(theEvent.type)
    {
        case ButtonPress:
/* Handle the buttonpress by button number */
            switch(theEvent.xbutton.button)
            {
                case Button1:
                    ...
                    break;
                case Button2:
                    ...
                    break;
                case Button3:
                    ...
                    break;
            }
            break;

/* Handle other events */
        ...
    }
}
```

You can use another `switch` statement to provide different functionality for different buttons when the application receives a buttonpress event.

XButtonEvent Data Structure

Detailed information on buttonpress and button-release events are available in the `xbutton` member of the `XEvent` union. The `xbutton` member is an `XButtonEvent` data structure that contains information, such as the button that was pressed and the coordinates of the pointer at the time of the buttonpress. The `XButtonEvent` structure is defined in `<X11/Xlib.h>` as follows:

```
typedef struct
{
    int             type;          /* Type of event            */
    unsigned long   serial;        /* Last processed request no.*/
    Bool            send_event;    /* True if from SendEvent   */
    Display         *display;      /* This display sent event  */
    Window          window;        /* Reported to this window  */
```

```
Window          root;          /* Root window               */
Window          subwindow;     /* Pointer is in this child  */
Time            time;          /* Timestamp in milliseconds */
int             x, y;          /* Position in event window  */
int             x_root, y_root; /* Position relative to root */
unsigned int    state;         /* State of key and buttons  */
unsigned int    button;        /* Which button is involved? */
Bool            same_screen;   /* True=grab on same screen  */
} XButtonEvent;
```

Most fields in the XButtonEvent structure have obvious meanings. The window field identifies the window that had requested this type of event. It may also be the window where the event occurred. Because buttonpress and button-release events propagate up the window hierarchy, the event may have occurred in a subwindow that did not request the event. In this case, the subwindow field identifies the subwindow. If the event actually occurred in window, the subwindow field is set to None. The root field contains the ID of the root window of this screen.

The location of the pointer at the time of occurrence of the event is reported in x and y. These values are in pixels with respect to the origin of window. The x_root and y_root fields give the location of the same point in the root window's coordinates.

The state field is a bit mask that indicates which mouse buttons and modifier keys (Shift, Ctrl, Meta, or Alt) were pressed just before the event occurred. Using the state, you can implement functions such as popping up a menu when the user presses the mouse button while holding down the Ctrl key. For example, to display a menu window, my_popup, when Button1 is pressed together with the Ctrl key, you can use this code:

```
Window my_popup;
     .
     .
    case Button1:
        if(theEvent.xbutton.state & ControlMask)
        {
/* Display pop-up menu window */
            XMapWindow(theDisplay, my_popup);
            .
            .
/* Unmap when menu selection is done */
        }
/* Handle regular Button1 press here */
        .
        .
        break;
```

The last field in the XButtonEvent, same_screen, is important for X displays with multiple screens. It has to do with the concept of grab, described next. The same_screen field becomes important in a scenario in which the user presses the mouse button in a window on one screen but releases it after moving the pointer to another screen. In this case, when reporting the button-release event, the server will set same_screen to False.

Automatic Grabs During *ButtonPress*

The term *grab* has a special meaning in X. Normally, the X server sends each event to a specific window that previously requested that type of event. However, for mouse buttonpresses, there are some problems with this method of dispatching events to windows. For example, suppose you select both `ButtonPress` and `ButtonRelease` events for window A. Your expectation is that once you receive a buttonpress followed by the release, you assume that the mouse button was clicked and you call some function in response to the click. The user, unaware of your intentions, presses the mouse button inside A, but decides to move the mouse outside the borders of A and into another window, B, before releasing the button. How should the events be delivered? The buttonpress clearly occurred in A, but what about the button-release? Should it be reported to B? What if the event handling loop is confused by a single stray button-release event in B?

To make matters simple, X provides the notion of a grab. When it makes sense, you can call `XGrabPointer` to grab the mouse pointer (or the keyboard) for the exclusive use by a single window. In other words, the events you specify when grabbing the pointer or the keyboard are reported only to the window of your choice even if the pointer moves outside the boundary of that window. Because a grab disrupts the normal delivery of events, you have to make sure that you call `XUngrabPointer` when it is time to end the grab.

If you must ensure the delivery of a matching button-release event for each buttonpress, you can start a grab after the buttonpress requesting that all further button-release events be reported to your window. When you receive notification of the button-release, you can end the grab.

Note that you do not have to grab and ungrab the pointer explicitly in response to buttonpress and button-release events. The designers of X felt that this situation is common with buttonpress and button-release, so they included a feature in the X server to grab the pointer automatically after a buttonpress event. The grab ends when the user releases the button.

Pointer Events During Automatic Grabs

If you call `XSelectInput` to select buttonpress events for a window with the `ButtonPressMask`, the server delivers all pointer events to that window during the automatic grab. Sometimes this may not be what you really want.

Consider the example of a menubar with pull-down menus. When the user presses a button in an item in the menubar, you want to display a menu that pops up under the item (a *pull-down menu*). Then you want the user to indicate a selection from the pull-down menu by moving the pointer into one of its items and releasing the button. This is clearly a case where you want the button-release event to go to a window different from the one where the buttonpress occurred. What you need is a way to stop the X server from automatically sending all button events to the window where the button is pressed. To do this, you have to select the buttonpress events on the menubar's window with an extra mask, `OwnerGrabButtonMask`. Here is how the code might look:

```
Window  menubar_item1;  /* Window for an item in the menubar */

XSelectInput(theDisplay, menubar_item1, ButtonPressMask |
                             OwnerGrabButtonMask);
```

When `OwnerGrabButtonMask` is specified with `ButtonPressMask`, the server reports all pointer events for your application as you normally expect. In particular, the button's release is reported to the window where the button is released by the user. You will see an example showing a menubar with pull-down menu where buttonpress events are solicited with `OwnerGrabButtonMask`.

Clicks and Double-Clicks

Rather than triggering an action when the user presses a mouse button, you may want to ask the user to click in a window (which represents a button) for the desired action. In this case, you have to look at the buttonpress and button-release events individually and decide when a click has occurred. One way to detect a button click is to select the events for the window with the masks (`ButtonPressMask ¦ ButtonReleaseMask ¦ OwnerGrabButtonMask`) and set a flag on buttonpress. When the button-release event occurs, if you find the flag set, you can call it a button click. The event handling loop for this case might look like this:

```
    int    button_pressed;

    switch (theEvent.type)
    {
        case ButtonPress:
            button_pressed = True;
            break;

        case ButtonRelease:
/* If button was pressed, this is a button click */
            if(button_pressed)
            {
/* Handle button. */
                .
                .
                .
                button_pressed = False;
            }
            break;
    }
```

Another type of interaction that many GUIs require is the double-click. On Apple Macintosh and Microsoft Windows, you start an application by double-clicking on its icon. You can have similar functionality in your X applications by following these steps:

1. To detect a double-click, use the preceding code to detect clicks.

2. When you detect a click, set a variable, `button_clicked`, for example, to `True`.

3. When you get the next click, check that the two clicks occurred at about the same location and that the elapsed time between the two clicks was less than some small value.

The following block of code illustrates how you might achieve this:

```
#include <stdlib.h>
#include <X11/Xlib.h>
    .
    .
    .
    int    button_pressed;    /* Has button been pressed?   */
    int    button_clicked;    /* True = clicked once        */
```

```
int    x_lastclick,        /* Position of last click     */
       y_lastclick;
Time   t_lastclick;        /* Time of click (milliseconds)*/
Time   DblClickTime = 500; /* Two clicks < .5 sec apart  */
int    DblClickSpace = 10; /* Clicks < 10 pixels apart   */

switch (theEvent.type)
{
    case ButtonPress:
        button_pressed = True;
        break;

    case ButtonRelease:

/* If button was clicked once, this may be a double-click.
 * We will call it a double-click if both clicks occurred
 * within 0.5 sec of each other and their locations are
 * within a 10-pixel-by-10-pixel area
 */
        if(button_clicked)
        {
            button_pressed = False;
            button_clicked = False;
            if(((theEvent.xbutton.time - t_lastclick) <=
                    DblClickTime) &&
               (abs(theEvent.xbutton.x - x_lastclick) <=
                    DblClickSpace) &&
               (abs(theEvent.xbutton.y - y_lastclick) <=
                    DblClickSpace) )
            {
/* It's a double-click. Call appropriate function to handle it */

                    .
                    .
            }
        }

/* If button was pressed, generate an XUI_BUTTON_CLICK message */
        if(button_pressed)
        {
/* A button click occurred. Remember position and time. */
            t_lastclick = theEvent.xbutton.time;
            x_lastclick = theEvent.xbutton.x;
            y_lastclick = theEvent.xbutton.y;
            button_clicked = True;
            button_pressed = False;
        }
        break;
}
```

Window Entry or Exit

Notification of the pointer entering and leaving a window is necessary for many tasks in a user interface. In a menu, you may want to somehow highlight the item (perhaps by displaying that window in reverse video) that currently contains the pointer. In an editor, you may change the cursor in the window displaying the text. For such tasks, you want to know when the mouse enters or leaves a window.

Window managers also may need these events. Many window managers assign input focus (which designates the window that gets all keyboard events) to the window that currently contains the pointer. Such window managers would want to change the focus as the pointer enters a window.

EnterNotify and *LeaveNotify* Events

You select these window crossing events by specifying EnterWindowMask and LeaveWindowMask in the call to XSelectInput. When EnterWindowMask is specified for a window, you receive an EnterNotify event when the pointer enters the specified window. With LeaveWindowMask, a LeaveNotify event is sent when the pointer leaves the window. Thus, changing the cursor, for instance, becomes easy. You change the cursor with an XDefineCursor in response to an EnterNotify event.

The server reports the information for EnterNotify and LeaveNotify events in the field named xcrossing in the XEvent union. This is an XCrossingEvent data structure, defined in <X11/Xlib.h> as the following:

```
typedef struct
{
    int            type;        /* EnterNotify or LeaveNotify   */
    unsigned long  serial;      /* Last processed request number */
    Bool           send_event;  /* True = if from a SendEvent   */
    Display        *display;     /* Display where event occurred  */
    Window         window;      /* Window to which event reported*/
    Window         root;        /* Root window in that screen    */
    Window         subwindow;   /* Child window involved in event*/
    Time           time;        /* Time in milliseconds          */
    int            x, y;        /* Final position in event window*/
    int            x_root,      /* Pointer's final position in   */
                   y_root;      /* root window's coordinate frame*/
    int            mode;        /* One of the three constants:   */
                                /*    NotifyNormal, NotifyGrab,  */
                                /*    NotifyUngrab               */
    int            detail;      /* One of the five constants:    */
                                /*    NotifyAncestor, NotifyVirtual, */
                                /*    NotifyInferior, NotifyNonLinear, */
                                /*    NotifyNonLinearVirtual     */
    Bool           same_screen; /* Pointer/window in same screen?*/
    Bool           focus;       /* Input focus on this window?   */
    unsigned int   state;       /* State of key and buttons      */
} XCrossingEvent;
```

Most of the fields in the XCrossingEvent structure are similar to those in XButtonEvent. The x, y coordinates always represent the final position of the pointer after the crossing event, and state gives you the state of the buttons and shift keys just before the event.

The focus field is True if the window identified by the field window or one of its ancestors owns the keyboard focus. This can be useful if you want to indicate (perhaps by changing the border color) which of your application's windows has the input focus (assuming your application uses multiple windows).

Crossing events can occur in three different ways: when the user moves the mouse, when the program starts a grab, or when the program ends a grab. When the pointer is grabbed, it can be forced to stay within a specified window. In this case, crossing events are generated with the mode field set to NotifyGrab. At the end of the grab, more crossing events are generated, this time with the mode field set to NotifyUngrab. The real, user-generated crossing events are reported with mode equal to NotifyNormal. If your application is not concerned with grabs (most applications are not), you have to process only those crossing events whose mode field is NotifyNormal.

Hierarchy Reflected in Crossing Events

The mode and detail fields are unique to crossing events. The mode tells you how the crossing event originated, and detail is there to help you determine the hierarchical relationship of windows involved in the crossing event. The X server tells you, in excruciating detail, how the pointer moved from one location to another. Each window in the path of the pointer gets an appropriate crossing event, with the detail field reflecting the exact nature of the crossing. Let's use the layout of the window shown in Figure 8.3 to explain several interesting cases.

When the pointer moves from window B.2.1 to its ancestor A, B.2.1 receives a LeaveNotify event with detail set to NotifyAncestor, and A gets an EnterNotify event with NotifyInferior in the detail field. Any intervening windows of the same hierarchy, lying in the path of the pointer—in this case, B.2—will receive LeaveNotify events with the detail field set to NotifyVirtual.

For the reverse situation, with the pointer moving from A to B.3.3, the ancestor A gets a LeaveNotify event with NotifyInferior in the detail field, and the destination window B.3.3 gets an EnterNotify event with NotifyAncestor as the detail. Because window B.3 lies in the path of the pointer's motion, it receives an EnterNotify event with the detail NotifyVirtual.

What happens if you move the pointer from one window to its sibling? When the pointer moves from B.2.2 to its sibling B.2.3, the first window receives a LeaveNotify event with detail set to NotifyNonlinear, and the second one gets an EnterNotify event with the same detail.

Finally, suppose the user moves the pointer from one window to another that is not in the same branch of the hierarchy. For example, for the layout shown in Figure 8.3, when the pointer moves from window B.1 to A.2, the first window gets a LeaveNotify event and the final destination window A.2 receives an EnterNotify event, both with the detail NotifyNonlinear. Additionally, the window B receives a LeaveNotify event and A receives an EnterNotify event, both with the detail NotifyNonlinearVirtual.

Hints for Processing Crossing Events

The mode and detail fields in the XCrossingEvent data structure reflect a problem you face when processing crossing events: how to handle all the possible combinations. Here are some hints:

✦ If you have a simple layout of windows, you can process the EnterNotify and LeaveNotify events without paying any attention to the mode and detail fields.

✦ For more complicated situations, the first simplification is to process only those crossing events with mode equal to NotifyNormal. The only case in which you cannot do this is when you are working with pointer grabs in your program.

♦ Check the detail field. If the detail is NotifyVirtual or NotifyNonlinearVirtual, the pointer is merely passing through the window. You can safely ignore these events.

Figure 8.3.
Window layout and hierarchy for illustrating pointer crossing events.

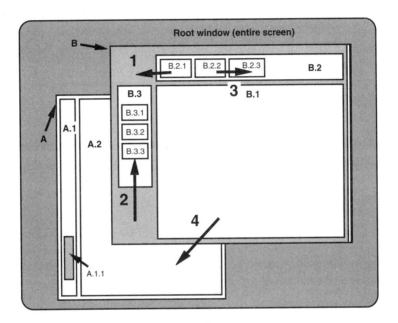

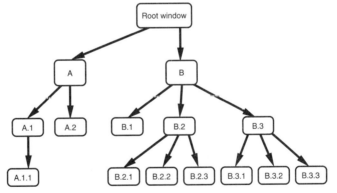

Pointer Motion Detection

Another type of mouse event reports the motion of the pointer. Suppose you are writing a general-purpose drawing program. You probably want to have the capability of drawing straight lines as well as free-style curves. For straight lines, the user may indicate the starting point by pressing the mouse button; then the user moves the mouse to the endpoint and releases the button to draw the line. As the user moves the mouse, you want the application to provide feedback in the form of a line drawn from the starting point to the current location of the pointer. The line must move as the pointer moves on the screen (this is known as *rubber-banding* because it is as if there is a rubber band between the starting point and the pointer).

For a free-style curve, you may want the user to press a button at the starting point and move the pointer along the outline of the path. As the pointer moves, your program joins the points to draw an arbitrary curve.

For both these requirements—straight lines and freestyle curves—you have to request and process pointer motion events.

MotionNotify Events

You can enable pointer motion events in several ways. If you want the motion of the pointer reported without regard to the state of the mouse buttons, use the `PointerMotionMask` with the `XSelectInput` function. If you want the events only when one of the mouse buttons is pressed, you should use the mask named `ButtonMotionMask`. If you want motion events only when a specific button is pressed, you can use the masks `Button1MotionMask` through `Button5MotionMask` to identify the button.

One problem with pointer motions is that if you are not careful, you can get too many of them. If you merely want to know when the user moves the pointer, you should use an additional mask, `PointerMotionHintMask`, when selecting this event. Thus, a typical selection of a motion event might be the following:

```
Display    *theDisplay;
Window     my_window;
.
.
.
XSelectInput(theDisplay, my_window, ExposureMask |
                         ButtonMotionMask |
                         PointerMotionHintMask |
                         ButtonPressMask |
                         OwnerGrabButtonMask);
```

You are asking the server to give you a hint when the pointer is moved with any button pressed. Note that you need to select the `ButtonPress` event also, and, to ensure delivery of the motion events during the buttonpress, you have to specify `OwnerGrabButtonMask`.

With this selection, your application is guaranteed to receive at least one `MotionNotify` event after the user presses any mouse button and moves the mouse pointer in the window my_window. Once you get the first `MotionNotify` event, read the position of the pointer by calling `XQueryPointer`. After you do this, the next movement of the mouse (provided the button is still pressed) will generate another `MotionNotify` event. This method stops your application from being swamped by too many motion events and tracks the pointer's position reasonably well.

XMotionEvent **Data Structure**

Information about motion events are returned in the xmotion field of the XEvent union. Like most of the fields in XEvent, xmotion is a data structure of the following form:

```
typedef struct
{
    int           type;        /* Event's type                 */
    unsigned long serial;      /* Last processed request number */
    Bool          send_event;  /* True = if from a SendEvent    */
    Display       *display;    /* Display where event occurred  */
    Window        window;      /* Window to which event reported*/
    Window        root;        /* Root window in that screen    */
    Window        subwindow;   /* Child window involved in event*/
    Time          time;        /* Time in milliseconds          */
    int           x, y;        /* Position in event window      */
    int           x_root,      /* Pointer's position in the     */
                  y_root;      /* root window's coordinate frame*/
    unsigned int  state;       /* State of key and buttons      */
    char          is_hint;     /* NotifyNormal or NotifyHint    */
    Bool          same_screen; /* Pointer/window in same screen?*/
} XMotionEvent;
```

The fields of the XMotionEvent structure are similar to identically named fields in XButtonEvent and XCrossingEvent. The only new field, is_hint, is a flag that is set to 1 if the MotionNotify event is generated as a hint that the pointer has moved. This happens only if you specify PointerMotionHintMask when selecting the event.

Motion History

One way to handle pointer motion events is to specify the PointerMotionHintMask and, after the first MotionNotify event is received, call XQueryPointer to get the pointer's position. This reenables delivery of another hint when the user moves the pointer again.

There is another way to determine the points that the pointer has passed through; some X servers maintain a history of pointer motion in a buffer. The Xlib function XDisplayMotionBufferSize returns the size of the motion history buffer as a long integer. If this size is nonzero, you can call XGetMotionEvents to retrieve the motion history in response to the MotionNotify event.

Because there is no guarantee that a server has the motion history available, a smart strategy is to first check the size of the history buffer. If the size is zero, set a flag to zero to indicate that motion history is not available. Then, in the event handling loop, call XGetMotionEvents only if the flag is nonzero. Otherwise, use XQueryPointer to get the pointer position. The following fragment of code illustrates this scheme:

```
Display  *theDisplay;
Window   my_window;
XEvent   theEvent;
GC       theGC;
int      use_mhistory = 1;
    .
    .
    .
/* Check size of motion history buffer and set flag */
```

```
            if(XDisplayMotionBufferSize(theDisplay) == 0)
                                      use_mhistory = 0;
       .
       .
       .
/* Event handling for my_window */
   switch(theEvent.type)
   {
       case MotionNotify:
           if(use_mhistory)
           {
               int nevents;
               XTimeCoord *xypos;

               xypos = XGetMotionEvents(theDisplay,
                           my_window, theEvent.xmotion.time,
                           CurrentTime, &nevents);
/* Here is how you might use the points */
               for (i=0; i<nevents; i++)
               {
                   XDrawPoint(theDisplay, my_window, theGC,
                           xypos[i].x, xypos[i].y);
               }
               XFree(xypos);
           }
           else
           {
/* No motion history available...use XQueryPointer */
               Window rw, cw;
               int xr, yr, xw, yw, kbstat;

               XQueryPointer(theDisplay,
                   theEvent.xmotion.window,
                   &rw, &cw, &xr, &yr, &xw, &yw, &kbstat);

               XDrawPoint(theDisplay, my_window, theGC,
                           xw, yw);
/* You should also save the point so that you can redraw
 * the window's contents in reponse to Expose events.
 */
           }
           break;

/* Other case statements... */

   }
```

XGetMotionEvents returns information about the pointer's position during the start and stop times specified in its third and fourth arguments, respectively. To specify these times, you can use the time reported by an event or the constant CurrentTime to denote the current time.

> **TIP:**
>
> Some X servers may not have a motion history buffer. Therefore, you should always check before relying on this mechanism. The approach that seems to work on most workstations is to specify PointerMotionHintMask when selecting motion events. In response to the MotionNotify event, call XQueryPointer to get the pointer's position.

XGetMotionEvents allocates an array of structures of type XTimeCoord, fills it with information received from the X server, and returns the address of that buffer to the calling program. The XTimeCoord structure is defined in <X11/Xlib.h> as follows:

```
typedef struct
{
    Time    time;  /* Milliseconds since the X server started */
    short   x, y;  /* Position relative to window specified in
                      the call to XGetMotionEvents          */
} XTimeCoord;
```

The last argument you provide to XGetMotionEvents is the address of an integer, wherein it returns the number of elements in the array holding the motion history. Each element of this array gives you the pointer's position at a certain time during its motion. The positions are relative to the origin of the window you specify in the second argument to XGetMotionEvents.

After you have used the positions reported in the motion history buffer, you have to remember to release the memory used by the buffer. You can do this by calling XFree.

Keyboard Events

The mouse is important for the point-and-click parts of a GUI; the keyboard is indispensable for text entry. Whether it is annotating a figure or typing in a program listing, a program must handle keyboard input to get the job done.

As with the mouse buttonpress and button-release events, the X server generates a KeyPress event when a key is pressed and a KeyRelease event when the key is released. All keys generate these events (including, for instance, Shift, Ctrl, Alt, Caps Lock, and the function keys). All workstations generate KeyPress events; some systems may not reliably report the KeyRelease event. Because there is usually no need to detect a KeyRelease, you should process keyboard input using the KeyPress event only. That enables the application to work with all X servers.

> **NOTE:**
>
> Keys such as Shift, Ctrl, Alt, and Caps Lock (or Shift Lock) keys are known as *modifier keys* because they modify the meaning of the other keys. X supports up to five system-dependent modifier keys.

Keyboard Event Processing

Unlike the mouse, which has a pointer to indicate the window in which a pointer event occurs, the keyboard has to rely on the concept of a focus window that gets the keyboard events. How the focus is assigned and how to ensure that the designated subwindow in your application gets the keystrokes are discussed in later sections. For now, you can proceed under the assumption that somehow the window of your choice has the input focus.

You can request KeyPress events for the window by using KeyPressMask as the event mask when calling XSelectInput.

XKeyEvent Data Structure

Once selected, KeyPress and KeyRelease events are reported in an XKeyEvent data structure, which is defined in <X11/Xlib.h> as follows:

```
typedef struct
{
    int          type;        /* Event's type                 */
    unsigned long serial;     /* Last processed request number */
    Bool         send_event;  /* True = if from a SendEvent    */
    Display      *display;     /* Display where event occurred  */
    Window       window;      /* Window to which event reported*/
    Window       root;        /* Root window in that screen    */
    Window       subwindow;   /* Child window involved in event*/
    Time         time;        /* Time in milliseconds          */
    int          x, y;        /* Position in event window      */
    int          x_root,      /* Pointer's position in the     */
                 y_root;      /* root window's coordinate frame*/
    unsigned int state;       /* State of key and buttons      */
    unsigned int keycode;     /* detail */
    Bool         same_screen;/* Pointer/window in same screen?*/
} XKeyEvent;
```

You can access the fields of XKeyEvent through the xkey member of the XEvent union. For example, if the event is received in a variable named theEvent of type XEvent, refer to the keycode after a KeyPress event as theEvent.xkey.keycode.

Most of the fields in the XKeyEvent structure have the same meaning as identically named members in other event data structures. The two most important fields for processing keystrokes are state and keycode. The state indicates the state (pressed or released) of the modifier keys, such as Shift, Ctrl, and Alt, as well as any system-dependent modifiers. The keycode is an integer with values between 8 and 255 that uniquely identifies the key. You have to translate this code into ASCII characters (or the ISO Latin-1 code of which ASCII is a subset) before using it.

Keycode Mapping to *keysym* and Character String

The X server decides the keycode to generate for a specific physical key. Each key, including the modifiers, has a unique keycode. Although the keycode generated for the common alphanumeric keys may be the same for many workstations, it is not guaranteed to be so. Therefore, applications do not use the raw keycode. Instead, this server-dependent keycode is translated to meaningful characters by a two-step process:

1. As shown in Figure 8.4, the first step involves translating the keycode to a symbolic name, known as keysym. All meaningful combinations of a key and the modifiers have unique keysyms, which are constants defined in the header file <X11/keysym.h>. The keysym resulting from a single keypress depends on the state of the modifier keys as well as the key itself. For example, if you press the A key alone, you should get a lowercase a, but if you

press A while the Shift key is down, the result should be an uppercase A. The keysym differentiates between these cases and assigns the names XK_a and XK_A, respectively, for lowercase and uppercase A.

2. Convert the keysym to an ASCII text string that you can use for displaying (and for saving in files or buffers). For most keys, this would be a string with a single character, but function keys, especially programmable ones, may generate a multicharacter string.

Figure 8.4.

Translating keycode to keysym and ASCII characters.

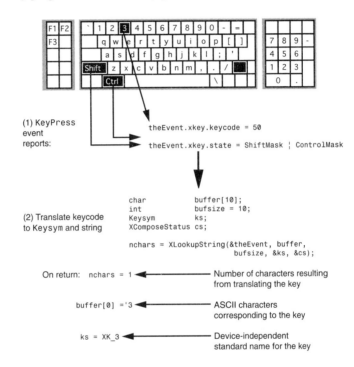

Keycode Translation with *XLookupString*

You can use a single function, XLookupString, to complete both steps of translating a keycode to a keysym as well as to an ASCII text string (see Figure 8.4). A typical use of this function might be as follows:

```
#include <X11/keysym.h>
.
XEvent        theEvent;
char          xlat[20];    /* Room for string  */
int           nchar = 20;  /* Size of xlat     */
int           count;       /* Chars. returned  */
KeySym        key;         /* keysym on return */
XComposeStatus cs;         /* Compose key status*/

.
.
XNextEvent(p_disp, &theEvent);
```

```
         .
         .

/* In the event processing section */

    switch(theEvent.type)
    {
        case KeyPress:
        {
            count = XLookupString(&theEvent, xlat, nchar
                                  &key, &cs);
/* Add null byte to make [sq]xlat[sq] a valid C string */
            xlat[count] = [sq]\0[sq];

/* Print out translated string... */
            printf("Keypress %s received on window %x, \
subwindow %x\n",    xlat, theEvent.xkey.window,
                      theEvent.xkey.subwindow);

/* Keysym may be used like this... */
            if(key == XK_Q ¦¦ key == XK_q)
            {
/* User has pressed [sq]q[sq]. Exit? */
                    .
                    .
                    exit(0);
            }
        }
        break;

/* Other events... */
    }
```

To use XLookupString, you have to have a buffer for the characters (xlat in the example). You have to pass the address of the event that contains the keycode you want translated. The event must be of type KeyPress or KeyRelease. XLookupString takes into account the state of the Shift key when translating the keycode to a keysym.

The string returned by XLookupString is not null-terminated. To convert it to a null-terminated C-style string, you should insert a null character as shown in the example.

What you do with the keysym or the text string generated by XLookupString is up to your application. If you are accepting text from the user, you will probably use the text string only, perhaps saving it in a buffer. On the other hand, if you want the application to quit when the user presses the Q key, you can compare the returned keysym with the ones for uppercase and lowercase Q, (including, for instance, Shift, Ctrl, Alt, Caps Lock, and the function keys)—XK_q and XK_Q, respectively.

The XComposeStatus structure passed to XLookupString is used to store certain status information to support composing multiple key sequences. For example, the user might press a designated Compose key, then a backquote (`'`), and finally an E to construct the capital letter È with the grave accent. If you do not care about multikey characters, you can provide a NULL pointer in place of the argument.

Translation of *keysym* to String

With the function XRebindKeysym, you can assign an arbitrary ASCII text string to any key. Note that this binding of a string to a key is local to your application. It does not affect the other applications sharing the display. Therefore, you can use it without any apprehension.

Here is an example of binding the string HELP to the function key F1 and HELP INDEX to Ctrl-F1:

```
    Display  *theDisplay;
    KeySym   modkeys[2];
    .
    .
/* Bind "HELP" to the F1 key */
    XRebindKeysym(theDisplay, XK_F1, NULL, 0, "HELP", 4);

/* Bind "HELP INDEX" to Control-F1 */
    modkeys[0] = XK_Control_L;
    XRebindKeysym(theDisplay, XK_F1, modkeys, 1,
                "HELP INDEX", 10);
```

As you can see, the second argument to XRebindKeysym is the key (indicated by its keysym) whose string equivalent is being changed. Next comes an array of keysyms representing the modifiers to be associated with this binding. Use NULL if no modifiers are needed. The number of modifier keysyms comes next. The last two arguments are the string and its length.

Keyboard Mapping Refresh

The X server manages the translation of keycodes to keysym. Applications can change this mapping by calling the function XChangeKeyboardMapping. An application should not do this on its own, but the user may run a utility program such as xmodmap to alter the mapping of one or more keys. When this happens, your application will receive a MappingNotify event. Future mappings of keycodes to keysyms will work properly as long as your application calls XRefreshKeyboardMapping each time it receives a MappingNotify event.

Input Focus

The server can associate a pointer event with a specific window by noting which window contains the pointer. There is no good way to decide the window that should receive the keyboard events. To solve the problem, X uses the concept of *focus*. The window with the focus gets all the keypresses, regardless of the pointer's location (unless, of course, the pointer's location also controls the focus).

Because all applications displaying in a workstation have to share the keyboard, it is important to have a well-defined mechanism for transferring the input focus from one application's window to another. In fact, such conventions do exist, in the form of the *Inter-Client Communication Conventions Manual (ICCCM)*. These conventions have been followed earnestly since the release of X11R4 in January 1990. What you need is a window manager that follows the ICCCM. Then you can give the window manager an appropriate hint about your application's need for input focus. After that, your application should get the focus when the user selects your application's top-level window. The exact mechanism for transferring the focus depends on the window manager. If the window manager uses a *click-to-type* model, the user indicates the focus window by clicking on it. Some window managers may follow the model whereby the input focus is always on the top-level window with the pointer in it.

Hints to the Window Manager

Application programs that need keyboard input should so indicate by setting the input field of the XWMHints structure to True before calling XSetWMHints (or XSetWMProperties). Here is how this might be done:

```
    XWMHints            *p_xwmh;

    if((p_xwmh = XAllocWMHints()) == NULL)
    {
        fprintf(stderr, "Error allocating Window \
Manager hints!\n");
        exit(1);
    }

/* Tell the window manager to put the window in its normal
 * state and to transfer input focus to our window when
 * the user does so. Use XSetWMProperties or XSetWMHints to
 * inform the window manager.
 */
    p_xwmh->flags = (InputHint|StateHint);
    p_xwmh->input = True;
    p_xwmh->initial_state = NormalState;

    XSetWMHints(theDisplay, theMain, p_xwmh);
```

FocusChange Events

The window manager will take care of setting the focus to your application's top-level window. Suppose your application handles all text input in a single subwindow and you want to give the focus to this subwindow when the top-level window receives the focus. You can do this by requesting FocusChange events on the topmost window. When you get notification of focus being on your main window (through a FocusIn event), you can call XSetInputFocus to give the focus to the subwindow that needs it. Having done this, you can place all code for handling the keyboard events in the section that processes events for that subwindow. This simplifies keyboard inputs in your application.

Although the suggested scheme is straightforward, the FocusIn and FocusOut events are somewhat like the crossing events—a window can get one even if it is not the ultimate recipient of the input focus. The trick is to look at the mode and detail fields of the XFocusChangeEvent data structure, which is defined in <X11/Xlib.h> as follows:

```
typedef struct
{
    int          type;      /* FocusIn or FocusOut           */
    unsigned long serial;    /* Last processed request number */
    Bool         send_event; /* True = if from a SendEvent    */
```

```
    Display        *display;     /* Display where event occurred  */
    Window         window;       /* Window to which event reported*/
    int            mode;         /* One of the three constants:
                                    NotifyNormal, NotifyGrab,
                                    NotifyUngrab                   */
    int            detail;       /* One of the five constants:
                                    NotifyAncestor, NotifyVirtual,
                                    NotifyInferior, NotifyNonLinear,
                                    NotifyNonLinearVirtual          */
} XFocusChangeEvent;
```

You care about getting the focus because of an assignment by the user; therefore, you should care about only those FocusIn events with mode equal to NotifyNormal. Furthermore, the focus always changes from another application's window to your application's top-level window. For this case, the detail field will be NotifyNonlinear. Thus, you can assign focus to a selected subwindow of your application:

```
    Display *theDisplay;
    Window  theMain, kb_win;
    XSelectInput(theDisplay, theMain, ExposureMask |
                                      FocusChangeMask);
        .
        .
/* In event handling loop... */
    switch (theEvent.type)
    {
        case FocusIn:
/* Give focus to our keyboard handling subwindow */
            if(theEvent.xfocus.mode == NotifyNormal &&
                theEvent.xfocus.detail == NotifyNonlinear)
            XSetInputFocus(theDisplay, kb_win, RevertToParent,
                        CurrentTime);
            break;

/* Handle other events ... */
    }
```

Always use the constant RevertToParent as the third argument to XSetInputFocus. This argument specifies what to do if the subwindow receiving the input focus becomes obscured. The constant RevertToParent specifies that, in this case, the focus should revert back to the parent window.

Keyboard Control

Xlib includes routines to control some aspects of the keyboard, such as the status of the LED (light-emitting diode) lamps on the keyboard, the volume and pitch of the bell, and the rate at which keys are automatically repeated (if pressed continuously).

A structure of type XKeyboardControl is used to specify the values of the parameters. The XKeyboardControl structure is defined in <X11/Xlib.h> as follows:

```
typedef struct
{
    int key_click_percent; /* 0 (silent) to 100 (loudest) */
    int bell_percent;      /* 0 (silent) to 100 (loudest) */
```

```
    int bell_pitch;            /* 20 Hz to 20 Khz          */
    int bell_duration;         /* milliseconds for bell    */
    int led;                   /* Which LED? (1 to 32)     */
    int led_mode;              /* LedModeOn or LedModeOff   */
    int key;                   /* Keycode for next field    */
    int auto_repeat_mode;      /* 0 (off) or 1 (on)        */
} XKeyboardControl;
```

The approach used to specify the values in this structure is similar to that used in specifying other X data structures. You set up the fields you want, set up a bit mask to indicate which fields are being changed, and call XChangeKeyboardControl with the mask and a pointer to the XKeyboardControl structure. Note that a -1 as value sets the parameter back to its default.

Applications should not have any reason to change the keyboard parameters. These items are usually set by the user by running the utility program xset. You can see the current settings by typing xset q at the shell prompt in an xterm window.

Other X Events

In addition to the mouse and keyboard events, the X server also sends events to alert your application of situations that may require some action. Of these events, the Expose event is the most important. As explained earlier in this chapter, the server sends Expose events when any of your application's windows that were previously obscured become visible again. To handle this event, your application should draw whatever was being displayed in that window. If you display anything in a window, you must request and process Expose events; otherwise, the contents of the windows will not be maintained when the user moves around any overlapping windows.

Several notification events are generated when windows are moved and resized, and their hierarchy and stacking order are changed. As usual, there are many more events than you may care to handle (at least, in the beginning), but all the possible notification events are there, in case someone needs them.

Window Notification Events

Nine events report changes in a window's position, size, and other state. Here is a summary of these events:

✦ CirculateNotify. This event indicates that the window's position in the stacking order of its siblings has changed.

✦ ConfigureNotify. The server sends this event when the window is moved, resized, or its position in the stacking order is changed. You have to request this event if you want to resize the windows in your application when the user alters the size of the top window. Use StructureNotifyMask in the call to XSelectInput.

✦ CreateNotify. The server sends this event when a subwindow is created. You can request this event using the SubStructureNotifyMask when selecting events for your top-level window to get reports of creation of subwindows. This event is used by window managers because they can request this event for the root window and get notification when an application creates its top-level window.

◆ `DestroyNotify`. This event reports the destruction of a window.

◆ `GravityNotify`. If a window is moved because its parent's size has changed, the server sends this event.

◆ `MapNotify`. This event is generated when the window is mapped.

◆ `ReparentNotify`. The server sends this event when a window's parent is changed by a call to the function `XReparentWindow`. When a window manager places its own decorative frame around a window, it reparents your application's top-level window.

◆ `UnmapNotify`. This event is sent to indicate that the window is unmapped.

◆ `VisibilityNotify`. If the window's visibility changes (it becomes visible or invisible), the server sends this event.

ConfigureNotify **Events**

Of the events that notify you about changes in a window's state, the `ConfigureNotify` event may be the most important. This event reports changes in position, size, and stacking order of a window. You probably care most about the report in the change of size of your application's top-level window because this may require changes to other subwindows.

If you have a simple hierarchy of windows, you should request the `ConfigureNotify` event by using the event mask `StructureNotifyMask` for your program's main window. When you receive the `ConfigureNotify` events, you can resize the subwindows manually.

If you want to receive a `ConfigureNotify` event when any of the subwindows are reconfigured, you can also use the event mask `SubStructureNotifyMask` for the main window.

XConfigureEvent **Data Structure**

The information for a `ConfigureNotify` event is reported in a data structure of type `XConfigureEvent`, which is present as the member `xconfigure` in the `XEvent` union. The `XConfigureEvent` data structure is defined in `<X11/Xlib.h>` as follows:

```
typedef struct
{
    int         type;        /* ConfigureNotify              */
    unsigned long serial;    /* Last processed request number */
    Bool        send_event;  /* True = if from a SendEvent    */
    Display     *display;     /* Display where event occurred  */
    Window      event;        /* Window to which event reported*/
    Window      window;       /* Window that was reconfigured  */
    int         x, y;         /* New position in parent's frame*/
    int         width,        /* New width of window           */
                height;       /* New height of window          */
    int         border_width;/* New border width of window    */
    Window      above;        /* Set to: Sibling or None       */
    Bool        override_redirect; /* If True, window manager
                             will not intervene with the
                             reconfiguration of this window*/
} XConfigureEvent;
```

As you can see from the comments in the definition of the structure, most of the fields have straight-forward meaning. The last field, `override_redirect` has a special significance. The value in this field comes from the `override_redirect` attribute of the window that was reconfigured. Window managers usually intercept the `ConfigureNotify` events so that they can decide the placement and size of each application's top-level windows. When window managers see that the `override_redirect` field is set to `True`, they do not interfere with that window's location and size. Applications use this feature when creating pop-up windows (that are children of the root). They set the `override_redirect` attribute of pop-up windows to `True`. That way, the window manager does not place any decorative frame around the pop-up, nor does it try to prompt the user for placement of the window (only some window managers do this).

Another word of caution is in order. In the presence of a window manager, the x and y positions reported for your application's top-level windows may not be with respect to the root window (which is what you probably expect), because the window managers usually reparent the top-level windows.

Window Size Changes

The reaction to a change in size of your application's main window depends on the exact nature of the application. For example, if you are developing a text editor, and you have a single subwindow displaying the text, all you have to do is change this window by using the function `XResizeWindow`. Assuming that this is the case, the `ConfigureNotify` event might be selected and handled as follows:

```
    Display *theDisplay;
    Window  w;
    XEvent  theEvent;

    XSelectInput(theDisplay, w, ExposureMask |
                               StructureNotifyMask);
    .
    .
    .
/* In the event handling loop ... */

/* Get the next event from Xlib */
    XNextEvent(theDisplay, &theEvent);

    if(theEvent.xany.window == w &&
       theEvent.type == ConfigureNotify)
    {
        XResizeWindow(theDisplay, w, theEvent.xconfigure.width,
                    theEvent.xconfigure.height);
    }
```

Because `ConfigureNotify` events are generated for a variety of reasons, of which size change is one, you should save the old size of the window and compare it with the size reported in the event.

Events for Graphics and Interclient Communications

There are several other X events that play important roles in X applications. Of these, the `ColorMapNotify` event reports installation of a new colormap for a window. Applications can request this event by specifying the mask `ColormapChangeMask`. Also, if the X server encounters certain problems during graphics copy operations, it generates `GraphicsExpose` events. Both of these events are described in detail in Chapter 9.

The other group of events are meant for exchanging information between X clients. (Your application must work with at least one client, the window manager.) The events in this category are `ClientMessage`, `PropertyNotify`, `SelectionClear`, `SelectionNotify`, and `SelectionRequest`. These events are described in Chapter 16.

Example with Menubar and Pull-Down Menus

You have seen many small fragments of code illustrating various aspects of event handling in X applications. The next example illustrates how you can implement a sophisticated graphical interface using the low-level event reporting mechanism of X. You reuse the routines `initapp.c` (Chapter 7, Listing 7.2) and `xbutton.c` (Listing 8.3) to build the program.

The example program implements a menubar with pull-down menus. Keyboard event handling is not shown here because if the application accepts text input, it also must display the text. Chapter 10 discusses displaying text, and this example is expanded to include text editing and display.

Menu Window

The first step in displaying a menubar is to implement the menu. Each menu shows a number of items in a window. The program has to initiate some action when the user presses the mouse button with the pointer inside one of the items. In the beginning of this chapter, you developed a button window, multiple copies of which can be handled easily, as shown in Listing 8.4. You will reuse that code and build the menu as an outer window with a number of buttons as subwindows.

The same code can handle a menubar as well as a pull-down menu. The difference between the two is that the individual button windows are laid out horizontally in the menubar, but they are arranged vertically in the pull-down menu.

In keeping with the design of `xbutton.c` (Listing 8.3), the menu has a private data structure in which information about each copy of the menu is stored. The menu's data structure is divided into two parts:

✦ Information about each menu item is stored in a structure of type `D_ITEM`.

✦ Information about the entire menu is stored in a structure of type `D_MENU`.

Listing 8.7 shows the file `xmenu.c`, which implements the menu window. The data structures `D_ITEM` and `D_MENU` appear in that file.

Listing 8.7. xmenu.c—Implementing menubars and pull-down menus.

```
/*----------------------------------------------------------*/
/* File: xmenu.c
 *
 * Implement a "menu"—a window that displays a number
 * of buttons and calls an "action" routine when the
 * user presses any mouse button inside one of the buttons.
 *
 */
/*----------------------------------------------------------*/
#include <stdio.h>
#include <varargs.h>  /* Variable-length argument list macros */
#include "xwins.h"
#include "app_glob.c"

#define GAP    2    /* Separation between buttons, in pixels  */

typedef int    (*P_FUNC)();
typedef char   *P_CHAR;

typedef struct D_ITEM
{
    int            item_number; /* This item's index     */
    int            width;       /* Width of button       */
    int            height;      /* Height of button      */
    char           *item_text;  /* Label for this item   */
    P_FUNC         item_action; /* Ptr to Action routine*/
    caddr_t        action_args; /* Argument for action   */
    XWIN           *p_button;   /* This item's window    */
    struct D_ITEM *next;        /* Pointer to next item */
} D_ITEM;

typedef struct D_MENU
{
    int     nitems;          /* How many items in menu */
    int     max_item_width;  /* Max. width in pixels   */
    int     max_item_height; /* Max. height in pixels  */
    int     style;           /* Menu style             */
#define MENUBAR_STYLE  0
#define PULLDOWN_STYLE 1
    D_ITEM  *item_list;      /* Start of list of items */
} D_MENU;

static int menu_handler();          /* Event handler for menu */
/*----------------------------------------------------------*/
/* M a k e X m e n u
 *
 * A "menu" with a number of items (each implemented as a
 * button that you can press to perform an "action")
 * Uses the UNIX calling convention for functions
 * requiring a variable number of arguments.
 *
 * In this function,   ...    represents a list of:
 *
 * char *item_text, int (*item_action)(), caddr_t action_args
 *
 * A NULL marks end of list.
```

```
   */
XWIN *MakeXMenu(va_alist)
va_dcl  /* Macro must appear without semicolon */
{
    va_list      argp;          /* Used to access arguments */
    XWIN         *new_menu;
    D_MENU       *p_data;
    D_ITEM       *p_item, *p_i;
    char         *item_text;
    int          xb, yb, char_height;
    unsigned     width, height, bdwidth;
    int          x, y, style;
    unsigned long bdcolor, bgcolor;
    Window       parent;

    va_start(argp);
    x = va_arg(argp, int);
    y = va_arg(argp, int);
    bdwidth = va_arg(argp, unsigned int);
    bdcolor = va_arg(argp, unsigned long);
    bgcolor = va_arg(argp, unsigned long);
    parent = va_arg(argp, Window);
    style = va_arg(argp, int);

    char_height = theFontStruct->max_bounds.ascent +
                  theFontStruct->max_bounds.descent + 4;

/* Allocate memory for the menu */
    if((p_data = (D_MENU*)calloc(1, sizeof(D_MENU))) == NULL)
    {
        fprintf(stderr, "No memory for menu's data");
        exit(1);
    }

/* Allocate an XWIN structure */
    if((new_menu = (XWIN*)calloc(1, sizeof(XWIN))) == NULL)
    {
        fprintf(stderr, "No memory for the menu");
        exit(1);
    }

/* Initialize the menu's data */
    p_data->max_item_height = char_height;
    p_data->style = style;

/* Get rest of the items one by one and compute sizes of buttons */
    while((item_text = va_arg(argp, P_CHAR)) != NULL)
    {
/* Allocate memory for this menu item */
        if((p_item = (D_ITEM*)calloc(1, sizeof(D_ITEM))) == NULL)
        {
            fprintf(stderr, "No memory for menu items");
            exit(1);
        }
```

continues

Listing 8.7. continued

```
/* Save the pointer in the list */
        if(p_data->item_list == NULL)
            p_data->item_list = p_item;
        else
        {
/* Get to the end of the list using an empty for loop */
            for(p_i = p_data->item_list; p_i->next != NULL;
                p_i = p_i->next) ;
            p_i->next = p_item;
        }
/* Set up contents of item data structure */
        p_item->item_number = p_data->nitems++;
        p_item->item_text = item_text;
        p_item->width = XTextWidth(theFontStruct, item_text,
                            strlen(item_text)) + 4;
        p_item->height = char_height;
        if(p_data->max_item_width < p_item->width)
            p_data->max_item_width = p_item->width;

        p_item->item_action = va_arg(argp, P_FUNC);
        p_item->action_args = va_arg(argp, caddr_t);
    }
    va_end(argp);

    if(style == MENUBAR_STYLE)
    {
        height = p_data->max_item_height + 2 * GAP;
        width  = GAP;
        for(p_i = p_data->item_list; p_i != NULL;
            p_i = p_i->next) width += p_i->width + GAP;
    }
    if(style == PULLDOWN_STYLE)
    {
        width = p_data->max_item_width + 2 * GAP;
        height = GAP;
        for(p_i = p_data->item_list; p_i != NULL;
            p_i = p_i->next) height += p_i->height + GAP;
    }

/* Create the menu shell—the outer window */
    new_menu->xid = XCreateSimpleWindow(theDisplay, parent,
                        x, y, width, height, bdwidth, bdcolor,
                        bgcolor);
    new_menu->data = p_data;
    new_menu->event_handler = menu_handler;
    new_menu->parent = parent;

/* Save new_menu as data associated with this window ID
 * and the context "xwin_context"
 */
    if(XSaveContext(theDisplay, new_menu->xid, xwin_context,
                (caddr_t) new_menu) != 0)
    {
        fprintf(stderr, "Error saving xwin_context data");
        exit(1);
    }
```

```
/* Select ButtonRelease events. No need to select
 * Expose events because we don't draw in the menu shell.
 */
    XSelectInput(theDisplay, new_menu->xid, ButtonReleaseMask);

/* Create the buttons for all menu items */
    xb = GAP;
    yb = GAP;
    for(p_i = p_data->item_list; p_i != NULL; p_i = p_i->next)
    {
        if(style == PULLDOWN_STYLE)
            width = p_data->max_item_width;
        else
            width = p_i->width;
        p_i->p_button = MakeXButton(xb, yb, width-1,
                p_i->height-1, 1, bdcolor, bgcolor, new_menu->xid,
                p_i->item_text, p_i->item_action,
                p_i->action_args);
        if(style == MENUBAR_STYLE) xb += p_i->width +  GAP;
        if(style == PULLDOWN_STYLE) yb += p_i->height + GAP;

/* Select additional events for each button */
        AddNewEvent(p_i->p_button->xid,
                EnterWindowMask | LeaveWindowMask |
                OwnerGrabButtonMask);
    }

/* Map menubars, but not pull-down menus */
    if(style == MENUBAR_STYLE)
        XMapWindow(theDisplay, new_menu->xid);

    return (new_menu);
}
/*------------------------------------------------------------*/
/* m e n u _ h a n d l e r
 *
 * Event handler for the "menu"
 */
static int menu_handler(p_xwin)
XWIN *p_xwin;
{
    int    real_enter;
    D_ITEM *p_i;
    D_MENU *p_data = (D_MENU *) p_xwin->data;

/* Handle events delivered to this window */
    switch(theEvent.type)
    {
        case ButtonRelease:
            if(p_data->style == PULLDOWN_STYLE &&
               theEvent.xbutton.subwindow != None)
            {
                for(p_i = p_data->item_list; p_i != NULL;
                    p_i = p_i->next)
                {
```

continues

Listing 8.7. continued

```
                    if(p_i->p_button->xid ==
                       theEvent.xbutton.subwindow)
                    {
                        if (*(p_i->item_action) != NULL)
                            (*(p_i->item_action))
                                    (p_i->action_args);
                    }
                }
            }
            break;
    }
    return 0;
}
```

A menu can have a variable number of items. In implementing the menu window, let's allow a variable number of arguments in the function that creates and initializes the menu. The prototype of this function, MakeXMenu, is as follows:

```
XWIN *MakeXMenu(int x, int y, unsigned bdwidth,
    unsigned long bdcolor, unsigned long bgcolor,
    Window parent, int style,...);
```

The ellipsis (. . .) in the prototype indicates that the function takes a variable number of arguments. For each menu item, you have to provide the item's label (a char * variable), the address of the function to call when that item is selected (what you might call the *action routine*), and a generic pointer that will be passed to that action routine. A NULL marks the end of the list. For example, to create a menubar with the items File, Edit, and Utilities, you call MakeXMenu:

```
#define MENUBAR_STYLE  0

XWIN *menubar;

menubar = MakeXMenu(0, 0, 1, theFGpix, theBGpix,
        theMain, MENUBAR_STYLE,
/* List the menu entries one by one, end with a NULL */
        "File",      disp_menu, (caddr_t)&menu_0,
        "Edit",      disp_menu, (caddr_t)&menu_1,
        "Utilities", disp_menu, (caddr_t)&menu_2,
        NULL);
```

The style is indicated by a defined constant, MENUBAR_STYLE. All three menu items use the same action routine, disp_menu, which displays the pop-up menu specified by the argument passed to that routine.

Note that MakeXMenu handles a variable number of arguments, using the UNIX approach to variable-length argument lists.

Menubar with Pull-Down Menus: *menudemo.c*

As with `xbutton.c`, `xmenu.c` implements a reusable menu object. You can create as many menus as you want by calling `MakeXMenu`. To implement a menubar with pull-down menus, you first create the menubar and the individual pull-down menus. By default, the pull-down menus are not mapped. To create the effect of pulling down a menu, all you have to do is provide an action routine for the menubar that will map the appropriate pull-down menu on buttonpress. The file `menudemo.c` in Listing 8.8 implements a program that creates a user interface with the desired effects.

To build the program `menudemo`, you need these files:

+ `app_glob.c` (Chapter 7, Listing 7.1)
+ `initapp.c` (Chapter 7, Listing 7.2)
+ `xwins.h` (Listing 8.1)
+ `xwinutil.c` (Listing 8.2)
+ `xbutton.c` (Listing 8.3)
+ `xmenu.c` (Listing 8.7)

You also need to insert the utility routines `AddNewEvent` and `IgnoreEvent` (Chapter 7, Listing 7.3) into the file `xwinutil.c` before building `menudemo`. You can use the following makefile (after some minor modifications to account for your system) to build `menudemo`:

```
# Some definitions...

RM = rm -f
CC = cc

# Compiler flags, paths for include files and libraries

CFLAGS =
INCLUDES = -I. -I/usr/include -I/usr/include/X11
LIBS = -lX11

# Rule to create .o files from .c files
.c.o:
    $(RM) $@
    $(CC) -c $(CFLAGS) $(INCLUDES) $*.c

# Targets...

all::    menudemo

menudemo.o: menudemo.c app_glob.c xwins.h

initapp.o: initapp.c app_glob.c

xwinutil.o: xwinutil.c app_glob.c xwins.h

xbutton.o: xbutton.c app_glob.c xwins.h

xmenu.o: xmenu.c app_glob.c xwins.h
```

```
menudemo: menudemo.o initapp.o xwinutil.o xbutton.o \
      xmenu.o
   $(RM) $@
   $(CC) -o $@ $(CFLAGS) menudemo.o initapp.o \
       xwinutil.o xbutton.o xmenu.o \
       $(LIBS)
```

Figure 8.5 shows the initial result of running menudemo. In Figure 8.6, the user has pressed the mouse button on the File item of the menubar and moved the mouse (while holding down the button) into the Open item of the pull-down menu. The button is highlighted by monitoring the EnterNotify and LeaveNotify events.

Figure 8.5.

The menubar from menudemo.

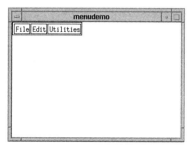

Figure 8.6.

The pull-down menu displayed when a mouse button is pressed on the File item.

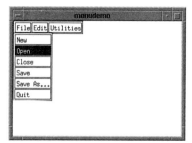

Listing 8.8. menudemo.c—A menubar with pull-down menus.

```
/*------------------------------------------------------------*/
/*  File: menudemo.c
 *
 *  Demonstrates a menubar with several pull-down menus.
 *  Uses the button window implemented in "xbutton.c" and
 *  the menu window from "xmenu.c" Also needs utility
 *  routine "AddNewEvent" which appears in Chapter 7.
 *
 */
/*------------------------------------------------------------*/
#include <stdio.h>
```

```c
#include <X11/Xlib.h>
#include <X11/Xutil.h>

#include "xwins.h"
#include "app_glob.c"

/* Menu styles */
#define MENUBAR_STYLE    0
#define PULLDOWN_STYLE   1

static int one=1, two=2, three=3, four=4;

static  int     menu_0 = 0, menu_1 = 1, menu_2 = 2;
static  int     PullDownOn = 0;
static  GC      invertGC;
static  Window  pulldown_id;

/* Function prototypes */

void initapp(/* int, char **, int, int, unsigned, unsigned */);
XWIN *MakeXButton(/* int x, int y,
        unsigned width, unsigned height, unsigned bdwidth,
        unsigned long bdcolor, unsigned long bgcolor,
        Window parent, char *text, int (*button_action)(),
        caddr_t action_data */);

XWIN *MakeXMenu(/* int x, int y, unsigned bdwidth,
        unsigned long bdcolor, unsigned long bgcolor,
        Window parent, int style,... */);

static void process_event(/* void */);
static void hilite_button(/* XWIN * */);
static int  disp_menu(/* caddr_t */);
static int  quit_app(/* caddr_t */);
static int  do_nothing(/* caddr_t */);


/* Windows in the application */
XWIN  *menubar, *PullDown[3];
/*-----------------------------------------------------------*/
main(argc, argv)
int argc;
char **argv;
{
    Window  parent;
    int     yp, xp1, xp2, xp3;

    xwin_init();

/* Create the main window */
    initapp(argc, argv, 10, 10, 300, 200);

/* Create the menubar */
    menubar = MakeXMenu(0, 0, 1, theFGpix, theBGpix,
                theMain, MENUBAR_STYLE,
```

continues

Listing 8.8. continued

```
/* List the menu entries one by one, end with a NULL */
            "File",      disp_menu, (caddr_t)&menu_0,
            "Edit",      disp_menu, (caddr_t)&menu_1,
            "Utilities", disp_menu, (caddr_t)&menu_2,
            NULL);

    yp = theFontStruct->max_bounds.ascent +
        theFontStruct->max_bounds.descent + 8;

    xp1 = XTextWidth(theFontStruct,
                    "File", strlen("File")) + 8;

    xp2 = xp1 + XTextWidth(theFontStruct,
                    "Edit", strlen("Edit")) + 8;

/* Create the pull-down menus */
    PullDown[0] = MakeXMenu(0, yp, 1, theFGpix, theBGpix,
                    theMain, PULLDOWN_STYLE,
                    "New",        do_nothing, (caddr_t)&one,
                    "Open",       do_nothing, (caddr_t)&two,
                    "Close",      do_nothing, (caddr_t)&three,
                    "Save",       do_nothing, (caddr_t)&four,
                    "Save As...", do_nothing, NULL,
                    "Quit",       quit_app,   NULL,
                    NULL);

    PullDown[1] = MakeXMenu(xp1, yp, 1, theFGpix, theBGpix,
                    theMain, PULLDOWN_STYLE,
                    "Undo",       do_nothing, (caddr_t)&one,
                    "Cut",        do_nothing, (caddr_t)&two,
                    "Copy",       do_nothing, (caddr_t)&three,
                    "Paste",      do_nothing, (caddr_t)&four,
                    NULL);

    PullDown[2] = MakeXMenu(xp2, yp, 1, theFGpix, theBGpix,
                    theMain, PULLDOWN_STYLE,
                    "Find",       do_nothing, (caddr_t)&one,
                    "Help",       do_nothing, (caddr_t)&two,
                    NULL);

/* Set up a GC to highlight the buttons */

    invertGC = XCreateGC(theDisplay, theMain, 0, 0);
    XCopyGC(theDisplay, theGC, GCForeground | GCBackground,
            invertGC);
    XSetFunction(theDisplay, invertGC, GXinvert);
    XSetPlaneMask(theDisplay, invertGC, theFGpix^theBGpix);

/* Add ButtonRelease to the event selection of the main
 * window so that we can detect when the user releases
 * the button without selecting any menu item.
 */
    AddNewEvent(theMain, ButtonReleaseMask);
```

```
/* Event handling loop—keep processing events until done */

    while (!AppDone)
        process_event();

/* Close connection to display and exit */

    XCloseDisplay(theDisplay);
    exit(0);
}
/*------------------------------------------------------------*/
/*  p r o c e s s _ e v e n t
 *
 *  Ask for an event and process it...
 */
static void process_event()
{
    XWIN        *which_xwin;

/* Get the next event from Xlib */
    XNextEvent(theDisplay, &theEvent);

/* Next, retrieve the XWIN data from Xlib using the
 * context manager routine XFindContext
 */
    if(XFindContext(theDisplay, theEvent.xany.window,
            xwin_context, (caddr_t *) &which_xwin) == 0)
    {
/* Call the event handler of this XWIN structure */
        if (*(which_xwin->event_handler) != NULL)
            (*(which_xwin->event_handler))(which_xwin);
    }

/* Handle EnterNotify and LeaveNotify events for the buttons */
    if(theEvent.type == EnterNotify ||
        theEvent.type == LeaveNotify)
                            hilite_button(which_xwin);

    if(PullDownOn && theEvent.type == ButtonRelease)
        PullDownOn = 0;
}
/*------------------------------------------------------------*/
static int disp_menu(data)
caddr_t data;
{
    XWIN    *which_xwin;
    int     menu_number;

/* Display the PullDown menu and process events until a
 * choice is made
 */
    menu_number = * ((int *) data);
    pulldown_id = PullDown[menu_number]->xid;
    XMapRaised(theDisplay, pulldown_id);
    PullDownOn = 1;
```

continues

Listing 8.8. continued

```
    while(PullDownOn)
        process_event();

/* Unmap the pull-down menu window */
    XUnmapWindow(theDisplay, pulldown_id);

    return 1;
}
/*------------------------------------------------------------*/
static int do_nothing(data)
caddr_t data;
{
    PullDownOn = 0;
printf("Menu selection: %d\n", *((int *)data));
    return 1;
}
/*------------------------------------------------------------*/
static int quit_app(data)
caddr_t data;
{
    PullDownOn = 0;
    AppDone = 1;         /* This will cause the program to exit */
    return 1;
}
/*------------------------------------------------------------*/
/*  h i l i t e _ b u t t o n
 *
 *  Highlight a button window by inverting it
 */
static void hilite_button(p_xwin)
XWIN *p_xwin;
{
    int i, go_on = 0;
/* Check if window's parent is one of the pull-down menus */
    for(i = 0; i < 3; i++)
    {
        if(p_xwin->parent == PullDown[i]->xid)
        {
            go_on = 1;
            break;
        }
    }
    if (!go_on) return;

/* Invert a rectangle large enough so that the button window
 * gets highlighted
 */
    XFillRectangle(theDisplay, p_xwin->xid, invertGC,
                    0, 0, 1024, 1024);
    XFlush(theDisplay);
}
```

Summary

In the X Window System, all user interactions occur through events. The user's actions at the keyboard or the mouse are reported by the X server through events. Each event identifies the window in which the event occurred and the type of event. In addition to events initiated by the user, the X server can report many other types of events. One of these is the Expose event, which plays an important role in maintaining the on-screen appearance of windows. In X, the application that owns a window is responsible for its contents. The X server does not keep track of what appears in a window. If requested, it sends an Expose event to the application when any of that application's windows has to be redrawn.

The event reporting mechanism is very flexible. Using the XSelectInput function, you can inform the X server to report only specific types of events occurring inside a window. You indicate the selected events by the bitwise-OR of event masks that are defined in the header file <X11/Xlib.h>. The events you select for a window depend on how that window is used in your application. For example, if a window is used to display a text string, you have to handle Expose events only. On the other hand, if that window is supposed to be a pushbutton (which means some task is performed when the user presses a mouse button with the pointer inside that window), you also have to select and process ButtonPress events for that window.

If you use a large number of windows in your application, you need a way to organize the event handling. You can use the context manager in Xlib to implement a smart event handling strategy. In this scheme, each window has a data structure including a member that is a pointer to the event handling routine for that window. As windows are created, the window's data structures are stored, and indexed by the window ID calling the context-management routine, XSaveContext. Later on, in the main event processing loop, this data structure can be retrieved using XFindContext, which takes the window ID as an argument. With this event handling scheme, you can build reusable components for creating complex user interfaces.

## Part Three

Drawing in
an X Window

Chapter 9

Drawing Graphics

After you create the windows and set up the event handling code, to complete your application, you need to arrange to display text and graphics in the windows. Although an X display is an array (or *raster*) of pixels, you do not always have to draw one pixel at a time. The Xlib library includes many drawing functions; those functions can be grouped into three broad categories:

✦ Functions to draw graphical objects such as lines, rectangles, and circles

✦ Functions to draw text

✦ Functions to display and manipulate images

This chapter describes the graphics drawing functions. Chapters 10, "Drawing Text," and 12, "Pixmaps, Bitmaps, and Images," cover the topics of text output and image manipulation, respectively. These chapters do not discuss color, except to point out how the current foreground and background colors affect the output. Chapter 11, "Using Color in X," explores the topic of how color is handled in X.

This chapter starts with a discussion of the *graphics context* (GC). Recall that a GC is a data structure (a resource) maintained in the server to store graphics attributes such as background and foreground colors, line style, and font. The appearance of graphics and text is controlled by these attributes. After describing GCs and the functions that manipulate GCs, this chapter presents the Xlib functions you can use to draw graphical objects, such as points, lines, rectangles, polygons, arcs, and circles. Advanced drawing techniques such as drawing rubber-band lines and changing fill styles and clipping are also covered. An example program illustrates how to use the graphics drawing functions in Xlib.

Graphics Contexts

From the moment you begin displaying output in a window, the graphics context (GC) becomes the focal point of your attention. A GC must be specified as an argument for each Xlib function that draws in a window. Through the GC, you specify attributes such as color, font, patterns, and line styles. As with other X resources, you have to create a GC, initialize it, and then use it. Before getting into those topics, consider the process of drawing in X and see where the GC fits into the scheme.

Purpose of a *GC*

The X server goes through a number of steps before altering the appropriate pixels in a window or a pixmap (a drawable) to generate a requested output, such as a line of a specified width and style (dashed, for instance). The GC is the repository of information needed to complete the drawing process.

> **NOTE:**
>
> In X, a *drawable* refers to a window or a pixmap. Both represent a raster of pixels, one on screen (window) and the other, off screen (pixmap). Conceptually, each drawable is a two-dimensional array of memory locations where each location can hold a number of bits of information representing a pixel value (see Figure 9.1). The number of bits in each pixel value gives the drawable its *depth*. You can also think of the two-dimensional drawable as being organized into a number of *bit planes*, in which each bit plane has a depth of one (see Figure 9.1).

Figure 9.1.

A drawable in X.

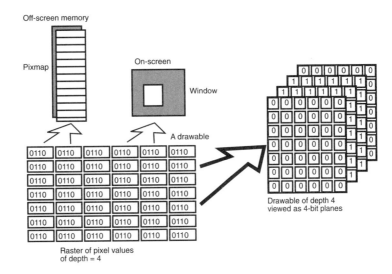

To create a drawing, follow these steps (see Figure 9.2):

1. Select pixels that should be altered to "paint" the graphical object.
2. Apply the pixel values to the selected pixels, using a pattern specified in the GC.
3. Use the *clip rectangles*, specified in the GC, as a stencil through which the drawing occurs.
4. Use another stencil defined by the visible region of the window where the output will appear.
5. Alter the values of these pixels according to the function and plane_mask attributes in the GC.

The two stenciling steps determine the final set of pixels that have to be changed. The GC controls each step of the rendering process shown in Figure 9.2.

Figure 9.2.

Steps involved in rendering graphics in X.

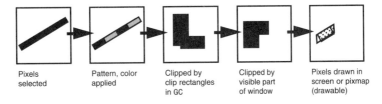

| Pixels selected | Pattern, color applied | Clipped by clip rectangles in GC | Clipped by visible part of window | Pixels drawn in screen or pixmap (drawable) |

NOTE:

The concept of GC was introduced in X11. In X10, drawing functions provided all graphics attributes (such as line width and foreground pixel) in each call. This was inefficient because the parameters had to be sent to the server for each drawing request, even if you never changed the attributes. X11 takes the more efficient approach of setting up a GC once and referring to it by a single resource ID in each drawing request.

Creating and Destroying *GCs*

You have to create at least one GC before your application can draw anything in its windows. You use the Xlib function XCreateGC to create a GC. This function takes four arguments in the following order:

1. A pointer to the Display
2. The ID of a drawable (a Window or a Pixmap variable)
3. An unsigned long bit mask
4. The address of an XGCValues structure

You specify various graphics attributes in the XGCValues structure and use the bit mask to indicate which members of the structure have valid values. The syntax of calling XCreateGC is as follows:

```
Display        *p_disp;
Drawable        win_or_pix;
unsigned long  mask;
XGCValues       xgcv;
GC              new_GC;
.
.
.

new_GC = XCreateGC(p_disp, win_or_pix, mask, &xgcv);
```

> **NOTE:**
>
> It is common practice in Xlib to use a structure with a bit mask to indicate the valid fields in that structure.

If you want to create a GC with the default settings (which is described soon), call XCreateGC with a 0 value for the bit mask and the pointer to the XGCValues structure:

```
Display        *p_disp;
Window          my_window;
GC              my_GC;

my_GC = XCreateGC(p_disp, my_window, 0, NULL);
```

Once a GC is created this way, you can alter specific attributes of that GC by using the Xlib function XChangeGC or by using convenience functions such as XSetForeground and XSetBackground.

One *GC* for Many Drawables

Although you specify the ID of a window or a pixmap (a drawable) when creating a GC, there is no requirement that the GC be used with that specific drawable. What matters is the number of bit planes in the drawable—its depth. Thus, you can use a single GC with any window or pixmap as long as they both have the same depth and are on the same screen.

It is common practice to create as many GCs as required by the distinct drawing styles (determined by sets of graphics attributes) used in an application. For example, if your application requires several different types of dashed lines, you can set up several GCs, one for each style, and use them as needed. An alternative approach is to create a single GC and change attributes as needed by calling XChangeGC. Because this involves making an X protocol request for each change, frequent changes may degrade the performance of your applications. Therefore, it is generally better to create and use multiple GCs.

GC Attribute Specification

Instead of accepting the default values, you can create a GC with some or all of its attributes set to values of your choice. You specify the values of a GC's attributes through an XGCValues structure, which is defined in <X11/Xlib.h> as follows:

```
typedef struct
{
    int             function;        /* Operation on pixels    */
    unsigned long   plane_mask;      /* Bit planes affected    */
    unsigned long   foreground;      /* Foreground pixel value */
    unsigned long   background;      /* Background pixel value */
    int             line_width;      /* Line width (0 or more) */
    int             line_style;      /* One of: LineSolid,
                                        LineOnOffDash,
                                        LineDoubleDash          */
    int             cap_style;       /* One of: CapNotLast,
                                        CapButt, CapRound,
                                        CapProjecting           */
    int             join_style;      /* One of: JoinMiter,
                                        JoinRound, JoinBevel    */
    int             fill_style;      /* One of: FillSolid,
                                        FillTiled, FillStippled,
                                        FillOpaqueStippled      */
    int             fill_rule;       /* One of: EvenOddRule,
                                        WindingRule             */
    int             arc_mode;        /* One of: ArcChord,
                                        ArcPieSlice             */
    Pixmap          tile;            /* Pixmap for tiling      */
    Pixmap          stipple;         /* Bitmap for stippling   */
    int             ts_x_origin;     /* x and y offset for tile*/
    int             ts_y_origin;     /* or stipple operations  */
    Font            font;            /* Default font           */
    int             subwindow_mode;  /* One of: ClipByChildren,
                                        IncludeInferiors        */
    Bool            graphics_exposures;/* True=generate exposures*/
    int             clip_x_origin;   /* Origin of clip_mask    */
    int             clip_y_origin;
    Pixmap          clip_mask;       /* Bitmap for clipping    */
    int             dash_offset;     /* Controls dashed line   */
    char            dashes;          /* Pattern of dashes      */
} XGCValues;
```

The members of the XGCValues structure include all graphics attributes necessary to control the appearance of text and graphics output in X. Table 9.1 shows the default values of the members of the XGCValues structure. The table also lists the value of the bit mask that identifies each member of the XGCValues structure.

Table 9.1. Default Values and Selection Masks for Members of the XGCValues Structure

Member Name	Purpose	Bit Mask Value to Select Member	Default Value
function	Operation on pixels	GCFunction	GXcopy
plane_mask	Bit planes affected	GCPlaneMask	All Planes
foreground	Foreground pixel	GCForeground	0
background	Background pixel	GCBackground	1
line_width	Line width	GCLineWidth	0
line_style	Line style	GCLineStyle	LineSolid
cap_style	Line endings	GCCapStyle	CapButt
join_style	Line joinings	GCJoinStyle	JoinMiter
fill_style	Filling style	GCFillStyle	FillSolid
fill_rule	Pixels to be filled	GCFillRule	EvenOddRule
arc_mode	Arcs to be filled as pie slices or closed with a chord	GCArcMode	ArcPieSlice
tile	Pixmap for tiling	GCTile	Pixmap filled with foreground pixel
stipple	Bitmap for stippling	GCStipple	Bitmap of all 1s
ts_x_	x-offset for tiling or stippling	GCTileStipXOrigin	0
ts_y_origin	y-offset for tiling or stippling	GCTileStipYOrigin	0
font	Default font for text output	GCFont	Server-dependent
subwindow_mode	Whether to draw into children	GCSubwindowMode	ClipByChildren
graphics_exposures	Exposure events generated if True	GCGraphicsExposures	True
clip_x_origin	x-origin of clip_mask	GCClipXOrigin	0
clip_y_origin	y-origin of clip_mask	GCClipYOrigin	0
clip_mask	Bitmap for clipping	GCClipMask	None
dash_offset	Starting point in dash pattern	GCDashOffset	0
dashes	Pattern of dashes	GCDashList	{4,4}

Here is how you can use this information. Suppose you want a GC with all default attributes except the foreground and background pixel values. To set up the GC, this is what you do:

1. Define an XGCValues structure.

2. In that structure, set the foreground and background members to desired values.

3. Set the unsigned long bit mask variable to the bitwise-OR of GCForeground and GCBackground, the constants from Table 9.1 that identify these particular members of the XGCValues structure.

4. Create the GC by calling XCreateGC:

```
Display        *p_disp;
Window         window_1;
unsigned long  gc_mask;
XGCValues      xgcv;
GC             new_GC;

/* Set values of selected members of xgcv, as needed.
 * Then set gc_mask. This example sets the foreground and the
 * background pixels to the default white and black colors
 * for the screen.
 */
xgcv.foreground = WhitePixel(p_disp, DefaultScreen(p_disp));
xgcv.background = BlackPixel(p_disp, DefaultScreen(p_disp));
gc_mask = GCForeground | GCBackground;

new_GC = XCreateGC(p_disp, window_1, gc_mask, &xgcv);
```

GC Destruction

Because a GC is a resource, it consumes memory in the X server. Therefore, you should free a GC when it is no longer needed. You can do so with the XFreeGC function:

```
Display *p_disp;
GC      my_GC;

XFreeGC(p_disp, my_GC);
```

All your application's resources (including GCs) are automatically freed when the application exits, so you need to destroy a GC explicitly when you have created one for a temporary purpose.

GC Manipulation

After you create a GC, you can modify the attributes by calling the XChangeGC function:

```
Display        *p_disp;
GC             old_GC;
unsigned long  gc_mask;
XGCValues      xgcv;
```

```
/* Set values in xgcv and set up gc_mask */
...
XChangeGC(p_disp, old_GC, gc_mask, &xgcv);
```

The bit mask gc_mask and the XGCValues structure xgcv are used in the same way as they are in the XCreateGC function: you set the values of selected members of the XGCValues structure and indicate these members through the mask.

XChangeGC is not the only way to alter graphics attributes in a GC. Xlib includes a number of convenience functions to help set specific attributes. Table 9.2 summarizes these functions. You will see these functions used and mentioned again in the rest of the chapter.

Table 9.2. Convenience Functions for Setting Attributes in a GC

Function Name	XGCValues Member Set by Function	Summary Description
XSetArcMode	arc_mode	Determines whether filled arcs are drawn as pie slices or a chord closes the arc
XSetBackground	background	Sets background pixel value
XSetClipmask	clip_mask	Specifies bitmap against which drawings are clipped
XSetClipOrigin	clip_x_origin clip_y_origin	Controls position of the clip mask in the GC
XSetClipRectangles	clip_mask clip_x_origin clip_y_origin	Sets clip_mask to be a collection of rectangles and alters origin
XSetDashes	dash_offset dashes	Specifies dashed line style
XSetFillRule	fill_rule	Specifies rule used to determine pixels to be filled
XSetFillStyle	fill_style	Determines how areas are filled
XSetFont	font	Sets font for text output
XSetForeground	foreground	Sets foreground pixel value
XSetFunction	function	Specifies how old and new pixel values are combined
XSetGraphicsExposures	graphics_exposures	Determines whether GraphicsExpose and NoExpose events are generated
XSetLineAttributes	line_width, line_style cap_style, join_style	Determines appearance of lines

Function Name	*XGCValues Member Set by Function*	*Summary Description*
XSetPlaneMask	plane_mask	Specifies which bit planes are affected by a drawing request
XSetRegion	clip_mask	Sets `clip_mask` to a region
XSetState	background, foreground, function, plane_mask	Sets four attributes in a single call
XSetStipple	stipple	Specifies bitmap that determines the pattern of foreground and background pixels
XSetSubwindowMode	subwindow_mode	Determines whether graphics are clipped by the subwindows
XSetTile	tile	Sets pixmap used for tiling
XSetTSOrigin	ts_x_origin ts_y_origin	Sets origin of a stipple or tile relative to drawable

In addition to changing attributes in a GC, you also can copy selected attributes from one GC to another (both GCs must already exist). Use the XCopyGC function to do this. For example, to copy the foreground and background colors from oldGC to newGC, you write this:

```
XCopyGC(p_disp, oldGC, GCForeground ¦ GCBackground, newGC);
```

As with XCreateGC and XChangeGC, the attributes that XCopyGC copies from oldGC to newGC are identified by a mask.

Now that you have seen the functions used to manipulate GCs, it's time to take a look at the specific graphics attributes affected by these functions.

Display Functions

Because the pixels in a drawable's raster (window or pixmap) already have existing values, the server has to be told how to change the value—should it overwrite the old value with the new one or combine the old and new values in some way? You indicate this through the function member of the XGCValues structure. Sometimes this attribute is known as *raster operation* or *display function* because it indicates the bitwise logical operations between old and new pixel values in a drawable's raster and, consequently, determines the final appearance of the graphics output.

X supports sixteen distinct raster operations. Table 9.3 lists those operations and shows the symbolic name for each operation in Xlib (defined in <X11/Xlib.h>).

Table 9.3. Display Functions in X

Symbolic Name of Function	Final Pixel Value (old = existing pixel, new = new pixel)
GXClear	0
GXand	new AND old
GXandReverse	new AND (NOT old)
GXcopy	new
GXandInverted	(NOT new) AND old
GXnoop	old
GXxor	new XOR old
GXor	new OR old
GXnor	NOT (new OR old)
GXequiv	(NOT new) XOR old
GXinvert	NOT old
GXorReverse	new OR (NOT old)
GXcopyInverted	NOT new
GXorInverted	(NOT new) OR old
GXnand	NOT (new AND old)
GXset	1

The default value of function is GXcopy, which means that the new pixel values overwrite the old ones. Another important display function is GXxor which performs an exclusive-OR (XOR) of the old pixel value with the new. This function is useful in erasing drawings because of the following property of the XOR operation:

```
(x XOR y)  XOR  y  ==  x
```

which says that if you exclusive-OR a pixel value x with y you can get back x by repeating the exclusive-OR with y. Thus, if you use the GXxor function, you can erase a figure by simply redrawing over the old one. You can use this property of GXxor to animate drawings in X by erasing at the old location and drawing at the new one. A common use of the GXxor display function is in rubber-banding, where a figure such as a line or a rectangle is stretched and shrunk as the user moves the mouse. (You will see an example of rubber-banding later in this chapter.)

The GXinvert function is useful for highlighting an area in a black and white drawing by changing white pixels to black and vice versa.

You can set the function attribute of a GC by calling XSetFunction. For example, to set the display function in a GC to GXxor, write the following:

```
XSetFunction(p_disp, this_GC, GXxor);
```

Plane Mask

After the logical operation specified by the `function` attribute has been performed, another step is still required before any pixels in the raster are altered. The `plane_mask` attribute in the `GC` specifies which bit planes in the raster are altered by a graphics operation. The plane mask has a 1 in each bit position that may be modified. If a bit in `plane_mask` is 0, the corresponding bit in the raster's existing pixel values is not changed. For example, in a display with four bit planes, the least-significant four bits in the `plane_mask` attribute control how the planes are altered. If you want only bits 1 and 3 (0 being the least significant bit) of each pixel value affected by a graphics operation, you can set the `plane_mask` attribute to the binary pattern 1010 (0x0a in C's notation for hexadecimal numbers). You can set this in a `GC` by calling `XSetPlaneMask`:

```
XSetPlaneMask(p_disp, this_GC, 0x0a);
```

After this is done, if a pixel value of 0110 is to be copied to the raster, only bit 1 of each affected pixel will be set to 1.

If you want a graphics operation to affect all bit planes, you can set `plane_mask` to the constant `AllPlanes`, which is a macro that refers to all the bit planes. The default value of the plane mask is `AllPlanes`.

Foreground and Background Pixels

The `foreground` and `background` graphics attributes specify the foreground and background colors used for graphics operations. You can use the functions `XSetForeground` and `XSetBackground` to set these attributes. Each attribute is a pixel value, so the colormap associated with the window determines the actual colors displayed. The default values for `foreground` and `background` depend on the X server. If you want black and white drawings, you can use the macros `BlackPixel` and `WhitePixel` (they take the display and screen as arguments) as pixel values that map to black and white colors on the screen.

> **NOTE:**
>
> The background pixel specified in a `GC` is used differently from the background attribute of a window.

Line Attributes

There are four attributes in a `GC` that determine the appearance of lines:

- `line_width`
- `line_style`
- `cap_style`
- `join_style`

The `line_width` attribute specifies the width of lines in pixels, the default being **0**. If the width is **0**, the X protocol enables the server to draw lines that are one pixel wide using an implementation-dependent algorithm. There is no guarantee that lines drawn with `line_width` set to **0** will appear the same on all displays but such lines are drawn quickly. You can assure uniformity by explicitly setting `line_width` to **1**.

The `line_style` attribute controls whether lines are solid or dashed. You can have one of three values for this attribute (see Figure 9.3):

✦ `LineSolid`, the default value, specifies that a solid line be drawn in the foreground color.

✦ `LineOnOffDash` indicates that lines are drawn using the current dashed style (set by `XSetDashes`) with odd-numbered segments drawn in foreground color and even-numbered segments skipped.

✦ `LineDoubleDash` also draws dashed lines, but with odd-numbered segments in foreground color and even-numbered ones in background color.

Figure 9.3.

Line styles defined by the `line_style` *attribute.*

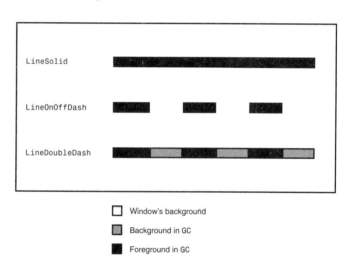

The `cap_style` attribute determines how the server draws the endpoints of a line. As illustrated in Figure 9.4, there are four types of endcaps, each identified by one of the following constants:

✦ `CapNotLast`. For a line width of **0** or **1**, the endpoints are not drawn. For wider lines, the line ends squarely at the endpoints.

✦ `CapButt`. The line ends squarely at the endpoint. This is the default setting.

✦ `CapRound`. The endcap is a circle with its diameter equal to the width.

✦ `CapProjecting`. The line ends squarely, but projects half a `line_width` beyond the endpoint.

For line widths of `0` or 1, the `CapRound` and `CapProjecting` styles are equivalent to `CapButt`.

Figure 9.4.
Endcap styles defined by the
cap_style attribute.

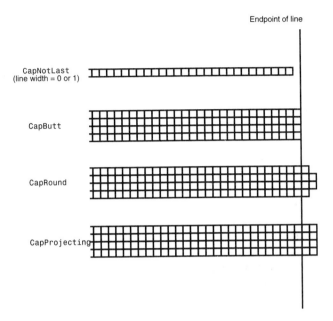

The `join_style` member in the `XGCValues` structure specifies how two wide lines (`line_width` greater than one) should be joined. The three possible styles are illustrated in Figure 9.5. The default join style is `JoinMiter`.

Figure 9.5.
Join styles defined by the
join_style attribute.

You can set all four line attributes with the convenience function `XSetLine Attributes`. The following is a sample call:

```
Display *p_disp;
GC       thisGC;
unsigned line_width = 4;
int      line_style = LineOnOffDash;
int      cap_style = CapRound;
int      join_style = JoinRound;

XSetLineAttributes(p_disp, thisGC, line_width, line_style,
                   cap_style, join_style);
```

Dashed Lines

In addition to the four attributes that control the appearance of lines, the pattern of dashes is another attribute that affects the appearance when the line style is LineOnOffDash or LineDoubleDash.

Unlike most other attributes, you cannot specify the pattern of dashes through the XGCValues structure. You have to use the XSetDashes function to do this. XSetDashes expects the following arguments:

```
Display  *p_disp;
GC        thisGC;
int       offset;      /* Where to start in dash pattern */
char      dash_list[]; /* Count of pixels on and off     */
int       num_dashes;  /* Number of elements in dash_list */

XSetDashes(p_disp, thisGC, offset, dash_list, num_dashes);
```

You specify the pattern of dashes through the values in the dash_list array. Each element of the array is interpreted as the length of a line segment. The server draws the even segments—dash_list[0], dash_list[2], and so on—using the foreground pixel value. The odd segments are drawn in the background color for lines of style LineDoubleDash, and are not drawn at all if the style is LineOnOffDash. Because dash_list is an array of char variables, each segment of the pattern can be a maximum of 255 pixels long.

The server repeats the dash pattern along the length of the line. You can use the offset argument to control further how the dash pattern is applied to a line. At the beginning of a new line, the server skips the first offset pixels before starting to apply the pattern. Figure 9.6 illustrates how dash patterns are set and used in lines.

Figure 9.6.

Examples of setting dash patterns in GCs.

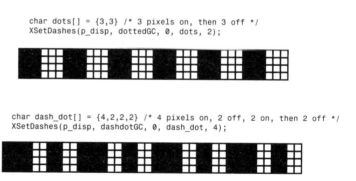

```
char dots[] = {3,3} /* 3 pixels on, then 3 off */
XSetDashes(p_disp, dottedGC, 0, dots, 2);
```

```
char dash_dot[] = {4,2,2,2} /* 4 pixels on, 2 off, 2 on, then 2 off */
XSetDashes(p_disp, dashdotGC, 0, dash_dot, 4);
```

Fill Rules

Often you want to fill a figure—a rectangle or circle, for instance—with a color or a pattern. Several attributes control how a figure is filled. When filling an arbitrary shape, the X server has to determine which points lie inside the figure. It does so using the rule specified by the fill_rule graphics attribute. The fill rule can be one of `EvenOddRule` or `WindingRule`. To apply `EvenOddRule` at a point, you have to imagine a line drawn from that point to a far point outside the figure. A point is inside if this line crosses the edges of the figure an odd number of times (see Figure 9.7). This is the default fill rule.

Figure 9.7.
Fill rules in X.

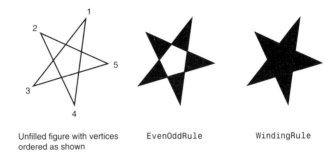

| Unfilled figure with vertices ordered as shown | EvenOddRule | WindingRule |

To apply `WindingRule`, you also need to know the order of the vertices in the figure. Once you know this, follow these steps:

1. Draw an imaginary line from the test point to each vertex, starting with the first one and continuing until you return to the first one again. As you do this, that line will rotate.

2. Count the number of complete clockwise and counterclockwise rotations. A point is inside if the difference between these two counts is nonzero. Figure 9.7 illustrates the effect of this fill rule.

You can set the fill rule using the function `XSetFillRule`. For example, you can set the fill rule to `WindingRule` with the following call:

```
Display  *p_disp;
GC       thisGC;

XSetFillRule(p_disp, thisGC, WindingRule);
```

Stipples, Tiles, and Fill Styles

The appearance of a filled area depends on the `fill_style`. The default fill style, `FillSolid`, specifies that the pixels inside the figure are to be filled with the current foreground color.

The other fill styles, `FillStippled`, `FillOpaqueStippled`, and `FillTiled` use a stipple or a tile for the fill operation. In the X Window System, the term *stipple* refers to a pixmap of depth one—a bitmap that serves as a mask through which foreground and background colors are applied during the fill operation. The stipple pixmap is of fixed size, usually 8x8 or 16x16. To cover arbitrary areas, the stipple pattern is repeated in *x* and *y* directions. If a stipple is being used, the `fill_style` attribute is either `FillStippled` or `FillOpaqueStippled`. Figure 9.8 shows the effect of these two fill styles. In the `FillStippled` style, the server fills, with the foreground color, the pixels corresponding to locations where the stipple pattern has a 1. For the `FillOpaqueStippled` style, the foreground color is applied to the pixels where the stipple pattern has a 1, and the background to those where the stipple has a 0.

Figure 9.8.

Filling with stipples.

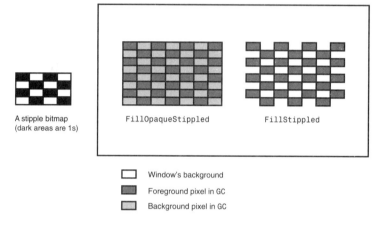

A stipple bitmap
(dark areas are 1s)

FillOpaqueStippled   FillStippled

☐ Window's background
■ Foreground pixel in GC
▨ Background pixel in GC

A *tile* is a pixmap—a two-dimensional array of pixel values with the same depth (number of bits per pixel) as the drawable for which the graphics context was created. A stipple pixmap has a unity depth and serves as a mask through which colors are applied, but a tile pixmap has the same depth as the drawable and is applied directly to the area being filled (see Figure 9.9). A tile pixmap also has a fixed size, usually 8x8 or 16x16. Larger areas are filled by replicating the tile along the x and y coordinate axes. To use a tile as a fill pattern, you have to set the `fill_style` to `FillTiled`.

Figure 9.9.

Filling with tiles.

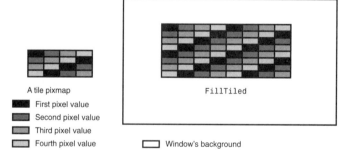

A tile pixmap
■ First pixel value
▨ Second pixel value
▨ Third pixel value
☐ Fourth pixel value

FillTiled

☐ Window's background

You can use the `XSetFillStyle` function to set the fill style. For example, to use the `FillStippled` style in a `GC`, the call would be as follows:

```
XSetFillStyle(p_disp, thisGC, FillStippled);
```

Use the functions `XSetStipple` and `XSetTile` to set the `stipple` and `tile` attributes of a `GC`. Before using either of these functions, you have to prepare a pixmap to be used as the stipple or tile. Chapter 12 shows how to define bitmaps and pixmaps.

When the pixmap is ready, it is easy to set the stipple by calling the function `XSetStipple`:

```
Pixmap stipple_pattern;

/* Prepare pixmap to be used as stipple (see Chapter 12) */
...
XSetStipple(p_disp, thisGC, stipple_pattern);
```

Similarly, you specify a tile pixmap by calling `XSetTile`.

Clip Masks

By default, the server clips all graphics output against the boundaries of the drawable (window or pixmap). Also, the graphics operations do not affect any subwindows. Most of the time, this default behavior suffices. However, the `GC` has provisions to alter the default behavior. For example, if you want to draw into subwindows, you can do so by altering the `subwindow_mode` attribute from the default `ClipByChildren` to `IncludeInferiors`. Call `XSetSubwindowMode` as follows:

```
XSetSubwindowMode(p_disp, thisGC, IncludeInferiors);
```

You also can clip the graphics output against a bitmap you specify in the `clip_mask` attribute. The default setting for this attribute is `None`, but you can define a pixmap of depth one and set `clip_mask` to this pixmap by calling `XSetClipMask`:

```
Display *p_disp;
GC      thisGC;
Pixmap  clip_stencil;

/* Set up 'clip_stencil' pixmap (see Chapter 12) */
...
XSetClipMask(p_disp, thisGC, clip_stencil);
```

Unlike stipples and tiles, the `clip_mask` pixmap is not a repetitive pattern. You have to define a pixmap of the size you want. The X server will restrict graphics output only to those pixels where the clip mask has a value of 1. The server also refrains from drawing outside the boundaries of the clip mask. Thus, the clip mask acts as a stencil that the server applies to the final drawing.

As you might expect, the server has to do extra work—and the graphics output appears slower than usual—if you specify a `clip_mask` other than `None`. Therefore, you should use this feature sparingly.

Collection of Rectangles as Clip Mask

Apart from an arbitrary pixmap, you also can set the `clip_mask` to a collection of nonintersecting rectangles. For example, suppose you want to confine all output to two rectangles in a window. You can do this with the `XSetClipRectangles` function:

```
Display    *p_disp;
GC         thisGC;
XRectangles rect[2];
int        xoffset = 0,
           yoffset = 0,
           numrect = 2,
           ordering;
/* Prepare the clip rectangles */
rect[0].x = 100;
rect[0].y = 10;
rect[0].width = 200;
rect[0].height = 100;

rect[1].x = 10;
rect[1].y = 150;
rect[1].width = 500;
rect[1].height = 100;

/* Set up the clip mask */
ordering = YXSorted;
XSetClipRectangles(p_disp, thisGC, xoffset, yoffset,
                   rect, numrect, ordering);
```

This is a contrived example, but it shows several important items. The rectangles are specified in an array of XRectangle structures. The XRectangle structure is defined in <X11/Xlib.h> as the following:

```
typedef struct
{
    short          x, y;
    unsigned short width, height;
} XRectangle;
```

The xoffset and yoffset in the call to XSetClipRectangles can be used to position the clipping rectangles with respect to the origin of the drawable. The ordering argument is there to help the server perform the clipping efficiently. Depending on what you know about the clipping rectangles, you can specify one of the following four values:

✦ Unsorted is for use when you do not know the order.

✦ YSorted specifies that the rectangles are sorted by the y-origin in ascending order.

✦ YXSorted implies the YSorted ordering and also that rectangles of equal y-origins have nondecreasing x-origins.

✦ YXBanded implies YXSorted and that all rectangles intersected by a horizontal line have identical y-origins and heights.

If you call XSetClipRectangles with None as the list of rectangles, the X server will not generate any graphics output at all.

Regions as Clip Mask

Another way to specify a clip mask is to use a *region*, which is an arbitrary collection of pixels. (Contrast this with a pixmap which is a rectangular array of pixels.) Xlib provides a number of utility routines to create and manipulate regions. Internally, a region is maintained as a number of nonintersecting rectangles. When referring to regions, use a `Region` data type defined in the header file `<X11/Xutil.h>` as a pointer to an internal data structure. You can treat `Region` the same way you do the `FILE` data type used in the standard I/O routines in C. You do not need to know the details of the data structure—merely use the type where required.

You create regions in two ways. The first approach is to start with an empty `Region`, created by calling `XCreateRegion`:

```
Region new_region;

new_region = XCreateRegion();
```

Then you add rectangles to the region by using the `XUnionRectWithRegion` function:

```
/* A 100x50 pixel rectangle at (10,10) */
XRectangle rect = { 10, 10, 100, 50 };

/* Add the rectangle to the region "new_region" */
XUnionRectWithRegion(&rect, new_region, new_region);
```

The other approach is to create a region from the points that lie inside a polygon. Use the `XPolygonRegion` function to do this:

```
Region new_region;

XPoint points[3] =    /* Vertices of a polygon */
{
    { 100, 100 },
    { 50,   150 },
    { 150, 150 }
};
int numpoints = sizeof(points) / sizeof(XPoint);

new_region = XPolygonRegion(points, numpoints, WindingRule);
```

An array of `XPoint` structures defines the vertices of the polygon (a triangle, in this example). The last argument to `XPolygonRegion` is the fill rule used to determine which points belong to the region. You can use `EvenOddRule` or `WindingRule` as the fill rule.

After a region is created by `XPolygonRegion`, you can add rectangles to it with `XUnionRectWithRegion` as you would to any other region.

After a region has been defined, you can use it as the clip mask in a `GC` by calling the `XSetRegion` function:

```
XSetRegion(p_disp, thisGC, new_region);
```

After setting a region as the clip mask, you can destroy the region by calling `XDestroyRegion`.

Basic Drawing Functions

You have learned how a `GC` embodies all attributes that affect graphics output in X. You also have gotten an overview of what the various attributes are and how you can use Xlib functions to manipulate them. The next logical step is to learn how to draw simple graphical shapes and see how the `GC`s affect the appearance of these graphics.

Xlib includes functions to draw points, rectangles, arcs, and polygons. By varying the arguments to the arc drawing function, you can draw ellipses and circles. There are separate functions for drawing filled rectangles, polygons, and arcs. The first three arguments to all drawing functions are the same:

+ Pointer to the `Display`
+ The ID of a `Drawable`
+ A `GC` that controls the appearance of the figure being drawn

Xlib provides separate functions for drawing several figures at once. For example, `XDrawPoint` draws one point, but `XDrawPoints` draws an entire array of points. The reason for the special plural versions of the functions is efficiency. Because X applications draw by sending protocol requests to the X server, it is more efficient to send a single request for drawing several figures (of the same type) rather than sending a separate drawing request for each figure.

Drawing Points

The simplest of graphics operations in X is to draw a point in a window or pixmap. You can draw a single point at the coordinates (x,y) with the following call:

```
Display *p_disp; /* The connection to the X server   */
Window  window_1; /* The drawable--a window          */
GC      thisGC;  /* Graphics context for the drawing */
int     x, y;    /* Point to be drawn                */

XDrawPoint(p_disp, window_1, thisGC, x, y);
```

The pixel at the location is set to the foreground color specified in the `GC`. Other attributes in the `GC` also control the final appearance of the point. For example, the point is not drawn if it lies outside the clip mask.

Drawing Multiple Points

If you want to draw a large number of points, all using the same `GC`, you can use the `XDrawPoints` function to draw them all at once with a single X protocol request. You store the points in an array of `XPoint` structures. The `XPoint` structure is defined in `<X11/Xlib.h>` as the following:

```
typedef struct
{
    short x, y;   /* x and y coordinates of the point */
} XPoint;
```

You call `XDrawPoints` in the usual manner with a display, a drawable, and a `GC` as the first three arguments:

```
XPoint  pt[10];
int     numpt = 10;
...
XDrawPoints(p_disp, window_1, thisGC, pt, numpt,
            CoordModeOrigin);
```

The three standard arguments are followed by the array of points and number of points. The last argument tells the server how to interpret the coordinates of the points in the array. You can specify one of the following constants:

✦ `CoordModeOrigin` means the coordinates are relative to the origin of the window or the pixmap.

✦ `CoordModePrevious` is used when the coordinate of each point is given in terms of the x and y displacements from the previous point. The first point is assumed to be relative to the origin of the window.

Drawing with Points: An Example

Consider a simple example that uses `XDrawPoints` to display an interesting pattern of points. Listing 9.1, `xpoints`, follows a seemingly random process that results in the pattern shown in Figure 9.10.

Figure 9.10.
An interesting pattern with points.

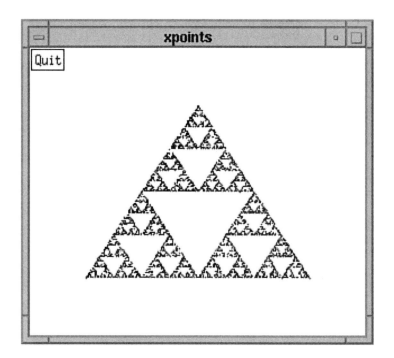

Listing 9.1. `xpoints.c`—Drawing an interesting pattern of points.

```
/*----------------------------------------------------------*/
/*  File: xpoints.c
 *
 *  Draw an interesting pattern using a seemingly random
 *  process (illustrates use of XDrawPoint and XDrawPoints)
```

continues

Listing 9.1. continued

```
 *
 */
/*-----------------------------------------------------------*/
#include <stdio.h>          /* For definition of NULL       */
#include <stdlib.h>         /* For srand, and rand          */

#include <X11/Xlib.h>
#include <X11/Xutil.h>

#include "xwins.h"
#include "app_glob.c"

#ifndef RAND_MAX
/* Assume 2**31 -1 */
#define RAND_MAX 0x7fffffff
#endif

#define MAXPTS     5000

/* Array of points */
XPoint pt[MAXPTS];
int    cpt;

/* Starting points used to generate the rest */
XPoint pseed[3] = { { 50, 200 }, { 150, 50 }, { 250, 200 } };
XPoint pnow = { 200, 200 };

char *quit_label = "Quit";

/* Function prototypes */

void initapp(/* int, char **, int, int, unsigned, unsigned */);
int  quit_action(/* caddr_t */);
void compute_points();
/*-----------------------------------------------------------*/
main(argc, argv)
int  argc;
char **argv;
{
    XWIN    *QuitButton, *which_xwin;
    unsigned quit_width, quit_height;

    xwin_init();

    initapp(argc, argv, 20, 20, 300, 250);

/* Create the "Quit" button */
    quit_width = XTextWidth(theFontStruct, quit_label,
                         strlen(quit_label)) + 4;
    quit_height = theFontStruct->max_bounds.ascent +
              theFontStruct->max_bounds.descent + 4;

    QuitButton = MakeXButton(1, 1, quit_width, quit_height,
                          1, theFGpix, theBGpix, theMain,
                          quit_label, quit_action, NULL);
```

```
/* Compute the points to plot */
    compute_points();

/* Event handling loop */

    while (!AppDone)
    {
        XNextEvent(theDisplay, &theEvent);

/* Main window is handled here */
        if(theEvent.xany.window == theMain)
        {
            if(theEvent.type == Expose &&
               theEvent.xexpose.count == 0)
            {
/* Clear the window and draw the points in the "pt" array */
                XClearWindow(theDisplay, theMain);
                XDrawPoints(theDisplay, theMain,
                        theGC, pseed, 3, CoordModeOrigin);
                XDrawPoints(theDisplay, theMain,
                        theGC, pt, cpt, CoordModeOrigin);
            }
        }

/* For all other windows, retrieve the XWIN data from
 * Xlib using the context manager routine XFindContext
 */
        if(XFindContext(theDisplay, theEvent.xany.window,
            xwin_context, (caddr_t *) &which_xwin) == 0)
        {
/* Call the event handler of this XWIN structure */
            if(*(which_xwin->event_handler) != NULL)
              (*(which_xwin->event_handler))(which_xwin);
        }
    }

/* Close connection to display and exit */

    XCloseDisplay(theDisplay);
    exit(0);
}
/*------------------------------------------------------------*/
/*  q u i t _ a c t i o n
 *
 *  This routine is called when a ButtonPress event occurs in
 *  the quit window.
 */
int quit_action(data)
caddr_t data;
{
/* Set the done flag */
    AppDone = 1;
    return 1;
}
/*------------------------------------------------------------*/
/*  c o m p u t e _ p o i n t s
```

continues

Listing 9.1. continued

```
 *
 *  This routine computes the points to be drawn
 */
void compute_points()
{
    int     i;
    unsigned long num, num1 = RAND_MAX / 3, num2 = 2*num1;

/* Set seed for random number generator */
    srand((unsigned)time(NULL));

    for(cpt = 0; cpt <  MAXPTS; cpt++)
    {
/* Pick a random index between 0 and 2 */
        num = rand();
        if(num < num1) i = 0;
        else
            if(num < num2) i = 1;
            else i = 2;

/* Pick a point halfway between the seed point with that
 * index and the current point (pnow)
 */
        pt[cpt].x = (pseed[i].x + pnow.x) / 2;
        pt[cpt].y = (pseed[i].y + pnow.y) / 2;
/* Make this the current point */
        pnow.x = pt[cpt].x;
        pnow.y = pt[cpt].y;
    }
}
```

The steps for generating the points are the following:

1. Pick three "seed" points and store them in an array (the pseed array in Listing 9.1).
2. Pick a point and call it the current point (the pnow point in Listing 9.1).
3. Pick a random number between 0 and 2.
4. Compute the coordinates of the point halfway between the current point and the point pseed[*n*] where *n* is the random number generated in step 3.
5. Call this new point the current point (this is the point to be drawn).
6. If you have as many points as you need, stop. Otherwise, go to step 3.

The compute_points function in Listing 9.1 performs these steps and generates the array named pt consisting of 5,000 XPoint structures. The drawing is done in the event handling loop by calling XDrawPoints.

Adapt (change the compiler options and libraries, if necessary) the following makefile to your system and use it to build the xpoints program on your system:

```
# Makefile for "xpoints" shown in Listing 9.1
#
# Some common definitions...

RM = rm -f
CC = cc

# Compiler flags, paths for include files and libraries

CFLAGS =
INCLUDES = -I. -I/usr/include -I/usr/include/X11
LIBS = -lX11

# Rule to create .o files from .c files
.c.o:
        $(RM) $@
        $(CC) -c $(CFLAGS) $(INCLUDES) $*.c

# Targets...

all::    xpoints

xpoints.o: xpoints.c  app_glob.c xwins.h

initapp.o: initapp.c app_glob.c

xwinutil.o: xwinutil.c app_glob.c xwins.h

xbutton.o: xbutton.c app_glob.c xwins.h

xpoints: xpoints.o initapp.o xwinutil.o xbutton.o
        $(RM) $@
        $(CC) -o $@ $(CFLAGS) xpoints.o initapp.o \
            xwinutil.o xbutton.o \
            $(LIBS)
```

In addition to `xpoints.c` (Listing 9.1), you need the following files from Chapters 7, "Creating and Managing Windows," and 8, "Handling Events," to build the `xpoints` program:

- ◆ `app_glob.c` (Chapter 7, Listing 7.1)
- ◆ `initapp.c` (Chapter 7, Listing 7.2)
- ◆ `xwins.h` (Chapter 8, Listing 8.1)
- ◆ `xwinutil.c` (Chapter 8, Listing 8.2)
- ◆ `xbutton.c` (Chapter 8, Listing 8.3)

Drawing Lines

There are three line-drawing functions:

- ◆ XDrawLine
- ◆ XDrawSegments
- ◆ XDrawLines

This function:

```
XDrawLine(p_disp, window, thisGC, x1, y1, x2, y2);
```

draws a line between the points (x1, y1) and (x2, y2) in the drawable, window, using the line attributes specified in the GC, thisGC.

XDrawSegments draws several possibly disjointed line segments using the same graphics attributes. The segments are specified using the XSegment structure, which is defined in <X11/Xlib.h> as the following:

```
typedef struct
{
    short x1, y1;   /* Coordinates of start-point of segment */
    short x2, y2;   /* Coordinates of end-point of segment   */
} XSegment;
```

An array of segments is passed as an argument to XDrawSegments:

```
Display    *p_disp;
Window     window_1;
GC         thisGC;
XSegment   lines[] =
{
    {100, 100, 200, 200},
    {10,   20,  35,  60},
    {300,  10, 300, 100}
};
int numsegs = sizeof(lines) / sizeof(XSegment);
.
.
.
XDrawSegments(p_disp, window_1, thisGC, lines, numsegs);
```

The XDrawLines function is similar to XDrawPoints with one difference: XDrawPoints draws points, and XDrawLines connects them with a line. You call XDrawLines with the same arguments as you do XDrawPoints.

When you draw a line using XDrawLine or XDrawSegments, the server also draws endcaps for each line segment. For XDrawLines, the endcaps appear only at the very beginning and at the very end.

Drawing and Filling Rectangles

Xlib includes several functions to draw rectangles. The XDrawRectangle function is for drawing a rectangle given the coordinates of its upper-left corner and its width and height. The following is the function call:

```
XDrawRectangle(p_disp, window, thisGC, x, y, width, height);
```

To draw the outline around the rectangle, this function draws the following lines:

```
(x, y)               to (x+width, y)
(x+width, y)         to (x+width, y+height)
(x+width, y+height)  to (x, y+height)
(x, y+height)        to (x,y)
```

You can draw several rectangles using the same GC by calling XDrawRectangles, which expects an array of rectangles and their number as arguments:

```
XRectangle rect[];  /* Array of rectangles  */
int        nrect;   /* Number of rectangles */

XDrawRectangles(p_disp, window, thisGC, rects, nrects);
```

In this example, XRectangle is a structure for storing the parameters of a rectangle and is defined in <X11/Xlib.h> as follows:

```
typedef struct
{
    short         x, y;            /* Upper-left corner */
    unsigned short width, height; /* Width and height  */
} XRectangle;
```

You can draw a filled rectangle by calling the XFillRectangle function. Call this function the same way you do XDrawRectangle, with exactly the same arguments. When you draw a filled rectangle, the width and height of the filled area is exactly the width and height specified in the call to XFillRectangle.

XFillRectangles is the function for drawing multiple filled rectangles. It is analogous to XDrawRectangles and is called with the same arguments.

Drawing Polygons

A polygon is a figure enclosed by multiple lines. To draw the outline of a polygon, use the XDrawLines function. For filled polygons, Xlib provides the XFillPolygon function:

```
int shape; /* One of: Convex, NonConvex, or Complex      */
int mode;  /* One of: CoordModeOrigin or CoordModePrevious */

XPoint points[];  /* Vertices of the polygon */
int    numpoints; /* How many vertices       */

XFillPolygon(p_disp, window, thisGC, points, numpoints,
             shape, mode);
```

You specify the vertices of the polygon in an array of XPoint structures just as you do when drawing multiple points with XDrawPoints (see example program in Listing 9.1). The mode argument is also interpreted the same way as it is for XDrawPoints.

The shape argument helps the server optimize the filling algorithm. Specify Convex for this argument only if your polygon is such that a line drawn between any two internal points lies entirely inside the polygon. For example, triangles and rectangles are convex shapes.

If the shape is not convex, but none of the edges intersect each other, you should use NonConvex as the shape argument. For polygons with intersecting edges, use Complex. Note that if you are not sure about a polygon, you can safely specify Complex as the shape. The drawing may be a bit slower, but the result will be correct.

The fill rule in the GC determines which points are filled by XFillPolygon. You can set the fill rule by calling XSetFillRule.

Drawing Arcs, Circles, and Ellipses

In X, arcs, ellipses, and circles are handled by the arc drawing functions: XDrawArc and XDrawArcs. Use the first one for a single arc, the latter for a number of arcs.

You can think of the arc as a part of an ellipse. As shown in Figure 9.11, drawing the arc involves specifying the *bounding rectangle*, which is the smallest rectangle that completely encloses the ellipse to which the arc belongs. Specify the rectangle with the coordinates of the upper-left corner, (x,y), and the dimensions of the rectangle, width and height. Indicate the angle where the arc starts, angle1, as well as its angular extent, angle2.

Figure 9.11.

Specifying an arc in X.

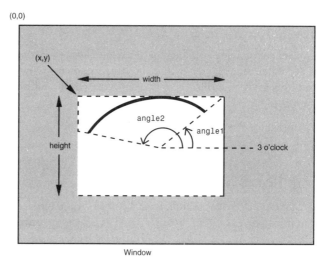

XDrawArc(display, window, gc, x, y, width, height, angle1, angle2);

The X server draws the arc:

1. The start angle, angle1, measured counterclockwise, with 0 degrees along the three o'clock line, defines the point where the arc begins.

2. The server starts tracing over the ellipse from this point on, in a counterclockwise direction, until it covers the angular extent given by angle2.

The angles angle1 and angle2 are integer values that specify angles in units of 1/64-degree. Thus, to draw an arc 60 degrees wide, starting at 30 degrees from the three o'clock direction, you call the following:

```
XDrawArc(p_disp, window, thisGC, x, y, width, height,
         30*64, 60*64);
```

You can draw an ellipse by starting at 0 degrees and specifying an extent of 360x64. If the width and height of the bounding rectangle are equal, you get a circle.

Drawing Multiple Arcs

If you have to draw more than one arc, use the XDrawArcs function. This function is used like its counterparts XDrawPoints and XDrawRectangles. Each arc is specified in an XArc structure, which is defined in <X11/Xlib.h> as follows:

```
typedef struct
{
    short           x, y;          /* Parameters of the  */
    unsigned short width, height;  /* bounding rectangle */
    short           angle1, angle2; /* Start and extent   */
} XArc;
```

As you might guess, the XDrawArcs function is called in the following manner:

```
XArc  arcs[];  /* The arcs (maybe ellipses or circles) */
int   numarcs; /* How many arcs in the array...       */

XDrawArcs(p_disp, window, thisGC, arcs, numarcs);
```

Drawing Filled Arcs

You can use XFillArc to draw a filled arc. The filling is done using the foreground color and fill style specified in the GC. The filled arc looks like a pie-shaped wedge if the arc_mode graphics attribute is set to ArcPieSlice. If the arc_mode is ArcChord, the X server fills the area within the curved edge of the arc and the chord joining its endpoints. You can alter the arc_mode by calling the XSetArcMode function.

For filling multiple arcs, use the XFillArcs function. You call XFillArc and XFillArcs the same way you call XDrawArc and XDrawArcs, respectively.

Creating a Simple Drawing Program

The simple drawing program, xfigures, shown in Listing 9.2, enables the user to draw one of five basic figures: line, rectangle, ellipse, filled rectangle, and filled ellipse. The choices are presented in a menubar implemented using the xmenu.c file shown in Listing 8.7. The user selects a figure and starts drawing by moving the cursor to the drawing area and pressing down a mouse button to indicate the starting point of the figure. The drawing is completed by moving the mouse to the desired endpoint (with the button pressed) and releasing the button.

Drawing Rubber-Band Figures

In xfigures (as in most drawing programs for the Macintosh or Microsoft Windows), rubber-banding occurs when the user moves the mouse while pressing a button. That is, the figure expands or contracts in keeping with the mouse movements.

The key to rubber-banding is to set up a GC with the function attribute set to GXxor. Here is how it is done in xfigures.c:

```
/* Set up GC for rubber-band drawing */
    xgcv.foreground = theFGpix ^ theBGpix;
    xgcv.background = theBGpix;
    xgcv.function = GXxor;
    xorGC = XCreateGC(theDisplay, theMain, GCForeground |
                    GCBackground | GCFunction, &xgcv);
```

In addition to the `function` attribute set to `GXxor`, the `foreground` is set to the exclusive-OR of the foreground and background pixels to be used for the drawing. This ensures that drawing the figure twice at the same spot will erase it and restore the background.

To handle rubber-banding, you also have to request pointer-motion events. You can do this by calling `XSelectInput`:

```
XSelectInput(theDisplay, dWin, ExposureMask |
                    PointerMotionHintMask |
                    ButtonPressMask|OwnerGrabButtonMask|
                    ButtonReleaseMask| ButtonMotionMask);
```

Once this is done, you can have rubber-band drawings by starting a drawing in response to a `ButtonPress` event and redrawing when the mouse moves. In `xfigures.c`, the functions `start_rubberband` and `continue_rubberband` implement the rubber-banding (see Listing 9.2).

Building *xfigures*

To compile and link `xfigures`, you can use the following makefile:

```
# Some common definitions...

RM = rm -f
CC = cc

# Compiler flags, paths for include files and libraries

CFLAGS =
INCLUDES = -I. -I/usr/include -I/usr/include/X11
LIBS = -lX11

# Rule to create .o files from .c files
.c.o:
    $(RM) $@
    $(CC) -c $(CFLAGS) $(INCLUDES) $*.c

# Targets...

all::    xfigures

xfigures.o: xfigures.c app_glob.c xwins.h

initapp.o: initapp.c app_glob.c

xwinutil.o: xwinutil.c app_glob.c xwins.h

xbutton.o: xbutton.c app_glob.c xwins.h

xmenu.o: xmenu.c app_glob.c xwins.h
```

```
xfigures: xfigures.o initapp.o xwinutil.o xbutton.o \
      xmenu.o
    $(RM) $@
    $(CC) -o $@ $(CFLAGS) xfigures.o initapp.o \
        xwinutil.o xbutton.o xmenu.o \
        $(LIBS)
```

The other source files appear in Chapters 7 and 8, and the makefile is similar to the one for the `menudemo` program shown in Listing 8.8.

After the program is built, you can try it out by typing `xfigures &` at the shell prompt. Figure 9.12 shows a sample drawing created with `xfigures`.

Figure 9.12.

A sample drawing from `xfigures`.

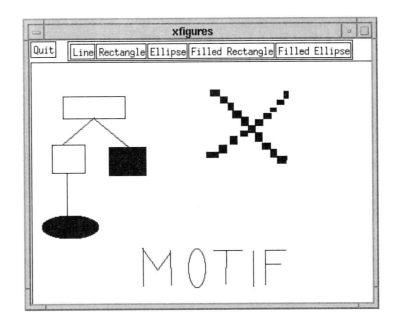

Listing 9.2. `xfigures.c`—Drawing rubber-band figures.

```
/*------------------------------------------------------------*/
/*  File: xfigures.c
 *
 *  Demonstrate drawing of figures (including rubber-banding).
 */
 /*-----------------------------------------------------------*/
#include <stdio.h>

#include <X11/Xlib.h>
#include <X11/Xutil.h>
#include <X11/cursorfont.h>

#include "xwins.h"
#include "app_glob.c"
```

continues

Listing 9.2. continued

```
#define MENUBAR_STYLE  0

#define MAXFIGURES     100

typedef struct FIGURE
{
    short    type;       /* What type of figure        */
#define LINE             0
#define RECT             1
#define ELLIPSE          2
#define FILLRECT         3
#define FILLELLIPSE      4
    short    x1, y1;     /* Corners of bounding rectangle */
    short    x2, y2;     /* or end-points of line         */
} FIGURE;

/* Array of figures */

FIGURE  figures[MAXFIGURES];
int     numfigures = 0;
int     curfig = 0,
        figtype = 0;

static int zero=0, one=1, two=2, three=3, four=4;

GC   xorGC;       /* GC used for rubber-band drawing */

char *quit_label = "Quit";

Cursor xhair_cursor;
Window dWin;
XWIN   *fig_menu;

/* Function prototypes */

void initapp(/* int, char **, int, int, unsigned, unsigned */);
int  quit_action(/* caddr_t */);
void start_rubberband(/* int x, int y */);
void continue_rubberband(/* int x, int y */);
int  figure_select(/* caddr_t */);
static void draw_figure(/* Display *d, Window w, GC gc, int fig */);

/*-----------------------------------------------------------*/
main(argc, argv)
int argc;
char **argv;
{
    XWIN     *QuitButton, *which_xwin;
    unsigned quit_width, quit_height;
    XGCValues xgcv;

    xwin_init();

    initapp(argc, argv, 20, 20, 400, 300);

/* Create the "Quit" button */
```

```
    quit_width = XTextWidth(theFontStruct, quit_label,
                            strlen(quit_label)) + 4;
    quit_height = theFontStruct->max_bounds.ascent +
                  theFontStruct->max_bounds.descent + 4;

    QuitButton = MakeXButton(1, 1, quit_width, quit_height,
                             1, theFGpix, theBGpix, theMain,
                             quit_label, quit_action, NULL);

/* Create a menu that lists the figures that we can draw */
    fig_menu = MakeXMenu(quit_width+16, 1, 1, theFGpix, theBGpix,
                 theMain, MENUBAR_STYLE,
                 "Line",             figure_select, (caddr_t)&zero,
                 "Rectangle",        figure_select, (caddr_t)&one,
                 "Ellipse",          figure_select, (caddr_t)&two,
                 "Filled Rectangle", figure_select, (caddr_t)&three,
                 "Filled Ellipse",   figure_select, (caddr_t)&four,
                 NULL);

/* Create and map a window that serves as the drawing area */
    dWin = XCreateSimpleWindow(theDisplay, theMain, 1,
            quit_height+8, 500, 400, 1, theFGpix, theBGpix);

    XSelectInput(theDisplay, dWin, ExposureMask |
                         PointerMotionHintMask |
                         ButtonPressMask|OwnerGrabButtonMask|
                         ButtonReleaseMask| ButtonMotionMask);
    XMapRaised(theDisplay, dWin);

/* Set up GC for rubber-band drawing */
    xgcv.foreground = theFGpix ^ theBGpix;
    xgcv.background = theBGpix;
    xgcv.function = GXxor;
    xorGC = XCreateGC(theDisplay, theMain, GCForeground |
                    GCBackground | GCFunction, &xgcv);

/* A crosshair cursor for line drawing */
    xhair_cursor = XCreateFontCursor(theDisplay, XC_crosshair);

/* Event handling loop */

    while (!AppDone)
    {
        XNextEvent(theDisplay, &theEvent);

/* Events for the dWin window are handled here */
        if(theEvent.xany.window == dWin)
        {
            switch(theEvent.type)
            {
                case Expose:
                    if(theEvent.xexpose.count == 0)
                    {
                        int i;
```

continues

Listing 9.2. continued

```
/* Clear the window and draw the figures in the "figures" array*/
                    XClearWindow(theDisplay, dWin);
                    if(numfigures > 0)
                        for(i=0; i<numfigures; i++)
                            draw_figure(theDisplay, dWin,
                                        theGC, i);
                }
                break;

            case ButtonPress:
                XDefineCursor(theDisplay, dWin,
                              xhair_cursor);
/* Crude check to ensure that we don't exceed array's capacity */
                if(numfigures > MAXFIGURES-1)
                    numfigures = MAXFIGURES-1;
                curfig = numfigures;
                numfigures++;
                start_rubberband(theEvent.xbutton.x,
                                 theEvent.xbutton.y);
                break;

            case ButtonRelease:
                XUndefineCursor(theDisplay, dWin);
                break;

            case MotionNotify:
            {
                Window rw, cw;
                int xr, yr, xw, yw, kbstat;

                XQueryPointer(theDisplay,
                              theEvent.xmotion.window,
                    &rw, &cw, &xr, &yr, &xw, &yw, &kbstat);

                continue_rubberband(xw, yw);
                break;
            }
        }
    }

/* For all other windows, retrieve the XWIN data from
 * Xlib using the context manager routine XFindContext
 */
    if(XFindContext(theDisplay, theEvent.xany.window,
       xwin_context, (caddr_t *) &which_xwin) == 0)
    {
/* Call the event handler of this XWIN structure */
        if(*(which_xwin->event_handler) != NULL)
            (*(which_xwin->event_handler))(which_xwin);
    }
  }

/* Close connection to display and exit */

    XCloseDisplay(theDisplay);
    exit(0);
```

```
}
/*----------------------------------------------------------*/
/*  q u i t _ a c t i o n
 *
 *  This routine is called when a ButtonPress event occurs in
 *  the quit window.
 */
int quit_action(data)
caddr_t data;
{
/* Set the done flag */
    AppDone = 1;
    return 1;
}
/*----------------------------------------------------------*/
/*  s t a r t _ r u b b e r b a n d
 *
 *  Start of rubber-band line
 */
void start_rubberband(x, y)
int x, y;
{
    figures[curfig].type = figtype;
    figures[curfig].x1 = x;
    figures[curfig].y1 = y;
    figures[curfig].x2 = x;
    figures[curfig].y2 = y;
    draw_figure(theDisplay, dWin, xorGC, curfig);
}
/*----------------------------------------------------------*/
/*  c o n t i n u e _ r u b b e r b a n d
 *
 *  Handle mouse movement while drawing a rubber-band line
 */
void continue_rubberband(x, y)
int x, y;
{
/* Draw once at old location (to erase line) */
    draw_figure(theDisplay, dWin, xorGC, curfig);

/* Now update end-point and redraw */
    figures[curfig].x2 = x;
    figures[curfig].y2 = y;
    draw_figure(theDisplay, dWin, xorGC, curfig);
}

/*----------------------------------------------------------*/
static int figure_select(data)
caddr_t data;
{
/* Set figure type and return */
    figtype = *((int *)data);
    return 1;
```

continues

Listing 9.2. continued

```
}
/*------------------------------------------------------------*/
static void draw_figure(d, w, gc, curfig)
Display *d;
Window  w;
GC      gc;
int     curfig;
{
    int x1 = figures[curfig].x1, y1 = figures[curfig].y1,
        x2 = figures[curfig].x2, y2 = figures[curfig].y2, t;

/* Make sure x2 >= x1 and y2 >= y1 */
    if(figures[curfig].type != LINE && x1 > x2)
    {
        t = x1;
        x1 = x2;
        x2 = t;
    }
    if(figures[curfig].type != LINE && y1 > y2)
    {
        t = y1;
        y1 = y2;
        y2 = t;
    }
    switch(figures[curfig].type)
    {
        case LINE:
            XDrawLine(d, w, gc, x1, y1, x2, y2);
            break;
        case RECT:
            XDrawRectangle(d, w, gc, x1, y1, x2-x1, y2-y1);
            break;
        case ELLIPSE:
            XDrawArc(d, w, gc, x1, y1, x2-x1, y2-y1, 0, 360*64);
            break;
        case FILLRECT:
            XFillRectangle(d, w, gc, x1, y1, x2-x1, y2-y1);
            break;
        case FILLELLIPSE:
            XFillArc(d, w, gc, x1, y1, x2-x1, y2-y1, 0, 360*64);
            break;
    }
}
```

Handling *Expose* Events

Because handling Expose events are an important part of displaying output in a window, this section includes a discussion of the Expose, GraphicsExpose, and NoExpose events. You have encountered Expose events in the example programs. GraphicsExpose and NoExpose events become necessary when copying a rectangular region from one window to another.

Generation of *Expose* Events

The server generates `Expose` events when any of your application's windows need redrawing. This can happen when the window is first mapped, when an obscuring window is moved, or when you clear an area of a window by calling `XClearArea`.

In most applications, all drawing occurs in reponse to `Expose` events. This is because you cannot draw in a window until it is ready and there is no good way of knowing when it is ready. However, when you receive an `Expose` event for a window, you can be sure that it is ready for use.

When parts of a window need redrawing, the server generates an `Expose` event for every rectangular region that is exposed. When you retrieve an `Expose` event by calling one of Xlib's event retrieval functions (`XNextEvent`, for instance), the relevant information is in an `XExposeEvent` data structure (accessed as the `xexpose` member of the `XEvent` union):

```
typedef struct
{
    int             type;        /* Event's type                 */
    unsigned long   serial;      /* Last processed request number */
    Bool            send_event;  /* True means from a SendEvent  */
    Display         *display;    /* Display where event occurred */
    Window          window;      /* Window that needs redrawing  */
    int             x, y;        /* Origin and dimensions of the */
    int             width,       /* rectangle that has been      */
                    height;      /* "exposed"                    */
    int             count;       /*Number of Expose events to come*/
} XExposeEvent;
```

The members `x`, `y`, `width`, and `height` identify the rectangle whose contents are lost and have to be redrawn. The last member of the structure, `count`, tells you how many more `Expose` events for the same window are yet to arrive. Knowing this, you can devise a simple strategy for handling `Expose` events.

Wait for the `Expose` event with `count` equal to 0. Then, clear the entire window and redraw everything in the window. In other words, you are ignoring the information about the specific parts that need refreshing and simply updating the whole window.

Handling `Expose` events on `count` 0 works well for simple drawings, but for complex drawings, it is better to make use of the information on the rectangle that needs redrawing. One method is to use a region. You can use `XUnionRectWithRegion` to add all the rectangles in a region. Set the clipping mask of the drawing `GC` with `XSetRegion`. Then redraw when the `Expose` event with `count` 0 arrives. For maximum efficiency, your application's drawing function must be smart enough to draw only within the regions. Because the server clips against the region, there is no harm in drawing everything, but that sends unnecessary graphics requests and wastes time. The `viewfile` program in Chapter 10 demonstrates the use of this technique.

Clearing Windows and Areas

If you have all output operations in the block of code that handles `Expose` events, how do you handle the need to refresh the window on purpose? The server sends `Expose` events only when some previously hidden parts of a window become visible again. One way to redraw the window is to clear an area and force an `Expose` event. You can use the `XClearArea` function for this purpose:

```
Bool expose_flag = 1;  /* if flag = 1 generate Expose event */

XClearArea(p_disp, window, x, y, width, height, expose_flag);
```

The arguments `x`, `y`, `width`, and `height` specify the rectangular area to be cleared. The server generates an `Expose` event for this rectangle if the last argument is nonzero (`True`).

If you specify 0s for the `width` and `height`, the server clears the entire window. Thus, a common method of forcing a redrawing of a window is to call `XClearArea`:

```
XClearArea(p_disp, window, 0, 0, 0, 0, True);
```

If the last argument in the call is `False`, the server clears the window without generating an `Expose` event. The function call, `XClearWindow(p_disp, window)`, serves the same purpose.

Area Copying

Xlib provides two functions for copying parts of one drawable to another. You can use `XCopyPlane` to copy one or more selected bit planes from one rectangle to another.

The `XCopyArea` function, on the other hand, copies all pixel values from one rectangular area to another. You can copy from a window to a pixmap and vice versa. The source rectangle (the one you are copying from) can overlap the destination. Thus, you can use `XCopyArea` to move the contents of a window up, for instance. The `viewfile` program in Chapter 10 shows how to implement scrolling using the `XCopyArea` function.

The `XCopyArea` function is often used to copy the contents of a window to a pixmap and to scroll windows. `XCopyPlane` can be used to overlay images.

GraphicsExpose Events

One consequence of the graphics copy operation is that sometimes the contents of the entire source rectangle may not be available. For instance, consider Case A of Figure 9.13, which shows copying from one rectangle to another in Window 1. Windows 2 and 3 are overlapping Window 1. More importantly, Windows 2 and 3 are obscuring parts of the source rectangle. If you attempt an `XCopyPlane` or `XCopyArea` for the geometry shown in Case A of Figure 9.13, the server cannot copy anything into the hatched areas of the destination rectangle because those parts of the `source` are obscured. In this case, the server generates a `GraphicsExpose` event for the hatched rectangles. This is the server's way of informing your application that the contents of those areas in the destination have to be redrawn in some other way.

For the situation shown in Case B of Figure 9.13, there are no problems because all visible areas of the destination can be filled by the server. In this case, the server sends a `NoExpose` event indicating that copy is successful.

Figure 9.13.

GraphicsExpose and NoExpose events.

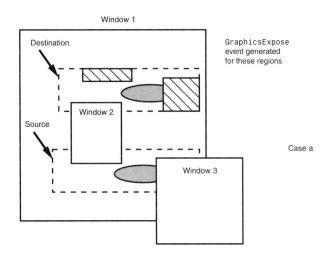

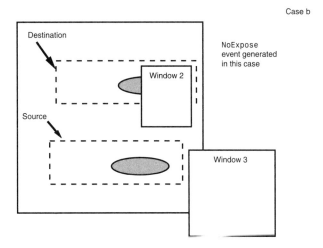

The graphics_exposures attribute in a GC controls whether GraphicsExpose events are sent by the server. They are enabled by default, but you can turn them off by using the XSetGraphicsExposures function. For example, to turn them off in a specific GC, call the following:

```
XSetGraphicsExposures(p_display, thisGC, False);
```

Summary

In X, the graphics context (GC) controls the appearance of drawings in windows. Colors, styles, fonts, and other attributes used by graphics and text drawing primitives are stored in GCs. GCs are maintained by the X server and referenced by applications through a resource ID. Xlib provides a large number of functions to manipulate the attributes of a GC. All drawing functions in Xlib take a GC as an argument. Applications typically create several GCs—one for each unique drawing style.

Xlib provides many functions you can use to draw graphical objects, such as points, lines, rectangles, polygons, arcs, and circles. It also enables advanced drawing techniques, such as drawing rubber-band figures and clipping.

Chapter 10

Drawing Text

Displaying text is an important function in all computer systems. Prior to the emergence of graphical user interfaces, text-based interfaces were the norm, and users interacted with computers through text display terminals. Even now, most users spend their time reading and entering textual information. X provides ample facilities for displaying text. However, unlike text display terminals, X displays can show text in varying sizes and shapes (fonts). This chapter describes how to display text in X, and includes an example program that illustrates how to handle text output in X applications.

Fonts

The X server draws characters using a rectangular bitmap for each character. The term *font* refers to a collection of such rectangular bitmaps representing a set of printable characters of given shape, size, weight, and style. These bitmaps in a font are also known as *glyphs*.

Fonts are generally identified by their *typeface*, a term for a collection of fonts of similar shape but differing sizes, styles, and weights. Helvetica, Courier, Time, and Symbol are some of the commonly used typefaces.

The size, weight, and style determine the appearance of a specific font in a typeface. The size is expressed in terms of the height of the glyphs in the font. Usually, sizes are expressed in *points*, each point being approximately 1/72-inch. Some common sizes are 10 and 12 points.

If you think of each character being drawn by a curved line, the weight of the font is equivalent to the thickness of the curved line. For example, a bold version of a font provides thicker characters than the regular version.

The style or slant of a font indicates the vertical orientation of each character in the font. Typical styles are *roman* for upright characters and *italic* for characters tilted to the right.

You can think of a font as an array of glyphs indexed by the character's code. To draw a character, the X server extracts the bitmap corresponding to that character's code from the font's glyph array and applies foreground and background colors using the bitmap as a mask.

The character code, on the other hand, depends on the encoding used to represent the characters in the alphabet of a language. ASCII (American Standard Code for Information Interchange) and ISO Latin-1 (International Standards Organization) are examples of commonly used character codes.

Font Names

When you prepare a document with any graphical word processor (or desktop publishing software), you usually indicate a specific font by naming its typeface, size, weight, and style. For example, *14-point Helvetica Bold* refers to a specific font. Starting with X11R3, names of fonts are constructed in a similar manner. The font name includes information on the font's designer and the typeface, weight, style, and size. There is other information as well, such as the character set encoding to be used with the font, intercharacter spacings (monospaced or proportional), and the screen resolution (in pixels per inch) at which the font should be used. For instance, you can identify a 14-point Helvetica Bold font with the following name (see Chapter 3, "Exploring X Applications," for information on X11R3 and X11R6 font naming conventions):

```
-adobe-helvetica-bold-r-normal--14-140-75-75-p-82-iso8859-1
```

Although the name looks complicated, it is easy enough for a program to construct it from the parts. Here, `adobe` refers to Adobe Corporation which donated the font. The typeface is `helvetica` in `bold` weight and regular style (represented by `r`). The `normal` refers to normal-sized characters.

Size information follows the two dashes after `normal`. The `14` indicates the font's size in pixels, the `140` refers to the size of the font in tenths of a point. The next two numbers (`75-75`) indicate the horizontal and vertical screen resolutions for which the font was designed. In this case, the font is designed for a screen with 75 dpi (dots per inch) resolution. Next comes the spacing information—`m` indicates monospaced font (equal spacing between any two characters), and `p` denotes proportionally spaced font (spacings vary from one letter to another). The name here includes a `p` because Helvetica is a proportionally spaced typeface.

The next number (`82`) is the average width of the character glyphs in units of tenths of a pixel. The last part in the font's name is the character encodings used to index into the font. The `iso8859-1` refers to the ISO Standard 8859/1 character set, also known as the ISO Latin-1 set.

If the font size and width are zero, the font is a scalable one; you can use a scalable font at any size. Font scaling capability and support for scaling fonts was introduced in X11R5.

Although the font names are complicated, you do not have to specify full names when specifying a font. The Xlib functions that accept font names have been designed to handle incomplete font names.

You can use asterisks (*) as wildcard characters for parts of the name that can be arbitrary. For example, if you want only Adobe's 14-point Helvetica Bold font, you can specify it with the following name:

```
-adobe-helvetica-bold-r-*--*-180-*-*-*-*-iso8859-1
```

As you will see in the `viewfile` program shown in Listing 10.1, the capability of using wildcards in a font's name helps you devise a good scheme for handling multiple fonts in an X application.

Font Listing and Examination

The X distribution comes with two utility programs that enable you to determine which fonts are available on a server and how a specific font looks.

Listing Fonts with *xlsfonts*

The first utility, `xlsfonts`, lists the names of all available fonts. You can run it by typing `xlsfonts` at the shell prompt. If you want to see the names of all 14-point Helvetica typefaces in bold weight, for instance, you can do so with the following command:

```
xlsfonts "*helvetica*bold*140*"
```

which generates the following in a typical system:

```
-adobe-helvetica-bold-o-normal--14-140-75-75-p-82-iso8859-1
-adobe-helvetica-bold-o-normal--20-140-100-100-p-103-iso8859-1
-adobe-helvetica-bold-r-normal--14-140-75-75-p-82-iso8859-1
-adobe-helvetica-bold-r-normal--20-140-100-100-p-105-iso8859-1
```

You can get more detailed information on a font by using the `-l` option with `xlsfonts`.

Viewing Fonts with *xfd*

You can use the `xfd` utility to view a font. To see a specific font, type `xfd -fn <fontname>` at the shell prompt. The `<fontname>` argument should be the name of an actual font (with wildcards, if necessary). For example, to view Roman 14-point Helvetica Bold font, use this command:

```
xfd -fn "*helvetica*bold-r*140*" &
```

Figure 10.1 shows the resulting display. Character sizes may be different from 14-point type because the font is being displayed on a screen with resolution different from the 75 dpi for which the screen is designed.

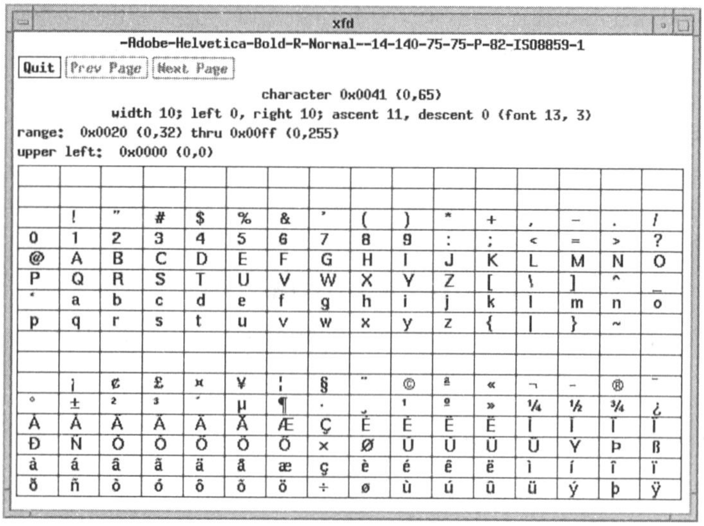

Figure 10.1.

Bold Roman Helvetica font displayed by xfd.

Font Loading and Unloading

In X, fonts are resources residing in the server. Applications have to load a font before using it. When the server successfully loads a font, it returns a resource ID that the application subsequently uses to refer to that font. Once the name is known, you can load a font by calling the XLoadFont function like this:

```
Display *p_disp; /* Identifies the connection to the X server */
char    fontname[] = "*helvetica-bold-r*140*";  /* Font name */
Font    helvb14;                                /* Font ID   */
    .
    .
    .
if((helvb14 = XLoadFont(p_disp, fontname)) == None)
{
    fprintf(stderr, "Cannot load font: %s\n", fontname);
    exit(1);
}
```

where the program exits if the font cannot be loaded. (XLoadFont returns a 0 when it fails.) When successful, you can start using the 14-point bold Helvetica font, shown in the example, by setting the font attribute of a GC. To do this, call XSetFont:

```
XSetFont(p_disp, thisGC, helvb14);
```

Subsequently, when any text is drawn with this GC, the output will be in 14-point bold Helvetica font.

Because fonts are server-resident resources, when your application no longer needs a font, you should release the font with the XUnloadFont function. This function call has the following form:

```
XUnloadFont(p_disp, helvb14);
```

If you have a `GC` with `helvb14` as the font and you unload that font, the X server refrains from unloading the font until the `GC` is destroyed.

Font Characteristics

A font is a set of bitmaps. When writing text output, the X server draws each character by painting the pixels in a rectangle matching the size of that character's bitmap. Because you have to specify where the server should start drawing the characters, you need to know the size of each character's bitmap—at the very least, the maximum size of a character's bitmap in a font. Xlib includes functions that enable you to obtain such information.

If you have loaded a font using `XLoadFont`, you can use `XQueryFont` to obtain a pointer to an `XFontStruct` structure that contains aggregate information about the font. For example, if you have obtained a valid font ID, `helvb14`, you can get information on this font by calling `XQueryFont`:

```
Font        helvb14;        /* A valid font ID        */
XFontStruct *info_helvb14; /* Pointer to returned info */

info_helvb14 = XQueryFont(p_disp, helvb14);
```

When you call `XQueryFont`, Xlib allocates an `XFontStruct` structure, fills it with information retrieved from the X server, and returns a pointer. Save the pointer for subsequent use, and when you no longer need the font, call `XFreeFont` to unload the font and, at the same time, free the memory allocated by Xlib for the `XFontStructure` structure.

Rather than calling `XLoadFont` followed by `XQueryFont`, you can call the `XLoadQueryFont` function to load a font and get the font information with a single request to the server. Like `XQueryFont`, `XLoadQueryFont` returns a pointer to an `XFontStruct` structure. Use the following:

```
Display     *p_disp;
char        fontname[] =  "*helvetica-bold-r*140*";
XFontStruct *info_helvb14;
    .
    .
    .
if((info_helvb14 = XLoadQueryFont(p_disp, fontname)) == NULL)
{
    fprintf(stderr, "Cannot load font: %s\n", fontname);
    exit(1);
}
```

The `XFontStruct` structure that contains aggregate information about a font is defined in `<X11/Xlib.h>` as follows:

```
typedef struct
{
    XExtData    *ext_data;       /* Room for future expansion */
    Font        fid;             /* Font ID for this font     */
    unsigned    direction;       /* One of: FontLeftToRight or*/
                                 /*         FontRightToLeft   */
    unsigned    min_char_or_byte2;/* First defined character  */
    unsigned    max_char_or_byte2;/* Last defined character   */
    unsigned    min_byte1;       /* First row that exists     */
    unsigned    max_byte1;       /* Last row that exists       */
```

```
    Bool       all_chars_exist;  /* True = all characters have*/
                                 /*        nonzero size       */
    unsigned   default_char;     /* Character to print for    */
                                 /* undefined character       */
    int        n_properties;     /* Total number of properties*/
    XFontProp  *properties;      /* Pointer to array of       */
                                 /* additional properties     */
    XCharStruct min_bounds;      /* Info on smallest character*/
    XCharStruct max_bounds;      /* Info on largest character */
    XCharStruct *per_char;       /* Info on all characters    */
    int        ascent;           /* Pixels above baseline     */
    int        descent;          /* Pixels below baseline     */
} XFontStruct;
```

You can safely ignore some of the members of the XFontStruct structure. An important member is fid which is the font ID. The direction flag may be important if your application handles languages that expect characters to go from right to left rather than left to right.

The ascent and descent members are the number of pixels that the font extends above and below a baseline (see Figure 10.2). You can use these values to decide how far apart you position lines of text.

Figure 10.2.
Font size information in XFontStruct and XCharStruct structures.

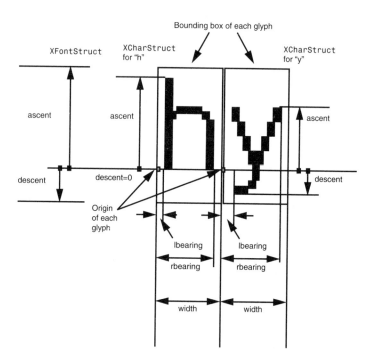

The per_char in the XFontStruct structure is an array of XCharStruct structures that contain further information on each character in the font. This structure is defined in <X11/Xlib.h> as the following:

```
typedef struct
{
    short    lbearing;  /* Distance to left edge of bitmap   */
    short    rbearing;  /* Distance to right edge of bitmap  */
    short    width;     /* Distance to next char's origin    */
    short    ascent;    /* Baseline to top edge of bitmap    */
    short    descent;   /* Baseline to bottom edge of bitmap */
    unsigned short attributes; /* Other font-specific info   */
} XCharStruct;
```

To understand the meaning of the fields in this structure, refer to Figure 10.2 where the information is shown for two different characters.

Text Output

Xlib provides three functions for text output:

◆ XDrawString

◆ XDrawImageString

◆ XDrawText

Each function draws a number of characters on a single line. The first two functions draw all the characters using the font specified in the GC which you provide as an argument. They are called in the same way:

```
char  string[];  /* String to be displayed        */
int   nchars;    /* Number of characters in string */

XDrawString(p_disp, window, thisGC, x, y, string, nchars);
XDrawImageString(p_disp, window, thisGC, x, y, string, nchars);
```

You specify a starting position—that is, where the server places the origin of the first character's bitmap (see Figure 10.2). Then it copies the foreground pixel value (from the GC) to all pixels corresponding to 1s in the bitmap. XDrawString does not alter the pixels if the bitmap is 0. XDrawImageString, on the other hand, also fills the pixels corresponding to 0s in each character's bitmap with the GC's background color. Figure 10.3 shows the appearance of strings displayed with these two functions. In this case, the window's background is white, and the GC's foreground and background are black and light gray, respectively. As you can see, XDrawImageString fills in the background of each character's bounding rectangle.

Figure 10.3.

Text output from
XDrawString *and*
XDrawImageString.

XDrawString

XDrawImageString

Multiple Fonts on the Same Line

If you want to use more than one font on the same line of text, use the XDrawText function. This function accepts the information about the string segments in an XTextItem structure, which is defined in <X11/Xlib.h> as the following:

```
typedef struct
{
    char *chars; /* Pointer to the string to be drawn       */
    int  nchars; /* Number of characters in string           */
    int  delta;  /* Distance from last char of prev. string  */
    Font font;   /* Font to be used (None means use GC's font) */
} XTextItem;
```

Each XTextItem structure contains information about one chunk of text. The first two members identify the string and its length. The member named delta is an offset in pixels that is applied before drawing this string. The last member in the XCharStruct structure, font, specifies the font to be used when drawing this string. When calling XDrawText, you provide the usual Display pointer, Drawable, and GC:

```
XTextItem   text_chunks[]; /* Array of strings to be displayed */
int         numchunks;     /* Number of XTextItem structures    */

/* Initialize "text_chunks" ... */
    .
    .
XDrawText(p_disp, window, thisGC, x, y, text_chunks, numchunks);
```

Additionally, you provide the strings in an array of XTextItem structures, the number of such structures, and the coordinates (x,y) (with respect to the origin of the drawable) where the first character of the first string is displayed.

XDrawText displays each string using the font specified in the font field of the XTextItem structure. It does this by loading the font into the GC that you provide in the function call. If the font field in the XTextItem is set to None, XDrawText uses whatever font the GC happens to have.

Figure 10.4 shows a sample output generated with XDrawText. Here are the relevant lines of code that produce the output:

```
Display     *p_disp;
Window      Main;
XTextItem   line[3];
XFontStruct *p_ncsb14, *p_courb14, *p_helvo14;
char        n_ncsb14[]  = "*new century schoolbook-medium-r*140*",
            n_courb14[] = "*courier-bold-r*140*",
            n_helvo14[] = "*helvetica-medium-o*140*";

    .
    .
    .
/* Load the fonts...    */

    if ((p_ncsb14 = XLoadQueryFont(p_disp, n_ncsb14)) == NULL)
        exit(1);
    if ((p_courb14 = XLoadQueryFont(p_disp, n_courb14)) == NULL)
        exit(1);
    if ((p_helvo14 = XLoadQueryFont(p_disp, n_helvo14)) == NULL)
        exit(1);

    line[0].chars = "XDrawText";
    line[0].nchars = strlen("XDrawText");
    line[0].delta = p_courb14->max_bounds.width/2;
    line[0].font  = p_courb14->fid;
```

```
    line[1].chars = "lets you";
    line[1].nchars = strlen("lets you");
    line[1].delta = p_helvo14->max_bounds.width/2;
    line[1].font =  p_helvo14->fid;

    line[2].chars = "mix fonts on a line.";
    line[2].nchars = strlen("mix fonts on a line.");
    line[2].delta = p_ncsb14->max_bounds.width/2;
    line[2].font =  p_ncsb14->fid;
/* In the event processing loop...*/
    if(theEvent.xany.window == Main &&
       theEvent.type == Expose &&
       theEvent.xexpose.count == 0)
    {
        XClearWindow(p_disp, Main);
        XDrawText(p_disp, Main, theGC, 30, 30, line, 3);
    }
        .
        .
        .
```

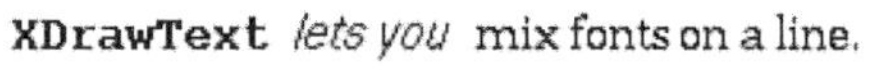

Figure 10.4.
*Mixing fonts on the same
line with XDrawText.*

XDrawText *lets you* mix fonts on a line.

As you can see, once the XTextItem structures are ready, displaying them is easy—just call XDrawText. In a real application (for example, a word processing program), you allocate the XTextItem structures dynamically and initialize them as the user types in text and selects a font.

Text Positioning

When drawing text, you have to decide where to position the string. Unlike a text display terminal, the X server does not automatically handle carriage returns or linefeeds. You have to position each line of text explicitly and draw it by calling one of these functions: XDrawString, XDrawText, or XDrawImageString. To help you position each line, Xlib provides the functions XTextWidth and XTextExtents that compute the dimensions (in pixels) of a text string when it is displayed in a specified font. When calling these functions, you have to provide a pointer to an XFontStruct structure that contains information about the font. Thus, you have to use XLoadQueryFont (or XLoadFont followed by XQueryFont) before calling XTextWidth and XTextExtents.

String Width Computation

XTextWidth is the simpler of the two dimension-computing functions. It accepts a pointer to the array of characters and returns the width of a string in pixels:

```
XFontStruct *p_font;         /* Structure with info on font */
char        text[] = "Hello";
int         text_width;

text_width = XTextWidth(p_font, text, strlen(text));
```

You can use this width for horizontal placement of text. For vertical spacing, use the sum of the ascent and descent fields of the XFontStruct structure pointed by p_font.

String Extent Computation

The XTextExtents function provides more information about the area occupied by a text string when displayed in a particular font. This function returns the information by filling in an XCharStruct whose address you provide as an argument. The calling syntax is the following:

```
XFontStruct *p_font;          /* Structure with info on font   */
char        text[] = "Hello";
int         direction,        /* Font direction returned here  */
            ascent,           /* Font's ascent returned here   */
            descent;          /* Font's descent returned here  */
XCharStruct text_sizes;       /* Sizes returned in this struct */

XTextExtents(p_font, text, strlen(text),
    &direction, &ascent, &descent, &text_sizes);
```

You can interpret the information returned in the variables ascent and descent, and the XCharStruct structure text_sizes, by consulting Figure 10.2. The figure illustrates the information in an XCharStruct structure for individual characters; remember that the fields of the text_sizes structure pertain to the entire string.

The server is not involved when you call XTextWidth or XTextExtents to compute the sizes of text being displayed. The XFontStruct structure specified in the function calls has all the information needed by the functions to perform the calculations. Thus, you pay no significant penalty if you make frequent calls to these functions.

> **NOTE:**
>
> Functions that make no server requests do not need a Display pointer as an argument.

File Viewing: A Sample Program

Now that you have an idea about the fonts, text positioning, and text output functions, this section provides a complete example that consolidates these concepts with some ideas (copying areas) from the last chapter.

The application is a program named viewfile that enables you to view the contents of a file in a font of your choice. For example, you can view the file viewfile.c by typing the following command at the shell prompt:

```
viewfile -file viewfile.c&
```

When started this way, viewfile first opens and reads the contents of the file. Then it displays the first part of the file in a window under a menubar.

The menubar has three items:

◆ Font (which really lists the typefaces)

◆ Weight

◆ Size

To the left of this menubar is a box labeled Quit. Clicking on this box causes `viewfile` to exit.

Pressing the mouse button on the items in the menubar displays pull-down menus from which the user can select a new font (typeface), alter the size of the font, or change the font's weight. For example, Figure 10.5 shows the appearance of the display for 14-point Courier Bold.

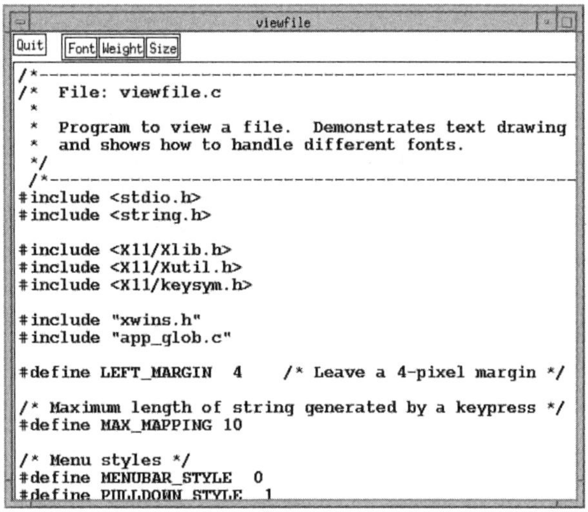

Figure 10.5.

Viewing `viewfile.c` *in 14-point Courier Bold.*

```
/*---------------------------------------------
/*  File: viewfile.c
 *
 *  Program to view a file.  Demonstrates text drawing
 *  and shows how to handle different fonts.
 */
 /*---------------------------------------------
#include <stdio.h>
#include <string.h>

#include <X11/Xlib.h>
#include <X11/Xutil.h>
#include <X11/keysym.h>

#include "xwins.h"
#include "app_glob.c"

#define LEFT_MARGIN  4      /* Leave a 4-pixel margin */

/* Maximum length of string generated by a keypress */
#define MAX_MAPPING 10

/* Menu styles */
#define MENUBAR_STYLE   0
#define PULLDOWN_STYLE  1
```

The `viewfile` program also enables the user to scroll the file up or down using the arrow keys. Before these keys can work, the user has to transfer the input focus to `viewfile`'s text window. Depending on the window manager, this requires either moving the mouse pointer into the window or clicking on the window.

The program also interprets the Ctrl+U and Ctrl+D key combinations the same way that the `vi` editor does in UNIX, and enables the user to refresh the display (by pressing Ctrl+L) if something goes wrong with the scrolling.

All in all, `viewfile` does quite a lot for a program its size. The next section explains how it does all this. As you explore the program, you may find it convenient to refer to Listing 10.1 for the source code of `viewfile`.

Listing 10.1. `viewfile.c`—Viewing a file.

```c
/*-------------------------------------------------------*/
/*  File: viewfile.c
 *
 *  Program to view a file.  Demonstrates text drawing functions
 *  and shows how to handle different fonts.
 */
 /*-------------------------------------------------------*/
#include <stdio.h>
#include <string.h>

#include <X11/Xlib.h>
#include <X11/Xutil.h>
#include <X11/keysym.h>

#include "xwins.h"
#include "app_glob.c"

#define LEFT_MARGIN  4    /* Leave a 4-pixel margin */

/* Maximum length of string generated by a keypress */
#define MAX_MAPPING 10

/* Menu styles */
#define MENUBAR_STYLE  0
#define PULLDOWN_STYLE  1

#define SCROLL_UP    0
#define SCROLL_DOWN  1

#define MAXCHARS   512    /* Maximum length of a line    */

typedef struct D_LINE    /* Holds info on each line     */
{
    struct D_LINE *prev;  /* Pointer to previous line    */
    struct D_LINE *next;  /* Pointer to next line        */
    char          *line;  /* Null-terminated line        */
    short         length; /* Number of characters in line*/
    short         lbearing;/* Left and right edges of    */
    short         rbearing;/* rectangle covered by line   */
    short         height; /* Height of text string       */
} D_LINE;

typedef struct D_LBUF    /* Info on entire buffer       */
{
    D_LINE        *lines; /* First line in buffer        */
    D_LINE        *lstart;/* First line in window        */
    GC            gc;     /* GC used to display text      */
    Region        rexp;   /* Current exposed region       */
    XFontStruct   *fstruct;/* Info on current font        */
    int           font;   /* Currently selected font      */
    int           weight; /* weight and                   */
    int           size;   /* size                         */
    unsigned      dwidth; /* Width of text display area   */
    unsigned      dheight;/* Height of text display area */
    long          count;  /* How many lines in buffer     */
} D_LBUF;
```

```
static D_LBUF fbuf = { NULL,NULL, None, None, None, 0, 0, 0,
                       0, 0, 0};

static int zero=0, one=1, two=2, three=3, four=4;

static  GC      invertGC;   /* GC used for highlighting    */
static  int     PullDownOn = 0,
                full_update = 0;
static  Window pulldown_id;
static  unsigned quit_width, quit_height;

/* Information necessary to construct X font names    */
static char *fontname[] =
{
  "courier", "helvetica", "new century schoolbook", "times"
};
static char *weight[] = { "medium", "bold" };
static char *size[] = {"100", "120", "140", "180", "240"};

char *quit_label = "Quit";

/* File to be opened */
char *file_name;

/* Function prototypes */

void initapp(/* int, char **, int, int, unsigned, unsigned */);
static int  disp_menu(/* caddr_t */);
static int  quit_action(/* caddr_t */);
static void process_event();
static void hilite_button(/* XWIN * */);

static int  font_select(/* caddr_t */);
static int  wt_select(/* caddr_t */);
static int  size_select(/* caddr_t */);

static void load_file(/* char *filename */);
static void apply_font();
static void display_lines();
static void scroll_lines(/* int direction, int numlines */);

/* Windows in the application */

Window dWin;
XWIN    *menubar, *PullDown[3];

/*-----------------------------------------------------------*/
main(argc, argv)
int argc;
char **argv;
{
    XWIN       *QuitButton, *which_xwin;
    XGCValues xgcv;
    int        i, yp, xp1, xp2;

    xwin_init();
```

continues

Listing 10.1. continued

```
    initapp(argc, argv, 20, 20, 500, 400);

/* Get file name from command line */
    for (i = 1; i < argc; i += 2)
    {
        if(strcmp("-file", argv[i]) == 0)
        {
            file_name = argv[i+1];
            break;
        }
    }
    if(i >= argc)
    {
        fprintf(stderr, "Need: viewfile -file <file_name>\n");
        exit(1);
    }

/* Create the "Quit" button */
    quit_width = XTextWidth(theFontStruct, quit_label,
                            strlen(quit_label)) + 4;
    quit_height = theFontStruct->max_bounds.ascent +
                  theFontStruct->max_bounds.descent + 4;

    QuitButton = MakeXButton(1, 1, quit_width, quit_height,
                             1, theFGpix, theBGpix, theMain,
                             quit_label, quit_action, NULL);

/* Create a menubar */
    menubar = MakeXMenu(quit_width+16, 1, 1, theFGpix, theBGpix,
                theMain, MENUBAR_STYLE,
                "Font",   disp_menu, (caddr_t)&zero,
                "Weight", disp_menu, (caddr_t)&one,
                "Size",   disp_menu, (caddr_t)&two,
                NULL);

    yp = quit_height + 10;

    xp1 = quit_width+16 + XTextWidth(theFontStruct,
                "Font", strlen("Font")) + 8;

    xp2 = xp1 + XTextWidth(theFontStruct,
                "Weight", strlen("Weight")) + 8;

/* Create the pull-down menus */
    PullDown[0] = MakeXMenu(0, yp, 1, theFGpix, theBGpix,
                theMain, PULLDOWN_STYLE,
                "Courier",    font_select, (caddr_t)&zero,
                "Helvetica",  font_select, (caddr_t)&one,
                "New Century Schoolbook",
                              font_select, (caddr_t)&two,
                "Times",      font_select, (caddr_t)&three,
                NULL);

    PullDown[1] = MakeXMenu(xp1, yp, 1, theFGpix, theBGpix,
                theMain, PULLDOWN_STYLE,
```

```
                          "Medium",   wt_select, (caddr_t)&zero,
                          "Bold",     wt_select, (caddr_t)&one,
                          NULL);

        PullDown[2] = MakeXMenu(xp2, yp, 1, theFGpix, theBGpix,
                          theMain, PULLDOWN_STYLE,
                          " 10pt",        size_select, (caddr_t)&zero,
                          " 12pt",        size_select, (caddr_t)&one,
                          " 14pt",        size_select, (caddr_t)&two,
                          " 18pt",        size_select, (caddr_t)&three,
                          " 24pt",        size_select, (caddr_t)&four,
                          NULL);

/* Set up a GC to display text */

    fbuf.gc = XCreateGC(theDisplay, theMain, 0, 0);
    XCopyGC(theDisplay, theGC, GCForeground | GCBackground |
            GCFont, fbuf.gc);

/* Set up a GC to highlight the buttons */

    invertGC = XCreateGC(theDisplay, theMain, 0, 0);
    XCopyGC(theDisplay, theGC, GCForeground | GCBackground,
            invertGC);
    XSetFunction(theDisplay, invertGC, GXinvert);
    XSetPlaneMask(theDisplay, invertGC, theFGpix^theBGpix);

/* Add ButtonRelease to the event selection of the main
 * window so that we can detect when the user releases
 * the button without selecting any menu item.
 */
    AddNewEvent(theMain, ButtonReleaseMask|StructureNotifyMask);

/* Create and map a window that serves as the file display area */
    dWin = XCreateSimpleWindow(theDisplay, theMain, 1,
            quit_height+8, 500, 400, 1, theFGpix, theBGpix);

    XSelectInput(theDisplay, dWin, ExposureMask |
                ButtonPressMask|OwnerGrabButtonMask|
                ButtonReleaseMask | StructureNotifyMask |
                KeyPressMask);

    XMapRaised(theDisplay, dWin);

/* Load the file */
    load_file(file_name);
    fbuf.lstart = fbuf.lines;
    apply_font();
    fbuf.rexp = XCreateRegion();

/* Event handling loop--keep processing events until done */

    while (!AppDone)
        process_event();

/* Close connection to display and exit */
```

continues

Listing 10.1. continued

```
    XCloseDisplay(theDisplay);
    exit(0);
}
/*------------------------------------------------------------*/
/*  p r o c e s s _ e v e n t
 *
 *  Retrieve an event and process it...
 */
static void process_event()
{
    XWIN        *which_xwin;

/* Get the next event from Xlib */
    XNextEvent(theDisplay, &theEvent);

/* If main window is resized, we must resize dWin */
    if(theEvent.xany.window == theMain &&
        theEvent.type == ConfigureNotify)
    {
        XResizeWindow(theDisplay, dWin, theEvent.xconfigure.width,
                theEvent.xconfigure.height - quit_height - 8);
    }

/* Handle events for the dWin, the text display window */
    if(theEvent.xany.window == dWin)
    {
        switch (theEvent.type)
        {
            case Expose:
            {
/* Accumulate exposed areas in a region */
                XRectangle r;
                r.x = theEvent.xexpose.x;
                r.y = theEvent.xexpose.y;
                r.width = theEvent.xexpose.width;
                r.height = theEvent.xexpose.height;

                XUnionRectWithRegion(&r, fbuf.rexp, fbuf.rexp);
                if(fbuf.dwidth == 0 ¦¦ fbuf.dheight == 0)
                {
                    Window rid;
                    int junk;
/* Get dimensions of this window */
                    XGetGeometry(theDisplay, theMain, &rid, &junk,
                &junk, &fbuf.dwidth, &fbuf.dheight, &junk, &junk);
                    fbuf.dheight -= (quit_height+8);
                }
                if(theEvent.xexpose.count == 0) display_lines();
                break;
            }

            case KeyPress:
            {
                char    xlat[MAX_MAPPING];
                KeySym  key;
                int     count;
```

```
/* Translate keycode into keysym and string */
                count = XLookupString(&theEvent, xlat,
                            MAX_MAPPING, &key, None);
/* Up and Down arrows */
                if(key == XK_Up)
                    scroll_lines(SCROLL_DOWN, 1);

                if(key == XK_Down)
                    scroll_lines(SCROLL_UP, 1);

/* Is it Ctrl+D or Ctrl+U? */
                if(theEvent.xkey.state & ControlMask)
                {
                    if(key == XK_l)
/* Refresh display */    XClearArea(theDisplay, dWin,
                                0,0,0,0,True);
                    if(key == XK_u)
                        scroll_lines(SCROLL_DOWN,
                            fbuf.dheight/fbuf.lstart->height-1);
                    if(key == XK_d)
                        scroll_lines(SCROLL_UP,
                            fbuf.dheight/fbuf.lstart->height-1);
                }
            }
            break;
        case ConfigureNotify:
            fbuf.dwidth = theEvent.xconfigure.width;
            fbuf.dheight = theEvent.xconfigure.height;
            XClearArea(theEvent.xany.display, dWin,
                0, 0, 0, 0, True);
        break;
    }
}
/************* Process events for other windows  *************/
/* Next, retrieve the XWIN data from Xlib using the
 * context manager routine XFindContext
 */
    if(XFindContext(theDisplay, theEvent.xany.window,
            xwin_context, (caddr_t *) &which_xwin) == 0)
    {
/* Call the event handler of this XWIN structure */
        if (*(which_xwin->event_handler) != NULL)
            (*(which_xwin->event_handler))(which_xwin);
    }

/* Handle EnterNotify and LeaveNotify events for the buttons */
    if(theEvent.type == EnterNotify ||
        theEvent.type == LeaveNotify)
                        hilite_button(which_xwin);

    if(PullDownOn && theEvent.type == ButtonRelease)
        PullDownOn = 0;

}
/*-----------------------------------------------------------*/
static int disp_menu(data)
caddr_t data;
```

continues

Listing 10.1. continued

```
{
    XWIN    *which_xwin;
    int     menu_number;

/* Display the PullDown menu and process events until a
 * choice is made
 */
    menu_number = * ((int *) data);
    pulldown_id = PullDown[menu_number]->xid;
    XMapRaised(theDisplay, pulldown_id);
    PullDownOn = 1;

    while(PullDownOn)
        process_event();

/* Unmap the pull-down menu window */
    XUnmapWindow(theDisplay, pulldown_id);

    return 1;
}
/*-----------------------------------------------------------*/
/*  q u i t _ a c t i o n
 *
 *  This routine is called when a ButtonPress event occurs in
 *  the quit window.
 */
static int quit_action(data)
caddr_t data;
{
/* Set the done flag */
    AppDone = 1;
    return 1;
}
/*-----------------------------------------------------------*/
/*  h i l i t e _ b u t t o n
 *
 *  Highlight a button window by inverting it
 */
static void hilite_button(p_xwin)
XWIN *p_xwin;
{
    int i, go_on = 0;
/* Check whether window's parent is one of the pull-down menus */
    for(i = 0; i < 3; i++)
    {
        if(p_xwin->parent == PullDown[i]->xid)
        {
            go_on = 1;
            break;
        }
    }
    if (!go_on) return;

/* Invert a rectangle large enough so that the button window
 * gets highlighted
 */
```

```
    XFillRectangle(theDisplay, p_xwin->xid, invertGC,
                   0, 0, 1024, 1024);
    XFlush(theDisplay);
}
/*-------------------------------------------------------------*/
/*  f o n t _ s e l e c t
 *
 *  Process a font selection
 *
 */
static int font_select(data)
caddr_t data;
{
    int font = *((int *)data);
    PullDownOn = 0;
    if(font != fbuf.font)
    {
        fbuf.font = font;
        apply_font();
/* Clear the display window so that text is displayed again */
        XClearArea(theDisplay, dWin, 0, 0, 0, 0, True);
    }
    return 1;
}
/*-------------------------------------------------------------*/
/*  w t _ s e l e c t
 *
 *  Font weight changed.
 *
 */
static int wt_select(data)
caddr_t data;
{
    int weight = *((int *)data);
    PullDownOn = 0;
    if(weight != fbuf.weight)
    {
        fbuf.weight = weight;
        apply_font();
/* Clear the display window so that text is displayed again */
        XClearArea(theDisplay, dWin, 0, 0, 0, 0, True);
    }
    return 1;
}
/*-------------------------------------------------------------*/
/*  s i z e _ s e l e c t
 *
 *  New size font selected
 *
 */
static int size_select(data)
caddr_t data;
{
    int size = *((int *)data);
    PullDownOn = 0;
    if(size != fbuf.size)
    {
```

continues

Listing 10.1. continued

```
        fbuf.size = size;
        apply_font();
/* Clear the display window so that text is displayed again */
        XClearArea(theDisplay, dWin, 0, 0, 0, 0, True);
    }
    return 1;
}
/*--------------------------------------------------------*/
/*  l o a d _ f i l e
 *
 *  Read in file to be displayed
 *
 */
static void load_file(filename)
char *filename;
{
    FILE    *fp;
    D_LINE *p_l = NULL, *p_l_prev = NULL;
    char    buf[MAXCHARS];

/* Open the file */
    if((fp = fopen(filename, "r")) == NULL)
    {
        fprintf(stderr, "Cannot open: %s\n", filename);
        exit(1);
    }

/* Read each line and store in linked list of D_LINE structs  */
    while((fgets(buf, MAXCHARS, fp)) != NULL)
    {
        if((p_l = (D_LINE *) calloc(1, sizeof(D_LINE))) != NULL)
        {
            if(fbuf.lines == NULL)
            {
                fbuf.lines = p_l;
            }
            else
            {
                p_l_prev->next = p_l;
                p_l->prev = p_l_prev;
            }
        }
        else
        {
/* Allocation failed...*/
            fprintf(stderr, "Failed to allocate memory for\
line data structure...\n");
            exit(1);
        }
        p_l->length = strlen(buf) - 1; /* Exclude newline */
        buf[p_l->length] = [sq]\0[sq];
        if((p_l->line = malloc(p_l->length+1)) == NULL)
        {
            fprintf(stderr, "Failed to allocate memory for\
line:\n%s\n", buf);
            exit(1);
```

```
        }
        strcpy(p_l->line, buf);
        p_l_prev = p_l;
        fbuf.count++;
    }
    printf("%d lines loaded from %s\n", fbuf.count, filename);

/* Close the file */
    fclose(fp);
}
/*-----------------------------------------------------------*/
/*  a p p l y _ f o n t
 *
 *  Set up a new font for use. Also compute screen areas
 *  occupied by each line.
 */
static void apply_font()
{
    D_LINE     *p_l;
    int        dir, ascent, descent;
    char       fname[120];       /* Room for font's name */
    XCharStruct cinfo;
    int        font = fbuf.font,
               wt = fbuf.weight,
               sz = fbuf.size;
/* Construct font's name */
    sprintf(fname, "*adobe-%s-%s-r*%s*", fontname[font],
            weight[wt], size[sz]);

    printf("Font = %s\n", fname);

/* Free the font, if necessary */
    if(fbuf.fstruct != NULL && fbuf.fstruct != theFontStruct)
        XFreeFont(theDisplay, fbuf.fstruct);

/* Load the new font */
    if ((fbuf.fstruct = XLoadQueryFont(theDisplay, fname))
        == NULL)
    {
        fprintf(stderr, "%s: display %s cannot load font %s\n",
            theAppName, DisplayString(theDisplay), fname);

/* Set fbuf.fstruct to our default font */
        fbuf.fstruct = theFontStruct;
    }

/* Compute bounding box of each line in the buffer */
    for(p_l = fbuf.lines; p_l != NULL; p_l = p_l->next)
    {
        XTextExtents(fbuf.fstruct, p_l->line, p_l->length,
            &dir, &ascent, &descent, &cinfo);
        p_l->lbearing = cinfo.lbearing;
        p_l->rbearing = cinfo.rbearing;
        p_l->height = ascent + descent;
    }

/* Set the font in the GC */
```

continues

Listing 10.1. continued

```
    XSetFont(theDisplay, fbuf.gc, fbuf.fstruct->fid);
}
/*------------------------------------------------------------*/
/* d i s p l a y _ l i n e s
 *
 * Displays the lines in the text window
 */
static void display_lines()
{
    int    xpos, ypos = 0, width;
    D_LINE *p_l;

/* If a full update is needed, alter the exposed region */
/*    if(full_update)
    {
        XRectangle r;
        r.x = r.y = 0;
        r.width = fbuf.dwidth;
        r.height = fbuf.dheight;

        XUnionRectWithRegion(&r, fbuf.rexp, fbuf.rexp);
        full_update = False;
    }
*/

/* Set the accumulated exposed regions as the clip mask */
    XSetRegion(theDisplay, fbuf.gc, fbuf.rexp);

/* Display the lines starting with the first one. Draw
 * a string ONLY if it falls in the exposed region.
 */

    for(p_l = fbuf.lstart; p_l != NULL && ypos < fbuf.dheight;
        p_l = p_l->next)
    {
        xpos = LEFT_MARGIN - p_l->lbearing;
        ypos += p_l->height;
        if(XRectInRegion(fbuf.rexp, xpos, ypos - p_l->height,
                    p_l->lbearing + p_l->rbearing,
                    p_l->height) != RectangleOut)
        {
/* Yes. String's rectangle is partially in region. Draw it */
            XDrawImageString(theDisplay, dWin, fbuf.gc,
                    xpos, ypos, p_l->line, p_l->length);
        }
    }

/* Destroy current region and create a new "empty" one */
    XDestroyRegion(fbuf.rexp);
    fbuf.rexp = XCreateRegion();
}
/*------------------------------------------------------------*/
/* s c r o l l _ l i n e s
 *
 * Scroll the text display by a specified amount.
 */
```

```
static void scroll_lines(direction, numlines)
int direction;
int numlines;
{
    int i, ysrc, yclr, numpix = 0;
    D_LINE *p_l;

/* Figure out how many pixels to scroll */

    switch(direction)
    {
        case SCROLL_UP:
            for(i = 0, p_l = fbuf.lstart;
                i < numlines && p_l->next != NULL;
                i++, p_l = p_l->next) numpix += p_l->height;
            ysrc = numpix;
            yclr = fbuf.dheight - numpix;
            break;

        case SCROLL_DOWN:
            for(i = 0, p_l = fbuf.lstart;
                i < numlines && p_l->prev != NULL;
                i++, p_l = p_l->prev) numpix += p_l->height;
            ysrc = 0;
            yclr = 0;
            break;
    }
    if(numpix == 0)
    {
/* No need to scroll */
        XBell(theDisplay, 0);
        return;
    }
/* Adjust first line to display */
    fbuf.lstart = p_l;

/* Copy area */
    XSetClipMask(theDisplay, fbuf.gc, None);
    XCopyArea(theDisplay, dWin, dWin, fbuf.gc,
              0, ysrc, fbuf.dwidth, fbuf.dheight - numpix,
              0, numpix - ysrc);

/* Clear new rectangle so that it is redrawn */

    XClearArea(theDisplay, dWin, 0, yclr,
               fbuf.dwidth, numpix, True);
}
```

Data Structures in *viewfile*

The viewfile program assumes that it is reading a text file with lines terminated by newline ('\n') characters. The function load_file reads the lines using the C library routine fgets. The lines are stored in doubly-linked D_LINE structures in which each structure includes pointers to the previous and the next structure. The D_LINE structure is defined as follows:

```
typedef struct D_LINE      /* Holds info on each line    */
{
    struct D_LINE *prev;   /* Pointer to previous line   */
    struct D_LINE *next;   /* Pointer to next line       */
    char          *line;   /* Null-terminated line       */
    short         length;  /* Number of characters in line*/
    short         lbearing;/* Left and right edges of     */
    short         rbearing;/* rectangle covered by line   */
    short         height;  /* Height of text string       */
} D_LINE;
```

The last three members of each D_LINE structure are initialized later by the apply_font function. These hold information about the bounding box of each line for the current font.

The aggregate information about the file's text and information necessary to display the lines are stored in a statically allocated D_LBUF structure named fbuf:

```
typedef struct D_LBUF      /* Info on entire buffer     */
{
    D_LINE      *lines;  /* First line in buffer        */
    D_LINE      *lstart; /* First line in window        */
    GC          gc;      /* GC used to display text      */
    Region      rexp;    /* Current exposed region       */
    XFontStruct *fstruct;/* Info on current font         */
    int         font;    /* Currently selected font      */
    int         weight;  /* weight and                   */
    int         size;    /* size                         */
    unsigned    dwidth;  /* Width of text display area   */
    unsigned    dheight; /* Height of text display area  */
    long        count;   /* How many lines in buffer     */
} D_LBUF;

static D_LBUF fbuf = { NULL,NULL, None, None, None, 0, 0, 0,
                       0, 0, 0};
```

The lines field in fbuf points to the first D_LINE structure holding the first line of the file, and lstart is the first line being displayed in the window. The width and height of the text display window and information on the currently selected font are also part of this structure.

Smart Handling of *Expose* Events

Chapter 9, "Drawing Graphics," mentions that a smart way to handle Expose events is to keep track of the exposed rectangular regions and handle the event when the Expose event with 0 count arrives. The Region in the D_LBUF structure is used to implement this strategy.

As shown in the process_event function of Listing 10.1, the XUnionRectWithRegion function is used to add each rectangle from the Expose events (for the text-display window dWin) to the region rexp in the fbuf structure. When the Expose event with a 0 count arrives, the display_lines function is called to update the window.

The display_lines function also uses a smart way to draw the text. First it calls XSetRegion to set the accumulated region, fbuf.rexp, as the clip mask of the GC. Then it uses the following code to draw the text:

```
/*-- From: "display_lines" function --*/

    int    xpos, ypos;
    D_LINE *p_l;

/* Display the lines starting with the first one. Draw
 * a string ONLY if it falls in the exposed region.
 */

    for(p_l = fbuf.lstart; p_l != NULL && ypos < fbuf.dheight;
        p_l = p_l->next)
    {
        xpos = LEFT_MARGIN - p_l->lbearing;
        ypos += p_l->height;
        if(XRectInRegion(fbuf.rexp, xpos, ypos - p_l->height,
                     p_l->lbearing + p_l->rbearing,
                     p_l->height) != RectangleOut)
        {
/* Yes. String's rectangle is partially in region. Draw it */
            XDrawImageString(theDisplay, dWin, fbuf.gc,
                     xpos, ypos, p_l->line, p_l->length);
        }
    }
```

This function starts with the line pointed by `fbuf.lstart` and loops until there are no more lines or until the current line goes outside the display window. For each line, the `display_lines` function tests whether the line's bounding box (which is precomputed and saved in that line's `D_LINE` structure) intersects the exposed region. It draws only those lines that partially lie in the exposed region. The string is displayed using `XDrawImageString` so that the foreground and background are altered at the same time.

Before returning, `display_lines` uses the following code to destroy the current exposed region and create an empty region for the next `Expose` event:

```
/* Destroy current region and create a new "empty" one */
    XDestroyRegion(fbuf.rexp);
    fbuf.rexp = XCreateRegion();
```

Scrolling the Text

Scrolling is another new idea introduced in Listing 10.1. As shown in Figure 10.6, scrolling can be implemented by copying from one rectangle to another. For example, to scroll a window down, you can use `XCopyArea` to copy part of the window (see Figure 10.6), then clear the area to be redrawn with a call to `XClearArea`. Pressing the arrow keys sets the amount to be scrolled to the height of a line in pixels. When Ctrl+D and Ctrl+U are pressed, the contents of the window are scrolled by an amount that roughly equals the height of all lines in the window.

In `viewfile.c`, scrolling is implemented by the last function in Listing 10.1, `scroll_lines`. You can see how it is done by studying this function. The contents of the window are not explicitly redrawn; an `Expose` event is generated by clearing the area that needs redrawing.

Figure 10.6.
Scrolling by copying the area.

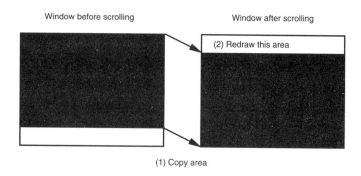

Window before scrolling   Window after scrolling

(2) Redraw this area

(1) Copy area

Font Selections

The `viewfile` program enables the user to set the typeface (under the Font menu item), the weight, and the size of a font. Font names in X can be constructed from these components. Because Xlib allows asterisk wildcard characters (*) in font names, the name of the font is constructed from these three components using asterisks for undefined fields.

The `apply_font` function takes care of changing fonts. It checks to make sure that the font has really changed (because the user can always select the same typeface again). If there is a change of font, `apply_font` first constructs the name of the font. Then it frees the `XFontStruct` of the old font, loads the new font, and computes the sizes of the bounding boxes of all lines in the list of `D_LINE` structures. Finally, it sets the new font in the `GC` to be used for text output.

You can use the `viewfile` program's technique for handling multiple fonts as a role model for your application. This method still relies on a standard set of fonts (Adobe and Bitstream) being available in all servers.

Construction of the *viewfile* Program

As with the example programs in the last chapter, `viewfile` builds upon the tools developed in Chapters 7, "Creating and Managing Windows," and 8, "Handling Events." You can build the `viewfile` program by adapting the following makefile to suit your system's needs:

```
# Some common definitions...

RM = rm -f
CC = cc

# Compiler flags, paths for include files and libraries

CFLAGS =
INCLUDES = -I. -I/usr/include -I/usr/include/X11
LIBS = -lX11

# Rule to create .o files from .c files
.c.o:
    $(RM) $@
    $(CC) -c $(CFLAGS) $(INCLUDES) $*.c
```

```
# Targets...

all::    viewfile

viewfile.o: viewfile.c app_glob.c xwins.h

initapp.o: initapp.c app_glob.c

xwinutil.o: xwinutil.c app_glob.c xwins.h

xbutton.o: xbutton.c app_glob.c xwins.h

xmenu.o: xmenu.c app_glob.c xwins.h

viewfile: viewfile.o initapp.o xwinutil.o xbutton.o \
      xmenu.o
    $(RM) $@
    $(CC) -o $@ $(CFLAGS) viewfile.o initapp.o \
        xwinutil.o xbutton.o xmenu.o \
        $(LIBS)
```

Summary

X draws text the same way it draws any graphics—using all the graphics attributes specified in a GC. Text output differs from arbitrary graphics only in what is drawn. Text is specified by an array of characters, each encoded according to some standard such as ASCII or ISO Latin 1. The character shapes are stored in an array of bitmaps (or glyphs) called a font. X draws each character indexing into the font, retrieving its bitmap, and filling the pixels with foreground and background colors, using the bitmap as a mask.

Fonts are resources stored in the X server. A font has several characteristics, such as typeface, weight, size, and style. In X, the name of a font can be constructed from the names of these components. This can be used to handle a selection of fonts in an application.

Applications have to load a font before using it. Xlib includes functions to load a font and get information on the sizes of the characters when displayed in that font. Xlib also provides utility functions that compute the sizes of the rectangular area that will be occupied by a text string when displayed in a specific font.

There are three text drawing functions in Xlib: XDrawString, XDrawImageString, and XDrawText. The first two functions draw single strings using the font specified in a GC. XDrawText enables you to draw several strings in varying fonts on the same line.

This chapter includes an example program, viewfile, that enables users to view the contents of a text file in a selected font. The program illustrates how to handle multiple fonts in an application and how to scroll the contents of a window.

## Chapter 11

Using Color in X

Previous chapters describe how to create windows in X and how to display graphics and text in them. From these discussions, you know that each window has a background color and a border color. You also know that the graphics context (GC), which controls the appearance of all output, includes foreground and background colors as attributes that are used by the graphics and text output functions. You know that pixel values are the values used when specifying colors in a GC or for a window's background. In Chapter 3, "Exploring X Applications," you learned how to name colors, so that as a user you can set the colors in an application.

Workstations differ significantly in the way they handle color. Luckily, X11 incorporates an abstract color model that captures most of the commonly encountered color handling capabilities. To use color in an X application, you need to understand the color model used by X. This chapter describes this model and how you can use color in your X applications.

Color in Display Hardware

Let's begin with a discussion of how color is handled by most workstations. Most graphics displays consist of two components:

- ✦ A graphics adapter that is either a plug-in card or some circuitry built into the system's motherboard
- ✦ A monitor that usually is a cathode ray tube (CRT, often referred to as the display screen or, simply, screen) where the graphics output appears

Grayscale Raster Displays and Frame Buffer

Most grayscale displays used in X workstations and X terminals are raster displays that construct an image by sweeping an electron beam back and forth across the face of the monitor. As shown in Figure 11.1, each horizontal sweep across the screen constitutes a *raster line* and a large number of such raster lines make up one *frame* of the image.

Figure 11.1.
Raster scan CRT.

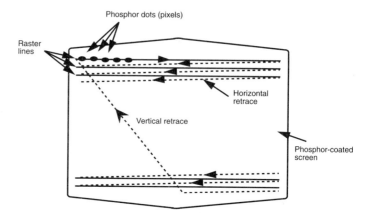

The source of the electron beam is called the *electron gun.* The screen itself is coated with an array of dots of phosphors (the physical pixels) that glow when hit by the electron beam. The intensity of the electron beam controls the brightness of the phosphor it hits. Thus, a line of the image can be generated by controlling the intensity of the beam as it scans across the screen. The phosphor fades in a short while, but if the lines are redrawn repeatedly, your persistence of vision creates an illusion of a steady image. Most display monitors redraw an entire screenful of raster lines 50 to 70 times a second.

Frame Buffer

Because the image corresponds to an intensity level for each pixel on the screen, you can think of a raster image as a two-dimensional array of values. Indeed, graphics adapters store the intensity level of each pixel (the gray level) in a block of memory known as the *frame buffer* or *video memory.* Recall that these values are known as pixel values.

Each pixel value is represented by a fixed number of bits—usually 4 or 8, even 24 or 32 in higher-performance displays. Conceptually, you can think of the frame buffer organized as a number of bit planes with as many planes as there are bits in each pixel value (see Figure 11.2). The number of bit planes is also known as the depth of the display.

Figure 11.2.

A 4-bit plane frame buffer with a 16-bit wide look-up table.

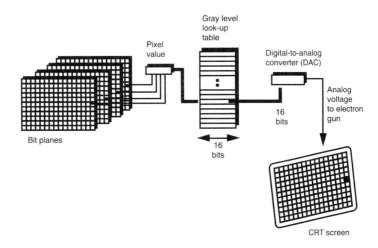

Look-Up Tables

The graphics adapter generates the signals that control the intensity of the beam. It does this in accordance with the contents of the frame buffer location that corresponds to the current pixel on the screen. If a 4- or 8-bit pixel value is used directly as the intensity of the on-screen pixel, there can be only 16 (2^4) or 256 (2^8) fixed levels of gray in the image.

A smarter approach is to allow many more gray levels, but use only $2n$ of these at any time, where n is the number of bits in the pixel value. As shown in Figure 11.2, this can be done by using the pixel value as an index into a look-up table. If each entry in the look-up table is a 16-bit value, there will be $2^{16} = 65,536$ possible gray levels. Of course, with 4-bit pixel values, only 16 of these levels can be used at any time.

Figure 11.2 shows an additional component, a digital-to-analog converter (DAC), that converts the digital gray level from the look-up table into a continuously varying voltage that can be used to control the CRT's electron guns. This is necessary because the CRTs in most workstations are analog devices that expect a continuous electrical voltage for the intensity level.

Color Raster Displays

Color displays represent any color by a combination of the three primary colors: red (R), green (G), and blue (B). A color CRT uses three electron beams—one for each primary color.

The screen in a color CRT has a repeated triangular pattern of red, green, and blue phosphor dots. Each phosphor glows in its color when the electron beam impinges on it. As shown in Figure 11.3, a perforated metal screen, known as the *shadow mask*, ensures that each electron beam excites the correct phosphor. By varying the intensity of the electron beams, many shades of colors can be displayed.

Figure 11.3.

Phosphors and shadow mask in a color CRT.

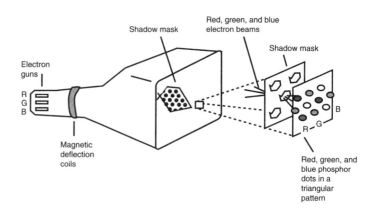

Color Frame Buffers

As in a grayscale display, the frame buffer of a color display stores the information that controls the intensity of each electron beam. There are two ways of using the information stored in the frame buffer:

✦ Directly, as intensity levels of R, G, and B colors

✦ Indirectly, as indices in a color look-up table

Figure 11.4 shows the situation for a 24-bit color frame buffer. In this case, 8-bit planes are assigned to each primary color. Each 8-bit value drives an 8-bit digital-to-analog circuit (DAC) whose output is used as the intensity of one of the electron guns. This scheme allows 256 (2^8) intensity levels for each of the red, green, and blue colors. Thus, the display can show 256x256x256 = 16,777,216 (16 million) distinct colors at once. Such high-performance frame buffers are often known as *full color frame buffers* because the entire range of allowable colors is available for use any time.

Figure 11.4.

A 24-bit full color frame buffer.

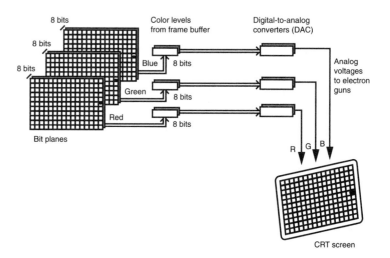

Colormaps

In color displays with fewer bit planes, the full color scheme is more appropriate with intermediate look-up tables for each primary color. These look-up tables are called *color look-up tables* or *colormaps*. There are two types of colormaps:

✦ Each entry of the colormap specifies the intensity of one of the R, G, and B colors. In this case, there are three colormaps, one for each of the R, G, and B colors.

✦ Each entry in the colormap specifies a single combination of R, G, and B intensities. In this case, a single colormap defines the available colors.

Figure 11.5 illustrates the first type of colormap; in this case, each 12-bit pixel value is decomposed into three 4-bit values, one each for the red, green, and blue components. These 4-bit values are used as indices into three colormaps containing 8-bit intensity values for each color. The intensity value from the colormaps go to digital-to-analog converters whose outputs control the intensities of the red, green, and blue guns. With this scheme, there can be 4,096 (2^{12}) simultaneous colors out of a possible 256x256x256 = 16,777,216 (because each colormap is 8 bits wide). Without the colormaps, there would be only 4,096 distinct colors.

Figure 11.5.

A 12-bit full color frame buffer with an 8-bit colormap for red, green, and blue.

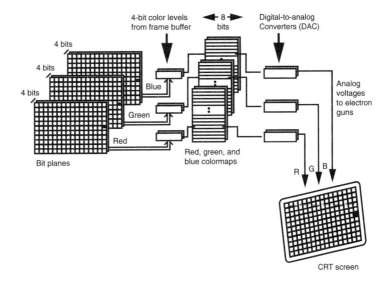

The second kind of colormap, often employed in displays with 4- or 8-bit frame buffers, uses the entire pixel value as an index into a single colormap that defines the RGB levels. In this case, each colormap entry decomposes into intensity levels of the red, green, and blue electron guns. Figure 11.6 shows a 4-bit frame buffer that indexes into an 18-bit wide colormap. The 18-bit value in each colormap cell is interpreted as three 6-bit quantities, one each for the R, G, and B components. Because each component can have 64 (2^6) possible values, this approach allows a total of 262,144 (64x64x64) possible colors, of which only 16 (2^4) can be used at any one time.

Figure 11.6.

A 4-bit color frame buffer with an 18-bit wide colormap (6 bits each for red, green, and blue).

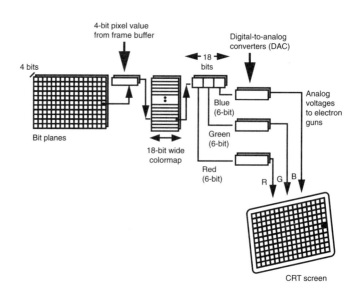

NOTE:

Colormap entries specifying R, G, B levels are called *RGB values.*

Most color workstations use this approach and they typically provide an 8-bit frame buffer with a 24-bit wide colormap (8 bits each per R, G, and B). Such color displays support 256 simultaneous colors from a palette of over 16 million (256x256x256 = 16,777,216) colors.

Concept of Color in X

There are several ways to implement a color frame buffer in hardware. Nevertheless, enough commonality exists among the color handling schemes to allow an abstract model that can handle a wide variety of color and grayscale displays. This section describes the X color model, many aspects of which are directly related to the hardware implementations of frame buffers.

Common Features of Frame Buffers

If you look carefully at the various ways frame buffers are implemented in hardware, you immediately notice that all graphics displays with multiple bit planes fall into one of two categories: color or grayscale.

Furthermore, in color frame buffers, the pixel values can be used in two ways:

♦ Decomposing the bits in each pixel value into fields that are used to look up the R, G, and B levels from three separate colormaps (see Figure 11.5)

✦ Using the entire pixel value as an index for a single colormap, which yields the RGB components of the desired color (see Figure 11.6)

Because grayscale displays control only the intensity of the pixels, the entire pixel value is used to look up the gray level from a single colormap.

You can think of all color and grayscale displays as frame buffers that store pixel values that are used to look up color or gray levels from one or more colormaps. Even the full-color display of Figure 11.4 falls into this category because that display implicitly assumes a fixed colormap that maps an index to itself.

Color displays are further classified on the basis of the number of colormaps: a single colormap indexed by the pixel value or three separate colormaps (one each for R, G, and B) indexed by specific bits of the pixel value.

Visuals

X encapsulates the common features of the display hardware in a data structure called the `Visual`. However, it adds an important twist to encourage sharing of colormaps: X allows colormaps to be read-only or read-write. Cells in the read-write colormaps can be changed dynamically; read-only colormaps are fixed.

Each screen in an X display has a `Visual` structure that characterizes its capabilities. The `class` member of the `Visual` structure indicates these capabilities. Figure 11.7 shows the classification of color and grayscale displays based on the common features of the hardware together with X's notion of read-write and read-only colormaps. As shown in the figure, this classification of displays results in six distinct classes of `Visual`, identified by the following constants (defined in `<X11/X.h>`):

✦ `DirectColor` visual class models the display shown in Figure 11.5, in which the pixel value is decomposed into bit fields that index into individual colormaps for the R, G, and B components. The colormap entries can be changed dynamically. This visual class is common among displays with 8 or more bit planes.

✦ `TrueColor` displays are the same as `DirectColor`, but their colormaps are fixed. The full-color display illustrated in Figure 11.4 is modeled by this visual class.

✦ `PseudoColor` visual class models a commonly encountered display hardware—one wherein each pixel value looks up an RGB value and the colormap can be modified any time.

✦ `StaticColor` displays are similar to `PseudoColor` except that the colormap cannot be modified.

✦ `GrayScale` visual class models a grayscale monitor that enables the intensity map to be modified. It is the grayscale equivalent of the `PseudoColor` visual.

✦ `StaticGray` is similar to `GrayScale`, but with a fixed gray level map. Black-and-white (monochrome) displays are modeled by a `StaticGray` visual with a unity depth.

Figure 11.7.
Visual classes in X.

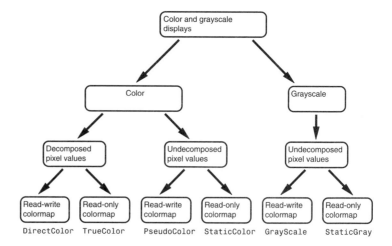

Each screen in an X display has at least one associated Visual structure. Many servers provide more than one visual for a screen. For instance, the server for an 8-bit display might provide a PseudoColor visual of depth 8 and a StaticGray visual of depth 1. Thus, the same screen can be used as a color screen or, in the case of StaticGray, as a monochrome one. Later in this chapter you learn how you can select an appropriate visual for your application.

Even if a server supports multiple visuals, one of them is the default visual. You can refer to this default visual by the macro DefaultVisual(display,screen), which returns a pointer to the Visual structure of the specified screen in the X display identified by display.

Note that when creating a window, you have to specify an associated Visual. If you use the XCreateSimpleWindow function to create a window, the window is automatically created for the default visual—the visual of the root window.

Using the DefaultVisual macro, you can easily determine the visual class of your X display screen:

```
Display    *p_disp;
int        screen;
.

.

.
display = XOpenDisplay("");
screen = DefaultScreen(p_disp);

visual = DefaultVisual(p_disp, screen);
depth = DefaultDepth(p_disp, screen); /* same as visual->depth */

printf ("Display type: \n");
if (depth == 1)
    printf("Monochrome\n");
else
{
    switch (visual->class)
    {
```

```
        case PseudoColor:
            printf("PseudoColor\n");
            break;
        case GrayScale:
            printf("GrayScale\n");
            break;
        case DirectColor:
            printf("DirectColor\n");
            break;
        case TrueColor:
            printf("TrueColor\n");
            break;
        default:
            printf("Unknown...ERROR\n");
            break;
    }
}
```

> **TIP:**
>
> The `switch` statement in this example directly uses the class member of the screen's `Visual`. Because the details of the `Visual` data structure are supposed to be hidden from the programmer, this example violates the data-hiding principle. One approach to minimize the code's dependence on the definition of `Visual` is to use a macro to access its members. For example, you might define the following:
>
> ```
> #define ClassOfVisual(v)    ((v)->class)
> ```
>
> and use `ClassOfVisual(visual)` in place of `visual->class`. That way, you can accommodate changes in the definition of `Visual` by simply redefining the macro.

Colormaps in X

As with hardware frame buffers, the X color model also uses a colormap. In X, each window has an associated colormap that determines how the pixel values are translated into colors (or gray levels in grayscale monitors). Although the hardware might allow only one colormap, X allows each window to have its own colormap—as long as the visual class of the screen is not one of TrueColor, StaticColor, or StaticGray. Before the pixel values in a window are interpreted according to such a *virtual colormap*, it has to be installed into the hardware colormap. You need a window manager to take care of this chore. By convention, most window managers implement a policy of installing a window's colormap into the hardware as soon as the window gains input focus.

A colormap is a resource of the X server. Normally, you do not have to create a new colormap for your application. When the server is started, it creates and installs a default colormap. The server usually defines only two color cells in this default colormap. The rest of the cells can be allocated and used by any X application.

Sharing the Default Colormap

Often, the default colormap has enough color cells to provide all the colors that a simple application needs. All the examples used so far in this book use the default colormap. Before using this colormap, you should understand how X expects you to share colors in a colormap.

To use colors from a colormap, you first have to find the colormap's identifier, which is a variable of type `Colormap`. When you create a new colormap, you get back an ID. For the default colormap, the colormap's ID is returned by the macro `DefaultColormap(display,screen)`, which requires you to identify the `display` and the `screen`. You can use `DefaultScreen(display)` as the `screen` argument to `DefaultColormap`.

Allocating Color Cells

When you use color in X, you have to specify a pixel value. This value implies a particular color depending on the contents of the colormap cell that it references. The first step in using a color in X is to obtain the index of a colormap cell that contains the red, green, and blue intensities appropriate for the color you want. To do this, you request that the X server allocate a colormap cell (in a specified colormap) with your color. When requesting a colormap cell, you provide the desired red, green, and blue levels; the X server returns an index that you can use as the pixel value corresponding to that color.

Because many applications may use similar colors, X provides two ways to allocate colormap cells:

+ Asking for shared read-only cells
+ Asking for private read-write cells

You can allocate shared read-only cells in any visual class, but to allocate read-write cells, the visual class must allow the colormap to be altered. That means the visual class has to be `DirectColor`, `PseudoColor`, or `GrayScale`.

For each colormap, the X server keeps track of cells currently in use. When the server receives a request for a shared read-only cell in a colormap, it determines the closest color the hardware can support. Then it searches any previously allocated read-only cells in that colormap for one that may already contain that color. If the server finds such a cell, it returns the information about that cell. Otherwise, if the visual class permits writing to the colormap, the server allocates a new cell for read-only use, loads the requested color into the cell, and returns that information.

The nice thing about shared, read-only colormap cells is that you can use them on any visual; but to allocate private, read-write colormap cells, you have to make sure the visual is `DirectColor`, `PseudoColor`, or `GrayScale`.

Private, read-write cells also have some advantages. They enable you to alter the mapping of pixels to color any time. This can be useful when displaying images—you can change the colors of an image by altering the colormap entries—without having to redraw the image with new pixel values. Also, private colormap cells can be allocated in a single contiguous block so that the pixel values are in sequence. This can be useful if the application requires that the displayed colors relate to the pixel values in a well-defined way.

When allocating colors or defining new colormap entries, you provide information about the color in an XColor structure, which is defined in <X11/Xlib.h> as the following:

```
typedef struct
{
    unsigned long  pixel; /* Pixel value (after allocation) */
    unsigned short red,   /* Red intensity   (0 - 65,535)   */
                   green, /* Green intensity (0 - 65,535)   */
                   blue;  /* Blue intensity  (0 - 65,535)   */
    char           flags; /* Used when storing colors       */
    char           pad;   /* Just so structure size is even */
};
```

You specify a color by indicating the intensities of the RGB components in the fields red, green, and blue. These intensities range from 0 to 65,535, where 0 implies no intensity and 65,535 means full intensity. The server automatically scales these values to the range of intensities needed by the display screen's hardware.

The member named pixel is the pixel value you use to display the color corresponding to the RGB value in red, green, and blue. When allocating a color, you provide the RGB values for the color and the server returns the pixel value corresponding to the colormap cell with that color.

Allocating Shared Colormap Cells

Xlib provides two functions for allocating shared, read-only colormap cells: XAllocColor and XAllocNamedColor. The XAllocColor function requires that you define an XColor structure and fill the red, green, and blue fields with the RGB levels appropriate for the color you want. You also have to specify the colormap in which you want to allocate the color. Typically, you use XAllocColor in conjunction with XParseColor, which accepts the name of a color and sets up the corresponding RGB values in an XColor structure.

To allocate a light cyan color in the default colormap and use it as the background of a window, you might use this code:

```
    Display       *p_disp;
    XColor        color;
    Colormap      default_cmap;
    unsigned long bgpixel;

    default_cmap = DefaultColormap(p_disp,
                            DefaultScreen(p_disp));

/* Try to allocate a "light cyan" colormap cell */

    if (XParseColor(p_disp, default_cmap, "light cyan",
                 &color) == 0 ||
        XAllocColor(p_disp, default_cmap, &color) == 0)
    {
/* Use white background in case of failure */
        bgpixel = WhitePixel(p_disp, DefaultScreen(p_disp));
    }
    else
    {
/* Colormap cell successfully allocated */
```

```
        bgpixel = color.pixel;
    }
    .
    .
    .
/* Use "bgpixel" as background when creating the window */
```

(See Chapter 3 for information on naming colors in X applications.)

First, `XParseColor` sets up the RGB values in `color` for the color named `light cyan`. Then, `XAllocColor` requests a read-only color cell with that RGB value. If all goes well, both functions return nonzero values and the `pixel` member of `color` contains the pixel value that you should use wherever you need the `light cyan` color. If the functions fail, you must include some means of handling the situation. In this example, if the allocation fails, the `white` is used as the background color. The server always allocates the `white` and `black` colors in the default colormap. You can refer to these colors by the macros `WhitePixel(display,screen)` and `BlackPixel(display,screen)`, respectively.

> **NOTE:**
>
> The X server provides a color database that applications can use to translate textual names of colors into red, green, and blue intensities appropriate for that particular display screen. The functions `XParseColor` and `XAllocNamedColor` use this database.

`XAllocNamedColor` is similar to `XAllocColor` except that it directly takes the name of a color as a string. For instance, when you use `XAllocNamedColor`, the earlier example of allocating a `light cyan` color cell becomes the following:

```
    XColor exact;  /* Exact RGB definition of color */

    if (XAllocNamedColor(p_disp, default_cmap, "light cyan",
                &exact, &color) == 0)
    {
/* Use white background in case of failure */
        bgpixel = WhitePixel(p_disp, DefaultScreen(p_disp));
    }
    else
    {
/* Colormap cell successfully allocated */
        bgpixel = color.pixel;
    }
```

`XAllocNamedColor` requires two `XColor` arguments. In `exact`, it returns the exact RGB value for the requested color (from the database) and in `color`, it returns the closest color supported by hardware and the pixel value corresponding to the allocated colormap cell (when allocation succeeds).

Allocating Private Colormap Cells

Some applications need colors to be allocated in the colormap in a specific way. For instance, you can display a two-dimensional array of data points as an image, wherein the color of each pixel represents a data point. When displaying such an image, you may want all pixel values in sequence so that it is easy to map the data into colors. You may also want to alter the mapping of data to colors to bring out features of the data. This type of need is best handled by allocating a contiguous block of private, read-write colormap cells.

XAllocColorCells

The `XAllocColorCells` function is a convenient way to allocate read-write color cells. Of course, before you use this function, you must make sure that the screen's visual class allows alterations to the colormap (the class must be `DirectColor`, `PseudoColor`, or `GrayScale`).

You call `XAllocColorCells` as follows:

```
Display        *p_disp;
Colormap       cmap;      /* Colormap where cells are allocated*/
Bool           contig;    /* True = allocate contiguous planes */
unsigned long planes[];  /* Array to hold plane masks         */
unsigned int  nplanes;   /* Number of planes to allocate      */
unsigned long pixels[];  /* Array to hold pixel values        */
unsigned int  npixels;   /* Number of pixels to allocate      */

XAllocColorCells(p_disp, cmap, contig, planes, nplanes, pixels,
                 npixels);
```

X requires you to specify the read-write colormap cells in a unique manner. You specify the number of pixel values, *npixels*, and the number of planes, *nplanes*. *npixels* must be positive; *nplanes* can be 0 or positive. In return, the server reserves *npixels*2nplanes colormap cells and returns the information about the usable cells in the arrays `pixels` and `planes`. There will be *npixels* values returned in `pixels` and *nplanes* bitmasks returned in the `planes` array.

The *npixels* argument to `XAllocColorCells` is *not* the total number of pixel values that you can use. To determine the pixel values that your application can use, consider the following example.

Suppose, for an 8-bit visual, you call `XAllocColorCells` requesting three pixel values and two color planes (*npixels* = 3 and *nplanes* = 2). On return from `XAllocColorCells`, the three entries in the `pixels` array and the two entries in the `planes` array are as follows (in binary):

```
pixels:    1010 0000     planes:    0000 0100
           0110 0000                0000 0001
           0001 0010
```

To arrive at the list of usable pixel values, first form the four possible combinations of masks by OR-ing together zero or more entries in the `planes` array with each other:

```
All possible combinations of plane masks:

    0000 0000
    0000 0001
    0000 0100
    0000 0101
```

Next, OR each entry in the `pixels` array with these masks. There are three entries and four masks, so you get the following 12 pixel values for your use:

```
12 pixel values:
```

```
1010 0000
1010 0001
1010 0100
1010 0101

0110 0000
0110 0001
0110 0100
0110 0101

0001 0000
0001 0001
0001 0100
0001 0101
```

If the `contig` flag is `True`, the allocated planes will be contiguous.

If you ask for too many color cells, `XAllocColorCells` is likely to fail. When it fails, `XAllocColorCells` returns 0; otherwise, it returns a nonzero status.

Color Storage

Once you have allocated private, read-write color cells, you must store colors in these cells before using them. Use `XStoreColor` to change the RGB value corresponding to a single pixel value. You have to use an `XColor` structure to do this. Set the `red`, `green`, and `blue` fields to the desired levels of the primary color. Set `pixel` to the pixel value of an allocated (read-write) cell. Then call `XStoreColor`:

```
    Colormap  colormap;
    XColor    color;
/* Assume that colorcell is a previously allocated read-write
 * cell. The following code stores "red" in this cell
 */
    color.pixel = colorcell;
    color.red = 65535;
    color.green = 0;
    color.blue = 0;
    color.flags = DoRed | DoGreen | DoBlue;
    XStoreColor(p_disp, colormap, &color);
```

The `flags` field in `color` indicates which of the primary color levels in the colormap cell should be updated.

To set a single colormap cell with a color identified by a name rather than the RGB components, you can use `XStoreNamedColor`. For example, to set pixel value `colorcell` to `red`, use the following:

```
XStoreNamedColor(p_disp, colormap, "red", colorcell,
                 DoRed | DoGreen | DoBlue);
```

If you have several read-write colormap cells to initialize, you can use `XStoreColors` to store colors into them at once. As expected, this function takes an array of `XColor` structures and the number of such structures as arguments:

```
XColor colors[];  /* Array of colors       */
int    ncolors;   /* Number in colors array */
.
.
/* Set up the "colors" array before calling XStoreColors */

XStoreColors(p_disp, colormap, colors, ncolors);
```

Usage Strategies

The specification of private colormap cells—with the number of pixels and planes—seems rather complicated, but this flexibility enables you to use the facility in several different ways.

One specific use is to obtain a number of colormap entries that need not be related in any way. For this case, simply specify *n*pixels as the cells you need and provide 0 as the number of planes.

If you want a number of contiguous cells for an image processing application, you can get the cells by specifying *n*pixels as 1, and *n*planes as the logarithm (to the base 2) of the required colormap cells.

Another way to use private cells is for drawing overlays. For example, suppose you want to draw some figures in four colors, but sometimes you want to display all the figures in a fifth color. Use the following steps to do this:

1. Call XAllocColorCells with *n*pixels set to 4 and *n*planes set to 1. This gives you a total of 8 pixel values—4 *base* pixel values returned in the pixels array and another 4 *alternate* values obtained by OR-ing each of the base values with the planemask.

2. Define the base pixel values to the RGB colors you want.

3. Define all the alternate pixels to the same fifth overlay color.

4. Convert everything into the overlay color by setting, in all the figures, the bit indicated by planemask.

Here is an example with two colors and one plane:

```
Display       *p_disp;
Colormap      cmap;
unsigned long colorcells[2];
unsigned long planemask;
.
.
colormap = DefaultColormap(p_disp, DefaultScreen(p_disp));

if(XAllocColorCells(p_disp, colormap, True, &planemask, 1,
                    colorcells, 2))
{
/* Define "base" pixel values */

    color.pixel = colorcells[0];
    color.red = 65535;
    color.green = 0;
    color.blue = 0;
```

```
        color.flags = DoRed | DoGreen | DoBlue;
        XStoreColor(p_disp, xswa.colormap, &color);

        color.red = 0;
        color.green = 65535;
        color.blue = 0;
        color.pixel = colorcells[1];
        color.flags = DoRed|DoGreen|DoGreen;
        XStoreColor(p_disp, xswa.colormap, &color);

/* Define "alternate" pixel values */

        color.pixel = colorcells[0] | planemask;
        color.red = 65535;
        color.green = 65535;
        color.blue = 0;
        color.flags = DoRed|DoGreen|DoGreen;
        XStoreColor(p_disp, xswa.colormap, &color);

        color.pixel = colorcells[1] | planemask;
        color.red = 65535;
        color.green = 65535;
        color.blue = 0;
        color.flags = DoRed|DoGreen|DoGreen;
        XStoreColor(p_disp, xswa.colormap, &color);
}
else
{
/* Handle failure to allocate colorcells */
        fprintf("Colorcell allocation failed...\n");
        .
        .
}
        .
        .
        .
/* In "Expose" event handler... Draw using "base" colors */

XSetForeground(p_disp, theGC, colorcells[0]);
XFillRectangle(p_disp, Main, theGC, 10, 10, 20, 20);

XSetForeground(p_disp, theGC, colorcells[1]);
XFillRectangle(p_disp, Main, theGC, 30, 30, 20, 20);
        .
        .
        .
/* When you want to change to "overlay" color */

XSetFunction(p_disp, theGC, GXor);
XSetForeground(p_disp, theGC, planemask);
XFillRectangle(p_disp, Main, theGC, 0,0,50,50);
XSetFunction(p_disp, theGC, GXcopy);
```

The first part of the code shows the color cell allocation and setup. The last part shows how to switch to the alternate color.

Freeing Colormap Cells

Whether you are using shared or private colormap cells, you should free the colors when they are no longer needed. When an application terminates, the X server automatically frees the colors used by that application. However, if your application allocates colors often (for example, every time an image is displayed in a window), you should call XFreeColors to free the colors you no longer need:

```
Display        *p_disp;
Colormap        colormap;    /* Cells freed in this colormap  */
unsigned long pixels[];      /* Identifies cells being freed  */
int            numpix;       /* Number of cells being freed   */
unsigned long planes;        /* Identifies planes being freed */

XFreeColors(p_disp, colormap, pixels, numpix, planes);
```

XFreeColors frees colors allocated by any one of these functions: XAllocColor, XAllocNamedColor, XAllocColorCells, or XAllocColorPlanes. When freeing one or more read-only cells allocated by XAllocColor or XAllocNamedColor, provide the array of pixel values, their number, and a 0 for the planes argument.

For private, read-write cells, use a logical OR of the plane masks that were returned by an earlier call to XAllocColorCells.

Colormap Manipulation

Sometimes your application needs more colors than there are free entries in the default colormap. To display a multicolored image, you may need all available color cells supported by the display hardware. In these cases, you have to create and set up your own colormap.

Using Your Own Colormap

The first step in setting up a colormap is to select a visual. The visual is required as an argument to the XAllocColormap function that you use to create a colormap. As with any resource in X, when you create a colormap, you receive a resource identifier that you can use to identify the colormap in subsequent function calls that manipulate colors. After a colormap is created, you have to set up the color cells using a function such as XStoreColors.

When the colormap is ready, you have to associate the colormap with the window in which you plan to use the colors. Because most displays support only one colormap at a time, you have to install your colormap before its effects can be seen. The X Window System's rules of etiquette dictate that applications should not install colormaps haphazardly. Instead, a window manager should decide when to install the colormap—usually when the window in question has the input focus.

> **NOTE:**
>
> Consult your window manager's documentation and the *Inter-Client Communication Conventions Manual (ICCCM)* for information on using multiple colormaps.

Selecting a Visual

The first step in creating a colormap is to pick a visual. In particular, the visual's class determines how the color cells in the colormap are interpreted and used; its depth determines the number of entries in the colormap. This is the number of colors you can display simultaneously. If the default visual meets your needs (it has enough depth and is of the right class), you can use the `DefaultVisual` macro wherever you have to specify a visual.

Visual Matching

If the default visual does not meet your needs, you do not have to give up. Many X displays provide more than one visual. If you know the exact depth and class of visual you want, you can use the `XMatchVisualInfo` function to locate a matching visual. This function returns a nonzero value if a matching visual is found and fills in certain fields in an `XVisualInfo` structure, which is defined in `<X11/Xutil.h>` as the following:

```
typedef struct
{
    Visual      *visual;     /* Pointer to Visual struct */
    VisualID    visualid;    /* Visual resource ID       */
    int         screen;      /* Screen number.        */
    int         depth;       /* Bits per pixel value    */
    int         class;       /* One of: DirectColor,    */
                             /* TrueColor, PseudoColor, */
                             /* StaticColor, GrayScale, */
                             /* or StaticGray           */
    unsigned long red_mask;   /* Identifies bits in pixel */
    unsigned long green_mask; /* value used for the red,  */
    unsigned long blue_mask;  /* green, and blue levels   */
    int         colormap_size; /* Max. colormap cells     */
    int         bits_per_rgb; /* Hardware uses these many */
                             /* bits to store each of red*/
                             /* green and blue levels    */
} XVisualInfo;
```

For example, if you want a `PseudoColor` visual of depth 4, you can call `XMatchVisualInfo`:

```
Display    *p_disp;
XVisualInfo vis_info;

screen = DefaultScreen(display);
.
.
if(XMatchVisualInfo(p_disp, screen, 4, PseudoColor, &xvis_info))
{
```

```
/* Successfully matched a visual... Use it. */
    .
    .
    .
}
else
{
/* Failed to find a visual. Exit, if application cannot do
 * without this visual.
 */
    .
    .
    .
}
```

After returning from XMatchVisualInfo, the vis_info structure will have the necessary information to use the matched visual. In particular, when a function needs a Visual * argument, you should use vis_info.visual.

Visual Selection from a List

One problem with XmatchVisualInfo is that it fails if both the depth and the class do not exactly match one of the visuals supported by the display. In many instances, all you need is a visual that is better than some minimum acceptable level. For example, if you want to handle an image with 3-bit pixel values, a visual of depth greater than 3 will suffice. For these situations, you can use another approach to determine a suitable visual:

1. Use XGetVisualInfo to retrieve a list of visuals supported by the screen you plan to use. To do this, set the screen member in an XVisualInfo structure and call XGetVisualInfo:

    ```
    XVisualInfo *vis_list, vis_template;
    int         num_visuals,

    /* Get a list of all visuals for this screen */
        vis_template.screen = theScreen;
        vis_list = XGetVisualInfo(theDisplay,
                        VisualScreenMask, &vis_template,
                        &num_visuals);
        if(num_visuals == 0)
        {
            fprintf(stderr, "No visuals found!\n");
            exit(0);
        }
    ```

    Here, the VisualScreenMask constant in the argument list asks XGetVisualInfo to return all visuals for the screen specified by vis_template.screen. The number of visuals is returned in the integer whose address you provide as the last argument to XGetVisualInfo. The return value from XGetVisualInfo is a pointer to an array of XVisualInfo structures.

2. Search through this list and locate a visual that meets your needs. For example, here is the `pick_visual` function used in the `viewpcx` program of Chapter 12, "Pixmaps, Bitmaps, and Images," to pick a visual with `class` matching `class_wanted` and `depth` greater than or equal to `depth_wanted`:

```
XVisualInfo  *vis_list;   /* List of visuals returned by    */
                          /* prior call to: XGetVisualInfo  */
int          num_visuals; /* Number of visuals in vis_list  */
Visual       theVisual;   /* Selected visual                */
int          vis_depth;   /* Depth of selected visual       */
 .
 .
 .

/*------------------------------------------------------------*/
/*  p i c k _ v i s u a l
 *
 *  Select a visual of appropriate "class" and "depth" from
 *  the list of visuals. Return 1 if successful, 0 if no
 *  matching visuals found.
 */
static int pick_visual(int depth_wanted, int class_wanted)
{
    XVisualInfo *p_visinfo;
    int         i, status = 0;

    for(i = 0, p_visinfo = vis_list; i < num_visuals;
        i++, p_visinfo++)
    {
        if(p_visinfo->class == class_wanted  &&
           p_visinfo->depth > depth_wanted)
        {
            theVisual = p_visinfo->visual;
            vis_depth = p_visinfo->depth;
            status = 1;
            break;
        }
    }
    return (status);
}
```

Setting Up the Colormap

Once you have a visual, you should first set up an array of `XColor` structures with information for the colormap cells of your colormap. Then you can call `XCreateColormap` to set up the colormap.

Suppose you want a copy of the default colormap (assume that the default visual meets your needs). You can create such a colormap with the following block of code:

```
Display  *p_disp;
int      screen, i;
XColor   *colors;
Colormap new_colormap;

screen = DefaultScreen(p_disp);
colormap_size = DisplayCells(p_disp, screen);
```

```
/* Allocate the XColor array for the colormap */

    if((colors = (XColor *)calloc(colormap_size,
                        sizeof(XColor))) == NULL)
    {
        fprintf(stderr, "No memory for setting \
up colormap\n");
        exit(1);
    }
```

```
/* Initialize parts of the colors array */
    for(i = 0; i < colormap_size; i++)
    {
        colors[i].pixel = i;
        colors[i].flags = DoRed | DoGreen | DoBlue;
    }
```

```
/* Get RGB values from default colormap */
    XQueryColors(p_disp, DefaultColormap(p_disp, screen),
                colors, colormap_size);
```

```
/* Create the new colormap */
    new_colormap = XCreateColormap(p_disp,
                        RootWindow(p_disp, screen),
                        DefaultVisual(p_disp, screen),
                        AllocAll);
```

```
/* Store the colors in the new colormap */
    XStoreColors(p_disp, new_colormap, colors, colormap_size);
```

```
/* Now we can release the memory used by the colors
 * because the X server already has this information.
 */
    free(colors);
```

Associating the Colormap with a Window

After you have a visual and a colormap, use them to create the window in which you will use the colors. When you create a window with the XCreateSimpleWindow function, the newly created window uses its parent's visual. To use a visual other than the parent's, you have to use XCreateWindow. You can associate the colormap with the window as you create it:

```
Display         *display;
Visual          *visual;
Colormap        new_colormap;
```

```
    Window              new_win, theMain;
    XSetWindowAttributes xswa;

/* Visual selected and colormap prepared */
    .
    .
    .
/* Set up window's attributes */

    xswa.colormap = new_colormap;
    xswa.background_pixel = WhitePixel(p_disp,
                        DefaultScreen(p_disp));

    xswa.border_pixel = BlackPixel(p_disp,
                        DefaultScreen(p_disp));

/* Window at (xpos, ypos) with dimensions width x height
 * with border width bdwidth. Visual's depth is vis_depth.
 * The parent window's ID "theMain"
 */
    new_win = XCreateWindow(p_disp, theMain, xpos, ypos,
                        width, height, bdwidth, vis_depth,
                        InputOutput, visual,
                        CWColormap ¦ CWBackPixel ¦ CWBorderPixel,
                        &xswa);
```

Informing the Window Manager

If you associate a new colormap with a top-level window (a window whose parent is the root window), most window managers will install the colormap when your window gains the input focus. If you have colormaps associated with subwindows, the situation becomes complicated. In fact, you have to check with your window manager's documentation to see how you can ensure a switching of the colormap when you are displaying in that subwindow.

The Motif window manager, mwm, pays attention to a subwindow's colormap, provided that subwindow's ID is listed in a property named WM_COLORMAP_WINDOWS in the application's top window. Properties are described later, but here is some sample code that sets up the property in a top-level window with the ID theMain:

```
#include <X11/Xatom.h>        /* For definition of XA_WINDOW */

    Display    *p_disp;
    Colormap   new_colormap;
    Window     new_win, theMain;
    int        screen;
    Atom       ATOM_WM_COLMAP_WIN;
    .
    .
    screen = DefaultScreen(p_disp);

/* Set the WM_COLORMAP_WINDOWS property so that the OSF/Motif
 * window manager knows about windows with their
 * own colormap. In this case, we have only 1 such window.
 */
    if(new_colormap != DefaultColormap(p_disp, screen))
    {
```

```
    ATOM_WM_COLMAP_WIN = XInternAtom(p_disp,
                        "WM_COLORMAP_WINDOWS", False);
    XChangeProperty(p_disp, theMain, ATOM_WM_COLMAP_WIN,
                XA_WINDOW, 32, PropModeReplace,
                (unsigned char *)&new_win, 1);
}
```

(For further discussion of properties, see Chapter 16, "Advanced Topics in X.")

Once this property has been defined, mwm also enables you to switch colormaps interactively. To do this, bind the function f.next_cmap to one of the keys or mouse buttons. This is done in the .mwmrc file in your home directory. (See Chapter 2, "Clients, Servers, and Window Managers," for more information on the OSF/Motif window manager.)

Suppose you want the colormaps to switch when you press the Alt key together with the third mouse button, with the mouse pointer in the subwindow that has its own colormap. For this to work, make sure the following line appears in the button-binding section of the .mwmrc file (in the DefaultButtonBindings, ExplicitButtonBindings, and PointerButtonBindings sections):

```
Alt<Btn3Down>        window          f.next_cmap
```

Remember to restart mwm for the new bindings to take effect.

> **NOTE:**
>
> Using a new colormap for your application may seem enticing, but it does have one drawback: when the window manager switches colormaps to satisfy your application's need, the other windows on the screen will be in the wrong color. By the same token, when your application does not have the focus, the colors in your application's windows will not look right. Another problem is the flashing that occurs when colormaps are switched rapidly. This is more of a problem when the focus is determined by the location of the pointer. As the user moves the mouse, the windows gain and lose focus rapidly with attendant changes in the colormap. This causes considerable flashing. In cases where the user has to click on a window to change focus (the default behavior in OSF/Motif), the situation is better because mere movement of the mouse does not cause switching of colormaps.

Summary

This chapter describes how you can use color in your X applications. Although X displays vary in how color is handled internally, all have certain common features:

✦ They use frame buffers with one or more bit planes.

✦ Colors are composed from different intensities of the primary colors: red, green, and blue (RGB).

✦ The hardware uses a colormap or a grayscale map to convert pixel values in the frame buffer into colors or intensities on the screen.

X encapsulates the color capabilities of displays in a visual, which contains all the information that characterizes the display. A visual has depth and class. The depth corresponds to the number of bit planes in the frame buffer; the class indicates how the colormap is used. Six classes of visuals exist: three with modifiable colormaps (`DirectColor`, `PseudoColor`, and `GrayScale`) and three with immutable colormaps (`TrueColor`, `StaticColor`, and `StaticGray`).

Applications use color as foreground and background pixel values in windows and in graphics contexts (`GCs`). Before using a color, you have to allocate the colors from a colormap. The process of allocation involves specifying an RGB color and getting back a pixel value that can be used wherever a color is needed. You can allocate shared, read-only color cells and private, read-write ones. It is best to use shared color cells because they are supported by all classes of visuals. Xlib provides several functions for allocating colors.

For the most part, you can get by with the default visual and the default colormap; however, many displays support more than one class of visual. You can use Xlib functions to locate a suitable visual and create a colormap for the selected visual. Both the visual and the colormap are associated with a window in which the colors will be used.

Although windows can have their own colormaps, most displays support only one colormap in the hardware. The window manager is supposed to take care of the chore of installing a window's colormap in the hardware when the window has the input focus.

This chapter includes small blocks of code to illustrate the use of color. Chapter 12 provides a complete example program (`viewpcx`) that displays color images (stored in the PC Paintbrush .PCX format) using the ideas presented in this chapter.

## Chapter 12

Pixmaps, Bitmaps, and Images

Previous chapters describe how to draw graphical shapes and display text in X. This chapter describes another category of drawing functions: those used to display and manipulate images. The X server supports images through pixmaps and bitmaps, and Xlib supports the XImage structure that enables you to manipulate images locally—on the system where your application is running, not at the server. This chapter introduces the Xlib functions for creating and manipulating pixmaps, bitmaps, and XImage structures. The chapter ends with a complete example program, viewpcx, that displays images stored in the PC Paintbrush (.PCX) format—a popular format for images in the MS-DOS world.

Pixmaps

Earlier chapters often used the term *drawable* to refer to an X resource that can serve as the destination of drawing requests. Windows are one type of drawable—the kind that you can see on the screen. A pixmap is also a drawable. Like windows, pixmaps can be thought of as a rectangular array of pixels (a raster), each location capable of holding a pixel value. You also can view a pixmap as a number of rectangular bit planes, with as many planes as there are bits in the pixel value (see Figure 9.1 in Chapter 9, "Drawing Graphics").

For windows, the pixel values in the raster are constantly being displayed. The hardware reads the pixel values and translates them into colors or gray levels, depending on the capabilities of the display. (Chapter 11, "Using Color in X," describes how pixel values are mapped into on-screen colors and gray levels.)

In contrast to this, the contents of a pixmap are not visible until copied into a window. Thus, you can think of a pixmap as an off-screen drawing area—an area of memory where you can save a drawing or an image. In fact, you can even prepare drawings in a pixmap and display them when needed by using the XCopyArea function.

Pixmaps are used primarily to draw images and to store patterns for tiling. Pixmaps used as tiles are small, usually no larger that 32x32 pixels, but those used to store images might be quite large.

Using a Pixmap

Like windows, pixmaps are resources maintained at the X server. Before using a pixmap, you have to create it by calling the Xlib function, XCreatePixmap. This function returns a resource identifier of type Pixmap that you use when referring to the pixmap in subsequent drawing requests.

Suppose you want to create a pixmap to draw some figures off screen. You can create a pixmap with the following:

```
Display      *p_disp;  /* Identifies the X display  */
Window       root_win; /* Root window's ID          */
Pixmap       pmap1;    /* Pixmap being created      */
unsigned int width,    /* Width of pixmap (pixels)  */
             height,   /* Height of pixmap (pixels) */
             depth;    /* Bits per pixel value      */
.
.
.
/* Create a pixmap */
    width = 100;
    height = 50;
    depth = DefaultDepth(p_disp, DefaultScreen(p_disp));
    root_win = RootWindow(p_disp, DefaultScreen(p_disp));

    pmap1 = XCreatePixmap(p_disp, root_win, width,
                          height, depth);
```

When creating a pixmap, you specify its dimensions (width and height) and its depth (the number of bits in the pixel values that the pixmap should be able to store).

The second argument to XCreatePixmap must be an identifier of a previously created drawable. The X server uses this argument to determine the screen for which you are creating the pixmap. You can use the ID of any valid window or pixmap. A simple solution is to use the root window's ID.

In X, every window and pixmap is created for a specific screen. In a multiscreen X display, you cannot copy a pixmap from one screen to a window in another, even if both have the same depth.

Drawing into a Pixmap

When a valid pixmap is available, you can draw into it exactly as you would in a window. For example, here is how you draw some figures in a pixmap:

```
/* Draw into the pixmap (assume the GC is already set up  */

    XFillRectangle(p_disp, pmap1, theGC, 10, 10, 20, 20);
    XFillArc(p_disp, pmap1, theGC, 30, 30, 20, 20, 0, 360*64);
```

As with windows, you have to provide a graphics context (GC) with all the graphics attributes, such as foreground and background colors. You use the same coordinate system with pixmaps as with windows. (Chapter 7, "Creating and Managing Windows," explains the coordinate system and geometry of windows.)

A few minor differences exist between drawing in pixmaps and drawing in windows. The differences stem from the fact that windows are always displayed on the screen but pixmaps are never displayed. One of the main differences is that windows have an associated background color but pixmaps do not. Thus, you cannot fill the pixmap with the background color by calling XClearArea. Instead, you must use XFillRectangle to fill all pixels in the pixmap to the current background color. When you first create a pixmap, its contents are undefined, so you should always fill it with a known value, such as the background color.

Pixmaps do not generate any events other than GraphicsExpose and NoExpose that occur when copying between windows and pixmaps (see Chapter 9).

Handling Errors in Allocating Pixmaps

When you create a pixmap, the X server has to allocate some off-screen memory for the raster of pixel values. Many X servers do not have much off-screen memory to spare. Thus, you should not use too many large pixmaps in your applications. Even when you use only a few, you should include code to handle failure to create a pixmap. The exact approach for handling failures depends on how you plan to use the pixmaps. For example, if you use a pixmap for off-screen storage for fast screen updates and the server fails to provide a pixmap, you can always redraw the screen from scratch—it will work, albeit slower.

One problem with handling pixmap-creation failures is that the XCreatePixmap function cannot return any status because the actual creation of the pixmap is done by the server. XCreatePixmap returns the ID that it has requested for the pixmap   remember that all resource identifiers are set up when your application first connects to a server. If the server does not have enough memory to allocate the pixmap, it returns a BadAlloc error. You can set up your own error handler as follows to take appropriate actions if the error was due to a failure to create a pixmap:

```
#include <X11/Xproto.h>   /* For definition of X_CreatePixmap */

/* Prototype of error handling function */

int myXErrorHandler(Display *p_disp, XErrorEvent *p_error);
    .
    .
    .
/* In main...*/
    XSetErrorHandler(myXErrorHandler);
    .
    .
```

```
int myXErrorHandler(Display *p_disp, XErrorEvent *p_error)
{
    char err_msg[80];

/* Check whether error occurred on a "create pixmap" request */
    if(p_error->error_code == BadAlloc &&
       p_error->request_code == X_CreatePixmap))
       {
           fprintf(stderr, "Failed to allocate pixmap\n");
/* Return if you are taking corrective action, else exit */
             .
             .
             .
       }
    else
    {
        XGetErrorText(p_disp, p_error->error_code, err_msg, 80);
        fprintf(stderr, "Error detected:\n  %s\n", err_msg);
        fprintf(stderr, "  Protocol request: %d\n",
                                  p_error->request_code);
        fprintf(stderr, "  Resource ID:     0x%x\n",
                                  p_error->resourceid);

/* Perform necessary clean-ups (close files etc.) and exit */
        fprintf(stderr, "\nCleaning up and exiting...\n");
        exit(1);
    }
}
```

(See Chapter 6, "The Xlib Programming Model," for information on handling errors in X.)

Because the error handler is called only when the error event arrives, it does not help much in taking corrective action. You can call the XGetGeometry function with the newly created pixmap's ID immediately after calling XCreatePixmap. This function makes a request to the server, asking for the size of the pixmap, and waits for a reply. If the server did not create the pixmap, the function returns a 0 to indicate failure. At this point, you can fall back on some other way of handling the situation. Here is a typical section of code:

```
    Display *p_disp;
    Pixmap  pmap1;
/* Create the pixmap */
      .
      .
      .
/* Check whether pixmap was successfully created */
    {
    Window       r;
    int          x, y;
    unsigned int w, h, bdw, depth;

        if(!XGetGeometry(p_disp, pmap1, &r, &x, &y, &w, &h,
                    &bdw, &depth))
        {
/* Pixmap creation failed. Take corrective action */
            fprintf(stderr, "Failed to allocate pixmap!\n");
              .
              .
              .
        }
    }
```

With this code, you still need to catch the error in your own error handler and return because the server always sends back a `BadAlloc` error event on failing to allocate a pixmap. If you do not install your own handler, the default error handler prints a message and exits.

Freeing Pixmaps

Because most X displays have limited off-screen memory, you should release pixmap resources as soon as you are finished with them. You can free a pixmap by calling `XFreePixmap`:

```
Pixmap pmap1;

/* Create pixmap "pmap1" and use it */
.
.
.
XFreePixmap(p_disp, pmap1);
```

All resources (including pixmaps) used by your application are automatically freed when your application exits. You have to do this explictly only if you use several large pixmaps.

Bitmaps

Recall that a bitmap is a pixmap of depth 1. In fact, you create a bitmap by specifying depth of 1 when you call the `XCreatePixmap` function. Because there is only 1 bit in each location of the bitmap, a bitmap is a pattern of 1s and 0s.

Bitmaps are used somewhat differently. Because pixmaps store the entire pixel value, they are usually copied directly into windows and displayed. Bitmaps, however, are used mostly as a *stencil* (or, stipple) through which the background and foreground pixel values are applied to a drawable's raster. First, the bitmap is laid down over the raster of the drawable (repeating the bitmap, if necessary, to cover the entire raster). Then, the foreground color is applied to all pixels where the bitmap (the stencil) has a 1.

Another use of bitmaps is as a clip mask. The operation is similar to using the bitmap as a stencil, except that the graphics operations are performed only for those pixels in the raster that have a 1 in the bitmap pattern being used as stencil.

Because of the special use of bitmaps, they are widely used even when the displays may support more than one plane.

To facilitate use of bitmaps, Xlib includes functions that can read and write *bitmap files*, which are text files containing a definition of bitmaps suitable for use in C programs. On UNIX systems, you will find a collection of bitmap files in the directory `/usr/include/X11/bitmaps`. The standard X software distribution comes with a utility program named `bitmap` which you can use to edit one of these bitmaps or to create new ones.

A bitmap file is a text file with information about the size of the bitmap and the bitmap itself in the form of an array of characters. For example, the file `/usr/include/X11/bitmaps/left_ptr` defines the bitmap shown in Figure 12.1:

```
#define left_ptr_width 16
#define left_ptr_height 16
#define left_ptr_x_hot 3
#define left_ptr_y_hot 1
static char left_ptr_bits[] =
{
    0x00, 0x00, 0x08, 0x00, 0x18, 0x00, 0x38, 0x00,
    0x78, 0x00, 0xf8, 0x00, 0xf8, 0x01, 0xf8, 0x03,
    0xf8, 0x07, 0xf8, 0x00, 0xd8, 0x00, 0x88, 0x01,
    0x80, 0x01, 0x00, 0x03, 0x00, 0x03, 0x00, 0x00
};
```

Figure 12.1.

The 16x16 left_ptr bitmap showing individual pixels.

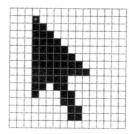

The file defines five items, each prefixed with the name of the bitmap and an underscore, `left_ptr_` in this case. These items have the following meanings:

`width` and `height`	Definition of the width and the height of the bitmap in number of pixels
`x_hot` and `y_hot`	Coordinates of the hotspot, with `(0,0)` being the upper-left corner of the bitmap
`bits`	Array of bytes that defines the bitmap

Notice from Figure 12.1 that for the `left_ptr` bitmap, the hotspot is the tip of the pointer. The hotspot is useful when a bitmap is used as a cursor—it defines exactly where the cursor is pointing.

You can construct these values by traversing the bitmap's grid row by row, from left to right and from top to bottom, starting with the upper-left corner (see Figure 12.1). For each row, start copying the bits from the grid into a byte, starting with the least-significant bit and advancing toward the most-significant one. When a byte fills up, start with the next byte. Always start a row in a new byte. The bitmap of Figure 12.1 contains 16 rows, each 16 bits wide. Each row fits into 2 bytes. Thus, there are a total of 32 bytes in the `bits` array. To verify the encoding scheme, look at the third row of Figure 12.1. Verify that traversing the row from left to right yields the following bits arranged in 2 bytes (shown in the order the bytes are constructed):

```
0001 1000
0000 0000
```

You can write these bytes in hexadecimal notation as `0x18 0x00`, which are bytes 5 and 6 of the `left_ptr_bits` array.

Reading a Bitmap File

If you want to use one of the predefined bitmaps from /usr/include/X11/bitmaps (or one that you have created with the bitmap program), you do not have to decode the information. You can read the file and construct a bitmap directly by using the XReadBitmapFile function. For instance, here is an example of creating a bitmap out of the information in a file named lnblogo (which contains a 64x64 bitmap used as a logo):

```
Display      p_disp;          /* Identifies the X display   */
Window       root_win;        /* Root window's ID           */
Pixmap       logo_bmap;       /* Bitmap created by function */
int          xh_logo, yh_logo; /* Coordinates of hotspot    */
unsigned int w_logo, h_logo;  /* Width and height of bitmap */

root_win = RootWindow(p_disp, DefaultScreen(p_disp));

/* Read bitmap file and load data into a bitmap */

if(XReadBitmapFile(p_disp, root_win, "lnblogo",
               &w_logo, &h_logo, &logo_bmap,
               &xh_logo, &yh_logo) != BitmapSuccess)
{
    fprintf(stderr, "Failed to read bitmap file!\n");
/* Exit if you cannot proceed */
    .
    .
}
/* Bitmap "logo_bmap" is ready to be used */
    .
    .
```

The XReadBitmapFile opens the bitmap file, creates a pixmap of depth 1, and initializes the bitmap using the data from the bits array in the file. The second argument to XReadBitmapFile should be an existing window or pixmap on the same screen. The server creates the new bitmap for the same screen.

Copying a Bitmap into a Drawable

Bitmaps are often used as stipples and clip masks in GCs. You also can display a bitmap directly in a window or copy it into a pixmap. Because the bitmap is of depth 1 and the drawable (pixmap or window) may have depth greater than 1, you cannot use the XCopyArea function to do this. Xlib provides another function, XCopyPlane, for this purpose.

XCopyPlane requires you to specify a rectangular area in a source bitmap and a destination drawable. The server copies the bitmap into the destination pixmap by using the bitmap as a stencil, and draws using the foreground color (specified in a GC) of those pixels in the drawable where the bitmap has 1s.

You can identify the bitmap as one of the planes in an arbitrary pixmap. To do this, you specify a mask with exactly one bit set to 1. That mask identifies a bit plane in the source pixmap. This is the bit plane that is used as the stencil for the copy operation.

As an example, here is some code that copies the bitmap that was read by `XReadBitmapFile` into a window using the current foreground color in a GC:

```
Display       p_disp;         /* Identifies the X display   */
Window        Main;           /* Destination window         */
GC            theGC;          /* GC used for copying         */
Pixmap        logo_bmap;      /* Bitmap created by function */
unsigned int  w_logo, h_logo; /* Width and height of bitmap */
unsigned long planemask;      /* Identifies source bitmap   */
int           xsrc, ysrc;     /* Corner of source rectangle */
int           xdest, ydest;   /* Copy to this point         */
.
.
.
/* Read in bitmap using "XReadBitmapFile" */
.
.
xsrc = 0;
ysrc = 0;
xdest = 10;
ydest = 10;
planemask = 1;

XCopyPlane(p_disp,logo_bmap, Main, theGC, xsrc, ysrc,
           w_logo, h_logo, xdest, ydest, planemask);
```

Note that the mask identifying the bitmap from `logo_bmap` is set to 1 because `logo_bmap` is already a bitmap and as such has only one bit plane.

You can copy the bitmap into a pixmap using an identical function call: merely replace the window with the pixmap. If you have the pixmap ready, you can use `XCopyArea` to copy the pixmap into the window to display it. Here is the preceding example drawn via a pixmap:

```
Pixmap  pmap1;
.
/* Create the pixmap */
.
.
/* Fill pixmap with "white" */

XSetForeground(p_disp, theGC, WhitePixel(p_disp,
                            DefaultScreen(p_disp)));
XFillRectangle(p_disp, pmap1, theGC, 0, 0, 200, 200);

/* Copy "logo_bmap" in "black" */

XSetForeground(p_disp, theGC, BlackPixel(p_disp,
                            DefaultScreen(p_disp)));
XCopyPlane(p_disp, logo_bmap, pmap1, theGC, 0, 0,
           w_logo, h_logo, 0, 0, 1);
.
.
```

Including Bitmap Files in C Programs

Bitmap files are set up so that you can include them in your programs. Reading from a bitmap file gives the user the flexibility to alter the bitmap, although you can include the bitmap in your program without providing the bitmap file. If you decide to include the bitmap file, you can use the `XCreateBitmapFromData` function to create a bitmap directly from the data. Here is an example of including the bitmap `lnblogo`:

```
#include "lnblogo"            /* The bitmap file           */

Display      p_disp;          /* Identifies the X display  */
Window       root_win;        /* Root window's ID          */
Pixmap       logo_bmap;       /* Bitmap created by function */
unsigned int w_logo, h_logo;  /* Width and height of bitmap */

root_win = RootWindow(p_disp, DefaultScreen(p_disp));

/* Create bitmap from data. By convention, the bitmap's width
 * height, and data are in "width", "height", and "bits"
 * prefixed by the bitmap's name followed by an underscore,
 * "lnblogo_" in this case.
 */

w_logo = lnblogo_width;
h_logo = lnblogo_height;

if((logo_bmap = XCreateBitmapFromData(p_disp, root_win,
                    lnblogo_bits, w_logo, h_logo)) == None)
{
    fprintf(stderr, "Failed to create bitmap!\n");
/* Exit if you cannot proceed */
    .
    .
    .
}
/* Bitmap "logo_bmap" is ready to be used */
.
.
```

When the bitmap is ready, you can use it for any purpose—as a cursor, a stipple, or a clip mask.

Creating Pixmaps from Bitmap Data

Xlib also includes another function, `XCreatePixmapFromBitmapData`, that enables you to create a pixmap directly from bitmap data. This function is equivalent to using `XCreateBitmapFromData` followed by an `XCopyPlane` into the pixmap. Here is an example of creating a pixmap with the `lnblogo` bitmap:

```
#include "lnblogo"            /* The bitmap file            */

Display       p_disp;         /* Identifies the X display   */
Window        root_win;       /* Root window's ID           */
Pixmap        pmap1;          /* Pixmap created by function */
unsigned int  depth;          /* Depth of the pixmap        */
unsigned int  w_logo, h_logo; /* Width and height of bitmap */
unsigned long fgpix;          /* Foreground pixel value     */
unsigned long bgpix;          /* Background pixel value     */
```

```
root_win = RootWindow(p_disp, DefaultScreen(p_disp));
depth = DefaultDepth(p_disp, DefaultScreen(p_disp));

/* Create the logo in black over a white background */

bgpix = WhitePixel(p_disp, DefaultScreen(p_disp));
bgpix = BlackPixel(p_disp, DefaultScreen(p_disp));

/* Directly create pixmap from bitmap data */

if((pmap1 = XCreatePixmapFromBitmapData(p_disp, root_win,
                               lnblogo_bits, w_logo, h_logo,
                               fgpix, bgpix, depth)) == None)
{
    fprintf(stderr, "Failed to create bitmap!\n");
/* Exit if you cannot proceed */
    .
    .
}
/* Pixmap "pmap1" is ready to be used */
    .
    .
```

After the pixmap is successfully created, you can display it using the XCopyArea function. For example, to display the pixmap in the window Main at coordinates (20,10), you would write this:

```
/* Copy drawing from pixmap to the window */
   XCopyArea(p_disp, pmap1, Main, theGC, 0, 0,
             w_logo, h_logo, 20, 10);
```

Images

Image refers to a raster of pixels. Therefore, bitmaps and pixmaps are examples of images. These images reside in the X server. Because images typically involve a lot of data, copying an image into a pixmap requires Xlib to send a large amount of data to the server. Another problem is that the pixel values are usually packed into 8-, 16-, or 32-bit quantities, and servers may vary in the way they interpret these packed images.

To solve these problems, Xlib includes some facilities to handle images locally at your application, using XImage structures. Xlib includes functions to create an image, retrieve an image from the server, send an image to the server, and alter individual pixel values through utility functions. This section summarizes these functions and the following section presents an example program that creates and displays images using these facilities.

Examining the *XImage* Structure

All information about an image, its format and its data, is stored in an XImage structure, which is defined in <X11/Xlib.h> as follows:

```
typedef struct _XImage
{
    int         width, height;    /* Size of image in pixels */
    int         xoffset;          /* Number of pixels to      */
                                  /* ignore at the beginning */
                                  /* of each row (scan line) */
    int         format;           /* One of: XYBitmap,        */
                                  /*     XYPixmap, ZPixmap */
    char        *data;            /* Pointer to image data    */
    int         byte_order;       /* LSBFirst or MSBFirst      */
    int         bitmap_unit;      /* "Chunk size" of image     */
                                  /* data:  8, 16, or 32      */
    int         bitmap_bit_order; /* LSBFirst, or MSBFirst    */
    int         bitmap_pad;       /* Scan lines are multiples*/
                                  /* of these many bits:      */
                                  /* usually 8, 16, or 32    */
    int         depth;            /* Depth of image           */
    int         bytes_per_line;   /* Bytes between start of   */
                                  /* consecutive scan lines   */
    int         bits_per_pixel;   /* Bits used for each pixel*/
                                  /* in ZPixmap format (may   */
                                  /* be larger than "depth"   */
    unsigned long red_mask;       /* Identifies red, green,   */
    unsigned long green_mask;     /* and blue parts of pixel */
    unsigned long blue_mask;      /* for DirectColor and      */
                                  /* TrueColor visuals        */
    char        *obdata;          /* Room for future routines*/
    struct funcs                  /* Pointers to image        */
    {                             /* manipulation routines    */
        struct _XImage *(*create_image)();
        int            (*destroy_image)();
        unsigned long  (*get_pixel)();
        int            (*put_pixel)();
        struct _XImage *(*sub_image)();
        int            (*add_pixel)();
    } f;
} XImage;
```

Figure 12.2 shows the components of a complete image. The XImage structure holds information about the image's size and format. The actual image data has to be allocated and prepared separately. The XImage structure holds a pointer to this data.

The meanings of most of the members of the XImage structure are obvious from the comments next to each member. If you plan to create your own raster images, you have to know about the image formats. As indicated next to the format field in the XImage structure, Xlib supports three forms of image data:

✦ XYBitmap

✦ XYPixmap

✦ ZPixmap

Figures 12.3, 12.4, and 12.5 graphically illustrate these three image formats.

Figure 12.2.

XImage structure and image data.

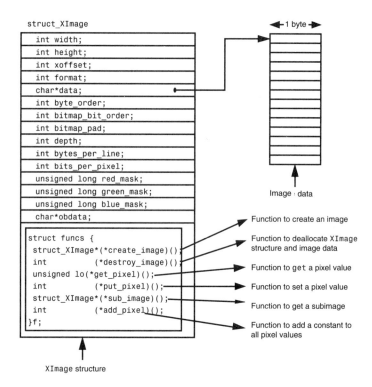

```
struct_XImage
    int width;
    int height;
    int xoffset;
    int format;
    char*data;
    int byte_order;
    int bitmap_bit_order;
    int bitmap_pad;
    int depth;
    int bytes_per_line;
    int bits_per_pixel;
    unsigned long red_mask;
    unsigned long green_mask;
    unsigned long blue_mask;
    char*obdata;

    struct funcs {
    struct_XImage*(*create_image)();
    int           (*destroy_image)();
    unsigned lo(*get_pixel)();
    int           (*put_pixel)();
    struct_XImage*(*sub_image)();
    int           (*add_pixel)();
    }f;
```

1 byte

Image data

Function to create an image

Function to deallocate XImage structure and image data

Function to get a pixel value

Function to set a pixel value

Function to get a subimage

Function to add a constant to all pixel values

XImage structure

Figure 12.3.

Byte-organized image data in XYBitmap format with LSBFirst bit order within each byte.

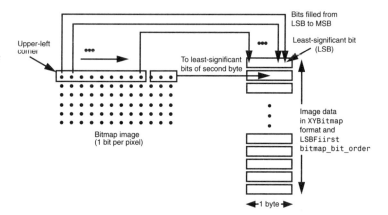

Upper-left corner

Bits filled from LSB to MSB

Least-significant bit (LSB)

To least-significant bits of second byte

Bitmap image (1 bit per pixel)

Image data in XYBitmap format and LSBFiirst bitmap_bit_order

1 byte

The XYBitmap format is meant for data representing pixmaps of depth 1—bitmaps. The bits are packed into bytes, and their order is indicated by the bitmap_bit_order field in XImage. For example, the bitmap files shown earlier use an LSBFirst bit order (see Figure 12.3 for clarification).

Figure 12.4.

Byte-organized image data in XYPixmap *format with* LSBFirst *bit order within each byte.*

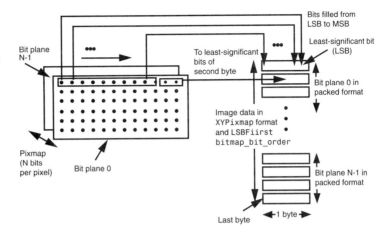

The XYPixmap format stores each bit plane in a pixmap using the format specified by XYBitmap. As shown in Figure 12.4, the data is laid out one plane after another, starting with plane 0 and ending with the plane depth-1.

Figure 12.5.

Byte-organized image data in ZPixmap *format with* MSBFirst *byte order.*

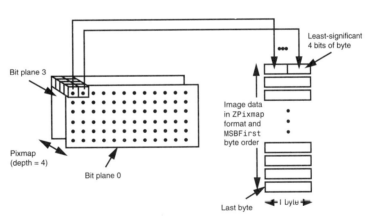

The ZPixmap format is also for storing images of any depth. In this format, data is organized as an array of pixels (see Figure 12.5). The bits_per_pixel field indicates how many bits are used to store each pixel value. Although this field is usually equal to depth, it can be larger than depth. If bits_per_pixel is 1, 2, or 4, the pixel values are packed 8, 4, or 2 pixels per byte. In Figure 12.5, bits_per_pixel is equal to the depth, which is 4. Thus, the pixel values are packed 2 to a byte.

Creating *XImages*

To prepare an image that can be displayed at an X display, you have to first allocate enough memory and set up the image's data packed according to one of three accepted formats. When the data is ready, you can call XCreateImage to create an XImage structure. The function accepts arguments that define all the characteristics of the image data that you have prepared.

Here is an example call of the XCreateImage function call, illustrating its syntax:

```
Display       p_disp;        /* Identifies the X display    */
Visual        *p_visual;     /* Identifies the visual       */
XImage        *image;        /* Newly created image         */
unsigned int  depth;         /* Depth of the image          */
int           format;        /* Format of image's data      */
int           offset;        /* Pixels to skip at start of  */
                             /* each scan line              */
char          *image_data;   /* Pointer to image data       */
unsigned int  width, height; /* Width and height of image   */
int           bitmap_pad;    /* Each line padded to         */
                             /* multiples of these many bits */
int           bytes_per_line;/* Number of bytes between start*/
                             /* of successive scan lines    */

depth = DefaultDepth(p_disp, DefaultScreen(p_disp));
p_visual = DefaultVisual(p_disp, DefaultScreen(p_disp));
format = ZPixmap;
offset = 0;          /* No pixels to skip at start of line */
bitmap_pad = 8;      /* Data is byte-organized             */
bytes_per_line = 0;  /* Means: scan lines are contiguous   */

/* Assume that "image_data" has been allocated and
 * initialized in ZPixmap format.
 */
image = XCreateImage(p_disp, p_visual, depth, format, offset,
                     image_data, width, height, bitmap_pad,
                     bytes_per_line);

/* Indicate that pixels are packed in MSBFirst order */
image->byte_order = MSBFirst;
```

The visual provided to XCreateImage is used only if the format is ZPixmap and the visual's class is DirectColor or TrueColor. In this case, XCreateImage derives the red_mask, green_mask, and blue_mask fields of the XImage structure from the visual.

You can specify a 0 for the bytes_per_line argument, provided that the scan lines are contiguous in the image's data. In this case, XCreateImage computes the value of bytes_per_line.

Sending Images to the X Server

You can display an image in a window or copy it to a pixmap by using the Xlib function XPutImage. The function is similar to XCopyArea: you specify a rectangular region of your image and a point in a destination drawable. The rectangular region of the image is copied to the drawable with the rectangle's upper-left corner positioned at that point in the drawable.

Here is how you might copy an image to a pixmap:

```
Display *p_disp;/* Identifies the X display                */
Pixmap  pmap1;  /* Destination pixmap (same depth as image) */
GC      imageGC;/* GC used for the copy operation          */
XImage  *image; /* Image being copied                      */
int     x_im,
```

```
        y_im;   /* Upper-left corner of image rectangle    */
int     x_pmap,
        y_pmap; /* Where to place image rectangle in pixmap */

/* Copy entire image into a pixmap. Assume pixmap of proper
 * size and matching depth has been created.
 */
x_im = y_im = 0;
x_pmap = y_pmap = 0;

XPutImage(p_disp, pmap1, image_gc, image, x_im, y_im,
          x_pmap, y_pmap, image->width, image->height);
```

To display the image in a window, merely substitute the pixmap ID in the call to XPutImage with a window ID.

Copying Images from the X Server

Sometimes you may want to copy an image from a window or a pixmap and manipulate it locally. Xlib provides the XGetImage function for this purpose. XGetImage creates an XImage structure, copies a specified rectangular area from a drawable into the image, and returns a pointer to the XImage structure. For example, to copy a 200x100 pixel rectangle at (30, 15) from the window Main into a ZPixmap format image, write the following:

```
XImage  *scr_image;

scr_image = XGetImage(p_disp, Main, 30, 15, 200, 100,
                      AllPlanes, ZPixmap);
```

The last-but-one argument to XGetImage specifies how many planes of the drawable you want copied. Specifying AllPlanes means you want all the bit planes copied. You can extract any combination of bit planes by specifying an unsigned long mask as this argument. You should set to 1 the bits that correspond to the bit planes you want copied by XGetImage.

Manipulating Images

Xlib provides several utility functions to manipulate any image maintained in an XImage structure:

+ Destroy an image.
+ Get or set individual pixels.
+ Extract a subimage (using XGetSubImage).
+ Add a constant value to every pixel in an image.

All these manipulations are performed by calling functions through pointers stored in the f structure within the XImage structure (see Figure 12.2). Xlib sets up these pointers appropriately when an XImage structure is allocated.

When manipulating images, you do not have to access these pointers to functions; you call certain convenience functions that perform the necessary manipulations.

Getting and Setting Pixels

The XGetPixel function retrieves the pixel value at a specified location in the image. The pixel is identified by its *x* and *y* coordinates. The coordinate system is the same as that used by windows and pixmaps—the origin is at the upper-left corner of the image, with the *x* and *y* coordinates increasing from left to right and from top to bottom, respectively.

As an example, you can obtain the pixel at (20,10) in an image by writing this:

```
XImage *image;
long    pixval;

pixval = XGetPixel(image, 20, 10);
```

Similarly, to set that pixel to the pixel value 4, you write this:

```
if(!XSetPixel(image, 20, 10, 4))
    fprintf(stderr, "Failed to set pixel\n");
```

These functions do not need a Display pointer as the first argument because these functions manipulate the image locally without sending any protocol requests to the X server.

Destroying Images

The XDestroyImage function deallocates both the XImage structure and its image data (the pointer stored in the data member of the XImage structure):

```
XImage *image;
.
.
XDestroyImage(image);
```

If you want to preserve the image data, and free only the XImage structure, you can do so by using XFree.

An Image Viewing Program: *viewpcx*

One good example of using X's image handling capabilities is to display raster images. For example, many MS-DOS drawing programs save image files in a format originated by ZSoft Corporation and used in its PC Paintbrush program. These image files are often referred to as *.PCX files* because they are usually stored in files with that extension. This section presents a complete program, viewpcx, that reads a .PCX image file, prepares the data in the ZPixmap format, and uses Xlib's image handling functions to display the .PCX image in a window.

Building *viewpcx*

Listing 12.1 shows the source code for the complete program viewpcx.c. To compile and link this program, you need the following files from previous chapters:

✦ app_glob.c (Listing 7.1)
✦ initapp.c (Listing 7.2)

✦ `xwins.h` (Listing 8.1)

✦ `xwinutil.c` (Listing 8.2)

✦ `xbutton.c` (Listing 8.3)

To build the program, use the following makefile with appropriate changes to suit your system's requirements:

```
# Some common definitions...

RM = rm -f
CC = cc

# Compiler flags, paths for include files and libraries

CFLAGS =
INCLUDES = -I. -I/usr/include -I/usr/include/X11
LIBS = -lX11

# Rule to create .o files from .c files
.c.o:
    $(RM) $@
    $(CC) -c $(CFLAGS) $(INCLUDES) $*.c

# Targets...

all::    viewpcx

viewpcx.o: viewpcx.c app_glob.c xwins.h

initapp.o: initapp.c app_glob.c

xwinutil.o: xwinutil.c app_glob.c xwins.h

xbutton.o: xbutton.c app_glob.c xwins.h

viewpcx: viewpcx.o initapp.o xwinutil.o xbutton.o
    $(RM) $@
    $(CC) -o $@ $(CFLAGS) viewpcx.o initapp.o \
        xwinutil.o xbutton.o \
        $(LIBS)
```

Using *viewpcx*

To use `viewpcx`, type this command:

```
viewpcx -file <filename>
```

where `<filename>` is the name of the .PCX image file you want to view. For example, to view the file `dog.pcx`, use this command:

```
viewpcx -file dog.pcx
```

Figure 12.6 shows a sample .PCX image displayed by `viewpcx`.

Figure 12.6.

Viewing a .PCX image file with `viewpcx`.

Dissecting *viewpcx.c*

Now that you know what `viewpcx` does, you must be curious about its inner details. This section provides an overview of the program and summarizes some of the important steps in decoding an image format and displaying an image in X.

The first task in `viewpcx` is to open the .PCX image file and decode the image data. The `load_file` function in Listing 12.1 does this job. The .PCX image file provides information about the width, height, and depth of the image and the colormap used by the image. Based on this information, the `setup_disp` function picks a visual and creates a colormap initialized with the colormap obtained from the .PCX image file. (Chapter 11 describes how to pick a visual and set up a colormap.)

Next, a window is created with the selected visual, depth, and colormap. Then the `setup_ximage` function (Listing 12.1) is called to set up the image data in `ZPixmap` format with the `MSBFirst` byte order (see Figure 12.5). The image is immediately copied to a pixmap. The image is displayed by copying the pixmap to the window in response to an `Expose` event (see the `process_events` function in Listing 12.1).

Because the program was written in an environment with the Motif window manager, `mwm`, it also sets the `WM_COLORMAP_WINDOWS` property so that the colormap can be installed properly. (See Chapter 11 for a discussion of colormap handling under the Motif window manager.)

.PCX File Format

The first step in viewing a .PCX image is to decode the contents of the .PCX image file. The file format is straightforward:

1. Each file starts with a 128-byte header (described later). The header is followed by encoded scan lines.

2. Each scan line is created by first laying out the scan lines of individual bit planes one after another.

3. Then the entire line is encoded using a run-length encoding scheme that works like this: if the 2 highest-order bits of a byte are set, the low-order 6 bits indicate how many times the following byte must be repeated. If the 2 highest-order bits are not both 1, the byte represents the bitmap data.

The function `load_file` in Listing 12.1 illustrates this format.

.PCX File Header

All .PCX files start with a 128-byte header that can be described by the following `PCX_HEADER` structure:

```
typedef struct PCX_HEADER
{
    unsigned char   manufacturer;
    unsigned char   version;
    unsigned char   encoding;
    unsigned char   bits_per_pixel_per_plane;
    short           xmin;
    short           ymin;
    short           xmax;
    short           ymax;
    unsigned short  hresolution;
    unsigned short  vresolution;
    unsigned char   colormap[48];
    unsigned char   reserved;
    unsigned char   nplanes;
    unsigned short  bytes_per_line;
    short           palette_info;
    unsigned char   filler[58];
} PCX_HEADER;
```

The `viewpcx` program uses information from only the following fields in the file's header:

xmin, ymin, xmax, and ymax	Specify the image's dimensions. The width is xmax - xmin + 1 and the height is ymax - ymin + 1.
nplanes	Specify the number of bit planes in the image.
bits_per_pixel_per_plane	Indicate the number of bits for each pixel in each plane. For example, a 256-color PCX image has a single plane (nplanes = 1) but 8 bits_per_pixel_per_plane.
bytes_per_line	Indicate the number of bytes in each scan line of a single bit plane.
colormap	Specify the colormap for images with up to 16 colors. For 256-color images, the colormap is appended to the image data at the end of the file (see the load_file function in Listing 12.1 for further details).

> **NOTE:**
>
> The .PCX file's header contains 2-byte integers. These are stored with the least-significant byte first—in the little-endian format. On big-endian systems (such as Motorola 680x0-based systems or Sun workstations), the bytes must be swapped before the value is interpreted as a short integer.

Listing 12.1. `viewpcx.c`—Viewing .PCX image files in X.

```c
/*------------------------------------------------------------*/
/*  File: viewpcx.c
 *
 *  Program to view images stored in .PCX format.  Demonstrates
 *  how to select a visual, set up a colormap, store colors,
 *  create an image, and display it.
 *
 *  NOTES: (1)  On big-endian machines, uncomment the line
 *                    #define BIG_ENDIAN
 *         so that information from the PCX file's header
 *         is interpreted properly.
 *
 *         (2) Sets up the property "WM_COLORMAP_WINDOWS" to
 *         allow colormap switching under the Motif window
 *         manager. Edit the .mwmrc file to bind a button
 *         press to "f.next_cmap" (for instance, you can
 *         bind Alt<Btn3Down> to this function). That
 *         way you can switch the colormap on the fly and
 *         see the results.
 *
 *         (3) Uses colormap from the header of the .PCX file,
 *         but that does not display the image in its true
 *         colors.  Modify colormap, if you have better
 *         information on colormaps used by the .PCX files.
 */
/*------------------------------------------------------------*/
#include <stdio.h>
#include <string.h>             /* ANSI standard string library */
#include <stdlib.h>             /* Prototype of "calloc"        */

#include <X11/Xlib.h>
#include <X11/Xatom.h>          /* For definition of XA_WINDOW  */

#include "xwins.h"
#include "app_glob.c"

/****************************************************************/
#define BIG_ENDIAN              /* Uncomment on Suns, for instance */
/****************************************************************/

#ifndef SEEK_END
#define SEEK_END 2
#endif

/* Scaling factor for colormap entries */
```

```
#define   CSCALE 255

/* Data types of reading .PCX files */

typedef struct PCX_HEADER
{
    unsigned char    manufacturer;
    unsigned char    version;
    unsigned char    encoding;
    unsigned char    bits_per_pixel_per_plane;
    short            xmin;
    short            ymin;
    short            xmax;
    short            ymax;
    unsigned short   hresolution;
    unsigned short   vresolution;
    unsigned char    colormap[48];
    unsigned char    reserved;
    unsigned char    nplanes;
    unsigned short   bytes_per_line;
    short            palette_info;
    unsigned char    filler[58];
} PCX_HEADER;

typedef char       *SCANLINE;
typedef SCANLINE *PLANE;


PCX_HEADER      header;
unsigned short image_width, image_height;
PLANE          *image = NULL;
int            bits_per_pixel;

/* Screen, visual and colormap */
int          theScreen;
Visual       *theVisual;
XVisualInfo *vis_list;
int          num_visuals,
             vis_depth;
int          colormap_size;
Colormap     theColormap;

static GC   image_gc;

/* Image to be displayed by X server */
XImage          *theXImage = NULL;
unsigned char   *image_data = NULL;
XColor          *colors = NULL;
Pixmap          thePixmap;

/* File to be opened */
char *file_name;

/* Variables for the "quit" button */
static   char     *quit_label = "Quit";
static   unsigned quit_width, quit_height;

/* Function prototypes */
```

continues

Listing 12.1. continued

```
void initapp(/* int, char **, int, int, unsigned, unsigned */);
static int  quit_action(/* caddr_t */);
static void process_event();

static void swap2bytes(/* unsigned short *x */);
static int  adjust_index(/* int *bi, int *li, int *pi */);

static void load_file(/* char *filename */);
static void setup_disp();
static int  pick_visual(/* int depth_wanted, int class_wanted */);
static void setup_ximage();

/* Windows in the application */
Window dWin;

/*------------------------------------------------------------*/
main(argc, argv)
int argc;
char **argv;
{
    XWIN                *QuitButton, *which_xwin;
    XGCValues           xgcv;
    XSetWindowAttributes xswa;
    int                 i, win_depth;
    Atom                ATOM_WM_COLMAP_WIN;

    xwin_init();

    initapp(argc, argv, 20, 20, 500, 400);

/* Get filename from command line */
    for (i = 1; i < argc; i += 2)
    {
        if(strcmp("-file", argv[i]) == 0)
        {
            file_name = argv[i+1];
            break;
        }
    }
    if(i >= argc)
    {
        fprintf(stderr, "Need: viewpcx -file <file_name>\n");
        exit(1);
    }

/* Load the image file */
    load_file(file_name);

/* Check whether image file format is acceptable. */
    if(header.manufacturer != 0x0a) exit(1);

/* Exit if we are not prepared to handle the image */
/* We only handle 1, 4, or 8-bit images */

    if(bits_per_pixel != 1 &&
       bits_per_pixel != 4 &&
       bits_per_pixel != 8)
```

```
        {
            fprintf(stderr, "Cannot handle %d bits per pixel\n",
                    bits_per_pixel);
            exit(1);
        }

/* Select a Visual and colormap for displaying the image */
    setup_disp();

/* Create the "Quit" button */
    quit_width = XTextWidth(theFontStruct, quit_label,
                            strlen(quit_label)) + 4;
    quit_height = theFontStruct->max_bounds.ascent +
                    theFontStruct->max_bounds.descent + 4;

    QuitButton = MakeXButton(1, 1, quit_width, quit_height,
                             1, theFGpix, theBGpix, theMain,
                             quit_label, quit_action, NULL);

/* Create and map a window for displaying the image */
    if(bits_per_pixel == 1)
        win_depth = CopyFromParent;
    else
        win_depth = vis_depth;

    xswa.colormap = theColormap;
    xswa.background_pixel = theBGpix;
    xswa.border_pixel = theFGpix;

    dWin = XCreateWindow(theDisplay, theMain, 1,
            quit_height+8, image_width, image_height, 1,
            win_depth, InputOutput, theVisual,
            CWColormap | CWBackPixel | CWBorderPixel,
            &xswa);

    XSelectInput(theDisplay, dWin, ExposureMask);

    XMapRaised(theDisplay, dWin);

/* Set the WM_COLORMAP_WINDOWS property so that the Motif
 * window manager knows about the windows that have their
 * own colormap. In this case, we have only one such window.
 */
    if(theColormap != DefaultColormap(theDisplay, theScreen))
    {
        ATOM_WM_COLMAP_WIN = XInternAtom(theDisplay,
                            "WM_COLORMAP_WINDOWS", False);
        XChangeProperty(theDisplay, theMain, ATOM_WM_COLMAP_WIN,
                    XA_WINDOW, 32, PropModeReplace,
                    (unsigned char *)&dWin, 1);
    }

/* Set up a GC to display image */
    image_gc = XCreateGC(theDisplay, dWin, 0, 0);
    XSetForeground(theDisplay, image_gc, theFGpix);
    XSetBackground(theDisplay, image_gc, theBGpix);
```

continues

Listing 12.1. continued

```
/* Prepare the image */
    setup_ximage();

/* Event handling loop--keep processing events until done */

    while (!AppDone)
        process_event();

/* Close connection to display and exit */

    XCloseDisplay(theDisplay);
    exit(0);
}
/*-------------------------------------------------------------*/
/* p r o c e s s _ e v e n t
 *
 *  Retrieve an event and process it...
 */
static void process_event()
{
    XWIN     *which_xwin;

/* Get the next event from Xlib */
    XNextEvent(theDisplay, &theEvent);

/* Handle events for the dWin, the text display window */
    if(theEvent.xany.window == dWin)
    {
        switch (theEvent.type)
        {
            case Expose:
            {
/* Copy the exposed area from the pixmap to the window */
                XCopyArea(theDisplay, thePixmap, dWin, image_gc,
                    theEvent.xexpose.x, theEvent.xexpose.y,
                    theEvent.xexpose.width,
                    theEvent.xexpose.height,
                    theEvent.xexpose.x, theEvent.xexpose.y);
                break;
            }
        }
    }
/************** Process events for other windows  ************/
/* Retrieve the XWIN data from Xlib using the context
 * management routine XFindContext
 */
    if(XFindContext(theDisplay, theEvent.xany.window,
        xwin_context, (caddr_t *) &which_xwin) == 0)
    {
/* Call the event handler of this XWIN structure */
        if (*(which_xwin->event_handler) != NULL)
            (*(which_xwin->event_handler))(which_xwin);
    }
}
/*-------------------------------------------------------------*/
/* q u i t _ a c t i o n
 *
```

```
 *  This routine is called when a ButtonPress event occurs in
 *  the quit window.
 */
static int quit_action(data)
caddr_t data;
{
/* Set the done flag */
    AppDone = 1;
    return 1;
}
/*-------------------------------------------------------------*/
/*  l o a d _ f i l e
 *
 *  Read in .PCX image file to be displayed
 *
 */
static void load_file(filename)
char *filename;
{
    FILE    *p_file;
    int     numread=0, byte, i, j,
            byteindex, lineindex, planeindex, count;
    long    imbytes, pcx_image_size;

/* Open the file */
    if((p_file = fopen(filename, "r")) == NULL)
    {
        fprintf(stderr, "Cannot open: %s\n", filename);
        exit(1);
    }

/* Read header */

    if((numread = fread(&header, 1, sizeof(PCX_HEADER), p_file))
         < sizeof(PCX_HEADER))
    {
        fprintf(stderr,
                "Incomplete file header (%d bytes). Exiting...\n",
                numread);
        exit(1);
    }

/* Swap bytes in "big-endian" systems (not needed in 80x86-based
 * systems.
 */
#ifdef BIG_ENDIAN
    swap2bytes((unsigned short *) &header.xmin);
    swap2bytes((unsigned short *)&header.ymin);
    swap2bytes((unsigned short *)&header.xmax);
    swap2bytes((unsigned short *)&header.ymax);
    swap2bytes(&header.hresolution);
    swap2bytes(&header.vresolution);
    swap2bytes(&header.bytes_per_line);
    swap2bytes((unsigned short *)&header.palette_info);
#endif

/* Allocate storage for decoding image */
    image_width = header.xmax - header.xmin + 1;
```

continues

Listing 12.1. continued

```
    image_height = header.ymax - header.ymin + 1;
    pcx_image_size = (long) header.nplanes *
                            (long) image_height *
                            (long) header.bytes_per_line;

    if((image = (PLANE *) calloc(header.nplanes,
                        sizeof(PLANE))) == NULL)
    {
        fprintf(stderr,
                "Error allocating image...%d planes, %d bytes\n",
                header.nplanes, sizeof(PLANE));
        exit(1);
    }
    for(i = 0; i < header.nplanes; i++)
    {
        if((image[i] = (SCANLINE *) calloc(image_height,
                            sizeof(SCANLINE))) == NULL)
        {
            fprintf(stderr, "Error allocating plane %d...\n", i);
            exit(1);
        }

        for(j = 0; j < image_height; j++)
        {
            if((image[i][j] = (SCANLINE)
                        calloc(header.bytes_per_line,
                            sizeof(unsigned char))) == NULL)
            {
                fprintf(stderr,
                        "Error allocating line %d in plane %d\n",
                        j, i);
                exit(1);
            }
        }
    }

/* Decode run-length encoded image data */
    lineindex = 0;
    byteindex = 0;
    planeindex = 0;
    imbytes = 0;
    while ((byte = getc(p_file)) != EOF)
    {
        byte &= 0xff;
        if((byte & 0xc0) == 0xc0)
        {
            count = byte & 0x3f;
            if((byte = getc(p_file)) != EOF)
                for(i = 0; i < count; i++)
                {
                    image[planeindex][lineindex][byteindex] = byte;
                    imbytes++;
                    if(adjust_index(&byteindex, &lineindex, &planeindex))
                        break;
                }
        }
        else
```

```
            {
                image[planeindex][lineindex][byteindex] = byte;
                imbytes++;
                if(adjust_index(&byteindex, &lineindex, &planeindex))
                    break;
            }
            if(imbytes >= pcx_image_size) break;
        }

/* Read the colormap. */
    colormap_size = 16;
    bits_per_pixel = header.nplanes *
                        header.bits_per_pixel_per_plane;
    if(bits_per_pixel == 1) colormap_size = 2;

    if(header.version >= 5 && bits_per_pixel > 4)
    {
/* Go back 769 bytes from the end of the file. */
        fseek(p_file, -769L, SEEK_END);
        if(getc(p_file) == 12)
        {
/* There is a 256-color colormap following this byte. */
            colormap_size = 256;
        }
    }
/* If image has more than 256 colors then there is no colormap. */
    if(bits_per_pixel > 8) colormap_size = 0;

/* Set up the colormap. */
    if(colormap_size > 0)
    {
        int cindex;

/* Create the XColor entries for the colormap */
        if((colors = (XColor *)calloc(colormap_size,
                            sizeof(XColor))) == NULL)
        {
            fprintf(stderr, "No memory for setting \
up colormap\n");
            exit(1);
        }
        for(cindex = 0; cindex < colormap_size; cindex++)
        {
            if(colormap_size == 256)
            {
/* Read colors from file. */
                colors[cindex].red     = CSCALE * getc(p_file);
                colors[cindex].green   = CSCALE * getc(p_file);
                colors[cindex].blue    = CSCALE * getc(p_file);
                colors[cindex].pixel   = cindex;
                colors[cindex].flags   = DoRed | DoGreen | DoBlue;
            }
            if(colormap_size == 16)
            {
/* 16-color colors from PCX header. */
                colors[cindex].red = CSCALE *
                                    header.colormap[3*cindex];
```

continues

Listing 12.1. continued

```
                    colors[cindex].green = CSCALE *
                                header.colormap[3*cindex+1];
                    colors[cindex].blue = CSCALE *
                                header.colormap[3*cindex+2];
                    colors[cindex].pixel    = cindex;
                    colors[cindex].flags    = DoRed ¦ DoGreen ¦ DoBlue;
                }
            }
        }

/* Close file and return */
    fclose(p_file);
}
/*------------------------------------------------------------*/
/*  s w a p 2 b y t e s
 *
 *  Swaps the bytes in a 2-byte short integer.
 */
static void swap2bytes(x)
unsigned short *x;
{
    union
    {
        unsigned short s;
        unsigned char  b[2];
    } b2;
    unsigned char t;

    b2.s = *x;
    t = b2.b[0];
    b2.b[0] = b2.b[1];
    b2.b[1] = t;
    *x = b2.s;
}
/*------------------------------------------------------------*/
/*  a d j u s t _ i n d e x
 *
 *  Adjusts the indices as image data is decoded.
 *
 */
static int adjust_index(bi, li, pi)
int *bi, *li, *pi;
{
    int status = 0;
    *bi += 1;
    if(*bi == header.bytes_per_line)
    {
        *bi = 0;
        *pi += 1;
        if(*pi == header.nplanes)
        {
            *pi = 0;
            *li += 1;
            if(*li == image_height)
            {
                printf("%d raster lines read.\n", *li);
                status = 1;
```

```
                }
            }
        }
        return (status);
}
/*------------------------------------------------------------*/
static void setup_disp()
{
    XVisualInfo vis_template;
    int         i;

    theScreen = DefaultScreen(theDisplay);

    if(bits_per_pixel != 1)
    {
/* Get a list of all visuals for this screen */
        vis_template.screen = theScreen;
        vis_list = XGetVisualInfo(theDisplay,
                        VisualScreenMask, &vis_template,
                        &num_visuals);
        if(num_visuals == 0)
        {
            fprintf(stderr, "No visuals found!\n");
            exit(0);
        }

/* Search for a PseudoColor visual with depth >= image depth.
 * You may want other strategies here--for visuals such
 * as "DirectColor" or for StaticColor with 8 or more
 * bit planes.
 */
        if(!pick_visual(bits_per_pixel, PseudoColor))
        {
            fprintf(stderr, "No appropriate visual...Exiting\n");
            exit(0);
        }

/* Create the colormap */
        theColormap = XCreateColormap(theDisplay,
                        RootWindow(theDisplay, theScreen),
                        theVisual, AllocAll);

/* Store the colors in the colormap */
        XStoreColors(theDisplay, theColormap, colors,
                        colormap_size);

/* Now we can release the memory used by the colors
 * because the X server already has this information.
 */
        free(colors);
    }
    else
    {
/* Image is monochrome. Handle using default visual */
        theVisual = DefaultVisual(theDisplay, theScreen);
        theColormap = DefaultColormap(theDisplay, theScreen);
        vis_depth = DefaultDepth(theDisplay, theScreen);
```

continues

Listing 12.1. continued

```
    }
}
/*------------------------------------------------------------*/
/*  p i c k _ v i s u a l
 *
 *  Select a visual of appropriate "class" and "depth" from
 *  the list of visuals. Return 1 if successful, 0 if no
 *  matching visuals found.
 */
static int pick_visual(depth_wanted, class_wanted)
int depth_wanted, class_wanted;
{
    XVisualInfo *p_visinfo;
    int         i, status = 0;

    for(i = 0, p_visinfo = vis_list; i < num_visuals;
        i++, p_visinfo++)
    {
        if(p_visinfo->class == class_wanted  &&
           p_visinfo->depth >= depth_wanted)
        {
            theVisual = p_visinfo->visual;
            vis_depth = p_visinfo->depth;
            status = 1;
            break;
        }
    }
    return (status);
}
/*------------------------------------------------------------*/
/*  s e t u p _ x i m a g e
 *
 *  Yes, we already have the decoded image in memory, but now
 *  we need it in a form usable by Xlib. This function creates
 *  the image data and sets up an XImage. It creates a Pixmap
 *  in the server and copies the image over using XPutImage.
 *  Once this is done, the image can be drawn by copying from
 *  the pixmap into the window (using XCopyArea).
 *
 *  Note that whether monochrome or not, the image is created
 *  at the depth of the selected visual.
 *
 */
static void setup_ximage()
{
    int            i, j, k, l, planeindex, select,
                   bytes_per_vis_depth, pixval_per_byte,
                   xim_width, pixpac_count = 0, curbyte = 0,
                   bits_copied = 0;
    unsigned long  pixval;
    unsigned int   image_bytes;

/* Compute some sizes */
    bytes_per_vis_depth = (vis_depth + 7) / 8;
    pixval_per_byte = (8/vis_depth);
    xim_width = 8 * ((image_width+7)/8);
```

```
        image_bytes = xim_width * bytes_per_vis_depth * image_height;

        if(pixval_per_byte > 1) image_bytes /= pixval_per_byte;

/* Allocate room for image's data */
    if((image_data = (unsigned char *)
                    calloc(image_bytes,
                            sizeof(unsigned char) )) == NULL)
    {
        fprintf(stderr, "Error allocating room for image...\n");
        exit(1);
    }

/* Set up image data in MSBFirst, ZPixmap format */
    if(header.nplanes == 1 &&
        header.bits_per_pixel_per_plane == 8)
    {
/* Handle 8-bit images in straightforward manner */
        for(j=0; j < image_height; j++)
    {
            for(i = 0; i < image_width; i++)
        {
                image_data[curbyte] = image[0][j][i];
                curbyte++;
        }
            if(xim_width > image_width)
            {
                for(k = image_width; k < xim_width; k++)
                    curbyte++;
            }
    }
    }
    else
    {
        for(j = 0; j < image_height; j++)
        {
            for(i = 0; i< (image_width+7)/8; i++)
            {
                select = 0x80;
/* The following for loop extracts bits from each byte */
                for(k = 0; k < 8; k++)
                {
/* First construct the pixel value */
                    pixval =  (image[0][j][i] & select) > 0;

                    if(header.nplanes  == 1)
                    {
/* For monochrome images, translate 1 and 0 into White and
 * Black pixel values
 */
                        if(pixval == 0)
                            pixval = theFGpix;
                        else
                            pixval = theBGpix;
                    }
                    if(header.nplanes  > 1)
                    {
```

continues

Listing 12.1. continued

```
                        for(planeindex=1;
                            planeindex < header.nplanes;
                            planeindex++)
                        {
/* Add other planes to the pixel value */
                            pixval = pixval << 1;
                            pixval ¦=  (image[planeindex][j][i] &
                                    select) > 0;
                        }
                    }

/* Copy pixel value into image's data array */
                    for(l = 0; l < bytes_per_vis_depth; l++)
                    {
                        if(pixval_per_byte > 1)
                        {
/* CASE A: more than one pixel value fits in a byte */
                            image_data[curbyte] ¦=
                                (pixval & 0xff) <<
                                (8 - pixpac_count * vis_depth);
                            pixpac_count++;
                            if(pixpac_count == pixval_per_byte)
                            {
                                pixpac_count = 0;
                                curbyte++;
                            }
                        }
                        else
                        {
/* CASE B: more than one byte per pixel value */
                            if(bits_copied + 8 <= vis_depth)
                            {
                                image_data[curbyte] = pixval & 0xff;
                                bits_copied += 8;
                            }
                            else
                            {
                                image_data[curbyte] =
                                    (pixval & 0xff) <<
                                    (vis_depth - bits_copied);
                                bits_copied = 0;
                            }
                            pixval >>= 8;
                            curbyte++;
                        }
                    }
/* Go to next bit in current byte from each bit plane */
                    select = select >> 1;
                }
            }
        }
    }

/* Set up an XImage structure in ZPixmap format */
    theXImage = XCreateImage(theDisplay, theVisual, vis_depth,
                ZPixmap, 0, (char *)image_data, xim_width,
```

```
                 image_height, 8, 0);

    theXImage->byte_order = MSBFirst;

/* Create a Pixmap and copy image into it */
    thePixmap = XCreatePixmap(theDisplay, dWin, theXImage->width,
                 theXImage->height, vis_depth);

    XPutImage(theDisplay, thePixmap, image_gc, theXImage,
            0, 0, 0, 0, theXImage->width, theXImage->height);

/* Now we can destroy the image because the information is in
 * the pixmap in the X server
 */
    XDestroyImage(theXImage);
}
```

Summary

In addition to basic graphical shapes and text, X also handles raster images. The X server supports images through the pixmap resource, a block of off-screen memory that stores a rectangular array of pixel values. The bits used for each pixel value equal the depth of the pixmap. Pixmaps are used as tiles and to store drawings. A pixmap is like a window, except that its contents are not displayed on the screen. You can draw into a pixmap as you would in a window. For this reason, X uses the generic term *drawable* to refer to both windows and pixmaps.

Because a pixmap is a resource, you have to create it before using it. When a pixmap is created, its contents are undefined. You can set up a pixmap by drawing into it using Xlib's drawing functions. A pixmap can be displayed by copying into a window.

Pixmaps of depth 1 are called bitmaps. Bitmaps are often used as stencils through which the X server draws into a drawable. Bitmaps also serve as clip masks. Xlib supports a text file format for bitmaps and provides special functions to read and create bitmaps.

Because raster images typically involve large amounts of data, Xlib provides the XImage structure to enable handling of images locally at the client application. The XImage structure encapsulates all information about an image and it includes a pointer to the image data. Xlib supports several formats of image data and includes functions to manipulate the pixel values in an image.

The last part of this chapter presents an example program, viewpcx, that reads, decodes, and displays images stored in the PC Paintbrush .PCX format. The source code of this program illustrates how to select a visual, set up a colormap, create image data in Xlib's ZPixmap format, and display the resulting image in an X window.

## Part Four

Developing
X Applications

Chapter 13

X Toolkits

You have seen Xlib—the C programming language interface to the X Window System—in action. You have seen how Xlib functions help you build graphical user interfaces with menus and buttons, using a hierarchy of windows. And you have seen how graphics, text, and images are displayed in these windows.

You can do a lot with Xlib, but you need some planning and organization before you build complete programs using Xlib functions. Even the examples in the preceding chapters rely on some homegrown utility routines. For example, Chapter 7, "Creating and Managing Windows," introduces some utility routines to set up the top-level window in a program, and Chapter 8, "Handling Events," presents a scheme for handling events in an organized manner using the context management functions in Xlib. With these tools available, you could write complete programs that handle user-defined resources and command-line options.

Chapter 8 also develops a few reusable components—buttons (Listing 8.3) and menus (Listing 8.7). The button displays a string in a window, and its event handling function calls a predefined function when the user presses a mouse button with the pointer inside the window. The menu is built from a number of buttons laid out next to one another. The buttons and menus are reusable components because you can create multiple copies and use them to build complicated user interfaces, just as the buttons are used to build a menu. You can think of each component as a collection of windows organized in a hierarchy, which is exactly what the X Window System supports.

To build user interfaces without being bogged down in details, you need utility functions and a collection of prefabricated user-interface components, such as buttons, menus, and scrollbars. X toolkits provide the tools that help you build user interfaces easily.

Most X toolkits consist of two parts:

+ X Toolkit Instrinsics (Xt Intrinsics, for short)
+ User-interface components, commonly referred to as widgets

Xt Intrinsics is a set of high-level utility functions and data structures upon which the widgets are built.

There are several common X toolkits. One well-known public-domain toolkit is the Athena widget set developed at MIT. The other prominent commercial toolkits are the Open Software Foundation's OSF/Motif toolkit and the OPEN LOOK toolkit from Sun and AT&T.

Because you are likely to use a toolkit to build your applications, this chapter and the next two discuss the OSF/Motif toolkit, which is based on the Xt Intrinsics. This chapter describes how to create and manipulate widgets through the functions provided by the Xt Intrinsics. Chapter 14, "OSF/ Motif Widgets," presents an overview of the OSF/Motif widget set. Chapter 15, "Toolkit-Based Applications," explains how to use widgets with Xlib functions to build applications.

NOTE:

X toolkits are like the standard C library. Someone has carefully designed and implemented the functions for many common tasks that you have to handle in a C program. For example, to open a file, all you have to do is call `fopen` and, irrespective of the underlying operating system, the file is opened. As with the C library, the X toolkit provides a standard and efficient way to do your job—build a graphical user interface.

Aside from keeping the size of the source code manageable, a well-designed X toolkit makes efficient use of the X protocol requests by sending requests only when necessary. One drawback is the size of toolkit-based applications—they tend to be much larger than comparable applications built using Xlib alone. Another drawback is that more than one X toolkit exists and each has its own unique programming interface. The current crop of X toolkits includes Open Software Foundation's OSF/Motif toolkit, AT&T's XT+ OPEN LOOK widget set, Sun's XView, and the Athena Widgets, to name but a few. This book covers the OSF/Motif toolkit, which is the dominant commercial standard among X toolkits.

Xt Intrinsics

Xt Intrinsics is a library of functions and data structures layered on top of Xlib. There are two ways of looking at the Xt Intrinsics:

+ It provides a set of utility functions for one-step initialization of an application's main window, for reading and interpreting user-defined resource files, for handling events, and for creating and manipulating widgets. This is the view of Xt Intrinsics that you see when developing applications. (See Chapter 3, "Exploring X Applications," for information on specifying the resources of X applications via resource files.)

✦ The basic data structures of the Xt Intrinsics can be used to develop new widgets. For instance, the design of these data structures is such that you can pick an existing widget and extend its functionality to create a specialized version of the widget. For this widget-writing role, you have to understand the architecture of the toolkit. (Some of this is covered in Chapter 14.)

The following sections explain the Xt programming model and how you use it to build user interfaces with existing widgets.

X Toolkit Programming Model

When using an Xt Intrinsics-based toolkit, you write your application in a specific manner prescribed by Xt Intrinsics. The programming model is closely related to that for Xlib, with some crucial differences. As shown in Figure 13.1, your application can make use of functions from Xlib, the Xt Intrinsics layer, and the toolkit itself. The toolkit also calls functions from your application.

Figure 13.1.

The X toolkit programming model.

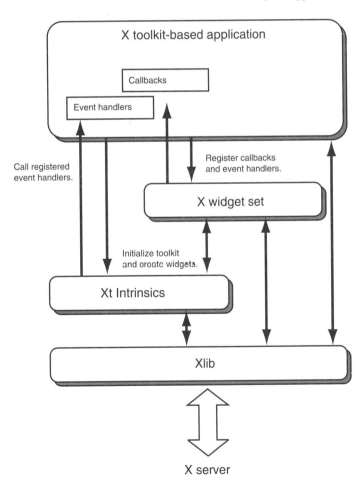

Event Handlers

With Xlib you set up your windows and enter a loop where the program continually retrieves events and processes them. With an X toolkit, the event handling loop is simplified:

1. Initialize the toolkit, create the widgets, and set up their internal parameters (the resources).

2. Write small routines for handling specific events, such as a mouse buttonpress occurring in a PushButton widget.

3. Register these event handlers with the toolkit by calling the XtAddEventHandler function.

4. Call the XtAppMainLoop function and let the toolkit handle all events. The toolkit, in turn, calls your registered event handlers at the appropriate time.

Callback Functions

Most of the time, however, you do not have to handle events by installing event handlers. Instead, each widget handles the X events and, based on a sequence of events, decides when to use a callback function. Callback functions are registered by calling XtAddCallback. Most of an application's work is done in one or more callback routines. The exact number and type of callback routine depends on the widget. For example, a PushButton widget may accept a callback routine that will be invoked when the left mouse button is pressed and released with the pointer inside the PushButton widget's window. Typically, a widget accepts a list of callback functions so that you can have a number of functions called in response to a single event. The callback functions are called one after another according to the order in which they were registered.

X Toolkit-Based Programming

Use the following steps when writing programs that use widgets based on the Xt Intrinsics:

1. Include the header files. For the OSF/Motif toolkit, use the following:

   ```
   #include <Xm/Xm.h>

   /* Include header file of each widget you plan to use
    * This is for the Form, Label, and PushButton widgets
    */
   #include <Xm/Form.h>
   #include <Xm/Label.h>
   #include <Xm/PushB.h>
   ```

2. Initialize the toolkit and create a top-level widget by calling the XtAppInitialize function. This returns an identifier for the top-level widget.

3. Create each widget, using XtVaCreateManagedWidget and setting resources as necessary. Add callbacks, using XtAddCallback, and add event handlers, if any. Usually, all application-specific work is handled in the callback functions.

4. Realize the widgets by calling the `XtRealizeWidget`, with the identifier of the top-level widget as the argument.

5. Start the main event processing loop with a call to the `XtAppMainLoop` function.

Listing 13.1 shows a short example, xmdemo, that illustrates the steps involved in writing a program that uses the OSF/Motif toolkit. A more substantial example appears at the end of this chapter.

Listing 13.1. `xmdemo.c`—An example of X toolkit programming.

```
/*--------------------------------------------------------------*/
/*  File:  xmdemo.c
 *
 *  An example program that displays a PushButton widget.
 *
 */

/* STEP 1:  Include the header files */

#include <Xm/Xm.h>
#include <Xm/PushB.h>

/* Label for the pushbutton */
static char quit_label[] = "Press here to exit...";

/* Room for setting up arguments passed to widgets */
static Arg args[10];

/* Prototype of callback function */

static void button_pushed( /* Widget w, XtPointer client_data,
                    XmAnyCallbackStruct *call_data */ );


/*--------------------------------------------------------------*/
void main(argc, argv)
int argc;
char **argv;
{
    XtAppContext app;
    Widget      main_widget, quit_button;
    XmString    xmlabel;

/* STEP 2: Initialize toolkit and create the top-level widget */
    main_widget = XtAppInitialize(&app, "XMdemo", NULL, 0,
                            &argc, argv, NULL, NULL, 0);

/* STEP 3: Create the pushbutton widget, setting its label
 *         at the same time. Create the label and free it
 *         after the widget is created.
 */
    xmlabel = XmStringCreateLtoR(quit_label,
                            XmSTRING_DEFAULT_CHARSET),
    quit_button = XtVaCreateManagedWidget("Exit",
                        xmPushButtonWidgetClass, main_widget,
                        XmNlabelString, xmlabel,
```

continues

Listing 13.1. continued

```
                        NULL);
    XmStringFree(xmlabel);

/* Install the callback function for this pushbutton */
    XtAddCallback(quit_button, XmNactivateCallback,
                    button_pushed, NULL);

/* STEP 4: Realize the widgets */
    XtRealizeWidget(main_widget);

/* STEP 5: Start the main event handling loop */
    XtAppMainLoop(app);
}
/*------------------------------------------------------------*/
/* b u t t o n _ p u s h e d
 *
 * Function to be called when user presses and releases button
 * in the "exit" pushbutton.
 */
static void button_pushed(w, client_data, call_data)
Widget w;
XtPointer client_data;
XmAnyCallbackStruct *call_data;
{
    XtCloseDisplay(XtDisplay(w));
    exit(0);
}
```

In the callback function `button_pushed`, you close the display by calling `XtCloseDisplay`. This function requires a pointer to a `Display` as the argument. You use `XtDisplay(w)` to obtain a pointer to the `Display` structure used by the widget w. Similarly, the ID of widget w's window is given by the following:

```
XtWindow(w)
```

The exact steps for compiling and linking an X toolkit-based application depend on the toolkit and on your operating system. On the author's Sun SPARCstation IPC running Solaris 4.1.3 and X11R6, the following command line compiles and links the example shown in Listing 13.1:

```
cc -o xmdemo xmdemo.c -lXm -lXt -lXmu -lX11
```

The X11R6 version of `Xt` requires you to link with two additional libraries: `SM` and `ICE`. You can either link with these libraries explicitly with the option `-lSM -lICE`, or link with the `Xmu` library, which then links with the SM and ICE libraries.

On other UNIX systems, you may have to link with additional libraries (such as networking libraries on 386 UNIX systems) or contend with other nuances (such as the nonstandard location of the libraries and include files under HP-UX 9.x).

Once xmdemo is built, you can run it from the UNIX shell—from an xterm window, for instance. Figure 13.2 shows the output generated by the xmdemo program. When you click on the pushbutton (by pressing and releasing the left mouse button with the pointer inside the pushbutton's window), the program exits.

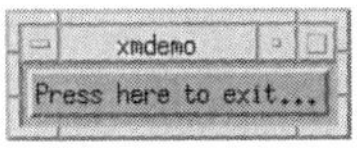

Figure 13.2.
Output of the xmdemo program.

Step-by-Step Toolkit Programming

Now that you have seen the basic structure of a toolkit-based program, let's examine each of the steps in detail. This introduces you to the convenience functions in Xt Intrinsics that help you create and manipulate widgets.

Including the Header Files

In addition to C header files such as `<stdio.h>`, programs that use the OSF/Motif toolkit must include the header file `<Xm/Xm.h>`. This header file includes other necessary header files that define symbolic names for standard widget resources (such as foreground and background colors) and structures used to initialize and use widgets.

Following the header file `<Xm/Xm.h>` are the header files for each type of widget you use in the program. For example, if a program uses `ScrolledWindow`, `ScrollBar`, and `PushButton` widgets, the sequence of header files is as follows:

```
#include <Xm/Xm>
#include <Xm/PushB.h>
#include <Xm/ScrolledW.h>
#include <Xm/ScrollBar.h>
```

Initializing the Toolkit

From the preceding chapters on Xlib programming, you know that all X applications must start by opening a connection to the X server. Once the connection is established, you have to create a top-level window for your application. This step involves working with the window manager to set up the initial position and size (geometry) of the top-level window. If the user specifies the geometry on the command line, you are supposed to use that information to set up the top-level window. The initapp.c function in Chapter 7, Listing 7.2, shows the chores that have to be handled by an X application at startup.

The Xt Intrinsics provides the `XtAppInitialize` function to take care of these steps. This function initializes an application context (information associated with an instance of the application), opens a connection to the X display, parses the command-line options, and creates a top-level widget with an associated top-level window that serves as the parent of all other widgets in your application. This top-level widget is known as a `Shell` widget.

The XtAppInitialize function has the following prototype:

```
Widget XtInitialize(
XtAppContext    *app_context,/* Application context         */
String          app_class,   /* Class name of application   */
XrmOptionDescRec options[],   /* List of acceptable options  */
Cardinal        num_options, /* Number of options in list   */
Cardinal        *argc,       /* Pointer to number of        */
                             /* command-line arguments      */
String          *argv,       /* Array of command-line       */
                             /* arguments to be processed   */
String          *fallbacks,  /* Predefined resource list    */
ArgList         *args,       /* Argument list and number    */
Cardinal        nargs);      /* arguments for toplevel shell */
```

The data types Cardinal and String are defined in the header file <X11/Intrinsic.h>, which is included in <Xm/Xm.h>.

The first argument to XtAppInitialize is the address of an XtAppContext structure that will be initialized with information about the current instance of the program. Xt uses the context information to manage the event loops when multiple copies of the application are running.

The second argument is the class name of the application. By convention, Xt-based applications use the name of the application with the first letter capitalized for the class name. When the first letter of the application's name is an X, the first two letters are capitalized in the class name. Thus, for the xmdemo program shown in Listing 13.1, the application name is xmdemo and the conventional class name is XMdemo.

The options array of XrmOptionDescRec structures describes the options accepted by the application. You learn more about options later in this chapter.

The next two arguments are &argc and argv; argc is the number of command-line arguments and argv is the array of actual command-line arguments. You have to provide the address of argc because XtAppInitialize alters argc after removing applicable options from argv.

The next parameter, fallbacks, is an array of strings in which each string specifies a resource and its value (see Chapter 3 for the format of specifying resource values in X). Xt uses these resource settings if expected resource files cannot be found when the application runs.

The last two arguments, args and nargs, enable you to provide an argument list to set various resources of the top-level shell.

For most applications, a typical call to XtAppInitialize is the following:

```
/* Program's name is "demo"-- thus class-name is "Demo" */

void main(int argc, char **argv)
{
    Widget toplevel;
    XtAppContext app;

/* Initialize toolkit and create the top-level widget */
```

```
toplevel = XtAppInitialize(&app, "Demo", NULL, 0,
                           &argc, argv, NULL, NULL, 0);


   ...
}
```

Creating and Initializing Widgets

You can think of a widget as a window with some relevant data. Chapter 14 covers the details of the data structures used by a widget. To get a rough idea of a widget's data structure, consider a `Label` widget that displays some text in a window. Clearly, this widget needs a window to display the label. Additionally, it needs a text string and a `GC` to display the string. The window's size must be remembered and a procedure is needed to draw the label when an `Expose` event is reported for its window. As you will see in Chapter 14, the Xt Intrinsics provides the necessary data structures to store the information for a widget, and the Intrinsics has a standard method of handling tasks, such as drawing in response to `Expose` events.

Setting a Widget's Resources

When using a widget in an application, you do not need to know the details of the widget's data structure. You do need information about the arguments that each widget accepts. These arguments, also known as the widget's resources, control its appearance and behavior.

> **NOTE:**
>
> The term *resource* has two different meanings in X. The resource of an application or a widget means any configurable data used by that application or widget. When used in the context of the X server, the resource implies things such as windows, `GC`s, colormaps, and fonts that applications create and use to display output.

To be useful as a building block of user interfaces, a widget must be highly configurable. For instance, a widget that enables the programmer to pick the foreground and background colors is much more useful than one that hard-wires the values. The best solution is to set a widget's resources from a resource database—a text file that defines values of parameters in a specific syntax. (Chapter 3 describes how you can specify an application's resources in a text file.)

The next best approach to setting a widget's resources is to set them with an argument list. To do this, first consult the widget's documentation and determine the names of the resources you want to set. The resource names are constants defined in a header file (`<Xm/Xm.h>` for the OSF/Motif widgets). For example, `XmNwidth`, `XmNheight` are defined in `<Xm/Xm.h>` as the following:

```
#define XmNwidth    "width"
#define XmNheight   "height"
```

You use the constants XmNwidth and XmNheight to refer to the width and height resources of a widget. The value of each resource is specified in an Arg structure, which is defined in <X11/Intrinsic.h> as follows:

```
typedef struct
{
    String    name;  /* Name of resource */
    XtArgVal  value; /* Its value        */
} Arg, *ArgList;
```

The value of the named resource is stored as an XtArgVal—a system-dependent data type capable of holding a pointer to any C variable. If the value of a resource is less than the size of XtArgVal, it is stored directly in the value field of Arg. Otherwise, the value field is a pointer to the resource's value.

> **NOTE:**
>
> Xlib, the Xt Intrinsics, and the OSF/Motif toolkit follow standard naming conventions for variables and functions. Xlib uses an X as the prefix for all functions and data types. The Xt Intrinsics uses the Xt prefix for functions and macros. The Intrinsics defines names of resources and resource classes with the prefixes XtN and XtC, respectively. OSF/Motif uses Xm as the prefix for functions and for names of widgets, and widget class pointers start with xm and have the suffix WidgetClass. Thus, the Label widget's name is XmLabel and its class pointer is xmLabelWidgetClass. Names of resources use the XmN prefix, and each resource's class name begins with an XmC.

When creating a widget, you can specify an array of Arg structures with values of the resources that you wish to set. You can prepare the array of resource values in two ways:

✦ By using a statically initialized array

✦ By assigning values at run-time using the XtSetArg macro

To see how to set resources, consider the OSF/Motif PushButton widget. Suppose you want to set the pushbutton's width and height as well as the label to be displayed in it. The documentation of the XmPushButton widget provides the names of the resources XmNwidth, XmNheight, and XmNlabelString. You also have to know that the string for XmNlabelString is not a simple C character array—it is a *compound string*, a special data type that you create by passing the string as an argument to a utility routine (XmStringCreateLtoR).

With the information about the resources in hand, you can set the values in the following manner:

```
Arg       args[20];
Cardinal nargs;
XmString xms;
.
.
xms = XmStringCreateLtoR("Press for help",
        XmSTRING_DEFAULT_CHARSET);
XtSetArg(args[nargs], XmNwidth, 300);        nargs++;
```

```
XtSetArg(args[nargs], XmNheight, 100);        nargs++;
XtSetArg(args[nargs], XmNlabelString, xms);  nargs++;
XmStringFree(xms);
```

There is a reason why nargs++ is not used in XtSetArg to increment the count of arguments—XtSetArg is defined as a macro in such a way that it uses the first argument twice. If you use nargs++ in the first argument, the macro increments nargs twice in each call. Thus, most toolkit applications define the argument list as shown.

Creating a Widget

When the argument list is ready, you can create a widget and set its resources by calling the XtCreateManagedWidget function:

```
Widget   toplevel,  /* Previously-created top-level shell */
         button1;   /* New pushbutton                     */

button1 = XtCreateManagedWidget("HelpButton",
                 xmPushButtonWidgetClass, toplevel,
                 (ArgList) args, nargs);
```

This creates a new pushbutton named HelpButton whose parent widget is toplevel and whose initial resource settings are in the array args.

The name of the widget is used to retrieve from the resource database any resource meant for this widget. Chapter 3 explains how users can specify the resources of the widgets in the resource database.

One-Step Widget Creation

There is a way to avoid the tedious steps of specifying the resources one by one and then creating the widget. The Xt Intrinsics library includes the XtVaCreateManagedWidget function, which enables you to specify the resources and create the widget with a single function call. For instance, you can create a pushbutton of specified width, height, and label by using the following call to XtVaCreateManagedWidget:

```
Widget   toplevel,  /* Previously-created top-level shell */
         h_button;  /* New pushbutton                     */
XmString xmlabel;   /* Compound string to store label     */

/* First, create the compound string for the label */
xmlabel = XmStringCreateLtoR("Press for help",
                        XmSTRING_DEFAULT_CHARSET),

h_button = XtVaCreateManagedWidget("HelpButton",
                 xmPushButtonWidgetClass, toplevel,
                 XmNwidth,      200,
                 XmNheight,     100,
                 XmNlabelString, xmlabel,
                 NULL);

/* Free the compound string (the Motif toolkit makes a copy) */
XmStringFree(xmlabel);
```

As you can see, `XtVaCreateManagedWidget` accepts a variable number of arguments; the first three arguments are required and are the same as those required by `XtCreateManagedWidget`. Following the three compulsory arguments, `XtVaCreateManagedWidget` expects a list of resource specifications. Each specification is in the form of a resource name followed by the value of that resource. A NULL resource name marks the end of this list.

Registering Callbacks

Many widgets include a class of resources known as callbacks that are pointers to functions. You can set such a resource to one of your functions and have the widget call the function in response to one or more events. Recall that callback functions are so named because the X toolkit calls them back when appropriate. A widget may have more than one type of callback resource, with each type meant for functions to be called under a specific situation. A widget's callback resource is actually a list of functions rather than a single function. The widget calls all the callbacks when the conditions for that callback resource are met. The calling order is the same as the order in which you register the callbacks.

In Listing 13.1, the function `button_pushed` is set to be a callback function for the `PushButton` widget's `XmNactivateCallback` resource. According to the documentation of the `XmPushButton` widget, the widget calls the functions in the `XmNactivateCallback` resource when the user presses and releases the left mouse button (this can be changed to another button) with the pointer inside the pushbutton's window. The `XmPushButton` widget has two more callback resources:

✦ `XmNarmCallback` functions, called when the user presses the button

✦ `XmNdisarmCallback` list, called when the user releases the button

Adding to a Callback List

As shown in Listing 13.1, you use the `XtAddCallback` function to add a function to the callback list of a widget. To add the `button_pushed` function to the callback list specified by the `XmNactivateCallback` resource of the `XmPushButton` widget `quit_button`, write the following:

```
XtAddCallback(quit_button, XmNactivateCallback,
              button_pushed, NULL);
```

The last argument to `XtAddCallback`—defined to be of type `XtPointer`—is a pointer to data that you want passed to the callback function when the widget calls it. The callback function, `button_pushed`, has the following prototype:

```
static void button_pushed(Widget w, XtPointer client_data,
                XmAnyCallbackStruct *call_data);
```

When the widget calls this function, the second argument is whatever you had passed to `XtAddCallback` as the last argument. The last argument passed to the callback function is an `XmAnyCallbackStruct` structure, which is defined in `<Xm/Xm.h>` as follows:

```
typedef struct
{
    int     reason;    /* Indicates why callback was called   */
```

```
    XEvent  *event;     /* Information on event that triggered */
                        /* the callback                        */
} XmAnyCallbackStruct;
```

The reason field indicates why the widget called the callback function. You have to consult the widget's documentation to interpret the value of this field. The event field is a pointer to an XEvent structure with information on the event that triggered the callback.

Registering Event Handlers

Suppose you want to catch a mouse buttonpress in a widget's window. The designers of the Xt Intrinsics thoughtfully provided for this, using a method similar to the callback resources used by widgets. Essentially, you can register your own event handler for selected events on a widget's window. Thereafter, when these events occur, the Xt Intrinsics call the registered event handler, giving you a chance to take the desired action.

Suppose you want to alter the xmdemo program (Listing 13.1) so that when the user presses any mouse button in the pushbutton window, the label changes. Then on the next buttonpress, the program terminates. You can do this by adding your own handler for the ButtonPress event. Listing 13.2 shows the modified version of the program.

You use the Intrinsics function XtAddEventHandler to add the handler. To add a function named my_event_handler as the handler for ButtonPress events in the quit_button widget, you write the following:

```
XtAddEventHandler(quit_button, ButtonPressMask, FALSE,
                  my_event_handler, NULL);
```

The second argument to XtAddEventHandler is an event mask that determines for which events the handler is invoked. The mask is used in the same way as you do when calling XSelectInput (see Chapter 6, "The Xlib Programming Model").

The third argument is a Boolean that should be set to True if you are setting the event handler for one of the events for which there is no event mask—ClientMessage, MappingNotify, SelectionClear, or SelectionRequest. In this case, set the second argument to NoEventMask.

As in XtAddCallback, the last argument is a pointer to any data that you want passed back to the event handler when it is called.

Writing the Event Handler

You have to write the event handler my_event_handler according to the following prototype:

```
static void my_event_handler(Widget w, XtPointer client_data,
                             XEvent *p_event);
```

Xt Intrinsics calls the event handler with three arguments. The first argument is the widget's ID and the second one is the same pointer that you had passed as the last argument of XtAddEventHandler when registering this event handler. The third argument is a pointer to the XEvent structure that triggered the function call.

In Listing 13.2, the event handler creates a new label and sets it with the following code:

```
/* Room for setting up arguments passed to widgets */
    static Arg args[10];

    XmString xmlabel;

/* Create a new label and set it */
    xmlabel = XmStringCreateLtoR("Press again please",
                                  XmSTRING_DEFAULT_CHARSET);
    XtSetArg(args[0], XmNlabelString, xmlabel);
    XtSetValues(w, args, 1);

/* Free the compund string */
    XmStringFree(xmlabel);
```

When you set the XmPushButton widget's label string to a new value by calling XtSetValues, the widget automatically clears its window and generates an Expose event that subsequently causes the window to be redrawn with the new label.

Listing 13.2. `xmdemo_e.c`—Pushbutton with event handler.

```
/*-------------------------------------------------------------*/
/* File:  xmdemo_e.c
 *
 * An example program that displays a PushButton widget and
 * uses an event handler to change the message when user
 * presses the left mouse button.
 *
 */

#include <Xm/Xm.h>
#include <Xm/PushB.h>

static int quit_now = 0;

/* Label for the pushbutton */
static char quit_label[] = "Press here to exit...";

/* Room for setting up arguments passed to widgets */
static Arg args[10];

/* Prototype of callback function */

static void my_event_handler( /* Widget w, XtPointer client_data,
                                  XEvent *p_event */ );
/*-------------------------------------------------------------*/
void main(argc, argv)
int argc;
char **argv;
{
    XtAppContext app;
    Widget       main_widget, quit_button;
    XmString     xmlabel;

/* Create the top-level widget */
    main_widget = XtAppInitialize(&app, "XMdemo", NULL, 0,
```

```
                                  &argc, argv, NULL, NULL, 0);

/* Create the pushbutton widget and set its label */
    xmlabel = XmStringCreateLtoR(quit_label,
                                 XmSTRING_DEFAULT_CHARSET),
    quit_button = XtVaCreateManagedWidget("Exit",
                        xmPushButtonWidgetClass, main_widget,
                        XmNlabelString, xmlabel,
                        NULL);
    XmStringFree(xmlabel);

/* Install an event handler for ButtonPress events */
    XtAddEventHandler(quit_button, ButtonPressMask, FALSE,
                      my_event_handler, NULL);

/* Realize the widgets and start event processing loop */

    XtRealizeWidget(main_widget);
    XtAppMainLoop(app);
}
/*------------------------------------------------------------*/
/*  m y _ e v e n t _ h a n d l e r
 *
 *  Function to be called when the user presses a mouse button
 *  in the "exit" pushbutton.
 */
static void my_event_handler(w, client_data, p_event)
Widget w;
XtPointer client_data;
XEvent *p_event;
{

/* Exit if the quit flag is set */
    if(quit_now)
        exit(0);
    else
    {
        XmString xmlabel;

/* Create a new label and set it */
        xmlabel = XmStringCreateLtoR("Press again please",
                            XmSTRING_DEFAULT_CHARSET);
        XtSetArg(args[0], XmNlabelString, xmlabel);
        XtSetValues(w, args, 1);
        XmStringFree(xmlabel);

/* Set flag so that we quit on next ButtonPress */
        quit_now = 1;
    }
}
```

Realizing the Widgets

After all the widgets are created, you have to display their windows on the screen. You do this by calling the XtRealizeWidget function with the top-level widget as the sole argument:

```
Widget top-level;   /* The top-level widget */
.
.
/* Create the widget hierarchy */
.
.
/* Display the windows */
XtRealizeWidget(top_level);
```

Calling XtRealizeWidget is similar to calling XMapWindow in Xlib programming. Although the widgets are created, they are not visible until XtRealizeWidget is called.

Using the Event Handling Loop

When programming with Xlib alone, you have to retrieve events and process each one—even if the processing for certain events is to simply ignore them. In fact, much of the complexity of Xlib-based programs comes from the need to process events for a large number of windows in an X application. Xt Intrinsics greatly simplifies event handling. Each widget in an X toolkit-based application has an associated window and an event handling function. The arrangement is not unlike the event handling scheme outlined in Chapter 8 that uses Xlib's context management functions to store the event handler for a window, with the window ID as an index.

In Xt Intrinsics, you can retrieve an event and process it with the following sequence of function calls:

```
XtAppContext app;   /* Application context of this app. */
XEvent theEvent;    /* Structure for retrieving event   */


XtAppNextEvent(app, &theEvent);
XtDispatchEvent(&theEvent);
```

Because X applications usually work by repeatedly retrieving and processing events, you can code the entire event handling loop:

```
XtAppContext app;   /* Application context of this app. */
XEvent theEvent;    /* Structure for retrieving event   */
.
.
do
{
    XtAppNextEvent(app, &theEvent);
    XtDispatchEvent(&theEvent);
} while(app->exit_flag == FALSE);
```

Xt Intrinsics simplifies event handling even further by providing the function XtAppMainLoop, which embodies this loop. You call this function with the application's context as argument. After you call XtAppMainLoop, you have no way of exiting the application except through a callback function or a registered event handler, as illustrated in Listings 13.1 and 13.2.

Hello, World! with OSF/Motif Widgets

You have seen the basic functions of the Xt Intrinsics and how they are used to create and manage widgets. The next few sections present a longer example than the one in Listing 13.1. The example is xmhello, the OSF/Motif version of the Xlib-based xhello program shown in Listing 5.1 in Chapter 5, "A Simple X Application." You can compare the two and see how an X toolkit reduces the drudgery of writing X applications. xmhello also displays the Hello, World! message in a window. To provide a convenient way of exiting xmhello, you include a pushbutton labeled Quit. The program ends when the user clicks on this button.

Widget Selection

In writing xmhello to use the OSF/Motif toolkit, the first step is to identify appropriate widgets to accomplish the job. You can display the Hello, World! message in an XmLabel widget and use an XmPushButton widget for the Quit button, but you need some way to position these two widgets in the application's main window. The XmForm widget is a good candidate for this. Thus, your widget hierarchy will be a top-level shell with a Form widget as the only child. The Form widget will have a label and a pushbutton as children. Figure 13.3 illustrates the widget tree for xmhello.

Figure 13.3.

The widget hierarchy in xmhello.

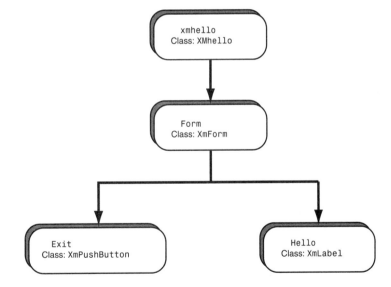

Application-Specific Resources

Widgets in X toolkits retrieve their resources automatically from one or more resource files—usually, a file with the same name as the application's class in the directory /usr/lib/X11/app-defaults or the .Xdefaults file in the user's login directory. Chapter 3 describes how to specify resources in a resource file.

In addition to the resources used by the widgets, you may need additional resources for parameters used by your application. In xmhello, you want to enable the user to specify the message and the label for the Quit button. Accordingly, you will use two resources, mtext and etext, which are the strings to be displayed in the label and in the pushbutton, respectively.

NOTE:

Applications created with the OSF/Motif toolkit automatically load resources from several sources. Resources from all the sources are merged—new specifications override older ones encountered earlier. For an application such as xmhello of class XMhello, the typical sequence is the following (in order of precedence):

1. Use any hard-coded resource values specified in the application's code.

2. Use any resource values specified on the command line through options such as -geometry, -bg, and -xrm.

3. Load resources from the file specified in the XENVIRONMENT environment variable. If XENVIRONMENT is not defined, look for the file $HOME/.Xdefaults-*host*, where *host* is the name of the system on which the client application (not the X server) is running.

4. Load data in the RESOURCE_MANAGER property on the root window, provided the property exists. In the absence of the RESOURCE_MANAGER property, load the file .Xdefaults in the home directory of the user.

5. If the XUSERFILESEARCHPATH environment variable is defined (as a colon-separated list of resource pathnames), load resources from that file. Otherwise, load the file XMhello from the directory specified in the XAPPLRESDIR environment variable. If XAPPLRESDIR is not defined, load the file XMhello from the user's login directory ($HOME).

6. If the XFILESEARCHPATH environment variable is defined, load the file XMhello from one of the directories specified in XFILESEARCHPATH. Otherwise, load the file /usr/lib/X11/app-defaults/XMhello.

7. If none of the previous steps provide the resources, load the fallback resources specified in the call to XtAppInitialize.

Most X toolkits follow these basic steps. Because the command-line options take precedence over all but the hard-coded resources, the user can always override resources from the command line.

To use application-specific resources, you define a data structure to hold the values of these resources. Then you create an array of XtResource structure with information about the resources and where each resource's value should be loaded. The XtResource structure is defined in <X11/Intrinsic.h> as follows:

```
typedef struct _XtResource
{
    String    resource_name;   /* Name of resource              */
    String    resource_class;  /* Class name of resource        */
    String    resource_type;   /* Type of resource              */
    Cardinal  resource_size;   /* Size of its value in bytes    */
    Cardinal  resource_offset; /* Offset from base of structure */
                               /* that will hold resource values*/
    String    default_type;    /* Type of default value         */
    XtPointer default_addr;    /* Address of default value      */
} XtResource;
```

The following sample code from `xmhello` clarifies the meaning of the different fields in an `XtResource` structure:

```
typedef struct APP_DATA   /* Application's data     */
{
    char    *mtext;       /* Message string         */
    char    *etext;       /* Label on exit button   */
} APP_DATA, *P_APP_DATA;


/* Resources specific to this application */
static XtResource resources[] =
{
    {"mtext", "Mtext", XtRString, sizeof(String),
     XtOffset(P_APP_DATA, mtext), XtRString, "Hello, World!"},

    {"etext", "Etext", XtRString, sizeof(String),
     XtOffset(P_APP_DATA, etext), XtRString, "Quit"}
};

Widget    main_widget;   /* Top-level shell widget      */
APP_DATA  data;          /* Application's data structure */

    .
    .
    .
/* Later, in main program...Get the resources */

XtGetApplicationResources(main_widget, &data, resources,
                          XtNumber(resources), NULL, 0);
```

This code sets up the `resources` array with two `XtResource` structures initialized with information necessary to retrieve and interpret the values. The type of resource is specified using the defined constant `XtRString`, defined in `<X11/StringDefs.h>`. Other common representation types, such as `XtRInt` for integers and `XtRColor` for colors, are also defined in this header file.

To retrieve and load the resources, you call the `XtGetApplicationResources` function as shown in the code. This function converts the value of each resource from a string to the specified type and places the value at a specified offset in the data structure whose address you provide as the second argument (`data` in the example). The offset for each resource is indicated in the `resource_offset` field of that resource's `XtResource` structure. You use the `XtOffset` macro to indicate the offset to the location within the structure where the resource's value is to be placed.

Command-Line Options

All toolkit-based applications accept a standard complement of command-line options. The common ones are foreground (-fg) and background (-bg) colors and the geometry of the top-level window (-geometry). Parameters specified in the command line usually have corresponding resources.

Your application can have command-line options in addition to those already supported by the Xt Intrinsics. In xmhello, you enable the user to specify the strings for the label and the pushbutton on the command line. As with the resources, you specify the acceptable command-line options in an array of XrmOptionDescRec structures. This structure and its pointer types are defined in <X11/Xresource.h> as follows:

```
typedef struct
{
    char            *option;     /* Option string in command line */
    char            *specifier;  /* Corresponding resource name    */
    XrmOptionKind   argKind;     /* The "style" of option          */
    XtPointer       value;       /* Pointer to value if argKind    */
                                 /* is XrmoptionNoArg              */
} XrmOptionDescRec, *XrmOptionDescList;
```

The argKind field indicates how the value of an option is given on the command line. This can be one of the enumerated constants shown in Table 13.1.

Table 13.1. Argument Styles for Command-Line Options

Argument Style	Description
XrmoptionNoArg	Value is specified in value field of the XrmOptionDescRec structure
XrmoptionIsArg	Value is the option string itself
XrmoptionStickyArg	Value immediately follows option without any intervening space
XrmoptionSepArg	Value is the next argument in command line
XrmoptionResArg	A resource and its value appear in the next argument in the command line
XrmoptionSkipArg	Ignore this option and the next argument in the command line
XrmoptionSkipLine	Ignore this option and the rest of the command line
XrmoptionSkipNArgs	Ignore this option and the next *n* arguments where *n* is equal to the value field of the XrmOptionDescRec structure

For xmhello, the option strings are -mtext and -etext; each requires the string to follow the option. Thus, its options array is defined as follows:

```
/* Command-line options specific to this application */

static XrmOptionDescRec options[] =
{
    {"-mtext", "*mtext", XrmoptionSepArg, NULL},
    {"-etext", "*etext", XrmoptionSepArg, NULL}
};
```

Each command-line option requires the name of the corresponding resource's name. When you call XtAppInitialize to create the top-level Shell widget and initialize the toolkit, it loads the value of each option specified in the command line into the structure where its corresponding resource's value is supposed to go. For example, in xmhello, the options array is provided to XtAppInitialize as follows:

```
void main(argc, argv)
int argc;
char **argv;
{
    XtAppContext    app;
    Widget          main_widget;

/* Create and initialize the top-level widget. Also parse
 * the command line and accept any specified options.
 */
    main_widget = XtAppInitialize(&app, "XMhello", options,
                        XtNumber(options), &argc, argv,
                        NULL, NULL, 0);

        .
        .
        .
}
```

Putting Together *xmhello*

Listing 13.3 shows xmhello.c—the OSF/Motif application that displays a string in a label and provides a button so that the user can exit the program by clicking on it.

The only part of the program left unexplained is how you control the placement of the Label and PushButton widget inside the Form widget. This requires learning about the resources of the Form widget XmForm. Chapter 14 describes some of the OSF/Motif widgets, including the Form widget.

On the author's Sun SPARCstation IPC running SunOS 4.1.3 and X11R6, the following command line compiles and links the xmhello program:

```
cc -o xmhello xmhello.c -lXm -lXt -lXmu -lX11
```

Some variation of this should work on your system. You may need to modify or add some more library specifications.

Listing 13.3. xmhello.c—Saying Hello, World! with OSF/Motif widgets.

```
/*------------------------------------------------------------*/
/* File: xmhello.c
 *
 * Motif version of the "Hello, World!" program
 * with an exit button. Uses Motif's Form,
 * PushButton, and Label widgets.
 *
 */
#include <Xm/Xm.h>
#include <Xm/Form.h>
#include <Xm/Label.h>
#include <Xm/PushB.h>

typedef struct APP_DATA    /* Application's data   */
{
    char   *mtext;         /* Message string       */
    char   *etext;         /* Label on exit button */
} APP_DATA, *P_APP_DATA;

/* Command-line options specific to this application */

static XrmOptionDescRec options[] =
{
    {"-mtext", "*mtext", XrmoptionSepArg, NULL},
    {"-etext", "*etext", XrmoptionSepArg, NULL}
};

/* Resources specific to this application */

static XtResource resources[] =
{
    {"mtext", "Mtext", XtRString, sizeof(String),
     XtOffset(P_APP_DATA, mtext), XtRString, "Hello, World!"},

    {"etext", "Etext", XtRString, sizeof(String),
     XtOffset(P_APP_DATA, etext), XtRString, "Quit"}
};

/* Prototype of callback function */

static void quit_action(/* Widget w, XtPointer client_data,
                    XmAnyCallbackStruct *call_data */ );

/*------------------------------------------------------------*/
void main(argc, argv)
int argc;
char **argv;
{
    APP_DATA    data;
    XtAppContext app;
    Widget      main_widget, form_widget, hello_message,
                exit_button;
    XmString    xmlabel;

/* Create and initialize the top-level widget */
    main_widget = XtAppInitialize(&app, "XMhello", options,
```

```
                         XtNumber(options), &argc, argv,
                         NULL, NULL, 0);

/* Get the resources from the resource file */
    XtGetApplicationResources(main_widget, &data, resources,
                         XtNumber(resources), NULL, 0);

    printf("mtext = %s\netext = %s\n", data.mtext, data.etext);

/* Next, create the Form widget that will hold the exit
 * pushbutton and the label widget.
 */
    form_widget = XtCreateManagedWidget("Form",
                    xmFormWidgetClass, main_widget);

/* Create the exit button */
    xmlabel =  XmStringCreateLtoR(data.etext,
                             XmSTRING_DEFAULT_CHARSET);

    exit_button = XtVaCreateManagedWidget("Exit",
                    xmPushButtonWidgetClass, form_widget,
                    XmNtopAttachment,  XmATTACH_FORM,
                    XmNleftAttachment, XmATTACH_FORM,
                    XmNlabelString,    xmlabel,
                    NULL);
    XmStringFree(xmlabel);

/* Install the callback function for this pushbutton */
    XtAddCallback(exit_button, XmNactivateCallback,
                 quit_action, NULL);

/* Now, create the message label */
    xmlabel =  XmStringCreateLtoR(data.mtext,
                             XmSTRING_DEFAULT_CHARSET);

    hello_message = XtVaCreateManagedWidget("Hello",
                    xmLabelWidgetClass, form_widget,
                    XmNtopAttachment,    XmATTACH_WIDGET,
                    XmNtopWidget,        exit_button,
                    XmNleftAttachment,   XmATTACH_FORM,
                    XmNrightAttachment,  XmATTACH_FORM,
                    XmNbottomAttachment, XmATTACH_FORM,
                    XmNlabelString,      xmlabel,
                    NULL);

    XmStringFree(xmlabel);

/* Realize the widgets and start processing events */
    XtRealizeWidget(main_widget);
    XtAppMainLoop(app);
}
/*------------------------------------------------------------*/
/* q u i t _ a c t i o n
 *
 * Function to be called when user presses and releases button
 * in the "exit" pushbutton.
 */
```

continues

Listing 13.3. continued

```
static void quit_action(w, client_data, call_data)
Widget w;
XtPointer client_data;
XmAnyCallbackStruct *call_data;
{
    XtCloseDisplay(XtDisplay(w));
    exit(0);
}
```

Running *xmhello*

To run xmhello, type its name at the shell prompt. You can specify resources for xmhello in one of two places: in the file /usr/lib/X11/app-defaults/XMhello or in the XMhello file in your login directory. For instance, to specify a font, an initial size and position for xmhello's main window, and its foreground and background colors, you can place the following lines in the file XMhello file in your login directory:

```
*fontList:          "*helvetica-bold*-r-*140*"
*foreground:        black
*background:        white
*geometry:          200x100+10+10
```

Figure 13.4 shows the result of running xmhello after specifying these resources.

Figure 13.4.

*Hello, World! from
xmhello.*

If you want xmhello to display some other message than Hello, World! and a different string for the pushbutton, you can use the command-line options -mtext and -etext, respectively. The following is an example:

```
xmhello -mtext "File creation succeeded." -etext " OK "
```

Using Translation Manager

When you run the xmhello program, you might be surprised to see that resources such as foreground, background, and geometry are automatically handled in a toolkit-based application. In addition to handling certain resources automatically, the Xt Intrinsics also includes a *translation manager* that enables users to specify a mapping between the user's actions and the functions provided by a widget. The translation manager provides a powerful mechanism for users to customize the behavior of an application without recompiling the program.

In response to a user's actions (a combination of keystrokes and mouse button events), a widget performs an action, either by default or by calling functions in its callback list. You can use the translation manager to specify which callback to activate when certain keystrokes and mouse button events occur.

As an example, consider the PushButton widget in xmhello. Usually, when you press the left mouse button (Button1) in this widget, it calls the callbacks registered under the XmNactivateCallback resource. Suppose a user wants the pushbutton to call these callback functions when the Ctrl key is pressed together with Button1. This user can modify the behavior of xmhello by adding the following lines to the file XMhello in the login directory:

```
*XmPushButton.translations: #replace\n\
                    Ctrl<Btn1Down>: ArmAndActivate()
```

This specifies the translations resource for the pushbutton. The exact specification is in a format specified by the translation manager. In this case, it says that the action ArmAndActivate() should be bound to the event: Button1 of the mouse pressed while the Ctrl key is down. The names of the actions are specified by each widget's documentation.

Once this is done, you can exit from xmhello only by pressing the left button of the mouse (with the pointer inside the Quit button) while pressing the Ctrl key.

Adding Actions

As an application developer, you can also add your own list of actions that can be bound by the user to a combination of keystrokes and mouse events. Consider adding to xmhello a function that can be invoked by a user-defined sequence of keystrokes. Here are the steps to follow:

1. Define the function that will be called when the user-defined keystrokes occur, for example, quit. The function, which must accept four arguments, has the following prototype:

```
static void quit(Widget w, XEvent *ev,  String *params,
                Cardinal *num_params)
{
    printf("Quit() called\n");

/* Print out the parameters, if any */
    if(num_params)
    {
        int i;
        printf("num_params = %d\n", *num_params);
        for(i = 0; i < *num_params; i++)
            printf("Parameter %d = %s\n", i, params[i]);
    }
```

```
        XtCloseDisplay(XtDisplay(w));
        exit(0);
    }
```

In this case, when this function is called, xmhello quits. (Soon you will see how parameters are passed to this function.)

2. Prepare an array of XtActionsRec structures for which each structure is initialized with two fields: the name by which you want the user to refer to this action, and the function that performs the action. Here is the table for the quit function:

```
/* Function prototype */
static void quit(Widget w, XEvent *ev,  String *params,
                    Cardinal *num_params);


/* Actions table */
static XtActionsRec actions[] =
{
    {"Quit",   quit}
};
```

This table performs the crucial step of binding the name of an action to a function. In this case, the user will refer to this action by the name Quit.

3. Prepare a default binding for the action. This is merely a string that looks like a resource specification for the translation manager. For example, to bind the letter q to the action Quit, write the following:

```
static char default_translation[] = "<Key>q: Quit()";
```

4. In the program, after the toolkit has been initialized, call XtAppAddActions to register the new actions and parse the default binding from the string default_translation:

```
XtAppContext   app;  /* Context for this application */
XtTranslations translations;

        .

        .

XtAppAddActions(app, actions, XtNumber(actions));
translations = XtParseTranslationTable(default_translation);
```

5. After the PushButton widget exit_button has been created, call XtAugmentTranslations to add the default bindings to the translation table for this widget:

```
XtAugmentTranslations(exit_button, translations);
```

6. Recompile the program and run it.

7. Exit from the program by pressing the Q key. The program prints the following on the console:

```
Quit() called
num_params = 0
```

8. Add the following to the file XMhello in your home directory:

```
*XmPushButton.translations: #replace\n\
                       Ctrl<Key>z:  Quit(Goodbye, 10)
```

This binds Control-Z to the Quit action. Additionally, it passes two arguments to the function called to handle this action.

9. After modifying the resource file, you can exit from the modified xmhello by pressing either q or Control-Z. When you exit using Control-Z, the program prints the following on the console:

```
Quit() called
num_params = 2
Parameter 0 = Goodbye
Parameter 1 = 10
```

As you can see, the arguments specified in the resource file are passed to the quit function (which is bound to the action named Quit). These arguments appear like command-line arguments, each as a string. How you use them in the function is up to you.

Summary

Although you can develop applications using Xlib alone, you can be much more productive if you work with an X toolkit. Even if you work with Xlib only, you need a set of utility routines and a way of managing the complexity arising from handling events occurring in the windows of the application. Toolkits include these facilities. They provide widgets—labels, pushbuttons, and dialog boxes—that can be thought of as predefined software components used to construct user interfaces.

There are several popular toolkits available. The most prominent ones are the OSF/Motif toolkit from the Open Software Foundation and Sun's OPEN LOOK Intrinsics Toolkit (OLIT). These widget sets are layered on top of the Xt Intrinsics, which is a set of utility routines and data structures that enable you to create and manage widgets. This chapter describes how this is done through several small examples. The examples use the widgets provided by the OSF/Motif toolkit and illustrate the use of callbacks, event handlers, and the translation manager.

Xt Intrinsics not only reduces the event handling loop to a single function call, it also provides many ways for the user to customize an application. Users can specify values for configurable parameters known as resources, in a text file, using a specific format. Xt Intrinsics automatically loads these resources during initialization. Additionally, applications can call functions from Xt Intrinsics to load new resources and accept values specified through the command line.

Effective use of widgets requires that you know the widget set. Chapter 14 gives you an overall view of the OSF/Motif widget set.

OSF/Motif Widgets

Chapter 13, "X Toolkits," shows how to use the facilities of Xt Intrinsics to build user interfaces with widgets. However, to make productive use of the widgets, you need to know what widgets are available, what they do, and what their configurable resources are. Accordingly, this chapter describes the widgets available in the OSF/Motif toolkit. Because of limited space, this chapter does not cover each available widget in the toolkit; it focuses on the general features of the OSF/Motif widgets—their object-oriented architecture and the way it is implemented. Then it describes the major categories of widgets and presents short example programs that illustrate how to create and use some of them.

Basic Architecture of Xt Intrinsics-Based Widgets

You can use the OSF/Motif widgets without knowing the internal details of any of them. All you need to know is the functionality provided by a widget and how to configure the widget's parameters—the resources. However, knowing the basic architecture of the widgets helps. For example, knowing the object-oriented design of the widgets helps you understand what it means to say, for instance, that the XmPushButton inherits from the XmLabel widget or that XmNwidth is a part of the Core resource set. The following sections describe the object-oriented nature of Xt Intrinsics-based widgets and explains how a widget inherits from its parent.

> **NOTE:**
>
> The names of the OSF/Motif widgets start with an Xm, but the widgets are often referred to by their name without the prefix. Thus, XmPushButton and PushButton refer to the same widget.

Xt Intrinsics and Object-Oriented Programming (OOP)

Xt Intrinsics provides the basic data structures on which all OSF/Motif widgets are built. The designers of Xt Intrinsics used an *object-oriented programming (OOP)* model for the widgets. In particular, the widgets are designed to support the concepts of data abstraction and inheritance.

Objects and Data Abstraction

To understand data abstraction, consider the file I/O routines in the C run-time library. These routines enable you to view the file as a stream of bytes and perform various operations on this stream. For example, you can open a file (fopen), close it (fclose), read a character from it (getc), write a character to it (putc), and so on. This abstract model of a file is implemented by defining the FILE data type using C's typedef facility.

To use the FILE data type, you do not have to know the C data structure that defines the FILE data type. In fact, FILE's underlying data structure can vary from one system to another. The C file I/O routines work in the same manner on all systems, however. This is what is known as *information hiding* or *data hiding*.

Data abstraction is the combination of defining a data type and data hiding. Thus, C's FILE data type is an example of data abstraction.

You can use the idea of data abstraction to create an *object* by defining a block of data together with the functions necessary to operate on that data. The data represents the information contained in the object, and the functions define the operations that can be performed on that object.

In C, you can represent an object by a structure. Because an object's data is not accessible to the outside world, a basic tenet of OOP is that you must access and manipulate the object's data by calling functions provided by that object. Although object-oriented programming languages such as C++ enforce this principle, implementing object-oriented techniques in a C program requires discipline on the part of the programmer because C does not prohibit code that directly accesses members of an object's data structure.

Classes and Methods

In OOP terminology, the template defining an object's data type is usually called a `class`—the term may differ from one object-oriented programming language to another. Thus, each object is an instance of a class. In C, a `class` can be implemented by defining a new data type (based on a `struct`) with `typedef`.

The functions that operate on an object have a special name—they are known as `methods` because that was the name used in the object-oriented language Smalltalk. The methods define the behavior of an object. When applying OOP techniques in C, the methods are usually pointers to functions.

Another important concept of OOP, also from Smalltalk, is the idea of sending messages to an object to perform an action by invoking one of its methods. In C, this is done by calling a function through the pointer stored in the object's class.

Inheritance

A real-world object is often an extension of an existing object. Consequently, you often describe a real-world object by pointing out how it differs from an existing one—a square is a rectangle whose sides are all equal, for example. OOP uses the term *inheritance* for this concept because you can think of one object inheriting the properties from another. Inheritance imposes a parent-child hierarchical relationship among classes where a child inherits from its parent. The parent class is often called the *super class* (or *base class* in C++).

Widgets as Objects

Widgets based on Xt Intrinsics implement OOP techniques in C using `structs` and `typedefs`. The approach is to define two types of data structures for a specific type (class) of widget:

+ Class structure
+ Instance structure

The methods of the widget are represented by pointers to functions. These are stored in the class data structure. Also included in the class structure are variables common to all widgets of this type as well as a pointer to the parent or super class.

The instance data structure contains information unique to each copy of the widget. By design, each widget has a window. The ID of this window is stored in the widget's instance data structure because each copy of the widget must have its own window. Also, because X supports a hierarchy of windows, the widgets are also used in a hierarchy. The widget's instance record stores the ID of its parent. When you create a widget, Xt Intrinsics allocates a new copy of the instance structure and initializes it.

The information in a widget's class data structure is the same for all widgets in that class. Thus, only one copy of the class structure is needed for each type of widget. Figure 14.1 shows a widget class with several instances.

Figure 14.1.

A widget class with several instances.

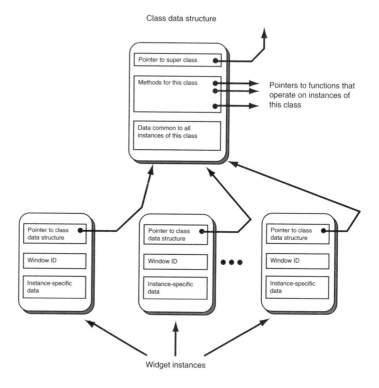

Class data structure

Pointer to super class

Methods for this class

Pointers to functions that operate on instances of this class

Data common to all instances of this class

Pointer to class data structure

Window ID

Instance-specific data

Pointer to class data structure

Window ID

Instance-specific data

Pointer to class data structure

Window ID

Instance-specific data

Widget instances

Inheritance in Widgets

A widget can employ inheritance to use, extend, or replace all or part of another widget's characteristics and functions. Basically, inheritance involves altering the class and instance data structures. Figure 14.2 illustrates the technique used in Xt Intrinsics. Here, a newly defined class of widgets (class B) inherits data and functions from class A. B's class structure is defined by appending B's new data to copy A's structure. The instance structure is defined similarly. Later, if class C inherits from B, the same process is repeated for C's new data structures.

Note that the structures shown in Figure 14.2 illustrate how Xt Intrinsics implements inheritance; however, they are not the actual data structures used in Xt Intrinsics.

Instance Hierarchy versus Class Hierarchy

The parent-child relationship among widget classes controls the inheritance of properties; the widget instances have their own parent-child hierarchy. This hierarchy is similar to the hierarchy of windows in the X Window System. In fact, because each widget in Xt Intrinsics has an associated window, the widget instance hierarchy is the same as the window hierarchy.

Figure 14.2.

A widget inheriting from another.

Keep in mind this notion of two distinct hierarchies. The *class hierarchy* defines the properties of a widget, and the *instance hierarchy* controls the placement of its window and handling of the events. The class hierarchy is necessary because of the object-oriented design of the widgets, and the instance hierarchy is there to take advantage of the hierarchical arrangement of windows supported by the X Window System.

By design, Xt Intrinsics provides a fixed class hierarchy. The instance hierarchy, on the other hand, can be anything you want. Each application has its own unique instance hierarchy that defines the unique screen layout of the widget's windows.

Basic Widgets in Xt Intrinsics

Xt Intrinsics does not define a complete hierarchy of widget classes. Rather, it defines several basic classes. Widget sets such as the OSF/Motif toolkit and OLIT build new classes by inheriting from these basic classes. In fact, you rarely have to use the widgets provided by Xt Intrinsics directly. These widgets are used only as the foundation of other widgets.

Class and Instance Records

Xt Intrinsics uses two C structures for each widget class: one for the class information and the other for instance-specific data. The class structure is commonly referred to as the *class record*, and the instance-specific structure is called the *instance record*. The class record is allocated as static data, and most of its members are initialized at compile-time. The instance record, on the other hand, has to be allocated dynamically when a widget of that class is created.

The class record contains pointers to the methods—functions for all operations that the widget can perform, including creating, initializing, and destroying the widget.

Core Widgets

Xt Intrinsics defines the Core class as the basis of all widgets in a toolkit. Thus, the class record of the Core class embodies information common to all widgets. You need to know the members of Core's class record only when you are writing a new widget. Right now, you will focus on how to use all existing OSF/Motif widgets. Therefore, let's look at the Core widget's configurable parameters—its resources.

> **NOTE:**
>
> The Core class is, in fact, built from the classes Object, RectObj, and WindowObj. The Object class is really the most basic class. The RectObj class adds the concept of a rectangle, and the WindowObj class brings an X window into the widget. In fact, some toolkits provide a kind of object called a gadget that does not have an associated window. The gadget classes, such as OSF/Motif's XmGadget, are derived from RectObj and Object only. Unless you are designing new gadgets, you can continue to think of Core as the basic class for all widgets in any toolkit built using Xt Intrinsics.

The resources of the Core widget are important to programmers because every widget in a toolkit inherits these resources. In fact, when you want to use a new widget, you have to know what types of resources (parameters) are used by the widget. Because all widgets are derived from Core, its resources are available in every widget.

Table 14.1 lists Core's resources, showing how a widget's documentation tabulates them. The table does not show the class names of the resources. You should be familiar with the Core resource set because these resources are available in all widgets.

Table 14.1. The Core Resource Set in OSF/Motif

Name	*Type*	*Default1*	*Set/Get2*
XmNaccelerators	XtAccelerators	*	CSG
XmNancestorSensitive	Boolean	*	G
XmNbackground	Pixel	*	CSG

Name	Type	Default1	Set/Get2
XmNbackgroundPixmap	Pixmap	XmUNSPECIFIED_PIXMAP	CSG
XmNborderColor	Pixel	*	CSG
XmNborderPixmap	Pixmap	XmUNSPECIFIED_PIXMAP	CSG
XmNborderWidth	Dimension	1	CSG
XmNcolormap	Colormap	*	CG
XmNdepth	int	*	CG
XmNdestroyCallback	XtCallbackList	NULL	C
XmNheigh	Dimension	*	CSG
XmNmappedWhenManaged	Boolean	True	CSG
XmNscreen	Screen*	*	CG
XmNsensitive	Boolean	True	CSG
XmNtranslations	XtTranslations	*	CSG
XmNwidth	Dimension	*	CSG
XmNx	Position	0	CSG
XmNy	Position	0	CSG

[1]A * in the Default column indicates that the default is determined at run-time.

[2]Interpret the Set/Get column as follows:

    C = Resource can be set at time of widget's creation.

    S = Resource can be set with XtSetValues.

    G = Resource value returned by XtGetValues.

NOTE:

Data types such as Boolean, Pixel, Dimension, Position, and XtCallbackList are defined by C typedef statements.

The Core resources shown in Table 14.1 are important enough that you should know their meanings. You can interpret them as follows:

XmNaccelerators	Translation table that binds a sequence of keyboard and mouse events to specific actions. (See example in Chapter 13 for more information on translation tables.)
XmNancestorSensitive	Boolean variable that indicates whether the immediate parent of a widget receives input events. You can alter this resource setting by calling the XtSetSensitive function.

XmNbackground	Background pixel value for the widget's window.
XmNbackgroundPixmap	Pixmap used to tile the widget's window.
XmNborderColor and XmNborderPixmap	Color and pixmap for the border of the widget's window.
XmNborderWidth	Width of the border around the widget's window.
XmNcolormap	Colormap to be used by the widget's window.
XmNdepth	Number of bits used for each pixel value in the widget's window. This value is set by Xt Intrinsics when the window is initially created.
XmNdestroyCallback	List of functions that are called when you destroy the widget by calling the XtDestroyWidget function.
XmNheight and XmNwidth	Height and width of the widget's window, excluding the border width.
XmNmappedWhenManaged	Flag that, when set to True, maps the widget's window as soon as the widget is realized and managed (the XtCreateManagedWidget function manages the widget). You can alter this flag by calling the XtSetMappedWhenManaged function.
XmNscreen	Pointer to the Screen data structure that contains information about the physical display screen where the widget's window is displayed.
XmNsensitive	Boolean variable, when True, that causes Xt Intrinsics to dispatch mouse and keyboard events to the widget. To alter this resource, use the function XtSetSensitive.
XmNTranslations	Translation table—a list of events with corresponding functions that are called when the specified events occur. (Chapter 13 shows an example that uses the translation table.)
XmNx and XmNy	The *x* and *y* coordinates of the upper-left corner of the widget's window, excluding the border. The coordinates are specified in the parent widget's coordinate frame.

> **NOTE:**
>
> Every widget in Xt Intrinsics has a window. Thus, you often use the terms *widget* and *window* interchangeably. For example, a widget's coordinate frame means the coordinate frame of its associated window.

Composite Widgets

Xt Intrinsics includes only a few basic widgets besides `Core`. The `Composite` widget inherits directly from `Core` and is meant to be used as a container for other widgets. Because many user-interface components consist of a number of widgets contained in an outer shell, the `Composite` class comes in handy when you have to build a widget that manages the positions of several child widgets. Any widget class that manages the layout of a number of child widgets is a subclass of the `Composite` class.

When a child widget is managed by its parent, the child cannot resize or move itself. To change its geometry, the child makes a request to its parent by calling `XtMakeGeometryRequest`. The parent widget decides what to do depending on its policy.

Other Widgets in Xt Intrinsics

Another basic widget in Xt Intrinsics is the `Shell` widget. As you know from the Xlib programming experience of the previous chapters, you have to take special care when setting up the top-level window of an X application. Because the X display is shared among different applications, your application has to work with a window manager to establish the position and size of the top-level window. Although this step is tedious, it is quite standard. Chapter 7, "Creating and Managing Windows," shows a utility function `initapp` that takes care of this chore. In Xt Intrinsics, the `Shell` class sets up the top-level window of an application.

The `Constraint` widget is a subclass of `Composite`. The `Composite` class uses a fixed management policy to lay out the child widgets, but the `Constraint` class handles the layout of child widgets based on information associated with each child. The name of the class comes from the fact that the layout information is specified in the form of constraints, such as `the "OK" button is to the left of the "Cancel" button with both below the message area`. The `Constraint` class attaches extra information to each child widget's instance record to store the layout constraints. The `xmhello` program shown in Chapter 13, Listing 13.3, uses the OSF/Motif `XmForm` widget, a class that inherits from `Constraint`. In that example you can see how certain resources in each child of the `XmForm` widget are set to indicate its layout inside the `Form` widget.

OSF/Motif Widget Set

As an application programmer, you cannot do much with the widgets defined in Xt Intrinsics. These widgets provide the framework for writing other widgets that can be directly used in your application. Many widget sets are built upon the Xt Intrinsics' widget architecture. Of these, the OSF/Motif widget set is a good example. Another popular widget set is the OPEN LOOK Intrinsic Toolkit. The following sections describe the OSF/Motif widgets.

OSF/Motif Class Hierarchy

All OSF/Motif widget classes are subclasses of the `Core`, `Composite`, and `Shell` widgets of Xt Intrinsics. As you can see from Figure 14.3, OSF/Motif adds more scaffolding to the class tree before defining the classes that you commonly use in your applications. Specifically, it adds the class `XmPrimitive` under `Core` and `XmManager` under `Composite`. There are new additions under the `Shell` class also. As such, Xt Intrinsics also defines several subclasses of `Shell`.

A widget set is like any toolbox—before using the tools you have to know what each one does. The key to understanding and using the OSF/Motif widgets is to study the class hierarchy, identify the broad categories, and learn what each category can do (see Figure 14.3). After that, you should learn about the individual widgets in each category. Then you can pick the widgets that meet your needs and set up the instance hierarchy for your application. To see what resources (parameters) of a widget you should set, look up the detailed documentation of the widget. (Appendix L, "Motif Quick Reference," provides a quick reference guide.) Finally, you can use the knowledge you gained from the examples in Chapter 13 to create and realize the widgets and use them in your application.

Figure 14.3.

The class hierarchy of OSF/Motif widgets.

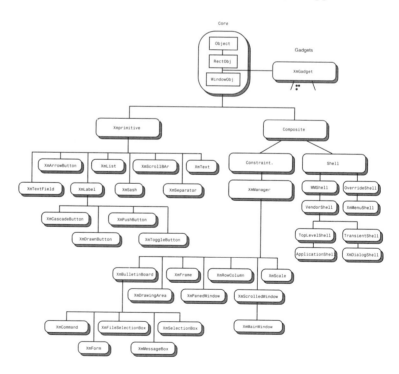

Figure 14.3 features three distinct categories of widgets:

✦ Shell widgets are meant for creating widgets whose window is a child of the root window. In other words, these widgets are for creating top-level windows. An example of a Shell widget is the top-level widget that you create in any toolkit-based application by calling XtAppInitialize (see example programs in Chapter 13). Other examples include pop-up menus.

✦ Primitive widgets include all stand-alone widgets, such as labels, pushbuttons, and scrollbars.

✦ Manager widgets include the widgets that manage the layout of several child widgets. In this category you find forms, message boxes, and scrolled windows.

Shell Widgets

Shell widgets are a special subclass of the Composite widgets. A Shell widget manages only one child. Its primary purpose is to set up the top-level window of an application. Xt Intrinsics provides several classes of Shell widgets, the important ones being TopLevelShell, OverrideShell, and TransientShell.

When you call XtAppInitialize, Xt Intrinsics creates an instance of ApplicationShell widget, a subclass of TopLevelShell. The ApplicationShell and TopLevelShell widgets are used for normal top-level windows of applications. These windows interact with the window manager.

TransientShell Widgets

The TransientShell class is used for top-level windows that can be manipulated via the window manager but that cannot be reduced to an icon. Pop-up dialog boxes use this type of shell. OSF/Motif provides a subclass, XmDialogShell, just for this purpose. A number of convenience functions in the Motif toolkit create an XmDialogShell widget and place another widget, such as a SelectionBox or a MessageBox, inside it. These functions have names that start with XmCreate and end with Dialog. You will see examples of these functions in later sections of this chapter.

OverrideShell Widgets

The OverrideShell widget, derived from the Shell widget, completely bypasses the window manager. It does so by setting the override_redirect attribute of its window to True. This causes the window manager to ignore the window and not attempt to put frames around it or position it by prompting the user. The OverrideShell is primarily used to display pop-up menus. OSF/Motif defines a subclass XmMenuShell for this purpose. As you will see in the following sections, you can use the function XmCreatePopupMenu to create an XmMenuShell with a menu inside it.

Primitive Widgets

All OSF/Motif Primitive widgets are derived from the XmPrimitive class, which is defined as a subclass of the Core class. You never create an instance of the XmPrimitive class. It is there to define a standard set of resources that are inherited by all Primitive widgets. In particular, the

XmPrimitive class is responsible for the three-dimensional shadowing effect of OSF/Motif widgets. This class also provides support for *keyboard traversal*—the concept of transferring keyboard focus from one widget to another.

NOTE:

The process of moving the keyboard focus from one widget to another is known as *keyboard traversal.* An added benefit of using a toolkit such as OSF/Motif is that the transfer of focus is handled automatically. Each Primitive widget indicates, through the XmNtraversalOn resource setting, whether or not the widget accepts input focus. The Manager widgets use this information to transfer focus to child widgets. The Motif toolkit includes the XmProcessTraversal function that you can call to change the keyboard focus under your application's control.

Eight widgets are derived directly from the XmPrimitive class:

- ✦ XmArrowButton
- ✦ XmLabel
- ✦ XmList
- ✦ XmSash
- ✦ XmScrollBar
- ✦ XmSeparator
- ✦ XmText
- ✦ XmTextField

The functionality of the XmLabel class is further specialized by the following subclasses:

- ✦ XmCascadeButton
- ✦ XmDrawnButton
- ✦ XmPushButton
- ✦ XmToggleButton

The next sections describe some of these widget classes. In general, the Primitive widgets appear as components inside other Manager widgets described later in this chapter.

The *XmPrimitive* Class

Because all Primitive widgets inherit the resources of the XmPrimitive class, you should be familiar with the resources of this class (see Table 14.2). Several resources are used to control the three-dimensional look of the Motif widgets. The colors used for the shading that imparts the three-dimensional look are set at run-time, depending on the type of display (monochrome or color).

The last resource, XmNuserData, can store a pointer to any data that you may want to associate with a Primitive widget. This pointer is not used internally by the widgets—its sole purpose is to enable you to store your own data in a widget.

Another innovative idea in the Motif widget set is the use of a *help callback* resource. By setting the XmNhelpCallback resource, you can have your help function called by the toolkit when the user presses the help key sequence. The user specifies the key sequence through a translation table.

Table 14.2. Resources of the XmPrimitive Class in OSF/Motif

Name	Type	Default1	Set/Get2
XmNbottomShadowColor	Pixel	*	CSG
XmNbottomShadowPixap	Pixmap	XmUNSPECIFIED_PIXMAP	CSG
XmNforeground	Pixel	*	CSG
XmNhelpCallback	XtCallbackList	NULL	C
XmNhighlightColor	Pixel	*	CSG
XmNhighlightOnEnter	Boolean	False	CSG
XmNhighlightPixmap	Pixmap	*	CSG
XmNhighlightThickness	Dimension	2	CSG
XmNnavigationType	XmNavigationType	XmNONE	CSG
XmNshadowThickness	Dimension	2	CSG
XmNtopShadowColor	Pixel	*	CSG
XmNtopShadowPixmap	Pixmap	*	CSG
XmNtraversalOn	Boolean	True	CSG
XmNunitType	unsigned char	*	CSG
XmNuserData	XtPointer	NULL	CSG

[1]A * in the Default column indicates that the default is determined at run-time.

[2]Interpret the Set/Get column as follows:

> C = Resource can be set at time of widget's creation.
>
> S = Resource can be set with XtSetValues.
>
> G = Resource value returned by XtGetValues.

You can interpret the resources of the XmPrimitive class as follows:

> XmNbottomShadowColor. Pixel value used to draw the bottom and right side of a Primitive widget's shadow (see Figure 14.4). These two sides are collectively called the *bottom shadow*.
> XmNbottomShadowPixMap. Pixmap used to draw the bottom shadow (see Figure 14.4).
> XmNforeground. Foreground color to be used in the Primitive widgets.

XmNhelpCallback. List of callbacks that can be bound to functions that provide context-sensitive help.

XmNhighlightColor. Color used to highlight the widget's window. For example, a pushbutton is highlighted when the user presses the mouse button with the pointer on it.

XmNhighlightOnEnter. Boolean variable that, when set to True, asks the widget to highlight its window when the cursor enters the window (provided the focus policy of the shell containing the widget is XmPOINTER). This resource is ignored if the focus policy of the shell containing the widget is XmEXPLICIT.

XmNhighlightPixmap. Pixmap used to highlight the widget's window.

XmNhighlightThickness. Thickness of the rectangle used to highlight the widget's window.

XmNnavigationType. Constant that specifies how focus is assigned to the widget during keyboard traversal. Can be XmNONE, XmTAB_GROUP, XmSTICKY_TAB_GROUP, or XmEXCLUSIVE_TAB_GROUP.

XmNshadowThickness. Thickness of the shadow (see Figure 14.4).

XmNtopShadowColor. Color for the top shadow (see Figure 14.4). Used only if is XmNtopShadowPixmap NULL.

XmNtopShadowPixmap. Pixmap for the top shadow (see Figure 14.4).

XmNtraversalOn. Boolean to indicate whether the widget accepts keyboard inputs.

XmNunitType. Measurement unit used for all values specifying dimensions in the widget. The default value is copied from a manager that owns the widget. Usually, the default unit is pixels (specified by the constant XmPIXELS).

XmNuserData. Pointer that is not used internally. You can store the pointer to your own widget-specific data in this resource.

Figure 14.4.
Shadows in Motif widgets.

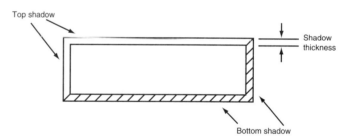

Xm1000TH_INCHES for 1/1000 of an inch, and Xm100TH_POINTS for 1/100 of a point where a point is 1/72 inch. Use Xm100TH_FONT_UNIT to indicate that all dimensions are in terms of 1/100 of a font's unit, which is taken from the font's QUAD_WIDTH property. You can also explicitly set the font unit with the XmSetFontUnits function.

A Common Main Program

In writing programs to illustrate the use of one or more OSF/Motif widgets, you have to repeat a number of steps in each program. Rather than duplicating the code for each example, you can create a common main function. As Listing 14.1 shows, this main function takes care of the standard steps of initializing the Motif toolkit, realizing the widgets, and initiating the event handling loop. The main function also calls another function named MakeWidgets. With this arrangement, you can test new widgets by writing a MakeWidgets function for each type of widget. The next section shows an example that uses this main function to test an XmPushButton widget. Once you see that example, you will understand the idea behind this common main function.

**Listing 14.1. xm_main.c—Common main function
for sample programs that illustrate widgets.**

```
/*------------------------------------------------------------*/
/*  File:  xm_main.c
 *
 *  Main program for demonstrating OSF/Motif widgets.
 *  The function "MakeWidgets" creates the widgets being
 *  demonstrated.
 *
 */
#include <Xm/Xm.h>

extern Widget MakeWidgets();

/*------------------------------------------------------------*/
void main(argc, argv)
int   argc;
char **argv;
{
    Widget       main_widget;
    XtAppContext app;

/* Create and initialize the top-level widget */
    main_widget = XtAppInitialize(&app, "XM_main", NULL, 0,
                                  &argc, argv, NULL, NULL, 0);

/* Now call MakeWidgets to create the widgets */
    MakeWidgets(main_widget);

/* Realize the widgets and start processing events */
    XtRealizeWidget(main_widget);
    XtAppMainLoop(app);
}
```

Label and *PushButton* Widgets

The XmLabel widget is one of the simplest widgets: it displays a string or a pixmap inside a window. You have seen the Label widget used in Chapter 13. As the name implies, labels are used to display a fixed text string or a pixmap. Nothing happens when you click on a Label widget.

Another class of widgets, derived from the XmLabel class, invokes a callback function when the user presses a mouse button inside the widget. The XmPushButton widget is one such widget.

As explained in Chapter 13, the PushButton widget calls any registered callback with three arguments:

✦ The widget's ID

✦ A pointer that you passed when registering the callback

✦ A pointer to an XmAnyCallbackStruct structure

The reason field of the XmAnyCallbackStruct structure indicates why the callback was invoked. The XmPushButton class supports three callback resources:

> XmNarmCallback. List of callback functions that are called when the button is *armed*— when the user presses the mouse button while the pointer is inside the pushbutton's window. The reason field of the XmAnyCallbackStruct is set to the constant XmCR_ARM, and the button is inverted if the XmNinvertOnArm resource (a Boolean) is set to True.
> XmNactivateCallback. List of functions called (with XmCR_ACTIVATE as the reason) when the user activates the pushbutton by pressing and releasing the mouse button with the pointer inside the window.
> XmNdisarmCallback. List of functions called when the pushbutton is *disarmed* by releasing the mouse button (not necessarily inside the widget). In this case, the reason field of the XmAnyCallbackStruct structure is set to XmCR_DISARM.

Of course, in addition to these callback resources, XmPushButton inherits the label string and the pixmap from its super class, XmLabel. Figure 14.5 shows a typical instance of a PushButton widget. Listing 14.2 shows the MakeWidget function that creates the XmPushButton widget.

Listing 14.2. `pushb.c`—Function to create an `XmPushButton` widget.

```
/*-------------------------------------------------------*/
/*  File:  pushb.c
 *
 *  Demonstrates an XmPushButton widgeti.
 *
 */
#include <Xm/Xm.h>

#include <Xm/PushB.h>

static char message[] =
"The XmPushButton widget is \n\
useful for initiating actions.\n\
CLICK here to EXIT.";
```

```
static void action();

/*----------------------------------------------------------*/
Widget MakeWidgets(parent)
Widget parent;
{
    Widget w;
    XmString xmlabel =  XmStringCreateLtoR(message,
                           XmSTRING_DEFAULT_CHARSET);


    w = XtVaCreateManagedWidget("PushButton",
                    xmPushButtonWidgetClass, parent,
                    XmNlabelString,          xmlabel,
                    XmNwidth,                200,
                    NULL);

    XmStringFree(xmlabel);

/* Add a callback function */
    XtAddCallback(w, XmNarmCallback, action, NULL);
    return w;
}
/*----------------------------------------------------------*/
static void action(w, client_data, call_data)
Widget            w;
XtPointer         client_data;
XmAnyCallbackStruct *call_data;
{
    XtCloseDisplay(XtDisplay(w));
    exit(0);
}
```

Figure 14.5.

The XmPushButton widget.

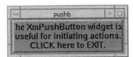

To create an executable program from Listing 14.2, you must compile this listing and link it with the main function shown in Listing 14.1. The makefile shown in Listing 14.3 illustrates the steps necessary to compile and link the files pushb.c and xm_main.c.

Listing 14.3. Makefile to build the example programs that use the main function shown in Listing 14.1.

```
#################################################################
# Makefile for building sample programs that use the main
# function from the file "xm_main.c"
#################################################################

# Some common definitions...
RM = rm -f
CC = cc
```

continues

Listing 14.3. continued

```
# Compiler flags, paths for include files and libraries

CFLAGS = -g
LDFLAGS=
DEFINES =
INCLUDES = -I. -I/usr/include -I/usr/include/X11
LIBS = -lX11
XMLIBS = -lXm -lXt -lXmu -lX11

# Rule to create .o files from .c files
.c.o:
        $(RM) $@
        $(CC) -c $(CFLAGS) $(INCLUDES) $*.c

REQUIRED =      xm_main.o

# Add names of example programs on the next line
ALL =           pushb

all::           ${ALL}

$(ALL):         $$@.o $(REQUIRED)
        $(RM) $@
        $(CC) -o $@ $@.o $(CFLAGS) \
            $(LDFLAGS) $(REQUIRED) $(XMLIBS)
```

With this makefile, you can build the program pushb by entering the make command at the UNIX shell prompt. In subsequent sections, when you see example programs for other widgets, you can create the programs for those widgets by adding the name of the program to the definition of the symbol named ALL in Listing 14.3.

ToggleButton Widgets

The XmToggleButton class is also derived from XmLabel. It displays a string or a pixmap next to a small button. The button represents a state with two values—selected or unselected—that you can interpret as being on or off. When selected, the button is highlighted. As the name indicates, the state of the button toggles from one value to the other with every press of the mouse button on the widget.

Toggle buttons are not meant to be used alone; you should use them as child widgets of a RowColumn widget. The RowColumn widget has built-in capabilities to manage a list of ToggleButton widgets and provide the user a choice of *one-out-of-many* or *many-out-of-many* selections. Listing 14.4 shows an example that sets up a RowColumn widget with three toggle buttons.

Listing 14.4. Program to demonstrate the use of toggle buttons.

```
/*------------------------------------------------------------*/
/*  File: toggle.c
 *
```

```
 *   Demonstrates the use of ToggleButton widgets in a
 *   RowColumn widget.
 *
 */
#include <Xm/Xm.h>

#include <Xm/ToggleB.h>
#include <Xm/RowColumn.h>

/* Labels for the ToggleButtons */
static char* choices[] =
{
    "Xlib", "OPEN LOOK Widgets", "Motif Widgets"
};

/* Callbacks */
static void button_set();
static void button_unset();

/*-----------------------------------------------------------*/
Widget MakeWidgets(parent)
Widget parent;
{
    Widget   w, b;
    int      i;
    XmString xms;

/* Create the RowColumn widget that serves as container for
 * the ToggleButtons
 */
    w = XtVaCreateManagedWidget("ManyOfMany",
                     xmRowColumnWidgetClass, parent,
                     XmNorientation,    XmVERTICAL,
                     NULL);

/* Add the ToggleButton widgets */
    for(i = 0; i < XtNumber(choices); i++)
    {
        xms = XmStringCreateLtoR(choices[i],
                           XmSTRING_DEFAULT_CHARSET);

        b = XtVaCreateManagedWidget("TButton",
                     xmToggleButtonWidgetClass, w,
                     XmNlabelString,   xms,
                     NULL);
        XmStringFree(xms);

        XtAddCallback(b, XmNarmCallback, button_set,
                      (XtPointer)choices[i]);
        XtAddCallback(b, XmNdisarmCallback, button_unset,
                      (XtPointer)choices[i]);
    }
    return w;
}
/*-----------------------------------------------------------*/
static void button_set(w, client_data, call_data)
Widget    w;
XtPointer         client_data;
XmAnyCallbackStruct *call_data;
```

continues

Listing 14.4. continued

```
{
    printf("%s SET\n", (char*) client_data);
}
/*----------------------------------------------------------*/
static void button_unset(w, client_data, call_data)
Widget      w;
XtPointer            client_data;
XmAnyCallbackStruct *call_data;
{
    printf("%s UNSET\n", (char*) client_data);
}
```

To build the test program for the file `toggle.c` shown in Listing 14.4, add the name `toggle` following `pushb` in the definition of the symbol `ALL` in the makefile of Listing 14.3. Running the `make` utility after this change to the makefile creates a program named `toggle`. Figure 14.6 shows the widgets created by this program. In Figure 14.6, the first and third toggle buttons are selected.

Figure 14.6.

Three `ToggleButton`
widgets inside a
`RowColumn` *widget.*

The `RowColumn` widget's `XmNradioBehavior` resource controls whether you can select more than one toggle button. As the name suggests, when `XmNradioBehavior` is `True`, the group of buttons acts as "radio buttons"—you can only "push in" (select) one button at a time. In this case, the shape of each button changes to a diamond. By default, `XmNradioBehavior` is `False` and the `RowColumn` widget allows many-out-of-many selections.

Separator Widgets

The `XmSeparator` widget is a special type of label that draws a line whose orientation is specified by the `XmNorientation` resource. The default value is `XmHORIZONTAL` for a horizontal line. You can set this resource to `XmVERTICAL` for a vertical separator. Separators are used to separate items in a display, particularly to delineate different groups of items in a menu. Figure 14.7 shows a separator drawn between two labels. Listing 14.5 shows the `MakeWidget` function that sets up the widgets displayed in Figure 14.7.

Listing 14.5. `sep.c`—Example of the `Separator` widget.

```
/*----------------------------------------------------------*/
/* File:  sep.c
 *
 * Demonstrates the use of Separator widgets to separate
 * labels displayed in a RowColumn widget.
 *
```

```
 */
#include <Xm/Xm.h>
#include <Xm/Label.h>
#include <Xm/Separator.h>
#include <Xm/RowColumn.h>


/*-------------------------------------------------------------*/
Widget MakeWidgets(parent)
Widget parent;
{
    Widget   w, b;
    int      i;

/* Create the RowColumn widget that serves as container for
 * the other widgets.
 */
    w = XtVaCreateManagedWidget("Separators",
                    xmRowColumnWidgetClass, parent,
                    XmNorientation,    XmVERTICAL,
                    NULL);

/* Add two labels with a separator in between */
    (void) XtVaCreateManagedWidget("Item 1",
                                    xmLabelWidgetClass, w,
                                    NULL);

    (void) XtVaCreateManagedWidget("Sep",
                                    xmSeparatorWidgetClass, w,
                                    NULL);

    (void) XtVaCreateManagedWidget("Item 2 is below a separator",
                                    xmLabelWidgetClass, w,
                                    NULL);
    return w;
}
```

Figure 14.7.

A Separator widget.

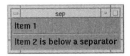

Scrollbar Widgets

The XmScrollBar widget, derived from the XmPrimitive class, is used to enable users to view data that extends beyond the limits of a widget's window. The scrollbar is usually attached to a widget displaying the data. Through the use of callback functions, you can scroll the data as the user interacts with the scrollbar.

Scrollbars can be horizontal or vertical. The orientation is controlled by the XmNorientation resource, which can be either XmHORIZONTAL or XmVERTICAL. As Figure 14.8 shows, the scrollbar consists of an elongated rectangle with an arrow at each end. Another rectangle, called a *slider*, appears inside the larger rectangle. The slider is meant to give an indication of how much of the total data is visible in the widget being controlled by the scrollbar. For example, if 50 percent of available data is visible, the slider should be half the size of the larger rectangle.

Figure 14.8.

A ScrollBar widget.

Listing 14.6 shows the file scroll.c, which demonstrates a ScrollBar widget. You can get indication of the slider's movement through a callback function registered for the callback resource named XmNvalueChangedCallback. When the ScrollBar widget calls this callback, the call_data argument (the third argument of the callback) points to an XmScrollBarCallbackStruct structure, defined in the header file <Xm/Xm.h> as follows:

```
typedef struct
{
    int      reason;  /* Indicates why callback was invoked */
    XEvent   *event;  /* Event that triggered the callback  */
    int      value;   /* New value of slider's location     */
    int      pixel;   /* x or y coord of pixel where mouse   */
                      /* click occurred. Used only for       */
                      /* XmNtoTopCallback and                */
                      /* XmNtoBottomCallback.                */
} XmScrollBarCallbackStruct;
```

Listing 14.6. scroll.c—Example of the ScrollBar widget.

```
/*-----------------------------------------------------------*/
/*  File:  scroll.c
 *
 *  Demonstrates the use of the ScrollBar widget.
 *
 */
#include <Xm/Xm.h>

#include <Xm/ScrollBar.h>

/* Callback */
static void slider_moved();
static int current_value = 0;
/*-----------------------------------------------------------*/
Widget MakeWidgets(parent)
Widget parent;
{
    Widget w;
    int    min_value = 0, max_value = 500, step_size = 25,
           slider_size = 300;

/* Create the Scrollbar widget */
    w = XtVaCreateManagedWidget("Scrollbar1",
                    xmScrollBarWidgetClass, parent,
                    XmNwidth,          200,
                    XmNorientation,    XmHORIZONTAL,
                    XmNminimum,        min_value,
                    XmNmaximum,        max_value,
                    XmNvalue,          current_value,
                    XmNincrement,      step_size,
                    XmNsliderSize,     slider_size,
                    NULL);

/* Add callback for the XmNvalueChangedCallback resource. */
```

```
        XtAddCallback(w, XmNvalueChangedCallback, slider_moved,
                               (XtPointer)&current_value);
        return w;
}
/*----------------------------------------------------------*/
static void slider_moved(w, client_data, call_data)
Widget                  w;
XtPointer               client_data;
XmScrollBarCallbackStruct *call_data;
{
/* Here call_data is a pointer to an XmScrollBarCallbackStruct
 * structure, which has the new value in the member named
 * value. In client_data we have have passed the address
 * of a value being maintained through this scrollbar. So we
 * simply copy the new value into *client_data.
 */
    printf("Old value = %d\n", *(int *)client_data);

    *(int *)client_data = call_data->value;
    printf("New value = %d\n", *(int *)client_data);
}
```

The `ScrollBar` widget provides the user interface for scrolling the contents of a widget, but it does not perform the scrolling. You have to implement scrolling yourself by placing appropriate code in the `XmNvalueChangedCallback` function. The `xmbrowse.c` program shown in Listing 15.3 shows one way of scrolling text in a window.

List Widgets

The `XmList` widget is another `Primitive` widget that displays a list of items in a window and enables the user to pick one or more items from the list. Figure 14.9 shows a list displayed with the `List` widget. Listing 14.7 shows the code that generates this display.

Figure 14.9.
A List *widget.*

Listing 14.7. `list.c`—Function demonstrating the `List` widget.

```
/*----------------------------------------------------------*/
/*  File:  list.c
 *
 *  Demonstrates the use of a List widget.
 *
 */
#include <Xm/Xm.h>
```
continues

Listing 14.7. continued

```c
#include <Xm/List.h>

#define LIST_MARGIN_WIDTH  30
#define LIST_SPACING        5

/* List entries */
static char *list_items[] =
{
    "Ada", "BASIC", "C", "C++", "FORTRAN", "Pascal", "Lisp"
};

static XmStringTable  compound_strings;

/* Callback */
static void select();

/*--------------------------------------------------------------*/
Widget MakeWidgets(parent)
Widget parent;
{
    Widget  w;
    int     i;

/* Allocate memory for the compound strings */
    compound_strings = (XmStringTable)XtMalloc(
                        XtNumber(list_items) * sizeof(XmString*));

/* Convert the array of strings into compound strings */
    for(i = 0; i < XtNumber(list_items); i++)
    {
        compound_strings[i] =
            XmStringCreateSimple(list_items[i]);
    }

/* Create the List widget */
    w = XtVaCreateManagedWidget("List",
                        xmListWidgetClass,          parent,
                        XmNlistSpacing,      LIST_SPACING,
                        XmNmarginWidth,      LIST_MARGIN_WIDTH,
                        XmNitemCount,        XtNumber(list_items),
                        XmNvisibleItemCount, XtNumber(list_items),
                        XmNitems,            compound_strings,
                        NULL);

/* Free the compound string list */
    for(i = 0; i < XtNumber(list_items); i++)
        XmStringFree(compound_strings[i]);

    XtFree(compound_strings);

/* Function to be called when an item is "double-clicked"     */
    XtAddCallback(w, XmNdefaultActionCallback, select, NULL);
    return w;
}
/*--------------------------------------------------------------*/
static void select(w, client_data, call_data)
Widget              w;
```

```
XtPointer             client_data;
XmListCallbackStruct *call_data;
{
    char *str;

    if(call_data->reason == XmCR_DEFAULT_ACTION)
    {
/* Convert compound string to C string */
        XmStringGetLtoR(call_data->item,
                        XmSTRING_DEFAULT_CHARSET, &str);
        printf("Double click on item: %s\n", str);

/* Remember to free memory allocated by Motif toolkit for
 * the returned C string.
 */
        XtFree(str);
    }
}
```

The List widget is most useful when combined with a ScrolledWindow widget. OSF/Motif provides a convenience function XmCreateScrolledList to do exactly this. The combination of a List widget inside a ScrolledWindow allows you to display a list with more elements than fit in a viewing area. The user can use an attached scrollbar to scroll through the list.

The Motif toolkit provides a number of utility functions for manipulating the contents of a List widget. Table 14.3 provides a summary of these functions.

Table 14.3. Functions for Manipulating the Contents of a **List** Widget

Function	Purpose
XmListAddItem	Adds an XmString item to a list
XmListAddItemUnselected	Adds an item but does not select it
XmListAddItems	Adds an array of XmString items to a list
XmListAddItemsUnselected	Adds an array of items but does not select any of them
XmListDeleteAllItems	Deletes all items from a list
XmListDeleteItem	Deletes an item from a list
XmListDeleteItems	Deletes an array of items
XmListDeleteItemsPos	Deletes one or more items starting at a given position
XmListDeletePos	Deletes an item at a specified position
XmListDeletePositions	Deletes items specified through an array of positions
XmListDeselectAllItems	Unhighlights all but one item
XmListDeselectItem	Deselects a specified item
XmListDeselectPos	Deselects an item at a given position
XmListGetKbdItemPos	Returns position of item at the location cursor

continues

Table 14.3. continued

Function	Purpose
XmListGetMatchPos	Returns all instances of an item in the list
XmListGetSelectedPos	Returns the position of every selected item in the list
XmListItemExists	Returns True if a specified item is in the list
XmListItemPos	Returns position of an item in the list
XmListPosSelected	Returns True if the item at a specified position is selected
XmListPosToBounds	Returns the coordinates of the bounding box for an item at a specified position
XmListReplaceItems	Replaces specified items in the list with new ones
XmListReplaceItemsPos	Replaces one or more items starting at a specified position
XmListReplaceItemsPosUnselected	Replaces items without selecting the new ones
XmListReplaceItemsUnselected	Replaces specified items with new ones but does not select the new ones
XmListReplacePositions	Replaces items based on an array of positions
XmListSelectItem	Selects (highlights) a specified item from list
XmListSelectPos	Selects an item at a specified position in the list
XmListSetAddMode	Turns "add mode" on or off (when "add mode" is on, new selections are added to the list of selected items)
XmListSetBottomItem	Makes the specified item the last visible item in the list
XmListSetBottomPos	Makes the item at the specified position the last visible item in the list
XmListSetHorizPos	Scrolls horizontally to the specified position
XmListSetItem	Makes the specified item the first visible item in list
XmListSetKbdItemPos	Sets the location cursor at the specified position
XmListSetPos	Makes the item at the specified position the first visible item in the list
XmListUpdateSelectedList	Updates the list of selected items (XmNselectedItems resource)
XmListYToPos	Returns position of item at a specified y-coordinate

Text Widgets

The XmText widget is another powerful and useful widget in the OSF/Motif repertoire. This is essentially a self-contained text editor that you can use to accept keyboard input. You can use the XmNeditMode resource to configure the XmText widget for editing single or multiple lines. The default value of this resource is XmSINGLE_LINE_EDIT, which indicates that the Text widget should accept a single line only. For multiline editing, set this resource to the constant XmMULTI_LINE_EDIT. Listing 14.8 shows how to set up a Text widget for multiline text input with word-wrap enabled. Figure 14.10 shows the resulting Text widget after the user has entered some text.

Listing 14.8. list.c—Function demonstrating the List widget.

```
/*-----------------------------------------------------------*/
/*  File:   text.c
 *
 *  Demonstrates the use of a Text widget.
 *
 */
#include <Xm/Xm.h>

#include <Xm/Text.h>

/*-----------------------------------------------------------*/
Widget MakeWidgets(parent)
Widget parent;
{
    Widget   w;
    int      i;

/* Create the Text widget */
    w = XtVaCreateManagedWidget("Text",
                        xmTextWidgetClass,   parent,
                        XmNeditable,         True,
                        XmNeditMode,         XmMULTI_LINE_EDIT,
                        XmNcolumns,          40,
                        XmNrows,             10,
                        XmNwordWrap,         True,
                        NULL);
    return w;
}
```

Figure 14.10.

A Text *widget.*

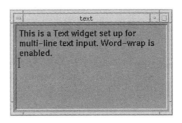

A convenient way to use the Text widget, as with the List widget, is to use it as a child of a ScrolledWindow. You can do this with the XmCreateScrolledText function.

If you are using a Text widget to read text entered by the user, you need a way to retrieve the text. The OSF/Motif toolkit includes a number of utility functions for manipulating the contents of a Text widget (see Table 14.4). The XmTextGetString function, in particular, returns the contents of the text buffer maintained by the Text widget. Here is some example code to retrieve the string from a Text widget:

```
    Widget  text;
    char    *contents;

    contents = XmTextGetString(text);
     .
     .
     .
/* Use "contents" as needed */
     .
/* You are responsible for freeing the storage */
    XtFree(contents);
```

Getting the text string is straightforward. The Text widget allocates storage for the string, copies its contents to that space, and returns a pointer to that location. After you are finished with the string, you are responsible for freeing the memory by calling the XtFree function.

> **NOTE:**
>
> The Motif toolkit provides the TextField widget, which is specifically meant for single-line text entry and editing. The TextField widget has resources and routines that correspond closely to the ones provided for the more general-purpose Text widget.

Table 14.4. Functions for Manipulating the Contents of Text Widgets

Function	Purpose
XmTextClearSelection	Clears the primary selection in the Text widget
XmTextCopy	Copies the primary selection to the clipboard
XmTextCut	Copies the selected text (the primary selection) to the clipboard and deletes the selected text
XmTextDisableRedisplay	Disables visual update of the Text widget
XmTextEnableRedisplay	Enables visual update of widget
XmTextFindString	Finds the beginning position of a specified text string
XmTextFindStringWcs	Finds the beginning position of a wide-character text string
XmTextGetAddMode	Returns the setting of the "add mode" (when "add mode" is True, the text insertion cursor can be moved around without affecting the selection)
XmTextGetBaseline	Returns the x position of the first baseline in the widget

Function	Purpose
XmTextGetCursorPosition	Returns the cursor position
XmTextGetEditable	Returns True if the contents of the Text widget can be edited
XmTextGetInsertionPosition	Returns the position of the text insertion cursor
XmTextGetLastPosition	Returns the last position in the text buffer of the Text widget
XmTextGetMaxLength	Returns maximum allowable length of text string accepted by the widget
XmTextGetSelection	Returns a pointer to the primary selection
XmTextGetSelectionPosition	Provides the starting and ending position of the selection
XmTextGetSelectionWcs	Returns the primary selection as a wide-character string
XmTextGetSource	Returns the text source of the Text widget
XmTextGetString	Returns the text string representing the contents of the Text widget
XmTextGetStringWcs	Returns contents of the Text widget as a wide-character string
XmTextGetSubstring	Retrieves a specified portion of the internal text buffer
XmTextGetSubstringWcs	Retrieves a portion of the internal text buffer as a wide-character string
XmTextGetTopCharacter	Returns the position of the first character being displayed (the first position in the buffer is zero)
XmTextInsert	Inserts a C-style string at a specified position
XmTextInsertWcs	Inserts a wide-character string at a specified position
XmTextPaste	Inserts the clipboard selection at the current insertion point
XmTextPosToXY	Provides the (x,y) coordinates of a character at a specified position in the text buffer
XmTextRemove	Deletes the primary selection
XmTextReplace	Replaces a specified portion of the text buffer with a new string
XmTextReplaceWcs	Replaces part of a wide-character string in the text buffer
XmTextScroll	Scrolls the text in the Text widget by a specified number of lines
XmTextSetAddMode	Sets the "add mode" (when "add mode" is True, the insertion point can be moved without disturbing the primary selection)
XmTextSetCursorPosition	Sets the cursor position

continues

Table 14.4. continued

Function	*Purpose*
XmTextSetEditable	Sets widget's mode to "editable" or "not editable"
XmTextSetHighlight	Highlights text between two specified positions
XmTextSetInsertionPosition	Sets the position of the insertion point
XmTextSetMaxLength	Sets the maximum allowable length of a text string that can be entered from the keyboard
XmTextSetSelection	Sets the primary selection to be the text between two specified positions
XmTextSetSource	Sets the text source for the widget
XmTextSetString	Sets the text string to the one specified by a null-terminated C-style string
XmTextSetStringWcs	Sets the wide-character string value of the widget
XmTextSetTopCharacter	Sets the position of the first character to be displayed
XmTextShowPosition	Forces the text at a specified position to be displayed
XmTextXYToPos	Returns the position of the character nearest to a specified (x,y) coordinate in the widget

Gadgets

In addition to the widgets, OSF/Motif includes another type of user-interface component called *gadgets*. As shown in Figure 14.3, the gadgets inherit from two components of the Core class—the Object and the RectObj. The difference between widgets and gadgets is that every widget has a window whereas gadgets do not have any window of their own. A gadget must have a parent widget so that it can display its output in the parent widget's window.

As a programmer, you can use gadgets the same way you do widgets. You use the XtCreateManagedWidget or XtVaCreateManagedWidget function, providing the gadget's class pointer as an argument. For example, the following code creates a label gadget whose class pointer is xmLabelGadgetClass:

```
Widget main_widget, label_gadget;
.
.
.
label_gadget = XtCreateManagedWidget("label_1",
                  xmLabelGadgetClass, main_widget, NULL, 0);
```

Gadgets are included in OSF/Motif for situations where you may not want to have many windows. Because of its lack of a window, a gadget does not support event handlers, key translations, and pop-up child windows. Gadgets do support callback functions. OSF/Motif includes gadget versions of several Primitive widgets. Table 14.5 shows the supported gadgets as well as the equivalent widget for each gadget and indicates the header file that you have to include when using the gadget. The gadgets have the same appearance as the corresponding widgets.

Table 14.5. OSF/Motif Gadgets

Gadget Name	Equivalent Widget Name	Header File Gadget
XmArrowButtonGadget	XmArrowButton	<Xm/ArrowBG.h>
XmCascadeButtonGadget	XmCascadeButton	<Xm/CascadeBG.h>
XmLabelGadget	XmLabel	<Xm/LabelG.h>
XmPushButtonGadget	XmPushButton	<Xm/PushBG.h>
XmSeparatorGadget	XmSeparator	<Xm/SeparatoG.h>
XmToggleButtonGadget	XmToggleButton	<Xm/ToggleBG.h>

> **TIP:**
>
> You can derive the name of a widget or gadget's class pointer from its name (see Figure 14.3). For widgets, simply change the Xm prefix to xm and append the string WidgetClass to the widget's name. For a gadget, change the first letter to lowercase and append the string Class. Thus, the class pointer for the XmLabel widget is xmLabelWidgetClass and for the XmLabelGadget is xmLabelGadgetClass.

Manager Widgets

All OSF/Motif Manager widgets are derived from the XmManager class, which is a subclass of Constraint and which, in turn, inherits from the Composite class. These widgets are meant to be containers for other widgets and they manage the layout of their children according to specified constraints. This section describes several interesting Manager widgets.

The *XmManager* Class

All Manager widgets inherit from the XmManager class. As you can see from Table 14.6, these resources are similar to those for XmPrimitive class (Table 14.2) except that everything in Table 14.6 applies to the Manager widgets. Several of these resources are devoted to supporting the unique three-dimensional look of the OSF/Motif widgets.

Table 14.6. Resources of the **XmManager** Class in OSF/Motif

Name	Type	Default1	Set/Get2
XmNbottomShadowColor	Pixel	*	CSG
XmNbottomShadowPixap	Pixmap	XmUNSPECIFIED_PIXMAP	CSG

continues

Table 14.6. continued

Name	Type	Default1	Set/Get2
XmNforeground	Pixel	*	CSG
XmNhelpCallback	XtCallbackList	NULL	C
XmNhighlightColor	Pixel	*	CSG
XmNhighlightPixmap	Pixmap	*	CSG
XmNinitialFocus	Widget	NULL	CSG
XmNnavigationType	XmNavigationType	XmTAB_GROUP	CSG
XmNshadowThickness	Dimension	0	CSG
XmNtopShadowColor	Pixel	*	CSG
XmNtopShadowPixmap	Pixmap	*	CSG
XmNtraversalOn	Boolean	True	CSG
XmNunitType	unsigned char	*	CSG
XmNuserData	XtPointer	NULL	CSG

[1]A * in the Default column indicates that the default is determined at run-time.

[2]Interpret the Set/Get column as follows:

   C = Resource can be set at time of widget's creation.

   S = Resource can be set with XtSetValues.

   G = Resource value returned by XtGetValues.

SelectionBox Widgets

The SelectionBox widget is meant to display a list of items in a scrollable box and provide an area where the current selection is displayed. There are three buttons labelled OK, Cancel, and Help. A fourth button, Apply, can be turned on or off. A typical setup and display is shown in Listing 14.9. The resulting selection box is shown in Figure 14.11.

Figure 14.11.

A SelectionBox *widget.*

Listing 14.9. sbox.c—Function for demonstrating a SelectionBox widget.

```c
/*------------------------------------------------------------*/
/* File:  sbox.c
 *
 * Demonstrates an XmSelectionBox widget.
 *
 */
#include <Xm/Xm.h>

#include <Xm/SelectioB.h>

#define VISIBLE_ITEMS  5

/* List of items to be displayed in selection box */

static char *list_items[] =
{
    "X Protocol", "Xlib", "Xt Intrinsics", "Athena Widgets",
    "OSF/Motif", "OPEN LOOK", "XView", "XT+"
};

/* Callback */
static void sbox_cb();
/*------------------------------------------------------------*/
Widget MakeWidgets(parent)
Widget parent;
{
    int          i;
    Widget       w;
    XmStringTable compound_strings;

/* Allocate memory for the compound strings */
    compound_strings = (XmStringTable)XtMalloc(
                    XtNumber(list_items) * sizeof(XmString*));

/* Convert the array of strings into compound strings */
    for(i = 0; i < XtNumber(list_items); i++)
    {
        compound_strings[i] =
            XmStringCreateSimple(list_items[i]);
    }

/* Create the List widget */
    w = XtVaCreateManagedWidget("SelectionBox",
                xmSelectionBoxWidgetClass,  parent,
                XmNlistItemCount,          XtNumber(list_items),
                XmNlistVisibleItemCount, VISIBLE_ITEMS,
                XmNlistItems,              compound_strings,
                XmNdialogType,             XmDIALOG_SELECTION,
                NULL);

/* Free the compound string list */
    for(i = 0; i < XtNumber(list_items); i++)
        XmStringFree(compound_strings[i]);

    XtFree(compound_strings);
```

continues

Listing 14.9. continued

```
/* Function to be called when OK or Cancel button is clicked */
    XtAddCallback(w, XmNcancelCallback, sbox_cb, NULL);
    XtAddCallback(w, XmNokCallback, sbox_cb, NULL);

    return w;
}
/*--------------------------------------------------------------*/
static void sbox_cb(w, client_data, call_data)
Widget                      w;
XtPointer                   client_data;
XmSelectionBoxCallbackStruct *call_data;
{
    char *str;
    switch(call_data->reason)
    {
        case XmCR_OK:
/* Convert compound string to C string */
            XmStringGetLtoR(call_data->value,
                            XmSTRING_DEFAULT_CHARSET, &str);
            printf("Selected item: %s\n", str);

/* Remember to free memory allocated by Motif toolkit for
 * the returned C string.
 */
            XtFree(str);
            break;

        case XmCR_CANCEL:
/* User clicked on Cancel button. Exit program. */
            exit(0);
            break;
    }
}
```

If you want to display a `SelectionBox` widget in a pop-up dialog shell, you can use the `XmCreateSelectionDialog` function to do the job. You call `XmCreateSelectionDialog` the same way you do `XmCreateSelectionBox`.

FileSelectionBox Widgets

A special type of selection box is the `FileSelectionBox` widget represented by the `XmFileSelection` class in OSF/Motif. This widget is similar to the selection box, except that it is used to display a list of filenames in a list box. There is an area where the user can enter a file filter, which is a search string used to locate the files of interest (use `*.c` to see all files ending with `.c`). The user's current selection is displayed in another box. At the bottom of the widget, there are four buttons labeled `OK`, `Filter`, `Cancel`, and `Help`. Figure 14.12 shows a typical file selection box. As shown in Listing 14.10, you can use the `XtVaCreateManagedWidget` with `xmFileSelectionBoxWidgetClass` as the class name to create this widget. Listing 14.10 also demonstrates how to retrive the filename once the user clicks on the OK button (see the `fs_ok` callback function).

Figure 14.12.

A FileSelectionBox widget.

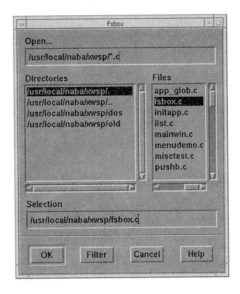

Listing 14.10. fsbox.c—Function for demonstrating a FileSelectionBox widget.

```
/*-----------------------------------------------------------*/
/*  File:  fsbox.c
 *
 *  Demonstrates an XmFileSelectionBox widget.
 *
 */
#include <Xm/Xm.h>
#include <Xm/FileSB.h>

/* Callbacks */
static void fs_ok();
static void fs_cancel();
/*-----------------------------------------------------------*/
Widget MakeWidgets(parent)
Widget parent;
{
    Widget w;
    XmString  title, dir_mask;

    title = XmStringLtoRCreate("Open...",
                        XmSTRING_DEFAULT_CHARSET);
    dir_mask = XmStringLtoRCreate("*.c",
                          XmSTRING_DEFAULT_CHARSET);

    w = XtVaCreateManagedWidget("File Selection",
                    xmFileSelectionBoxWidgetClass, parent,
                    XmNdirMask,              dir_mask,
                    XmNfilterLabelString,    title,
                    XmNwidth,                200,
                    NULL);
```

continues

Listing 14.10. continued

```
/* Free the XmStrings */
    XmStringFree(title);
    XmStringFree(dir_mask);

/* Add callbacks for the "OK" and "Cancel" buttons */
    XtAddCallback(w, XmNcancelCallback, fs_cancel, NULL);
    XtAddCallback(w, XmNokCallback, fs_ok, NULL);

    return w;
}
/*-------------------------------------------------------------*/
/*  f s _ o k
 *
 *  Callback for the "OK" button on the file selection box
 */
static void fs_ok(w, client_data, call_data)
Widget                     w;
XtPointer                  client_data;
XmSelectionBoxCallbackStruct *call_data;
{
    char *file_name;

/* Get filename from user's selection */
    if(XmStringGetLtoR(call_data->value,
                       XmSTRING_DEFAULT_CHARSET, &file_name))
    {
        printf("File selected: %s\n", file_name);
        XtFree(file_name);
    }
}
/*-------------------------------------------------------------*/
/*  f s _ c a n c e l
 *
 *  Callback for the "Cancel" button in the file selection box
 */
static void fs_cancel(w, client_data, call_data)
Widget                     w;
XtPointer                  client_data;
XmSelectionBoxCallbackStruct *call_data;
{
/* Usually, this should get rid of the dialog box that
 * displays the FileSelectionBox, but here we simply exit.
 */
    exit(0);
}
```

Scale Widgets

The Scale widget displays an elongated rectangle with a slider that allows the user to enter a numerical value. You can set the minimum and maximum values for the scale; for floating-point values, you can specify the number of digits to follow the decimal point. Figure 14.13 shows a scale capable of displaying values between 0.0 and 10.0, in steps of 0.1. As shown in Listing 14.11, you can create a `Scale` widget by calling the `XtVaCreateManagedWidget` function with `xmScaleWidgetClass` as the class name. The callback function `scale_cb` demonstrates how to retrieve the value corresponding to the current location of the slider.

Figure 14.13.
A Scale widget.

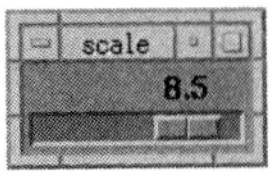

Listing 14.11. `scale.c`—Function that demonstrates a `Scale` widget.

```
/*--------------------------------------------------------*/
/*  File:  scale.c
 *
 *  Demonstrates an XmScale widget.
 *
 */
#include <Xm/Xm.h>
#include <Xm/Scale.h>

/* Minmum and maximum values for scale */
#define SCALE_MIN_VALUE      0
#define SCALE_MAX_VALUE      100
#define SCALE_DECIMAL_POINT  1

static void scale_cb();
/*--------------------------------------------------------*/
Widget MakeWidgets(parent)
Widget parent;
{
    Widget w;

    w = XtVaCreateManagedWidget("Scale",
                    xmScaleWidgetClass, parent,
                    XmNorientation,     XmHORIZONTAL,
                    XmNborderWidth,     1,
                    XmNminimum,         SCALE_MIN_VALUE,
                    XmNmaximum,         SCALE_MAX_VALUE,
                    XmNdecimalPoints,   SCALE_DECIMAL_POINT,
                    XmNshowValue,       True,
                    NULL);

/* Add a callback function */
    XtAddCallback(w, XmNvalueChangedCallback, scale_cb, NULL);
    XtAddCallback(w, XmNdragCallback, scale_cb, NULL);
    return w;
}
/*--------------------------------------------------------*/
static void scale_cb(w, client_data, call_data)
Widget                  w;
XtPointer               client_data;
XmScaleCallbackStruct *call_data;
{
/* Value has one decimal point */
    printf("Value = %.1f\n", (double)(call_data->value)/10.0);
}
```

Command Widgets

The `Command` widget is a subclass of `SelectionBox` widget. Its purpose is to provide a command history mechanism. There is a command entry area where the user can type in commands. Once a command is entered, that command string is saved in a history buffer that is displayed in a scrollable list area. You can use the `Command` widget to accept user input for your command-driven applications. Figure 14.14 shows a typical `Command` widget. Listing 14.12 shows how to create and use the `Command` widget.

Figure 14.14.

A Command widget.

Listing 14.12. `command.c`—Function that demonstrates a `Command` widget.

```
/*-----------------------------------------------------------*/
/*  File:  command.c
 *
 *  Demonstrates an XmCommand widget.
 *
 */
#include <Xm/Xm.h>
#include <Xm/Command.h>

static void command_cb();
/*-----------------------------------------------------------*/
Widget MakeWidgets(parent)
Widget parent;
{
    Widget   w;
    XmString prompt = XmStringCreateSimple("Enter command:");

    w = XtVaCreateManagedWidget("Command",
                    xmCommandWidgetClass, parent,
                    XmNpromptString,  prompt,
                    NULL);
    XmStringFree(prompt);

/* Add a callback function */
    XtAddCallback(w, XmNcommandEnteredCallback, command_cb, NULL);

    return w;
}
/*-----------------------------------------------------------*/
```

```
static void command_cb(w, client_data, call_data)
Widget                  w;
XtPointer               client_data;
XmCommandCallbackStruct *call_data;
{
    char *command;
/* Convert compound string to C string */
    XmStringGetLtoR(call_data->value,
                    XmSTRING_DEFAULT_CHARSET, &command);
    printf("Command received: %s\n", command);

/* Remember to free memory allocated by Motif toolkit for
 * the returned C string.
 */
    XtFree(command);
}
```

> **NOTE:**
>
> The OSF/Motif Command widget is very different from the widget with the same name that
> appears in the Athena Widgets. Athena's Command widget is actually similar to OSF/Motif's
> PushButton widget.

MessageBox Widgets and Message Dialogs

The OSF/Motif toolkit includes a MessageBox widget that you can use to display messages. For
your convenience, there are special-purpose functions that create a DialogShell widget and display the message box in that shell. Figure 14.15 shows a generic message box created by the
XmCreateMessageDialog function.

Figure 14.15.

*A pop-up message box
created by
XmCreateMessageDialog.*

Creating a message dialog is straightforward. For instance, the dialog box of Figure 14.15 is displayed when the user clicks on the pushbutton labeled Message Dialog from a column of
pushbuttons displayed by the program shown in Listing 14.13 (see Figure 14.16). Consult the code
in the callback function pop_msgdlg to see how the message dialog of Figure 14.15 is created and
displayed. You create the dialog only once; after the first time, you can display the dialog by calling
XtManageChild.

Figure 14.16.

*Pushbuttons to display
various message dialogs.*

Listing 14.13. `msgbox.c`—Program that demonstrates message dialogs.

```
/*-----------------------------------------------------------*/
/*  File:  msgbox.c
 *
 *  Program to demonstrate message dialogs.
 */
#include <Xm/Xm.h>
#include <Xm/RowColumn.h>
#include <Xm/DialogS.h>
#include <Xm/MessageB.h>
#include <Xm/PushB.h>

/* Callbacks */

static void mbox_cb(/* Widget w, caddr_t client_data,
                   XmAnyCallbackStruct *call_data */);
static void pop_msgdlg();
static void pop_warndlg();
static void pop_infodlg();
static void pop_workdlg();

static Widget  msgdlg = 0, warndlg = 0, infodlg = 0, workdlg = 0;
/*-----------------------------------------------------------*/
void main(argc, argv)
int  argc;
char **argv;
{
    Widget        main_widget, rowcol, b;
    XtAppContext app;

/* Create and initialize the top-level widget */
    main_widget = XtAppInitialize(&app, "Msgbox", NULL, 0,
                              &argc, argv, NULL, NULL, 0);

/* Set up a row of buttons that enables user to pop up the dialogs */
    rowcol = XtVaCreateManagedWidget("rowcol",
                     xmRowColumnWidgetClass, main_widget,
                     NULL);

    b = XtVaCreateManagedWidget("Message Dialog",
                     xmPushButtonWidgetClass, rowcol,
                     NULL);
    XtAddCallback(b, XmNarmCallback, pop_msgdlg, NULL);

    b = XtVaCreateManagedWidget("Warning Dialog",
                     xmPushButtonWidgetClass, rowcol,
                     NULL);
    XtAddCallback(b, XmNarmCallback, pop_warndlg, NULL);
```

```
        b = XtVaCreateManagedWidget("Info Dialog",
                        xmPushButtonWidgetClass, rowcol,
                        NULL);
        XtAddCallback(b, XmNarmCallback, pop_infodlg, NULL);

        b = XtVaCreateManagedWidget("Working Dialog",
                        xmPushButtonWidgetClass, rowcol,
                        NULL);
        XtAddCallback(b, XmNarmCallback, pop_workdlg, NULL);


/* Realize the widgets and start processing events */
    XtRealizeWidget(main_widget);
    XtAppMainLoop(app);
}
/*------------------------------------------------------------*/
/* p o p _ m s g d l g
 * Display a message dialog box.
 */
static void pop_msgdlg(w, client_data, call_data)
Widget w;
XtPointer client_data, call_data;
{
    if(msgdlg == (Widget)0)
    {
        XmString xms;
        Arg      args[10];
        Cardinal argcount;

/* Create the pop-up dialog widget */
/* Convert message string to a Motif compound string */
        xms = XmStringCreateSimple(
                        "From XmCreateMessageDialog()");
/* Set up arguments and create the message box dialog */
        argcount = 0;
        XtSetArg(args[argcount], XmNmessageString, xms);
                                        argcount++;
        msgdlg = XmCreateMessageDialog(w, "Message",
                                args, argcount);
        XmStringFree(xms);

/* Add callbacks for OK and Cancel buttons. */
        XtAddCallback(msgdlg, XmNcancelCallback, mbox_cb,
                    (XtPointer)msgdlg);
        XtAddCallback(msgdlg, XmNokCallback, mbox_cb,
                    (XtPointer)msgdlg);
        XtManageChild(msgdlg);
    }
    else
    {
/* Simply manage the dialog box again */
        XtManageChild(msgdlg);
    }
}
/*------------------------------------------------------------*/
/* p o p _ w a r n d l g
 * Display a warning dialog box.
```

continues

Listing 14.13. continued

```
    */
static void pop_warndlg(w, client_data, call_data)
Widget w;
XtPointer client_data, call_data;
{
    if(warndlg == (Widget)0)
    {
        XmString xms;
        Arg      args[10];
        Cardinal argcount;

/* Create the pop-up dialog widget */
/* Convert message string to a Motif compound string */
        xms = XmStringCreateSimple(
                        "From XmCreateWarningDialog()");
/* Set up arguments and create the message box dialog */
        argcount = 0;
        XtSetArg(args[argcount], XmNmessageString, xms);
                                           argcount++;
        warndlg = XmCreateWarningDialog(w, "Warning",
                                        args, argcount);
        XmStringFree(xms);

/* Add callbacks for OK and Cancel buttons. */
        XtAddCallback(warndlg, XmNcancelCallback, mbox_cb,
                      (XtPointer)warndlg);
        XtAddCallback(warndlg, XmNokCallback, mbox_cb,
                      (XtPointer)warndlg);
        XtManageChild(warndlg);
    }
    else
    {
/* Simply manage the dialog box again */
        XtManageChild(warndlg);
    }
}
/*--------------------------------------------------------------*/
/* p o p _ i n f o d l g
 * Display an information dialog box.
 */
static void pop_infodlg(w, client_data, call_data)
Widget w;
XtPointer client_data, call_data;
{
    if(infodlg == (Widget)0)
    {
        XmString xms;
        Arg      args[10];
        Cardinal argcount;

/* Create the pop-up dialog widget */
/* Convert message string to a Motif compound string */
        xms = XmStringCreateSimple(
                        "From XmCreateInformationDialog()");
/* Set up arguments and create the message box dialog */
        argcount = 0;
```

```
            XtSetArg(args[argcount], XmNmessageString, xms);
                                        argcount++;
            infodlg = XmCreateInformationDialog(w, "Information",
                                    args, argcount);
            XmStringFree(xms);

/* Add callbacks for OK and Cancel buttons. */
            XtAddCallback(infodlg, XmNcancelCallback, mbox_cb,
                        (XtPointer)infodlg);
            XtAddCallback(infodlg, XmNokCallback, mbox_cb,
                        (XtPointer)infodlg);
            XtManageChild(infodlg);
    }
    else
    {
/* Simply manage the dialog box again */
            XtManageChild(infodlg);
    }
}
/*------------------------------------------------------------*/
/* p o p _ w o r k d l g
 * Display a "working" dialog box.
 */
static void pop_workdlg(w, client_data, call_data)
Widget w;
XtPointer client_data, call_data;
{
    if(workdlg == (Widget)0)
    {
        XmString xms;
        Arg      args[10];
        Cardinal argcount;

/* Create the pop-up dialog widget */
/* Convert message string to a Motif compound string */
            xms = XmStringCreateSimple(
                        "From XmCreateWorkingDialog()");
/* Set up arguments and create the message box dialog */
            argcount = 0;
            XtSetArg(args[argcount], XmNmessageString, xms);
                                        argoount++;
            workdlg = XmCreateWorkingDialog(w, "Working...",
                                    args, argcount);
            XmStringFree(xms);

/* Add callbacks for OK and Cancel buttons. */
            XtAddCallback(workdlg, XmNcancelCallback, mbox_cb,
                        (XtPointer)workdlg);
            XtAddCallback(workdlg, XmNokCallback, mbox_cb,
                        (XtPointer)workdlg);
            XtManageChild(workdlg);
    }
    else
    {
/* Simply manage the dialog box again */
            XtManageChild(workdlg);
    }
```

continues

Listing 14.13. continued

```
}
/*-------------------------------------------------------*/
/*  m b o x _ c b
 *
 *  Callback for the message dialogs.
 */
static void mbox_cb(w, client_data, call_data)
Widget w;
XtPointer client_data, call_data;
{
/* Simply unmanage the widget whose ID is provided in the
 * the "client_data" argument.
 */
    XtUnmanageChild((Widget)client_data);
}
```

The OK, Cancel, and Help buttons can invoke lists of callbacks when pressed. The mbox_cb function in Listing 14.13 is an example of a callback function. It hides the message dialog and its children by calling XtUnmanageChild with the dialog widget's ID as the argument.

In addition to the generic message dialog, the OSF/Motif toolkit provides several styles of message boxes meant for specific situations. Figure 14.17 shows a warning dialog created by calling the XmCreateWarningDialog function. The appearance of this dialog is similar to that of the standard message dialog except for the exclamation mark preceding the message. As the name implies, this dialog is meant for displaying warnings and cautions. The pop_warndlg callback function in Listing 14.13 creates and displays this dialog.

Figure 14.18 shows an information dialog with an *i*-shaped icon in the message area. You can use this icon to display informative messages. The function that creates this dialog is XmCreateInformationDialog. The pop_infodlg callback function in Listing 14.13 creates and displays this dialog.

Figure 14.17.
*Message dialog
created by the
XmCreateWarningDialog
function.*

Figure 14.18.
*Message dialog
created by the
XmCreateInformationDialog
function.*

The XmCreateWorkingDialog function creates a dialog box of the style shown in Figure 14.19. This dialog, with an hourglass icon, is meant for displaying messages that tell the user that a lengthy operation is in progress. The pop_workdlg callback function in Listing 14.13 shows how to create and display this dialog.

Figure 14.19.

Message dialog created by the XmCreateWorkingDialog function.

Menus and Main Windows

GUIs use a wide variety of menus, from a simple array of pushbuttons to the more elaborate ones with a menubar incorporating cascading pull-down submenus. The OSF/Motif toolkit supports a number of widgets for creating and displaying menus.

You create the basic menu pane (a number of menu entries arranged in column or row) with a RowColumn widget. Menu entries are buttons, either PushButton or ToggleButton widgets. You can use the CascadeButton widget for buttons that trigger a submenu. Label widgets are used to display nonselectable text or a pixmap in a menu, and the Separator widget draws the lines delineating groups of items.

Figure 14.20 shows a type of menu known as the option menu that consists of a menu title followed by a box in which the current selection is displayed. If you press the left mouse button with the pointer in the box, a pull-down menu is displayed. You can pick another item from this menu by moving the pointer to the selected item and releasing the mouse button.

You create option menus using the XmCreateOptionMenu function. Before you call this function, you have to prepare a pull-down menu using the XmCreatePulldownMenu function. The pull-down menu, in turn, requires a number of pushbuttons that serve as the menu items. Listing 14.14 shows the code used to generate the option menu of Figure 14.20.

Figure 14.20.

An option menu showing the selections in its associated pull-down menu.

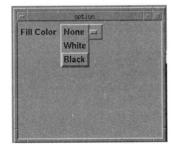

Listing 14.14. `option.c`—Function that demonstrates an option menu.

```
/*------------------------------------------------------------*/
/*  File:  option.c
 *
 *  Demonstrates an option menu.
 *
 */
#include <Xm/Xm.h>
#include <Xm/BulletinB.h>
#include <Xm/RowColumn.h>
#include <Xm/PushB.h>

static void action();
/*------------------------------------------------------------*/
Widget MakeWidgets(parent)
Widget parent;
{
    Widget   w, sub_menu, entry1, entry2, entry3;
    XmString option_menu_title;
    Arg      args[20];
    Cardinal argcount;

/* Create the Pulldown menu to be displayed by option menu */
    sub_menu = XmCreatePulldownMenu(parent, "PullDown", NULL, 0);

/* Pulldown menu entries--implemented by pushbuttons */
    entry1 = XmCreatePushButton(sub_menu, "None", NULL, 0);
    XtManageChild(entry1);
    XtAddCallback(entry1, XmNactivateCallback, action,
                (XtPointer)"None");

    entry2 = XmCreatePushButton(sub_menu, "White", NULL, 0);
    XtManageChild(entry2);
    XtAddCallback(entry2, XmNactivateCallback, action,
                (XtPointer)"White");

    entry3 = XmCreatePushButton(sub_menu, "Black", NULL, 0);
    XtManageChild(entry3);
    XtAddCallback(entry3, XmNactivateCallback, action,
                (XtPointer)"Black");

/* Now we create the actual option menu */
    option_menu_title = XmStringCreateSimple("Fill Color");

    argcount = 0;
    XtSetArg(args[argcount], XmNy, 100);                  argcount++;
    XtSetArg(args[argcount], XmNlabelString, option_menu_title);
                                                          argcount++;
    XtSetArg(args[argcount], XmNsubMenuId, sub_menu); argcount++;
    XtSetArg(args[argcount], XmNmenuHistory, entry1); argcount++;
    w = XmCreateOptionMenu(parent, "Options", args, argcount);
    XtManageChild(w);

    return w;
}
/*------------------------------------------------------------*/
static void action(w, client_data, call_data)
Widget              w;
```

```
XtPointer          client_data;
XmAnyCallbackStruct *call_data;
{
    printf("Current selection: %s\n", (char*)client_data);
}
```

OSF/Motif also provides functions to create a main window with a menubar and cascading panes such as the one shown in Figure 14.21. As you might expect, the steps you follow to create such a menu are considerably more detailed than those for a simple option menu. Still, with the power of a toolkit, generating such a menu is merely a matter of following the steps. Listing 14.15 shows the code that prepares the main window, attaches the menubar to it, and adds the cascading menus.

Figure 14.21.

A main window with menubar and cascading menus.

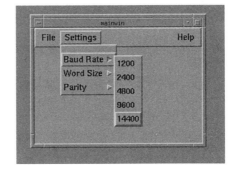

Listing 14.15. `mainwin.c`—Function that demonstrates a main window with a menubar and cascading menus.

```
/*------------------------------------------------------------*/
/* File:  mainwin.c
 *
 * Demonstrates a main window with a menubar.
 *
 */
#include <Xm/Xm.h>

#include <Xm/RowColumn.h>
#include <Xm/MainW.h>
#include <Xm/PushB.h>
#include <Xm/CascadeB.h>


#define MAX_ENTRIES  16

/* Information on individual menu items */
typedef struct ITEM_ACTION
{
    char           *label;    /* Label for the item    */
    XtCallbackProc callbacks; /* Callbacks for the item */
    XtPointer      data;      /* Data for callback     */
```

continues

Listing 14.15. continued

```
} ITEM_ACTION;

/* Data structure to hold Pulldown menu information */
typedef struct PULLDOWN_MENU_INFO
{
   int   size;      /* Number of entries in menu */
   char  *name;         /* Name of menu            */
   ITEM_ACTION items[MAX_ENTRIES];
} PULLDOWN_MENU_INFO;

/* Information for cascade buttons */
typedef struct CASCADE_ITEM
{
   char              *label;  /* Cascade button's label */
   PULLDOWN_MENU_INFO *submenu; /* Menu to be pulled down */
} CASCADE_ITEM;

/* Structure to hold cascade menu information */
typedef struct CASCADE_MENU_INFO
{
   int            size;   /* Number of entries in menu */
   char           *name;      /* Name of cascade menu    */
   CASCADE_ITEM   items[MAX_ENTRIES];
} CASCADE_MENU_INFO;

/* Callbacks */
/*------------------------------------------------------------*/
void parity(w, y, x)
Widget w;
XtPointer y;
XmAnyCallbackStruct *x;
{
    printf("parity = %s\n", (char*)y);
}
/*------------------------------------------------------------*/
void baud_rate(w, y, x)
Widget w;
XtPointer y;
XmAnyCallbackStruct *x;
{
    printf("Baud rate = %d\n", (int)y);
}
/*------------------------------------------------------------*/
void word_size(w, y, x)
Widget w;
XtPointer y;
XmAnyCallbackStruct *x;
{
    printf("word_size = %d\n", (int)y);
}
/*------------------------------------------------------------*/
static PULLDOWN_MENU_INFO sub_menu1_data =
{
    5, "Baud Rate",
    {
        {"1200",  baud_rate, (XtPointer)1200},
```

```
            {"2400",  baud_rate, (XtPointer)2400},
            {"4800",  baud_rate, (XtPointer)4800},
            {"9600",  baud_rate, (XtPointer)9600},
            {"14400",  baud_rate, (XtPointer)14400}
    }
};

static PULLDOWN_MENU_INFO sub_menu2_data =
{
    2, "Word Size",
    {
        {"1",  word_size, (XtPointer)1},
        {"2",  word_size, (XtPointer)2},
    }
};

static PULLDOWN_MENU_INFO sub_menu3_data =
{
    4,  "Parity",
    {
        { "None",  parity,  (XtPointer)"none"},
        { "Even",  parity,  (XtPointer)"even"},
        { "Odd",   parity,  (XtPointer)"odd"},
        { "Mark",  parity,  (XtPointer)"mark"}
    }
};

/* Continue with other submenus, if any. */

/* Define the Cascade Menu (for second button on menubar) */
static CASCADE_MENU_INFO menu2_data =
{
    3, "Settings",
    {
        {"Baud Rate",  &sub_menu1_data},
        {"Word Size",  &sub_menu2_data},
        {"Parity",     &sub_menu3_data}
    }
};
/*-----------------------------------------------------------*/
/* Callback function for the simple Pulldown menu */
void menu_cb(w, item_number, call_data)
Widget   w;
int      item_number;
XtPointer call_data;
{
    printf("Item number = %d\n", item_number);
    if(item_number == 2) exit(0);
}
/*-----------------------------------------------------------*/
Widget MakeWidgets(parent)
Widget parent;
{
    Widget              w, help_button, menu2, menu_tmp,
                        button, cbutton;
    int                 count=0, subcount;
    XmString            xm_new, xm_open, xm_exit;
    Widget              main_window, menu_bar;
```

continues

Listing 14.15. continued

```
    Arg                 args[20];
    Cardinal            argcount;
    PULLDOWN_MENU_INFO *menu_data;

/* Create and manage a main window */
    argcount = 0;
    XtSetArg(args[argcount], XmNwidth, 300);   argcount++;
    XtSetArg(args[argcount], XmNheight, 200);   argcount++;
    main_window = XmCreateMainWindow(parent, "MainWin",
                                     args, argcount);
    XtManageChild(main_window);

/* Create the menubar */
    menu_bar = XmCreateMenuBar(main_window, "MenuBar", NULL, 0);
    XtManageChild(menu_bar);

/* Add the menubar to the main window */
    XmMainWindowSetAreas(main_window, menu_bar, NULL, NULL,
                         NULL, NULL);

/* Create the first cascade button on the menubar */
    (void)XtVaCreateManagedWidget("File",
                    xmCascadeButtonWidgetClass, menu_bar,
                NULL);

/* Create a simple Pulldown menu that is attached to the first
 * cascade button on the menubar.
 */
    xm_new = XmStringCreateSimple("New...");
    xm_open = XmStringCreateSimple("Open...");
    xm_exit = XmStringCreateSimple("Exit");

    (void)XmVaCreateSimplePulldownMenu(menu_bar,
                "file_menu",
                0,          /* Attach to first cascade button */
                menu_cb,    /* Menu callback                  */
                XmVaPUSHBUTTON, xm_new,  'N', NULL, NULL,
                XmVaPUSHBUTTON, xm_open, 'O', NULL, NULL,
                XmVaSEPARATOR,
                XmVaPUSHBUTTON, xm_exit, 'x', NULL, NULL,
                NULL);

/* Remember to free the XmStrings */
    XmStringFree(xm_new);
    XmStringFree(xm_open);
    XmStringFree(xm_exit);

/* Now create another Pulldown menu */
    argcount = 0;
    XtSetArg(args[argcount], XmNtearOffModel, XmTEAR_OFF_ENABLED);
                                                argcount++;

    menu2 = XmCreatePulldownMenu(menu_bar, "Settings",
                            args, argcount);

/* Create the entries that will activate further submenus */
```

```
        for(count = 0; count < menu2_data.size; count++)
        {
/* Build the submenu to be attached to the second cascade
 * button.
 */
        menu_tmp = XmCreatePulldownMenu(menu2,
                        menu2_data.items[count].label, NULL, 0);

/* Add entries to the submenu */
        menu_data =  (menu2_data.items[count]).submenu;

        for(subcount = 0; subcount < menu_data->size; subcount++)
        {
/* Create an entry (can be a pushbutton, toggle button, label,
 * or a separator. Here we use pushbuttons.
 */
            button = XmCreatePushButton(menu_tmp,
                        menu_data->items[subcount].label, NULL, 0);
            if(menu_data->items[subcount].callbacks)
                XtAddCallback(button, XmNactivateCallback,
                            menu_data->items[subcount].callbacks,
                            menu_data->items[subcount].data);
            XtManageChild (button);
        }
/* Now create the cascade button and attach the submenu */
        argcount = 0;
        XtSetArg(args[argcount], XmNsubMenuId, menu_tmp);
        argcount++;
        cbutton = XmCreateCascadeButton(menu2,
                    menu2_data.items[count].label, args, argcount);
        XtManageChild(cbutton);
    }

/* Create the cascade buttons on the menubar */
    (void) XtVaCreateManagedWidget("Settings",
                        xmCascadeButtonWidgetClass, menu_bar,
                        XmNsubMenuId, menu2,
                NULL);

/* Create a "Help" button */
    help_button = XtVaCreateManagedWidget("Holp",
                        xmCascadeButtonWidgetClass, menu_bar,
                NULL);
    XtVaSetValues(menu_bar, XmNmenuHelpWidget, help_button,
                NULL);

    return w;
}
```

The first step is to create a main window and a menubar. The main window is created by calling XmCreateMainWindow, and the menubar is created by the utility function XmCreateMenuBar. You add entries to the menubar after it has been created. Each entry must be a CascadeButton widget. In Figure 14.21, there are three items labeled File, Settings, and Help. Each cascade button can have an associated pull-down menu that is to be displayed when the user presses on the cascade button. Because the buttons in the pull-down menu can also be cascade buttons requiring further pull-down menus, you have to prepare all the menus before adding entries to the menubar. Figure 14.22 shows the hierarchy of cascade buttons and menus in the example shown in Figure 14.21.

Figure 14.22.

Widget hierarchy for the menu shown in Figure 14.21.

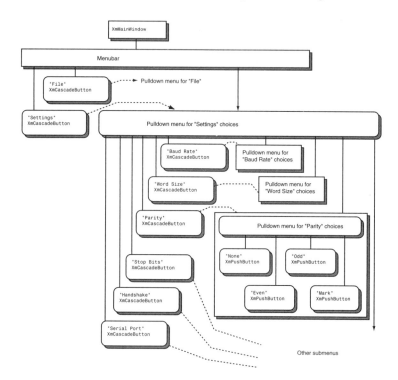

It is convenient to store the menu definitions in a data structure so that you can create all the submenus mechanically. This example uses the data structures ITEM_ACTION, PULLDOWN_MENU_INFO, CASCADE_ITEM, and CASCADE_MENU_INFO to organize and store the information needed to build the menus.

The term *cascade menu* refers to a pull-down menu whose items are all CascadeButton widgets, each capable of displaying another pull-down menu. Figure 14.21 shows a cascade menu (with entries Baud Rate, Word Size, and Parity) with a pull-down menu displayed by an activated cascade button.

Next, you have to prepare the cascading menu panes—each as a pull-down menu with CascadeButton widgets as menu items. Once you have all the submenus ready, you can create the cascade buttons for the menubar and attach the appropriate menus to each button.

In the menubar of Figure 14.21, the Help button appears at the right edge of the menubar, which is what is recommended in the OSF/Motif Style Guide. To get the recommended placement for the Help button, set the XmNmenuHelpWidget resource on the menubar. For instance, here is how you can create a Help button and attach it to a menubar whose widget ID is menu_bar:

```
/* Create a "Help" button */
   help_button = XtVaCreateManagedWidget("Help",
                        xmCascadeButtonWidgetClass, menu_bar,
                NULL);
/* Make sure the Help button appears in its proper place */
   XtVaSetValues(menu_bar, XmNmenuHelpWidget, help_button,
                NULL);
```

Another interesting feature of menus, introduced in OSF/Motif 1.2, is the concept of tear-off menus. These are menus from which you can tear off the menubar and make them stay visible. Motif introduced the tear-off menus in answer to OPEN LOOK's *pushpin* feature, which also enables a user to pin a menu on the screen and keep it visible. It is easy to make any pull-down menu a tear-off menu; all you have to do is set the `XmNtearOffModel` resource of the pull-down menu to `XmTEAR_OFF_ENABLED`. (You must use this resource at the time of creating the menu.) Here is an example of how to create a tear-off menu:

```
Widget menu_bar, menu2;

argcount = 0;
XtSetArg(args[argcount], XmNtearOffModel, XmTEAR_OFF_ENABLED);
                                        argcount++;

menu2 = XmCreatePulldownMenu(menu_bar, "Settings",
                        args, argcount);
```

Form Widgets

The `Form` widget is a general-purpose container widget like `RowColumn`. However, instead of simply laying out its children in rows and columns the way `RowColumn` does, `Form` supports much more complex layouts that are specified by the values of certain resources that the `Form` widget attaches to each of its children. These resources are known as *constraint resources* and they, in effect, provide a layout language that you can use to indicate how the child widgets are placed in the `Form` widget. Each constraint resource indicates the spatial relationship of a child widget to the `Form` widget and to another existing child widget. Table 14.7 lists the specific constraint resources that the `Form` widget provides for each child.

Table 14.7. Meanings of Constraint Resources of a `Form` Widget

Resource Name	Meaning
XmNbottomAttachment	Specifies how the bottom edge of the child widget is attached to the form (some possible values are XmATTACH_NONE, XmATTACH_FORM, XmATTACH_WIDGET, XmATTACH_SELF, XmATTACH_POSITION)
XmNbottomOffset	Spacing between the bottom side of the child widget and the object to which it is attached

continues

Table 14.7. continued

Resource Name	Meaning
XmNbottomPosition	Position of the bottom side of the child when XmNbottomAttachment is XmATTACH_POSITION
XmNbottomWidget	Widget to which the bottom edge of the child widget is attached (used when XmNbottomAtttachment is XmATTACH_WIDGET or XmATTACH_OPPOSITE_WIDGET)
XmNleftAttachment	Specifies how the left edge of the child widget is attached to the form
XmNleftOffset	Spacing between the left side of the child widget and the object to which it is attached
XmNleftPosition	Position of the left side of the child widget when XmNleftAttachment is XmATTACH_POSITION
XmNleftWidget	Widget to which the left edge of the child widget is attached (used when XmNleftAtttachment is XmATTACH_WIDGET or XmATTACH_OPPOSITE_WIDGET)
XmNresizable	If True, the child widget may be resized when the form is resized
XmNrightAttachment	Specifies how the right edge of the child widget is attached to the form
XmNrightOffset	Spacing between the right side of the child widget and the object to which it is attached
XmNrightPosition	Position of the right side of the child when XmNrightAttachment is XmATTACH_POSITION
XmNrightWidget	Widget to which the right edge of the child widget is attached (used when XmNrightAtttachment is XmATTACH_WIDGET or XmATTACH_OPPOSITE_WIDGET)
XmNtopAttachment	Specifies how the top edge of the child widget is attached to the form
XmNtopOffset	Spacing between the top side of the child widget and the object to which it is attached
XmNtopPosition	Position of the top side of the child when XmNtopAttachment is XmATTACH_POSITION
XmNtopWidget	Widget to which the top edge of the child widget is attached (used when XmNtopAtttachment is XmATTACH_WIDGET or XmATTACH_OPPOSITE_WIDGET)

Figure 14.23 shows a sample layout created by placing a menubar and a `ScrolledWindow` widget inside a Form. The `ScrolledWindow` widget contains a `Text` widget as a child. The user can exit the program by selecting the Exit option from the File menu on the menubar.

Figure 14.23.

A sample layout using the Form widget.

Listing 14.16 shows the example program (`form.c`) that creates the layout shown in Figure 14.23. Notice that you do not have to specify any resources when creating the Form widget. All the constraint resources are specified when creating the children—the menubar and `ScrolledWindow` widgets. In this case, the menubar's top, left, and right edges are attached to the Form widget (indicated by the `XmATTACH_FORM` setting of the attachment resources). The `ScrolledWindow` widget sets `XmNtopAttachment` to `XmATTACH_WIDGET` and lists the menubar widget as its `XmNtopWidget`, so it is positioned below the menubar widget. The `ScrolledWindow` widget is also attached to the bottom, left, and right edges of the Form widget. Additionally, the `ScrolledWindow` widget is made resizable in x and y directions. Thus, when the user resizes the window shown in Figure 14.23, the Form widget resizes the `ScrolledWindow` widget to match the new size of the Form widget's window.

Listing 14.16. `form.c`—Typical layout of widgets that uses the `Form` widget.

```
/*-----------------------------------------------------------*/
/*  File:  form.c
 *
 *  Demonstrates the use of the Form widget.
 *
 */
#include <Xm/Xm.h>
#include <Xm/Form.h>
#include <Xm/RowColumn.h>
#include <Xm/ScrolledW.h>
#include <Xm/Text.h>
#include <Xm/CascadeB.h>

/* Callback */
static void button_select();
/*-----------------------------------------------------------*/
```

continues

Listing 14.16. continued

```
Widget MakeWidgets(parent)
Widget parent;
{
    Widget   w, mbar, swin, tw;
    XmString xm_new, xm_open, xm_exit;
    Arg      args[20];
    int      n;

/* Create the Form widget */
    w = XtVaCreateManagedWidget("form",
                    xmFormWidgetClass, parent,
                    NULL);

/* Add other widgets to the Form. First an area for menu */
    n = 0;
    XtSetArg(args[n], XmNleftAttachment, XmATTACH_FORM); n++;
    XtSetArg(args[n], XmNrightAttachment, XmATTACH_FORM); n++;
    XtSetArg(args[n], XmNtopAttachment, XmATTACH_FORM); n++;
    mbar = XmCreateMenuBar(w, "menubar", args, n);
    XtManageChild(mbar);

/* Add a Pulldown menu to the menubar */
/* Create the first cascade button on the menubar */
    (void)XtVaCreateManagedWidget("File",
                    xmCascadeButtonWidgetClass, mbar,
                NULL);

/* Create a simple Pulldown menu that is attached to the first
 * cascade button on the menubar.
 */
    xm_new = XmStringCreateSimple("New...");
    xm_open = XmStringCreateSimple("Open...");
    xm_exit = XmStringCreateSimple("Exit");

    (void)XmVaCreateSimplePulldownMenu(mbar,
                "file_menu",
                0,              /* Attach to first cascade button */
                button_select,  /* Menu callback              */
                XmVaPUSHBUTTON, xm_new, 'N', NULL, NULL,
                XmVaPUSHBUTTON, xm_open, 'O', NULL, NULL,
                XmVaSEPARATOR,
                XmVaPUSHBUTTON, xm_exit, 'x', NULL, NULL,
                NULL);

/* Remember to free the XmStrings */
    XmStringFree(xm_new);
    XmStringFree(xm_open);
    XmStringFree(xm_exit);

/* Add a ScrolledWindow and within it a Text widget */

    swin = XtVaCreateManagedWidget("scrollwin",
                    xmScrolledWindowWidgetClass, w,
                    XmNtopAttachment,    XmATTACH_WIDGET,
                    XmNtopWidget,        mbar,
                    XmNbottomAttachment, XmATTACH_FORM,
```

```
                    XmNleftAttachment,     XmATTACH_FORM,
                    XmNrightAttachment,    XmATTACH_FORM,
                    XmNresizable,          True,
                    XmNscrollingPolicy,    XmAUTOMATIC,
                    NULL);

    tw = XtVaCreateManagedWidget("text",
                    xmTextWidgetClass, swin,
                    XmNeditable,       True,
                    XmNeditMode,       XmMULTI_LINE_EDIT,
                    XmNwordWrap,       True,
                    XmNheight,         500,
                    XmNwidth,          500,
                    NULL);
    return w;
}
/*------------------------------------------------------------*/
/* Callback function for the simple Pulldown menu */

static void button_select(w, item_number, call_data)
Widget    w;
int       item_number;
XtPointer call_data;
{
    printf("Item number = %d\n", item_number);
    if(item_number == 2) exit(0);
}
```

Summary

All Xt Intrinsics-based toolkits, including OSF/Motif and the OPEN LOOK Intrinsics Toolkit, share a common object-oriented structure. Instead of working with individual windows, as Xlib does, the toolkits define higher-level objects such as labels and pushbuttons, called widgets, that are used as components to build user interfaces for applications. Each widget encapsulates one or more windows with other data and includes functions that provide some predefined functionality.

An Xt Intrinsics-based widget has a class data structure and an instance data structure. There is only one class structure for each class; each copy of a widget has its own private instance data. The class data structure includes data common to all instances and provides the functions that draw the widget and handle events occurring in the windows associated with that widget. The widget class is organized in a hierarchy so that child widgets can share data and functions with their parents—this is known as inheritance. The widget instances also have their hierarchy, which is similar to the hierarchy of windows in X.

The class hierarchy of the OSF/Motif widget set is built upon a basic set of widgets defined in Xt Intrinsics. This base set consists of the Core, Composite, Constraint, and Shell widgets. Motif adds a few more base classes such as XmPrimitive and XmManager. All other Motif widgets are derived from these base widgets. You can broadly classify the Motif widgets into three categories:

✦ The stand-alone `Primitive` widgets such as labels and pushbuttons

✦ The `Manager` widgets such as `RowColumn` and `Form` that can contain other widgets

✦ The `Shell` widgets for setting up the top-level windows of applications

This chapter describes several representative members of each class of widget. It includes example code to create these widgets and corresponding figures to illustrate their visual appearance.

Chapter 15

Toolkit-Based Applications

A toolkit-based X application can use that toolkit's widget set to build most of its user interface, but some parts of the application cannot be constructed from the widgets alone. For example, if your application is a utility for browsing through text files, you can use various widgets to prompt for the filename and prepare a scrollable viewing area to display the contents of the file. The file browser, however, also has to manage the file's contents in memory and display the text in a window. For these tasks, you have to design your own data structures, open and load the file, and use Xlib functions to draw the text strings in the viewing area provided by the widgets.

No matter how versatile the toolkit, most realistic applications require you to mix Xlib calls with toolkit functions. This chapter illustrates how you can use Xlib functions for graphics and text output in widgets based on the OSF/Motif toolkit. Two example programs—a simple drawing program and a file viewer—show how you can do this. These examples are based on the Xlib-based `viewfile` and `xfigures` programs described in Chapters 9, "Drawing Graphics," and 10, "Drawing Text," respectively. The latter part of the book describes facilities such as workprocs and input callbacks that can be useful in X applications.

Xlib and Xt Intrinsics

The approach for mixing Xlib functions with those in an X toolkit are the same for all toolkits based on Xt Intrinsics. Essentially, to use Xlib functions in any application, you need the `Display` pointer, the window ID, and, for drawing functions, a `GC`. Xt Intrinsics provides macros and functions to get these parameters for any widget.

Identifying the Display and Windows

Xt Intrinsics and toolkits based on Intrinsics work with widgets, but most Xlib functions require a pointer to the `Display` structure and a window identifier as arguments. Given a widget ID, you can get the pointer to its `Display` structure with the `XtDisplay` function. Similarly, the `XtWindow` function returns the ID of the window associated with a widget. As an example, suppose you want to use the Xlib function `XClearWindow` to clear a widget's window. Given the widget ID `w`, you can use the following:

```
#include <X11/Intrinsics.h>
.
.

Widget   w;
Display  *p_disp;
Window   win;

p_disp = XtDisplay(w);
win = XtWindow(w);
XClearWindow(p_disp, win);
```

The window ID returned by `XtWindow` will be `NULL` if the widget has not been realized. The `Display` pointer, however, is valid immediately after the widget is created by calling `XtCreateWidget` or another equivalent function.

Creating a *GC*

From Chapter 9, you know that in X the appearance of text and graphics is controlled by attributes stored in a `GC`. When you program using a toolkit, one of the common tasks is to draw text and graphics in a widget's window. You have to create `GC`s for this. When using Xlib alone, you use functions such as `XCreateGC`, `XCopyGC`, and `XChangeGC` to create and manipulate `GC`s. Xt Intrinsics provides the function `XtGetGC` for creating `GC`s. This function tries to minimize the number of `GC` creations by keeping track of the `GC`s created by all the widgets in an application. Xt Intrinsics creates a new `GC` only when none of the existing ones has attributes matching what you request in the `XtGetGC` call.

When creating a `GC` for a widget, you should get the foreground and background pixel values from the widget's resources. That way, you will be using the foreground and background colors that the user might have specified for that widget in a resource file.

You get the value of a widget's resources by calling `XtGetValues`. The steps are similar to those involved in setting resource values. For example, suppose you want the foreground and background colors for the widget `drawing_area`. Here is how you can get these values and set up a `GC` with these attributes:

```
    Arg         args[20];
    Cardinal    argcount;
    Widget      drawing_area;
    XGCValues   xgcv;
    GC          theGC;
    int         fg, bg;

/* Retrieve the background and foreground
 * colors from the widget's resources.
 */
    argcount = 0;
    XtSetArg(args[argcount], XmNforeground, &fg); argcount++;
    XtSetArg(args[argcount], XmNbackground, &bg); argcount++;
    XtGetValues(drawing_area, args, argcount);

/* Now, define a GC with these colors */
    xgcv.foreground = fg;
    xgcv.background = bg;
    theGC = XtGetGC(drawing_area, GCForeground | GCBackground,
                    &xgcv);
```

When retrieving a resource's value, you provide the address of a variable in which `XtGetValues` places the value.

Once you have created the `GC`, you can manipulate it with Xlib functions (as explained in Chapter 9). The `GC` returned by `XtGetGC` is read-only, however; you cannot change it. Use `XCreateGC` if you need a `GC` that you can change.

An OSF/Motif Drawing Program: *xmfigure*

Chapter 9 shows an Xlib-based drawing program, `xfigures` (Listing 9.2). In this chapter, you will build `xmfigure`—an OSF/Motif version of that drawing program. Like the Xlib-based program, `xmfigure` displays a menubar with two menus—`File` and `Figures`—and has a drawing area under the menubar. As shown in Figure 15.1, when the user presses the mouse buttton on the `Figures` item, a pull-down menu appears. This menu lists five types of figures that the program can draw—line, rectangle, ellipse, filled rectangle, and filled ellipse. To draw a figure, the user selects the type of figure and starts drawing in the drawing area.

The program can draw rubber-band figures. When the user first presses the left mouse button in the drawing area, it marks one corner of the figure. As the user moves the mouse while keeping the button pressed, the figure grows and shrinks in keeping with the mouse movement. The final figure is drawn when the user releases the button. (Chapter 9 shows how to draw rubber-band figures.)

Figure 15.1.

Output from xmfigure—
*a simple drawing program
that uses the OSF/Motif
toolkit.*

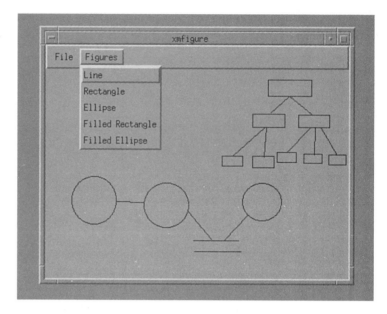

Selecting the Widgets

Selecting the appropriate widgets is the first step in implementing the drawing program with the OSF/Motif toolkit. A good candidate is the MainWindow widget. This is a composite widget that allows for a menubar, a drawing area, and scrollbars. You have to create the component widgets individually, and the components are optional. For xmfigure, you will use a MainWindow with a menubar and a drawing area.

To create the widgets, you have to start with a call to XtAppInitialize to set up a top-level shell widget. Next, you call a convenience function named XmCreateMainWindow to create the main window. This window is a child of the top-level shell.

The menubar is actually a RowColumn widget of type XmMENU_BAR (a constant defined in <Xm/Xm.h>) configured to hold the CascadeButton widgets that control the pull-down menus. You can call another convenience function, XmCreateMenuBar, to create the menubar.

Setting Up Menus

To set up the menubar, you have to create a pull-down menu for a cascade button and then attach that menu to the button. Because these steps tend to be repetitive, these are prime candidates for utility functions. You set up the functions MakeMenuPane and AttachToCascade to create a menu pane and attach it to a cascade button. Listing 15.1 shows the file xmutil.c containing these two functions. The menu pane is constructed by laying out a number of pushbutton widgets, one after another. Each pushbutton has a callback function, which is called when that menu item is selected.

Listing 15.1. xmutil.c—Utility functions for OSF/Motif programming.

```c
/*------------------------------------------------------------*/
/* File: xmutil.c
 *
 * Utility functions for building menus with the OSF/Motif
 * toolkit
 */
 /*-----------------------------------------------------------*/
#include <stdio.h>
#include <varargs.h>  /* UNIX-standard variable argument macros */

#include <Xm/Xm.h>
#include <Xm/RowColumn.h>
#include <Xm/PushB.h>
#include <Xm/CascadeB.h>

typedef void    (*P_FUNC)();
typedef char    *P_CHAR;


/*-----------------------------------------------------------*/
/*  M a k e M e n u P a n e
 *
 * Make a menu pane (uses variable number of arguments)
 * Each menu entry is a pair of the form: label, action_proc
 * A NULL marks the end.
 */
Widget MakeMenuPane(va_alist)
va_dcl  /* Macro must appear without semicolon */
{
    va_list  argp;          /* Used to access arguments */
    Widget   new_menu, button, parent;
    char     *item_label;
    P_FUNC   item_action;
    caddr_t  action_args;
    char     *name;

/* First retrieve the Pulldown menu's name and the ID of
 * the parent widget.
 */
    va_start(argp);
    name = va_arg(argp, P_CHAR);
    parent = va_arg(argp, Widget);

/* Create the Pulldown menu */
    new_menu = XmCreatePulldownMenu(parent, name, NULL, 0);

/* Add entries (pushbuttons) to this submenu */
/* Get items one by one and prepare the pushbuttons */

    while((item_label = va_arg(argp, P_CHAR)) != NULL)
    {
/* Create an entry (can be a pushbutton, toggle button, label,
 * or a separator). Here we use pushbuttons.
 */
        button = XmCreatePushButton(new_menu, item_label,
                                    NULL, 0);
```

continues

Listing 15.1. continued

```
/* Register callback for this menu button */

        item_action = va_arg(argp, P_FUNC);
        action_args = va_arg(argp, caddr_t);

        XtAddCallback(button, XmNactivateCallback,
                      item_action, action_args);
        XtManageChild (button);
    }
    va_end(argp);
    return(new_menu);
}
/*------------------------------------------------------------*/
/*  A t t a c h T o C a s c a d e
 *
 *  Attach a Pulldown menu to a cascade button.
 */
void AttachToCascade(parent, label, sub_menu)
Widget parent;
char    *label;
Widget sub_menu;
{
    Arg       args[10];
    Cardinal argcount;
    Widget    cbutton;

/* Create the cascade button and attach the submenu to it */
    argcount = 0;
    XtSetArg(args[argcount], XmNsubMenuId, sub_menu);
    argcount++;
    cbutton = XmCreateCascadeButton(parent, label,
                                    args, argcount);
    XtManageChild(cbutton);
}
```

With these two utility functions, setting up menus becomes very easy. For instance, to create the Figures menu in xmfigure, use the following:

```
/* "figure_select" is a callback. zero, one, two, ... are
 *  integers indicating figure to be drawn.
 */

    Widget menu_bar, new_menu;
      .
      .
/* Create the "Figures" menu --------------------------------*/
    new_menu = MakeMenuPane("Figures", menu_bar,
             "Line",              figure_select, (XtPointer)&zero,
             "Rectangle",         figure_select, (XtPointer)&one,
             "Ellipse",           figure_select, (XtPointer)&two,
             "Filled Rectangle", figure_select, (XtPointer)&three,
             "Filled Ellipse",   figure_select, (XtPointer)&four,
             NULL);

/* Now create the cascade button and attach this submenu to it */
    AttachToCascade(menu_bar, "Figures", new_menu);
```

Setting Up the Main Window

Once the menubar is ready, create a `DrawingArea` widget that will be used as the drawing area. You can use the `XmCreateDrawingArea` function to set up this widget. The last step in setting up the interface is to attach the menubar and the drawing area to the main window. You can do this by calling `XmMainWindowSetAreas`:

```
    Widget main_window, menu_bar, drawing_area;

/* Attach the menubar and the drawing area to main window */
    XmMainWindowSetAreas(main_window, menu_bar, NULL, NULL,
                         NULL, drawing_area);
```

Building *xmfigure*

The source code for the application, `xmfigure.c`, appears in Listing 15.2. You can use the following makefile to compile and link `xmfigure`:

```
# Some common definitions...

RM = rm -f
CC = cc

# Compiler flags, paths for include files and libraries

CFLAGS =
DEFINES =
INCLUDES = -I. -I/usr/include -I/usr/include/X11
LIBS = -lXm -lXt -lXmu -lX11

# Rule to create .o files from .c files
.c.o:
    $(RM) $@
    $(CC) -c $(CFLAGS) $(DEFINES) $(INCLUDES) $*.c

# Targets...

all::    xmfigure

xmfigure: xmfigure.o xmutil.o
    $(RM) $@
    $(CC) -o $@ $(CFLAGS) xmfigure.o xmutil.o $(LIBS)
```

This makefile should work as is in most UNIX systems running X11R6.

Listing 15.2. `xmfigure.c`—OSF/Motif version of drawing program.

```
/*----------------------------------------------------------*/
/*  File: xmfigure.c
 *
 *  OSF/Motif version of simple drawing program
 */
/*----------------------------------------------------------*/
#include <stdio.h>
```

continues

Listing 15.2. continued

```c
#include <X11/Xlib.h>
#include <X11/Xutil.h>
#include <X11/cursorfont.h>

#include <Xm/Xm.h>
#include <Xm/RowColumn.h>
#include <Xm/MainW.h>
#include <Xm/DrawingA.h>

#define MAXARGS     20
#define MAXFIGURES  100

#define WIDTH       400
#define HEIGHT      300

typedef struct FIGURE
{
    short   type;       /* What type of figure         */
#define LINE         0
#define RECT         1
#define ELLIPSE      2
#define FILLRECT     3
#define FILLELLIPSE  4
    short   x1, y1;   /* Corners of bounding rectangle */
    short   x2, y2;   /* or endpoints of line          */
} FIGURE;

/* Array of figures */

FIGURE  figures[MAXFIGURES];
int     numfigures = 0;
int     curfig = 0,
        figtype = 0;

static int zero=0, one=1, two=2, three=3, four=4;

GC   theGC;     /* GC for regular drawing */
GC   xorGC;     /* GC used for rubber-band drawing */

Cursor xhair_cursor;

/* Function prototypes */

/* These are callbacks */
void start_rubberband(/* Widget w, XtPointer data,
                    XEvent *p_event */);
void continue_rubberband(/* Widget w, XtPointer data,
                    XEvent *p_event */);
void end_rubberband(/* Widget w, XtPointer data,
                    XEvent *p_event */);

void figure_select(/* Widget w, XtPointer data,
                    XmAnyCallbackStruct *call_data */);

void handle_expose(/* Widget w, XtPointer client_data,
                    XmDrawingAreaCallbackStruct *call_data */);
```

```
void quit_action(/* Widget w, XtPointer client_data,
                    XmAnyCallbackStruct *call_data */);


/* This function draws the figures */
static void draw_figure(/* Display *d, Window w, GC gc,
                           int fig */);


/* This function, defined in file "xmutil.c" prepares menus */
Widget MakeMenuPane(/* char *name, Widget parent, ... */);


/* This function, also in xmutil.c, attaches a menu to a
 * cascade button
 */
void AttachToCascade(/* Widget parent, char *label,
                        Widget sub_menu */);
/*-----------------------------------------------------------*/
void main(argc, argv)
int  argc;
char **argv;
{
    Widget      top_level, main_window, menu_bar, drawing_area,
                new_menu;
    Arg         args[MAXARGS];
    Cardinal    argcount;
    int         fg, bg;
    XGCValues   xgcv;
    XtAppContext app;

/* Create the top-level shell widget and initialize the toolkit*/
    top_level = XtAppInitialize(&app, "XMfigure", NULL, 0,
                                  &argc, argv, NULL, NULL, 0);
/* Next, the main window widget */
    argcount = 0;
    XtSetArg(args[argcount], XmNwidth, WIDTH);   argcount++;
    XtSetArg(args[argcount], XmNheight, HEIGHT); argcount++;
    main_window = XmCreateMainWindow(top_level, "Main",
                                     args, argcount);
    XtManageChild(main_window);

/* Create the menubar */
    menu_bar = XmCreateMenuBar(main_window, "Menubar", NULL, 0);
    XtManageChild(menu_bar);

/* Create the drawing area */
    argcount = 0;
    XtSetArg(args[argcount], XmNresizePolicy, XmRESIZE_ANY);
    argcount++;
    drawing_area = XmCreateDrawingArea(main_window,
                                  "drawing_area", args, argcount);
    XtManageChild(drawing_area);

/* Attach the menubar and the drawing area to main window */
    XmMainWindowSetAreas(main_window, menu_bar, NULL, NULL,
                         NULL, drawing_area);
```

continues

Listing 15.2. continued

```
/* Create the GCs. First retrieve the background and foreground
 * colors from the widget's resources.
 */
    argcount = 0;
    XtSetArg(args[argcount], XmNforeground, &fg); argcount++;
    XtSetArg(args[argcount], XmNbackground, &bg); argcount++;
    XtGetValues(drawing_area, args, argcount);

/* Define a GC with these colors */
    xgcv.foreground = fg;
    xgcv.background = bg;
    theGC = XtGetGC(drawing_area, GCForeground | GCBackground,
                    &xgcv);
/* Set up a GC with exclusive-OR mode (for rubber-band drawing)*/
    xgcv.foreground = fg ^ bg;
    xgcv.background = bg;
    xgcv.function = GXxor;
    xorGC = XtGetGC(drawing_area, GCForeground |
                    GCBackground | GCFunction, &xgcv);

/* Add callback to handle expose events for the drawing area */
    XtAddCallback(drawing_area, XmNexposeCallback, handle_expose,
                  &drawing_area);

/* Create the "File" menu --------------------------------------*/
    new_menu = MakeMenuPane("File", menu_bar,
                            "Quit", quit_action, NULL,
                            NULL);
/* Create the "File" cascade button and attach new_menu to it */
    AttachToCascade(menu_bar, "File", new_menu);

/* Create the "Figures" menu --------------------------------------*/
    new_menu = MakeMenuPane("Figures", menu_bar,
                "Line",             figure_select, (XtPointer)&zero,
                "Rectangle",        figure_select, (XtPointer)&one,
                "Ellipse",          figure_select, (XtPointer)&two,
                "Filled Rectangle", figure_select, (XtPointer)&three,
                "Filled Ellipse",   figure_select, (XtPointer)&four,
                NULL);

/* Now create the cascade button and attach this submenu to it */
    AttachToCascade(menu_bar, "Figures", new_menu);

/* Create a crosshair cursor for the drawing area */
    xhair_cursor = XCreateFontCursor(XtDisplay(drawing_area),
                                     XC_crosshair);

/* Add event handlers for button events to handle the drawing */
    XtAddEventHandler(drawing_area, ButtonPressMask, False,
                      start_rubberband, NULL);
    XtAddEventHandler(drawing_area, ButtonMotionMask, False,
                      continue_rubberband, NULL);
    XtAddEventHandler(drawing_area, ButtonReleaseMask, False,
                      end_rubberband, NULL);

/* Realize all widgets */
    XtRealizeWidget(top_level);
```

```
/* Set up a grab so that the cursor changes to a crosshair and
 * is confined to the drawing_area while the mouse button is
 * pressed. This is done through what is known as a "grab"
 */
    XGrabButton(XtDisplay(drawing_area), AnyButton, AnyModifier,
                XtWindow(drawing_area), True, ButtonPressMask|
                ButtonMotionMask | ButtonReleaseMask,
                GrabModeAsync, GrabModeAsync,
                XtWindow(drawing_area), xhair_cursor);

/* Start the main event handling loop */
    XtAppMainLoop(app);
}
/*-------------------------------------------------------------*/
/*  q u i t _ a c t i o n
 *
 *  This routine is called whenever the "Quit" item is selected from
 *  the "File" menu.
 */
void quit_action(w, client_data, call_data)
Widget               w;
XtPointer            client_data;
XmAnyCallbackStruct *call_data;
{
    XtCloseDisplay(XtDisplay(w));
    exit(0);
}
/*-------------------------------------------------------------*/
/*  s t a r t _ r u b b e r b a n d
 *
 *  Start of rubber-band figure
 */
void start_rubberband(w, data, p_event)
Widget      w;
XtPointer data;
XEvent    *p_event;
{
    int x = p_event->xbutton.x,
        y = p_event->xbutton.y;

/* Crude check to ensure that we don't exceed array's capacity */
    if(numfigures > MAXFIGURES-1)
        numfigures = MAXFIGURES-1;
    curfig = numfigures;
    numfigures++;

    figures[curfig].type = figtype;
    figures[curfig].x1 = x;
    figures[curfig].y1 = y;
    figures[curfig].x2 = x;
    figures[curfig].y2 = y;
    draw_figure(XtDisplay(w), XtWindow(w), xorGC, curfig);
}
/*-------------------------------------------------------------*/
/*  c o n t i n u e _ r u b b e r b a n d
 *
```

continues

Listing 15.2. continued

```
 *   Handle mouse movement while drawing a rubber-band figure
 */
void continue_rubberband(w, data, p_event)
Widget     w;
XtPointer data;
XEvent     *p_event;
{
    int x = p_event->xbutton.x,
        y = p_event->xbutton.y;

/* Draw once at old location (to erase figure) */
    draw_figure(XtDisplay(w), XtWindow(w), xorGC, curfig);

/* Now update endpoint and redraw */
    figures[curfig].x2 = x;
    figures[curfig].y2 = y;
    draw_figure(XtDisplay(w), XtWindow(w), xorGC, curfig);
}
/*------------------------------------------------------------*/
/*  e n d _ r u b b e r b a n d
 *
 *   End of rubber-band drawing
 */
void end_rubberband(w, data, p_event)
Widget     w;
XtPointer data;
XEvent     *p_event;
{
    int x = p_event->xbutton.x,
        y = p_event->xbutton.y;

/* Draw once at old location (to erase figure) */
    draw_figure(XtDisplay(w), XtWindow(w), xorGC, curfig);

/* Now update endpoint and redraw in normal GC */
    figures[curfig].x2 = x;
    figures[curfig].y2 = y;
    draw_figure(XtDisplay(w), XtWindow(w), theGC, curfig);
}
/*------------------------------------------------------------*/
/*  f i g u r e _ s e l e c t
 *
 *   Callback for "Figure" menu
 */
void figure_select(w, data, call_data)
Widget                w;
XtPointer             data;
XmAnyCallbackStruct *call_data;
{
/* Set figure type and return */
    figtype = *((int *)data);
}
/*------------------------------------------------------------*/
/*  h a n d l e _ e x p o s e
 *
 *   Expose event handler for the drawing area
```

```
    */
void handle_expose(w, client_data, call_data)
Widget                      w;
XtPointer                   client_data;
XmDrawingAreaCallbackStruct *call_data;
{
    XEvent *p_event = call_data->event;
    Window win = call_data->window;
    Display *p_display = XtDisplay(w);

    if(p_event->xexpose.count == 0)
    {
        int i;
/* Clear the window and draw the figures in the "figures" array*/
        XClearWindow(p_display, win);

        if(numfigures > 0)
        {
            for(i=0; i<numfigures; i++)
            {
                draw_figure(p_display, win, theGC, i);
            }
        }
    }
}
/*--------------------------------------------------------*/
/*  d r a w _ f i g u r e
 *
 *  Draw a specified figure
 */
static void draw_figure(d, w, gc, curfig)
Display *d;
Window  w;
GC      gc;
int     curfig;
{
    int x1 = figures[curfig].x1, y1 = figures[curfig].y1,
        x2 = figures[curfig].x2, y2 = figures[curfig].y2, t;

/* Make sure x2 >= x1 and y2 >= y1 */
    if(figures[curfig].type != LINE && x1 > x2)
    {
        t = x1;
        x1 = x2;
        x2 = t;
    }
    if(figures[curfig].type != LINE && y1 > y2)
    {
        t = y1;
        y1 = y2;
        y2 = t;
    }
    switch(figures[curfig].type)
    {
        case LINE:
            XDrawLine(d, w, gc, x1, y1, x2, y2);
            break;
```

continues

Listing 15.2. continued

```
        case RECT:
            XDrawRectangle(d, w, gc, x1, y1, x2-x1, y2-y1);
            break;
        case ELLIPSE:
            XDrawArc(d, w, gc, x1, y1, x2-x1, y2-y1, 0, 360*64);
            break;
        case FILLRECT:
            XFillRectangle(d, w, gc, x1, y1, x2-x1, y2-y1);
            break;
        case FILLELLIPSE:
            XFillArc(d, w, gc, x1, y1, x2-x1, y2-y1, 0, 360*64);
            break;
    }
}
```

Specifying Resources

As with any toolkit-based application, xmfigure enables you to specify resources. Because the class name of this program is Xmfigure (specified in the XtAppInitialize call), you can provide the resources in the file Xmfigure in your login directory. For instance, you can specify an initial geometry and the foreground and background colors:

```
################################################################
#  Xmfigure: Resources for the xmfigure program
################################################################
*foreground:                black
*background:                white
*geometry:                  400x300+10+10
```

An OSF/Motif File Browser: *xmbrowse*

As a second example of an OSF/Motif-based application, let's write a program that enables you to open a text file and browse through its contents. The program, called xmbrowse, is an improved version of the Xlib-based viewfile program of Chapter 10. As shown in Figure 15.2, xmbrowse sports a menubar, a text display area, and a scrollbar. The text is drawn in a user-selected font of specific size and weight, and the user selects these items from pull-down menus. These menus are created in the same way that you create the menus for xmfigure (Listing 15.2).

As with xmfigure, xmbrowse also uses a main window widget for the text display. However, in addition to the menubar and the text display area, it also uses a vertical scrollbar to enable the user to scroll through the file.

Figure 15.2.

Browsing xmbrowse.c *in 12-point Courier Bold.*

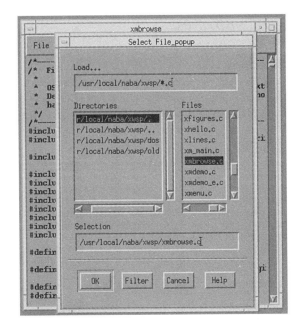

File Selection Dialog

The underlying design of xmbrowse is similar to that of viewfile in Chapter 10. A major difference between the two programs is that viewfile requires a filename on the command line, and xmbrowse displays a file selection dialog box when the user selects Open from the File menu. This is possible because the OSF/Motif toolkit provides the FileSelectionBox widget that displays a list of files and enables the user to select one (see Figure 15.2).

The function open_file in Listing 15.3 shows how the file selection box is created. The filename is extracted in the callback fs_ok which is called when the user presses the OK button in the dialog. As shown in fs_ok, the filename is provided as a compound string in the value field of an XmSelectionBoxCallbackStruct structure. You can convert this into a null-terminated C string by using the XmStringGetLtoR utility function. Here is an outline of the fs_ok callback:

```
char *file_name;

void fs_ok(Widget w, caddr_t client_data,
                  XmSelectionBoxCallbackStruct *call_data)
{
/* Get filename from user's selection */
    if(XmStringGetLtoR(call_data->value,
                       XmSTRING_DEFAULT_CHARSET, &file_name))
/* Open and load file */
    .
    .
    .
}
```

Building *xmbrowse*

Listing 15.3 shows `xmbrowse.c`, the complete source file for the `xmbrowse` application. To build the application, you also need the file `xmutil.c` from Listing 15.1. You can build `xmbrowse` using the same makefile as the one used to build `xmfigure`. You need to compile `xmbrowse.c` and `xmutil.c` and link them, at a minimum, with the libraries `-1Xm -1Xt -1Xmu -1X11`. There may be additional libraries necessary for interprocess communication between the X server and the program.

Listing 15.3. `xmbrowse.c`—OSF/Motif-based file browser.

```
/*-------------------------------------------------------------*/
/*  File: xmbrowse.c
 *
 *  OSF/Motif version of a program for browsing text files.
 *  Demonstrates text drawing functions and shows how to
 *  handle different fonts.
 */
/*-------------------------------------------------------------*/
#include <stdio.h>
#include <string.h>             /* ANSI standard string library */

#include <X11/Xlib.h>

#include <Xm/Xm.h>
#include <Xm/RowColumn.h>
#include <Xm/MainW.h>
#include <Xm/CascadeB.h>
#include <Xm/DrawingA.h>
#include <Xm/BulletinB.h>
#include <Xm/FileSB.h>
#include <Xm/ScrollBar.h>

#define MAXARGS       20

#define LEFT_MARGIN    4    /* Leave a 4-pixel margin */

#define SCROLL_UP      0
#define SCROLL_DOWN    1

#define MAXCHARS     512     /* Maximum length of a line    */

typedef struct D_LINE      /* Holds info on each line      */
{
    struct D_LINE *prev;   /* Pointer to previous line     */
    struct D_LINE *next;   /* Pointer to next line         */
    char          *line;   /* Null-terminated line         */
    short         length;  /* Number of characters in line */
    short         lbearing;/* Left and right edges of      */
    short         rbearing;/* rectangle covered by line    */
    short         height;  /* Height of text string        */
} D_LINE;

typedef struct D_LBUF      /* Info on entire buffer        */
{
    D_LINE        *lines;  /* First line in buffer         */
```

```
      D_LINE        *lstart; /* First line in window        */
      GC            gc;      /* GC used to display text      */
      Region        rexp;    /* Current exposed region       */
      XFontStruct   *fstruct;/* Info on current font         */
      int           font;    /* Currently selected font      */
      int           weight;  /* weight and                   */
      int           size;    /* size                         */
      Dimension     dwidth;  /* Width of text display area   */
      Dimension     dheight; /* Height of text display area  */
      long          count;   /* How many lines in buffer     */
} D_LBUF;

static D_LBUF fbuf = { NULL,NULL, None, None, None, 0, 0, 0,
                       0, 0, 0};

static int zero=0, one=1, two=2, three=3, four=4;

static  GC      theGC;   /* GC used for text output */

/* Information necessary to construct X11R3 font names    */
static char *fontname[] =
{
  "courier", "helvetica", "new century schoolbook", "times"
};
static char *weight[] = { "medium", "bold" };
static char *size[] = {"100", "120", "140", "180", "240"};

/* File to be opened */
char *file_name = NULL;

/* Window id of text area */
static Window  dWin;

/* Dialog box that displays a file selection box */
static Widget file_dialog = (Widget)0, file_sel_box,
              vsbar, text_area;

/* Name of application */
static char *theAppName;

static int last_slider_pos = 0;
static int file_not_loaded = True;

/* Variables for setting resources */
static Arg       args[MAXARGS];
static Cardinal argcount;

/* Function prototypes */

void handle_expose(/* Widget w, XtPointer client_data,
                   XmDrawingAreaCallbackStruct *call_data */);

void quit_action(/* Widget w, XtPointer client_data,
                 XmAnyCallbackStruct *call_data */);

void font_select(/* Widget w, XtPointer data,
                 XmAnyCallbackStruct *call_data */);
```

continues

Listing 15.3. continued

```
void wt_select(/* Widget w, XtPointer data,
                   XmAnyCallbackStruct *call_data */);
void size_select(/* Widget w, XtPointer data,
                   XmAnyCallbackStruct *call_data */);

void open_file(/* Widget w, XtPointer client_data,
                   XmAnyCallbackStruct *call_data */);

void fs_ok(/* Widget w, XtPointer client_data,
               XmSelectionBoxCallbackStruct *call_data */);

void fs_cancel(/* Widget w, XtPointer client_data,
               XmSelectionBoxCallbackStruct *call_data */);

void scroll_text(/* Widget w, XtPointer client_data,
                   XmScrollBarCallbackStruct *call_data */);

void resize_text(/* Widget w, XtPointer client_data,
                   XmAnyCallbackStruct *call_data */);

static void load_file(/* char *filename */);
static void apply_font(/* Widget w */);
static void display_lines(/* Widget w */);
static void scroll_lines(/* Widget w, int direction,
                             int numlines */);

/* This function, defined in file xmutil.c, prepares menus */
Widget MakeMenuPane(/* char *name, Widget parent, ... */);

/* This function, also in xmutil.c, attaches a menu to a
 * cascade button
 */
void AttachToCascade(/* Widget parent, char *label,
                     Widget sub_menu */);
/*-------------------------------------------------------------*/
void main(argc, argv)
int  argc;
char **argv;
{
    Widget       top_level, main_window, menu_bar, new_menu;
    int          fg, bg;
    XGCValues    xgcv;
    XtAppContext app;

/* Create the top-level shell widget and initialize the toolkit*/
    top_level = XtAppInitialize(&app, "XMbrowse", NULL, 0,
                               &argc, argv, NULL, NULL, 0);
    theAppName = argv[0];

/* Next, the main window widget */
    argcount = 0;
    XtSetArg(args[argcount], XmNwidth, 400);   argcount++;
    XtSetArg(args[argcount], XmNheight, 300); argcount++;
    main_window = XmCreateMainWindow(top_level, "Main",
                                    args, argcount);
    XtManageChild(main_window);
```

```
/* Create the menubar */
    menu_bar = XmCreateMenuBar(main_window, "Menubar", NULL, 0);
    XtManageChild(menu_bar);

/* Create the text area */
    argcount = 0;
    XtSetArg(args [argcount], XmNresizePolicy, XmRESIZE_ANY);
    argcount++;
    text_area = XmCreateDrawingArea(main_window,
                            "text_area", args, argcount);
    XtManageChild(text_area);

/* Create a vertical scrollbar for controlling the text area.*/
    vsbar = XmCreateScrollBar(main_window, "scroll_bar",
                            NULL, 0);
    XtManageChild(vsbar);

/* Add callbacks to the scrollbar to handle buttonpresses
 * in the arrows and the slider
 */
    XtAddCallback(vsbar, XmNvalueChangedCallback,
                scroll_text, NULL);
    XtAddCallback(vsbar, XmNdragCallback,
                scroll_text, NULL);

/* Attach the menubar, the text area, and the scrollbar
 * to main window
 */
    XmMainWindowSetAreas(main_window, menu_bar, NULL, NULL,
                        vsbar, text_area);

/* Add callback to handle expose events for the drawing area */
    XtAddCallback(text_area, XmNexposeCallback, handle_expose,
                NULL);

/* Another to handle any resizes... */
    XtAddCallback(text_area, XmNresizeCallback, resize_text,
                NULL);

/* Create the "File" menu --------------------------------*/
    new_menu = MakeMenuPane("File", menu_bar,
                        "Open", open_file, (XtPointer)top_level,
                        "Quit", quit_action, NULL,
                        NULL);
    AttachToCascade(menu_bar, "File", new_menu);

/* Create the "Font" menu --------------------------------*/
    new_menu = MakeMenuPane("Font", menu_bar,
                    "Courier",      font_select, (XtPointer)&zero,
                    "Helvetica",    font_select, (XtPointer)&one,
                    "New Century Schoolbook",
                                    font_select, (XtPointer)&two,
                    "Times",        font_select, (XtPointer)&three,
                    NULL);

    AttachToCascade(menu_bar, "Font", new_menu);
```

continues

Listing 15.3. continued

```
/* Create the "Weight" menu --------------------------------*/
    new_menu = MakeMenuPane("Weight", menu_bar,
                    "Medium",  wt_select, (XtPointer)&zero,
                    "Bold",    wt_select, (XtPointer)&one,
                    NULL);
    AttachToCascade(menu_bar, "Weight", new_menu);

/* Create the "Size" menu --------------------------------*/
    new_menu = MakeMenuPane("Size", menu_bar,
                    " 10pt",        size_select, (XtPointer)&zero,
                    " 12pt",        size_select, (XtPointer)&one,
                    " 14pt",        size_select, (XtPointer)&two,
                    " 18pt",        size_select, (XtPointer)&three,
                    " 24pt",        size_select, (XtPointer)&four,
                    NULL);
    AttachToCascade(menu_bar, "Size", new_menu);

/* Set up a GC to display text. First retrieve the background
 * and foreground colors from the widget's resources.
 */
    argcount = 0;
    XtSetArg(args [argcount], XmNforeground, &fg); argcount++;
    XtSetArg(args [argcount], XmNbackground, &bg); argcount++;
    XtGetValues(text_area, args, argcount);

/* Define a GC with these colors */
    xgcv.foreground = fg;
    xgcv.background = bg;
    fbuf.gc = XtGetGC(text_area, GCForeground | GCBackground,
                    &xgcv);
/* Realize all widgets */
    XtRealizeWidget(top_level);

/* dWin is a global variable that holds the Window id of
 * the text display area
 */
    dWin = XtWindow(text_area);

/* Event handling loop--keep processing events until done */
    XtAppMainLoop(app);
}
/*-------------------------------------------------------------*/
/* h a n d l e _ e x p o s e
 *
 * Expose event handler for the text display area
 */
void handle_expose(w, client_data, call_data)
Widget                    w;
XtPointer                 client_data;
XmDrawingAreaCallbackStruct *call_data;
{
    XRectangle r;

/* Do nothing, if no file has been loaded */
    if(file_not_loaded) return;
```

```
/* Accumulate exposed areas in a region */
    r.x = call_data->event->xexpose.x;
    r.y = call_data->event->xexpose.y;
    r.width = call_data->event->xexpose.width;
    r.height = call_data->event->xexpose.height;
    XUnionRectWithRegion(&r, fbuf.rexp, fbuf.rexp);

/* Handle the expose event only if 'count' is 0 */
    if(call_data->event->xexpose.count == 0) display_lines(w);
}
/*------------------------------------------------------------*/
/* q u i t _ a c t i o n
 *
 *  This routine is called when the "Quit" item is selected from
 *  the "File" menu.
 */
void quit_action(w, client_data, call_data)
Widget              w;
XtPointer           client_data;
XmAnyCallbackStruct *call_data;
{
    XtCloseDisplay(XtDisplay(w));
    exit(0);
}
/*------------------------------------------------------------*/
/* f o n t _ s e l e c t
 *
 *  Handle font selection
 *
 */
void font_select(w, data, call_data)
Widget              w;
XtPointer           data;
XmAnyCallbackStruct *call_data;
{
    int font = *((int *)data);

    if(font != fbuf.font)
    {
        fbuf.font = font;
        apply_font(w);
/* Clear the display window so that text is displayed again */
        XClearArea(XtDisplay(w), dWin, 0, 0, 0, 0, True);

/* Reset the scrollbar variables */
        resize_text(text_area, NULL, NULL);
    }
}
/*------------------------------------------------------------*/
/* w t _ s e l e c t
 *
 *  Font weight changed.
 *
 */
void wt_select(w, data, call_data)
Widget                 w;
```

continues

Listing 15.3. continued

```
XtPointer            data;
XmAnyCallbackStruct *call_data;
{
    int weight = *((int *)data);

    if(weight != fbuf.weight)
    {
        fbuf.weight = weight;
        apply_font(w);
/* Clear the display window so that text is displayed again */
        XClearArea(XtDisplay(w), dWin, 0, 0, 0, 0, True);
/* Reset the scrollbar variables */
        resize_text(text_area, NULL, NULL);
    }
}
/*------------------------------------------------------------*/
/*  s i z e _ s e l e c t
 *
 *   New size font selected
 *
 */
void size_select(w, data, call_data)
Widget              w;
XtPointer            data;
XmAnyCallbackStruct *call_data;
{
    int size = *((int *)data);

    if(size != fbuf.size)
    {
        fbuf.size = size;
        apply_font(w);
/* Clear the display window so that text is displayed again */
        XClearArea(XtDisplay(w), dWin, 0, 0, 0, 0, True);
/* Reset the scrollbar variables */
        resize_text(text_area, NULL, NULL);
    }
}
/*------------------------------------------------------------*/
/*  l o a d _ f i l e
 *
 *   Read in file to be displayed
 *
 */
static void load_file(filename)
char *filename;
{
    FILE   *fp;
    D_LINE *p_l = NULL, *p_l_prev = NULL, *p_l_next;
    char   buf[MAXCHARS];

/* If a file was already loaded, first release all memory */
    if(fbuf.lines != NULL)
    {
        p_l = fbuf.lines;
        while (p_l != NULL)
```

```
      {
          XtFree(p_l->line);
          XtFree(p_l);
          p_l_next = p_l->next;
          p_l = p_l_next;
      }
      fbuf.count = 0;
      fbuf.lines = NULL;
      fbuf.lstart = NULL;
      fbuf.rexp = NULL;
      file_not_loaded = True;
   }

/* Open the file */
   if((fp = fopen(filename, "r")) == NULL)
   {
       fprintf(stderr, "Cannot open: %s\n", filename);
       exit(1);
   }

/* Read each line and store in linked list of D_LINE structs   */
   while((fgets(buf, MAXCHARS, fp)) != NULL)
   {
       if((p_l = (D_LINE *) XtCalloc(1, sizeof(D_LINE)))
                                                    != NULL)

       {
           if(fbuf.lines == NULL)
           {
               fbuf.lines = p_l;
           }
           else
           {
               p_l_prev->next = p_l;
               p_l->prev = p_l_prev;
           }
       }
       else
       {
/* Allocation failed...*/
           fprintf(stderr, "Failed to allocate memory for\
line data structure...\n");
           exit(1);
       }
       p_l->length = strlen(buf) - 1; /* Exclude newline */
       buf[p_l->length] = '\0';
       if((p_l->line = XtMalloc(p_l->length+1)) == NULL)
       {
           fprintf(stderr, "Failed to allocate memory for\
line:\n%s\n", buf);
           exit(1);
       }
       strcpy(p_l->line, buf);
       p_l_prev = p_l;
       fbuf.count++;
   }
   printf("%d lines loaded from %s\n", fbuf.count, filename);
   file_not_loaded = False;
```

continues

Listing 15.3. continued

```
/* Close the file */
    fclose(fp);
}
/*--------------------------------------------------------------*/
/*  a p p l y _ f o n t
 *
 *  Set up a new font for use. Also compute screen areas
 *  occupied by each line.
 */
static void apply_font(w)
Widget w;
{
    D_LINE      *p_l;
    int         dir, ascent, descent;
    char        fname[120];         /* Room for font's name */
    XCharStruct cinfo;
    int         font = fbuf.font,
                wt = fbuf.weight,
                sz = fbuf.size;
/* Construct font's name */
    sprintf(fname, "*adobe-%s-%s-r*%s*", fontname[font],
            weight[wt], size[sz]);

    printf("Font = %s\n", fname);

/* Free the font, if necessary */
    if(fbuf.fstruct != NULL)
        XFreeFont(XtDisplay(w), fbuf.fstruct);

/* Load the new font */
    if ((fbuf.fstruct = XLoadQueryFont(XtDisplay(w), fname))
        == NULL)
    {
        fprintf(stderr, "%s: display %s cannot load font: %s\n",
            theAppName, DisplayString(XtDisplay(w)), fname);

/* Set fbuf.fstruct to the "fixed" font */
        if ((fbuf.fstruct = XLoadQueryFont(XtDisplay(w),
                                    "fixed")) == NULL)
        {
            fprintf(stderr, "%s: display %s cannot load \
\"fixed\" font\n", theAppName, DisplayString(XtDisplay(w)));
            exit(1);
        }
    }

/* Compute bounding box of each line in the buffer */
    for(p_l = fbuf.lines; p_l != NULL; p_l = p_l->next)
    {
        XTextExtents(fbuf.fstruct, p_l->line, p_l->length,
            &dir, &ascent, &descent, &cinfo);
        p_l->lbearing = cinfo.lbearing;
        p_l->rbearing = cinfo.rbearing;
        p_l->height = ascent + descent;
    }
```

```
/* Set the font in the GC */
    XSetFont(XtDisplay(w), fbuf.gc, fbuf.fstruct->fid);
}
/*-----------------------------------------------------------*/
/*  d i s p l a y _ l i n e s
 *
 *  Displays the lines in the text window
 */
static void display_lines(w)
Widget w;
{
    int    xpos, ypos = 0, width;
    D_LINE *p_l;

/* Set the accumulated exposed regions as the clip mask */
    XSetRegion(XtDisplay(w), fbuf.gc, fbuf.rexp);

/* Display the lines starting with the first one. Draw
 * a string ONLY if it falls in the exposed region.
 */

    for(p_l = fbuf.lstart; p_l != NULL && ypos < fbuf.dheight;
        p_l = p_l->next)
    {
        xpos = LEFT_MARGIN - p_l->lbearing;
        ypos += p_l->height;
        if(XRectInRegion(fbuf.rexp, xpos, ypos - p_l->height,
                         p_l->lbearing + p_l->rbearing,
                         p_l->height) != RectangleOut)
        {
/* Yes. String's rectangle is partially in region. Draw it */
            XDrawImageString(XtDisplay(w), dWin, fbuf.gc,
                     xpos, ypos, p_l->line, p_l->length);
        }
    }

/* Destroy current region and create a new "empty" one */
    XDestroyRegion(fbuf.rexp);
    fbuf.rexp = XCreateRegion();
}
/*             -------------------------------------------*/
/*  s c r o l l _ t e x t
 * Scroll text being displayed in the window.
 */
void scroll_text(w, client_data, call_data)
Widget                    w;
XtPointer                 client_data;
XmScrollBarCallbackStruct *call_data;
{
    int slider_pos = call_data->value;
    if(file_not_loaded | slider_pos == last_slider_pos) return;

    if(slider_pos > last_slider_pos)
    {
        scroll_lines(w, SCROLL_UP,
                     slider_pos - last_slider_pos);
```

continues

Listing 15.3. continued

```
    }
    else
    {
        scroll_lines(w, SCROLL_DOWN,
                          last_slider_pos - slider_pos);
    }

/* Update the last slider position */
    last_slider_pos = slider_pos;
}
/*-----------------------------------------------------------*/
/*  s c r o l l _ l i n e s
 *
 *  Scroll the text display by a specified amount.
 */
static void scroll_lines(w, direction, numlines)
Widget w;
int     direction;
int     numlines;
{
    int i, ysrc, yclr, numpix = 0;
    D_LINE *p_l;

/* Figure out how many pixels to scroll */

    switch(direction)
    {
        case SCROLL_UP:
            for(i = 0, p_l = fbuf.lstart;
                i < numlines && p_l->next != NULL;
                i++, p_l = p_l->next) numpix += p_l->height;
            ysrc = numpix;
            yclr = fbuf.dheight - numpix;
            break;

        case SCROLL_DOWN:
            for(i = 0, p_l = fbuf.lstart;
                i < numlines && p_l->prev != NULL;
                i++, p_l = p_l->prev) numpix += p_l->height;
            ysrc = 0;
            yclr = 0;
            break;
    }

    if(numpix == 0)
    {
/* No need to scroll */
        XBell(XtDisplay(w), 0);
        return;
    }
/* Adjust first line to display */
    fbuf.lstart = p_l;

/* Copy area */
    XSetClipMask(XtDisplay(w), fbuf.gc, None);
    XCopyArea(XtDisplay(w), dWin, dWin, fbuf.gc,
```

```
                    0, ysrc, fbuf.dwidth, fbuf.dheight - numpix,
                    0, numpix - ysrc);

/* Clear new rectangle so that it is redrawn */
    XClearArea(XtDisplay(w), dWin, 0, yclr,
                 fbuf.dwidth, numpix, True);
}
/*-----------------------------------------------------------*/
/*  o p e n _ f i l e
 *
 *  Display a "FileSelectionBox" and enable user to select the file
 *  to be loaded for browsing
 */
void open_file(w, client_data, call_data)
Widget                  w;
XtPointer               client_data;
XmAnyCallbackStruct *call_data;
{
    XmString  title, dir_mask;

/* Create dialog box, if not yet created */
    if(file_dialog == (Widget)0)
    {
        argcount = 0;
        XtSetArg(args[argcount], XmNdialogStyle,
                    XmDIALOG_MODELESS);                 argcount++;
        file_dialog = XmCreateBulletinBoardDialog(
                            (Widget)client_data, "Select File",
                            args, argcount);

        title = XmStringLtoRCreate("Load...",
                                XmSTRING_DEFAULT_CHARSET);
        dir_mask = XmStringLtoRCreate("*.c",
                                XmSTRING_DEFAULT_CHARSET);
        argcount = 0;
        XtSetArg(args[argcount], XmNdirMask, dir_mask); argcount++;
        XtSetArg(args[argcount], XmNfilterLabelString, title);
                                                        argcount++;
        file_sel_box = XmCreateFileSelectionBox(file_dialog,
                            "File Selection", args, argcount);

/* Add callbacks for the "OK" and "Cancel" buttons */
        XtAddCallback(file_sel_box, XmNcancelCallback, fs_cancel,
                    (XtPointer) file_dialog);
        XtAddCallback(file_sel_box, XmNokCallback, fs_ok,
                    (XtPointer) file_dialog);
        XmStringFree(title);
        XmStringFree(dir_mask);
        XtManageChild(file_sel_box);
    }
/* Display the dialog box */
    XtManageChild(file_dialog);
}
/*-----------------------------------------------------------*/
/*  f s _ o k
 *
 *  Callback for the "OK" button on the file selection box
```

continues

Listing 15.3. continued

```
    */
void fs_ok(w, client_data, call_data)
Widget                          w;
XtPointer                       client_data;
XmSelectionBoxCallbackStruct *call_data;
{
/* Get filename from user's selection */
    if(XmStringGetLtoR(call_data->value,
                       XmSTRING_DEFAULT_CHARSET, &file_name))
    {
        printf("File selected: %s\n", file_name);
/* Load the file */
        load_file(file_name);
        fbuf.lstart = fbuf.lines;
        apply_font(w);
        fbuf.rexp = XCreateRegion();
        resize_text(text_area, NULL, NULL);
/* Clear the display window so that text is displayed again */
        XClearArea(XtDisplay(w), dWin, 0, 0, 0, 0, True);
        XtFree(file_name);
    }
    else
    {
        printf("Nothing selected\n");
    }
    XtUnmanageChild((Widget)client_data);
}
/*------------------------------------------------------------*/
/*  f s _ c a n c e l
 *
 *  Callback for the "Cancel" button in the file selection box
 */
void fs_cancel(w, client_data, call_data)
Widget                          w;
XtPointer                       client_data;
XmSelectionBoxCallbackStruct *call_data;
{
    XtUnmanageChild((Widget)client_data);
}
/*------------------------------------------------------------*/
/*  r e s i z e _ t e x t
 *
 *  Callback to handle resizing of the text area
 */
void resize_text(w, client_data, call_data)
Widget              w;
XtPointer           client_data;
XmAnyCallbackStruct *call_data;
{
    int lines_visible, slider_size;

/* Determine the size of the text area */
    argcount = 0;
    XtSetArg(args[argcount], XmNheight, &fbuf.dheight);
                                        argcount++;
    XtSetArg(args[argcount], XmNwidth, &fbuf.dwidth);
                                        argcount++;
```

```
    XtGetValues(w, args, argcount);

/* Make sure scrollbar reflects size of the text display area */
    if(file_not_loaded) return;
    lines_visible = fbuf.dheight /
                (fbuf.fstruct->ascent + fbuf.fstruct->descent);
    if(lines_visible > fbuf.count) lines_visible = fbuf.count;
    slider_size = lines_visible / fbuf.count;
    if(slider_size < 1) slider_size = 1;
    if(slider_size > fbuf.count) slider_size = fbuf.count;

    argcount = 0;
    XtSetArg(args[argcount], XmNminimum, 0);          argcount++;
    XtSetArg(args[argcount], XmNmaximum, fbuf.count); argcount++;
    XtSetArg(args[argcount], XmNincrement, 1);        argcount++;
    XtSetArg(args[argcount], XmNpageIncrement, lines_visible);
                                                      argcount++;
    XtSetArg(args[argcount], XmNsliderSize, slider_size);
                                                      argcount++;
    XtSetValues(vsbar, args, argcount);
}
```

Other Toolkit Features

The two example programs, xmfigure and xmbrowse, illustrate how to mix Xlib functions with those from the OSF/Motif toolkit. However, there are several unique capabilities of the toolkit that have not been described. These include the idea of work procedures and input callbacks, described in the following sections.

WorkProcs

Xt Intrinsics supports a special type of callback function known as a WorkProc, or *work procedure,* that is called when there are no events pending. This enables you to perform some tasks in the background. Because normal event handling by Xt Intrinsics cannot proceed until the WorkProc returns, you should not include any time-consuming processing in a work procedure. As with other callbacks, you have to register a WorkProc. You do this with the XtAddWorkProc function:

```
XtWorkProcId wp_id;

/* ANSI-style prototype for the WorkProc */
Boolean do_work(caddr_t client_data);
.
.
/* Register the WorkProc. "my_data" is a pointer or any
 * value that will fit into a pointer-sized variable
 */
wp_id = XtAddWorkProc(do_work, my_data);
```

The return value of the WorkProc function determines whether it remains installed. If the function returns a True, it is removed after being called once. Return False if you want the function to be called repeatedly.

At any time, you can remove a WorkProc by calling XtRemoveWorkProc with the ID of the work procedure as the argument. This ID is returned by XtAddWorkProc when you register the procedure. Thus, to remove the work procedure, do_work, identified by the ID wp_id, you have to call the following:

```
XtRemoveWorkProc(wp_id);
```

Input Callbacks

Sometimes you want to handle more than just the stream of X events. For instance, you may have opened a connection to a network port and you want to accept input from that port when there is something available. At other times you want to go on processing X events. Xt Intrinsics provides an elegant way to do this. You can register an *input callback function* that will be called when there is input available from a specified file descriptor. For example, suppose you want to monitor stdin for any input and, when input is available, read it and display it in a scrolled text window. The inp_cb program in Listing 15.4 shows how this might be done. Figure 15.3 shows a sample output of this program. Note that the callback is triggered by input available at a file descriptor, not a file stream. This is why Listing 15.4 uses the fileno macro to obtain stdin's file descriptor as the first argument to the XtAppAddInput function.

Figure 15.3.

Output of a program that demonstrates input callbacks.

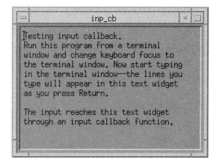

Listing 15.4. inp_cb.c—Program demonstrating input callbacks.

```
/*-------------------------------------------------------------*/
/* File:  inp_cb.c
 *
 * Demonstrates input callbacks. Run this program in the
 * foreground and type at the keyboard. When you press newline,
 * the text appears in the window.
 *
 */
#include <stdio.h>

#include <Xm/Xm.h>
#include <Xm/Text.h>

typedef struct XINPUT_DATA
{
    FILE    *stream;
```

```
        Widget widget;
} XINPUT_DATA;

#define MAXCHR 255

static XINPUT_DATA xpinfo;

/* Input callback */
static void read_input();

static char input[MAXCHR] = "Testing input callback.";
/*-------------------------------------------------------------*/
void main(argc, argv)
int  argc;
char **argv;
{
    Widget      main_widget, w;
    XtAppContext app;

/* Create and initialize the top-level widget */
    main_widget = XtAppInitialize(&app, "Inp_cb", NULL, 0,
                                  &argc, argv, NULL, NULL, 0);

/* Now create a Text widget to display input read from file */
    w = XtVaCreateManagedWidget("Text",
                        xmTextWidgetClass,   main_widget,
                        XmNeditable,         True,
                        XmNeditMode,         XmMULTI_LINE_EDIT,
                        XmNcolumns,          40,
                        XmNrows,             10,
                        XmNwordWrap,         True,
                        NULL);

/* Set up structure with information to be used by
 * the input callback and register the callback.
 */
    xpinfo.widget = w;
    xpinfo.stream = stdin;
    XtAppAddInput(app, fileno(stdin), XtInputReadMask,
              read_input, &xpinfo);

/* Realize the widgets and start processing events */
    XtRealizeWidget(main_widget);
    XtAppMainLoop(app);

}
/*-------------------------------------------------------------*/
/*  r e a d _ i n p u t
 *
 *  The "input callback" function. This function is called
 *  when input is available from the specified file.
 */
static void read_input(client_data, fid, id)
XtPointer client_data;
int       *fid;
XtInputId *id;
{
```

continues

Listing 15.4. continued

```
    int insertion_point;
    XINPUT_DATA *p_xp = (XINPUT_DATA *)client_data;

    if(fgets(input, MAXCHR, p_xp->stream) == NULL)
    {
        exit(1);
    }
/* Insert this line into the Text widget */
    insertion_point = XmTextGetLastPosition(p_xp->widget);
    XmTextInsert(p_xp->widget, insertion_point, input);
}
```

If you run inp_cb from a terminal window, you should change keyboard focus to the terminal window and type at the keyboard; the typed text appears in the window when you press the Enter key.

Timeouts

Another useful facility of Xt Intrinsics is the *timeout*, which allows you to specify a function that will be called after a specified interval of time. Use the XtAppAddTimeOut function to specify a timeout callback that should be called after a certain number of milliseconds. You can pass one argument to this timeout callback function. Xt Intrinsics calls this function only once. For periodic timeouts, you have to call XtAppAddTimeOut inside the function with another timeout delay.

You can use timeouts to build a clock, for instance. Listing 15.5 shows the program xmtime.c, which displays the current time using timeouts; Figure 15.4 illustrates the output of the program. This program gets the date and the time by executing the UNIX date command, and displays the string in a Label widget. All the work is done in the update_time function.

Listing 15.5. xmtime.c—Clock based on timeouts.

```
/*-------------------------------------------------------------*/
/*  File:  xmtime.c
 *
 *  Displays the current time using timeouts
 *
 */
/*-------------------------------------------------------------*/
#include <stdio.h>

#include <Xm/Xm.h>
#include <Xm/Label.h>

#define MAXCHR 80

static XtAppContext app;

void update_time(/* Widget w */);
/*-------------------------------------------------------------*/
void main(argc, argv)
```

```
int  argc;
char **argv;
{
    Widget        top_level, time_label;

/* Initialize the toolkit and create the top-level widget */
    top_level = XtAppInitialize(&app, "XMtime", NULL, 0,
                                &argc, argv, NULL, NULL, 0);

/* Set up a Label widget to display the time */
    time_label = XmCreateLabel(top_level, "Time", NULL, 0);
    XtManageChild(time_label);
    update_time(time_label);

/* Realize the widgets */
    XtRealizeWidget(top_level);

/* Start the main event handling loop */
    XtAppMainLoop(app);
}
/*------------------------------------------------------------*/
/*  u p d a t e _ t i m e
 *
 *  Updates the time by invoking the UNIX "date" command
 *  and reinstalls function using XtAddTimeOut
 */
void update_time(w)
Widget w;
{
    FILE    *fp;
    char    line[MAXCHR];
    Arg     args[2];
    XmString xms;

/* Run "date" to get time */

    if((fp = popen("/bin/date", "r")) == NULL)
    {
        perror("popen");
        exit(1);
    }
    if(fgets(line, MAXCHR, fp) == NULL)
    {
        perror("fgets");
        exit(1);
    }
    pclose(fp);

/* Display the time in the label widget */
    xms = XmStringLtoRCreate(line, XmSTRING_DEFAULT_CHARSET);
    XtSetArg(args[0], XmNlabelString, xms);
    XtSetValues(w, args, 1);
    XmStringFree(xms);

/* Make sure function is called again in 10 seconds */
    XtAppAddTimeOut(app, 10*1000, update_time, w);
}
```

Figure 15.4.

*Time displayed using
timeouts and the UNIX
date command.*

Summary

Toolkits are indispensable for real-world X applications. They enable you to control the complexity of Xlib calls, handle the routine chores of building a user interface, and focus on the application-specific tasks. For the latter, you have to rely on Xlib functions, especially the graphics and text drawing functions.

This chapter explains how to mix Xlib and toolkit calls for any Xt Intrinsics-based toolkits. It describes how to refer to a widget's window and its associated display and how to create GCs for use by the Xlib drawing functions.

Two example programs illustrate how to use the OSF/Motif toolkit to build applications. The xmfigure program illustrates the use of Xlib's graphics drawing functions, and xmbrowse is for browsing through text files. You can use these examples as starting points for other similar applications.

Xt Intrinsics-based toolkits also provide several other techniques for performing tasks in an application. Apart from the normal callback functions, you can have work procedures that are called when there are no events pending. Input callbacks enable you to monitor whether there is any data available from an open file, which, under UNIX, can be anything from a pipe to a network connection. For periodic calls to a function, you can use timeouts.

## Chapter 16

Advanced Topics in X

The previous chapters show what the X Window System can do and how you can use its facilities through the functions and data strutures defined in the Xlib library and the OSF/Motif toolkit. One important topic that is not covered in the previous chapters is X's built-in facilities for information sharing among different applications. This chapter starts by describing these interclient communication mechanisms that enable the user to cut and paste text and graphics information among X applications. The chapter closes with a discussion of some extensions to X and how, as a programmer, you can determine the extensions that a server supports.

Interclient Communication

The basic concepts of the X Window System are elegant and simple:

+ Separate the windowing system from the application.
+ Enable applications to generate output by sending appropriate requests in a predefined protocol using an interprocess communication mechanism.

Because of this design, an X server can display output from more than one client application on the same screen. Also, the X server and client applications can be on different systems communicating over a network. This enables a user to access applications on several systems from an X workstation (or X terminal), with output from each application organized in its own set of windows. Because the X server is shared by all applications displaying at the workstation, they can use the server as a conduit to pass information.

Indeed, X includes several facilities for sharing information among applications that are displaying at a specific X server. These *interclient communication* mechanisms are based on concepts of atoms, properties, and client messages. The following sections describe these concepts and illustrate how properties can be used to store information at the server and how client messages are used to establish direct communication and to coordinate the transfer of information among clients, especially among clients and the window manager.

NOTE:

The X server and X client applications need a protocol to work properly, and successful information sharing among clients also requires a well-defined convention outlining the steps that must be followed when exchanging data. The *Inter-Client Communication Conventions Manual (ICCCM)* describes these conventions. Even if your application does not plan to exchange any information (no cut-and-paste) with others, it has to interact with at least one other client—the window manager. The ICCCM provides detailed guidelines for interacting with the window manager and for exchanging data through the *selection* mechanism. The ICCCM is included in the documentation that comes with X software.

Atoms

In the X Window System's terminology, an *atom* is a unique identifier for a string. The X server has the facilities to maintain the relationship between a string and its identifier. As a programmer, you create the atom for a string by calling the XInternAtom function. In fact, the process of creating an atom for a string is often referred to as *interning*.

Interning an Atom

The XInternAtom function takes the display pointer, the string, and a Boolean flag—in that order—as arguments. For example, here is how you create an atom for the string WM_COLORMAP_WINDOWS:

```
#include <X11/Xlib.h>
.
.
Display  *theDisplay;
Atom     ATOM_WM_COLMAP_WIN;
.
.
ATOM_WM_COLMAP_WIN = XInternAtom(theDisplay,
                        "WM_COLORMAP_WINDOWS", False);
```

The value returned by XInternAtom is of type Atom, which is defined in the header file <X11/X.h>. You should save this atom and use it to refer to the string WM_COLORMAP_WINDOWS in the future. Note that if the last argument to XInternAtom is False, the server always returns an atom, creating a new one if that string was not previously interned. If you want an atom returned only for an existing string, specify True as the last argument.

When you intern an atom, it stays defined as long as the X server is running, and remains defined even if the application that creates the atom exits.

Converting an Atom to a String

You can use the `XGetAtomName` function to retrieve the string corresponding to an atom. For example, to get back the string corresponding to the atom ID `ATOM_WM_COLMAP_WIN`, you write the following:

```
Display  *theDisplay;
Atom     ATOM_WM_COLMAP_WIN;
char     *atom_def;
.
.
.
atom_def = XGetAtomName(theDisplay, ATOM_WM_COLMAP_WIN);
```

Xlib allocates memory for the string, copies to it the string returned by the server, and returns a pointer to you. After you are finished using the string, it is your responsibility to free the memory allocated by Xlib. You can free the string as follows:

```
XFree(atom_def);
```

Properties

In X, a *property* is a collection of three things: a name, a type, and a value that, depending on the type, can be a collection of data items. The name and type are expressed as strings, and the value is a collection of 8-bit bytes, 16-bit short integers, or 32-bit long integers whose interpretation depends on the type. The X Window System enables you to associate properties with windows. This means that applications can store data in windows and this data resides in the server.

Property Data Formats

In X, the *format* of a property's data refers to the size of each unit of the data. It can be 8, 16, or 32. In other words, you can store data as a sequence of 8-bit bytes, 16-bit short integers, or 32-bit long integers. If you store structures in properties, you must use one of these three data formats. If you use your own data structures to exchange data and if all fields in your structure have the same 8-, 16-, or 32-bit size, use that as the format.

When you store data in a property, you must specify both the type and the format of the data. When you retrieve the data, the server returns the format and type.

Byte-ordering can be a source of trouble when transferring your own data structures through properties. When transferring property data, the format (8-, 16-, or 32-bit) tells the server when and how to swap the bytes in the data. Potential problems arise only when you define your own data structure and store the structures in a property.

For example, if a structure has a mix of 8-, 16-, and 32-bit fields and you say that the format is 8-bit, the server does no swapping. If the client that receives the data expects a different byte order, its interpretation of all 16- and 32-bit fields will be wrong. For structures, the only safe approach is to ensure that all fields are the same size—8-, 16-, or 32-bit.

> **NOTE:**
>
> *Byte-ordering* refers to the ways in which 16- and 32-bit values can be stored in a computer with byte-addressable memory. Recall that there are little-endian systems (for example, the Intel 80x86-based systems), in which the least-significant byte of each value is the byte with the lower address. On the other side of the fence are the big-endian systems (for example, those based on the Motorola 680x0 microprocessors) that use the opposite convention. They store the high-order byte at the lower address. Usually, you need not worry about the exact ordering of bytes within the words in your computer's CPU, but X clients and servers can be on different systems. The X server is designed to take care of this problem and it swaps bytes, when necessary, to make sure that everything works right. Byte ordering can be a problem only when clients running on systems with differing byte orders directly exchange data.

Property Names and Types

Because the name and type of a property are strings, and because atoms provide a shorthand notation for strings interned at the server, X uses atoms as the name and type of properties.

To simplify matters, a number of property names and data types are predefined in X. In fact, these predefined atoms are part of the X protocol. These atoms have symbolic names that start with the prefix XA_, and the definitions appear in the header file <X11/Xatom.h>. Note that the string equivalent of each predefined atom is the same as its symbolic name without the XA_ prefix. For instance, if you use XGetAtomName to look up the string corresponding to the XA_WINDOW atom, you get back WINDOW as the result.

You will find the predefined atoms listed in Appendix G, "X Atoms." Table 16.1 shows the predefined atoms denoting data types.

> **TIP:**
>
> Use the xprop utility program to see what properties are defined for a window. For example, to see what properties are associated with the root window, type the following:
>
> xprop -root

Table 16.1. Predefined Atoms Denoting Data Types

Type Atom	Description
XA_ARC	XArc data structures
XA_ATOM	32-bit values denoting Atoms

Type Atom	Description
XA_BITMAP	32-bit values denoting bitmap IDs
XA_CARDINAL	Unsigned integers (the size of each integer depends on the format)
XA_COLORMAP	32-bit values denoting colormap IDs
XA_CURSOR	32-bit values denoting cursor IDs
XA_DRAWABLE	32-bit values denoting drawable IDs
XA_FONT	32-bit values denoting font IDs
XA_INTEGER	Signed integers (the size of each integer depends on the format)
XA_PIXMAP	32-bit values denoting pixmap IDs
XA_POINT	XPoint structures
XA_RECTANGLE	XRectangle structures
XA_RGB_COLOR_MAP	XStandardColormap structures
XA_STRING	8-bit values representing a text string
XA_VISUALID	32-bit values denoting visual IDs
XA_WINDOW	32-bit values denoting window IDs
XA_WM_HINTS	XWMHints data structures
XA_WM_SIZE_HINTS	XSizeHints data structures

Defining Properties

Some property names and data types are predefined in X, but that does not mean that any of these properties exist for any window. You have to store a property explicitly in a window by calling the Xlib function XChangeProperty. For example, the Motif window manager (mwm) expects the property named WM_COLORMAP_WINDOWS to be an array of data type XA_WINDOW, an array of IDs of windows that may need a colormap different from the one for the top-level window. This property is set on the top-level window. Here is an example of setting this property on the window main_win (to the lone window ID sub_win):

```
#include <X11/Xatom.h>  /* For definition of atom XA_WINDOW */

Display *theDisplay;
Window  main_win, sub_win;

/* Assume main_win and sub_win have been created and the atom
 * ATOM_WM_COLMAP_WIN is defined to be "WM_COLORMAP_WINDOWS"
 */
XChangeProperty(theDisplay, main_win, ATOM_WM_COLMAP_WIN,
                XA_WINDOW, 32, PropModeReplace,
                (unsigned char *)sub_win, 1);
```

Here, `XA_WINDOW` is a predefined atom indicating the data type of the property. The number `32` refers to the number of bits per data item. `PropModeReplace` is the mode. The following are valid modes:

- ✦ `PropModeReplace`. In this mode, the server replaces the old data of the property with the new value.

- ✦ `PropModePrepend`. In this mode, the server adds the new data to the beginning of any data existing in the property.

- ✦ `PropModeAppend`. In this mode, the server adds the new data to the end of any data existing in the property.

The last two arguments to `XChangeProperty` are the pointer to the data and the number of data elements, respectively.

Toolkits may contain utility functions to help you set specific properties. For example, the Xt Intrinsics includes the function `XtSetWMColormapWindows` that enables you to set the value of the `WM_COLORMAP_WINDOWS` property on a widget's window. See Appendix K, "Xt Intrinsics Quick Reference," for the calling syntax of the `XtSetWMColormapWindows` function.

Communicating with the Window Manager

Applications can use properties to communicate with the window manager. Of course, this is possible only if the application and the window manager follow the same conventions when interpreting the meaning of the properties. The ICCCM has simplified matters by specifying a minimal set of protocol for clients to communicate with the window manager. The basic mechanism is as follows:

- ✦ The window manager reads the properties listed on a client's top-level window when that window is mapped. Clients set these properties to provide information to the window manager. You will learn the names and types of these properties soon.

- ✦ The window manager watches for `PropertyNotify` events that the X server sends when a client changes any property. This is how clients can request service from the window manager at run-time.

- ✦ The window manager also sends `ClientMessage` events to clients that express an interest in such events through the property named `WM_PROTOCOLS`. The window manager uses this mechanism to send messages to clients. The following sections explain the details of this mechanism.

Once you know the names and purpose of the properties that the window manager uses for communicating with clients, you can set one or more of these properties on the window of your application's top-level widget by using the Xlib function `XChangeProperty`. If you need an atom to define a property, you can use `XInternAtom` to create the atom, as outlined earlier in this chapter.

ICCCM-Defined Properties

Table 16.2 shows a list of properties that the ICCCM defines for use in client-to-window manager communications.

Table 16.2. ICCCM-Defined Properties
Used in Client-to-Window Communications

Property	*Description*
WM_CLASS	This property contains the application's instance and class names.
WM_CLIENT_MACHINE	This property holds a string denoting the network node name of the system where the client is running.
WM_COLORMAP_WINDOWS	This is a list of windows for which the window manager should install colormaps.
WM_COMMAND	This is a string denoting a command that can restart the client.
WM_HINTS	This property, of type XA_WM_HINTS, is used by clients to indicate certain preferences to the window manager. These preferences include an indication of whether the client accepts keyboard input and where to place the client's icon.
WM_ICON_NAME	This property holds a string that is displayed when the client's top-level window is reduced to an icon.
WM_ICON_SIZE	The window manager stores the recommended dimensions of icons in this property. You can retrieve these dimensions by calling the Xlib function XGetWindowProperty.
WM_NAME	This property, of type XA_STRING, contains the title that the client wants the window manager to display in the header area of the top-level window's frame.
WM_NORMAL_HINTS	This property, of type XA_WM_SIZE_HINTS, is used by clients to indicate desired sizes for the top-level window.
WM_PROTOCOLS	This property contains a list of atoms through which a client indicates the types of ClientMessage events it wants to receive. This is the mechanism through which a window manager can communicate with clients using a private protocol.
WM_STATE	The window manager stores the window's state in this property on each top-level client window.
WM_TRANSIENT_FOR	This property, of type XA_WINDOW, is set on pop-up windows and is set to the ID of the top-level window that caused the pop-up window to appear.

Window Manager Protocols

An ICCCM-compliant window manager can provide its own protocol for communicating with clients through the WM_PROTOCOLS property. The window manager's documentation tells you the types of protocol messages the window manager provides and the purpose that each message serves. As the application developer, you select the protocol messages that you want to accept and place the names of these protocols in the WM_PROTOCOLS property of your application's top-level widget's window. Each protocol message is represented by an atom. Thus, all you have to do is create the necessary atoms and provide these as the value of the WM_PROTOCOLS property.

Although the WM_PROTOCOLS property can be used for private protocols unique to each window manager, the ICCCM does define the following three protocol messages that should be supported by all ICCCM-compliant window managers:

WM_DELETE_WINDOW	The window manager sends this protocol message when the user selects the Close option from the window menu. You can handle this message by performing necessary clean-up chores, displaying a notice to the user, and exiting the application, if the user confirms the action.
WM_SAVE_YOURSELF	When your application receives this message, you should set the WM_COMMAND property to a string that can be used to restart your application. ICCCM Version 2.0, released with X11R6, considers WM_SAVE_YOURSELF to be a depreciating convention whose use is expected to diminish over time.
WM_TAKE_FOCUS	If your application includes the WM_TAKE_FOCUS protocol in the WM_PROTOCOLS property, the window manager will send a ClientMessage event when your application's window should have the input focus.

If you indicate an interest in any of these protocols, the window manager will send a ClientMessage event at the appropriate time. Your application can take the necessary action in an event-handler for the ClientMessage event. To add an event-handler, you have to use the XtAddEventHandler function (see Chapter 13, "X Toolkits"). Appendix J, "X Event Reference," shows the information provided by the ClientMessage event.

An Example of Window Manager-Client Communication

As a concrete example of communicating with the window manager through the WM_PROTOCOLS property, consider a simple example program that handles the WM_DELETE_WINDOW protocol message. Listing 16.1 shows the file winprop.c, which illustrates how this is done. The basic steps are as follows:

1. For the top-level shell widget, set the XmNdeleteResponse resource to XmDO_NOTHING.
2. Use XInternAtom to create the atoms WM_PROTOCOLS and WM_DELETE_WINDOW.

3. Call `XtAddEventHandler` to add an event handler for `ClientMessage` events meant for the top-level widget. In Listing 16.1, `ClientMessage` events are handled by the function named `handle_wm_messages`.

4. Use the `XChangeProperty` function to set the `WM_PROTOCOLS` property to the atom `WM_DELETE_WINDOW`.

The function `handle_wm_messages` in Listing 16.1 illustrates how to handle the `ClientMessage` events sent by the window manager. The window manager sends the `WM_DELETE_WINDOW` message when the user selects Quit from the window menu. The example program's response is to display a dialog box requesting confirmation from the user. The application exits only if the user really wants to quit (see Figure 16.1).

Figure 16.1.

Dialog box displayed in response to `WM_DELETE_WINDOW` *protocol message.*

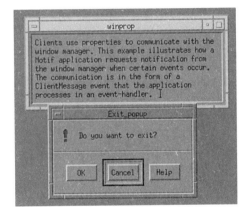

Listing 16.1. `winprop.c`—Handling protocol messages from the window manager.

```
/*------------------------------------------------------------*/
/*  File:  winprop.c
 *
 *  Shows how to WM_PROTOCOLS property to interact with the
 *  window manager.
 *
 */
#include <X11/Xatom.h>  /* For definition of XA_ATOM */
#include <Xm/Xm.h>

#include <Xm/DialogS.h>
#include <Xm/MessageB.h>
#include <Xm/Text.h>

/* ID of the top-level and warning dialog widget */
static Widget top_level, warndlg = (Widget)0;

static char message[] = "Clients use properties to communicate \
with the window manager. This example illustrates how a Motif \
application requests notification from the window manager \
```

continues

Listing 16.1. continued

```
when certain events occur. The communication is in the form of \
a ClientMessage event that the application processes in an \
event handler.  ";

/* Atoms used for interclient communication */
Atom ATOM_WM_PROTOCOLS, ATOM_WM_DELETE_WINDOW;

static void handle_wm_messages();
static void pop_warndlg();
static void cancel_cb();
static void do_exit();
/*------------------------------------------------------------*/
void main(argc, argv)
int    argc;
char **argv;
{
    Widget       w;
    XtAppContext app;

/* Create and initialize the top-level widget. To trap the
 * "Close" menu item, you have to make sure that the
 * XmNDeleteResponse resource is set to XmDO_NOTHING.
 */
    top_level = XtVaAppInitialize(&app, "Winprop", NULL, 0,
                            &argc, argv, NULL,
                            XmNdeleteResponse, XmDO_NOTHING,
                            NULL);

/* Create a Text widget */
    w = XtVaCreateManagedWidget("text",
                    xmTextWidgetClass, top_level,
                    XmNeditable,       False,
                    XmNeditMode,       XmMULTI_LINE_EDIT,
                    XmNwordWrap,       True,
                    XmNvalue,          message,
                    XmNwidth,          300,
                    XmNheight,         110,
                    NULL);

/* Intern the atoms */
    ATOM_WM_PROTOCOLS = XInternAtom(XtDisplay(w),
                                "WM_PROTOCOLS", False);
    ATOM_WM_DELETE_WINDOW = XInternAtom(XtDisplay(w),
                                "WM_DELETE_WINDOW", False);

/* Add an event handler to process ClientMessage events sent
 * by the window manager
 */
    XtAddEventHandler(top_level, NoEventMask, True,
                    handle_wm_messages, NULL);

/* Realize the widgets and start processing events */
    XtRealizeWidget(top_level);

/* Add WM_DELETE_WINDOW property to the definition of the
 * WM_PROTOCOLS property. This step requires the window ID
```

```
 * of the top-level widget. The window ID is valid only
 * after the widget is realized.
 */
    XChangeProperty(XtDisplay(top_level), XtWindow(top_level),
                    ATOM_WM_PROTOCOLS, XA_ATOM, 32,
                    PropModeReplace,
                    &ATOM_WM_DELETE_WINDOW, 1);

    XtAppMainLoop(app);
}
/*----------------------------------------------------------*/
static void handle_wm_messages(w, client_data, p_event)
Widget    w;
XtPointer client_data;
XEvent    *p_event;
{
    if(p_event->type == ClientMessage &&
       p_event->xclient.message_type == ATOM_WM_PROTOCOLS)
    {
        if(p_event->xclient.data.l[0] == ATOM_WM_DELETE_WINDOW)
        {
                pop_warndlg(w);
        }
    }
}
/*----------------------------------------------------------*/
/* p o p _ w a r n d l g
 * Display a warning dialog box.
 */
static void pop_warndlg(w)
Widget w;
{
    if(warndlg == (Widget)0)
    {
        XmString xms;
        Arg      args[10];
        Cardinal argcount;

/* Create the pop-up dialog widget */

/* Convert message string to a Motif compound string */
        xms = XmStringCreateSimple(
                     "Do you want to exit?");

/* Set up arguments and create the message box dialog */
        argcount = 0;
        XtSetArg(args[argcount], XmNmessageString, xms);
                                    argcount++;
        XtSetArg(args[argcount], XmNdefaultButtonType,
                              XmDIALOG_CANCEL_BUTTON);
                                    argcount++;
        warndlg = XmCreateWarningDialog(w, "Exit",
                                    args, argcount);
        XmStringFree(xms);

/* Add callbacks for OK and Cancel buttons. */
        XtAddCallback(warndlg, XmNcancelCallback, cancel_cb,
                      (XtPointer)warndlg);
```

continues

Listing 16.1. continued

```
        XtAddCallback(warndlg, XmNokCallback, do_exit,
                      (XtPointer)warndlg);
        XtManageChild(warndlg);
    }
    else
    {
/* Simply manage the dialog box again */
        XtManageChild(warndlg);
    }
}
/*------------------------------------------------------------*/
/*  c a n c e l _ c b
 *
 *  Callback for Cancel button.
 */
static void cancel_cb(w, client_data, call_data)
Widget w;
XtPointer client_data, call_data;
{
/* Simply unmanage the widget whose ID is provided in the
 * the "client_data" argument.
 */
    XtUnmanageChild((Widget)client_data);
}
/*------------------------------------------------------------*/
/*  d o _ e x i t
 *  Callback for the exit button.
 */
static void do_exit(w, call_data, client_data)
Widget    w;
XtPointer call_data, client_data;
{
    XCloseDisplay(XtDisplay(w));
    exit(0);
}
```

Data Transfer Through Properties

Properties play a major role in transferring data between X applications. To transfer data through a property, all you need is a window ID. Because applications do not know one another's window identifiers, the root window is the obvious choice for the common window. All that an application has to do is store data in a property on the root window. Any other application can get the data from that property. Of course, the applications have to use a prearranged name and data types for the property. As you will see in the next sections, this is how data transfer through cut buffers and selections works.

You can retrieve a property's data by using the Xlib function XGetWindowProperty. As an example, consider the following: the xterm terminal emulator stores the currently selected text in the root window's XA_CUT_BUFFER0 property. Suppose you want to retrieve the selected text from this property, if it exists. Listing 16.2 shows the file cbuf.c that illustrates how you can retrieve the value of the root window's `CUT_BUFFER0` property and monitor any changes in the value. To see the program in action, compile and link the program and run it from an `xterm` window. Then select text in the `xterm`—the selected text will appear in the `CUT_BUFFER0` property of the root window. When the property changes, X sends a `PropertyNotify` event to the program, and the program displays the new contents of the property. The next section further describes property events.

Listing 16.2. `cbuf.c`—Monitoring the `CUT_BUFFER0` property on the root window.

```c
/*------------------------------------------------------------*/
/*  File: cbuf.c
 *
 *  Monitor the CUT_BUFFER0 property.
 */
#include <stdio.h>
#include <X11/Xlib.h>
#include <X11/Xatom.h>


/*------------------------------------------------------------*/
void main(argc, argv)
int  argc;
char **argv;
{
    Display     *p_disp;        /* Connection to X display     */
    XEvent      theEvent;       /* Structure for current event */
    int         Done = 0;       /* Flag to indicate when done  */
    Atom        actual_type_atom;
    char        *property_data;
    int         actual_format, bytes_returned, bytes_remaining;

    if ((p_disp = XOpenDisplay(NULL)) == NULL)
    {
        fprintf(stderr, "Cannot open display!\n");
        exit(1);
    }

/* Select PropertyNotify event */
    XSelectInput(p_disp, DefaultRootWindow(p_disp),
                        ProportyChangeMask);

/* Get the current value of CUT_BUFFER0 property */

    if(XGetWindowProperty(p_disp, DefaultRootWindow(p_disp),
                        XA_CUT_BUFFER0, 0, 8192, False,
                        XA_STRING, &actual_type_atom,
                        &actual_format, &bytes_returned,
                        &bytes_remaining, &property_data)
        != Success)
    {
        printf("Error in XGetWindowProperty\n");
    }
    if(actual_format == 0)
    {
        printf("No such property\n");
```

continues

Listing 16.2. continued

```
        }
    else
    {
/* Display the value of the property */
        int i;
        printf("CUT_BUFFER0 contains %d bytes:\n",
                               bytes_returned);
        for(i=0; i < bytes_returned; i++)
            putchar(property_data[i]);
        printf("\n");
        XFree(property_data);
    }

/* Process PropertyNotify events */
    while (!Done)
    {
        XNextEvent(p_disp, &theEvent);

        if(theEvent.type == PropertyNotify &&
           theEvent.xany.window == DefaultRootWindow(p_disp) &&
           theEvent.xproperty.atom == XA_CUT_BUFFER0)
        {
            char    *buffer_contents;
            int     bytes_returned;
            if(theEvent.xproperty.state == PropertyDelete)
                printf("CUT_BUFFER0 has been deleted\n");

            if(theEvent.xproperty.state == PropertyNewValue)
            {
/* Use XFetchBytes to retrieve data from CUT_BUFFER0 */
                if((buffer_contents = XFetchBytes(p_disp,
                                 &bytes_returned)) != NULL)
                {
                    int i;
                    printf("--------------------------\n");
                    printf("CUT_BUFFER0 has a new %d-byte \
value:\n", bytes_returned);

/* Print the contents of the cut buffer */
                    for(i=0; i<bytes_returned; i++)
                        putchar(buffer_contents[i]);
                    printf("\n");
/* Now free memory allocated for the buffer's contents */
                    XFree(buffer_contents);

                }
                else
                {
                    printf("Nothing in CUT_BUFFER0\n");
                }
            }
        }
    }
}
```

> **NOTE:**
>
> Starting with X11R4, many properties that were previously of type XA_STRING have been changed to accommodate text strings that require more complicated encodings than the one-byte-per-character ASCII text. Text values are now stored in a new structure, XTextProperty, defined as follows:
>
> typedef struct
>
> ```
> {
>     unsigned char *value;    /* Value of the property      */
>     Atom          encoding; /* To interpret the value     */
>     int           format;    /* Property format: 8, 16, or 32 */
>     unsigned long nitems;    /* Number of data items in value */
> } XTextProperty;
> ```
>
> X includes utility routines such as XGetTextProperty, XSetTextProperty, XStringListToTextProperty, and XTextPropertyToStringList to help you manipulate text properties.

Property Events

One important aspect of exchanging data through properties is that there has to be a way to know if a property's data changes. For example, a pair of applications may be written to exchange a data item through a property. Suppose one application generates the data and stores it in a property on the root window, and the other monitors this property, retrieves the data, and plots it. How do you write the application that monitors the property? X provides a way to handle this situation through an event called PropertyNotify. You can request this event by using the PropertyChangeMask event mask in the call to the XSelectInput function (see Listing 16.2).

The data associated with the PropertyNotify event is in the xproperty field of the XEvent union. This field is an XPropertyEvent structure, defined in <X11/Xlib.h> as follows:

```
typedef struct
{
    int           type;       /* Type of event = PropertyNotify */
    unsigned long serial;     /* Last processed request number  */
    Bool          send_event; /* True if from SendEvent         */
    Display       *display;    /* This display sent event        */
    Window        window;     /* Window whose property changed  */
    Atom          atom;       /* Name of property involved      */
    Time          time;       /* Time when property changed     */
    int           state;      /* One of: PropertyNewValue  or   */
                              /*         PropertyDelete         */
} XPropertyEvent;
```

> **TIP:**
>
> You can force a PropertyNotify event without altering any property—the purpose being to get the server's current time from that event. To do this, call the XChangeProperty function with mode set to PropModeAppend and pass it zero-length data and any known property name. The result will be a PropertyNotify event with the server's current time.

ClientMessage Events

If you write two cooperating applications that need to coordinate their actions, you can do so by sending ClientMessage events. Because X applications do their work in response to events, it is convenient to communicate with other clients through an event. You send ClientMessage events by calling the XSendEvent function:

```
Display *p_disp;       /* Identifies the X server         */
Window  win;           /* Window that receives this event */
Bool    propagate_mask; /* True = Event is sent up the window */
                       /* hierarchy, False = Not sent     */
long    event_mask;    /* Mask used to decide whether window */
                       /* has selected the event being sent */
XEvent event;          /* Event structure with information */
                       /* pertinent to event being sent   */

/* Prepare the event structure and set the masks */
.
.
XSendEvent(p_disp, win, propagate_mask, event_mask, &event);
```

You do not have to request ClientMessage events explicitly (through a call to XSelectInput function). These events are nonmaskable and are always delivered by the X server.

In toolkit-based programs, you can add event handlers for ClientMessage events (see Chapter 13). Specify the constant NoEventMask as the second argument to the XtAddEventHandler function with the following:

```
Widget w;
void   msg_handler();

XtAddEventHandler(w, NoEventMask, TRUE, msg_handler, NULL);
```

where msg_handler is the function called when any nonmaskable event is received for the widget w. Because there are other nonmaskable events such as SelectionClear, SelectionNotify, and SelectionRequest, the msg_handler function should first make sure that the event type is ClientMessage before processing the event.

XClientMessageEvent Structure

Unlike other X events that deal with user inputs and repainting of windows, the ClientMessage event is meant to transmit a small amount of information from one client to another. The data for the ClientMessage event is in the xclient field of the XEvent union. This field is an XClientMessageEvent structure, defined in <X11/Xlib.h> as follows:

```
typedef struct
{
    int           type;         /* Type of event = ClientMessage*/
    unsigned long serial;       /* Last processed request number*/
    Bool          send_event;   /* Always True for ClientMessage*/
    Display       *display;      /* This display sent event     */
    Window        window;       /* Window to receive the event  */
    Atom          message_type; /* Atom for message type        */
    int           format;       /* Data format: 8, 16, or 32    */
    union                       /* You can pass up to 20 bytes   */
    {                           /* using ClientMessage events    */
        char b[20];             /* Data when format is  8        */
        short s[10];            /* Data when format is 16        */
        long l[5];              /* Data when format is 32        */
    } data;
} XClientMessageEvent;
```

Application Linkage with *ClientMessage* Events

Suppose you plan to establish a link between applications (which may be two copies of the same application) using ClientMessage events. The first problem you face is how to get the ID of a window so that events can be sent to it using XSendEvent. You can solve this problem by storing the identifier of the window in a property on the root window. The other client can check this property and extract the window ID by calling XGetWindowProperty.

The next problem is setting the event mask in the call to XSendEvent. A safe choice is to set it to zero. This causes the event to be delivered to the client that originally created the window specified in the call to XSendEvent.

You can send only 20 bytes at a time in a ClientMessage event. The meaning of this data depends on the atom message_type in the XClientMessageEvent structure. The sending and receiving clients have to agree on the meaning of this type and intrepret the data accordingly. Because of the small amount of data transferred by a ClientMessage event, the best use of this capability is to send a command from one application to another.

Cut Buffers

Cut buffers provide a simple mechanism for transferring data from one application to another. These are properties on the root window, eight of them in all, named by the predefined atoms XA_CUT_BUFFER0 through XA_CUT_BUFFER7.

The xterm terminal emulator uses cut buffers to copy text from one window to another. When the user selects text by pressing the left mouse and dragging, xterm copies this text to the XA_CUT_BUFFER0 property on the root window. If the user presses the middle mouse button in an xterm window, xterm retrieves the contents of XA_CUT_BUFFER0 from the server and inserts the text at the current location in its window. The xterm application assumes that the data in the cut buffers are ASCII bytes with lines separated by the newline (denoted by \n in C) character.

Storing Data

Xlib includes a number of utility routines to manipulate the cut buffers. To store data in cut buffer 0, you can use the `XStoreBytes` function as follows:

```
Display *p_disp;
char    text[] = "String being stored\n in cut buffer 0\n";
int     numchars = 39;

XStoreBytes(p_disp, text, numchars);
```

This puts the text in the `XA_CUT_BUFFER0` property on the root window of screen 0 in the X server specified by `p_disp`.

Retrieving Data

The retrieval is equally simple. You call `XFetchBytes` to get the current contents of cut buffer 0. Here is an example that fetches the contents of the `XA_CUT_BUFFER0` property on the root window:

```
#include <X11/Xatom.h>    /* For definition of XA_CUT_BUFFER0 */

Display *p_disp;
    .
    .
    .
/* Use XFetchBytes to retrieve data from CUT_BUFFER0 */
if((buffer_contents = XFetchBytes(p_disp,
                            &bytes_returned)) != NULL)
{
/* Print the contents of the cut buffer */
    int i;
    for(i=0; i<bytes_returned; i++)
            putchar(buffer_contents[i]);
    printf("\n");

/* Now free memory allocated for the buffer's contents */
    XFree(buffer_contents);
}
```

Selections

A *selection* is a more advanced way of transferring data from one X client to another. Although cut buffers are simple to use, they have two distinct drawbacks:

◆ The data in a cut buffer is always stored in the server, even if no client ever uses it.

◆ Cut buffers do not provide a flexible mechanism for storing a wide variety of data.

The best use of cut buffers is for transferring text between applications.

The *selection* mechanism in the X Window System overcomes the limitations of the cut buffers by using a different model of operation. A *selection* is also a property—there are two predefined ones, identified by the atoms `XA_PRIMARY` and `XA_SECONDARY`. Instead of using it to store data in a selection, it is used like a token. One of the clients always owns the selection. The owner is responsible for storing the data in a convenient format. Also, the owner must translate the data into other formats and store it in a specified property in reponse to a `SelectionRequest` event. After storing the data, the owner of the selection informs the requesting client of the availability of data by sending a `SelectionNotify` event.

Owning a Selection

If your application supports cut-and-paste operations, there will be some convention by which the user indicates that a selection has been made. At this point, the application has to claim ownership of a selection, usually the `XA_PRIMARY` selection. To do this, you call the `XSetSelectionOwner` function. Usually, there is some event that tells you that the user has completed selecting something. For instance, the user might drag across an item (text or a pixmap, for instance) and release the mouse button to indicate that the selection is complete. The application should assert ownership of the selection when handling the `ButtonRelease` event. Immediately after trying to own the `XA_PRIMARY` selection, you should call the `XGetSelectionOwner` function to get the current owner of the selection and see whether the owner is your window. Here is how this might be done:

```
#include <X11/Xatom.h>  /* For definition of XA_PRIMARY */

Display *p_disp;
Window  MainWin;
XEvent  theEvent;
.
.
/* Assume that the ButtonRelease event marks end of whatever
 * the user has been selecting
 */
.
.
/* In event handling loop */
XNextEvent(p_disp, &theEvent);
.
.
switch(theEvent.type)
{
    .
    .
    case ButtonRelease:
/* Own the selection. Note that we use time reported by the
 * ButtonPress event. ICCCM says you should not use CurrentTime.
 */
        XSetSelectionOwner(p_disp, XA_PRIMARY, MainWin,
                        thEvent.xbutton.time);
/* Check whether it worked */
        if(XGetSelectionOwner(p_disp, XA_PRIMARY) == MainWin)
        {
/* Success. Remember what has been selected so that we can honor
 * requests for this data. Also, give some visual feedback to
 * the user--by highlighting the selected item, for instance.
 */
            .
            .
        }
        else
        {
```

```
/* Indicate failure, for example, by beeping and not highlighting
 * the selected items.
 */
                .
                .
        }
    break;
        .
        .
        .
}
```

Coordinating Data Transfers with Selection Events

There are three events for coordinating the exchange of data through selections:

✦ SelectionClear

✦ SelectionRequest

✦ SelectionNotify

Applications do not have to solicit these events—they are sent automatically.

The X server sends a SelectionClear event to the current owner of a selection when the owner of the selection changes. The information for this event is in the xselectionclear field of the XEvent union. The xselectionclear field in this union is an XSelectionClearEvent structure, defined in <X11/Xlib.h> as follows:

```
typedef struct
{
    int           type;       /* Type of event = SelectionClear */
    unsigned long serial;     /* Last processed request number  */
    Bool          send_event; /* True if from SendEvent         */
    Display       *display;   /* This display sent event        */
    Window        window;     /* Window losing ownership        */
    Atom          selection;  /* Name of selection involved      */
    Time          time;       /* Time when ownership was lost    */
} XSelectionClearEvent;
```

When an application wants to receive the data corresponding to a selection, it calls the XConvertSelection function, which causes a SelectionRequest event to be sent to the current owner of the selection. The xselectionrequest field in the XEvent union contains information on this event. The event data structure is defined in <X11/Xlib.h> as follows:

```
typedef struct
{
    int           type;       /* Type of event = SelectionRequest*/
    unsigned long serial;     /* Last processed request number  */
    Bool          send_event; /* True if from SendEvent         */
    Display       *display;   /* This display sent event        */
    Window        owner;      /* Window that owns the selection */
    Window        requestor;  /* Window requesting data          */
    Atom          selection;  /* Name of selection involved      */
    Atom          target;     /* Data should be converted to     */
                              /* this type by the owner          */
```

```
    Atom          property;    /* Selection's owner should copy  */
                               /* data to this property          */
    Time          time;        /* Time when selection requested  */
} XSelectionRequestEvent;
```

When a selection's owner receives the `SelectionRequest` event, it should convert the data to the type specified by the `target` atom in the event and copy the converted data to the specified property on the requesting window. After that, the owner sends a `SelectionNotify` event to the requesting window to indicate the result of the request. The information for the `SelectionNotify` event is in the `xselection` field of the `XEvent` union. This field is a structure of type `XSelectionEvent`, defined in `<X11/Xlib.h>` as follows:

```
typedef struct
{
    int           type;        /* Type of event = SelectionNotify*/
    unsigned long serial;      /* Last processed request number  */
    Bool          send_event;  /* True if from SendEvent         */
    Display       *display;    /* This display sent event        */
    Window        requestor;   /* Window that had requested data */
    Atom          selection;   /* Name of selection involved     */
    Atom          target;      /* Data type of value in property */
    Atom          property;    /* Property where data has been   */
                               /* placed. "None" means failure   */
    Time          time;        /* Time when data stored          */
} XSelectionEvent;
```

If the owner of a selection cannot convert the data to the requested type or fails to store the data in the specified property, the owner sends a `SelectionNotify` event with the `property` field set to `None`. This tells the other party that the request for a selection's contents has failed.

Exchanging Data Through Selections

Applications that want to exchange data through a selection must follow a standard sequence of steps. For example, suppose window A currently owns the `XA_PRIMARY` selection and window B wants to get the contents of this selection as a string (`XA_STRING`). The two windows may be in the same client application or in different ones. Here is what should happen to complete the transfer of data from window A to window B:

Window B	Initiates the transfer by calling `XConvertSelection`. This sends a `SelectionRequest` event to the current owner of the selection, which happens to be window A. This application now waits for a `SelectionNotify` event from window A.
Window A	Receives the `SelectionRequest` event. It has to convert data to the type requested by window B. It calls `XChangeProperty` to store the converted data in the specified property on window B, then calls `XSendEvent` to send a `SelectionNotify` event to window B. In case of problems, it sets the `property` field in the event data structure to `None`.
Window B:	Receives the `SelectionNotify` event. If the `property` field is not `None`, it retrieves the data from that property and deletes the property.

To transfer large amounts of data, the clients have to follow further hand-shaking protocols to transfer the data in smaller-sized chunks. You should consult the ICCCM to learn how this is done.

NOTE:

Selections offer a powerful mechanism for transferring data from one application to another, but they can work properly *only* if all clients adhere to a common set of conventions. When developing X applications, it is important to read the ICCCM and be familiar with the conventions for exchanging data through selections. If you use a toolkit such as OSF/Motif, its own facilities (the Motif clipboard, for instance) can provide a simple way of implementing copy-and-paste operations in a way that maximizes the interoperability of your applications.

Data Transfer Through the Motif Clipboard

If you are writing application programs using the OSF/Motif toolkit, you can bypass most of the complexities of ICCCM-compliant data transfer by using the Motif clipboard. This is somewhat like the clipboard in Microsoft Windows or Apple Macintosh systems. It is a hidden storage location where applications can store data and from which they can later retrieve the data.

The use of the Motif clipboard is best illustrated by an example program. Listing 16.3 shows `xmnote.c`, the source code of the `xmnote` program. This program is a simple notepad where you can enter text, select it, copy it to the clipboard, and paste from it. Figure 16.2 shows an example with copying and pasting between two copies of `xmnote`.

Figure 16.2.

Copying between programs through the Motif clipboard.

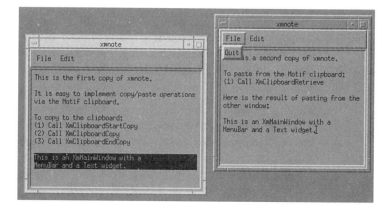

Listing 16.3. xmnote.c—A notepad program that illustrates the use of the Motif clipboard.

```
/*----------------------------------------------------------*/
/*  File: xmnote.c
 *
 *  An OSF/Motif program that illustrates how to implement
 *  copying and pasting between applications using the Motif
 *  clipboard.
 */
/*----------------------------------------------------------*/
#include <stdio.h>

#include <Xm/Xm.h>
#include <Xm/Text.h>
#include <Xm/RowColumn.h>
#include <Xm/MainW.h>
#include <Xm/CascadeB.h>
#include <Xm/BulletinB.h>
#include <Xm/PushB.h>
#include <Xm/CutPaste.h>

#define MAXCHR   1024

/* Function prototypes */
void quit_action(/* Widget w, XtPointer client_data,
                    XmAnyCallbackStruct *call_data */);
void copy(/* Widget w, XtPointer data,
                    XmAnyCallbackStruct *call_data */);
void paste(/* Widget w, XtPointer data,
                    XmAnyCallbackStruct *call_data */);

/* The following functions are defined in file xmutil.c */
Widget MakeMenuPane(/* char *name, Widget parent, ... */);
void AttachToCascade(/* Widget parent, char *label,
                    Widget sub_menu */);
/*----------------------------------------------------------*/
void main(argc, argv)
int  argc;
char **argv;
{
    Arg          args[20];
    Cardinal     argcount;
    XtAppContext app;
    Widget       main_widget, main_window, menu_bar, new_menu,
                 text_widget;

/* Initialize the toolkit and create the top-level widget */
    main_widget = XtAppInitialize(&app, "XMnote", NULL, 0,
                          &argc, argv, NULL, NULL, 0);

/* Next, the main window widget */
    main_window = XmCreateMainWindow(main_widget, "Main",
                                    NULL, 0);

    XtManageChild(main_window);
```

continues

Listing 16.3. continued

```
/* Create the menubar */
    menu_bar = XmCreateMenuBar(main_window, "Menubar", NULL, 0);
    XtManageChild(menu_bar);

/* Create the text area. Set up a text widget inside a
 * scrolled window. Make room for 15 rows of text with
 * 60 columns (characters).
 */
    argcount = 0;
    XtSetArg(args[argcount], XmNeditable, True);       argcount++;
    XtSetArg(args[argcount], XmNeditMode, XmMULTI_LINE_EDIT);
                                                       argcount++;
    XtSetArg(args[argcount], XmNcolumns, 60);          argcount++;
    XtSetArg(args[argcount], XmNrows, 15);             argcount++;
    XtSetArg(args[argcount], XmNx, 15);                argcount++;
    XtSetArg(args[argcount], XmNy, 15);                argcount++;
    text_widget = XmCreateText(main_window,
                               "TextWidget", args, argcount);
    XtManageChild(text_widget);

/* Attach the menubar, the text area, and the scrollbar
 * to main window
 */
    XmMainWindowSetAreas(main_window, menu_bar, NULL, NULL,
                         NULL, text_widget);

/* Create the "File" menu --------------------------------*/
    new_menu = MakeMenuPane("File", menu_bar,
                            "Quit", quit_action, NULL,
                            NULL);
    AttachToCascade(menu_bar, "File", new_menu);

/* Create the "Edit" menu --------------------------------*/
    new_menu = MakeMenuPane("Edit", menu_bar,
                    "Copy",  copy,  (XtPointer)text_widget,
                    "Paste", paste, (XtPointer)text_widget,
                    NULL);

    AttachToCascade(menu_bar, "Edit", new_menu);

/* Realize the widgets */
    XtRealizeWidget(main_widget);

/* Start the main event handling loop */
    XtAppMainLoop(app);
}
/*------------------------------------------------------------*/
/*  c o p y
 *
 *  Copies text from text widget to the Motif clipboard
 */
void copy(w, data, call_data)
Widget                  w;
XtPointer               data;
XmAnyCallbackStruct *call_data;
{
```

```
    char   *selection;
    long   item_id, data_id;
    XButtonEvent *p_event = (XButtonEvent *) call_data->event;
    Widget w_text = (Widget) data;

/* Do nothing if nothing selected in text widget */
    if((selection = XmTextGetSelection (w_text)) == NULL)
        return;

/* Otherwise, copy data to clipboard. First start the copy.
 * Loop until we succeed
 */
    while(XmClipboardStartCopy(XtDisplay(w), XtWindow(w_text),
              "XMNote", p_event->time, w_text, NULL,
              &item_id) != ClipboardSuccess)   ;

/* Next, do the actual copy */
    while(XmClipboardCopy(XtDisplay(w), XtWindow(w_text),
              item_id, XmRString, selection, strlen(selection),
              0, &data_id) != ClipboardSuccess)   ;

/* Finally, end the copy operation */
    while(XmClipboardEndCopy(XtDisplay(w), XtWindow(w_text),
              item_id) != ClipboardSuccess)   ;
}
/*-----------------------------------------------------------*/
/* p a s t e
 *
 * Retrieves text from Motif clipboard and inserts in text
 * widget.
 */
void paste(w, data, call_data)
Widget               w;
XtPointer            data;
XmAnyCallbackStruct *call_data;
{
    int    insertion_point, id, status, copy_done = FALSE,
           numchars;
    Widget w_text = (Widget) data;
    char   buf[MAXCHR];

    while(!copy_done)
    {
        status = XmClipboardRetrieve(XtDisplay(w),
                    XtWindow(w_text), XmRString, buf, MAXCHR,
                    &numchars, &id);

        switch(status)
        {
            case ClipboardLocked:    /* Locked...try again    */
                copy_done = TRUE;
                break;

            case ClipboardNoData:    /* Nothing to paste      */
                copy_done = TRUE;
                break;
```

continues

Listing 16.3. continued

```
              case ClipboardTruncate: /* Buffer size too small  */
                  XtWarning("Not enough room to retrieve data");
/* Fall through to the next step */
              case ClipboardSuccess:  /* Copy successful        */

/* Mark end of string with a null byte */
                  buf[numchars] = '\0';
/* Add text to scrolled text widget */
                  insertion_point =
                      XmTextGetInsertionPosition(w_text);
                  XmTextReplace(w_text, insertion_point,
                      insertion_point, buf);
                  copy_done = TRUE;
                  break;
          }
      }
}
/*------------------------------------------------------------*/
/*  q u i t _ a c t i o n
 *
 *  This routine is called when the "Quit" item is selected from
 *  the "File" menu.
 */
void quit_action(w, client_data, call_data)
Widget    w;
XtPointer client_data, call_data;
{
    XtCloseDisplay(XtDisplay(w));
    exit(0);
}
```

The copy function in Listing 16.3 shows how the copy operation is done. Before copying to the clipboard, you have to get the data that you are going to copy. In xmnote, this happens to be the current selection from the text widget. If there is something to copy, you start the operation by calling XmClipboardStartCopy to initialize the clipboard for the impending copy. This also locks out the clipboard from other clients. Next, you call XmClipboardCopy to perform the actual copying. The last step is to call XmClipboardEndCopy to release the clipboard to other clients.

Pasting involves calling the XmClipboardRetrieve function. The paste function in Listing 16.3 shows how this can be done. Of course, what you do with the retrieved data depends on your application. In xmnote, the retrieved text is inserted into the text widget.

Drag-and-Drop in Motif

Motif 1.2 introduced support for *drag-and-drop*—a style of user interaction in which the user initiates actions by dragging objects on the screen and dropping them on other objects. For instance, you can use the drag-and-drop feature to implement a user interface wherein users print documents by dragging and dropping an icon representing the document on an icon of a printer.

Built-In Support for Drag-and-Drop

Several Motif widgets come with built-in support for drag-and-drop. To see how drag-and-drop works, try the following steps:

1. Run the sample programs `list` and `text` from a shell window (Listings 14.7 and 14.8, respectively, from Chapter 14, "OSF/Motif Widgets"):

   ```
   list &
   text &
   ```

2. With the mouse pointer on an item in the list, press down the middle mouse button (or the button that is designated as the `BTransfer` button). The cursor shape should change to a *drag icon* to indicate that a drag operation is in progress. Drag the cursor over to the text window and release the mouse button. The cursor should appear to dissolve into the window and the item from the list should get inserted in the text window.

What you see is the `List` widget and `Text` widget's built-in support for drag-and-drop operations. In particular, the `List` widget can act as the source for drag operations and the `Text` widget can be a recipient of drop operations. In Motif terminology, the `List` widget can be a *drag source* and the `Text` widget can act as a *drop site*.

In addition to the `List` and `Text` widgets, the `Label` and `PushButton` widgets can also be drag sources. The `TextField` widget can be a drop site, and only the `Text` widget can be both a drag source and a drop site.

Implementing Drag-and-Drop Support

You can get the built-in drag-and-drop capabilities of the `Label`, `PushButton`, `List`, and `Text` widgets for free, but in many cases, your application's user interface may require you to implement drag-and-drop support for other widgets. The Motif toolkit (version 1.2 or later) includes new widgets and convenience functions that enable you to make any widget a drag source or a drop site.

To illustrate how to support drag-and-drop capabilities, the following sections present two programs that are designed to work together:

✦ The `tstamp` program (Listing 16.4) displays a label that can act as a drop site. If you drag a text string on the label, `tstamp` interprets that string as a filename, opens the file, and adds a line with the current time stamp into that file.

✦ The `Files` program (Listing 16.5) shows a list of files in the current directory. It acts as a drag source, so you can select a filename from the list and drag-and-drop the name on the label displayed by the `tstamp` program.

Figure 16.3 shows the windows of the `Files` and `tstamp` programs.

Figure 16.3.

The Files *and* tstamp
*programs illustrate drag-
and-drop capabilities of
Motif.*

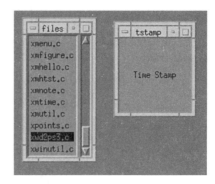

Setting Up a Drop Site

To set up a widget as a drop site, follow these steps:

1. Decide which data formats (called targets and identified by atoms) the widget
   should accept. A common format is compound text identified by the target atom
   COMPOUND_TEXT.

2. After creating the widgets, register a widget as the drop site by calling
   XmDropSiteRegister with the widget as argument. You have to specify a number of
   resources for XmDropSiteRegister. In particular, you have to specify the data format in
   terms of target atoms, the types of drop operations to be supported, and a *drop procedure*—
   a function that will be called to initiate the drop operation. In Listing 16.4, the drop site is
   registered by the following code fragment:

```
/* Make the label a drop site */
    n = 0;
    targets[0] = XmInternAtom(XtDisplay(main_widget),
                            "COMPOUND_TEXT", False);
    XtSetArg(args[n], XmNimportTargets, targets); n++;
    XtSetArg(args[n], XmNnumImportTargets, 1); n++;
    XtSetArg(args[n], XmNdropSiteOperations,
                                    XmDROP_COPY); n++;
    XtSetArg(args[n], XmNdropProc, accept_drop); n++;
    XmDropSiteRegister(w, args, n);
```

3. Write the drop procedure. In Listing 16.4, the accept_drop function is the drop
   procedure. The drop procedure takes the standard Motif callback arguments and
   has the following prototype:

```
void accept_drop(
    Widget              w,
    XtPointer           client_data,
    XmDropProcCallback drop);
```

The third argument to the drop procedure is a pointer to a structure of type
XmDropProcCallbackStruct (see Appendix L, "Motif Quick Reference,"
for a listing of this structure).

4. Inside the drop procedure, if the right type of data is available and the drop operation is a supported one, call XmDropTransferStart to initiate the transfer of data. When you call XmDropTransferStart, you have to specify a number of resources. At a minimum, you have to provide an XmDropTransferEntryRec with information on the type of data transfer and a *transfer procedure*—a function to be called to transfer the data from the drag source to the drop site.

5. Write the transfer procedure—it is of type XtSelectionCallbackProc (see Appendix K). In Listing 16.4, the function named transfer serves as the transfer procedure.

6. In the transfer procedure, copy the transferred data from the value argument of the function. In the example program of Listing 16.4, the transfer procedure gets the data (interpreted as a filename) and calls the function named time_stamp to add a timestamp to the specified file.

Listing 16.4. tstamp.c—Implementing a drop site.

```c
/*----------------------------------------------------------*/
/* File: tstamp.c
 *
 * Illustrates how to set up a drop site and handle a drop.
 * Accepts a filename (in COMPOUND_TEXT format), opens the
 * file, and adds a timestamp at the beginning of the file.
 */

#include <stdio.h>
#include <stdlib.h>
#include <string.h>
#include <Xm/Xm.h>
#include <Xm/Label.h>
#include <Xm/DragDrop.h>

/* Drop procedure */
void accept_drop(/* Widget w, XtPointer client_data,
                XmDropProcCallback drop */);

/* Transfer Procedure */
void transfer(/* Widget w, XtPointer client_data,
                Atom *selection, Atom *type, XtPointer value,
                unsigned long *length, int *format */);

/* Other functions */
void time_stamp(/* char *filename */);
/*----------------------------------------------------------*/
void main(argc, argv)
int   argc;
char **argv;
{
    Widget      main_widget, w;
    int         i, n;
    FILE        *fp;
    char        line[80];
    XmString    xms;
```

continues

Listing 16.4. continued

```
    XtAppContext app;
    Arg          args[10];
    Atom         targets[1];

/* Create and initialize the top-level widget */
    main_widget = XtAppInitialize(&app, "Tstamp", NULL, 0,
                            &argc, argv, NULL, NULL, 0);

/* Create a Label widget */
    w = XtVaCreateManagedWidget("Time Stamp",
                            xmLabelWidgetClass, main_widget,
                            XmNwidth,   100,
                            XmNheight,  100,
                            NULL);

/* Make the label a drop site */
    n = 0;
    targets[0] = XmInternAtom(XtDisplay(main_widget),
                            "COMPOUND_TEXT", False);
    XtSetArg(args[n], XmNimportTargets, targets); n++;
    XtSetArg(args[n], XmNnumImportTargets, 1); n++;
    XtSetArg(args[n], XmNdropSiteOperations,
                                    XmDROP_COPY); n++;
    XtSetArg(args[n], XmNdropProc, accept_drop); n++;
    XmDropSiteRegister(w, args, n);

/* Realize the widgets and start processing events */
    XtRealizeWidget(main_widget);
    XtAppMainLoop(app);
}
/*-------------------------------------------------------------*/
/* a c c e p t _ d r o p
 *
 * Accepts some text dropped on a widget.
 */
void accept_drop(w, client_data, drop)
Widget              w;
XtPointer           client_data;
XmDropProcCallback  drop;
{
    Arg                   args[10];
    int                   i, n;
    XmDropTransferEntryRec entries[1];
    Cardinal              nexports;
    Atom                  *exports;
    Atom ctext = XmInternAtom(XtDisplay(w), "COMPOUND_TEXT",
                            False);

/* See what types of targets are available */
    XtVaGetValues(drop->dragContext,
                    XmNexportTargets,    &exports,
                    XmNnumExportTargets, &nexports,
                    NULL);
    for(i = 0; i < nexports; i++)
    {
        if(exports[i] == ctext) break;
```

```
    }
    if(i > nexports)
    {
        printf("No exported target of COMPOUND_TEXT type!\n");
        exit(2);
    }
/*    XtFree(exports); */

/* See whether the operation is a supported one */
    if(drop->dropAction == XmDROP &&
        drop->operation == XmDROP_COPY)
    {
/* Set up transfer procedure */
        entries[0].target = ctext;
        entries[0].client_data = (XtPointer)w;
        n = 0;
        XtSetArg(args[n], XmNdropTransfers, entries); n++;
        XtSetArg(args[n], XmNnumDropTransfers, 1); n++;
        XtSetArg(args[n], XmNtransferProc, transfer); n++;
    }
    else
    {
        printf("Timestamp: Unknown drop operation!\n");
        n = 0;
        XtSetArg(args[n], XmNtransferStatus,
                        XmTRANSFER_FAILURE); n++;
    }
    XmDropTransferStart(drop->dragContext, args, n);
}
/*------------------------------------------------------------*/
/* t r a n s f e r
 *
 * This function gets the data transferred by the drop
 * operation.
 */
void transfer(w, client_data, selection, type, value,
                length, format)
Widget      w;
XtPointer   client_data;
Atom        *selection;
Atom        *type;
XtPointer   value;
unsigned long *length;
int         *format;
{
    XmString xms;
    char     *str;
    Atom     ctext;
    Widget   label = (Widget)client_data;

    ctext = XmInternAtom(XtDisplay(label), "COMPOUND_TEXT",
                            False);

    if(*type == ctext)
    {
        xms = XmCvtCTToXmString(value);
```

continues

Listing 16.4. continued

```
/* Convert XmString to C string */
        XmStringGetLtoR(xms,
                         XmSTRING_DEFAULT_CHARSET, &str);
        printf("Time stamp: received string: %s\n", str);

/* Call the time_stamp function with the filename as argument */
        time_stamp(str);

/* Remember to free memory allocated by Motif toolkit for
 * the returned C string.
 */
        XtFree(str);
        XmStringFree(xms);
    }
}
/*-------------------------------------------------------------*/
/* t i m e _ s t a m p
 *
 * Adds a line with a date and time at the beginning of a file.
 */
void time_stamp(filename)
char *filename;
{
    FILE *in, *out, *fp;
    char  line[256], dstr[40];
    int n = strlen(filename);
    char *bkup = malloc(sizeof(filename) + 2);

/* Get the timestamp by running the "date" command */
    if((fp = popen("/bin/date", "r")) == NULL)
    {
        printf("Error in popen\n");
        exit(1);
    }
    if(fgets(dstr, 40, fp) == NULL)
    {
        printf("Error getting date\n");
        exit(2);
    }

/* First create a backup copy of the file */
    strcpy(bkup, filename);
    strcat(bkup, "$");

    if((in = fopen(filename, "r")) != NULL)
    {
        if((out = fopen(bkup, "w")) != NULL)
        {
/* Copy the file over a line at a time */
            while(fgets(line, 256, in) != NULL)
                fputs(line, out);
            fclose(out);
        }
        fclose(in);
    }
```

```
/* Now overwrite original with an added timestamp line */
   if((in = fopen(bkup, "r")) != NULL)
   {
       if((out = fopen(filename, "w")) != NULL)
       {
           fprintf(out, "/* Time stamp: %s*/\n", dstr);

/* Now copy the entire file from backup to the original */
           while(fgets(line, 256, in) != NULL)
                               fputs(line, out);
           fclose(out);
       }
       fclose(in);
   }
}
```

Setting Up a Drag Source

The steps involved in setting up a drag source are similar to those involved in setting up the drop site:

1. Add an action that binds the event of pressing the middle mouse button to a function that starts the drag operation. This step involves setting up a translation table, an action table, and using the functions `XtAppAddActions` and `XtParseTranslationTable`. (Chapter 13 describes how to add actions and bind an action to a key or mouse event.)

2. Write the function that initiates the drag operation. In Listing 16.5, the `start_drag` function performs this step. This function sets up the target atoms indicating the format of the data being exported and calls `XmDragStart` to initiate the drag operation. The `XmDragStart` function creates an `XmDragContext` widget. You have to specify several resources for this widget—in particular, an array of target atoms and a convert procedure, a function that will be called to convert data to a specific format before the Motif toolkit can transfer the data to the drop site.

3. Write the convert procedure—it is of type `XtConvertSelectionProc` (see Appendix K). In Listing 16.5, the `text_convert` function serves as the convert procedure. In the convert procedure, you should allocate memory for the data being transferred and, if all goes well, copy the data in the requested format and return `True`. In case of any error in converting data, the convert procedure should return `False`.

Listing 16.5. `files.c`—Implementing a drag source.

```
/*-----------------------------------------------------------*/
/* File: files.c
 *
 * Illustrates how to set up a drag source. Displays a list
 * of filenames that can be dragged and dropped onto the
 * window of the "tstamp" program (that program inserts a
 * timestamp at the beginning of the file).
```

continues

Listing 16.5. continued

```
*
* Note: The List widget is already a Drag source, but we
* add another function to take care of the drag initiation
* to show how this is done.
*/

#include <stdio.h>
#include <string.h>
#include <Xm/Xm.h>
#include <Xm/List.h>
#include <Xm/DragDrop.h>

#define LIST_MARGIN_WIDTH  30
#define LIST_SPACING        5

/* Drag action callback */
void start_drag(/* Widget w, XEvent *event, String *params,
                   Cardinal *nparams */);

/* Data conversion procedure */
Boolean text_convert(/* Widget w, Atom *selection,
    Atom *target, Atom *type_return, XtPointer *value_return,
    unsigned long *length_return, int *format_return */);

static char translation_table[] =
    "#override <Btn2Down>: start_drag()";

static XtActionsRec action_table[] =
{
    { "start_drag", (XtActionProc)start_drag }
};
/*-----------------------------------------------------------*/
void main(argc, argv)
int  argc;
char **argv;
{
    Widget        main_widget, w;
    int           i, n;
    FILE          *fp;
    char          line[80];
    XmString      xms;
    XtAppContext  app;
    Arg           args[10];
    XtTranslations translations;

/* Create and initialize the top-level widget */
    main_widget = XtAppInitialize(&app, "Files", NULL, 0,
                                  &argc, argv, NULL, NULL, 0);

/* Add actions */
    XtAppAddActions(app, action_table, XtNumber(action_table));

    translations = XtParseTranslationTable(translation_table);

/* Create a ScrolledList widget */
    n = 0;
```

```
    XtSetArg(args[n], XmNvisibleItemCount, 10); n++;
    XtSetArg(args[n], XmNtranslations, translations); n++;
    w = XmCreateScrolledList(main_widget, "FileList", args, n);

/* Get a list of filenames (only "*.c" files are used) */
    if((fp = popen("/bin/ls -1 *.c", "r")) == NULL)
    {
        fprintf(stderr, "Error in popen. Exiting...\n");
        exit(1);
    }

    while(fgets(line, 80, fp) != NULL)
    {
/* Insert filename into the List widget */
/* First get rid of the newline character */
        n = strlen(line);
        line[n-1] = '\0';
        xms = XmStringCreateSimple(line);
        XmListAddItem(w, xms, 0);
        XmStringFree(xms);
    }

    XtManageChild(w);
/* Realize the widgets and start processing events */
    XtRealizeWidget(main_widget);
    XtAppMainLoop(app);
}
/*------------------------------------------------------------*/
/* s t a r t _ d r a g
 *
 * This is the drag start action callback routine.
 */
void start_drag(w, event, params, nparams)
Widget    w;
XEvent    *event;
String    *params;
Cardinal *nparams;
{
    Arg args[10];
    int n;
    Atom targets[1];

    targets[0] = XmInternAtom(XtDisplay(w), "COMPOUND_TEXT",
                              False);
    n = 0;
    XtSetArg(args[n], XmNexportTargets, targets); n++;
    XtSetArg(args[n], XmNnumExportTargets, 1); n++;
    XtSetArg(args[n], XmNconvertProc, text_convert); n++;
    XtSetArg(args[n], XmNclientData, (XtPointer)w); n++;
    XmDragStart(w, event, args, n);
}
/*------------------------------------------------------------*/
/* t e x t _ c o n v e r t
 *
 * Converts data to COMPOUND_TEXT format. Called during
 * drag-and-drop operations by the Motif toolkit to convert
```

continues

Listing 16.5. continued

```
 * data before transferring to the drop site.
 */
Boolean text_convert(w, selection, target, type_return,
    value_return, length_return, format_return)
Widget          w;
Atom            *selection;
Atom            *target;
Atom            *type_return;
XtPointer       *value_return;
unsigned long   *length_return;
int             *format_return;
{
    Widget          list;
    int             nsel;
    XmStringTable   xmsel;
    Atom            ctext;
    char            *ctsel;

/* List widget's ID is the clientData resource of the
 * DragContext widget w.
 */
    XtVaGetValues(w, XmNclientData, (XtPointer)&list, NULL);

/* Retrieve the selected item from the list, if any */
    XtVaGetValues(list,
                XmNselectedItemCount,   &nsel,
                XmNselectedItems,       &xmsel,
                NULL);
    if(nsel == 0)
    {
    printf("No items selected\n");
        return False;
    }

/* Check target */
    ctext = XmInternAtom(XtDisplay(list), "COMPOUND_TEXT",
                                            False);
    if(*target == ctext)
    {
        *type_return = ctext;
/* Use the first selected item */
        ctsel = XmCvtXmStringToCT(xmsel[0]);
        *value_return = (XtPointer)ctsel;
        *length_return = strlen(ctsel) + 1;
        *format_return = 8;
printf("%s  length = %ld\n", ctsel, *length_return);
/* Return True to indicate successful conversion */
        return True;
    }

/* Return False to indicate failure to convert */
    return False;
}
```

Extensions to X

The X protocol is designed to be extensible. Once an extension is available, applications can use the new features like the old ones. Xlib includes functions that enable you to determine whether any extensions are supported by a server. The following sections briefly describe the Xlib functions for querying about X extensions and PEX, an extension to X that supports 3-D graphics.

X Extensions

You can use the Xlib function, XListExtensions, to find out what extensions, if any, are available in an X server. If your application relies on whether a specific extension is available, you can go through this list to determine that. Another function, XQueryExtension enables you to get more information about the extension. This information includes the major opcode used by the extension and any new events and error codes it uses.

When you call XListExtensions, Xlib allocates memory for the list. When you are finished with the list, you should call XFreeExtensionList to release this memory.

Listing 16.6 shows an example program that lists the pertinent details of all the extensions available in the X server.

Listing 16.6. listex.c—Displaying all available extensions.

```
/*-----------------------------------------------------------*/
/*  File: listex.c
 *
 *  List the extensions supported by the X server.
 */
#include <stdio.h>
#include <X11/Xlib.h>


/*-----------------------------------------------------------*/
void main(argc, argv)
int  argc;
char **argv;
{
    Display    *p_disp;          /* Connection to X display    */
    char **extensions = NULL; /* List of extensions         */
    int  num_extensions,      /* Number of extensions       */
        major_opcode,        /* Major opcode for extension */
        first_event,         /* First custom event         */
        first_error;         /* First custom error code    */
    int  i;

/* Open connection to the X server */
    if ((p_disp = XOpenDisplay(NULL)) == NULL)
    {
        fprintf(stderr, "Cannot open display!\n");
        exit(1);
    }
```

continues

Listing 16.6. continued

```
/* Get the names of extensions supported by this server */
    extensions = XListExtensions(p_disp, &num_extensions);
    printf("There are %d extensions\n", num_extensions);

/* Get detailed information on each extension */
    if(num_extensions > 0)
        for(i = 0; i < num_extensions; i++)
        {
            printf("-----------------------------------\n");
            printf("Name: %s\n", extensions[i]);
            if(XQueryExtension(p_disp, extensions[i],
                    &major_opcode, &first_event, &first_error))
            {
                printf("Major Opcode: %d\n", major_opcode);
                if(first_event)
                    printf("First event: %d\n", first_event);
                if(first_error)
                    printf("First error: %d\n", first_error);
            }
        }

/* Free the memory allocated for the list of extensions */
    if(extensions != NULL)
        XFreeExtensionList(extensions);

    XCloseDisplay(p_disp);
}
```

On the author's Sun SPARstation system running SunOS 4.1.3 and the X Consortium's X11R6 server, the listex program (Listing 16.6) generates the following list of extensions:

```
There are 11 extensions
-----------------------------------
Name: SHAPE
Major Opcode: 128
First event: 64
-----------------------------------
Name: MIT-SHM
Major Opcode: 129
First event: 65
First error: 128
-----------------------------------
Name: X3D-PEX
Major Opcode: 130
First event: 66
First error: 129
-----------------------------------
Name: Multi-Buffering
Major Opcode: 131
First event: 67
First error: 144
-----------------------------------
Name: XTEST
Major Opcode: 132
```

```
- - - - - - - - - - - - - - - - - - - - - - - - - - - -
Name: BIG-REQUESTS
Major Opcode: 133
- - - - - - - - - - - - - - - - - - - - - - - - - - - -
Name: MIT-SUNDRY-NONSTANDARD
Major Opcode: 134
- - - - - - - - - - - - - - - - - - - - - - - - - - - -
Name: XIE
Major Opcode: 135
First event: 69
First error: 145
- - - - - - - - - - - - - - - - - - - - - - - - - - - -
Name: SYNC
Major Opcode: 136
First event: 74
First error: 152
- - - - - - - - - - - - - - - - - - - - - - - - - - - -
Name: XKEYBOARD
Major Opcode: 137
First event: 76
First error: 154
- - - - - - - - - - - - - - - - - - - - - - - - - - - -
Name: XC-MISC
Major Opcode: 138
```

The last opcode used by the basic X protocol is 127. Thus, the first extension, SHAPE, uses the next available opcode (128).

After you find out about an extension, you have to consult the documentation to use that extension. The extension should come with some functions to help you use the capabilities it offers. For example, the SHAPE extension supports arbitrarily shaped windows. The SHAPE extension comes with its own type of event (XShapeEvent) and a number of functions with which to use the new feature in programs.

The PHIGS Extension: PEX

PHIGS, the Programmer's Hierarchical Interactive Graphics System, is a sophisticated graphics system that enables you to define, modify, and display hierarchical graphics data structures, and that supports storage and display of two- (2-D) and three-dimensional (3-D) graphics. In contrast to this, X supports only 2-D graphics. PEX is an extension to the X protocol that enables you to mix standard X graphics with the 3-D capabilities of PHIGS. The X11R5 distribution included the first sample implementation of PEX.

Three-Dimensional Graphics in Xlib

You can display 3-D graphics using the basic Xlib drawing functions alone. To do this, you have to maintain the definitions of the 3-D objects (in terms of polygonal surfaces, for instance) in the client application. For a specified viewing angle, the client can transform the 3-D data and project them onto a plane to create a 2-D image, which it can draw using the 2-D Xlib drawing functions. One drawback to this approach is that any change in the viewing angle requires the client to go through the geometric transformations and redraw the 2-D image. Another problem is that this method does not enable the client to exploit the full capabilities of any advanced graphics hardware that can deal directly with 3-D shapes installed in an X server.

PEX Protocol

PEX extends the X protocol to enable client applications to exchange 3-D graphics data with an X server in a way that conforms to the PHIGS standard. It is worth emphasizing that PEX is only a protocol and not a set of routines for drawing 3-D graphics using PHIGS. The PEX sample implementation, also called the PEX-SI, includes an X server that understands the PEX protocol and PEXlib—a library (like Xlib for the existing standard X protocol) that sends PEX protocol requests to the X server. Although PEX began by implementing the capabilities of PHIGS, PEX is beginning to evolve beyond PHIGS as a mechanism to support 3-D application programs in general.

Three-Dimensional Graphics with PEXlib and Motif

Listing 16.7 shows `pexdemo.c`, a sample program that illustrates how to use PEXlib to display 3-D graphics in a Motif program. Figure 16.4 shows the output of the program—a 3-D line drawing displayed in a `DrawingArea` widget inside a `MainWindow`. The `pexdemo` program uses the Xt timeout callback to rotate the figure and redraw it every so often. Figure 16.4 shows a snapshot of the 3-D figure during the rotation.

Figure 16.4.

Three-dimensional graphics with PEXlib and Motif.

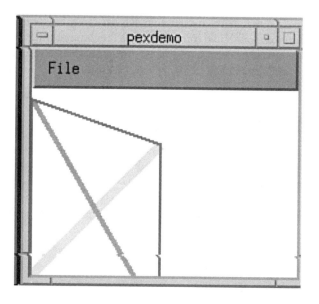

The example program in Listing 16.7 shows you the mechanics of combining PEXlib and Motif widgets. The program does not try to exploit the 3-D graphics capabilities of PEXlib. PEXlib is far too complex to describe fully in a short chapter such as this. For detailed information on 3-D programming with PEXlib, please consult a book such as the one by Tom Gaskins (*PEXlib Programming Manual*, O'Reilly & Associates, 1992).

To use PEXlib to display 3-D graphics in a Motif widget, you need to go through the following steps:

1. Check whether the X server on your workstation supports PEX. Use the utility program xdpyinfo or a program such as the one shown in Listing 16.6 to get a list of the extensions supported by the X server. If the list of extensions includes X3D-PEX, the X server supports PEX.

2. Include the necessary header files. To use PEXlib and to set up colormaps that PEXlib needs, you have to add the following #include directives:

```
#include <X11/PEX5/PEXlib.h>
#include <X11/Xutil.h>
#include <X11/Xatom.h>
#include <X11/Xmu/StdCmap.h>
```

Of these, the first header file is necessary for PEXlib, and the rest are for setting up the colors for PEX. You need these header files in addition to the standard header files for Motif.

3. Initialize the Xt Intrinsics the long way—rather than simply calling XtAppInitialize, call XtToolkitInitialize, XtCreateApplicationContext, XtOpenDisplay, and XtVaAppCreateShell, in that order. After opening the display, get a visual and set up a colormap for it. (See Chapter 11, "Using Color in X," for more information about visuals.) When creating the top-level application shell, explicitly set the visual, colormap, depth, background, and borderColor resources.

4. Initialize PEX by calling PEXInitialize. In Listing 16.7, the initPEX function performs the initialization.

5. Create the Motif widgets.

6. Initialize color information for PEX. This is a step required by PEXlib. The initPEXcolors function in Listing 16.7 illustrates how this is done. Much of the information needed to set up the color approximation information comes from a standard colormap, such as RGB_DEFAULT_MAP.

7. Call PEXCreateRenderer to create a PEX renderer for the window where PEX output should appear. The PEX renderer is used to draw the 3-D graphics in a window.

8. The actual drawing of 3-D graphics occurs in the expose callback function of the Motif widget where you want the output to appear. In Listing 16.7, the handle_expose function is responsible for displaying output in the DrawingArea widget's window. The handle_expose function, in turn, calls the renderPEX function (also in Listing 16.7) with the PEX renderer as an argument. The renderPEX function begins the rendering (another term for drawing) by calling PEXBeginRendering. Then renderPEX calls appropriate PEXlib functions to draw the output. You can call PEXlib functions that set attributes, such as PEXSetGlobalTransform, PEXSetLineWidth, and PEXSetLineColor, as well as actual drawing functions, such as PEXPolyline. PEX rendering ends with a call to PEXEndRendering. When you learn more about PEXlib, you can try out other 3-D primitives by embedding the appropriate PEXlib function calls in renderPEX.

**Listing 16.7. pexdemo.c—A Motif program
that displays 3-D graphics using PEXlib.**

```
/*------------------------------------------------------------*/
/* File: pexdemo.c
 *
 * A program that demonstrates how to use the 3-D graphics
 * capabilities of PEX in a Motif program.
 */
#include <X11/PEX5/PEXlib.h>
#include <X11/Xutil.h>
#include <stdio.h>

#include  <X11/Xatom.h>
#include  <X11/Xmu/StdCmap.h>

#include <Xm/Xm.h>
#include <Xm/RowColumn.h>
#include <Xm/MainW.h>
#include <Xm/DrawingA.h>

/* Some global variables */
XtAppContext  app;
PEXMatrix     pexmatrix;
int           sign = 1;
PEXCoord      from, to, up;

/* Function prototypes */
void handle_expose(/* Widget w, XtPointer client_data,
                   XmDrawingAreaCallbackStruct *call_data */);

void quit_action(/* Widget w, XtPointer client_data,
                 XmAnyCallbackStruct *call_data */);

int initPEX(/* Display* display, PEXExtensionInfo** pex_info */);
void initPEXcolors(/* Display* display, Window win,
                   XStandardColormap* stdcmap,
                   PEXRendererAttributes* attributes */);
void renderPEX(/* Display* display, Window window,
               PEXRenderer renderer */);
void rotate(/* Widget w */);

/* This function, defined in file "xmutil.c" prepares menus */
Widget MakeMenuPane(/* char *name, Widget parent, ... */);

/* This function, also in xmutil.c, attaches a menu to a
 * cascade button
 */
void AttachToCascade(/* Widget parent, char *label,
                     Widget sub_menu */);
/*------------------------------------------------------------*/
void main(argc, argv)
int  argc;
char **argv;
{
    Display          *display;
    int              screen;
    Visual*          visual;
```

```
    Colormap              colormap;
    unsigned long         bgpixel, bdpixel;
    XColor                hcolor, ecolor;
    int                   depth;
    XStandardColormap     stdcmap;
    PEXRenderer           renderer;
    PEXRendererAttributes PEXattributes;
    Widget                main_widget, main_window,
                          drawing_area, new_menu,
                          menu_bar;
    Arg                   args[20];
    Cardinal              argcount;
    PEXExtensionInfo      *PEXinfo;

/* Initialize the application the long way, starting with
 * a call to open the display connection.
 */
    XtToolkitInitialize();
    app = XtCreateApplicationContext();

    display = XtOpenDisplay(app, NULL, NULL, "Pexdemo",
                        (XrmOptionDescList) NULL, 0,
                        &argc, argv);
    if(display == NULL)
    {
        fprintf(stderr, "%s: can't open display!\n",
                argv[0]);
        exit(1);
    }

/* Initialize PEX. */
    if(initPEX(display, &PEXinfo) != True)
    {
        fprintf(stderr, "Error initializing PEX!\n");
        exit(2);
    }

/* Select an appropriate visual. Here, we use the default
 * visual.
 */
    screen = DefaultScreen(display);
    visual = DefaultVisual(display, screen);
    depth  = DefaultDepth(display, screen);

/* Get standard colormap for selected visual. */
    if(XmuLookupStandardColormap(display,
                screen, XVisualIDFromVisual(visual),
                depth, XA_RGB_DEFAULT_MAP,
                False, True) != 0)
    {
        int                i, number_colormaps;
        XStandardColormap* colormaps_returned;

        if(XGetRGBColormaps(display,
            RootWindow(display, screen),
            &colormaps_returned,
```

continues

Listing 16.7. continued

```
                &number_colormaps,
                XA_RGB_DEFAULT_MAP) != 0)
        {
            for (i = 0; i < number_colormaps; i++)
            {
                if (XVisualIDFromVisual(visual) ==
                    colormaps_returned[i].visualid)
                {
                    stdcmap = colormaps_returned[i];
                    colormap = stdcmap.colormap;
                    break;
                }
            }
            if(i >= number_colormaps)
            {
                printf("Error getting standard colormap!\n");
                exit(3);
            }
        }
    }
/* Now select the colors from the selected visual's colormap.
 * In this case, we are using the default visual, but
 * we show the steps anyway.
 */

/* Background color */
    if(XAllocNamedColor(display, colormap, "white",
                        &hcolor, &ecolor) != 0)
    {
        bgpixel = hcolor.pixel;
    } else
    {
/* Use white background in case of failure */
        bgpixel = WhitePixel(display, DefaultScreen(display));
    }

/* Border color */
    if(XAllocNamedColor(display, colormap, "black",
                        &hcolor, &ecolor) != 0)
    {
        bdpixel = hcolor.pixel;
    } else
    {
/* Use black border in case of failure */
        bdpixel = BlackPixel(display, DefaultScreen(display));
    }

/* Create the top-level shell. Remember to set the visual,
 * colormap, depth, background, and border colors,
 * especially if you use a nondefault visual.
 */
    main_widget = XtVaAppCreateShell(NULL, "Pexdemo",
                    applicationShellWidgetClass, display,
                    XmNallowResize,       True,
                    XmNwidth,             400,
                    XmNheight,            300,
```

```
                              XmNargc,              argc,
                              XmNargv,              argv,
                              XmNvisual,            visual,
                              XmNdepth,             depth,
                              XmNcolormap,          colormap,
                              XmNbackground,        bgpixel,
                              XmNborderColor,       bdpixel,
                              NULL);

/* Next, the main window widget */
    argcount = 0;
    main_window = XmCreateMainWindow(main_widget, "Main",
                              args, argcount);
    XtManageChild(main_window);

/* Create the menubar */
    menu_bar = XmCreateMenuBar(main_window, "Menubar", NULL, 0);
    XtManageChild(menu_bar);

/* Create the drawing area */
    argcount = 0;
    XtSetArg(args[argcount], XmNresizePolicy, XmRESIZE_ANY);
                                              argcount++;
    XtSetArg(args[argcount], XmNbackground,  bgpixel);
                                              argcount++;
    XtSetArg(args[argcount], XmNborderColor, bdpixel);
                                              argcount++;
    drawing_area = XmCreateDrawingArea(main_window,
                              "drawing_area", args, argcount);

/* Add callbacks to handle expose events for the drawing area */
    XtAddCallback(drawing_area, XmNexposeCallback, handle_expose,
                  (XtPointer)&renderer);

    XtManageChild(drawing_area);

/* Attach the menubar and the drawing area to main window */
    XmMainWindowSetAreas(main_window, menu_bar, NULL, NULL,
                         NULL, drawing_area);

/* Create the "File" menu ------------------------------------*/
    new_menu = MakeMenuPane("File", menu_bar,
                            "Quit", quit_action, NULL,
                            NULL);
/* Create the "File" cascade button and attach new_menu to it */
    AttachToCascade(menu_bar, "File", new_menu);


/* Realize the widgets */
    XtRealizeWidget(main_widget);

/* Set up the color approximations table */
    initPEXcolors(display, XtWindow(drawing_area),
                  &stdcmap, &PEXattributes);
```

continues

Listing 16.7. continued

```
/* Set up the PEX renderer. */
    renderer = PEXCreateRenderer(XtDisplay(main_widget),
                                 XtWindow(drawing_area),
                                 PEXRAColorApproxTable,
                                 &PEXattributes);
    if (renderer == 0)
    {
        printf("Error creating PEX renderer!\n");
        exit(4);
    }

/* Initialize the transformation matrix */
    from.x = 10.0;
    from.y = -10.0;
    from.z = 5.0;

    to.x = 0.0;
    to.y = 0.0;
    to.z = 0.0;

    up.x = 0.0;
    up.y = 0.0;
    up.z = 1.0;

    PEXLookAtViewMatrix(from, to, up, pexmatrix);

/* Set up a call to a routine that rotates the figure */
    XtAppAddTimeOut(app, 1000, rotate, drawing_area);

/* Start processing events */
    XtAppMainLoop(app);
}
/*-----------------------------------------------------------*/
/* h a n d l e _ e x p o s e
 *
 * Expose event handler for the drawing area
 */
void handle_expose(w, client_data, call_data)
Widget                          w;
XtPointer                       client_data;
XmDrawingAreaCallbackStruct *call_data;
{
    PEXRenderer  *renderer = (PEXRenderer *)client_data;
    XEvent       *p_event = call_data->event;

    switch(call_data->reason)
    {
        case XmCR_EXPOSE:
            if(p_event->xexpose.count == 0)
            {
/* Clear the window and "render" the PEX figures */
                XClearWindow(XtDisplay(w), XtWindow(w));
                renderPEX(XtDisplay(w), XtWindow(w), *renderer);
            }
            break;
    }
```

```
}
/*------------------------------------------------------------*/
void renderPEX(display, window, renderer)
Display     *display;
Window      window;
PEXRenderer renderer;
{
    PEXCoord coords[10];
    PEXColor pexcolor;

    PEXBeginRendering(display, window, renderer);

/* Set the transformation matrix */
    PEXSetGlobalTransform(display, renderer,
                          PEXOCRender, pexmatrix);

/* Draw lines along the edges of one face of a cube. Also
 * draw the diagonals. Start with the diagonal lines.
 */

/* Set line attributes for first diagonal */
    PEXSetLineWidth(display, renderer, PEXOCRender, 8.0);
/* Line color */
    pexcolor.rgb.red   = 1.0;   /* Floating-point values */
    pexcolor.rgb.green = 1.0;
    pexcolor.rgb.blue  = 0.0;
    PEXSetLineColor(display, renderer, PEXOCRender,
                    PEXColorTypeRGB, &pexcolor);
    coords[0].x = 0.0;
    coords[0].y = 0.0;
    coords[0].z = 0.0;

    coords[1].x = 1.0;
    coords[1].y = 0.0;
    coords[1].z = 1.0;

    PEXPolyline(display, renderer, PEXOCRender, 2, coords);

/* Next diagonal */
    PEXSetLineWidth(display, renderer, PEXOCRender, 4.0);
    pexcolor.rgb.red   = 1.0;
    pexcolor.rgb.green = 0.5;
    pexcolor.rgb.blue  = 0.5;
    PEXSetLineColor(display, renderer, PEXOCRender,
                    PEXColorTypeRGB, &pexcolor);

    coords[0].x = 0.0;
    coords[0].y = 0.0;
    coords[0].z = 1.0;

    coords[1].x = 1.0;
    coords[1].y = 0.0;
    coords[1].z = 0.0;

    PEXPolyline(display, renderer, PEXOCRender, 2, coords);
```

continues

Listing 16.7. continued

```
/* Rectangular border */
    PEXSetLineWidth(display, renderer, PEXOCRender, 2.0);
    pexcolor.rgb.red    = 0.5;
    pexcolor.rgb.green  = 0.5;
    pexcolor.rgb.blue   = 0.5;
    PEXSetLineColor(display, renderer, PEXOCRender,
                    PEXColorTypeRGB, &pexcolor);

    coords[0].x = 0.0;
    coords[0].y = 0.0;
    coords[0].z = 0.0;

    coords[1].x = 0.0;
    coords[1].y = 0.0;
    coords[1].z = 1.0;

    coords[2].x = 1.0;
    coords[2].y = 0.0;
    coords[2].z = 1.0;

    coords[3].x = 1.0;
    coords[3].y = 0.0;
    coords[3].z = 0.0;

    PEXPolyline(display, renderer, PEXOCRender, 4, coords);

    PEXEndRendering(display, renderer, True);
    XFlush(display);
}
/*------------------------------------------------------------*/
/* r o t a t e
 *
 * A time-out callback function that rotates the figures.
 */
void rotate(w)
Widget w;
{
/* Compute new transformation matrix */
    from.x += 2*sign;
    if(from.x >= 50.0) sign = -sign;
    if(from.x <= -5.0) sign = -sign;

    PEXLookAtViewMatrix(from, to, up, pexmatrix);

/* Invalidate the drawing area */
    XClearArea(XtDisplay(w), XtWindow(w), 0, 0, 0, 0, True);

/* Reinstall the timer */
    XtAppAddTimeOut(app, 200, rotate, w);
}
/*------------------------------------------------------------*/
/* q u i t _ a c t i o n
 *
 * This routine is called when the "Quit" item is selected from
 * the "File" menu.
 */
```

```
void quit_action(w, client_data, call_data)
Widget              w;
XtPointer           client_data;
XmAnyCallbackStruct *call_data;
{
    XtCloseDisplay(XtDisplay(w));
    exit(0);
}
/*------------------------------------------------------------*/
/* i n i t P E X
 *
 * Initialize PEX.
 */
int initPEX(display, PEXinfo)
Display*            display;
PEXExtensionInfo** PEXinfo;
{
    int    status;
    char   errmsg[PEXErrorStringLength+1];

    status = PEXInitialize(display, PEXinfo,
                           PEXErrorStringLength,
                           errmsg);
    if (status != 0) return False;

/* Check whether immediate mode is available */
    if(((((*PEXinfo)->subset_info & 0xFFFF) ==
        PEXCompleteImplementation) ||
        (*PEXinfo)->subset_info & PEXImmediateMode)
                                         return True;

/* Otherwise, return False to indicate failure */
    return False;
}
/*------------------------------------------------------------*/
/* i n i t P E X c o l o r s
 *
 * Set up color approximations table for PEX assuming that
 * we have a color visual.
 */
void initPEXcolors(display, win, stdcmap, attributes)
Display             *display;
Window              win;
XStandardColormap   *stdcmap;
PEXRendererAttributes *attributes;
{
    PEXColorApproxEntry acolor;

/* Set up the color approximations structure. The values
 * come from the standard colormap.
 */
    acolor.type       = PEXColorSpace;
    acolor.model      = PEXColorApproxRGB;
    acolor.dither     = PEXOn;
    acolor.base_pixel = stdcmap->base_pixel;
    acolor.max1       = stdcmap->red_max;
```

continues

Listing 16.7. continued

```
acolor.max2     = stdcmap->green_max;
acolor.max3     = stdcmap->blue_max;
acolor.mult1    = stdcmap->red_mult;
acolor.mult2    = stdcmap->green_mult;
acolor.mult3    = stdcmap->blue_mult;
acolor.weight1  = 0;
acolor.weight2  = 0;
acolor.weight3  = 0;

attributes->color_approx_table =
    PEXCreateLookupTable(display, win, PEXLUTColorApprox);

PEXSetTableEntries(display, attributes->color_approx_table,
                 0, 1, PEXLUTColorApprox, &acolor);
}
```

PEX supports two modes of graphics:

✦ *Stored structure mode.* In this mode, graphics primitives are stored in the server for later rendering.

✦ *Immediate mode.* In this mode, graphics primitives are sent to the PEX server one by one, and they are displayed immediately.

You can, of course, mix the two modes—store some complicated but relatively permanent graphics in the server and render simpler and more transient graphics in immediate mode. For simplicity, the pexdemo program of Listing 16.7 uses immediate mode only. The initPEX function shows how you can test for the availability of immediate mode capability in the PEX server.

Building *pexdemo*

To compile and link the pexdemo program (Listing 16.7), you have to link with the libPEX5.a library and the C math library (libm.a) in addition to the standard X and Motif libraries. Because pexdemo also relies on the the xmutil.c module (Listing 15.1), the following command should be adequate to build pexdemo on most UNIX systems:

```
cc -o pexdemo pexdemo.c xmutil.c pexdemo.c xmutil.c -lXm -lXt -lXmu -lX11 -lPEX5 -lm
```

Summary

Previous chapters cover the topics of using the X Window System and programming it via the functions in Xlib and the OSF/Motif toolkit. This closing chapter describes X's facilities for interclient communications and planned extensions to X.

Interclient communication refers to the exchange of data between X clients with the X server as an intermediary. Even if your application does not have to share any data with others, it has to deal with at least one other client, the window manager. The *Inter-Client Communication Conventions Manual (ICCCM)* specifies the proper way for clients to exchange data.

One way that X clients can share data is by placing it in a property on a specific window—the root window being a commonly used one. A property is identified by a name; the data in the property is simply a stream of bytes, interpreted according to their type. Both the name and type of a property are strings. Because strings can be many bytes in length, X uses atoms, which are fixed-length unique numbers that identify the strings. Applications call the Xlib function `XInternAtom` to register a string with the X server. All future references to the string are through its atom.

Applications can use properties to communicate with the window manager. For this communication to succeed, the applications and the window manager must follow the same conventions when interpreting the meaning of the properties. The ICCCM provides a minimal set of protocols for X clients to communicate with a window manager. Listing 16.1 is a sample program that illlustrates how to request and handle protocol messages such as the `WM_DELETE_WINDOW` message. The Motif window manager (`mwm`) sends that message when the user tries to quit an application by selecting the Quit option from the window menu.

Properties are also useful for exchanging data between applications. The cut buffers are properties on the root window that are often used to pass information from one application to another. In fact, the `xterm` terminal emulator uses the property named `XA_CUT_BUFFER0` for storing any selected text. An application can monitor changes in the property on a window by soliciting `PropertyNotify` events.

Selections are another way of sharing data. They are more efficient because data is not transferred until some application needs it. OSF/Motif provides another way of exchanging data by copying to and from a clipboard. Applications can also directly send events to each other to coordinate their actions.

Drag-and-drop is a relatively new user interface style that Motif supports. Several Motif widgets—`List`, `Label`, `PushButton`, `Text`, and `TextField`—have built-in support for drag-and-drop operations. Additionally, the Motif toolkit includes new widgets and routines that enable programmers to make any widget a drag source or a drop site. This chapter includes example programs that illustrate how to use the drag-and-drop capabilities of the Motif toolkit.

The chapter ends with a discussion of the extensibility of X and how your application can interrogate the server about any available extensions. A sample program illustrates how to use the 3-D graphics capabilities of PEX in a Motif program.

## Part Five

Appendixes

Xlib Functions

This appendix lists many commonly used Xlib functions in alphabetic order, showing the syntax, any return value, and a short description of how each function is used.

The syntax of each entry appears as a list of arguments followed by an actual function call. To conserve space, a number of common arguments are not listed. Instead, standard names are used for each so that you can infer the type directly from the name. For example, `display`, `gc`, and `w` are used for arguments of type `Display *`, `GC`, and `Window`, respectively. When in doubt, you can consult Table A.1 for the correspondence between a name and its type.

There is a reason for showing the function's syntax in the form of a sample call. Take for instance, the function XAllocColor. Its declaration in the form of an ANSI C function prototype is the following:

```
2Status XAllocColor(Display *display, Colormap cmap, XColor *color);
```

This does not tell you that you are supposed to declare the color structure yourself and pass its address to XAllocColor. An example call lists this as the following:

```
XColor  color;  /* Define the desired RGB values here */

if(XAllocColor(display, cmap, &color) == 0)
{
/* Allocation failed. Take corrective action. */
}
```

This clearly tells you that you have to declare the color structure, set the RGB fields, and pass its address in the call to the XAllocColor function.

Table A.1. Standard Names and Their Types

Name	Type	Description
cmap	Colormap	Colormap resource ID
cursor	Cursor	Cursor resource ID
depth	unsigned int	Depth of a pixmap or image
display	Display *	Identification of the X display
drawable	Drawable	A window or a pixmap
event_mask	unsigned int	Bits indicating events of interest
gc	GC	Graphics context
height	unsigned int	Height of windows and rectangles
time	Time	Time in milliseconds
value_mask	unsigned int	Indication of which entries of a structure are being changed
visual	Visual *	Pointer to a Visual structure
w	Window	Window resource ID
width	unsigned int	Width of windows and rectangles
x	int	x-coordinate
ximage	XImage *	Pointer to image structure in Xlib
y	int	y-coordinate

XActivateScreenSaver

Purpose:

Activates screen blanking.

Syntax:

```
XActivateScreenSaver(display);
```

See also:

XForceScreenSaver, XGetScreenSaver, XResetScreenSaver, XSetScreenSaver

XAddHost

Purpose:

Adds the specified host's network address to the access control list for the server.

Syntax:

```
XHostAddress *host;  /* Address of host to be added to list */
XAddHost(display, host);
```

See also:

XAddHosts, XDisableAccessControl, XEnableAccessControl, XListHosts, XRemoveHosts, XSetAccessControl

XAddHosts

Purpose:

Adds a number of hosts to the access control list of the server.

Syntax:

```
XHostAddress    *hosts;     /* Array of host addresses */
int             num_hosts;  /* Number of hosts in list */

XAddHosts(display, hosts, num_hosts);
```

See also:

XAddHost, XDisableAccessControl, XEnableAccessControl, XListHosts, XRemoveHosts, XSetAccessControl

XAddPixel

Purpose:

Adds a constant value to every pixel in an image.

Syntax:

```
unsigned long    value;   /* Constant to be added to each pixel */

int XAddPixel(ximage, value);
```

See also:

ImageByteOrder, XCreateImage, XDestroyImage, XGetImage, XGetPixel, XGetSubImage, XPutImage, XPutPixel, XSubImage

---

XAddToSaveSet

Purpose:

Adds a window w to the save set, which is a collection of windows that are reparented to the closest ancestor if the immediate parent is destroyed.

Syntax:

```
XAddToSaveSet(display, w);
```

See also:

XChangeSaveSet, XRemoveFromSaveSet

XAllocClassHint

Purpose:

Allocates an XClassHint structure; must be freed with XFree when no longer needed.

Syntax:

```
XClassHint  *cl_hint;

cl_hint = XAllocClassHint();
```

Returns:

A pointer to a newly allocated XClassHint structure or NULL if not enough memory is available.

See also:

XFree, XGetClassHint, XSetClassHint, XSetWMProperties

XAllocColor

Purpose:

Allocates a read-only colormap cell containing the closest RGB color supported by the hardware (see Chapter 11).

Syntax:

```
XColor  color;  /* Define the desired RGB values here */
                /* On return, it has the pixel value  */
```

```
if(XAllocColor(display, cmap, &color) == 0)
{
/* Allocation failed. Take corrective action. */
}
```

Returns:

Zero if the allocation fails.

See also:

XAllocColorCells, XAllocColorPlanes, XAllocNamedColor, XFreeColors, XLookupColor,
XParseColor, XQueryColor, XQueryColors, XStoreColor, XStoreColors, XStoreNamedColor

---

XAllocColorCells

Purpose:

Allocates private read-write cells from a specified colormap.

Syntax:

```
Bool          contig;        /* True = need contiguous planes */
unsigned long plane_masks[]; /* Plane masks returned here      */
unsigned int  nplanes;       /* Number of plane masks in array*/
unsigned long pixels[];      /* Pixel values returned here     */
unsigned int  ncolors;       /* Number of pixel values         */

if(XAllocColorCells(display, cmap, config, plane_masks,
                    nplanes, pixels, ncolors) == 0)
{
/* Allocation failed. Take appropriate action */
}
```

Returns:

Zero on failure.

See also:

XAllocColor, XAllocColorPlanes, XAllocNamedColor, XFreeColors, XLookupColor,
XParseColor, XQueryColor, XQueryColors, XStoreColor, XStoreColors, XStoreNamedColor

---

XAllocColorPlanes

Purpose:

Allocates private read-write color planes.

Syntax:

```
Bool          contig;        /* True = need contiguous planes*/
unsigned long pixels[];      /* Pixel values returned here     */
int           ncolors;       /* Number of colors in array      */
int           nreds, ngreens, nblues; /* Number of levels for */
                                      /* each of R, G, and B   */
unsigned long rmask, gmask, bmask;    /* R, G, B masks         */
```

```
if(XAllocColorPlanes(display, cmap, contig, pixels, ncolors,
       nreds, ngreens, nblues, &rmask, &gmask, &bmask) == 0)
{
/* Allocation failed. */
}
```

Returns:

Zero when allocation fails.

See also:

XAllocColor, XAllocColorCells, XAllocNamedColor, XFreeColors, XLookupColor,
XParseColor, XQueryColor, XQueryColors, XStoreColor, XStoreColors, XStoreNamedColor

---

XAllocIconSize

Purpose:

Allocates an XIconSize structure for use with XGetIconSizes or XSetIconSizes.

Syntax:

```
XIconSize *icon_size;

if((icon_size = XAllocIconSize()) == NULL)
{
/* Allocation failed */
}
```

Returns:

NULL when allocation fails due to lack of memory.

See also:

XGetIconSizes, XSetIconSizes

XAllocNamedColor

Purpose:

Allocates a shared read-only colormap cell for a color of specified name.

Syntax:

```
char    *colorname;    /* Name of color to be allocated    */
XColor  closest_color; /* Closest RGB in hardware returned  */
XColor  exact_color;   /* Exact RGB for color returned here */

if(XAllocNamedColor(display, cmap, colorname, closes_color,
                        exact_color) == 0)
{
/* Allocation failed */
}
```

Returns:

Zero to indicate failure.

See also:

XAllocColor, XAllocColorCells, XAllocColorPlanes, XFreeColors, XLookupColor,
XParseColor, XQueryColor, XQueryColors, XStoreColor, XStoreColors, XStoreNamedColor

XAllocSizeHints

Purpose:

Allocates an XSizeHints structure for use with XSetWMNormalHints or XGetWMNormalHints.

Syntax:

```
XSizeHints  *size_hints;

if((size_hints = XAllocSizeHints()) == NULL)
{
/* Not enough memory to allocate structure */
}
```

Returns:

If successful, pointer to a newly allocated XSizeHints structure. Otherwise, NULL to indicate
failure.

See also:

XFree, XGetWMNormalHints, XSetWMNormalHints

XAllocStandardColormap

Purpose:

Allocates an XStandardColormap structure.

Syntax:

```
XStandardColormap *xs_cmap;

if((xs_cmap = XAllocStandardColormap()) == NULL)
{
/* Not enough memory */
}
```

Returns:

Pointer to allocated structure or NULL, if allocation fails due to lack of memory.

See also:

XGetRGBColormap, XSetRGBColormap

XAllocWMHints

Purpose:

Allocates an XWMHints structure.

Syntax:

```
XWMHints *p_xwmhint;

if((p_xwmhint = XAllocWMHints()) == NULL)
{
/* Allocation failed */
}
```

Returns:

Pointer to allocated structure or NULL to indicate failure.

See also:

XGetWMHints, XSetWMHints

XAllowEvents

Purpose:

Allows keyboard or mouse events to be delivered after these devices are *frozen* by a grab.

Syntax:

```
int event_mode;   /* Indicates which events are delivered */
                  /* and how                             */

XAllowEvents(display, event_mode, time);
```

See also:

XGrabButton, XGrabKey, XGrabKeyboard, XGrabPointer

XAutoRepeatOff

Purpose:

Turns off the *auto-repeat* feature of the keyboard.

Syntax:

```
XAutoRepeatOff(display);
```

See also:

XAutoRepeatOn

XAutoRepeatOn

Purpose:

Turns on the *auto-repeat* feature of the keyboard.

Syntax:

```
XAutoRepeatOff(display);
```

See also:

```
XAutoRepeatOff
```

XBaseFontNameListOfFontSet

Purpose:

Returns a null-terminated string containing the comma-separated list of font names that were used to create the specified font set.

Syntax:

```
XFontSet font_set;  /* Font set whose base font list is sought */
char *font_list;

font_list = XBaseFontNameListOfFontSet(font_set);
```

Returns:

A null-terminated string with the font names. To free the memory allocated for the string, call `XFreeFontSet`.

See also:

```
XCreateFontSet, XFreeFontSet
```

XBell

Purpose:

Rings the bell.

Syntax:

```
int  percent; /* Volume of bell: -100 = off, 0 = normal, */
            /*                     100 = loudest      */
XBell(display, percent);
```

See also:

```
XChangeKeyboardControl, XGetKeyboardControl
```

XChangeActivePointerGrab

Purpose:

Changes the parameters of active grabs initiated by XGrabPointer or XGrabButton calls.

Syntax:

XChangeActivePointerGrab(display, event_mask, cursor, time);

See also:

XGrabButton, XGrabPointer

XChangeGC

Purpose:

Changes the members of a graphics context (GC).

Syntax:

XGCValues xgcv;   /* Structure with new values for GC */

XChangeGC(display, gc, value_mask, &xgcv);

See also:

XCopyGC, XCreateGC, XFreeGC, XGetGCValues

XChangeKeyboardControl

Purpose:

Changes parameters of the keyboard, such as the volume of key clicks and the bell.

Syntax:

XKeyboardControl kbval; /* Values of parameters being changed */

XChangeKeyboardControl(display, value_mask, &kbval);

See also:

XAutoRepeatOff, XAutoRepeatOn, XBell

XChangeKeyboardMapping

Purpose:

Changes the keyboard mapping—the correspondence between keycodes and keysyms (see Appendix E). Generates a MappingNotify event.

Syntax:

```
int    first_keycode;       /* First keycode to be changed    */
int    keysyms_per_keycode; /* No. of keysyms for each keycode */
KeySym keysyms[];           /* Array of keysyms               */
int    num_keycodes;        /* Number of keycodes being changed*/

XChangeKeyboardMapping(display, first_code, keysyms_per_code,
     keysyms, num_codes);
```

See also:

```
XGetKeyboardMapping, XRefreshKeyboardMapping
```

XChangePointerControl

Purpose:

Changes parameters such as acceleration and the acceleration threshold of the mouse pointer.

Syntax:

```
Bool do_accel,          /* True = Set acceleration        */
     do_threshold;      /* True = Set threshold           */
int  accel_numerator,   /* Acceleration is: numerator over */
     accel_denominator; /* denominator (should be > 0)    */
int  threshold;         /* Acceleration threshold (pixels) */

XChangePointerControl(display, do_accel, do_threshold,
    accel_numerator, accel_denominator, threshold);
```

See also:

```
XGetPointerControl
```

XChangeProperty

Purpose:

Changes the data stored in a property associated with a window. Generates PropertyNotify events.

Syntax:

```
Atom          property, /* Identifies property being changed  */
              type;     /* Type of data in the property       */
int           format;   /* Are they 8-, 16-, or 32-bit values */
int           mode;     /* PropModeAppend, PropModeReplace,    */
                        /* or PropModeReplace                  */
unsigned char *data;    /* Pointer to the data for property    */
int           nelements; /* Number of data elements in "data"  */

XChangeProperty(display, w, property, type, format, mode,
              data, nelements);
```

See also:

```
XDeleteProperty, XGetWindowProperty
```

XChangeSaveSet

Purpose:

Adds or removes a window from a save set.

Syntax:

```
int change_mode; /* SetModeInsert to add or SetModeDelete */
                 /* to remove a window from the save set  */

XChangeSaveSet(display, w, change_mode);
```

See also:

```
XAddToSaveSet, XRemoveFromSaveSet
```

XChangeWindowAttributes

Purpose:

Changes one or more attributes of a window.

Syntax:

```
XSetWindowAttributes xswa; /* Structure with new values */

XChangeWindowAttributes(display, w, value_mask, attributes);
```

See also:

```
XGetWindowAttributes
```

XCheckIfEvent

Purpose:

Checks the event queue for a matching event without blocking.

Syntax:

```
XEvent  event;        /* Event information returned here     */
Bool    (*call_me)(); /* Pointer to function called to       */
                      /* determine if the next event in the  */
                      /* queue meets your selection criteria */
char    *args;        /* Pointer to argument for function    */

if(XCheckIfEvent(display, &event, call_me, args))
{
/* Matching event found */
...
}
```

Returns:

True if the next event in the queue meets the criteria being tested by the function passed as the call_me argument.

See also:

XIfEvent, XPeekIfEvent, XNextEvent

XCheckMaskEvent

Purpose:

Gets the next event in the queue that matches the specified mask. Returns immediately if nothing matches.

Syntax:

```
XEvent  event;  /* Room for event's returned data */

Bool XCheckMaskEvent(display, event_mask, &event);
```

Returns:

True if an event matching event_mask is found in the queue.

See also:

XCheckTypedEvent, XMaskEvent, XNextEvent

XCheckTypedEvent

Purpose:

Removes the next event in the queue that matches the specified type. Returns immediately if no matching event found.

Syntax:

```
int     event_type; /* Type of event: ButtonPress, for example */
XEvent  event;      /* Room for returned event's information   */

if(XCheckTypedEvent(display, event_type, &event))
{
/* Event of specified type found */
}
```

Returns:

True if event of specified type found.

See also:

XCheckMaskEvent, XCheckTypedWindowEvent, XNextEvent

XCheckTypedWindowEvent

Purpose:

Returns the next event in the queue that matches the event type and window. Returns immediately if no matching event found.

Syntax:

```
int     event_type;
XEvent  event;

if(XCheckTypedWindowEvent(display, w, event_type, &event))
{
/* Event of matching window and type found */
}
```

Returns:

True if an event matching the specified window and type is found.

See also:

```
XCheckTypedEvent, XCheckWindowEvent, XNextEvent, XWindowEvent
```

XCheckWindowEvent

Purpose:

Returns the next event matching an event mask and a window. Returns immediately if no matching event found.

Syntax:

```
XEvent event; /* Room for returned event */

if(XCheckWindowEvent(display, w, event_mask, &event))
{
/* Matching event found */
}
```

Returns:

True if a matching event is found.

See also:

```
XCheckTypedWindowEvent, XNextEvent, XWindowEvent
```

XCirculateSubwindows

Purpose:

Rotates the position of subwindows in the stacking order.

Syntax:

```
int direction; /* One of: RaiseLowest  or LowerHighest */

XCirculateSubwindows(display, w, direction);
```

See also:

```
XCirculateSubwindowsDown, XCirculateSubwindowsUp, XRestackWindows
```

XCirculateSubwindowsDown

Purpose:

Moves the top subwindow to the bottom in the stacking order.

Syntax:

```
XCirculateSubwindowsDown(display, w);
```

See also:

```
XCirculateSubwindows, XCirculateSubwindowsUp
```

XCirculateSubwindowsUp

Purpose:

Moves the bottom subwindow to the top in the stacking order.

Syntax:

```
XCirculateSubwindowsUp(display, w)
```

See also:

```
XCirculateSubwindows, XCirculateSubwindowsDown
```

XClearArea

Purpose:

Clears a rectangular area (or entire window, if x, y, width, and height are all zero). Generates Expose events, if requested.

Syntax:

```
Bool exposures; /* True - generates expose event */

XClearArea(display, w, x, y, width, height, exposures);
```

See also:

```
XClearWindow, XFillRectangle
```

XClearWindow

Purpose:

Clears a window without generating any exposure event.

Syntax:

```
XClearWindow(display, w);
```

See also:

XClearArea, XFillRectangle

XClipBox

Purpose:

Computes the smallest rectangle enclosing a region.

Syntax:

```
Region     r;    /* Region whose enclosure is computed */
XRectangle rect; /* On return, rectangle enclosing r   */

XClipBox(r, &rect);
```

See also:

XCreateRegion, XDestroyRegion

XCloseDisplay

Purpose:

Closes the connection between the X application and the X server.

Syntax:

```
XCloseDisplay(display);
```

See also:

XOpenDisplay

XConfigureWindow

Purpose:

Changes window position, size, border width, or stacking order.

Syntax:

```
XWindowChanges xwcv; /* Structure with new values */

XConfigureWindow(display, w, value_mask, &xwcv);
```

See also:

XMoveWindow, XResizeWindow, XRestackWindows

XContextDependentDrawing

Purpose:

Indicates whether drawing functions include implicit text directionality or text drawn with the font set might include context-dependent drawing.

Syntax:

```
XFontSet font_set;

if(XContextDependentDrawing(font_set))
{
/* Yes, text drawing might be context-dependent */
}
```

Returns:

True if drawing functions include implicit text directionality or text drawn with the font set might include context-dependent drawing; False otherwise.

See also:

```
XContextualDrawing, XCreateFontSet, XDirectionalDependentDrawing, XFreeFontSet,
XLocaleOfFontSet
```

XContextualDrawing

Purpose:

Indicates whether text drawn with the font set might include context-dependent drawing.

Syntax:

```
XFontSet font_set;

if(XContextualDrawing(font_set))
{
/* Yes, text drawing might be context-dependent */
}
```

Returns:

True if text drawn with the font set might include context-dependent drawing; False otherwise.

See also:

```
XContextDependentDrawing, XCreateFontSet, XDirectionalDependentDrawing,
XFreeFontSet, XLocaleOfFontSet
```

XConvertCase

Purpose:

Converts a specified KeySym to its lowercase and uppercase forms.

Syntax:

```
KeySym keysym;     /* KeySym to convert          */
KeySym lowercase; /* Lowercase form returned here */
KeySym uppercase; /* Uppercase form returned here */

XConvertCase(keysym, &lowercase, &uppercase);
```

See also:

XLookupKeysym

XConvertSelection

Purpose:

Causes a `SelectionRequest` event to be sent to the current owner of the specified selection.

Syntax:

```
Atom    selection, /* Selection (usually XA_PRIMARY)  */
        target,    /* Target data type               */
        property;  /* Property where data returned    */
Window requestor;  /* Window on which property placed */

XConvertSelection(display, selection, target, property,
                requestor, time);
```

See also:

XGetSelectionOwner, XSetSelectionOwner

XCopyArea

Purpose:

Copies an area of a drawable from a source rectangle to a destination location.

Syntax:

```
Drawable      src, dest;     /* From and To drawables     */
int           src_x, src_y;  /* Source rectangle's origin */
unsigned int  width, height; /* Size of both rectangles   */
int           dest_x, dest_y; /* Destination point        */

XCopyArea(display, src, dest, gc, src_x, src_y, width,
        height, dest_x, dest_y);
```

See also:

XChangeGC, XCopyPlane

XCopyColormapAndFree

Purpose:

Copies a colormap and returns a new colormap ID.

Syntax:

```
Colormap old_cmap,  /* Colormap to copy       */
        new_cmap;  /* Newly created colormap ID */

new_cmap = XCopyColormapAndFree(display, old_cmap);
```

Returns:

Resource ID of newly created colormap.

See also:

XCreateColormap, XFreeColormap, XSetWindowColormap

XCopyGC

Purpose:

Copies selected fields of the source GC into the destination.

Syntax:

```
GC  src, dest; /* Source and destination GCs */

XCopyGC(display, src, value_mask, dest);
```

See also:

XCreateGC, XChangeGC, XFreeGC, XGetGCValues

XCopyPlane

Purpose:

Copies a rectangle from a single plane of a source drawable to a destination.

Syntax:

```
Drawable     src, dest;      /* FROM and TO drawables     */
int          src_x, src_y;   /* Origin of source rectangle */
unsigned int width, height;  /* Size of both rectangles    */
int          dest_x, dest_y; /* Destination point          */
unsigned long plane;         /* Source bit-plane to copy   */

XCopyPlane(display, src, dest, gc, src_x, src_y, width,
           height, dest_x, dest_y, plane);
```

See also:

XCopyArea

XCreateBitmapFromData

Purpose:

Creates a bitmap from data, bitmap data stored in X11's bitmap format (see Chapter 12).

Syntax:

```
char    *data; /* Bitmap data in X11 bitmap format    */
Pixmap  bmap;  /* Resource ID of bitmap being created */

bmap = XCreateBitmapFromData(display, drawable, data, width,
                             height);
```

Returns:

Bitmap ID if successful; zero if server could not create bitmap.

See also:

XCreatePixmap, XFreePixmap, XReadBitmapFile, XWriteBitmapFile

XCreateColormap

Purpose:

Creates a colormap for the specified visual type (see Chapter 11).

Syntax:

```
int       alloc;    /* Cells to allocate: AllocNone = none */
                    /* or AllocAll = allocate all cells    */
Colormap  new_cmap; /* To hold ID of new colormap          */

new_cmap = XCreateColormap(display, w, visual, alloc);
```

Returns:

Resource ID of new colormap.

See also:

XCopyColormapAndFree, XFreeColormap, XSetWindowColormap

XCreateFontCursor

Purpose:

Creates a cursor from a glyph in the standard cursor font.

Syntax:

```
#include <X11/cursorfont.h>
unsigned int shape;  /* Cursor shape (use constants from   */
                     /* cursorfont.h). Also see Appendix F */

cursor = XCreateFontCursor(display, shape);
```

Returns:

Resource ID of the cursor.

See also:

XCreateGlyphCursor, XCreatePixmapCursor, XDefineCursor, XFreeCursor, XRecolorCursor, XUndefineCursor

XCreateFontSet

Purpose:

Creates a font set for the current locale, using the specified comma-separated list of font names. Provides information on the *charsets* (character sets with associated encodings) for which there are no fonts.

Syntax:

```
XFontSet font_set;
char *base_font_list = "-misc-fixed-medium-r-normal-*";
char **missing_charsets;
int  num_missing;
char *default_string

if((font_set = XCreateFontSet(display, base_font_list,
                  &missing_charsets, &num_missing,
                  &default_string) == NULL)
{
/* Failed to create font set. Handle error here. */
}
```

Returns:

A valid XFontSet if successful; NULL otherwise.

See also:

XFreeFontSet, XFontsOfFontSet

XCreateGC

Purpose:

Creates a new graphics context for a screen, with the depth of the specified drawable (see Chapter 9).

Syntax:

```
XGCValues xgcv; /* Specify values for the new GC */

gc = XCreateGC(display, drawable, value_mask, &xgcv);
```

Returns:

Resource ID of a newly created GC.

See also:

XChangeGC, XCopyGC, XFreeGC, XGetGCValues

XCreateGlyphCursor

Purpose:

Creates a new cursor from specified source and mask glyphs from two fonts.

Syntax:

```
Font            source_font,      /* Font from which cursor    */
                                  /* shape will come           */
                mask_font;        /* Font from which mask char */
                                  /* comes. 0, if not used     */
unsigned int    source_char,      /* Cursor is this character  */
                mask_char;        /* Mask character (optional) */
XColor          foreground_color; /* RGB values for foreground */
XColor          background_color; /* RGB values for background */

cursor = XCreateGlyphCursor(display, source_font, mask_font,
              source_char, mask_char, &foreground_color,
              &background_color);
```

Returns:

Resource ID of cursor.

See also:

XCreateFontCursor, XCreatePixmapCursor, XDefineCursor, XFreeCursor, XRecolorCursor,
XUndefineCursor

XCreateImage

Purpose:

Allocates memory for XImage structure, used for manipulating images locally in the client (see
Chapter 12).

Syntax:

```
int  format;        /* Format of image: XYPixmap or ZPixmap */
int  offset;        /* Skip these many pixels at beginning  */
                    /* of each scanline                     */
char *data;         /* Actual image data (you have to       */
                    /* allocate this memory yourself        */
int  bitmap_pad,    /* Rows are multiples of these many     */
                    /* bits. Specify 8, 16, or 32           */
     bytes_per_line; /* Number of bytes per row of the image */

ximage = XCreateImage(display, visual, depth, format, offset,
          data, width, height, bitmap_pad, bytes_per_line);
```

Returns:

Pointer to XImage structure.

See also:

XDestroyImage, XGetImage, XInitImage, XPutImage, XSubImage

XCreatePixmap

Purpose:

Creates a pixmap of specified dimensions, with the depth of the `drawable`. Initial contents of pixmap are unspecified. You can draw into a pixmap as you do into a window.

Syntax:

```
Pixmap pmap;   /* ID of newly created pixmap */
pmap = XCreatePixmap(display, drawable, width, height,depth);
```

Returns:

Resource ID of pixmap.

See also:

```
XCreatePixmapFromBitmapData, XFreePixmap
```

XCreatePixmapCursor

Purpose:

Creates a cursor from two bitmaps (pixmaps of depth 1).

Syntax:

```
Pixmap         source, mask;      /* Source and mask bitmaps */
Xcolor         foreground_color,  /* RGB value of foreground */
               background_color;  /* RGB value of background */
unsigned int   x_hot, y_hot;      /* Hotspot of cursor       */

cursor = XCreatePixmapCursor(display, source, mask,
           &foreground_color, &background_color, x_hot, y_hot);
```

Returns:

Resource ID of cursor.

See also:

```
XCreateBitmapFromData, XCreateFontCursor, XCreateGlyphCursor, XDefineCursor,
XFreeCursor, XRecolorCursor, XUndefineCursor
```

XCreatePixmapFromBitmapData

Purpose:

Creates a pixmap of specified dimensions and depth from bitmap data.

Syntax:

```
char           *data;  /* Bitmap data in X11 bitmap format       */
unsigned long fg, bg;  /* Pixel values for fore- and background */
Pixmap         pmap;   /* ID of new pixmap                       */
```

```
pmap = XCreatePixmapFromBitmapData(display, drawable, data,
                            width, height, fg, bg, depth);
```

Returns:

Resource ID of pixmap.

See also:

XCreateBitmapFromData, XCreatePixmap, XFreePixmap

XCreateRegion

Purpose:

Creates an empty region (see Chapter 9).

Syntax:

```
Region r1;   /* New region */

r1 = XCreateRegion();
```

Returns:

New Region value (a pointer to a hidden data structure).

See also:

XDestroyRegion, XPolygonRegion

XCreateSimpleWindow

Purpose:

Creates an unmapped InputOutput window with visual and depth inherited from its parent. Uses XMapWindow to make the window visible.

Syntax:

```
Window       parent;     /* Parent window's ID        */
unsigned int border_width;/* Border width in pixels    */
unsigned long border,     /* Pixel value for border    */
             background;  /* Pixel value for background */
Window       new_win;    /* ID of new window           */

new_win = XCreateSimpleWindow(display, parent, x, y, width,
                height, border_width, border, background);
```

Returns:

Resource ID of the newly created window.

See also:

XCreateWindow, XDestroyWindow, XMapWindow

XCreateWindow

Purpose:

Creates a new window with a specified set of attributes.

Syntax:

```
Window              parent;      /* ID of parent window    */
unsigned int        border_width;/* Border width in pixels */
unsigned int        class;       /* InputOnly, InputOutput, */
                                 /* or CopyFromParent       */
XSetWindowAttributes xswa;       /* Attribute values       */
Window              new_win;     /* ID of new window       */

new_win = XCreateWindow(display, parent, x, y, width, height,
      border_width, depth, class, visual, value_mask, &xswa);
```

Returns:

Resource ID of newly created window.

See also:

```
XCreateSimpleWindow, XDestroyWindow, XMapWindow
```

XDefineCursor

Purpose:

Assigns a cursor to a window.

Syntax:

```
XDefineCursor(display, w, cursor);
```

See also:

```
XCreateFontCursor, XCreateGlyphCursor, XCreatePixmapCursor, XFreeCursor,
XRecolorCursor, XUndefineCursor
```

XDeleteContext

Purpose:

Deletes data of a context type belonging to a window (see Chapter 7 for an example use of contexts).

Syntax:

```
XContext context; /* Context to which data belongs */

if(XDeleteContext(display, w, context) == 0)
{
/* Success */
}
```

Returns:

Zero to indicate success; XCNOENT if specified context is not found.

See also:

XFindContext, XSaveContext, XUniqueContext

XDeleteModifiermapEntry

Purpose:

Deletes an entry from the specified XModifierKeymap structure (obtained by calling XGetModifierMapping).

Syntax:

```
XModifierKeymap *modmap;      /* Modifier map whose entry is   */
                             /* deleted.                      */
KeyCode          keysym_entry;/* Keycode of entry being deleted */
int              modifier;    /* Modifier being deleted        */
XModifierKeymap *new_modmap; /* Modifier map with the entry    */

new_modmap = XDeleteModifiermapEntry(modmap, keysym_entry,
                               modifier);
```

Returns:

Pointer to XModifierKeymap structure suitable for calling XSetModifierMapping.

See also:

XFreeModifiermap, XGetModifierMapping, XSetModifierMapping

XDeleteProperty

Purpose:

Deletes a property from a window (see Chapter 16).

Syntax:

```
Atom property; /* Identifies property being deleted */

XDeleteProperty(display, w, property);
```

See also:

XChangeProperty, XGetWindowProperty

XDestroyImage

Purpose:

Deallocates the specified XImage structure as well as the actual image data in that structure.

Syntax:

```
XDestroyImage(ximage);
```

See also:

```
XCreateImage, XGetImage, XPutImage, XSubImage
```

XDestroyRegion

Purpose:

Frees the memory allocated for a region (see Chapter 9).

Syntax:

```
Region r;   /* Region being destroyed */

XDestroyRegion(r);
```

See also:

```
XCreateRegion, XPolygonRegion
```

XDestroySubwindows

Purpose:

Destroys all subwindows of a window.

Syntax:

```
XDestroySubwindows(display, w);
```

See also:

```
XCreateSimpleWindow, XCreateWindow, XDestroyWindow
```

XDestroyWindow

Purpose:

Destroys the specified window and its subwindows. Does not destroy the root window.

Syntax:

```
XDestroyWindow(display, w);
```

See also:

```
XCreateSimpleWindow, XCreateWindow, XDestroySubWindow
```

XDirectionalDependentDrawing

Purpose:

Indicates whether text drawing functions implement implicit text directionality.

Syntax:

```
XFontSet font_set;

if(XDirectionalDependentDrawing(font_set))
{
/* Yes, drawing functions implement text directionality */
}
```

Returns:

True if text drawing functions implement implicit text directionality; False otherwise.

See also:

XContextualDrawing, XCreateFontSet, XFreeFontSet, XLocaleOfFontSet

XDisableAccessControl

Purpose:

Instructs the X server to allow connections from any host on the network.

Syntax:

```
XDisableAccessControl(display);
```

See also:

XAddHost, XAddHosts, XEnableAccessControl, XRemoveHost, XRemoveHosts, XSetAccessControl

XDisplayKeycodes

Purpose:

Gets a range of keycodes supported by the specified display.

Syntax:

```
int min_keycode, /* Minimum keycode returned here */
    max_keycode; /* Maximum keycode returned here */

XDisplayKeycodes(display, &min_keycode, &max_keycode);
```

See also:

XKeycodeToKeysym, XKeysymToKeycode

XDisplayMotionBufferSize

Purpose:

Returns the size of the motion buffer.

Syntax:

```
unsigned long size; /* Number of motion events remembered */

size = XDisplayMotionBufferSize(display);
```

Returns:

The number of motion events that the server saves.

See also:

```
XGetMotionEvents
```

XDisplayName

Purpose:

Obtains the name of the display.

Syntax:

```
char *string; /* If this is NULL, return the name from the */
              /* DISPLAY environment variable             */

printf("Attempting connection to: %s\n", XDisplayName(NULL));
```

Returns:

Name of display.

See also:

```
XOpenDisplay
```

XDrawArc

Purpose:

Draws an arc inside a bounding rectangle (see Chapter 9).

Syntax:

```
int angle1, angle2; /* Start and end of arc in */
                    /* 64ths of a degree       */

XDrawArc(display, drawable, gc, x, y, width, height,
        angle1, angle2);
```

See also:

XDrawArcs, XFillArc, XFillArcs

XDrawArcs

Purpose:

Draws a number of arcs.

Syntax:

```
XArc  arcs[]; /* List of arcs   */
int   narcs; /* Number of arcs */

XDrawArcs(display, drawable, gc, arcs, narcs);
```

See also:

XDrawArc, XFillArc, XFillArcs

XDrawImageString

Purpose:

Draws characters filling both foreground and background pixels in each glyph.

Syntax:

```
char string[]; /* The string to be drawn        */
int  length;   /* Number of characters in "string" */

XDrawImageString(display, drawable, gc, x, y, string, length);
```

See also:

XDrawString, XDrawText, XSetFont

XDrawImageString16

Purpose:

Draws 16-bit text characters filling both foreground and background of each glyph.

Syntax:

```
XChar2b string[]; /* Array of 16-bit characters     */
int     length;   /* Number of characters in string */

XDrawImageString16(display, drawable, gc, x, y, string, length);
```

See also:

XDrawString16, XDrawText16, XSetFont

XDrawLine

Purpose:

Draws a line between two points, using attributes from the specified `GC` (see Chapter 9).

Syntax:

```
int  x1, y1,  /* Coordinates of starting point */
     x2, y2;  /* Coordinates of endpoint       */

XDrawLine(display, gc, x1, y1, x2, y2);
```

See also:

XDrawLines, XDrawSegments, XSetLineAttributes

XDrawLines

Purpose:

Draws a number of lines using a single request to the server (see Chapter 9).

Syntax:

```
XPoint points[]; /* Array of points to be joined by line */
int    npoints,  /* Number of points in array            */
       mode;     /* CoordModeOrigin or CoordModePrevious */

XDrawLines(display, drawable, gc, points, npoints, mode);
```

See also:

XDrawLine, XDrawSegments, XSetLineAttributes

XDrawPoint

Purpose:

Draws a point.

Syntax:

```
int x, y; /* Coordinates of point being drawn */

XDrawPoint(display, drawable, gc, x, y);
```

See also:

XDrawPoints, XSetForeground

XDrawPoints

Purpose:

Draws a number of points with a single X protocol request.

Syntax:

```
XPoint points[]; /* Array of points to be drawn        */
int    npoints, /* Number of points in array           */
       mode;    /* CoordModeOrigin or CoordModePrevious */

XDrawPoints(display, drawable, gc, points, npoints, mode);
```

See also:

```
XDrawPoint, XSetForeground
```

XDrawRectangle

Purpose:

Draws the outline of a rectangle specified by (x,y) and the dimensions (width, height).

Syntax:

```
XDrawRectangle(display, drawable, gc, x, y, width, heigth);
```

See also:

```
XDrawRectangles, XFillRectangle, XFillRectangle
```

XDrawRectangles

Purpose:

Draws the outline of a number of rectangles (see Chapter 9).

Syntax:

```
XRectangle rectangles[]; /* Array of rectangles  */
int        nrectangles;  /* Number of rectangles */

XDrawRectangles(display, drawable, gc, rectangles, nrectangles);
```

See also:

```
XDrawRectangle, XFillRectangle, XFillRectangle
```

XDrawSegments

Purpose:

Draws multiple, disjoint lines (see Chapter 9).

Syntax:

```
XSegment segments[]; /* Array of line segments */
int      nsegments;  /* Number of segments     */

XDrawSegments(display, drawable, gc, segments, nsegments);
```

See also:

XDrawLine, XDrawLines, XSetLineAttributes

XDrawString

Purpose:

Draws a text string in foreground color only (see Chapter 10).

Syntax:

```
char string[]; /* The string being drawn            */
int  length;   /* Number of characters in the string */

XDrawString(display, drawable, gc, x, y, string, length);
```

See also:

XDrawImageString, XDrawString, XDrawText, XSetFont

XDrawString16

Purpose:

Draws a string of 16-bit characters in foreground color only.

Syntax:

```
XChar2b string[]; /* Array of 16-bit characters */
int     length;   /* Number of characters       */

XDrawString16(display, drawable, gc, x, y, string, length);
```

See also:

XDrawImageString16, XDrawText16, XSetFont

XDrawText

Purpose:

Draws several text strings on the same line (see Chapter 10).

Syntax:

```
XTextItem items[]; /* Array defining text strings  */
int        nitems; /* Number of strings in "items" */

XDrawText(display, drawable, gc, x, y, items, nitems);
```

See also:

XDrawImageString, XDrawString, XSetFont

XDrawText16

Purpose:

Draws a number of 16-bit character strings on the same line.

Syntax:

```
XTextItem16 items; /* Array of 16-bit character strings */
int         nitems;/* Number of strings being drawn    */

XDrawText16(display, drawable, gc, x, y, items, nitems);
```

See also:

XDrawImageString16, XDrawString16, XSetFont

XEmptyRegion

Purpose:

Indicates whether a specified region is empty.

Syntax:

```
Region r; /* Region being tested */

if(XEmptyRegion(r))
{
/* Region is empty. */
}
```

Returns:

True if region is empty; False otherwise.

See also:

XCreateRegion, XDestroyRegion, XPolygonRegion

XEnableAccessControl

Purpose:

Makes server use access control list when deciding whether to allow or deny access to a request for connection.

Syntax:

```
XEnableAccessControl(display);
```

See also:

XDisableAccessControl, XAddHost, XAddHosts, XRemoveHost, XRemoveHosts, XSetAccessControl

XEqualRegion

Purpose:

Checks whether two regions are equal.

Syntax:

```
Region r1, r2; /* Regions being compared */

if(XEqualRegion(r1, r2))
{
/* Regions are equal */
}
```

Returns:

True if r1 and r2 are equal; False otherwise.

See also:

XCreateRegion, XDestroyRegion, XEmptyRegion

XEventsQueued

Purpose:

Returns number of events in the queue without blocking (see Chapter 8).

Syntax:

```
int mode;/* Indicates whether Xlib's output buffer is flushed */
         /*QueuedAlready, QueuedAfterFlush, QueuedAfterReading*/
int nev; /* Number of events waiting to be processed        */

nev = XEventsQueued(display, QueuedAfterReading);
```

Returns:

Number of events in the queue.

See also:

XNextEvent, XPending

XExtendedMaxRequestSize

Purpose:

Gets the maximum size (in 4-byte units) of protocol requests that the X server can accept, provided the server supports extended-length protocol encoding.

Syntax:

```
long max_req_size_ext;
if((max_req_size_ext = XExtendedMaxRequestSize(display)) == 0)
{
/* Server does not support extended-length protocol requests */
}
```

Returns:

The maximum size (in 4-byte units) of protocol requests that the server can accept, if server supports extended-length protocol encoding; zero otherwise.

See also:

XMaxRequestSize

XFetchBuffer

Purpose:

Gets data from the specified cut buffer.

Syntax:

```
int  nbytes, /* On return: the number of bytes returned */
     buffer; /* Which cut buffer? can be 0 through 7    */
char *data;  /* Xlib allocates room and returns pointer */

data = XFetchBuffer(display, &nbytes, buffer);
```

Returns:

Pointer to data. Must be freed later (using XFree).

See also:

XFetchBytes, XFree, XStoreBuffer, XStoreBytes

XFetchBytes

Purpose:

Gets data from cut buffer 0 (see Chapter 16).

Syntax:

```
int  nbytes; /* On return: number of bytes returned */
char *data;  /* Pointer to returned data            */

data = XFetchBytes(display, nbytes);
```

Returns:

Pointer to returned data. Must be freed later (using XFree).

See also:

XFetchBuffer, XFree, XStoreBuffer, XStoreBytes

XFetchName

Purpose:

Gets a window's name from its XA_WM_NAME property.

Syntax:

```
char *window_name; /* On return: points to window's name */

if(XFetchName(display, w, &window_name) == 0)
{
/* Failed to get the name */
}
```

Returns:

Zero on failure; nonzero on success.

See also:

XGetWMHints, XStoreName

XFillArc

Purpose:

Draws a filled arc (see Chapter 9).

Syntax:

```
int angle1, angle2; /* Start and end of arc in */
                    /* 64ths of a degree      */

XFillArc(display, drawable, gc, x, y, width, height, angle1,
         angle2);
```

See also:

XDrawArc, XDrawArcs, XFillArcs, XSetForeground

XFillArcs

Purpose:

Draws several arcs using a single request to the server.

Syntax:

```
XArc  arcs[]; /* List of arcs   */
int   narcs;  /* Number of arcs */

XFillArcs(display, drawable, gc, arcs, narcs);
```

See also:

XDrawArc, XDrawArcs, XFillArc, XSetForeground

XFillPolygon

Purpose:

Draws a polygon filled with the color and pattern specified in a GC (see Chapter 9).

Syntax:

```
XPoint points;  /* Array of points denoting the vertices  */
int    npoints; /* Number of points in the array          */
int    shape;   /* Is shape complex, convex, or nonconvex */
                /* one of: Complex, Nonconvex, or Convex   */
int    mode;    /* CoordModeOrigin or CoordModePrevious    */

XFillPolygon(display, drawable, gc, points, npoints, shape, mode);
```

See also:

```
XDrawLine, XDrawLines, XSetForeground
```

XFillRectangle

Purpose:

Draws a rectangle filled with the foreground color specified in the GC (see Chapter 9).

Syntax:

```
XFillRectangle(display, drawable, gc, x, y, width, height);
```

See also:

```
XDrawRectangle, XDrawRectangles, XFillRectangles, XSetForeground
```

XFillRectangles

Purpose:

Fills several rectangles with a single request to the X server.

Syntax:

```
XRectangle rectangles[]; /* Array of rectangles  */
int        nrectangles;  /* Number of rectangles */

XFillRectangle(display, drawable, gc, rectangles, nrectangles);
```

See also:

```
XDrawRectangle, XDrawRectangles, XFillRectangle, XSetForeground
```

XFilterEvent

Purpose:

Filters X events for an input method that maps multiple keystrokes to a character (to enable entering characters for languages such as Japanese).

Syntax:

```
XEvent  event; /* Event to be filtered                  */
Window  w;     /* Window for which filter is to be applied */
```

```
if(!XFilterEvent(event, w))
{
/* If return value is False, event was not filtered.
 * Process it here.
 */
}
```

Returns:

True if event is filtered by an input method; False otherwise.

See also:

XNextEvent

XFindContext

Purpose:

Gets data associated with a particular context from Xlib's context management facility that enables you to store data indexed by windows. (See Chapter 7 for an example of using XFindContext.)

Syntax:

```
XContext  context; /* Context of the stored data          */
caddr_t   data;    /* The data is returned here. It is usually */
                   /* a pointer to storage you allocated   */

if(XFindContext(display, w, context, &data) == 0)
{
/* Data retrieved successfully */
}
```

Returns:

Zero if all goes well; otherwise, XCNOENT to indicate that the context was not found.

See also:

XDeleteContext, XSaveContext, XUniqueContext

XFlush

Purpose:

Sends all waiting X protocol requests to the server. Xlib queues requests and sends them only at certain times, but you can flush the queue with XFlush.

Syntax:

```
XFlush(display);
```

See also:

XNextEvent, XSync

XFlushGC

Sends all cached changes to a `GC` to the server.

Syntax:

```
XFlushGC(display, gc);
```

See also:

```
XChangeGC
```

XFontsOfFontSet

Purpose:

Gets the list of font names and corresponding `XFontStructs` for a specified font set.

Syntax:

```
XFontSet font_set; /* Font set for which information is sought */
XFontStruct** font_struct_list_returned;/* Font info returned */
char**  font_name_list_returned;        /* Font names returned */
int     nfonts;   /* Number of XFontStructs and names returned */

nfonts = XFontsOfFontSet(font_set, &font_struct_list_returned, &font_name_list_returned);
```

Returns:

Number of `XFontStruct` structures and font names returned in `font_struct_list_returned` and `font_name_list_returned`. To free the storage used by these arrays, call `XFreeFontSet`.

See also:

```
XCreateFontSet, XFreeFontSet, XLocaleOfFontSet
```

XForceScreenSaver

Purpose:

Turns the screen saver on or off.

Syntax:

```
int mode; /* ScreenSaverActive = on, ScreenSaverReset = off */

XForceScreenSaver(display, mode);
```

See also:

```
XActivateScreenSaver, XGetScreenSaver, XResetScreenSaver, XSetScreenSaver
```

XFree

Purpose:

Frees memory allocated by Xlib functions.

Syntax:

```
caddr_t data; /* Pointer to data */

XFree(data);
```

See also:

```
Xpermalloc
```

XFreeColormap

Purpose:

Destroys the specified colormap and installs the default colormap.

Syntax:

```
XFreeColormap(display, cmap);
```

See also:

```
XCopyColormapAndFree, XCreateColormap, XSetWindowColormap
```

XFreeColors

Purpose:

Frees colormap cells specified by pixels and planes (see Chapter 11).

Syntax:

```
unsigned long pixels[]; /* Array of pixel values              */
int            npixels;  /* Number of entries in "pixels" array */
unsigned long planes;    /* Planes indicated by set bits       */

XFreeColors(dsiplay, cmap, pixels, npixels, planes);
```

See also:

```
XAllocColor, XAllocColorCells, XAllocColorPlanes, XAllocNamedColor, XStoreColor,
XStoreColors
```

XFreeCursor

Purpose:

Destroys a cursor resource.

Syntax:

```
XFreeCursor(display, cursor);
```

See also:

XCreateFontCursor, XCreateGlyphCursor, XCreatePixmapCursor, XDefineCursor, XRecolorCursor, XUndefineCursor

---

XFreeExtensionList

Purpose:

Frees memory allocated by the XListExtensions function.

Syntax:

```
char **list; /* List that was returned by XListExtensions */

XFreeExtensionList(list);
```

See also:

XListExtensions, XQueryExtension

XFreeFont

Purpose:

Unloads a font and releases memory allocated for the font structure.

Syntax:

```
XFontStruct *font_struct; /* Font structure of font being freed */

XFreeFont(display, font_struct);
```

See also:

XLoadFont, XLoadQueryFont, XSetFont, XUnloadFont

XFreeFontInfo

Purpose:

Frees memory allocated by the XListFontsWithInfo function.

Syntax:

```
char        **names; /* Names from XListFontsWithInfo      */
XFontStruct *info;   /* Font info from XListFontsWithInfo */
int         count;   /* Number of fonts                    */

XFreeFontInfo(names, info, count);
```

See also:

XListFontsWithInfo

XFreeFontNames

Purpose:

Releases memory allocated by XListFonts.

Syntax:

```
char **list; /* List previously returned by XListFonts */

XFreeFontNames(list);
```

See also:

```
XListFonts
```

XFreeFontPath

Purpose:

Frees memory allocated by XGetFontPath.

Syntax:

```
char **list; /* Pointer previously returned by XGetFontPath */

XFreeFontPath(list);
```

See also:

```
XGetFontPath
```

XFreeFontSet

Purpose:

Frees the specified font set.

Syntax:

```
XFontSet font_set; /* Font set to be freed */

XFreeFontSet(font_set);
```

See also:

```
XCreateFontSet, XFontsOfFontSet
```

XFreeGC

Purpose:

Destroys a GC resource.

Syntax:

```
XFreeGC(display, gc);
```

See also:

XCreateGC, XChangeGC, XCopyGC

XFreeModifiermap

Purpose:

Frees memory originally allocated by XNewModifiermap or XGetModifierMapping.

Syntax:

XFreeModifierKeymap *modmap; /* Specifies structure being freed */

XFreeModifiermap(modmap);

See also:

XGetModifierMapping, XNewModifiermap

XFreePixmap

Purpose:

Frees a pixmap specified by a resource ID.

Syntax:

Pixmap pmap; /* Pixmap being freed */

XFreePixmap(display, pmap);

See also:

XCreatePixmap, XCreatePixmapFromBitmapData, XReadBitmapFile

XFreeStringList

Purpose:

Frees memory allocated by XTextPropertyToStringList for a list of text strings.

Syntax:

char **list; /* List returned by XTextPropertyToStringList */

XFreeStringList(list);

See also:

XGetTextProperty, XSetTextProperty, XStringListToTextProperty,
XTextPropertyToStringList

XGContextFromGC

Purpose:

Gets a `GContext` resource ID from a `GC`.

Syntax:

```
GContext gc_id;

gc_id = XGContextFromGC(gc);
```

Returns:

`GContext` field from the `GC` structure.

See also:

`XCreateGC, XFreeGC, XGetVisualInfo`

XGeometry   (Use XWMGeometry in X11R4 and later)

Purpose:

Computes position and size of a window, given a geometry string of type "200x100+20+10" (see Chapter 7).

Syntax:

```
int          screen;       /* Screen where window appears   */
char         *user_geom;   /* User-specified geometry       */
char         *default_geom;/* Default geometry string       */
unsigned int bwidth;       /* Border width in pixels        */
unsigned int fwidth, fheight;/* Font width and height in pixels*/
int          xadder, yadder; /* Additional padding in pixels  */
int          x, y;         /* Position returned here        */
int          width, height; /* Size returned here           */
int          ret_mask;     /* Mask indicating which return  */
                           /* values are valid              */

ret_mask = XGeometry(display, screen, user_geom, default_geom,
                 bwidth, fwidth, fheight, xadder, yadder,
                 &x, &y, &width, &height);
```

Returns:

Integer whose bits indicate which of the computed values are valid.

See also:

`XGetGeometry, XParseGeometry, XWMGeometry`

XGetAtomName

Purpose:

Gets the string corresponding to an atom.

Syntax:

```
Atom  atom;  /* Atom whose string equivalent is returned  */
char  *name; /* Returned string. Free with XFree when done */

if((name = XGetAtomName(display, atom)) != NULL)
{
/* Success */
}
```

Returns:

Pointer to string; NULL if atom is invalid.

See also:

XGetAtomNames, XInternAtom, XInternAtoms

XGetAtomNames

Purpose:

Gets the strings corresponding to an array of atoms. This is equivalent to calling XGetAtomName for each Atom, but more efficient.

Syntax:

```
Atom  atoms[];  /* Array of Atoms whose string equivalent
                   is returned                          */
int   natoms;   /* Number of Atoms in the "atoms" array */
char  *names[]; /* Array where strings are returned.    */

if(XGetAtomNames(display, atoms, natoms, names)
{
/* Success */
}
```

Returns:

Nonzero value if names are returned for all atoms; zero otherwise.

See also:

XGetAtomName, XInternAtom, XInternAtoms

XGetClassHint

Purpose:

Gets the XClassHint structure stored in the XA_WM_CLASS property on a window.

Syntax:

```
XClassHint class_hints;

if(XGetClassHint(display, w, &class_hints) == 0)
{
/* Failed to get property */
}
```

Returns:

Nonzero on success; zero on failure.

See also:

```
XAllocClassHint, XSetClassHint
```

XGetDefault

Purpose:

Gets the value of a specified option from the resource database (see Chapter 5).

Syntax:

```
char *app_name;     /* Name of application             */
char *option;       /* Option whose value is being retrieved */
cgar *value_string;/* Value returned by XGetDefault    */

if((value_string = XGetDefault(display, app_name, option))
   == NULL)
{
/* Option not in resource database */
}
```

Returns:

Pointer to string representing value of option. Do not free this string.

See also:

```
XResourceManagerString
```

XGetErrorDatabaseText

Purpose:

Gets error messages from an error database, the file /usr/lib/X11/XErrorDB in UNIX systems.

Syntax:

```
char *name,;
char *message;        /* Type of message: XProtError,    */
                      /* XlibMessage, or XRequestMajor   */
char *default_string; /* Default message                 */
char buffer[];        /* Buffer where message is returned */
int  length;          /* Size of buffer to hold message  */
```

```
XGetErrorDatabaseText(display, name, message, default_string,
                      buffer, legth);
```

See also:

XGetErrorText, XSetErrorHandler, XSetIOErrorHandler

XGetErrorText

Purpose:

Provides a string describing an error code.

Syntax:

```
int  code;     /* Error code such as BadWindow or BadValue */
char buffer[]; /* Buffer to hold the string               */
int  length;   /* Size of buffer (in bytes)               */

XGetErrorText(display, code, buffer, length);
```

See also:

XGetErrorDatabaseText, XSetErrorHandler, XSetIOErrorHandler

XGetFontPath

Purpose:

Gets the current font search path (list of directories where font data resides in the server's system).

Syntax:

```
int  npaths; /* On return: number of path strings       */
char **fpath; /* List of directories returned by XGetFontPath */

fpath = XGetFontPath(display, &npaths);
```

Returns:

List of directories that constitute the font search path. Free by calling XFreeFontPath when no longer needed.

See also:

XFreeFontPath

XGetFontProperty

Purpose:

Provides access to a font property specified by an atom. You provide an XFontStruct to identify the font whose property you want.

Syntax:

```
#include <X11/Xatom.h>      /* For predefined atoms        */

XFontStruct   *font_struct;/* Pointer to font structure    */
                          /* identifying font of interest  */
Atom          atom;       /* Specifies font property such as */
                          /* XA_UNDERLINE_POSITION         */
unsigned long value;      /* Place for the property's value */

if(XGetFontProperty(font_struct, atom, &value))
{
/* Specified font property found */
}
```

Returns:

True if font property is found; False otherwise.

See also:

```
XChangeProperty, XDeleteProperty
```

XGetGCValues

Purpose:

Provides access to values in a graphics context (GC). You cannnot get the clip mask or the dash list (see Chapter 9).

Syntax:

```
XGCValues xgcv; /* Structure where values are returned */

if(XGetGCValues(display, gc, value_mask, &xgcv))
{
/* Got GC values */
}
```

Returns:

Nonzero if successful; zero to indicate error.

See also:

```
XCreateGC, XChangeGC
```

XGetGeometry

Purpose:

Gets the current position and size of a drawable.

Syntax:

```
Window        root;      /* Root ID returned here      */
int           x, y;      /* Position returned here      */
unsigned int  width, height; /* Size returned here      */
```

```
unsigned int  border_width;  /* Border width on return    */
unsigned int  depth;         /* Depth of drawable on return */

if(XGetGeometry(display, drawable, &root, &x, &y, &width,
           &height, &border_width, &depth))
{
/* Success */
}
```

Returns:

Nonzero on success; zero on failure.

See also:

XGetWindowAttributes, XMoveWindow, XMoveResizeWindow, XResizeWindow

---

XGetIconName   (Use **XGetWMIconName** in X11R4 or later)

Purpose:

Gets the name displayed in an icon.

Syntax:

```
char *icon_name; /* On return: points to icon name  */
                 /* Use XFree(icon_name) when done  */

if(XGetconName(display, w, &icon_name))
{
/* Success */
}
```

Returns:

Nonzero if successful; zero on failure.

See also:

XGetWMIconName

XGetIconSizes

Purpose:

Gets icon sizes from the XA_WM_ICON_SIZE property that is set by the window manager.

Syntax:

```
XIconSize *size_list; /* On return: points to list of sizes */
int        count;     /* On return: number of icon sizes    */

if(XGetIconSizes(display, w, &size_list, &count))
{
/* Got icon sizes */
}
```

Returns:

Nonzero on success; zero otherwise.

See also:

XGetWMHints, XSetWMHints

XGetImage

Purpose:

Places contents of a rectangular region of a drawable into an XImage structure (see Chapter 12).

Syntax:

```
unsigned long plane_mask; /* Specifies planes to be obtained   */
int           format;     /* Image format: XYPixmap or ZPixmap */

if((ximage = XGetImage(display, drawable, x, y, width, height,
                    plane_mask, format)) != NULL)
{
/* Contents of drawable are now in ximage */
}
```

Returns:

Pointer to newly created XImage structure; NULL if something went wrong.

See also:

XCreateImage, XDestroyImage, XPutImage, XSubImage

XGetInputFocus

Purpose:

Gets the ID of the window that currently has the keyboard focus (all keyboard events are delivered to this window).

Syntax:

```
Window focus;      /* On return: ID of window with focus      */
int    revert_to; /* On return: constant to indicate who will */
                  /* get the focus if focus window is invisible*/

XGetInputFocus(display, &focus, &revert_to);
```

See also:

XSetInputFocus

XGetKeyboardControl

Purpose:

Gets current list of keyboard preferences.

Syntax:

```
XKeyboardState kbstate; /* Structure to hold current settings */

XGetKeyboardControl(display, &kbstate);
```

See also:

```
XBell, XGetPointerControl, XChangeKeyboardControl
```

XGetKeyboardMapping

Purpose:

Gets the keysyms corresponding to the specified keycodes.

Syntax:

```
KeyCode  first_keycode;        /* First keycode       */
int      keycode_count;        /* Number of keycodes  */
int      keysyms_per_keycode;  /* Value returned here */
KeySym   *keymap;              /* Returned mapping    */

keymap = XGetKeyboardMapping(display, first_keycode,
              keycode_count, &keysyms_per_keycode);
```

Returns:

Pointer to a list of keysyms. Free with XFree when no longer needed.

See also:

```
XChangeKeyboardMapping, XRefreshKeyboardMapping
```

XGetModifierMapping

Purpose:

Provides the mapping of the modifier keys, such as Control and Shift.

Syntax:

```
XModifierKeymap *modmap; /* Returned mapping */

modmap = XGetModifierMapping(display);
```

Returns:

Pointer to XModifierKeymap structure. Use XFreeModifiermap to free.

See also:

XDeleteModifiermapEntry, XFreeModifiermap, XInserModifiermapEntry, XNewModifiermap

XGetMotionEvents

Purpose:

Gets events from the motion history buffer.

Syntax:

```
Time    start, stop; /* Time interval for which events reported */
int     nevents;      /* Number of events returned here         */
XTimeCoord *mevents;/* Events returned by XGetMotionEvents      */

mevents = XGetMotionEvents(display, w, start, stop, &nevents);
```

Returns:

Pointer to array of XTimeCoord structures. Free using XFree.

See also:

XDisplayMotionBufferSize

XGetNormalHints   (Use XGetWMNormalHints in X11R4 or later)

Purpose:

Gets the XSizeHints structure stored in the XA_WM_NORMAL_HINTS property of a window.

Syntax:

```
XSizeHints hints;

if(XGetNormalHints(display, w, &hints))
{
/* Function succeeded */
}
```

Returns:

Nonzero on success; zero on failure.

See also:

XSetWMNormalHints

XGetPixel

Purpose:

Gets the pixel value at a specified point in an image.

Syntax:

```
unsigned long pixval; /* Pixel value at (x,y) in image */

pixval = XGetPixel(ximage, x, y);
```

Returns:

Pixel value at the specified point.

See also:

```
XCreateImage, XDestroyImage, XGetImage, XPutImage, XPutPixel
```

XGetPointerControl

Purpose:

Gets the current settings for the mouse pointer.

Syntax:

```
int  accel_numerator;   /* For numerator of acceleration   */
int  accel_denominator; /* For denominator of acceleration */
int  threshold;         /* For acceleration threshold      */

XGetPointerControl(display, &accel_numerator, &accel_denominator,
                 &threshold);
```

See also:

```
XGetKeyboardControl
```

XGetPointerMapping

Purpose:

Provides the mapping between the physical mouse buttons and the logical buttons `Button1` through `Button5` used in X programs.

Syntax:

```
unsigned char map[]; /* Array where the mapping is returned */
int           nmap;  /* Number of map entries in "map[]"    */
int           actual;/* Actual number of buttons available  */

actual = XGetPointerMapping(display, map, nmap);
```

Returns:

Actual number of button mappings.

See also:

```
XSetPointerMapping
```

XGetRGBColormaps

Purpose:

Gets the `XStandardColormap` structure stored in the specified property of type `RGB_COLOR_MAP` (see Chapter 16).

Syntax:

```
XStandardColormap *std_cmap; /* Returned colormap              */
int                num_cmap; /* Number of colormaps            */
Atom               cm_prop;  /* Identifies colormap property */

if(XGetRGBColormaps(display, w, &std_cmap, &num_cmap, cm_prop))
{
/* Found specified colormap property */
}
```

Returns:

Nonzero to indicate success; zero on failure.

See also:

XAllocStandardColormap, XGetStandardColormap, XSetRGBColormaps

XGetScreenSaver

Purpose:

Retrieves current settings of the screen saver.

Syntax:

```
                    /* Pass the addresses of these to get values*/
int timeout;        /*Seconds after which screen saver activates*/
int interval;       /* Seconds between calls to screen saver    */
int prefer_blanking;/* Blanking preference: DontPreferBlanking, */
                    /*      PreferBlanking, or DefaultBlanking  */
int allow_exposures;/* One of: Don't AllowExposures,            */
                    /*      AllowExposures or DefaultExposures  */

XGetScreenSaver(display, &timeout, &interval, &prefer_blanking,
              &allow_exposures);
```

See also:

XActivateScreenSaver, XForceScreenSaver, XResetScreenSaver, XSetScreenSaver

XGetSelectionOwner

Purpose:

Returns the ID of the current owner (window) of a selection specified by the atom (see Chapter 16).

Syntax:

```
Atom    selection; /* Which selection: XA_PRIMARY, for example */
Window owner;      /* Window that owns specified selection    */

owner = XGetSelectionOwner(display, selection);
```

Returns:

Window ID of selection's owner; None if no owner.

See also:

```
XSetSelectionOwner
```

XGetSizeHints   (Use XGetWMSizeHints in X11R4 or later)

Purpose:

Gets the XSizeHints structure stored in a property of type XA_SIZE_HINTS.

Syntax:

```
XSizeHints hints;     /* Value returned here                */
Atom       property; /* Identifies property: XA_WM_SIZE_HINTS, */
                     /* XA_WM_NORMAL_HINTS, or XA_WM_ZOOM_HINTS*/

if(XGetSizeHints(display, w, &hints, property))
{
/* Got property's value */
}
```

Returns:

Nonzero if successful; zero on failure.

See also:

```
XGetWMSizeHints, XSetSizeHints
```

XGetStandardColormap   (Use XGetRGBColormap in X11R4 or later)

Purpose:

Gets the standard colormap property (one of XA_RGB_BEST_MAP, XA_RGB_RED_MAP, XA_RGB_GREEN_MAP, XA_RGB_BLUE_MAP, XA_RGB_DEFAULT_MAP, or XA_RGB_GRAY_MAP).

Syntax:

```
XStandardColormap cmap_info; /* Colormap data returned here */
Atom              property;  /* One of predefined colormaps */

if(XGetStandardColormap(display, w, cmap_info, property))
{
/* Colormap retrieved */
}
```

Returns:

Nonzero if successful; zero on failure.

See also:

XCreateColormap, XFreeColormap, XGetRGBColormap, XSetWindowColormap

---

XGetSubImage

Purpose:

Copies a rectangular area from a drawable to a specified location in an existing image.

Syntax:

```
unsigned long plane_mask;      /* Planes being copied        */
int           format;          /* XYPixmap or ZPixmap        */
XImage        *dest_image;     /* Image to be updated        */
int           dest_x, dest_y;  /* Destination point in image */
XImage        *sub_image;      /* Returned pointer (dest_image) */

sub_image = XGetSubImage(display, drawable, x, y, width, height,
       plane_mask, format, dest_image, dest_x, dest_y);
```

Returns:

The dest_image pointer.

See also:

XCreateImage, XGetImage, XPutImage, XSubImage

XGetTextProperty

Purpose:

Retrieves text properties from a window.

Syntax:

```
XTextProperty xt_prop;
Atom          property;

if(XGetTextProperty(display, w, &xt_prop, property))
{
/* Text property retrieved */
}
```

Returns:

Nonzero if successful; zero on failure.

See also:

XFreeStringList, XSetTextProperty, XStringListToTextProperty, XTextPropertyToStringList

XGetTransientForHint

Purpose:

Gets the `XA_WM_TRANSIENT_FOR` property of a window. This property lists the windows that will appear temporarily and should not be decorated by the window manager with frames.

Syntax:

```
Window prop_window; /* Window ID in property is returned here */

if(XGetTransientForHint(display, w, &prop_window))
{
/* Property retrieved successfully */
}
```

Returns:

Nonzero on success; zero to indicate failure.

See also:

```
XSetTransientForHint
```

XGetVisualInfo

Purpose:

Finds an `XVisualInfo` structure matching a specified template.

Syntax:

```
long        vis_mask;    /* Fields (of template) to match    */
XVisualInfo *vis_template; /* Template structure             */
int         numvis;      /* No. of matching visuals returned */
XVisualInfo *vis_match;   /* Matching visual list            */

if((vis_match = XGetVisualInfo(display, vis_mask, vis_template,
                            &numvis)) == NULL)
{
/* No matching visuals */
}
```

Returns:

List of matching visuals.

See also:

```
XMatchVisualInfo
```

XGetWindowAttributes

Purpose:

Gets a window's attributes.

Syntax:

```
XWindowAttributes xwa; /* Structure where values are returned */

if(XGetWindowAttributes(display, w, &xwa))
{
/* Attributes retrieved successfully */
}
```

Returns:

Nonzero if successful; zero on failure.

See also:

```
XChangeWindowAttributes
```

XGetWindowProperty

Purpose:

Retrieves the data stored in a property of specified name and type (see Chapter 16 for more information). Use XFree to free memory allocated for the retrived data.

Syntax:

```
Atom           property;      /* Retrieve from this property  */
long           offset,        /* Starting point of data       */
long           length;        /* 32-bit values to retrieve    */
Bool           delete;        /* True = delete after retrieval*/
Atom           req_type;      /* Property type to retrieve    */
Atom           actual_type;   /* Type actually returned       */
int            actual_format; /* Format actually returned     */
unsigned long  nitems;        /* Items returned               */
unsigned long  bytes_remain;  /* Bytes remaining              */
unsigned char  *prop_value;   /* Pointer to retrieved data    */

if(XGetWindowProperty(display, w, property, offset,
    length, delete, req_type, &actual_type,
    &actual_format, &nitems, &bytes_remain, &prop) == Success)
{
/* Function executed successfully. Check values for validity */
...
}
```

Returns:

Success if the function executes properly.

See also:

```
XChangeProperty, XListProperties
```

XGetWMClientMachine

Purpose:

Retrieves the client machine's name from the XA_WM_CLIENT_MACHINE property.

Syntax:

```
XTextProperty txt_prop; /* Client machine's name returned here */

if(XGetWMClientMachine(display, w, &txt_prop))
{
/* Success */
}
```

Returns:

Nonzero if successful; zero otherwise.

See also:

```
XSetWMClientMachine
```

XGetWMColormapWindows

Purpose:

Retrieves a list of window IDs from the `XA_WM_COLORMAP_WINDOWS` property. This is a list of windows that need their own colormaps installed.

Syntax:

```
Window *cmap_windows; /* On return: points to list of windows */
int    count;         /* On return: number of entries in list */

if(XGetWMColormapWindows(display, w, &cmap_windows, &count))
{
/* Property value returned */
}
```

See also:

```
XSetWMColormapWindows
```

XGetWMHints

Purpose:

Gets the `XWMHints` structure stored in a window's `XA_WM_HINTS` property.

Syntax:

```
XWMHints *xwmh; /* Pointer to returned structure */

xwmh = XGetWMHints(display, w);
```

Returns:

Pointer to `XWMHints` structure, if successful; `NULL` on failure. Use `XFree` to free structure when you no longer need it.

See also:

```
XAllocWMHints, XSetWMHints
```

XGetWMIconName

Purpose:

Gets a window's XA_WM_ICON_NAME property.

Syntax:

```
XTextProperty xt_prop; /* Text property returned here */

if(XGetWMIconName(display, w, &xt_prop))
{
/* Value successfully retrieved */
}
```

Returns:

Nonzero on success; zero on failure.

See also:

XSetWMIconName

XGetWMName

Purpose:

Gets a window's XA_WM_NAME property.

Syntax:

```
XTextProperty xt_prop; /* Text property returned here */

if(XGetWMName(display, w, &xt_prop))
{
/* Value successfully retrieved */
}
```

Returns:

Nonzero on success; zero on failure.

See also:

XSetWMName

XGetWMNormalHints

Purpose:

Gets a window's XA_WM_NORMAL_HINTS property.

Syntax:

```
XSizeHints size_hints; /* Property's value returned here */
long      user_set;   /* Indicates fields set by user   */
```

```
if(XGetWMNormalHints(display, w, &size_hints, &user_set))
{
/* Value successfully retrieved */
}
```

Returns:

Nonzero on success; zero on failure.

See also:

```
XSetWMNormalHints
```

XGetWMProtocols

Purpose:

Gets the XA_WM_PROTOCOLS property of a window.

Syntax:

```
Atom   *protocols; /* On return: points to a list of protocols */
int    count;      /* Number of protocols in the list          */

if(XGetWMProtocols(display, w, &protocols, &count))
{
/* Success */
}
```

Returns:

Nonzero on success; zero on failure.

See also:

```
XSetWMProtocols
```

XGetWMSizeHints

Purpose:

Gets a window's XA_WM_SIZE_HINTS property.

Syntax:

```
XSizeHints size_hints; /* Property's value returned here */
long       user_set;   /* Indicates fields set by user   */
Atom       property;   /* Specifies property name        */

if(XGetWMSizeHints(display, w, &size_hints, &user_set,
                   property))
{
/* Value successfully retrieved */
}
```

Returns:

Nonzero on success; zero on failure.

See also:

XSetWMSizeHints

XGetZoomHints (Obsolete in X11R4 or later)

Purpose:

Gets the XSizeHints structure stored in the XA_WM_ZOOM_HINTS property of a window.

Syntax:

```
XSizeHints zoomh;

if(XGetZoomHints(display, w, &zoomh))
{
/* Success */
}
```

Returns:

Nonzero if successful; zero on failure.

See also:

XSetZoomHints

XGrabButton

Purpose:

Makes the X server report all pointer events to a specific window in your program. (This is called *grabbing*.)

Syntax:

```
unsigned int button;        /* Mouse button(s) being grabbed   */
unsigned int modifiers;     /* Specifies the modifier keys     */
Window       grab_window;   /* Window to receive all events    */
Bool         owner_events;  /* True = deliver this application's*/
                            /* events normally.                */
unsigned int event_mask;    /* Events to report during grab    */
int          pointer_mode;  /* Mode for pointer: GrabModeAsync  */
                            /* or GrabModeSync (freezes events) */
int          keyboard_mode;/* Mode for keyboard: GrabModeAsync */
                            /* or GrabModeSync (freezes events) */
Window       confine_to     /* Pointer is confined to this     */
                            /* window. None = not confined     */
Cursor       cursor;        /* Cursor displayed during grab    */

XGrabButton(display, button, modifiers, grab_window,
            owner_events, event_mask, pointer_mode,
            keyboard_mode, confine_to, cursor);
```

See also:

XAllowEvents, XGrabPointer, XUngrabButton, XUngrabPointer

XGrabKey

Purpose:

Grabs a specified key so that events corresponding to that key are delivered to a specific window.

Syntax:

```
int         keycode;      /* Keycode of key being grabbed    */
unsigned int modifiers;   /* Specifies the modifier keys     */
Window      grab_window;  /* Window to receive all events    */
Bool        owner_events; /* True = deliver this application's*/
                          /* events normally.                */
int         pointer_mode; /* Mode for pointer: GrabModeAsync  */
                          /* or GrabModeSync (freezes events) */
int         keyboard_mode;/* Mode for keyboard: GrabModeAsync */
                          /* or GrabModeSync (freezes events) */

XGrabKey(display, keycode, modifier, grab_window,
        owner_events, pointer_mode, keyboard_mode);
```

See also:

XGrabKeyboard, XUngrabKey, XUngrabKeyboard

XGrabKeyboard

Purpose:

Makes the server report all keyboard events to a specified window in your program.

Syntax:

```
Window      grab_window;  /* Window to receive all events    */
Bool        owner_events; /* True = deliver this application's*/
                          /* events normally.                */
int         pointer_mode; /* Mode for pointer: GrabModeAsync  */
                          /* or GrabModeSync (freezes events) */
int         keyboard_mode;/* Mode for keyboard: GrabModeAsync */
                          /* or GrabModeSync (freezes events) */
Time        time;         /* When to activate the grab       */

if(XGrabKeyboard(display, grab_window, owner_events,
      pointer_mode, keyboard_mode, time) == GrabSuccess)
{
/* Keyboard grabbed. Call XUngrabKeyboard as soon as possible */
}
```

Returns:

GrabSuccess if successful; otherwise, one of the following: AlreadyGrabbed, GrabNotViewable, GrabInvalidTime, or GrabFrozen.

See also:

XGrabKey, XUngrabKey, XUngrabKeyboard

XGrabPointer

Purpose:

Makes the X server send all pointer events to a specific window in your program. (This is called *grabbing* the pointer.)

Syntax:

```
Window       grab_window;   /* Window to receive all events   */
Bool         owner_events;  /* True = deliver this application's*/
                            /* events normally.               */
unsigned int event_mask;    /* Events to report during grab   */
int          pointer_mode;  /* Mode for pointer: GrabModeAsync */
                            /* or GrabModeSync (freezes events)*/
int          keyboard_mode; /* Mode for keyboard: GrabModeAsync*/
                            /* or GrabModeSync (freezes events)*/
Window       confine_to     /* Pointer is confined to this    */
                            /* window. None = not confined    */
Cursor       cursor;        /* Cursor displayed during grab   */
Time         time;          /* When to activate the grab      */

if(XGrabPointer(display, grab_window, owner_events, event_mask,
             pointer_mode, keyboard_mode, confine_to, cursor,
             time) == GrabSuccess)
{
/* Pointer grabbed. End with XUngrabPointer */
}
```

Returns:

GrabSuccess if successful; otherwise, one of the following: AlreadyGrabbed, GrabNotViewable, GrabInvalidTime, or GrabFrozen.

See also:

XChangeActivePointerGrab, XGrabButton, XUngrabButton, XUngrabPointer

XGrabServer

Purpose:

Forces the X server to act on your program's requests only. You should do this only when absolutely necessary.

Syntax:

```
XGrabServer(display);
```

See also:

XGrabButton, XGrabKey, XGrabKeyboard, XGrabPointer, XUngrabButton, XUngrabKey, XUngrabKeyboard, XUngrabPointer, XUngrabServer

XIconifyWindow

Purpose:

Attempts to iconify a top-level window.

Syntax:

```
int screen;  /* The screen on which the window appears */

if(XIconifyWindow(display, w, screen))
{
/* Window successfully iconified */
}
```

Returns:

Nonzero if successful (does not mean window is iconified—that depends on the window manager); zero on error.

See also:

XReconfigureWMWindow, XWithdrawWindow

XIfEvent

Purpose:

Waits until the application receives an event acceptable to a test function.

Syntax:

```
XEvent   event;         /* Matching event returned here */
Bool     (*predicate)(); /* Function that checks event   */
char     *args;         /* Arguments to function         */

XIfEvent(display, &event, predicate, args);
```

See also:

XCheckIfEvents, XPeekIfEvent

XInitImage

Purpose:

Initializes the internal image manipulation functions of the specified XImage structure whose other members are already initialized.

Syntax:

```
if(XInitImage(ximage))
{
/* Success */
}
```

Returns:

Nonzero if initialization is successful; zero otherwise.

See also:

```
XCreateImage
```

XInitThreads

Purpose:

Initializes Xlib support for concurrent threads. (A thread is a stream of execution within a process.) This function was introduced in X11R6.

Syntax:

```
if(XInitThreads())
{
/* Success */
}
```

Returns:

Nonzero if initialization is successful; zero otherwise.

See also:

```
XLockDisplay, XUnlockDisplay
```

XInsertModifiermapEntry

Purpose:

Adds a new entry to an XModifierKeymap structure.

Syntax:

```
XModifierKeymap *modmap,      /* Entry added to this structure */
KeyCode          keysym_entry; /* Keycode of key to be added    */
int              modifier;     /* Modifier to be mapped to above*/
                               /* keycode                       */
XModifierKeymap *new_map;      /* Modifier map with new entry   */

new_map = XInsertModifiermapEntry(modmap,
                        keysym_entry, modifier);
```

Returns:

Pointer to XModifierKeymap structure with new entry. You can use this with XSetModifierMapping.

See also:

```
XDeleteModifiermapEntry, XFreeModifiermap, XGetModifierMapping, XSetModifierMapping
```

XInstallColormap

Purpose:

Installs a virtual colormap into the hardware. This is usually done by a window manager.

Syntax:

```
XInstallColormap(display, cmap);
```

See also:

XCopyColormapAndFree, XCreateColormap, XFreeColormap, XSetWindowColormap,
XUninstallColormap

XInternAtom

Purpose:

Stores a string in the server and returns an Atom to be used for future references to that string.

Syntax:

```
char *string;        /* String being "interned"--stored    */
Bool only_if_exists; /* True = atom returned only if string */
                     /* already exists, False = create new atom*/
Atom atom;           /* Atom for the string                 */

atom = XInternAtom(display, string, only_if_exists);
```

Returns:

Atom used to refer to the specified string.

See also:

XGetAtomName, XGetAtomNames, XChangeProperty, XDeleteProperty, XInternAtoms

XInternAtoms

Purpose:

Stores an array of strings in the server and provides the corresponding Atoms in an array supplied by the calling program. This is equivalent to calling XInternAtom for each string, but more efficient.

Syntax:

```
char *strings[];     /* Array of strings to be "interned"--stored*/
int  nstrings;       /* Number of strings to be stored        */
Bool only_if_exists; /* True = atoms returned only if strings */
                     /* already exist, False = create new atom */
Atom atoms[];        /* Atoms for the strings                 */

if(XInternAtoms(display, strings, nstrings, only_if_exists, atoms))
{
/* Success */
}
```

Returns:

Nonzero value if Atoms are returned for all strings; zero otherwise.

See also:

XGetAtomName, XGetAtomNames, XChangeProperty, XDeleteProperty, XInternAtom

XIntersectRegion

Purpose:

Computes the intersection of two regions.

Syntax:

```
Region a, b; /* Regions being intersected */
Region iab; /* Resulting region          */

XIntersectRegion(a, b, iab);
```

See also:

XCreateRegion, XDestroyRegion, XUnionRegion, XXorRegion

XKeycodeToKeysym

Purpose:

Gets the keysym equivalent of a keycode.

Syntax:

```
KeyCode keycode; /* Keycode being converted    */
int     index;   /* Indicates which table:     */
                 /* unshifted (0) or shifted (1) */
KeySym  keysym;  /* Resulting keysym           */

keysym = XKeycodeToKeysym(display, keycode, index);
```

Returns:

Keysym corresponding to the specified keycode. NoSymbol indicates no keysym was found.

See also:

XKeysymToKeycode

XKeysymToKeycode

Purpose:

Retrieves the keycode for a specified keysym.

Syntax:

```
KeySym  keysym;  /* Keysym to be converted */
KeyCode keycode; /* Returned keycode       */

keycode = XKeysymToKeycode(display, keysym);
```

Returns:

Keycode corresponding to the specified keysym. A zero indicates no keycode was found.

See also:

```
XKeycodeToKeysym, XKeysymToString, XStringToKeysym
```

XKeysymToString

Purpose:

Gets the string equivalent of a keysym.

Syntax:

```
KeySym keysym;  /* Keysym being converted to string */
char   *string; /* String equivalent of the keysym  */

if((string = XKeysymToString(keysym)) != NULL)
{
/* A valid string has been returned */
}
```

Returns:

Pointer to string equivalent of the keysym. NULL if specified keysym is not defined.

See also:

```
XKeysymToKeycode, XLookupKeysym, XLookupStrung, XStringToKeysym
```

XKillClient

Purpose:

Destroys an X client application that created a specified resource. If the resource argument is AllTemporary, XKillClient also destroys the resources belonging to all clients that had exited in the RetainTemporary closedown mode.

Syntax:

```
XID resource; /* Resource of the client to be destroyed */

XKillClient(display, resource);
```

See also:

```
XSetCloseDownMode
```

XListDepths

Purpose:

Returns the depths (bits-per-pixel) supported by the specified screen.

Syntax:

```
int screen;  /* Which screen: 0, 1, ...               */
int count;   /* On return: number of supported depths  */
int *depths; /* List of depths returned by XListDepths */

if((depths = XListDepths(display, screen, &count)) == NULL)
{
/* Error getting depth list */
}
```

Returns:

A pointer to an array of integers denoting supported depths. Use XFree to release memory used by this array.

See also:

DefaultDepthOfScreen (macro)

XListExtensions

Purpose:

Gets a list of all extensions supported by an X server (see Chapter 16).

Syntax:

```
int   num_extensions; /* On return: number of extensions */
char  **extensions;   /* List of extensions              */

extensions = XListExtensions(display, &num_extensions);
```

Returns:

A pointer to an array of strings listing the names of extensions supported by the X server identified by display. Use XFreeExtensionList to free memory allocated for the list.

See also:

XFreeExtensionList, XQueryExtension

XListFonts

Purpose:

Provides a list of names of fonts available to an X server.

Syntax:

```
char *pattern; /* Names matching this pattern are returned */
               /* Example: "*courier*120*"                 */
```

```
int  maxnames; /* Maximum number of names to be returned   */
int  count;    /* On return: actual count of matched names */
char **fnames; /* Array of names                           */

if((fnames = XListFonts(display, pattern, maxnames, &count))
    == NULL)
{
/* No matching font names found... */
}
```

Returns:

A pointer to an array of names. NULL indicates no matching names found. Use XFreeFontNames to release the memory used by the list of names.

See also:

XFreeFontInfo, XFreeFontNames, XGetFontPath, XListFontsWithInfo, XSetFontPath

---

XListFontsWithInfo

Purpose:

Gets a list of fonts, with detailed information, available to the X server.

Syntax:

```
char *pattern; /* Names matching this pattern are returned */
               /* Example: "*adobe*courier*120*"           */
int  maxnames; /* Maximum number of names to be returned   */
int  count;    /* On return: actual count of matched names */
XFontStruct *info; /* On return: points to font info array */
char **fnames; /* Array of names                           */

if((fnames = XListFontsWithInfo(display, pattern, maxnames,
                            &count, &info)) == NULL)
{
/* No matching font names found... */
}
```

Returns:

A pointer to an array of names. NULL indicates no matching names found. Use XFreeFontNames and XFreeFontInfo to release the memory used by the list of names and XFontStruct structures, respectively.

See also:

XFreeFontInfo, XFreeFontNames, XGetFontPath, XListFonts, XSetFontPath

---

XListHosts

Purpose:

Gets a list of hosts that have access to the specified display.

Syntax:

```
int         numhosts; /* Number of hosts in returned list  */
Bool        control;  /* Access control status is returned */
                      /* True = access control enabled     */
XHostAddress *hosts;   /* List of hosts                     */

if((hosts = XListHosts(display, &numhosts, &control)) != NULL)
{
/* Successfully retrieved host list */
}
```

Returns:

Pointer to an array of XHostAddress structures. Use XFree to free the list.

See also:

XAddHost, XAddHosts, XDisableAccessControl, XEnableAccessControl, XRemoveHost, XRemoveHosts, XSetAccessControl

---

XListInstalledColormaps

Purpose:

Gets a list of installed colormap identifiers for the screen associated with the specified window.

Syntax:

```
int     num_cmaps; /* Number of colormap IDs returned */
Colormap *cmaps;    /* List of colormap IDs returned    */

if((cmaps = XListInstalledColormaps(display, w, num_cmaps))
    == None)
{
/* Failed to get list of installed colormaps */
}
```

Returns:

Pointer to array of colormap identifiers. Use XFree to free the memory used by the array.

See also:

XCreateColormap, XFreeColormap, XInstallColormap, XSetWindowColormap, XUninstallColormap

---

XListPixmapFormats

Purpose:

Gets a list of pixmap formats supported by a specified X server.

Syntax:

```
typedef struct              /* XPixmapFormatValues data type */
{
    int depth, bits_per_pixel, scanline_pad;
} XPixmapFormatValues;
```

```
int                count;  /* Number of supported formats */
XPixmapFormatValues *pflist; /* List of formats           */

if((pflist = XListPixmapFormats(display, &count)) != NULL)
{
/* Got the list */
}
```

Returns:

Pointer to an array of XPixmapFormatValues structures. Use Xfree to release memory used by array. A NULL return indicates failure.

See also:

XCreatePixmap, XListDepths

XListProperties

Purpose:

Gets an array of atoms identifying all properties on a window.

Syntax:

```
int  num_prop;    /* On return: number of properties */
Atom *prop_list;  /* Array of "property name" atoms   */

if((prop_list = XListProperties(display, w, num_prop))
    != NULL)
{
/* Got list of atoms... */
}
```

Returns:

A pointer to an array of atoms representing names of properties on the specified window. To free memory used by array, use XFree. A NULL return indicates error.

See also:

XChangeProperty, XDeleteProperty, XGetWindowProperty

XLoadFont

Purpose:

Loads a font, if not already loaded, and returns its font ID.

Syntax:

```
char *font_name; /* Name of font to be loaded */
Font fid;        /* Font ID returned          */

fid = XLoadFont(display, font_name);
```

Returns:

Font ID.

See also:

XFreeFont, XLoadQueryFont, XQueryFont, XUnloadFont

XLoadQueryFont

Purpose:

Loads a font and gets information about it.

Syntax:

```
char      *font_name; /* Name of font to be loaded */
XFontStruct *fstruct;    /* Returned font information */

if((fstruct = XLoadQueryFont(display, name)) != NULL)
{
/* Font has been successfully loaded */
}
```

Returns:

Pointer to XFontStruct structure with information about the font; NULL in case of error.

See also:

XFreeFont, XLoadFont, XQueryFont, XUnloadFont

XLocaleOfFontSet

Purpose:

Gets the name of the locale bound to the specified font set.

Syntax:

```
XFontSet font_set; /* Font set for which information is sought */
char*    locale_name;

locale_name = XLocaleOfFontSet(font_set);
```

Returns:

Null-terminated string containing the name of the locale bound to the specified font set. To free storage allocated for the locale name, call XFreeFontSet.

See also:

XCreateFontSet, XFreeFontSet

XLockDisplay

Purpose:

Locks out all other threads from using the specified display. (A thread is a stream of execution within a process.)

Syntax:

```
XLockDisplay(display);
```

See also:

```
XInitThreads, XUnlockDisplay
```

XLookUpColor

Purpose:

Gets RGB definition of a color, specified by name, from database (the /usr/lib/X11/rgb.txt file) as well as from the hardware colormap.

Syntax:

```
char    *colorname;  /* Name of color ("blue", for instance)  */
XColor  db_def;      /* RGB value from database returned here  */
XColor  hardware_def;/* Closest RGB value supported by hardware */

if(XLookUpColor(display, cmap, colorname, &db_def,
             &hardware_def))
{
/* Got RGB values */
}
```

Returns:

Nonzero if successful; zero on error.

See also:

```
XAllocNamedColor, XParseColor, XStoreNamedColor
```

XLookUpKeysym

Purpose:

Gets the keysym corresponding to the contents of an XEvent structure containing information for a KeyPress or KeyRelease event.

Syntax:

```
XKeyEvent event;   /* The event structure         */
int       index;   /* Indicates which table:      */
                   /* unshifted (0) or shifted (1) */
KeySym    keysym;  /* Resulting keysym            */

keysym = XLookUpKeysym(&event, index);
```

Returns:

Keysym corresponding to the keycode in the event structure. NoSymbol indicates no keysym was found.

See also:

XKeycodeToKeysym, XKeysymToString, XLookupString

XLookUpString

Purpose:

Translates a keyboard event directly into a string.

Syntax:

```
XKeyEvent      event;    /* KeyPress or KeyRelease event  */
char           buffer[]; /* Buffer where string is returned */
int            num_bytes;/* Size of buffer in bytes       */
KeySym         keysym;   /* Keysym returned here          */
XComposeStatus cstatus;  /* State for multikey character  */
                         /*composition. Not yet implemented.*/
int            count;    /* Number of chars. returned     */

count = XLookUpString(&event, buffer, num_bytes, &keysym,
                 &cstatus);
buffer[count] = '\0'; /* To make it a C-style string */
```

Returns:

Number of characters returned in buffer.

See also:

XKeycodeToKeysym, XKeysymToString, XLookupKeysym

XLowerWindow

Purpose:

Lowers the specified window in the stacking order of its siblings.

Syntax:

```
XLowerWindow(display, w);
```

See also:

XCirculateSubWindows, XRaiseWindow, XRestackWindows

XMapRaised

Purpose:

Maps a window and places it at the top of the stacking order.

Syntax:

XMapRaised(display, w);

See also:

XLowerWindow, XMapWindow, XRaiseWindow, XUnmapWindow

XMapSubwindows

Purpose:

Maps all subwindows of a window.

Syntax:

XMapSubwindows(display, w);

See also:

XMapWindow, XMapRaised, XUnmapSubwindows, XUnmapWindow

XMapWindow

Purpose:

Maps a window.

Syntax:

XMapWindow(display, w);

See also:

XMapRaised, XMapSubwindows, XUnmapSubwindows, XUnmapWindow

XMaskEvent

Purpose:

Waits until an event matching a specified mask is received.

Syntax:

XEvent event; /* Information on event is returned here */

XMaskEvent(display, event_mask, &event);

See also:

XCkeckMaskEvent, XCheckTypedEvent, XNextEvent

XMatchVisualInfo

Purpose:

Gets information on a visual of specified depth and class (see Chapter 11).

Syntax:

```
int        screen; /* Screen whose visual you want        */
int        depth;  /* Desired depth of visual: 4, for instance*/
int        class;  /* Desired class: PseudoColor, for instance*/
XVisualInfo vinfo;  /* Room for information on matching visual */

if(XMatchVisualInfo(display, screen, depth, class, &vinfo))
{
/* Matching visual's info is in "vinfo" */
}
```

Returns:

Nonzero on success; zero on failure.

See also:

DefaultVisual (macro), XGetVisualInfo

XMaxRequestSize

Purpose:

Gets the maximum size (in 4-byte units) of protocol requests that the X server can accept.

Syntax:

```
long max_req_size;

max_req_size = XMaxRequestSize(display);
```

Returns:

Maximum size (in 4-byte units) of protocol requests that the server can accept.

See also:

XExtendedMaxRequestSize

XMoveResizeWindow

Purpose:

Changes position and size of a window.

Syntax:

```
XMoveResizeWindow(display, w, x, y, width, height);
```

See also:

XMoveWindow, XResizeWindow

XMoveWindow

Purpose:

Moves a window.

Syntax:

```
XMoveWindow(display, w, x, y);
```

See also:

XMoveResizeWindow, XResizeWindow

XNewModifiermap

Purpose:

Provides a new XModifierKeymap structure.

Syntax:

```
int             keys_per_modifier; /* Max. keys per modifier  */
XModifierKeymap *new_modmap;       /* Pointer to new structure */

new_modmap = XNewModifiermap(keys_per_modifier);
```

Returns:

Pointer to new XModifierKeymap structure.

See also:

XDeleteModifiermapEntry, XFreeModifiermap, XGetModifierMapping, XInsertModifiermapEntry, XSetModifierMapping

XNextEvent

Purpose:

Waits until the next event from the X server. Also, sends any waiting protocol requests to the server.

Syntax:

```
XEvent  event; /* Information about event returned here */

XNextEvent(display, &event);
```

See also:

XEventsQueued, XMaskEvent, XPeekEvent, XSelectInput

XNoOp

Purpose:

Sends a do-nothing protocol request to exercise the connection with the X server.

Syntax:

```
XNoOp(display);
```

See also:

```
XCloseDisplay, XOpenDisplay
```

XOffsetRegion

Purpose:

Moves a region by a specified amount.

Syntax:

```
Region r;      /* Region being moved              */
int    dx, dy; /* Amount to move along x- and y-axis */

XOffsetRegion(r, dx, dy);
```

See also:

```
XCreateRegion, XDestroyRegion, XShrinkRegion
```

XOpenDisplay

Purpose:

Opens a connection to the X server that controls the named display (see Chapter 3 on conventions for naming displays and Chapter 5 for an example).

Syntax:

```
char    *display_name; /* Name of display or NULL        */
Display *display;      /* Pointer returned by XOpenDisplay */

if((display = XOpenDisplay(display_name)) == NULL)
{
    fprintf(stderr, "Could not open display: %s\n",
            XDisplayName(display_name));
    exit(1);
}
```

Returns:

Pointer to `Display` structure. You should save this pointer because it is a required argument for most Xlib function calls.

See also:

XCloseDisplay, XDisplayName,

XParseColor

Purpose:

Gets the RGB values corresponding to a color specified by a name ("cyan") or a hexadecimal number ("#00ffff").

Syntax:

```
char    *spec;    /* Color name or hexadecimal RGB value    */
XColor rgb_def; /* RGB values for color are returned here */

if(XParseColor(display, cmap, spec, &rgb_def))
{
/* Success */
}
```

Returns:

Nonzero if successful; zero on error.

See also:

XAllocNamedColor, XCreateColormap, XLookupColor

XParseGeometry

Purpose:

Gets position and size from a geometry specification string (for example, "300x200+20+15").

Syntax:

```
char        *geom_spec;    /* Geometry specification string */
int         x, y;          /* On return: the position       */
unsigned int width, height; /* On return: the size          */
int         bitmask;       /* Bits indicate valid values    */

bitmask = XParseGeometry(geom_spec, &x, &y, &width, &height);
```

Returns:

An integer whose bits indicate which of the computed values are valid.

See also:

XGeometry, XWMGeometry

XPeekEvent

Purpose:

Gets an event without removing it from the queue. Waits if no event is available.

Syntax:

```
XEvent  event;  /* Information on event returned here */

XPeekEvent(display, &event);
```

See also:

```
XNextEvent, XPeekIfEvent
```

XPeekIfEvent

Purpose:

Checks the event queue for a matching event without removing the event from the queue. You provide the function that is called to check whether an event meets your requirements for a match.

Syntax:

```
XEvent event;          /* Information on event returned here */
Bool   (*predicate)(); /* Function called to verify match   */
char   *args;          /* Arguments for the function        */

XPeekIfEvent(display, event, predicate, args);
```

See also:

```
XNextEvent, XPeekEvent
```

XPending

Purpose:

Flushes Xlib's output buffer and returns the number of events waiting to be processed.

Syntax:

```
int events_waiting;
events_waiting = XPending(display);
```

Returns:

Number of events waiting to be processed.

See also:

```
XEventsQueued
```

Xpermalloc

Purpose:

Permanently allocates memory (not freed until program exits).

Syntax:

```
unsigned int size; /* Number of bytes to allocate */
char          *mem; /* Pointer to allocated memory */

mem = Xpermalloc(size);
```

Returns:

A pointer to allocated memory.

XPointInRegion

Purpose:

Determines whether a point is inside a region.

Syntax:

```
Region r;    /* Is point in this region? */
int    x, y; /* Point being tested      */

if(XPointInRegion(r, x, y))
{
/* Yes. Point is in the region */
}
```

Returns:

True if point is in the region; False otherwise.

See also:

```
XCreateRegion, XDestroyRegion
```

XPolygonRegion

Purpose:

Generates a region from a polygon.

Syntax:

```
XPoint points[];  /* Array of points (vertices of the polygon)  */
int    npoints;   /* Number of points in the array             */
int    fill_rule; /* WindingRule or OddEvenRule (see Chapter 9) */
Region r;         /* Region created by XPolygonRegion          */

r = XPolygonRegion(points, n, fill_rule);
```

Returns:

A Region.

See also:

```
XCreateRegion, XDestroyRegion
```

XPutBackEvent

Purpose:

Puts an event back in the event queue so that the next call to XNextEvent returns this event.

Syntax:

```
XEvent event;

XPutBackEvent(display, &event);
```

See also:

XNextEvent

XPutImage

Purpose:

Copies a rectangular area of an image from an XImage structure to a drawable (window or pixmap).

Syntax:

```
int src_x, src_y; /* Corner of rectangle being copied */
int dst_x, dst_y; /* Destination point               */

XPutImage(display, drawable, gc, ximage, src_x, src_y,
        dst_x, dst_y, width, height);
```

See also:

XCreateImage, XDestroyImage, XGetImage, XGetSubImage

XPutPixel

Purpose:

Sets the pixel value at a specified point in an image.

Syntax:

```
unsigned long pixel; /* Pixel value being copied to (x,y) */

XPutPixel(ximage, x, y, pixel);
```

See also:

XAddPixel, XGetPixel

XQueryBestCursor

Purpose:

Gets the dimensions of the hardware-supported cursor that is closest to the size you want.

Syntax:

```
unsigned int width, height;    /* Desired size          */
unsigned int h_width, h_height;/* Hardware-supported size */

if(XQueryBestCursor(display, drawable, width, height,
                    &h_width, &h_height))
{
/* Found a cursor size */
}
```

Returns:

Nonzero if successful; zero on failure.

See also:

XCreateFontCursor, XCreatePixmapCursor, XDefineCursor, XFreeCursor, XQueryBestSize, XRecolorCursor, XUndefineCursor

---

XQueryBestSize

Purpose:

Gets the dimensions of a cursor, tile, or stipple that is supported by the hardware and is closest to the size you want.

Syntax:

```
int         class;             /* One of: TileShape,      */
                               /* CursorShape, or StippleShape */
unsigned int width, height;    /* Size you want           */
unsigned int h_width, h_height;/* Size supported by hardware */

if(XQueryBestSize(display, class, drawable, width, height,
                  &h_width, &h_height))
{
/* Found a "best" size */
}
```

Returns:

Nonzero if successful; zero if call fails.

See also:

XQueryBestCursor, XQueryBestStipple, XQueryBestTile

XQueryBestStipple

Purpose:

Gets the size of a stipple that is fastest for the hardware, yet closest to the size you want.

Syntax:

```
unsigned int width, height;    /* Size you want           */
unsigned int h_width, h_height;/* Best hardware-supported size */
```

```
if(XQueryBestStipple(display, drawable, width, height,
                 &h_width, &h_height))
{
/* Found a good stipple size */
}
```

Returns:

Nonzero if successful; zero if function fails.

See also:

```
XQueryBestSize
```

XQueryBestTile

Purpose:

Gets the tile size that is fastest for the hardware, yet closest to the size you want.

Syntax:

```
unsigned int width, height;     /* Size you want               */
unsigned int h_width, h_height;/* Best hardware-supported size */

if(XQueryBestTile(display, drawable, width, height,
                &h_width, &h_height))
{
/* Found best tile size */
}
```

Returns:

Nonzero if successful; zero if function fails.

See also:

```
XQueryBestSize
```

XQueryColor

Purpose:

Gets the RGB values for a specific cell in a colormap.

Syntax:

```
XColor cell;/* Set pixel value before call. RGB values returned */

XQueryColor(display, cmap, &cell);
```

See also:

```
XLookupColor, XParseColor, XQueryColors
```

XQueryColors

Purpose:

Gets the RGB values for an array of colormap cells.

Syntax:

```
XColor colors[]; /* Array of colormap cells. Set pixel values */
                 /* before call. Has RGB values on return    */
int    ncolors;  /* Number of colormap cells in "colors"     */

XQueryColors(display, cmap, colors, ncolors);
```

See also:

XLookupColor, XParseColor, XQueryColor

XQueryExtension

Purpose:

Gets information about a specific extension (call XListExtensions to get the names of extensions).

Syntax:

```
char *name;         /* Name of extension                          */
int  major_opcode;  /* On return: Major opcode used by extension */
int  first_event;   /* On return: First custom event code        */
int  first_error;   /* On return: First custom error code        */

if(XQueryExtension(display, name, &major_opcode,
                   &first_event, &first_error))
{
/* Got the information about this extension */
}
```

Returns:

True if function succeeds; False if the named extension is not found.

See also:

XFreeExtensionList, XListExtensions

XQueryFont

Purpose:

Gets information about a loaded font.

Syntax:

```
XID        id;       /* Resource ID of the font or the GContext */
XFontStruct *fstruct; /* Pointer to font information            */
```

```
if((fstruct = XQueryFont(display, font_ID)) != NULL)
{
/* Font information retrieved */
}
```

Returns:

Pointer to an XFontStruct structure. A NULL return means the font is not yet loaded.

See also:

XGContextFromGC, XLoadFont, XLoadQueryFont

XQueryKeymap

Purpose:

Gets a bit vector (returned in a 32-byte array) that describes the current state of the keyboard. (Each 1 bit denotes a key that is down.)

Syntax:

```
char keys[32]; /* Room for the state of the keys */

XQueryKeymap(display, keys);
```

See also:

XKeysymToString, XLookupString

XQueryPointer

Purpose:

Gets the current position of the pointer.

Syntax:

```
Window       root;        /* Root window ID returned here   */
Window       child;       /* Child window ID returned here  */
int          root_x, root_y;/* For position relative to root */
int          win_x, win_y;  /* For position in window 'w'    */
unsigned int keys_buttons;  /* For current state of modifiers */

if(XQueryPointer(display, w, &root, &child, &root_x, &root_y,
               &win_x, &win_y, &keys_buttons))
{
/* Retrieved pointer position */
}
```

Returns:

True to indicate success; False if pointer is not in the same screen as the window w.

See also:

XWarpPointer

XQueryTextExtents

Purpose:

Determines the bounding rectangle for a text string when displayed in a specified font. (See Chapter 10 for details of the XCharStruct structure.)

Syntax:

```
XID        font_ID;    /* Font ID or GContext ID                */
char       *string;    /* String whose bounding box is returned */
int        nchars;     /* Number of characters in the string    */
int        direction;  /* Direction of font returned here        */
int        ascent;     /* Maximum ascent returned here           */
int        descent;    /* Maximum descent returned here          */
XCharStruct overall;   /* Overall metric is returned here        */

XQueryTextExtents(display, font_ID, string, nchars, &direction,
            &ascent, &descent, &overall);
```

See also:

XGContextFromGC, XTextExtents, XTextWidth

XQueryTextExtents16

Purpose:

Determines the bounding rectangle for a string of 16-bit characters when displayed in a specified font.

Syntax:

```
XID        font_ID;    /* Font ID or GContext ID                */
XChar2b    *string;    /* String whose bounding box is returned */
int        nchars;     /* Number of characters in the string    */
int        direction;  /* Direction of font returned here        */
int        ascent;     /* Maximum ascent returned here           */
int        descent;    /* Maximum descent returned here          */
XCharStruct overall;   /* Overall metric is returned here        */

XQueryTextExtents16(display, font_ID, string, nchars, &direction,
            &ascent, &descent, &overall);
```

See also:

XGContextFromGC, XTextExtents16, XTextWidth16

XQueryTree

Purpose:

Gets the parent, root, and list of children of a window.

Syntax:

```
Window       root;      /* Root ID is returned here         */
Window       parent;    /* Parent window's ID returned here */
Window       *children; /* Points to list of children on    */
                        /* return. Free with XFree(children) */
unsigned int nchildren; /* Number of children returned here */

if(XQueryTree(display, w, &root, &parent, &children, &nchildren))
{
/* Query successful */
}
```

Returns:

Nonzero if successful; zero in case of problems.

See also:

```
XFree
```

XRaiseWindow

Purpose:

Raises a window to the top of the stacking order among its siblings.

Syntax:

```
XRaiseWindow(display, w);
```

See also:

```
XCirculateSubwindows, XLowerWindow, XRestackWindows
```

XReadBitmapFile

Purpose:

Reads bitmap from a file and prepares a bitmap (see Chapter 12 for file format).

Syntax:

```
char         *filename;    /* Name of bitmap file          */
unsigned int width, height; /* Sizes returned here          */
Pixmap       bitmap;       /* Bitmap ID returned here       */
int          x_hot, y_hot; /* Hotspot coords returned here */

if(XReadBitmapFile(display, drawable, filename, &width,
      &height, &bitmap, &x_hot, &y_hot) == BitmapSuccess)
{
/* Bitmap successfully prepared */
}
```

Returns:

BitmapSuccess if all goes well; otherwise, returns one of the following: BitmapOpenFailed, BitmapFileInvalid, or BitmapNoMemory.

See also:

XCreateBitmapFromData, XCreatePixmapFromBitmapData, XFreePixmap, XReadBitmapFileData, XWriteBitmapFile

---

XReadBitmapFileData

Purpose:

Reads bitmap data from a file and returns the data, but, unlike XReadBitmapFile, does not prepare the bitmap. The data is returned in data_return; you have to call XFree to free this storage when finished with the data.

Syntax:

```
char          *filename;      /* Name of bitmap file         */
unsigned int  width, height;  /* Sizes returned here         */
unsigned char *data;          /* Bitmap data returned here   */
int           x_hot, y_hot;   /* Hotspot coords returned here */

if(XReadBitmapFileData(filename, &width,
      &height, &data, &x_hot, &y_hot) == BitmapSuccess)
{
/* Bitmap successfully prepared */
}
```

Returns:

BitmapSuccess if all goes well; otherwise, returns one of the following: BitmapOpenFailed, BitmapFileInvalid, or BitmapNoMemory.

See also:

XCreateBitmapFromData, XCreatePixmapFromBitmapData, XFreePixmap, XReadBitmapFile, XWriteBitmapFile

---

XRebindKeysym

Purpose:

Binds an ASCII string to a keysym so that XLookupString returns that string when the user presses the key corresponding to that keysym.

Syntax:

```
KeySym        keysym;     /* Key to which string is bound  */
KeySym        mod_list[];/* Modifiers for the key          */
int           mod_count; /* Number of modifiers            */
unsigned char string[];  /* The string itself              */
int           slength;   /* Number of characters in string */

XRebindKeysym (display, keysym, mod_list, mod_count, string,
               slength);
```

See also:

XKeysymToString, XLookupString

XRecolorCursor

Purpose:

Changes the color of a cursor.

Syntax:

```
XColor foreground_color; /* RGB values for the foreground */
XColor background_color; /* RGB values for the background */

XRecolorCursor(display, cursor, &foreground_color,
               &background_color);
```

See also:

XCreateFontCursor, XCreatePixmapCursor, XDefineCursor, XUndefineCursor

XReconfigureWMWindow

Purpose:

Changes size and stacking order of a top-level window.

Syntax:

```
int            screen; /* Screen number where window appears */
XWindowChanges xwval;  /* New values for window's size, etc. */

if(XReconfigureWMWindow(display, w, screen, value_mask, &xwval))
{
/* Window reconfigured */
}
```

Returns:

Nonzero if no error; zero otherwise.

See also:

XIconifyWindow, XWithdrawWindow

XRectInRegion

Purpose:

Determines whether a rectangle is partly or completely inside a region.

Syntax:

```
Region r; /* Test if rectangle is in this region */

if(XRectInRegion(r, x, y, width, heigth) == RectanglePart)
{
/* Rectangle is partly inside the region */
}
```

Returns:

`RectangleIn` or `RectanglePart` if rectangle is completely or partially in the region. `RectangleOut` if rectangle is outside the region.

See also:

`XCreateRegion, XDestroyRegion, XUnionRectWithRegion`

XRefreshKeyboardMapping

Purpose:

Updates Xlib's internal keycode-to-keysym mapping tables by requesting information from the server. You should call this function in response to the `MappingNotify` event.

Syntax:

```
XMappingEvent event; /* New keyboard mapping information */

XRefreshKeyboardMapping(&event);
```

See also:

`XChangeKeyboardMapping, XGetKeyboardMapping`

XRemoveFromSaveSet

Purpose:

Removes a window from the save set, which is the list of windows that will be reparented if their immediate parent is destroyed.

Syntax:

```
XRemoveFromSaveSet(display, w);
```

See also:

`XAddToSaveSet, XChangeSaveSet`

XRemoveHost

Purpose:

Removes a host from the server's access-control list.

Syntax:

```
XHostAddress *host; /* Network address of host being removed */

XRemoveHost(display, host);
```

See also:

XAddHost, XAddHosts, XRemoveHosts, XSetAccessControl

XRemoveHosts

Purpose:

Removes a number of hosts from the server's access-control list.

Syntax:

```
XHostAddress host[];    /* List of network addresses of hosts */
int          num_hosts; /* Number of hosts in list            */

XRemoveHosts(display, host, num_hosts);
```

See also:

XAddHost, XAddHosts, XRemoveHost, XSetAccessControl

XReparentWindow

Purpose:

Changes the parent of a window.

Syntax:

```
Window parent;/* New parent's ID             */
int    x, y;  /* Position of "w" in "parent" */

XReparentWindow(display, win, parent, x, y);
```

See also:

XReconfigureWMWindow, XRestackWindows

XResetScreenSaver

Purpose:

Redisplays the screen if it was blanked.

Syntax:

```
XResetScreenSaver(display);
```

See also:

XActivateScreenSaver, XForceScreenSaver, XGetScreenSaver, XSetScreenSaver

XResizeWindow

Purpose:

Changes a window's size.

Syntax:

```
XResizeWindow(display, w, width, height);
```

See also:

```
XConfigureWindow, XMoveResizeWindow, XMoveWindow
```

XRestackWindows

Purpose:

Places the specified windows (all with a common parent) in the order listed, from top to bottom.

Syntax:

```
Window windows[]; /* New stacking order: top to bottom */
int     nwindows;  /* Number of window in array         */

XRestackWindows(display, windows, nwindows);
```

See also:

```
XCirculateSubWindows, XCirculateSubWindowsUp, XCirculateSubWindowsDown,
XLowerWindow, XRaiseWindow
```

XrmDestroyDatabase

Purpose:

Destroys a resource database.

Syntax:

```
XrmDatabase db; /* Database being destroyed */

XDestroyDatabase(db);
```

See also:

```
XrmMergeDatabases
```

XrmGetFileDatabase

Purpose:

Creates a new resource database and loads it with data read from a specified resource file. (See Chapter 3 for information on specifying resources.)

Syntax:

```
char        *res_filename; /* Resource filename   */
XrmDatabase new_db;        /* New resource database */

new_db = XrmGetFileDatabase(res_filename);
```

Returns:

An XrmDatabase value representing the new database. The return value is NULL if the file cannot be opened.

See also:

XrmDestroyDatabase, XrmGetResource, XrmPutFileDatabase

XrmGetResource

Purpose:

Gets a resource value (in an XrmValue structure) corresponding to specified class and resource names.

Syntax:

```
typedef struct
{
    unsigned int size; /* Number of characters in string */
    caddr_t      addr; /* Value in string form           */
} XrmValue;

XrmDatabase database; /* Resource database             */
char        *res_name; /* Resource name                */
char        *res_class;/* Class name                    */
char        *res_type; /* On return: resource's type   */
XrmValue    res_value; /* On return: resource's value  */

if(XrmGetResource(database, res_name, res_class,
              &res_type, &res_value))
{
/* Successfully retrieved resource's value */
}
```

Returns:

True if the resource is found; False otherwise.

See also:

XrmGetFileDatabase

XrmGetStringDatabase

Purpose:

Creates a resource database from a string (multiple lines separated by a new line).

Syntax:

```
char        *resource_spec; /* Resource specification */
XrmDatabase res_db;         /* Resource database      */

res_db = XrmGetStringDatabase(data);
```

Returns:

An XrmDatabase value representing the new database; NULL on error.

See also:

XrmDestroyDatabase, XrmGetFileDatabase, XrmPutFileDatabase

XrmInitialize

Purpose:

Initializes the X resource manager.

Syntax:

```
XrmInitialize();
```

See also:

XrmGetFileDatabase, XrmGetStringDatabase, XrmPutFileDatabase

XrmMergeDatabases

Purpose:

Combines the contents of the source database into the target.

Syntax:

```
XrmDatabase  source; /* Contents of this database are */
XrmDatabase  target; /* merged into this one          */

XrmMergeDatabases(source, &target);
```

See also:

XrmGetFileDatabase, XrmGetStringDatabase, XrmPutFileDatabase

XrmParseCommand

Purpose:

Loads resource database from command-line options (see Chapter 13, for example).

Syntax:

```
XrmDatabase      res_db;   /* Resource database             */
XrmOptionDescList table;   /* Table of command-line options */
int              noptions; /* Number of options in table    */
```

```
char                *app_name;/* Name of application       */
int                 argc;     /* Number of command-line arguments */
char                **argv;    /* The actual command-line arguments*/

XrmParseCommand(&res_db, table, table_count, name, &argc, argv);
```

See also:

```
XrmGetFileDatabase, XrmGetResource, XrmGetStringDatabase
```

XrmPutFileDatabase

Purpose:

Saves a resource database to a file.

Syntax:

```
XrmDatabase database;    /* Resource database to be saved     */
char        db_filename; /* Name of file where resources stored */

XrmPutFileDatabase(database, db_filename);
```

See also:

```
XrmGetFileDatabase, XrmGetResource, XrmGetStringDatabase
```

XrmPutLineResource

Purpose:

Adds a single line of a resource (for example, myapp.foreground: white) to a resource database.

Syntax:

```
XrmDatabase  database; /* Identifies resource database */
char         line[];   /* Resource specification       */

XrmPutLineResource(&database, line);
```

See also:

```
XrmGetFileDatabase, XrmPutFileDatabase, XrmPutResource
```

XrmPutResource

Purpose:

Stores a resource from an XrmValue structure into a resource database.

Syntax:

```
XrmDatabase database;  /* Resource database       */
char        *res_spec; /* Resource specification */
char        *res_type; /* Resource type          */
XrmValue    res_value; /* Resource's value       */

XrmPutResource(&database, res_spec, res_type, &res_value);
```

See also:

XrmGetFileDatabase, XrmPutFileDatabase, XrmPutLineResource

XrmPutStringResource

Purpose:

Adds to the database a resource specified by name and value.

Syntax:

```
XrmDatabase database;    /* Add to this resource database    */
char        resource[]; /* Resource name (left side of colon) */
char        value[];    /* Resource's value (right side)    */

XrmPutStringResource(&database, resource, value);
```

See also:

XrmGetFileDatabase, XrmGetStringDatabase, XrmPutLineResource, XrmPutResource

---

XrmQGetResource

Purpose:

Gets a resource's value when name and class are specified as *quarks*—integer identifiers for strings, used by the X resource manager.

Syntax:

```
XrmDatabase        database; /* Look for resource here     */
XrmNameList        quark_name;/* Resource name as a quark    */
XrmClassList       quark_list;/* Resource class as a quark   */
XrmRepresentation quark_type;/* Resource type is returned here */
XrmValue           value;    /* Resource value is returned here*/

if(XrmQGetResource(database, quark_name, quark_class,
                   &quark_type, &value))
{
/* Got resource value */
}
```

Returns:

True if named resource is found in database; False otherwise.

See also:

XrmGetFileDatabase, XrmQPutResource

XrmQGetSearchList

Purpose:

Prepares a search list for use by XrmQGetSearchResource.

Syntax:

```
XrmDatabase   database;     /* Resource database to search  */
XrmNameList   names;        /* Resource names of interest   */
XrmClassList  classes;      /* Resource classes of interest */
XrmSearchList search_list;  /* Room for search list (allocate) */
int           length;       /* Number of entries in search list*/

if(XrmQGetSearchList(database, names, classes, search_list,
                     length))
{
/* Search list returned */
}
```

Returns:

True if all goes well; False otherwise.

See also:

XrmGetFileDatabase, XrmQGetSearchResource

XrmQGetSearchResource

Purpose:

Searches for a resource, using a search list prepared by XrmQGetSearchList.

Syntax:

```
XrmSearchList      search_list; /* Search list to use in search */
XrmName            name;        /* Name of resource             */
XrmClass           class;       /* Class of resource            */
XrmRepresentation  type;        /* Room for representation type */
XrmValue           value;       /* Structure for returned value */

if(XrmQGetSearchResource(search_list, name, class, &type,
                         &value))
{
/* Got resource value */
}
```

Returns:

True if resource is found; False if not.

See also:

XrmGetFileDatabase, XrmQGetSearchList

XrmQPutResource

Purpose:

Stores a resource's value in a database when resource name and class are specified as *quarks*—integer identifiers for strings, used by the X resource manager.

Syntax:

```
XrmDatabase       database;  /* Store value in this database */
XrmBindingList    bindings;  /* Binding for the names       */
XrmQuarkList      quarks;    /* Complete or partial name    */
XrmRepresentation type;      /* Resource type as a quark    */
XrmValue          value;     /* Resource value              */

XrmQPutResource(&database, bindings, quarks, type, &value);
```

See also:

```
XrmGetFileDatabase, XrmQGetResource
```

XrmQPutStringResource

Purpose:

Adds to a database a resource specified by a quark representing the name.

Syntax:

```
XrmDatabase    database; /* Add resource to this database */
XrmBindingList bindings; /* Specify binding of names      */
XrmQuarkList   quarks;   /* Complete or partial name      */
char           *value;   /* Value in the form of a string */

XrmQPutStringResource(&database, bindings, quarks, value);
```

See also:

```
XrmGetFileDatabase, XrmPutStringResource
```

XrmQuarkToString

Purpose:

Converts a quark to a string.

Syntax:

```
XrmQuark quark;   /* Quark to be converted      */
char     *string; /* String equivalent of quark */

if((string = XrmQuarkToString(quark)) == NULL)
{
/* No such quark exists */
}
```

Returns:

Pointer to string equivalent of quark; NULL if no such quark exists.

See also:

```
XrmStringToQuark
```

XrmStringToBindingQuarkList

Purpose:

Converts a resource specification into two lists—one of quarks and one of bindings.

Syntax:

```
char          *string;   /* String (resource specification)  */ XrmBindingList
bindings; /* Bindings generated from string   */ XrmQuarkList    quarks;  /* Quarks
generated from string     */  XrmStringToBindingQuarkList(string, bindings, quarks);
```

See also:

XrmQuarkToString, XrmStringToQuark

XrmStringToQuark

Purpose:

Converts a string to a quark—an integer identifier.

Syntax:

```
char *string; /* String being converted */

XrmStringToQuark(string);
```

Returns:

A quark for the string.

See also:

XrmQuarkToString

XrmStringToQuarkList

Purpose:

Converts a resource name string (for example, xmh.toc.foreground) to a list of quarks.

Syntax:

```
char          *string; /* String being converted  */
XrmQuarkList  quarks;  /* List of quarks returned */

XrmStringToQuarkList(string, quarks);
```

See also:

XrmStringToBindingQuarkList, XrmStringToQuark

XrmUniqueQuark

Purpose:

Creates a new quark that is guaranteed not to represent any existing string.

Syntax:

```
XrmQuark quark; /* New quark */

quark = XrmUniqueQuark();
```

Returns:

A new quark.

See also:

```
XrmQuarkToString, XrmStringToQuark
```

XRotateBuffers

Purpose:

Rotates the cut buffers with contents of buffer 0 going to buffer first.

Syntax:

```
int first;  /* Contents of CUT_BUFFER0 goes to this buffer */

XRotateBuffers(display, first);
```

See also:

```
XFetchBuffer, XFetchBytes, XStoreBuffer, XStoreBytes
```

XRotateWindowProperties

Purpose:

Rotates the contents of an array of properties on a window.

Syntax:

```
Atom  properties[];/* Array of atoms identifying the properties */
int   num_prop;    /* Number of properties in array            */
int   npositions;  /* Rotated by these many positions          */

XRotateWindowProperties(display, w, properties, num_prop,
                        npositions);
```

See also:

```
XChangeProperty, XDeleteProperty, XGetWindowProperty
```

XSaveContext

Purpose:

Saves data corresponding to a window and a context. (See Chapter 7 for an example of using the context management facilities for efficient event processing.)

Syntax:

```
XContext  context;  /* Context of data                       */
caddr_t   data;     /* Data (usually a pointer to a structure) */

if(XSaveContext(display, w, context, data) != 0)
{
    fprintf(stderr, "Error saving context-sensitive data");
    exit(1);
}
```

Returns:

Zero if data successfully saved; XCNOMEM on error.

See also:

```
XFindContext, XUniqueContext
```

XSelectInput

Purpose:

Selects the types of events to be reported for a specific window.

Syntax:

```
XSelectInput(display, w, event_mask);
```

See also:

```
XNextEvent
```

XSendEvent

Purpose:

Sends an event to a window.

Syntax:

```
Bool  propagate; /* True = propagate event up the hierarchy */
XEvent event;    /* Data for event to be sent               */

if(XSendEvent(display, w, propagate, event_mask, event) != 0)
{
/* Event successfully sent */
}
```

Returns:

Nonzero if event successfully sent; zero on failure.

See also:

XNextEvent, XSelectInput

XSetAccessControl

Purpose:

Enables or disables access control. When enabled, X server accepts connections from hosts whose addresses appear in an access-control list.

Syntax:

```
int  mode; /* EnableAccess or DisableAccess */

XSetAccessControl(display, mode);
```

See also:

XAddHost, XAddHosts, XDisableAccessControl, XEnableAccessControl, XRemoveHost, XRemoveHosts

XSetAfterFunction

Purpose:

Sets a function that gets called after every protocol request to the server. You can use this for debugging X applications.

Syntax:

```
int (*func)(); /* Function called after each protocol request */
int (*last)(); /* Last "after" function                      */

last = XSetAfterFunction(display, func);
```

Returns:

Pointer to the previous "after" function.

See also:

XSynchronize

XSetArcMode

Purpose:

Sets the arc-drawing mode in a GC (see Chapter 9).

Syntax:

```
int arc_mode; /* Either ArcChord or ArcPieSlice */

XSetArcMode(display, gc, arc_mode);
```

See also:

XCreateGC, XChangeGC, XDrawArc, XFillArc, XFreeGC

XSetBackground

Purpose:

Sets the background pixel value in a GC. This is not the pixel value used to draw a window's background.

Syntax:

```
unsigned long background; /* Pixel value for background */

XSetBackground(display, gc, background);
```

See also:

XAllocColor, XCreateGC, XChangeGC, XFreeGC, XGetGCValues, XSetForeground

XSetClassHint

Purpose:

Sets the XA_WM_CLASS property of a window.

Syntax:

```
XClassHint class_hints; /* Specify value for property */

XSetClassHint(display, w, &class_hints);
```

See also:

XAllocClassHint, XGetClassHint

XSetClipMask

Purpose:

Sets the clip mask in a GC (see Chapter 9).

Syntax:

```
Pixmap clip_mask; /* Bitmap to be used as clip mask */

XSetClipMask(display, gc, clip_mask);
```

See also:

XCreateGC, XChangeGC, XFreeGC, XSetClipOrigin

XSetClipOrigin

Purpose:

Sets the origin of the clip mask in a GC (see Chapter 9).

Syntax:

```
int clip_x_origin, clip_y_origin; /* New origin */

XSetClipOrigin(display, gc, clip_x_origin, clip_y_origin);
```

See also:

XCreateGC, XChangeGC, XFreeGC, XSetClipMask

XSetClipRectangles

Purpose:

Sets the clip mask in a GC to a list of nonintersecting rectangles.

Syntax:

```
int        clip_x_origin, /* Origin of clip mask           */
           clip_y_origin;
XRectangle rectangles[];  /* List of rectangles            */
int        nrects;        /* Number of rectangles          */
int        ordering;      /* Ordering: UnSorted, YSorted,  */
                          /* YXSorted, or YXBanded (see Ch. 9)*/

XSetClipRectangles(display, gc, clip_x_origin, clip_y_origin,
                   rectangles, nrects, ordering);
```

See also:

XCreateGC, XChangeGC, XFreeGC, XSetClipMask, XSetClipOrigin

XSetCloseDownMode

Purpose:

Defines what happens to a client's resources after the connection to the X server is closed. Resources are retained if close_mode is RetainPermanent or RetainTemporary.

Syntax:

```
int close_mode; /* One of: DestroyAll, RetainPermanent, or */
                /* RetainTemporary                         */

XSetCloseDownMode(display, close_mode);
```

See also:

XKillClient

XSetCommand

Purpose:

Stores the command-line arguments in the XA_WM_COMMAND property of a window.

Syntax:

```
char **argv; /* Command-line arguments */
int  argc;   /* Number of arguments    */

XSetCommand(display, w, argv, argc);
```

See also:

XSetStandardProperties, XSetWMProperties

XSetDashes

Purpose:

Sets the style of dashes (for dashed lines) in a GC (see Chapter 9).

Syntax:

```
int  dash_offset; /* Where in the list to start              */
char dash_list[]; /* List of dashes to be repeated (see Ch.9) */
int  dash_length; /* Number of entries in dash_list          */

XSetDashes(display, gc, dash_offset, dash_list, dash_length);
```

See also:

XCreateGC, XFreeGC

XSetErrorHandler

Purpose:

Sets up a function to be called when nonfatal errors occur (see Chapter 6).

Syntax:

```
int (*handler)(Display *, XErrorEvent); /* Error handler */

XSetErrorHandler(handler)
```

Returns:

Starting with X11R4, XSetErrorHandler returns a pointer to the previous error handler.

See also:

XGetErrorDatabaseText, XGetErrorText, XSetIOErrorHandler

XSetFillRule

Purpose:

Sets the fill rule in a GC (see Chapter 9).

Syntax:

```
int  fill_rule; /* One of: EvenOddRule or WindingRule */

XSetFillRule(display, gc, fill_rule);
```

See also:

XCreateGC, XChangeGC, XFreeGC, XPolygonRegion

XSetFillStyle

Purpose:

Sets the fill style in a GC (see Chapter 9 for details).

Syntax:

```
int fill_style; /* FillSolid, FillTiled, FillStippled, or */
                /* FillOpaqueStippled (see Chapter 9)     */

XSetFillStyle(display, gc, fill_style);
```

See also:

XCreateGC, XChangeGC, XFreeGC, XSetStipple, XSetTile

XSetFont

Purpose:

Sets the font in a GC. You must load the font before using the GC to draw text.

Syntax:

```
Font font; /* ID of font to be set in the GC */

XSetFont(display, gc, font);
```

See also:

XLoadQueryFont, XUnloadFont

XSetFontPath

Purpose:

Sets the list of directories that the X server searches to locate fonts.

Syntax:

```
char  *directories[]; /* List of directory names */
int   ndirs;          /* Number of directories   */

XSetFontPath(display, directories, ndirs);
```

See also:

XFreeFontPath, XGetFontPath, XLoadFont, XLoadQueryFont, XQueryFont, XUnloadFont

XSetForeground

Purpose:

Sets the foreground pixel value in a GC. You must allocate a color to get a valid pixel value.

Syntax:

```
unsigned long foreground; /* Pixel value for foreground */

XSetForeground(display, gc, foreground);
```

See also:

XAllocColor, XCreateGC, XChangeGC, XFreeGC, XGetGCValues, XSetBackground

XSetFunction

Purpose:

Specifies in a GC the way the server should combine pixel values when drawing (see Chapter 9).

Syntax:

```
int  function; /* A bitwise logical function (use names such  */
               /* as GXcopy or GXxor, see Chapter 9 for list) */

XSetFunction(display, gc, function);
```

See also:

XCreateGC, XChangeGC, XCopyGC

XSetGraphicsExposures

Purpose:

Enables or disables generation of GraphicsExpose events by altering the graphics_exposure field of a GC (see Chapter 9).

Syntax:

```
Bool graphics_exposures; /* True = enable, False = disable */

XSetGraphicsExposures(display, gc, graphics_exposures);
```

See also:

XCreateGC, XChangeGC, XCopyGC

XSetIconName   (Use XSetWMIconName in X11R4)

Purpose:

Sets the name to be displayed in a window's icon.

Syntax:

```
char *icon_name; /* The name to be displayed in the icon */

XSetIconName(display, gc, icon_name);
```

See also:

XGetIconName, XSetStandardProperties, XSetWMIconName, XSetWMProperties

XSetIconSizes

Purpose:

Sets the value of the XA_WM_ICON_SIZE property of a window. This is used by window managers to set the range of preferred icon sizes.

Syntax:

```
typedef struct
{
    int min_width, min_height;
    int max_width, max_height;
    int width_inc, heigh_inc;
} XIconSize;

XIconSize size_list[]; /* Array of sizes               */
int       count;       /* Number of entries in size_list */

XSetIconSizes(display, w, size_list, count);
```

See also:

XAllocIconSize, XGetIconSizes

XSetInputFocus

Purpose:

Sets the keyboard focus to a window at a specified time.

Syntax:

```
int    revert_to; /* Indicates who gets focus if "w" is not  */
                  /* viewable. Use: RevertToParent,          */
                  /* RevertToPointerRoot, or RevertToNone    */

XSetInputFocus(display, w, revert_to, time);
```

See also:

XGetInputFocus, XSelectInput

XSetIOErrorHandler

Purpose:

Specifies a function that will be called when a fatal I/O error occurs (see Chapter 6).

Syntax:

```
int (*handler)(Display *); /* New fatal error handler */

XSetIOErrorHandler(handler);
```

Returns:

Starting with X11R4, XSetIOErrorHandler returns a pointer to the previous error handler.

See also:

XSetErrorHandler

XSetLineAttributes

Purpose:

Sets the line_width, line_style, cap_style, and join_style attributes in a GC. These affect the appearance of lines (see Chapter 9).

Syntax:

```
unsigned int line_width; /* Line width in pixels (0 allowed) */
int          line_style; /* One of: LineSolid, LineOnOffDash,*/
                         /*         LineDoubleDash            */
int          cap_style;  /* One of: CapNotLast, CapButt,     */
                         /*         CapRound, CapProjecting   */
int          join_style; /* JoinRound, JoinMiter, JoinBevel  */

XSetLineAttributes(display, gc, line_width, line_style,
                   cap_style, join_style);
```

See also:

XCreateGC, XChangeGC, XDrawLine, XSetDashes

XSetModifierMapping

Purpose:

Sets the keycodes used for the modifier keys, such as Shift, Control, and Meta.

Syntax:

```
XModifierKeymap mod_map; /* Specifies the modifier keycodes */

XSetModifierMapping(display, &mod_map);
```

See also:

XDeleteModifiermapEntry, XFreeModifiermap, XGetModifierMapping,
XInsertModifiermapEntry

XSetNormalHints   (Use XSetWMNormalHints in X11R4 or later)

Purpose:

Sets the value of an XA_WM_NORMAL_HINTS property of a window.

Syntax:

```
XSizeHints xsh; /* Specify the sizes in this structure */

XSetNormalHints(display, w, &xsh);
```

See also:

XGetNormalHints, XGetWMNormalHints, XSetWMNormalHints

XSetPlaneMask

Purpose:

Sets the plane_mask field of a graphics context. This determines the bit planes affected by a drawing request (see Chapter 9).

Syntax:

```
unsigned long plane_mask; /* Set bits indicate planes affected */

XSetPlaneMask(display, gc, plane_mask);
```

See also:

XCreateGC, XChangeGC, XGetGCValues

XSetPointerMapping

Purpose:

Defines the mapping from physical mouse buttons to the logical ones—Button1 through Button5—that are supported in X.

Syntax:

```
unsigned char map[]; /* Array of logical button numbers */
int       nmap;      /* Number of entries in "map"      */

if(XSetPointerMapping(display, map, nmap) == MappingSuccess)
{
/* Mapping changed and "MappingNotify" event generated */
}
```

Returns:

`MappingNotify` to indicate success; `MappingBusy` otherwise.

See also:

`XGetPointerMapping`

XSetRGBColormaps

Purpose:

Stores colormaps in a property of type `RGB_COLOR_MAP` on a window.

Syntax:

```
XStandardColormap std_cmap[];/* Colormaps being stored      */
int                num_cmap; /* Number of colormaps         */
Atom               cm_prop;  /* Identifies colormap property */

XSetRGBColormaps(display, w, std_cmap, num_cmap, cm_prop);
```

See also:

`XAllocStandardColormap`, `XSetRGBColormaps`

XSetRegion

Purpose:

Sets the `clip_mask` in a `GC` to a specified region.

Syntax:

```
Region r; /* Region to be used as a clip mask */

XSetRegion(display, gc, r);
```

See also:

`XSetClipMask`, `XSetClipOrigin`, `XSetClipRectangles`

XSetScreenSaver

Purpose:

Sets the parameters of the screen saver.

Syntax:

```
int timeout;       /*Seconds after which screen saver activates*/
int interval;      /* Seconds between calls to screen saver    */
int prefer_blanking;/* Blanking preference: DontPreferBlanking, */
                   /*      PreferBlanking, or DefaultBlanking   */
int allow_exposures;/* One of: Don't AllowExposures,           */
                   /*      AllowExposures or DefaultExposures   */
```

```
XSetScreenSaver(display, timeout, interval, prefer_blanking,
                allow_exposures);
```

See also:

XActivateScreenSaver, XForceScreenSaver, XGetScreenSaver, XResetScreenSaver

XSetSelectionOwner

Purpose:

Sets the owner of a selection identified by an atom (see Chapter 16).

Syntax:

```
Atom    selection; /* Which selection: XA_PRIMARY, for example */
Window owner;      /* New owner of the specified selection   */

XSetSelectionOwner(display, selection, owner, time);
```

See also:

XConvertSelection, XGetSelectionOwner

XSetSizeHints   (Use XSetWMSizeHints in X11R4)

Purpose:

Sets the value of any property of type XA_SIZE_HINTS.

Syntax:

```
XSizeHints xsh;     /* Specify new sizes here              */
Atom       property; /* Identifies property whose value is set */

XSetSizeHints(display, w, &xsh, property);
```

See also:

XGetSizeHints, XGetWMSizeHints, XSetWMSizeHints

XSetStandardColormap   (Use XSetRGBColormap in X11R4 or later)

Purpose:

Sets the value of a standard colormap property (XA_RGB_BEST_MAP, XA_RGB_RED_MAP, XA_RGB_GREEN_MAP, XA_RGB_BLUE_MAP, XA_RGB_DEFAULT_MAP, or XA_RGB_GRAY_MAP).

Syntax:

```
XStandardColormap cmap_value[]; /* Colormap data            */
Atom              property;     /* Predefined colormap property*/

XSetStandardColormap(display, w, cmap_value, property);
```

See also:

XGetRGBColormap, XGetStandardColormap, XSetRGBColormap

XSetStandardProperties   (Use XSetWMProperties in X11R4)

Purpose:

Sets a set of properties for the window manager.

Syntax:

```
char        *window_name; /* Name of window                 */
char        *icon_name;   /* Name displayed in window's icon */
Pixmap      icon_pixmap;  /* Bitmap for icon (or None)      */
char        **argv;       /* Command-line arguments         */
int         argc;         /* Number of command-line arguments */
XSizeHints xsh;           /* Size of window in normal state */

XSetStandardProperties(display, w, window_name, icon_name,
                    icon_pixmap, argv, argc, &xsh);
```

See also:

XSetWMProperties

XSetState

Purpose:

Sets the foreground and background pixel values and the logical function and plane mask in a GC.

Syntax:

```
ubsigned long   foreground, background; /* Pixel values  */
int             function;               /* Function code */
unsigned long   plane_mask;             /* Bit mask      */

XSetState(display, gc, foreground, background, function,
        plane_mask);
```

See also:

XSetBackground, XSetForeground, XSetFunction, XSetPlaneMask

XSetStipple

Purpose:

Specifies a bitmap to be used as a stipple pattern in a GC (see Chapter 9).

Syntax:

```
Pixmap stipple; /* Bitmap to be used as stipple */

XSetStipple(display, gc, stipple);
```

See also:

XSetFillStyle, XSetTSOrigin

XSetSubwindowMode

Purpose:

Indicates whether graphics output should be clipped against the subwindows (ClipByChildren) or drawn through them (IncludeInferiors).

Syntax:

```
int subwindow_mode; /* ClipByChildren or IncludeInferiors */

XSetSubwindowMode(display, gc, subwindow_mode);
```

See also:

XCreateGC, XChangeGC, XGetGCValues

XSetTextProperty

Purpose:

Sets a window's text property.

Syntax:

```
XTextProperty prop_value; /* Specify value of property here   */
Atom          txt_prop;   /* Identifies the property being set */

XSetTextProperty(display, w, &prop_value, txt_prop);
```

See also:

XGetTextProperty, XStringListToTextProperty, XTextPropertyToStringList

XSetTile

Purpose:

Sets the tile (a pixmap) in a GC. Tiles are used when fill style is FillTiled (see Chapter 9).

Syntax:

```
Pixmap    tile; /* The tile pixmap */

XSetTile(display, gc, tile);
```

See also:

XSetFillStyle, XSetTSOrigin

XSetTransientForHint

Purpose:

Sets the XA_WM_TRANSIENT_FOR property of a window.

Syntax:

```
Window prop_window; /* The property is set to this Window ID */

XSetTransientForHint(display, w, prop_window);
```

See also:

```
XGetTransientForHint
```

XSetTSOrigin

Purpose:

Sets the origin of tiles and stipples (see Chapter 9).

Syntax:

```
int  ts_x_origin, ts_y_origin; /* New origin */

XSetTSOrigin(display, gc, ts_x_origin, ts_y_origin);
```

See also:

```
XSetStipple, XSetTile
```

XSetWMClientMachine

Purpose:

Sets the XA_WM_CLIENT_MACHINE property.

Syntax:

```
XTextProperty txt_prop; /* Specify name of client's machine here */

XSetWMClientMachine(display, w, &txt_prop);
```

See also:

```
XGetWMClientMachine
```

XSetWMColormapWindows

Purpose:

Sets a window's XA_WM_COLORMAP_WINDOWS property. This list identifies the windows that need their own colormaps installed.

Syntax:

```
Window cmap_windows[]; /* List of windows that need colormaps */
int    count;          /* Number of entries in list          */

if(XSetWMColormapWindows(display, w, cmap_windows, count))
{
/* Property value set */
}
```

Returns:

Nonzero if successful; zero otherwise.

See also:

XGetWMColormapWindows

XSetWMHints

Purpose:

Sets a window's XA_WM_HINTS property. These are hints for the window manager.

Syntax:

```
XWMHints wm_hints; /* Specify hints here */

XSetWMHints(display, w, &wm_hints);
```

See also:

XGetWMHints, XSetWMProperties

XSetWMIconName

Purpose:

Sets the name to be displayed in a window's icon. This is in the XA_WM_ICON_NAME property.

Syntax:

```
XTextProperty text_prop; /* Icon name in a text property */

XSetWMIconName(display, w, &text_prop);
```

See also:

XGetWMIconName, XSetWMProperties

XSetWMName

Purpose:

Sets a window's name in its XA_WM_NAME property.

Syntax:

```
XTextProperty text_prop; /* Window's name in a text property */

XSetWMName(display, w, &text_prop);
```

See also:

```
XGetWMName, XSetWMProperties
```

XSetWMNormalHints

Purpose:

Sets a window's XA_WM_NORMAL_HINTS property.

Syntax:

```
XSizeHints size_hints; /* Property's value specified here */

XSetWMNormalHints(display, w, &size_hints);
```

See also:

```
XGetWMNormalHints, XSetWMProperties
```

XSetWMProperties

Purpose:

Sets a number of standard properties for the window manager.

Syntax:

```
XTextProperty window_name;    /* Window's name                */
XTextProperty icon_name;      /* Icon name                    */
char          **argv;         /* Command-line arguments       */
int           argc;           /* Number of arguments          */
XSizeHints    normal_hints;   /* For XA_WM_NORMAL_HINTS prop. */
XWMHints      wm_hints;       /* For XA_WM_HINTS property      */
XClassHint    class_hints;    /* For XA_WM_CLASS property      */

XSetWMProperties(display, w, &window_name, &icon_name, argv,
                &normal_hints, &wm_hints, &class_hints);
```

See also:

```
XSetClassHint, XSetWMHints, XSetWMIconName, XSetWMName, XSetWMNormalHints
```

XSetWMProtocols

Purpose:

Sets the XA_WM_PROTOCOLS property on a window. Protocols are used for interclient communications.

Syntax:

```
Atom   protocols[]; /* List of protocols   */
int    count;       /* Number of protocols */

if(XSetWMProtocols(display, w, protocols, count))
{
/* Success */
}
```

Returns:

Nonzero if successful; zero otherwise.

See also:

```
XGetWMProtocols
```

XSetWMSizeHints

Purpose:

Sets a property of type XA_WM_SIZE_HINTS on a window.

Syntax:

```
XSizeHints xsh;       /* Value of property   */
Atom       property; /* Identifies property */

XSetWMSizeHints(display, w, &xsh, property);
```

See also:

```
XGetWMSizeHints
```

XSetWindowBackground

Purpose:

Sets background pixel value of a window. This is the color that fills the window when it is cleared.

Syntax:

```
unsigned long background_pixel; /* Specify window's background */

XSetWindowBackground(display, w, background_pixel);
```

See also:

```
XChangeWindowAttributes, XClearWindow, XGetWindowAttributes, XSetWindowBackgroundPixmap
```

XSetWindowBackgroundPixmap

Purpose:

Specifies a pixmap to be used for tiling a window's background.

Syntax:

```
Pixmap background_tile; /* Pixmap for background tiling */

XSetWindowBackgroundPixmap(display, w, background_tile);
```

See also:

XChangeWindowAttributes, XCreatePixmap, XSetWindowBackground

XSetWindowBorder

Purpose:

Changes the pixel value used to paint a window's border.

Syntax:

```
unsigned long border_pixel; /* Specifies border color */

XSetWindowBorder(display, w, border_pixel);
```

See also:

XChangeWindowAttributes, XSetWindowBorderPixmap

XSetWindowBorderPixmap

Purpose:

Specifies a pixmap to be used to tile a window's border.

Syntax:

```
Pixmap border_tile; /* Pixmap for tiling window's border */

XSetWindowBorderPixmap(display, w, border_tile);
```

See also:

XChangeWindowAttributes, XSetWindowBorder

XSetWindowBorderWidth

Purpose:

Sets a window's border.

Syntax:

```
unsigned int width; /* Border width in pixels */

XSetWindowBorderWidth(display, w, width);
```

See also:

XChangeWindowAttributes, XCreateSimpleWindow

XSetWindowColormap

Purpose:

Sets a colormap to be used for drawing in a window. Starting with X11R4, the window manager is supposed to take care of installing a window's colormap, provided it is informed of the need through the XA_WM_COLORMAP_WINDOWS property.

Syntax:

```
Colormap  cmap; /* Resource ID of colormap */

XSetWindowColormap(display, w, cmap);
```

See also:

```
XGetWindowAttributes, XChangeWindowAttributes, XGetWMColormapWindows,
XSetWMColormapWindows
```

XSetWMHints   (Use XSetWMProperties in X11R4 or later)

Purpose:

Provides hints to the window manager for a top-level window's location and initial state.

Syntax:

```
XWMHints wmhints; /* Specify the hints in this structure */

XSetWMHints(display, w, &wmhints);
```

See also:

```
XAllocWMHints, XGetWMHints, XSetWMProperties
```

XSetZoomHints   (Obsolete in X11R4 or later)

Purpose:

Sets the XA_WM_ZOOM_HINTS property of a window.

Syntax:

```
XSizeHints zoomhint; /* Specify value of property here */

XSetZoomHints(display, w, &zoomhints);
```

See also:

```
XGetZoomHints
```

XShrinkRegion

Purpose:

Expands or shrinks a region by a specified amount.

Syntax:

```
Region  r;       /* Region whose size is being altered   */
int     dx, dy; /* Increment or decrement along x and y */

XShrinkRegion(r, dx, dy);
```

See also:

XCreateRegion, XdestroyRegion, XOffsetRegion, XPolygonRegion

XStoreBuffer

Purpose:

Stores an array of bytes (usually text) in a cut buffer.

Syntax:

```
char bytes[]; /* Data being stored in the cut buffer        */
int nbytes;   /* Number of bytes                            */
int buffer;   /* Cut buffer number in the range 0 through 7 */

XStoreBuffer(display, bytes, nbytes, buffer);
```

See also:

XFetchBuffer, XFetchBytes, XRotateBuffers, XStoreBytes

XStoreBytes

Purpose:

Stores an array of bytes in cut buffer 0 (property XA_CUT_BUFFER0 (see Chapter 16).

Syntax:

```
char bytes[]; /* Data being stored in the cut buffer 0 */
int nbytes;   /* Number of bytes                       */

XStoreBytes(display, bytes, nbytes);
```

See also:

XFetchBuffer, XFetchBytes, XRotateBuffers, XStoreBuffer

XStoreColor

Purpose:

Sets the RGB components of a read-write colormap cell (see Chapter 11).

Syntax:

```
Colormap cmap;    /* Identifies the colormap            */
XColor   rgb_def; /* Specify pixel value and RGB components */

XStoreColor(display, cmap, &rgb_def);
```

See also:

XAllocColorCells, XStoreColors, XStoreNamedColor

XStoreColors

Purpose:

Sets the RGB values of a number of read-write colormap cells (see Chapter 11).

Syntax:

```
Colormap cmap;       /* Colormap ID                */
XColor   rgb_defs[]; /* Array of colormap entries */
int      ncolors;    /* Number of entries          */

XStoreColors(display, cmap, rgb_defs, ncolors);
```

See also:

XAllocColorCells, XStoreColor, XStoreNamedColor

XStoreName   (Use XSetWMName in X11R4 or later)

Purpose:

Sets the name of a window. This is stored in the XA_WM_NAME property.

Syntax:

```
char *window_name; /* Window's name (a null-terminated string) */

XStoreName(dsiplay, w, window_name);
```

See also:

XFetchName, XSetWMName

XStoreNamedColor

Purpose:

Sets the RGB values of a read-write colormap cell with the color specified by a name.

Syntax:

```
Colormap      cmap;        /* Identifies the colormap        */
char          *colorname;  /*Name of color (for example, cyan) */
unsigned long pixel;       /* Identifies colormap entry      */
int           flags;       /* Which of R,G,B components to set */
                           /* Use OR of DoRed, DoBlue, DoGreen */


XStoreNamedColor(display, cmap, colorname, pixel, flags);
```

See also:

```
XAllocColorCells, XAllocNamedColor, XStoreColor, XStoreColors
```

XStringListToTextProperty

Purpose:

Sets up an XTextProperty structure containing a list of null-terminated strings.

Syntax:

```
char          *list[]; /* The array of strings          */
int           count;   /* Number of strings             */
XTextProperty txt_prop;/* Text property returned here */

if(XStringListToTextProperty(list, count, &txt_prop))
{
/* Successfully prepared text property structure */
}
```

See also:

```
XGetTextProperty, XSetTextProperty, XTextPropertyToStringList
```

XStringToKeysym

Purpose:

Converts a keysym name (for example, Shift) to a KeySym value (for example, XK_Shift).

Syntax:

```
char   *string; /* Keysym name      */
KeySym keysym;  /* Returned KeySym */
if((keysym = XStringToKeysym(string)) != NoSymbol)
{
/* Valid keysym returned */
}
```

Returns:

A KeySym value. In case of error, the return value is the constant NoSymbol.

See also:

```
XKeysymToString, XLookupString
```

XSubImage

Purpose:

Creates an `XImage` structure from a part of another image.

Syntax:

```
int          x, y;             /* Specifies origin and size of */
unsigned int subimage_width;   /* rectangular region that      */
unsigned int subimage_height;  /* defines the subimage         */
XImage       *subimage;        /* Returned subimage            */

subimage = XSubImage(ximage, x, y, subimage_width,
        subimage_height);
```

Returns:

Pointer to the subimage's `XImage` structure.

See also:

`XCreateImage, XDestroyImage, XGetImage, XPutImage`

XSubtractRegion

Purpose:

Subtracts one region from another.

Syntax:

```
Region a, b;   /* Subtract region b from a */
Region result; /* The result              */

XSubtractRegion(a, b, result);
```

See also:

`XCreateRegion, XDestroyRegion, XPolygonRegion, XUnionRegion, XUnionRectWithRegion,`
`XXorRegion`

XSync

Purpose:

Sends all waiting protocol requests to the X server and waits until everything is processed. Used for debugging.

Syntax:

```
int discard; /* If True, all input events are discarded */

XSync(display, discard);
```

See also:

`XFlush, XSynchronize`

XSynchronize

Enables or disables synchronized operations. This is equivalent to calling XSync after each protocol request. Used for debugging only.

Syntax:

```
int onoff;          /* True turns on synchronous operation */
int (*old_after)(); /* Returned pointer to "after" function */

old_after = XSynchronize(display, onoff);
```

Returns:

A pointer to the previous "after" function—a function called after each Xlib function.

See also:

```
XSetAfter
```

XTextExtents

Purpose:

Provides the dimensions of a text string when displayed in a specific font. This function does not involve any interaction with the server.

Syntax:

```
XFontStruct *fstruct;  /* Pointer to font information      */
char        *string;   /* String for which sizes computed */
int         nchars;    /* Number of characters in string   */
int         direction; /* Font direction returned here      */
int         ascent;    /* On return: font's ascent          */
int         descent;   /* On return: font's descent         */
XCharStruct overall;   /* Overall dimensions returned here*/

XTextExtents(fstruct, string, nchars, &direction,
             &ascent, &descent, &overall);
```

See also:

```
XLoadQueryFont, XQueryFont, XTextWidth
```

XTextExtents16

Purpose:

Provides the dimensions of a 16-bit text string when displayed in a specific font.

Syntax:

```
XFontStruct *fstruct;  /* Pointer to font information      */
XChar2b     *string;   /* String for which sizes computed */
int         nchars;    /* Number of characters in string   */
int         direction; /* Font direction returned here      */
```

```
int        ascent;    /* On return: font's ascent    */
int        descent;   /* On return: font's descent   */
XCharStruct overall;  /* Overall dimensions returned here*/

XTextExtents16(fstruct, string, nchars, &direction,
               &ascent, &descent, &overall);
```

See also:

XLoadQueryFont, XQueryFont, XTextWidth16

XTextPropertyToStringList

Purpose:

Provides a list of strings from a specified XTextProperty structure.

Syntax:

```
XTextProperty text_prop; /* Extract strings from this property */
char          **list;    /* Returned array of strings          */
int           count;     /* Number of strings returned         */

if(XTextPropertyToStringList(&text_prop, &list, &count))
{
/* Successfully retrieved strings from text property */
}
```

Returns:

Nonzero if successful; zero otherwise.

See also:

XFreeStringList, XGetTextProperty, XSetTextProperty, XStringListToTextProperty

XTextWidth

Purpose:

Gets the width (in pixels) of a text string when displayed in a specified font. Does not require any response from server.

Syntax:

```
XFontStruct *fstruct;  /* Pointer to font information    */
char        *string;   /* String for which sizes computed */
int         nchars;    /* Number of characters in string  */
int         width;     /* Width in pixels                 */

width = XTextWidth(font_struct, string, nchars);
```

Returns:

Width of the string in pixels.

See also:

XLoadQueryFont, XQueryFont, XTextExtents

XTextWidth16

Purpose:

Returns the width (in pixels) of a 16-bit text string when displayed in a specified font. Does not require any response from server.

Syntax:

```
XFontStruct *fstruct;  /* Pointer to font information   */
XChar2b     *string;   /* String for which sizes computed */
int         nchars;    /* Number of characters in string */
int         width;     /* Width in pixels               */

width = XTextWidth16(font_struct, string, nchars);
```

Returns:

Width of the string in pixels.

See also:

XLoadQueryFont, XQueryFont, XTextExtents16

XTranslateCoordinates

Purpose:

Converts coordinates of a point from the coordinate frame of one window to another.

Syntax:

```
Window src_w;          /* Coordinates known in this one's frame */
Window dest_w;         /* Coords. desired in this window's frame*/
int    src_x, src_y;   /* The coordinates in "src_w" window     */
int    dest_x, dest_y; /* Returned coords. in "dest_w" window    */
Window child;          /* Child of "dest_w" that contains point */

if(XTranslateCoordinates(display, src_w, dest_w, src_x,
                         src_y, &dest_x, &dest_y, &child))
{
/* Coordinate conversion successful */
}
```

Returns:

True if both src_w and dest_w are on the same screen; otherwise, the return value is False.

See also:

XGetGeometry, XQueryPointer

XUndefineCursor

Purpose:

Sets the cursor of a window to its parent's cursor.

Syntax:

```
XUndefineCursor(display, w);
```

See also:

```
XCreateFontCursor, XDefineCursor, XFreeCursor, XRecolorCursor
```

XUngrabButton

Purpose:

Cancels a passive grab of a button and key combination on a specified window.

Syntax:

```
unsigned int button;    /* Which button: Button1, Button2, ... */
unsigned int modifiers; /* Modifier keymasks: ShiftMask, etc. */

XUngrabButton(display, button, modifiers, w);
```

See also:

```
XGrabButton
```

XUngrabKey

Purpose:

Releases a key from a passive grab established by an earlier call to XGrabKey.

Syntax:

```
int          keycode;  /* Key being "ungrabbed"            */
unsigned int modifiers; /* Modifier mask such as ShiftMask */

XUngrabKey(display, keycode, modifiers, w);
```

See also:

```
XGrabKey, XGrabKeyboard
```

XUngrabKeyboard

Purpose:

Releases the keyboard from an active grab started by an earlier call to XGrabKeyboard.

Syntax:

```
Time time; /* Time when grab is released */

XUngrabKeyboard(display, time);
```

See also:

`XGrabKey, XGrabKeyboard, XUngrabKey`

XUngrabPointer

Purpose:

Releases the pointer from an active grab started by an earlier call to `XGrabPointer`.

Syntax:

```
Time time;  /* Time when pointer is released */

XUngrabPointer(display, time);
```

See also:

`XChangeActivePointerGrab, XGrabPointer`

XUngrabServer

Purpose:

Ends a *server grab* started by a previous call to `XGrabServer`. During a server grab, the server processes requests from only one client.

Syntax:

```
XUngrabServer(display);
```

See also:

`XGrabServer`

XUninstallColormap

Purpose:

Reverses the effects of an `XInstallColormap` call and resets the display system's colormap to the default colormap.

Syntax:

```
Colormap  cmap; /* Colormap being "uninstalled" */

XUninstallColormap(display, cmap);
```

See also:

`XCreateColormap, XInstallColormap, XSetWindowColormap, XStoreColors`

XUnionRectWithRegion

Purpose:

Computes a new region that is the union of a region and a rectangle.

Syntax:

```
XRectangle rect;    /* Rectangle to be added to region    */
Region     a;       /* Region to which rectangle is added */
Region     result; /* Resulting region                    */

XUnionRectWithRegion(rect, a, result);
```

See also:

XCreateRegion, XDestroyRegion, XPolygonRegion, XSubtractRegion, XUnionRegion, XXorRegion

XUnionRegion

Purpose:

Computes the union of two regions.

Syntax:

```
Region   a, b;    /* Compute union of these two regions */
Region   result; /* and return result in this region   */

XUnionRegion(a, b, result);
```

See also:

XCreateRegion, XDestroyRegion, XPolygonRegion, XSubtractRegion, XUnionRectWithRegion, XXorRegion

XUniqueContext

Purpose:

Creates a unique context ID for use by the context management utility of Xlib. (See Chapter 7 for an example of its use.)

Syntax:

```
XContext cid;

cid = XUniqueContext();
```

Returns:

An XContext value.

See also:

XDeleteContext, XFindContext, XSaveContext

XUnloadFont

Purpose:

Requests server to unload a font.

Syntax:

```
Font  font; /* ID of font being unloaded */

XUnloadFont(display, font);
```

See also:

XLoadFont, XLoadQueryFont, XQueryFont, XSetFont, XSetFontPath

XUnlockDisplay

Purpose:

Enables other threads to use the specified display again. (A thread is a stream of execution within a process.)

Syntax:

```
XUnlockDisplay(display);
```

See also:

XInitThreads, XLockDisplay

XUnmapSubwindows

Purpose:

Unmaps all subwindows of a specified window.

Syntax:

```
XUnmapSubwindows(display, w);
```

See also:

XMapSubwindows, XMapWindow, XUnmapWindow

XUnmapwindow

Purpose:

Unmaps a window.

Syntax:

```
XUnmapwindow(display, w);
```

See also:

XMapWindow, XMapSubwindows, XUnmapSubwindows

XVendorRelease

Purpose:

Returns the vendor's release number for the X Window System software.

Syntax:

```
int release;  /* The release number */
release = XVendorRelease(display);
```

Returns:

The release number. For example, for X11R5, the release number is 5.

XVisualIDFromVisual

Purpose:

Returns a visual ID from the pointer to a Visual structure.

Syntax:

```
VisualID  vid;

vid = XVisualIDFromVisual(display);
```

Returns:

A VisualID value.

See also:

```
XGetVisualInfo
```

XWarpPointer

Purpose:

Forcibly moves the mouse pointer to a specified location. Can be very disconcerting to the user.

Syntax:

```
Window       src_w;      /* Pointer starts out in this window */
Window       dest_w;     /* Pointer is moved to this window   */
int          src_x;      /* Pointer must be in rectangle      */
int          src_y;      /* defined by src_x, src_y,          */
unsigned int src_width;  /* src_width, src_height in order     */
unsigned int src_height; /* to be moved.                      */
int          dest_x;     /* Final location of pointer in the  */
int          dest_y;     /* coordinate frame of "dest_w"      */

XWarpPointer(display, src_w, dest_w, src_x, src_y,
             src_width, src_height, dest_x, dest_y);
```

See also:

```
XGrabPointer, XQueryPointer, XTranslateCoordinates, XUngrabPointer
```

XWindowEvent

Purpose:

Retrieves the next event that matches a specified event mask and window.

Syntax:

```
XEvent event; /* Event is returned in this structure */

XWindowEvent(display, w, event_mask, &event);
```

See also:

```
XCheckTypedWindowEvent, XCheckWindowEvent, XSelectInput
```

XWithdrawWindow

Purpose:

Informs a window manager that a top-level window and its icon should be unmapped.

Syntax:

```
int  screen; /* Window's screen number, 0, for example */

if(XWithdrawWindow(display, w, screen))
{
/* Success */
}
```

Returns:

Nonzero if successful; zero on failure.

See also:

```
XIconifyWindow, XReconfigureWindow
```

XWMGeometry

Purpose:

Gets the geometry specification of a window from a "geometry string" ("100x60+10+10").

Syntax:

```
int        screen;        /* Screen number of window        */
const char *user_geom;    /* User-specified geometry string */
const char *default_geom; /* Default geometry string        */
unsigned int bdwidth;     /* Border width of window         */
XSizeHints xsh;           /* Size hints for window          */
int        xr, yr;        /* Position returned here         */
int        width, height; /* Size returned in here          */
int        gravity;       /* Window gravity returned here   */
int        geom_mask;     /* Bitmask indicating the values  */
                          /* that were in "user_geom"       */
```

```
geom_mask = XWMGeometry(display, screen, user_geom, default_geom,
                bdwidth, &xsh, &xr, &yr, &width, &height, gravity);
```

Returns:

A bitmask whose set bits indicate which values (position, size) were specified in user's geometry string user_geom.

See also:

XGeometry, XParseGeometry, XSetWMProperties

XWriteBitmapFile

Purpose:

Writes a specified bitmap to a file, using the X11 bitmap file format (see Chapter 12).

Syntax:

```
char        *filename;      /* Write bitmap data to this file */
Pixmap       bitmap;        /* The bitmap being saved         */
unsigned int width, heigth; /* Bitmap's width and height      */
int          x_hot, y_hot;  /* Coords. of the hotspot         */

if(XWriteBitmapFile(display, filename, bitmap, width,
                    height, x_hot, y_hot) == BitmapSuccess)
{
/* Successfully saved bitmap to file */
}
```

Returns:

BitmapSuccess if all goes well; otherwise, return value is one of the following: BitmapOpenFailed or BitmapNoMemory.

See also:

XCreateBitmapFromData, XReadBitmapFile

XXorRegion

Purpose:

Computes a region that includes points that are either in a or b but not in both. This is equivalent to the difference between the union and intersection of the two regions a and b.

Syntax:

```
Region  a, b;   /* The regions involved in the computation */
Region  result; /* The result is returned here             */

XXorRegion(a, b, result);
```

See also:

XCreateRegion, XDestroyRegion, XPolygonRegion, XSubtractRegion, XUnionRegion

Appendix B

X Errors

This appendix lists the error codes returned by the X server in error events. The default error handler prints a message for each error code. In UNIX systems, you find these messages in the file /usr/lib/X11/XErrorDB. These error codes are defined in the header file <X11/X.h>.

Error Number	Symbolic Name	Description
0	Success	No error (ignore this error event)
1	BadRequest	Invalid request code or no such operation
2	BadValue	Integer parameter out of range for specified operation
3	BadWindow	Parameter is not a `Window`
4	BadPixmap	Parameter is not a `Pixmap`
5	BadAtom	Parameter is not an `Atom`
6	BadCursor	Parameter is not a `Cursor`
7	BadFont	Parameter is not a `Font`
8	BadMatch	Parameters do not match
9	BadDrawable	Parameter is not a `Pixmap` or `Window`
10	BadAccess	Attempt to access a resource is denied; reason depends on context: ✦ Key or button already grabbed ✦ Attempt to free an illegal colormap entry ✦ Attempt to store into a read-only colormap entry ✦ Attempt to modify the access control list from other than the local host
11	BadAlloc	Insufficient resources for operation
12	BadColor	No such `Colormap`
13	BadGC	Parameter is not a `GC`
14	BadIDChoice	Resource ID invalid for this connection
15	BadName	Named color or font does not exist
16	BadLength	Protocol request involving a poly-operation is too large, or internal Xlib length error
17	BadImplementation	Server does not implement operation

Appendix C

X Fonts

This appendix shows several representative fonts available in X11R6. Chapter 3, "Exploring X Applications," explains the font-naming conventions. You can list the fonts with the `xlsfonts` program and preview a font by using the utility program *xfd*.

Figure C.1.

*-misc-fixed-bold-r-
normal--15-120-100-
100-c-90-iso8859-1.*

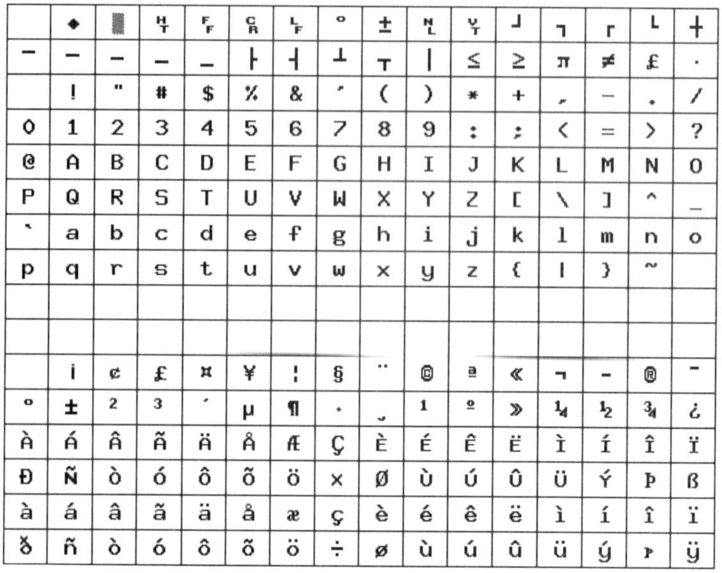

Figure C.2.

*-adobe-helvetica-
medium-r-normal--17-
120-100-100-p-88-
iso8859-1.*

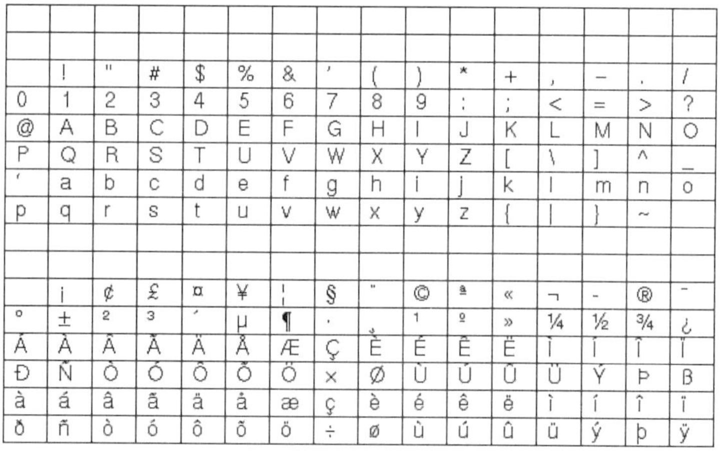

Figure C.3.

`-adobe-new century schoolbook-medium-i-normal--14-100-100-100-p-81-iso8859-1.`

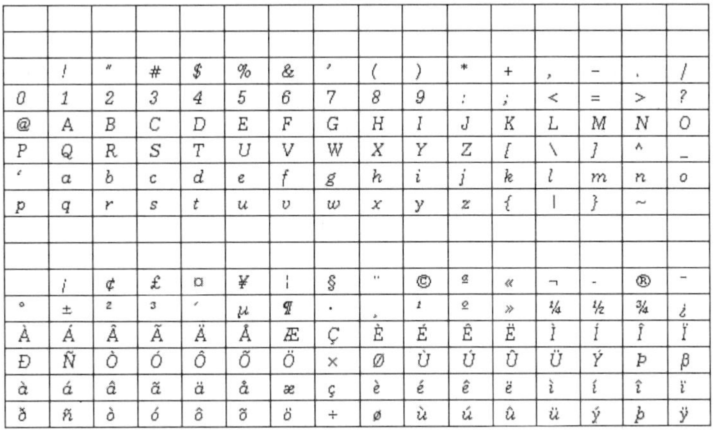

	!	"	#	$	%	&	'	(	)	*	+	,	-	.	/
0	1	2	3	4	5	6	7	8	9	:	;	<	=	>	?
@	A	B	C	D	E	F	G	H	I	J	K	L	M	N	O
P	Q	R	S	T	U	V	W	X	Y	Z	[	\	]	^	_
`	a	b	c	d	e	f	g	h	i	j	k	l	m	n	o
p	q	r	s	t	u	v	w	x	y	z	{	|	}	~	
	¡	¢	£	¤	¥	¦	§	¨	©	ª	«	¬	-	®	¯
°	±	²	³	´	µ	¶	·	¸	¹	º	»	¼	½	¾	¿
À	Á	Â	Ã	Ä	Å	Æ	Ç	È	É	Ê	Ë	Ì	Í	Î	Ï
Ð	Ñ	Ò	Ó	Ô	Õ	Ö	×	Ø	Ù	Ú	Û	Ü	Ý	Þ	ß
à	á	â	ã	ä	å	æ	ç	è	é	ê	ë	ì	í	î	ï
ð	ñ	ò	ó	ô	õ	ö	÷	ø	ù	ú	û	ü	ý	þ	ÿ

Figure C.4.

`-adobe-symbol-medium-r-normal--14-100-100-100-p-85-adobe-fontspecific.`

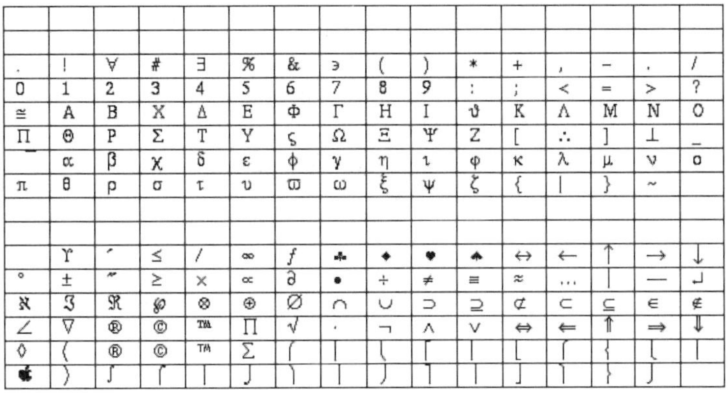

	!	∀	#	∃	%	&	∋	(	)	*	+	,	-	.	/
0	1	2	3	4	5	6	7	8	9	:	;	<	=	>	?
≅	Α	Β	Χ	Δ	Ε	Φ	Γ	Η	Ι	ϑ	Κ	Λ	Μ	Ν	Ο
Π	Θ	Ρ	Σ	Τ	Υ	ς	Ω	Ξ	Ψ	Ζ	[	∴	]	⊥	_
	α	β	χ	δ	ε	φ	γ	η	ι	φ	κ	λ	μ	ν	o
π	θ	ρ	σ	τ	υ	ϖ	ω	ξ	ψ	ζ	{	|	}	~	
	ϒ	′	≤	/	∞	ƒ	♣	♦	♥	♠	↔	←	↑	→	↓
°	±	″	≥	×	∝	∂	•	÷	≠	≡	≈	…	—		↵
ℵ	ℑ	ℜ	℘	⊗	⊕	∅	∩	∪	⊃	⊇	⊄	⊂	⊆	∈	∉
∠	∇	®	©	™	∏	√	·	¬	∧	∨	⇔	⇐	⇑	⇒	⇓
◊	⟨	®	©	™	∑										
	⟩	∫	⌈		⌋										

Figure C.5.

`-sony-fixed-medium-r-normal--16-120-100-100-c-80-jisx0201.1976-0.`

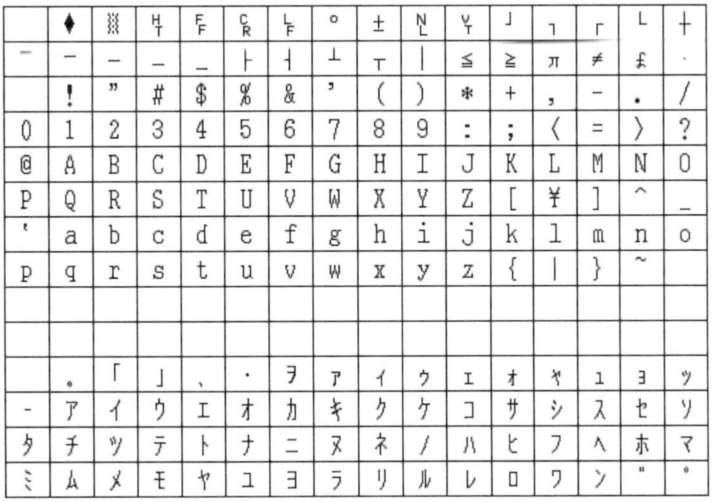

Figure C.6.

-schumacher-clean-medium-r-normal--16-160-75-75-c-80iso646.1991-irv.

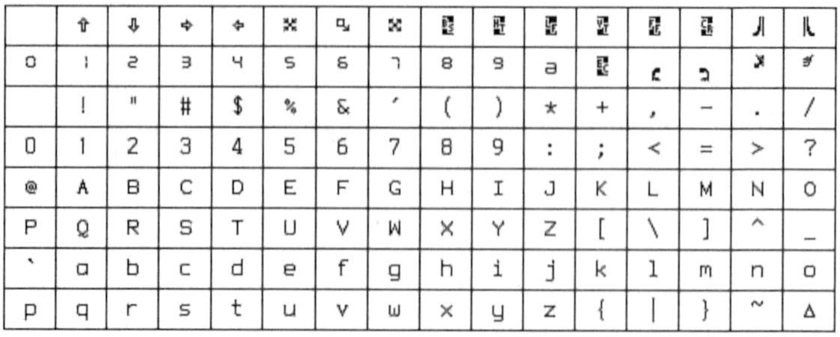

	0	1	2	3	4	5	6	7	8	9	A	B	C	D	E	F
0				!	"	#	$	%	&	'	(	)	*	+	,	-
1	.	/	0	1	2	3	4	5	6	7	8	9	:	;	<	=
2	>	?	@	A	B	C	D	E	F	G	H	I	J	K	L	M
3	N	O	P	Q	R	S	T	U	V	W	X	Y	Z	[	\	]
4	^	_	`	a	b	c	d	e	f	g	h	i	j	k	l	m
5	n	o	p	q	r	s	t	u	v	w	x	y	z	{	|	}
6	~	Δ														

Figure C.7.

-adobe-utopia-bold-r-normal--17-120-100-100-p-93-iso8859-1.

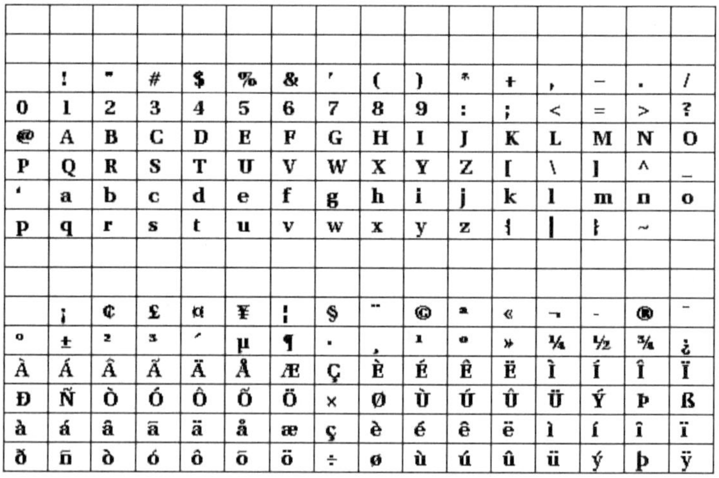

!	"	#	$	%	&	'	(	)	*	+	,	-	.	/
0	1	2	3	4	5	6	7	8	9	:	;	<	=	>	?
@	A	B	C	D	E	F	G	H	I	J	K	L	M	N	O
P	Q	R	S	T	U	V	W	X	Y	Z	[	\	]	^	_
'	a	b	c	d	e	f	g	h	i	j	k	l	m	n	o
p	q	r	s	t	u	v	w	x	y	z	{	|	}	~	
¡	¢	£	¤	¥	¦	§	¨	©	ª	«	¬		®	¯
°	±	²	³	´	µ	¶	·	¸	¹	º	»	¼	½	¾	¿
À	Á	Â	Ã	Ä	Å	Æ	Ç	È	É	Ê	Ë	Ì	Í	Î	Ï
Ð	Ñ	Ò	Ó	Ô	Õ	Ö	×	Ø	Ù	Ú	Û	Ü	Ý	Þ	ß
à	á	â	ã	ä	å	æ	ç	è	é	ê	ë	ì	í	î	ï
ð	ñ	ò	ó	ô	õ	ö	÷	ø	ù	ú	û	ü	ý	þ	ÿ

X Colors

This appendix lists the color names and their definitions available for use with the functions XAllocNamedColor, XLookupColor, XParseColor, and XStoreNamedColor. In UNIX systems, these definitions usually appear in the text file /usr/lib/X11/rgb.txt. You can use these names directly in Xlib functions that accept names of colors. You also can get a color by specifying the Red, Green, and Blue components shown in this list in the XColor structure passed to the color allocation functions. When directly using the RGB levels, remember that this list uses an 8-bit value for each component (full intensity of a component is 255), and the Xlib functions expect a 16-bit value (maximum intensity of each component is 65,535). See Chapter 11, "Using Color in X," for more information on specifying colors in X.

R	G	B	Color Name
255	250	250	snow
248	248	255	ghost white
248	248	255	GhostWhite
245	245	245	white smoke
245	245	245	WhiteSmoke
220	220	220	gainsboro
255	250	240	floral white
255	250	240	FloralWhite
253	245	230	old lace
253	245	230	OldLace
250	240	230	linen
250	235	215	antique white
250	235	215	AntiqueWhite
255	239	213	papaya whip
255	239	213	PapayaWhip
255	235	205	blanched almond
255	235	205	BlanchedAlmond
255	228	196	bisque
255	218	185	peach puff
255	218	185	PeachPuff
255	222	173	navajo white
255	222	173	NavajoWhite
255	228	181	moccasin
255	248	220	cornsilk
255	255	240	ivory
255	250	205	lemon chiffon
255	250	205	LemonChiffon
255	245	238	seashell
240	255	240	honeydew
245	255	250	mint cream
245	255	250	MintCream
240	255	255	azure
240	248	255	alice blue
240	248	255	AliceBlue

R	G	B	Color Name
230	230	250	lavender
255	240	245	lavender blush
255	240	245	LavenderBlush
255	228	225	misty rose
255	228	225	MistyRose
255	255	255	white
0	0	0	black
47	79	79	dark slate gray
47	79	79	DarkSlateGray
47	79	79	dark slate grey
47	79	79	DarkSlateGrey
105	105	105	dim gray
105	105	105	DimGray
105	105	105	dim grey
105	105	105	DimGrey
112	128	144	slate gray
112	128	144	SlateGray
112	128	144	slate grey
112	128	144	SlateGrey
119	136	153	light slate gray
119	136	153	LightSlateGray
119	136	153	light slate grey
119	136	153	LightSlateGrey
190	190	190	gray
190	190	190	grey
211	211	211	light grey
211	211	211	LightGrey
211	211	211	light gray
211	211	211	LightGray
25	25	112	midnight blue
25	25	112	MidnightBlue
0	0	128	navy

continues

R	G	B	Color Name
0	0	128	navy blue
0	0	128	NavyBlue
100	149	237	cornflower blue
100	149	237	CornflowerBlue
72	61	139	dark slate blue
72	61	139	DarkSlateBlue
106	90	205	slate blue
106	90	205	SlateBlue
123	104	238	medium slate blue
123	104	238	MediumSlateBlue
132	112	255	light slate blue
132	112	255	LightSlateBlue
0	0	205	medium blue
0	0	205	MediumBlue
65	105	225	royal blue
65	105	225	RoyalBlue
0	0	255	blue
30	144	255	dodger blue
30	144	255	DodgerBlue
0	191	255	deep sky blue
0	191	255	DeepSkyBlue
135	206	235	sky blue
135	206	235	SkyBlue
135	206	250	light sky blue
135	206	250	LightSkyBlue
70	130	180	steel blue
70	130	180	SteelBlue
176	196	222	light steel blue
176	196	222	LightSteelBlue
173	216	230	light blue
173	216	230	LightBlue
176	224	230	powder blue
176	224	230	PowderBlue

R	G	B	Color Name
175	238	238	pale turquoise
175	238	238	PaleTurquoise
0	206	209	dark turquoise
0	206	209	DarkTurquoise
72	209	204	medium turquoise
72	209	204	MediumTurquoise
64	224	208	turquoise
0	255	255	cyan
224	255	255	light cyan
224	255	255	LightCyan
95	158	160	cadet blue
95	158	160	CadetBlue
102	205	170	medium aquamarine
102	205	170	MediumAquamarine
127	255	212	aquamarine
0	100	0	dark green
0	100	0	DarkGreen
85	107	47	dark olive green
85	107	47	DarkOliveGreen
143	188	143	dark sea green
143	188	143	DarkSeaGreen
46	139	87	sea green
46	139	87	SeaGreen
60	179	113	medium sea green
60	179	113	MediumSeaGreen
32	178	170	light sea green
32	178	170	LightSeaGreen
152	251	152	pale green
152	251	152	PaleGreen
0	255	127	spring green
0	255	127	SpringGreen
124	252	0	lawn green
124	252	0	LawnGreen

continues

R	G	B	Color Name
0	255	0	green
127	255	0	chartreuse
0	250	154	medium spring green
0	250	154	MediumSpringGreen
173	255	47	green yellow
173	255	47	GreenYellow
50	205	50	lime green
50	205	50	LimeGreen
154	205	50	yellow green
154	205	50	YellowGreen
34	139	34	forest green
34	139	34	ForestGreen
107	142	35	olive drab
107	142	35	OliveDrab
189	183	107	dark khaki
189	183	107	DarkKhaki
240	230	140	khaki
238	232	170	pale goldenrod
238	232	170	PaleGoldenrod
250	250	210	light goldenrod yellow
250	250	210	LightGoldenrodYellow
255	255	224	light yellow
255	255	224	LightYellow
255	255	0	yellow
255	215	0	gold
238	221	130	light goldenrod
238	221	130	LightGoldenrod
218	165	32	goldenrod
184	134	11	dark goldenrod
184	134	11	DarkGoldenrod
188	143	143	rosy brown
188	143	143	RosyBrown
205	92	92	indian red

R	G	B	Color Name
205	92	92	IndianRed
139	69	19	saddle brown
139	69	19	SaddleBrown
160	82	45	sienna
205	133	63	peru
222	184	135	burlywood
245	245	220	beige
245	222	179	wheat
244	164	96	sandy brown
244	164	96	SandyBrown
210	180	140	tan
210	105	30	chocolate
178	34	34	firebrick
165	42	42	brown
233	150	122	dark salmon
233	150	122	DarkSalmon
250	128	114	salmon
255	160	122	light salmon
255	160	122	LightSalmon
255	165	0	orange
255	140	0	dark orange
255	140	0	DarkOrange
255	127	80	coral
240	128	128	light coral
240	128	128	LightCoral
255	99	71	tomato
255	69	0	orange red
255	69	0	OrangeRed
255	0	0	red
255	105	180	hot pink
255	105	180	HotPink
255	20	147	deep pink

continues

R	G	B	Color Name
255	20	147	DeepPink
255	192	203	pink
255	182	193	light pink
255	182	193	LightPink
219	112	147	pale violet red
219	112	147	PaleVioletRed
176	48	96	maroon
199	21	133	medium violet red
199	21	133	MediumVioletRed
208	32	144	violet red
208	32	144	VioletRed
255	0	255	magenta
238	130	238	violet
221	160	221	plum
218	112	214	orchid
186	85	211	medium orchid
186	85	211	MediumOrchid
153	50	204	dark orchid
153	50	204	DarkOrchid
148	0	211	dark violet
148	0	211	DarkViolet
138	43	226	blue violet
138	43	226	BlueViolet
160	32	240	purple
147	112	219	medium purple
147	112	219	MediumPurple
216	191	216	thistle
255	250	250	snow1
238	233	233	snow2
205	201	201	snow3
139	137	137	snow4
255	245	238	seashell1
238	229	222	seashell2

R	G	B	Color Name
205	197	191	seashell3
139	134	130	seashell4
255	239	219	AntiqueWhite1
238	223	204	AntiqueWhite2
205	192	176	AntiqueWhite3
139	131	120	AntiqueWhite4
255	228	196	bisque1
238	213	183	bisque2
205	183	158	bisque3
139	125	107	bisque4
255	218	185	PeachPuff1
238	203	173	PeachPuff2
205	175	149	PeachPuff3
139	119	101	PeachPuff4
255	222	173	NavajoWhite1
238	207	161	NavajoWhite2
205	179	139	NavajoWhite3
139	121	94	NavajoWhite4
255	250	205	LemonChiffon1
238	233	191	LemonChiffon2
205	201	165	LemonChiffon3
139	137	112	LemonChiffon4
255	248	220	cornsilk1
238	232	205	cornsilk2
205	200	177	cornsilk3
139	136	120	cornsilk4
255	255	240	ivory1
238	238	224	ivory2
205	205	193	ivory3
139	139	131	ivory4
240	255	240	honeydew1
224	238	224	honeydew2

continues

R	G	B	Color Name
193	205	193	honeydew3
131	139	131	honeydew4
255	240	245	LavenderBlush1
238	224	229	LavenderBlush2
205	193	197	LavenderBlush3
139	131	134	LavenderBlush4
255	228	225	MistyRose1
238	213	210	MistyRose2
205	183	181	MistyRose3
139	125	123	MistyRose4
240	255	255	azure1
224	238	238	azure2
193	205	205	azure3
131	139	139	azure4
131	111	255	SlateBlue1
122	103	238	SlateBlue2
105	89	205	SlateBlue3
71	60	139	SlateBlue4
72	118	255	RoyalBlue1
67	110	238	RoyalBlue2
58	95	205	RoyalBlue3
39	64	139	RoyalBlue4
0	0	255	blue1
0	0	238	blue2
0	0	205	blue3
0	0	139	blue4
30	144	255	DodgerBlue1
28	134	238	DodgerBlue2
24	116	205	DodgerBlue3
16	78	139	DodgerBlue4
99	184	255	SteelBlue1
92	172	238	SteelBlue2
79	148	205	SteelBlue3
54	100	139	SteelBlue4

R	G	B	Color Name
0	191	255	DeepSkyBlue1
0	178	238	DeepSkyBlue2
0	154	205	DeepSkyBlue3
0	104	139	DeepSkyBlue4
135	206	255	SkyBlue1
126	192	238	SkyBlue2
108	166	205	SkyBlue3
74	112	139	SkyBlue4
176	226	255	LightSkyBlue1
164	211	238	LightSkyBlue2
141	182	205	LightSkyBlue3
96	123	139	LightSkyBlue4
198	226	255	SlateGray1
185	211	238	SlateGray2
159	182	205	SlateGray3
108	123	139	SlateGray4
202	225	255	LightSteelBlue1
188	210	238	LightSteelBlue2
162	181	205	LightSteelBlue3
110	123	139	LightSteelBlue4
191	239	255	LightBlue1
178	223	238	LightBlue2
154	192	205	LightBlue3
104	131	139	LightBlue4
224	255	255	LightCyan1
209	238	238	LightCyan2
180	205	205	LightCyan3
122	139	139	LightCyan4
187	255	255	PaleTurquoise1
174	238	238	PaleTurquoise2
150	205	205	PaleTurquoise3
102	139	139	PaleTurquoise4

continues

R	G	B	Color Name
152	245	255	CadetBlue1
142	229	238	CadetBlue2
122	197	205	CadetBlue3
83	134	139	CadetBlue4
0	245	255	turquoise1
0	229	238	turquoise2
0	197	205	turquoise3
0	134	139	turquoise4
0	255	255	cyan1
0	238	238	cyan2
0	205	205	cyan3
0	139	139	cyan4
151	255	255	DarkSlateGray1
141	238	238	DarkSlateGray2
121	205	205	DarkSlateGray3
82	139	139	DarkSlateGray4
127	255	212	aquamarine1
118	238	198	aquamarine2
102	205	170	aquamarine3
69	139	116	aquamarine4
193	255	193	DarkSeaGreen1
180	238	180	DarkSeaGreen2
155	205	155	DarkSeaGreen3
105	139	105	DarkSeaGreen4
84	255	159	SeaGreen1
78	238	148	SeaGreen2
67	205	128	SeaGreen3
46	139	87	SeaGreen4
154	255	154	PaleGreen1
144	238	144	PaleGreen2
124	205	124	PaleGreen3
84	139	84	PaleGreen4
0	255	127	SpringGreen1

R	G	B	Color Name
0	238	118	SpringGreen2
0	205	102	SpringGreen3
0	139	69	SpringGreen4
0	255	0	green1
0	238	0	green2
0	205	0	green3
0	139	0	green4
127	255	0	chartreuse1
118	238	0	chartreuse2
102	205	0	chartreuse3
69	139	0	chartreuse4
192	255	62	OliveDrab1
179	238	58	OliveDrab2
154	205	50	OliveDrab3
105	139	34	OliveDrab4
202	255	112	DarkOliveGreen1
188	238	104	DarkOliveGreen2
162	205	90	DarkOliveGreen3
110	139	61	DarkOliveGreen4
255	246	143	khaki1
238	230	133	khaki2
205	198	115	khaki3
139	134	78	khaki4
255	236	139	LightGoldenrod1
238	220	130	LightGoldenrod2
205	190	112	LightGoldenrod3
139	129	76	LightGoldenrod4
255	255	224	LightYellow1
238	238	209	LightYellow2
205	205	180	LightYellow3
139	139	122	LightYellow4
255	255	0	yellow1

continues

R	G	B	Color Name
238	238	0	yellow2
205	205	0	yellow3
139	139	0	yellow4
255	215	0	gold1
238	201	0	gold2
205	173	0	gold3
139	117	0	gold4
255	193	37	goldenrod1
238	180	34	goldenrod2
205	155	29	goldenrod3
139	105	20	goldenrod4
255	185	15	DarkGoldenrod1
238	173	14	DarkGoldenrod2
205	149	12	DarkGoldenrod3
139	101	8	DarkGoldenrod4
255	193	193	RosyBrown1
238	180	180	RosyBrown2
205	155	155	RosyBrown3
139	105	105	RosyBrown4
255	106	106	IndianRed1
238	99	99	IndianRed2
205	85	85	IndianRed3
139	58	58	IndianRed4
255	130	71	sienna1
238	121	66	sienna2
205	104	57	sienna3
139	71	38	sienna4
255	211	155	burlywood1
238	197	145	burlywood2
205	170	125	burlywood3
139	115	85	burlywood4
255	231	186	wheat1
238	216	174	wheat2
205	186	150	wheat3

R	G	B	Color Name
139	126	102	wheat4
255	165	79	tan1
238	154	73	tan2
205	133	63	tan3
139	90	43	tan4
255	127	36	chocolate1
238	118	33	chocolate2
205	102	29	chocolate3
139	69	19	chocolate4
255	48	48	firebrick1
238	44	44	firebrick2
205	38	38	firebrick3
139	26	26	firebrick4
255	64	64	brown1
238	59	59	brown2
205	51	51	brown3
139	35	35	brown4
255	140	105	salmon1
238	130	98	salmon2
205	112	84	salmon3
139	76	57	salmon4
255	160	122	LightSalmon1
238	149	114	LightSalmon2
205	129	98	LightSalmon3
139	87	66	LightSalmon4
255	165	0	orange1
238	154	0	orange2
205	133	0	orange3
139	90	0	orange4
255	127	0	DarkOrange1
238	118	0	DarkOrange2
205	102	0	DarkOrange3
139	69	0	DarkOrange4

continues

R	G	B	Color Name
255	114	86	coral1
238	106	80	coral2
205	91	69	coral3
139	62	47	coral4
255	99	71	tomato1
238	92	66	tomato2
205	79	57	tomato3
139	54	38	tomato4
255	69	0	OrangeRed1
238	64	0	OrangeRed2
205	55	0	OrangeRed3
139	37	0	OrangeRed4
255	0	0	red1
238	0	0	red2
205	0	0	red3
139	0	0	red4
255	20	147	DeepPink1
238	18	137	DeepPink2
205	16	118	DeepPink3
139	10	80	DeepPink4
255	110	180	HotPink1
238	106	167	HotPink2
205	96	144	HotPink3
139	58	98	HotPink4
255	181	197	pink1
238	169	184	pink2
205	145	158	pink3
139	99	108	pink4
255	174	185	LightPink1
238	162	173	LightPink2
205	140	149	LightPink3
139	95	101	LightPink4
255	130	171	PaleVioletRed1

R	G	B	Color Name
238	121	159	PaleVioletRed2
205	104	137	PaleVioletRed3
139	71	93	PaleVioletRed4
255	52	179	maroon1
238	48	167	maroon2
205	41	144	maroon3
139	28	98	maroon4
255	62	150	VioletRed1
238	58	140	VioletRed2
205	50	120	VioletRed3
139	34	82	VioletRed4
255	0	255	magenta1
238	0	238	magenta2
205	0	205	magenta3
139	0	139	magenta4
255	131	250	orchid1
238	122	233	orchid2
205	105	201	orchid3
139	71	137	orchid4
255	187	255	plum1
238	174	238	plum2
205	150	205	plum3
139	102	139	plum4
224	102	255	MediumOrchid1
209	95	238	MediumOrchid2
180	82	205	MediumOrchid3
122	55	139	MediumOrchid4
191	62	255	DarkOrchid1
178	58	238	DarkOrchid2
154	50	205	DarkOrchid3
104	34	139	DarkOrchid4
155	48	255	purple1
145	44	238	purple2

continues

R	G	B	Color Name
125	38	205	purple3
85	26	139	purple4
171	130	255	MediumPurple1
159	121	238	MediumPurple2
137	104	205	MediumPurple3
93	71	139	MediumPurple4
255	225	255	thistle1
238	210	238	thistle2
205	181	205	thistle3
139	123	139	thistle4
0	0	0	gray0
0	0	0	grey0
3	3	3	gray1
3	3	3	grey1
5	5	5	gray2
5	5	5	grey2
8	8	8	gray3
8	8	8	grey3
10	10	10	gray4
10	10	10	grey4
13	13	13	gray5
13	13	13	grey5
15	15	15	gray6
15	15	15	grey6
18	18	18	gray7
18	18	18	grey7
20	20	20	gray8
20	20	20	grey8
23	23	23	gray9
23	23	23	grey9
26	26	26	gray10
26	26	26	grey10
28	28	28	gray11

R	G	B	Color Name
28	28	28	grey11
31	31	31	gray12
31	31	31	grey12
33	33	33	gray13
33	33	33	grey13
36	36	36	gray14
36	36	36	grey14
38	38	38	gray15
38	38	38	grey15
41	41	41	gray16
41	41	41	grey16
43	43	43	gray17
43	43	43	grey17
46	46	46	gray18
46	46	46	grey18
48	48	48	gray19
48	48	48	grey19
51	51	51	gray20
51	51	51	grey20
54	54	54	gray21
54	54	54	grey21
56	56	56	gray22
56	56	56	grey22
59	59	59	gray23
59	59	59	grey23
61	61	61	gray24
61	61	61	grey24
64	64	64	gray25
64	64	64	grey25
66	66	66	gray26
66	66	66	grey26
69	69	69	gray27
69	69	69	grey27

continues

R	G	B	Color Name
71	71	71	gray28
71	71	71	grey28
74	74	74	gray29
74	74	74	grey29
77	77	77	gray30
77	77	77	grey30
79	79	79	gray31
79	79	79	grey31
82	82	82	gray32
82	82	82	grey32
84	84	84	gray33
84	84	84	grey33
87	87	87	gray34
87	87	87	grey34
89	89	89	gray35
89	89	89	grey35
92	92	92	gray36
92	92	92	grey36
94	94	94	gray37
94	94	94	grey37
97	97	97	gray38
97	97	97	grey38
99	99	99	gray39
99	99	99	grey39
102	102	102	gray40
102	102	102	grey40
105	105	105	gray41
105	105	105	grey41
107	107	107	gray42
107	107	107	grey42
110	110	110	gray43
110	110	110	grey43
112	112	112	gray44

R	G	B	Color Name
112	112	112	grey44
115	115	115	gray45
115	115	115	grey45
117	117	117	gray46
117	117	117	grey46
120	120	120	gray47
120	120	120	grey47
122	122	122	gray48
122	122	122	grey48
125	125	125	gray49
125	125	125	grey49
127	127	127	gray50
127	127	127	grey50
130	130	130	gray51
130	130	130	grey51
133	133	133	gray52
133	133	133	grey52
135	135	135	gray53
135	135	135	grey53
138	138	138	gray54
138	138	138	grey54
140	140	140	gray55
140	140	140	grey55
143	143	143	gray56
143	143	143	grey56
145	145	145	gray57
145	145	145	grey57
148	148	148	gray58
148	148	148	grey58
150	150	150	gray59
150	150	150	grey59
153	153	153	gray60
153	153	153	grey60

continues

R	G	B	Color Name
156	156	156	gray61
156	156	156	grey61
158	158	158	gray62
158	158	158	grey62
161	161	161	gray63
161	161	161	grey63
163	163	163	gray64
163	163	163	grey64
166	166	166	gray65
166	166	166	grey65
168	168	168	gray66
168	168	168	grey66
171	171	171	gray67
171	171	171	grey67
173	173	173	gray68
173	173	173	grey68
176	176	176	gray69
176	176	176	grey69
179	179	179	gray70
179	179	179	grey70
181	181	181	gray71
181	181	181	grey71
184	184	184	gray72
184	184	184	grey72
186	186	186	gray73
186	186	186	grey73
189	189	189	gray74
189	189	189	grey74
191	191	191	gray75
191	191	191	grey75
194	194	194	gray76
194	194	194	grey76
196	196	196	gray77

R	G	B	Color Name
196	196	196	grey77
199	199	199	gray78
199	199	199	grey78
201	201	201	gray79
201	201	201	grey79
204	204	204	gray80
204	204	204	grey80
207	207	207	gray81
207	207	207	grey81
209	209	209	gray82
209	209	209	grey82
212	212	212	gray83
212	212	212	grey83
214	214	214	gray84
214	214	214	grey84
217	217	217	gray85
217	217	217	grey85
219	219	219	gray86
219	219	219	grey86
222	222	222	gray87
222	222	222	grey87
224	224	224	gray88
224	224	224	grey88
227	227	227	gray89
227	227	227	grey89
229	229	229	gray90
229	229	229	grey90
232	232	232	gray91
232	232	232	grey91
235	235	235	gray92
235	235	235	grey92
237	237	237	gray93
237	237	237	grey93

continues

R	G	B	Color Name
240	240	240	gray94
240	240	240	grey94
242	242	242	gray95
242	242	242	grey95
245	245	245	gray96
245	245	245	grey96
247	247	247	gray97
247	247	247	grey97
250	250	250	gray98
250	250	250	grey98
252	252	252	gray99
252	252	252	grey99
255	255	255	gray100
255	255	255	grey100
169	169	169	dark grey
169	169	169	DarkGrey
169	169	169	dark gray
169	169	169	DarkGray
0	0	139	dark blue
0	0	139	DarkBlue
0	139	139	dark cyan
0	139	139	DarkCyan
139	0	139	dark magenta
139	0	139	DarkMagenta
139	0	0	dark red
139	0	0	DarkRed
144	238	144	light green
144	238	144	LightGreen

X Keyboard Symbols

This appendix lists the symbolic names of keysyms—the portable representation of symbols appearing on keycaps—for the ISO Latin 1-character set and for certain miscellaneous keys. You can use the XLookupKeysym function to get the keysym from a KeyPress event. You have to include the header file <X11/keysym.h> before you can refer to these keysyms.

Keysym	Value
XK_space	0x020
XK_exclam	0x021
XK_quotedbl	0x022
XK_numbersign	0x023
XK_dollar	0x024
XK_percent	0x025
XK_ampersand	0x026
XK_apostrophe	0x027
XK_quoteright	0x027
XK_parenleft	0x028
XK_parenright	0x029
XK_asterisk	0x02a
XK_plus	0x02b
XK_comma	0x02c
XK_minus	0x02d
XK_period	0x02e
XK_slash	0x02f
XK_0	0x030
XK_1	0x031
XK_2	0x032
XK_3	0x033
XK_4	0x034
XK_5	0x035
XK_6	0x036
XK_7	0x037
XK_8	0x038
XK_9	0x039
XK_colon	0x03a
XK_semicolon	0x03b
XK_less	0x03c
XK_equal	0x03d
XK_greater	0x03e
XK_question	0x03f
XK_at	0x040

Keysym	Value
XK_A	0x041
XK_B	0x042
XK_C	0x043
XK_D	0x044
XK_E	0x045
XK_F	0x046
XK_G	0x047
XK_H	0x048
XK_I	0x049
XK_J	0x04a
XK_K	0x04b
XK_L	0x04c
XK_M	0x04d
XK_N	0x04e
XK_O	0x04f
XK_P	0x050
XK_Q	0x051
XK_R	0x052
XK_S	0x053
XK_T	0x054
XK_U	0x055
XK_V	0x056
XK_W	0x057
XK_X	0x058
XK_Y	0x059
XK_Z	0x05a
XK_bracketleft	0x05b
XK_backslash	0x05c
XK_bracketright	0x05d
XK_asciicircum	0x05e
XK_underscore	0x05f
XK_grave	0x060

continues

Keysym	Value
XK_quoteleft	0x060
XK_a	0x061
XK_b	0x062
XK_c	0x063
XK_d	0x064
XK_e	0x065
XK_f	0x066
XK_g	0x067
XK_h	0x068
XK_i	0x069
XK_j	0x06a
XK_k	0x06b
XK_l	0x06c
XK_m	0x06d
XK_n	0x06e
XK_o	0x06f
XK_p	0x070
XK_q	0x071
XK_r	0x072
XK_s	0x073
XK_t	0x074
XK_u	0x075
XK_v	0x076
XK_w	0x077
XK_x	0x078
XK_y	0x079
XK_z	0x07a
XK_braceleft	0x07b
XK_bar	0x07c
XK_braceright	0x07d
XK_asciitilde	0x07e
XK_nobreakspace	0x0a0
XK_exclamdown	0x0a1

Keysym	Value
XK_cent	0x0a2
XK_sterling	0x0a3
XK_currency	0x0a4
XK_yen	0x0a5
XK_brokenbar	0x0a6
XK_section	0x0a7
XK_diaeresis	0x0a8
XK_copyright	0x0a9
XK_ordfeminine	0x0aa
XK_guillemotleft	0x0ab
XK_notsign	0x0ac
XK_hyphen	0x0ad
XK_registered	0x0ae
XK_macron	0x0af
XK_degree	0x0b0
XK_plusminus	0x0b1
XK_twosuperior	0x0b2
XK_threesuperior	0x0b3
XK_acute	0x0b4
XK_mu	0x0b5
XK_paragraph	0x0b6
XK_periodcentered	0x0b7
XK_cedilla	0x0b8
XK_onesuperior	0x0b9
XK_masculine	0x0ba
XK_guillemotright	0x0bb
XK_onequarter	0x0bc
XK_onehalf	0x0bd
XK_threequarters	0x0be
XK_questiondown	0x0bf
XK_Agrave	0x0c0
XK_Aacute	0x0c1

continues

Keysym	*Value*
XK_Acircumflex	0x0c2
XK_Atilde	0x0c3
XK_Adiaeresis	0x0c4
XK_Aring	0x0c5
XK_AE	0x0c6
XK_Ccedilla	0x0c7
XK_Egrave	0x0c8
XK_Eacute	0x0c9
XK_Ecircumflex	0x0ca
XK_Ediaeresis	0x0cb
XK_Igrave	0x0cc
XK_Iacute	0x0cd
XK_Icircumflex	0x0ce
XK_Idiaeresis	0x0cf
XK_ETH	0x0d0
XK_Eth	0x0d0
XK_Ntilde	0x0d1
XK_Ograve	0x0d2
XK_Oacute	0x0d3
XK_Ocircumflex	0x0d4
XK_Otilde	0x0d5
XK_Odiaeresis	0x0d6
XK_multiply	0x0d7
XK_Ooblique	0x0d8
XK_Ugrave	0x0d9
XK_Uacute	0x0da
XK_Ucircumflex	0x0db
XK_Udiaeresis	0x0dc
XK_Yacute	0x0dd
XK_THORN	0x0de
XK_Thorn	0x0de
XK_ssharp	0x0df
XK_agrave	0x0e0

Keysym	Value
XK_aacute	0x0e1
XK_acircumflex	0x0e2
XK_atilde	0x0e3
XK_adiaeresis	0x0e4
XK_aring	0x0e5
XK_ae	0x0e6
XK_ccedilla	0x0e7
XK_egrave	0x0e8
XK_eacute	0x0e9
XK_ecircumflex	0x0ea
XK_ediaeresis	0x0eb
XK_igrave	0x0ec
XK_iacute	0x0ed
XK_icircumflex	0x0ee
XK_idiaeresis	0x0ef
XK_eth	0x0f0
XK_ntilde	0x0f1
XK_ograve	0x0f2
XK_oacute	0x0f3
XK_ocircumflex	0x0f4
XK_otilde	0x0f5
XK_odiaeresis	0x0f6
XK_division	0x0f7
XK_oslash	0x0f8
XK_ugrave	0x0f9
XK_uacute	0x0fa
XK_ucircumflex	0x0fb
XK_udiaeresis	0x0fc
XK_yacute	0x0fd
XK_thorn	0x0fe
XK_ydiaeresis	0x0ff

Miscellaneous Keysyms

Keysym	Value	Description
TTY Functions		
XK_BackSpace	0xFF08	
XK_Tab	0xFF09	
XK_Linefeed	0xFF0A	
XK_Clear	0xFF0B	
XK_Return	0xFF0D	
XK_Pause	0xFF13	
XK_Scroll_Lock	0xFF14	
XK_Escape	0xFF1B	
XK_Delete	0xFFFF	
International and Multikey Character Composition		
XK_Multi_key	0xFF20	Compose multikey character
Japanese Keyboard Support		
XK_Kanji	0xFF21	Kanji, Kanji convert
XK_Muhenkan	0xFF22	Cancel conversion
XK_Henkan_Mode	0xFF23	Start or stop conversion
XK_Henkan	0xFF23	Alias for Henkan_Mode
XK_Romaji	0xFF24	To Romaji
XK_Hiragana	0xFF25	To Hiragana
XK_Katakana	0xFF26	To Katakana
XK_Hiragana_Katakana	0xFF27	Toggle between Hiragana and Katakana
XK_Zenkaku	0xFF28	To Zenkaku
XK_Hankaku	0xFF29	To Hankaku
XK_Zenkaku_Hankaku	0xFF2A	Toggle between Zenkaku and Hankaku
XK_Touroku	0xFF2B	Add to dictionary
XK_Massyo	0xFF2C	Delete from dictionary
XK_Kana_Lock	0xFF2D	Kana Lock
XK_Kana_Shift	0xFF2E	Kana Shift
XK_Eisu_Shift	0xFF2F	Alphanumeric shift
XK_Eisu_toggle	0xFF30	Alphanumeric toggle
Cursor Control and Motion		
XK_Home	0xFF50	Home key
XK_Left	0xFF51	Left arrow

Keysym	*Value*	*Description*
XK_Up	0xFF52	Up arrow
XK_Right	0xFF53	Right arrow
XK_Down	0xFF54	Down arrow
XK_Prior	0xFF55	Go to previous line
XK_Next	0xFF56	Go to next line
XK_End	0xFF57	Go to end of line
XK_Begin	0xFF58	Go to beginning of line
Miscellaneous Functions		
XK_Select	0xFF60	Select, mark
XK_Print	0xFF61	Print
XK_Execute	0xFF62	Execute, run, do
XK_Insert	0xFF63	Insert, insert here
XK_Undo	0xFF65	Undo
XK_Redo	0xFF66	Redo
XK_Menu	0xFF67	
XK_Find	0xFF68	Find, search
XK_Cancel	0xFF69	Cancel, stop, abort, exit
XK_Help	0xFF6A	Help
XK_Break	0xFF6B	Break connection
XK_Mode_switch	0xFF7E	Character set switch
XK_script_switch	0xFF7E	Alias for mode_switch
XK_Num_Lock	0xFF7F	Num Lock key
Keypad Functions		
XK_KP_Space	0xFF80	Space
XK_KP_Tab	0xFF89	
XK_KP_Enter	0xFF8D	Enter key
XK_KP_F1	0xFF91	
XK_KP_F2	0xFF92	
XK_KP_F3	0xFF93	
XK_KP_F4	0xFF94	
XK_KP_Equal	0xFFBD	Equals
XK_KP_Multiply	0xFFAA	
XK_KP_Add	0xFFAB	

continues

Keysym	Value	Description
XK_KP_Separator	0xFFAC	Separator, usually comma
XK_KP_Subtract	0xFFAD	
XK_KP_Decimal	0xFFAE	
XK_KP_Divide	0xFFAF	
XK_KP_0	0xFFB0	
XK_KP_1	0xFFB1	
XK_KP_2	0xFFB2	
XK_KP_3	0xFFB3	
XK_KP_4	0xFFB4	
XK_KP_5	0xFFB5	
XK_KP_6	0xFFB6	
XK_KP_7	0xFFB7	
XK_KP_8	0xFFB8	
XK_KP_9	0xFFB9	

Auxiliary Functions
(Note the duplicate definitions for left and right function keys.)

XK_F1	0xFFBE	
XK_F2	0xFFBF	
XK_F3	0xFFC0	
XK_F4	0xFFC1	
XK_F5	0xFFC2	
XK_F6	0xFFC3	
XK_F7	0xFFC4	
XK_F8	0xFFC5	
XK_F9	0xFFC6	
XK_F10	0xFFC7	
XK_F11	0xFFC8	
XK_L1	0xFFC8	
XK_F12	0xFFC9	
XK_L2	0xFFC9	
XK_F13	0xFFCA	
XK_L3	0xFFCA	
XK_F14	0xFFCB	
XK_L4	0xFFCB	

Keysym	Value	Description
XK_F15	0xFFCC	
XK_L5	0xFFCC	
XK_F16	0xFFCD	
XK_L6	0xFFCD	
XK_F17	0xFFCE	
XK_L7	0xFFCE	
XK_F18	0xFFCF	
XK_L8	0xFFCF	
XK_F19	0xFFD0	
XK_L9	0xFFD0	
XK_F20	0xFFD1	
XK_L10	0xFFD1	
XK_F21	0xFFD2	
XK_R1	0xFFD2	
XK_F22	0xFFD3	
XK_R2	0xFFD3	
XK_F23	0xFFD4	
XK_R3	0xFFD4	
XK_F24	0xFFD5	
XK_R4	0xFFD5	
XK_F25	0xFFD6	
XK_R5	0xFFD6	
XK_F20	0xFFD7	
XK_R6	0xFFD7	
XK_F27	0xFFD8	
XK_R7	0xFFD8	
XK_F28	0xFFD9	
XK_R8	0xFFD9	
XK_F29	0xFFDA	
XK_R9	0xFFDA	
XK_F30	0xFFDB	
XK_R10	0xFFDB	
XK_F31	0xFFDC	

continues

Keysym	Value	Description
XK_R11	0xFFDC	
XK_F32	0xFFDD	
XK_R12	0xFFDD	
XK_R13	0xFFDE	
XK_F33	0xFFDE	
XK_F34	0xFFDF	
XK_R14	0xFFDF	
XK_F35	0xFFE0	
XK_R15	0xFFE0	
Modifiers		
XK_Shift_L	0xFFE1	Left Shift
XK_Shift_R	0xFFE2	Right Shift
XK_Control_L	0xFFE3	Left Control
XK_Control_R	0xFFE4	Right Control
XK_Caps_Lock	0xFFE5	Caps Lock
XK_Shift_Lock	0xFFE6	Shift Lock
XK_Meta_L	0xFFE7	Left Meta
XK_Meta_R	0xFFE8	Right Meta
XK_Alt_L	0xFFE9	Left Alt
XK_Alt_R	0xFFEA	Right Alt
XK_Super_L	0xFFEB	Left Super
XK_Super_R	0xFFEC	Right Super
XK_Hyper_L	0xFFED	Left Hyper
XK_Hyper_R	0xFFEE	Right Hyper

X Cursors

Figure F.1 shows the standard cursor shapes available in X. The table lists the values and symbolic names for the shapes. These definitions are in the header file <X11/cursorfont.h>. The row numbers in the table refer to the rows in Figure F.1. You can use the XCreateFontCursor function to create cursor resources with these shapes. See Chapter 8, "Handling Events," for more information on using this function.

Figure F.1.

Standard cursor font.

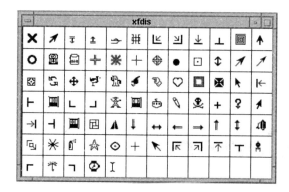

Value	Symbol
Row 1	
0	XC_X_cursor
2	XC_arrow
4	XC_based_arrow_down
6	XC_based_arrow_up
8	XC_boat
10	XC_bogosity
12	XC_bottom_left_corner
14	XC_bottom_right_corner
16	XC_bottom_side
18	XC_bottom_tee
20	XC_box_spiral
22	XC_center_ptr
Row 2	
24	XC_circle
26	XC_clock
28	XC_coffee_mug
30	XC_cross
32	XC_cross_reverse
34	XC_crosshair
36	XC_diamond_cross
38	XC_dot
40	XC_dotbox
42	XC_double_arrow
44	XC_draft_large

Value	Symbol
46	XC_draft_small
Row 3	
48	XC_draped_box
50	XC_exchange
52	XC_fleur
54	XC_gobbler
56	XC_gumby
58	XC_hand1
60	XC_hand2
62	XC_heart
64	XC_icon
66	XC_iron_cross
68	XC_left_ptr
70	XC_left_side
Row 4	
72	XC_left_tee
74	XC_leftbutton
76	XC_ll_angle
78	XC_lr_angle
80	XC_man
82	XC_middlebutton
84	XC_mouse
86	XC_pencil
88	XC_pirate
90	XC_plus
92	XC_question_arrow
94	XC_right_ptr
Row 5	
96	XC_right_side
98	XC_right_tee
100	XC_rightbutton
102	XC_rtl_logo

continues

Value	Symbol
104	XC_sailboat
106	XC_sb_down_arrow
108	XC_sb_h_double_arrow
110	XC_sb_left_arrow
112	XC_sb_right_arrow
114	XC_sb_up_arrow
116	XC_sb_v_double_arrow
118	XC_shuttle
Row 6	
120	XC_sizing
122	XC_spider
124	XC_spraycan
126	XC_star
128	XC_target
130	XC_tcross
132	XC_top_left_arrow
134	XC_top_left_corner
136	XC_top_right_corner
138	XC_top_side
140	XC_top_tee
142	XC_trek
Row 7	
144	XC_ul_angle
146	XC_umbrella
148	XC_ur_angle
150	XC_watch
152	XC_xterm

X Atoms

This appendix lists the predefined Atoms in X11R6. Chapter 16, "Advanced Topics in X," describes atoms and how they are used. These atoms are defined in the header file <X11/Xatom.h>. You can use the xprop utility program to see what properties are defined for a window. For example, to see the properties associated with the root window, use the following:

```
xprop -root
```

Selections

```
XA_PRIMARY
XA_SECONDARY
```

Data Types

```
XA_ARC
XA_ATOM
XA_BITMAP
XA_CARDINAL
XA_COLORMAP
XA_CURSOR
XA_DRAWABLE
XA_FONT
XA_INTEGER
XA_PIXMAP
XA_POINT
XA_RECTANGLE
XA_STRING
XA_VISUALID
XA_WINDOW
```

Cut Buffers

```
XA_CUT_BUFFER0
XA_CUT_BUFFER1
XA_CUT_BUFFER2
XA_CUT_BUFFER3
XA_CUT_BUFFER4
XA_CUT_BUFFER5
XA_CUT_BUFFER6
XA_CUT_BUFFER7
```

Resource Database

```
XA_RESOURCE_MANAGER
```

Standard Colormaps

```
XA_RGB_BEST_MAP
XA_RGB_BLUE_MAP
XA_RGB_COLOR_MAP
XA_RGB_DEFAULT_MAP
XA_RGB_GRAY_MAP
XA_RGB_GREEN_MAP
XA_RGB_RED_MAP
```

Window Manager Hints

```
XA_WM_CLASS
XA_WM_CLIENT_MACHINE
XA_WM_COMMAND
XA_WM_HINTS
XA_WM_ICON_NAME
XA_WM_ICON_SIZE
XA_WM_NAME
XA_WM_NORMAL_HINTS
XA_WM_SIZE_HINTS
XA_WM_TRANSIENT_FOR
XA_WM_ZOOM_HINTS
```

Font Properties

```
XA_CAP_HEIGHT
XA_COPYRIGHT
XA_END_SPACE
XA_FAMILY_NAME
XA_FONT_NAME
XA_FULL_NAME
XA_ITALIC_ANGLE
XA_MAX_SPACE
XA_MIN_SPACE
XA_NORM_SPACE
XA_NOTICE
XA_POINT_SIZE
XA_QUAD_WIDTH
```

```
XA_RESOLUTION
XA_STRIKEOUT_ASCENT
XA_STRIKEOUT_DESCENT
XA_SUBSCRIPT_X
XA_SUBSCRIPT_Y
XA_SUPERSCRIPT_X
XA_SUPERSCRIPT_Y
XA_UNDERLINE_POSITION
XA_UNDERLINE_THICKNESS
XA_WEIGHT
XA_X_HEIGHT
```

X Protocol Requests

This appendix shows the number (also known as the *major opcode*) and the name of each X protocol request. You can use this information to identify the operation that caused an error. (The error event indicates the major opcode of the failed request.) The symbolic names for the protocol requests are defined in the header file `<X11/Xproto.h>`. Extensions to the X protocol define their own opcodes.

Request Number	Symbolic Name
1	X_CreateWindow
2	X_ChangeWindowAttributes
3	X_GetWindowAttributes
4	X_DestroyWindow
5	X_DestroySubwindows
6	X_ChangeSaveSet
7	X_ReparentWindow
8	X_MapWindow
9	X_MapSubwindows
10	X_UnmapWindow
11	X_UnmapSubwindows
12	X_ConfigureWindow
13	X_CirculateWindow
14	X_GetGeometry
15	X_QueryTree
16	X_InternAtom
17	X_GetAtomName
18	X_ChangeProperty
19	X_DeleteProperty
20	X_GetProperty
21	X_ListProperties
22	X_SetSelectionOwner
23	X_GetSelectionOwner
24	X_ConvertSelection
25	X_SendEvent
26	X_GrabPointer
27	X_UngrabPointer
28	X_GrabButton
29	X_UngrabButton
30	X_ChangeActivePointerGrab
31	X_GrabKeyboard
32	X_UngrabKeyboard
33	X_GrabKey
34	X_UngrabKey

Request Number	Symbolic Name
35	X_AllowEvents
36	X_GrabServer
37	X_UngrabServer
38	X_QueryPointer
39	X_GetMotionEvents
40	X_TranslateCoords
41	X_WarpPointer
42	X_SetInputFocus
43	X_GetInputFocus
44	X_QueryKeymap
45	X_OpenFont
46	X_CloseFont
47	X_QueryFont
48	X_QueryTextExtents
49	X_ListFonts
50	X_ListFontsWithInfo
51	X_SetFontPath
52	X_GetFontPath
53	X_CreatePixmap
54	X_FreePixmap
55	X_CreateGC
56	X_ChangeGC
57	X_CopyGC
58	X_SetDashes
59	X_SetClipRectangles
60	X_FreeGC
61	X_ClearArea
62	X_CopyArea
63	X_CopyPlane
64	X_PolyPoint
65	X_PolyLine
66	X_PolySegment
67	X_PolyRectangle

continues

Request Number	Symbolic Name
68	X_PolyArc
69	X_FillPoly
70	X_PolyFillRectangle
71	X_PolyFillArc
72	X_PutImage
73	X_GetImage
74	X_PolyText8
75	X_PolyText16
76	X_ImageText8
77	X_ImageText16
78	X_CreateColormap
79	X_FreeColormap
80	X_CopyColormapAndFree
81	X_InstallColormap
82	X_UninstallColormap
83	X_ListInstalledColormaps
84	X_AllocColor
85	X_AllocNamedColor
86	X_AllocColorCells
87	X_AllocColorPlanes
88	X_FreeColors
89	X_StoreColors
90	X_StoreNamedColor
91	X_QueryColors
92	X_LookupColor
93	X_CreateCursor
94	X_CreateGlyphCursor
95	X_FreeCursor
96	X_RecolorCursor
97	X_QueryBestSize
98	X_QueryExtension
99	X_ListExtensions
100	X_ChangeKeyboardMapping

Request Number	Symbolic Name
101	X_GetKeyboardMapping
102	X_ChangeKeyboardControl
103	X_GetKeyboardControl
104	X_Bell
105	X_ChangePointerControl
106	X_GetPointerControl
107	X_SetScreenSaver
108	X_GetScreenSaver
109	X_ChangeHosts
110	X_ListHosts
111	X_SetAccessControl
112	X_SetCloseDownMode
113	X_KillClient
114	X_RotateProperties
115	X_ForceScreenSaver
116	X_SetPointerMapping
117	X_GetPointerMapping
118	X_SetModifierMapping
119	X_GetModifierMapping
127	X_NoOperation

Xlib Reference

Xlib Functions (X11R6)

```
XActivateScreenSaver(Display* display);
```
Activates screen blanking

```
XAddHost(Display* display, XHostAddress* host);
```
Offers a host access to X server

```
XAddHosts(Display* display, XHostAddress* hosts, int num_hosts);
```
Offers several hosts access to server

```
XAddPixel(XImage *ximage, unsigned long value);
```
Adds a constant to every pixel in an image

```
XAddToSaveSet(Display* display, Window w);
```
Adds a window to the save set

```
XClassHint *XAllocClassHint (void);
```
Allocates an XClassHint structure

```
Status XAllocColor(Display* display, Colormap colormap, XColor*
screen_in_out);
```
Allocates a read-only colormap cell

```
Status XAllocColorCells(Display* display, Colormap colormap, Bool
contig, unsigned long* plane_masks_return, unsigned int nplanes,
unsigned long* pixels_return, unsigned int npixels);
```
Allocates several read-write cells

```
Status XAllocColorPlanes(Display* display, Colormap colormap, Bool contig, unsigned long*
pixels_return, int ncolors, int nreds, int ngreens, int nblues, unsigned long*
rmask_return, unsigned long* gmask_return, unsigned long* bmask_return);
```
Allocates private read-write color planes

```
XIconSize *XAllocIconSize (void);
```
Allocates an XIconSize structure

```
Status XAllocNamedColor(Display* display, Colormap colormap, const char* color_name,
XColor* screen_def_return, XColor* exact_def_return);
```
Allocates a shared read-only colormap cell

```
XSizeHints *XAllocSizeHints (void);
```
Allocates an XSizeHints structure

```
XStandardColormap *XAllocStandardColormap (void);
```
Allocates an XStandardColormap structure

```
XWMHints *XAllocWMHints (void);
```
Allocates an XWMHints structure

```
XAllowEvents(Display* display, int event_mode, Time time);
```
Reenables event delivery after a grab

```
XAutoRepeatOff(Display* display);
```
Turns off the keyboard auto-repeat

```
XAutoRepeatOn(Display* display);
```
Turns on the keyboard auto-repeat

```
XBell(Display* display, int percent);
```
Rings the bell

```
char *XBaseFontNameListOfFontSet(XFontSet font_set);
```
Returns a null-terminated string containing the comma-separated list of font names that were used to create the specified font set

```
XChangeActivePointerGrab(Display* display, unsigned int event_mask, Cursor cursor, Time
time);
```
Changes the parameters of an active grab

```
XChangeGC(Display* display, GC gc, unsigned long valuemask, XGCValues* values);
```
Changes the members of a graphics context

```
XChangeKeyboardControl(Display* display, unsigned long value_mask, XKeyboardControl*
values);
```
Changes the parameters of the keyboard

```
XChangeKeyboardMapping(Display* display, int first_keycode, int keysyms_per_keycode,
KeySym* keysyms, int num_codes);
```

Changes the mapping of keycodes to keysyms

```
XChangePointerControl(Display* display, Bool do_accel, Bool do_threshold, int
accel_numerator, int accel_denominator, int threshold);
```

Changes the parameters of the mouse pointer

```
XChangeProperty(Display* display, Window w, Atom property, Atom type, int format, int
mode, const unsigned char* data, int nelements);
```

Changes the data stored in a window's property

```
XChangeSaveSet(Display* display, Window w, int change_mode);
```

Adds or removes a window from a save set

```
XChangeWindowAttributes(Display* display, Window w, unsigned long valuemask,
XSetWindowAttributes* attributes);
```

Changes one or more attributes of a window

```
Bool XCheckIfEvent(Display* display, XEvent* event_return, Bool (*) (Display* display,
XEvent* event, char* arg) predicate, char* arg);
```

Checks the event queue for a matching event (nonblocking)

```
Bool XCheckMaskEvent(Display* display, long event_mask, XEvent* event_return);
```

Gets the next event matching an event mask (nonblocking)

```
Bool XCheckTypedEvent(Display* display, int event_type, XEvent* event_return);
```

Gets the next event matching an event type (nonblocking)

```
Bool XCheckTypedWindowEvent(Display* display, Window w, int event_type, XEvent*
event_return);
```

Returns the event matching type and window (nonblocking)

```
Bool XCheckWindowEvent(Display* display, Window w, long event_mask, XEvent*
event_return);
```

Returns the event matching an event mask and window (nonblocking)

```
XCirculateSubwindows(Display* display, Window w, int direction);
```

Rotates the positions of subwindows in stacking order

```
XCirculateSubwindowsDown(Display* display, Window w);
```

Moves the top subwindow to bottom

```
XCirculateSubwindowsUp(Display* display, Window w);
```

Moves the bottom subwindow to top

```
XClearArea(Display* display, Window w, int x, int y, unsigned int width, unsigned int
height, Bool exposures);
```

Clears a rectangular area

```
XClearWindow(Display* display, Window w);
```

Clears a window (no exposure event)

```
XClipBox(Region r, XRectangle* rect_return);
```

Computes the smallest rectangle enclosing a region

```
XCloseDisplay(Display* display);
```

Closes the connection to the X server

```
XConfigureWindow(Display* display, Window w, unsigned int value_mask, XWindowChanges*
values);
```

Changes a window's position, size, and so forth

```
Bool XContextDependentDrawing(XFontSet font_set);
```

Returns True if drawing functions include implicit text directionality, or text drawn with the font set might include context-dependent drawing

```
Bool XContextualDrawing(XFontSet font_set);
```

Returns True if text drawn with the font set might include context-dependent drawing

```
void XConvertCase(KeySym key, KeySym* lowercase, KeySym* uppercase);
```

Converts a specified KeySym to its lowercase and uppercase forms

```
XConvertSelection(Display* display, Atom selection, Atom target, Atom property, Window
requestor, Time time);
```

Sends a SelectionRequest event to a selection's owner

```
XCopyArea(Display* display, Drawable src, Drawable dest, GC gc, int src_x, int src_y,
unsigned int width, unsigned int height, int dest_x, int dest_y);
```

Copies from one drawable to another

```
Colormap XCopyColormapAndFree(Display* display, Colormap colormap);
```

Copies a colormap and returns a new one

```
XCopyGC(Display* display, GC src, unsigned long valuemask, GC dest);
```

Copies selected fields from one GC to another

```
XCopyPlane(Display* display, Drawable src, Drawable dest, GC gc, int src_x, int src_y,
unsigned int width, unsigned int height, int dest_x, int dest_y, unsigned long plane);
```

Copies a single plane from one drawable to another

```
Pixmap XCreateBitmapFromData(Display* display, Drawable d, const char* data, unsigned int
width, unsigned int height);
```

Creates a bitmap from data stored in X11 bitmap format

```
Colormap XCreateColormap(Display* display, Window w, Visual* visual, int alloc);
```

Creates a colormap for a visual type

```
Cursor XCreateFontCursor(Display* display, unsigned int shape);
```

Creates a cursor from a glyph in the standard cursor font

```
XFontSet XCreateFontSet(Display* display, const char* base_font_name_list, char***
missing_charset_list_returned, int* missing_charset_count_returned, char**
default_string_returned);
```

Creates a font set for the current locale using the specified comma-separated list of font names, and provides information on the charsets (character sets with associated encodings) for which there are no fonts

```
GC XCreateGC(Display* display, Drawable d, unsigned long valuemask, XGCValues* values);
```

Creates a new graphics context

```
Cursor XCreateGlyphCursor(Display* display, Font source_font, Font mask_font, unsigned
int source_char, unsigned int mask_char, XColor* foreground_color, XColor*
background_color);
```

Creates a new cursor from source and mask glyphs

```
XImage *XCreateImage(Display* display, Visual* visual, unsigned int depth, int format,
int offset, char* data, unsigned int width, unsigned int height, int bitmap_pad, int
bytes_per_line);
```

Creates a new `XImage` structure

```
Pixmap XCreatePixmap(Display* display, Drawable d, unsigned int width, unsigned int
height, unsigned int depth);
```

Creates a new pixmap

```
Cursor XCreatePixmapCursor(Display* display, Pixmap source, Pixmap mask, XColor*
foreground_color, XColor* background_color, unsigned int x, unsigned int y);
```

Creates a cursor from a source and a mask bitmap

```
Pixmap XCreatePixmapFromBitmapData(Display* display, Drawable d, char* data, unsigned int
width, unsigned int height, unsigned long fg, unsigned long bg, unsigned int depth);
```

Creates a pixmap from bitmap data

```
Region XCreateRegion(void);
```

Creates an empty region

```
Window XCreateSimpleWindow(Display* display, Window parent, int x, int y, unsigned int
width, unsigned int height, unsigned int border_width, unsigned long border, unsigned
long background);
```

Creates an unmapped `InputOutput` window

```
Window XCreateWindow(Display* display, Window parent, int x, int y, unsigned int width,
unsigned int height, unsigned int border_width, int depth, unsigned int class, Visual*
visual, unsigned long valuemask, XSetWindowAttributes* attributes);
```
Creates an unmapped window with specified attributes

```
XDefineCursor(Display* display, Window w, Cursor cursor);
```
Assigns a cursor to a window

```
int XDeleteContext(Display* display, XID resource_id, XContext context);
```
Deletes data stored by context manager

```
XModifierKeymap *XDeleteModifiermapEntry(XModifierKeymap* modmap, KeyCode keycode_entry,
int modifier);
```
Deletes an entry from a modifier map

```
XDeleteProperty(Display* display, Window w, Atom property);
```
Deletes a property from a window

```
XDestroyImage(XImage *ximage);
```
Deallocates an XImage structure and its data

```
XDestroyRegion(Region r);
```
Deallocates a region

```
XDestroySubwindows(Display* display, Window w);
```
Destroys all subwindows of a window

```
XDestroyWindow(Display* display, Window w);
```
Destroys a window and its subwindows

```
Bool XDirectionalDependentDrawing(XFontSet font_set);
```
Returns True if text-drawing functions implement implicit text directionality

```
XDisableAccessControl(Display* display);
```
Enables any host to connect to X server

```
XDisplayKeycodes(Display* display, int* min_keycodes_return, int* max_keycodes_return);
```
Returns the range of supported keycodes

```
unsigned long XDisplayMotionBufferSize(Display* display);
```
Returns the size of the motion buffer

```
char *XDisplayName(const char* string);
```
Returns the name of the display

```
XDrawArc(Display* display, Drawable d, GC gc, int x, int y, unsigned int width, unsigned
int height, int angle1, int angle2);
```
Draws an arc

```
XDrawArcs(Display* display, Drawable d, GC gc, XArc* arcs, int narcs);
```
Draws several arcs

```
XDrawImageString(Display* display, Drawable d, GC gc, int x, int y, const char* string,
int length);
```
Draws characters using both foreground and background

```
XDrawImageString16(Display* display, Drawable d, GC gc, int x, int y, const XChar2b*
string, int length);
```
Draws 16-bit text characters using both foreground and background

```
XDrawLine(Display* display, Drawable d, GC gc, int x1, int x2, int y1, int y2);
```
Draws a line between two points

```
XDrawLines(Display* display, Drawable d, GC gc, XPoint* points, int npoints, int mode);
```
Draws several lines

```
XDrawPoint(Display* display, Drawable d, GC gc, int x, int y);
```
Draws a point

```
XDrawPoints(Display* display, Drawable d, GC gc, XPoint* points, int npoints, int mode);
```
Draws a number of points

```
XDrawRectangle(Display* display, Drawable d, GC gc, int x, int y, unsigned int width,
unsigned int height);
```
Draws an outline of a rectangle

```
XDrawRectangles(Display* display, Drawable d, GC gc, XRectangle* rectangles, int
nrectangles);
```
Draws an outline of several rectangles

```
XDrawSegments(Display* display, Drawable d, GC gc, XSegment* segments, int nsegments);
```
Draws multiple, disjoint lines

```
XDrawString(Display* display, Drawable d, GC gc, int x, int y, const char* string, int
length);
```
Draws a text string in foreground color only

```
XDrawString16(Display* display, Drawable d, GC gc, int x, int y, const XChar2b* string,
int length);
```
Draws a 16-bit string in foreground color only

```
XDrawText(Display* display, Drawable d, GC gc, int x, int y, XTextItem* items, int
nitems);
```
Draws several text strings on a line

```
XDrawText16(Display* display, Drawable d, GC gc, int x, int y, XTextItem16* items, int
nitems);
```
Draws several 16-bit strings on a line

```
XEmptyRegion(Region r);
```
Tests whether a region is empty

```
long XExtendedMaxRequestSize(Display* display)
```
Returns the maximum size (in 4-byte units) of protocol requests, if server supports extended-length protocol encoding

```
XEnableAccessControl(Display* display);
```
Makes the server use access control list

```
XEqualRegion(Region r1, Region r2);
```
Checks whether two regions are equal

```
int XEventsQueued(Display* display, int mode);
```
Returns the number of queued events (nonblocking)

```
XFontSetExtents *XExtentsOfFontSet(XFontSet font_set);
```
Returns an `XFontSetExtents` structure with information about the maximum extents of characters in the specified font set

```
char *XFetchBuffer(Display* display, int* nbytes_return, int buffer);
```
Gets data from cut buffer

```
char *XFetchBytes(Display* display, int* nbytes_return);
```
Gets data from cut buffer 0

```
Status XFetchName(Display* display, Window w, char** window_name_return);
```
Gets a window's name

```
XFillArc(Display* display, Drawable d, GC gc, int x, int y, unsigned int width, unsigned
int height, int angle1, int angle2);
```
Draws a filled arc

```
XFillArcs(Display* display, Drawable d, GC gc, XArc* arcs, int narcs);
```
Draws several filled arcs

```
XFillPolygon(Display* display, Drawable d, GC gc, XPoint* points, int npoints, int shape,
int mode);
```
Draws a filled polygon

```
XFillRectangle(Display* display, Drawable d, GC gc, int x, int y, unsigned int width,
unsigned int height);
```
Draws a filled rectangle

```
XFillRectangles(Display* display, Drawable d, GC gc, XRectangle* rectangles, int
nrectangles);
```
Fills several rectangles

```
Bool XFilterEvent(XEvent* event, Window window);
```
Filters X events for an input method that maps multiple keystrokes to a character to enable entering characters for languages such as Japanese

```
int XFindContext(Display* display, XID resource_id, XContext context, XPointer*
data_return);
```
Gets data stored using a context

```
XFlush(Display* display);
```
Sends out all queued X protocol requests

```
XFlushGC(Display* display, GC gc);
```
Sends all cached changes to the specified GC to the server

```
XForceScreenSaver(Display* display, int mode);
```
Turns the screen saver on or off

```
int XFontsOfFontSet(XFontSet font_set, XFontStruct*** font_struct_list_returned, char***
font_name_list_returned);
```
Gets the list of font names and corresponding XFontStructs for a specified font set

```
XFree(char* data);
```
Frees memory allocated by Xlib functions

```
XFreeColormap(Display* display, Colormap colormap);
```
Destroys a colormap

```
XFreeColors(Display* display, Colormap colormap, unsigned long* pixels, int npixels,
unsigned long planes);
```
Frees colormap cells

```
XFreeCursor(Display* display, Cursor cursor);
```
Destroys a cursor

```
XFreeExtensionList(char** list);
```
Frees memory allocated by XListExtensions

```
XFreeFont(Display* display, XFontStruct* font_struct);
```
Unloads a font

```
XFreeFontInfo(char** names, XFontStruct* free_info, int actual_count);
```
Frees memory allocated by XListFontsWithInfo

```
XFreeFontNames(char** list);
```
Frees memory allocated by `XListFonts`

```
XFreeFontPath(char** list);
```
Frees memory allocated by `XGetFontPath`

```
XFreeFontSet(Display* display, XFontSet font_set);
```
Frees the specified font set

```
XFreeGC(Display* display, GC gc);
```
Destroys a GC resource

```
XFreeModifiermap(XModifierKeymap* modmap);
```
Frees memory used by an `XModifierKeymap` structure

```
XFreePixmap(Display* display, Pixmap pixmap);
```
Frees a pixmap

```
void XFreeStringList(char** list);
```
Frees memory allocated by `XTextPropertyToStringList`

```
GContext XGContextFromGC(GC gc);
```
Gets a `GContext` ID from a `GC`

```
int XGeometry(Display* display, int screen, const char* position, const char*
default_position, unsigned int bwidth, unsigned int fwidth, unsigned int fheight, int
xadder, int yadder, int* x_return, int* y_return, int* width_return, int* height_return);
```
Computes position and size from a geometry string

```
char *XGetAtomName(Display* display, Atom atom);
```
Returns a string corresponding to an atom

```
Status *XGetAtomNames(Display* display, Atom* atoms, int count, char** atom_names);
```
Provides an array of strings corresponding to the entries in an array of atoms

```
Status XGetClassHint(Display* display, Window w, XClassHint* class_hints_return);
```
Gets the `XA_WM_CLASS` property

```
Status XGetCommand(Display* display, Window w, char*** argv_return, int* argc_return);
```
Gets the command line that started the application

```
char *XGetDefault(Display* display, const char* program, const char* option);
```
Gets the value of an option from the resource database

```
XGetErrorDatabaseText(Display* display, const char* name, const char* message, const
char* default_string, char* buffer_return, int length);
```
Gets an error message from a database

```
XGetErrorText(Display* display, int code, char* buffer_return, int length);
```

Gets a string describing an error code

```
char **XGetFontPath(Display* display, int* npaths_return);
```

Gets the current font search path

```
Bool XGetFontProperty(XFontStruct* font_struct, Atom atom, unsigned long* value_return);
```

Gets a font property

```
Status XGetGCValues(Display* display, GC gc, unsigned long valuemask, XGCValues* values_return);
```

Gets values from a GC

```
Status XGetGeometry(Display* display, Drawable d, Window* root_return, int* x_return,
int* y_return, unsigned int* width_return, unsigned int* height_return, unsigned int*
border_width_return, unsigned int* depth_return);
```

Gets the current position and size of a drawable

```
Status XGetIconName(Display* display, Window w, char** icon_name_return);
```

Gets the name displayed in a window's icon

```
Status XGetIconSizes(Display* display, Window w, XIconSize** size_list_return, int*
count_return);
```

Gets icon sizes from the XA_WM_ICON_SIZE property

```
XImage *XGetImage(Display* display, Drawable d, int x, int y, unsigned int width,
unsigned int height, unsigned long plane_mask, int format);
```

Copies from a drawable into an image

```
XGetInputFocus(Display* display, Window* focus_return, int* revert_to_return);
```

Returns the ID of the window with keyboard focus

```
XGetKeyboardControl(Display* display, XKeyboardState* values_return);
```

Returns a list of keyboard preferences

```
KeySym *XGetKeyboardMapping(Display* display, KeyCode first_keycode, int keycode_count,
int* keysyms_per_keycode_return);
```

Returns the keysyms corresponding to specific keycodes

```
XModifierKeymap *XGetModifierMapping(Display* display);
```

Returns mapping of modifier keys

```
XTimeCoord *XGetMotionEvents(Display* display, Window w, Time start, Time stop, int*
nevents_return);
```

Gets events from the motion history buffer

```
Status XGetNormalHints(Display* display, Window w, XSizeHints* hints_return);
```
Returns size hints for a window's normal state

```
unsigned long XGetPixel(XImage *ximage, int x, int y);
```
Returns the pixel value at a point in an image

```
XGetPointerControl(Display* display, int* accel_numerator_return, int*
accel_denominator_return, int* threshold_return);
```
Returns settings for the mouse pointer

```
int XGetPointerMapping(Display* display, unsigned char* map_return, int nmap);
```
Returns how physical mouse buttons map to logical ones

```
Status XGetRGBColormaps(Display* display, Window w, XStandardColormap** stdcmap_return,
int* count_return, Atom property);
```
Returns an XStandardColormap structure from a property

```
XGetScreenSaver(Display* display, int* timeout_return, int* interval_return, int*
prefer_blanking_return, int* allow_exposures_return);
```
Returns current settings of the screen saver

```
Window XGetSelectionOwner(Display* display, Atom selection);
```
Returns the ID of the window that owns a selection

```
Status XGetSizeHints(Display* display, Window w, XSizeHints* hints_return, Atom
property);
```
Returns an XSizeHints structure from a property

```
Status XGetStandardColormap(Display* display, Window w, XStandardColormap*
colormap_return, Atom property);
```
Returns a standard colormap property

```
XImage *XGetSubImage(Display* display, Drawable d, int x, int y, unsigned int width,
unsigned int height, unsigned long plane_mask, int format, XImage* dest_image, int
dest_x, int dest_y);
```
Copies from a drawable to an image

```
Status XGetTextProperty(Display* display, Window window, XTextProperty* text_prop_return,
Atom property);
```
Retrieves a text property from a window

```
Status XGetTransientForHint(Display* display, Window w, Window* prop_window_return);
```
Gets the XA_WM_TRANSIENT_FOR property of a window

```
XVisualInfo *XGetVisualInfo(Display* display, long vinfo_mask, XVisualInfo*
vinfo_template, int* nitems_return);
```
Finds a matching XVisualInfo structure

```
Status XGetWindowAttributes(Display* display, Window w, XWindowAttributes*
window_attributes_return);
```
Gets a window's attributes

```
int XGetWindowProperty(Display* display, Window w, Atom property, long long_offset, long
long_length, Bool delete, Atom req_type, Atom* actual_type_return, int*
actual_format_return, unsigned long* nitems_return, unsigned long* bytes_after_return,
unsigned char** prop_return);
```
Returns data stored in a property

```
Status XGetWMClientMachine(Display* display, Window w, XTextProperty* text_prop_return);
```
Returns the host machine's name

```
Status XGetWMColormapWindows(Display* display, Window w, Window** windows_return, int*
count_return);
```
Returns a list of windows that need colormaps installed

```
XWMHints *XGetWMHints(Display* display, Window w);
```
Gets an XWMHints structure from a property

```
Status XGetWMIconName(Display* display, Window w, XTextProperty* text_prop_return);
```
Gets a window's XA_WM_ICON_NAME property

```
Status XGetWMName(Display* display, Window w, XTextProperty* text_prop_return);
```
Gets a window's XA_WM_NAME property

```
Status XGetWMNormalHints(Display* display, Window w, XSizeHints* hints_return, long*
supplied_return);
```
Gets a window's XA_WM_NORMAL_HINTS property

```
Status XGetWMProtocols(Display* display, Window w, Atom** protocols_return, int*
count_return);
```
Gets a window's XA_WM_PROTOCOLS property

```
Status XGetWMSizeHints(Display* display, Window w, XSizeHints* hints_return, long*
supplied_return, Atom property);
```
Gets a window's XA_WM_SIZE_HINTS property

```
Status XGetZoomHints(Display* display, Window w, XSizeHints* zhints_return);
```
Returns size hints for a window's zoomed state

```
XGrabButton(Display* display, unsigned int button, unsigned int modifiers, Window
grab_window, Bool owner_events, unsigned int event_mask, int pointer_mode, int
keyboard_mode, Window confine_to, Cursor cursor);
```
Sets up a passive grab on the pointer

```
XGrabKey(Display* display, int keycode, unsigned int modifiers, Window grab_window, Bool
owner_events, int pointer_mode, int keyboard_mode);
```

Sets up a passive grab on a key

```
int XGrabKeyboard(Display* display, Window grab_window, Bool owner_events, int
pointer_mode, int keyboard_mode, Time time);
```

Grabs the keyboard

```
int XGrabPointer(Display* display, Window grab_window, Bool owner_events, unsigned int
event_mask, int pointer_mode, int keyboard_mode, Window confine_to, Cursor cursor, Time
time);
```

Actively grabs the server

```
XGrabServer(Display* display);
```

Forces the X server to act on your program's requests only

```
Status XIconifyWindow(Display* display, Window w, int screen_number);
```

Asks the window manager to iconify a top-level window

```
XIfEvent(Display* display, XEvent* event_return, Bool (*) (Display* display, XEvent*
event, char* arg) predicate, char* arg);
```

Waits until a matching event is received

```
Status XInitThreads();
```

Initializes Xlib support for concurrent threads (a thread is a stream of execution within a process)

```
Status XInitImage(XImage* image)
```

Initializes the internal image manipulation routines of an XImage structure based on the values of other members of the structure

```
long XMaxRequestSize(Display* display)
```

Returns the maximum size (in 4-byte units) of protocol requests that the server can accept

```
XModifierKeymap *XInsertModifiermapEntry(XModifierKeymap* modmap, KeyCode keycode_entry,
int modifier);
```

Adds a new entry to an XModifierKeymap structure

```
XInstallColormap(Display* display, Colormap colormap);
```

Installs a colormap into the hardware

```
Atom XInternAtom(Display* display, const char* atom_name, Bool only_if_exists);
```

Stores a string in the server and returns an Atom

```
Status XInternAtoms(Display* display, char** atom_names, Bool only_if_exists, Atom*
returned_atoms);
```

Stores a number of strings in the server and returns an array of Atoms

```
XIntersectRegion(Region sra, Region srb, Region dr_return);
```
Computes the intersection of two regions

```
KeySym XKeycodeToKeysym(Display* display,#if NeedWidePrototypes unsigned int
keycode,#else KeyCode keycode, int index);
```
Returns the `keysym` corresponding to a keycode

```
KeyCode XKeysymToKeycode(Display* display, KeySym keysym);
```
Returns the keycode corresponding to a `keysym`

```
char *XKeysymToString(KeySym keysym);
```
Returns the string equivalent of a `keysym`

```
XKillClient(Display* display, XID resource);
```
Destroys an X client application

```
int *XListDepths(Display* display, int screen_number, int* count_return);
```
Lists the supported depths (bits-per-pixel)

```
char **XListExtensions(Display* display, int* nextensions_return);
```
Lists the extensions supported by an X server

```
char **XListFonts(Display* display, const char* pattern, int maxnames, int*
actual_count_return);
```
Lists the fonts available in an X server

```
char **XListFontsWithInfo(Display* display, const char* pattern, int maxnames, int*
count_return, XFontStruct** info_return);
```
Returns a list of fonts with detailed information

```
XHostAddress *XListHosts(Display* display, int* nhosts_return, Bool* state_return);
```
Lists hosts with access to a display

```
Colormap *XListInstalledColormaps(Display* display, Window w, int* num_return);
```
Lists installed colormaps for a screen

```
XPixmapFormatValues *XListPixmapFormats(Display* display, int* count_return);
```
Lists pixmap formats supported by a server

```
Atom *XListProperties(Display* display, Window w, int* num_prop_return);
```
Lists all properties on a window

```
Font XLoadFont(Display* display, const char* name);
```
Loads a font, if not already loaded

```
XFontStruct *XLoadQueryFont(Display* display, const char* name);
```
Loads a font and returns information on it

```
char *XLocaleOfFontSet(XFontSet font_set);
```

Returns a null-terminated string containing the name of the locale bound to the specified font set

```
void XLockDisplay(Display* display);
```

Locks out all other threads from using the specified display (a thread is a stream of execution within a process)

```
Status XLookupColor(Display* display, Colormap colormap, const char* color_name, XColor*
exact_def_return, XColor* screen_def_return);
```

Returns the RGB definition of a named color

```
KeySym XLookupKeysym(XKeyEvent* key_event, int index);
```

Returns the keysym corresponding to a keyboard event

```
int XLookupString(XKeyEvent* event_struct, char* buffer_return, int bytes_buffer, KeySym*
keysym_return, XComposeStatus* status_in_out);
```

Translates a keyboard event into a string

```
XLowerWindow(Display* display, Window w);
```

Lowers a window in the stacking order

```
XMapRaised(Display* display, Window w);
```

Maps a window and places it at the top

```
XMapSubwindows(Display* display, Window w);
```

Maps all subwindows of a window

```
XMapWindow(Display* display, Window w);
```

Maps a window

```
XMaskEvent(Display* display, long event_mask, XEvent* event_return);
```

Waits until an event matching a mask arrives

```
Status XMatchVisualInfo(Display* display, int screen, int depth, int class, XVisualInfo*
vinfo_return);
```

Returns information on a visual of given depth and class

```
XMoveResizeWindow(Display* display, Window w, int x, int y, unsigned int width, unsigned
int height);
```

Changes the position and size of a window

```
XMoveWindow(Display* display, Window w, int x, int y);
```

Moves a window

```
XModifierKeymap *XNewModifiermap(int max_keys_per_mod);
```

Returns a new XModifierKeymap structure

```
XNextEvent(Display* display, XEvent* event_return);
```
Waits for the next event from the X server

```
XNoOp(Display* display);
```
Sends a do-nothing request to the server

```
XOffsetRegion(Region r, int dx, int dy);
```
Moves a region by a specified amount

```
Display *XOpenDisplay(const char* display_name);
```
Opens a connection to an X server

```
Status XParseColor(Display* display, Colormap colormap, const char* spec, XColor*
exact_def_return);
```
Gets the RGB values corresponding to a named color

```
int XParseGeometry(const char* parsestring, int* x_return, int* y_return, unsigned int*
width_return, unsigned int* height_return);
```
Extracts the position and size from a geometry specification

```
XPeekEvent(Display* display, XEvent* event_return);
```
Gets an event but does not remove it from the queue (blocking)

```
XPeekIfEvent(Display* display, XEvent* event_return, Bool (*) (Display* display, XEvent*
event, char* arg) predicate, char* arg);
```
Checks the event queue for a matching event without removing it

```
int XPending(Display* display);
```
Returns the number of waiting events

```
char *Xpermalloc(unsigned int size);
```
Allocates permanent memory (not freed until program exits)

```
Bool XPointInRegion(Region r, int x, int y);
```
Determines whether a point is inside a region

```
Region XPolygonRegion(XPoint* points, int n, int fill_rule);
```
Creates a region from a polygon

```
XPutBackEvent(Display* display, XEvent* event);
```
Puts an event back in the event queue

```
XPutImage(Display* display, Drawable d, GC gc, XImage* image, int src_x, int src_y, int
dest_x, int dest_y, unsigned int width, unsigned int height);
```
Copies from an image to a drawable

```
XPutPixel(XImage *ximage, int x, int y, unsigned long pixel);
```
Sets the pixel value at a specified point in an image

```
Status XQueryBestCursor(Display* display, Drawable d, unsigned int width, unsigned int
height, unsigned int* width_return, unsigned int* height_return);
```
Returns the dimensions of the hardware-supported cursor

```
Status XQueryBestSize(Display* display, int class, Drawable which_screen, unsigned int
width, unsigned int height, unsigned int* width_return, unsigned int* height_return);
```
Returns the best dimensions of a cursor, tile, or stipple

```
Status XQueryBestStipple(Display* display, Drawable which_screen, unsigned int width,
unsigned int height, unsigned int* width_return, unsigned int* height_return);
```
Returns the stipple size that is fastest for the hardware

```
Status XQueryBestTile(Display* display, Drawable which_screen, unsigned int width,
unsigned int height, unsigned int* width_return, unsigned int* height_return);
```
Returns the tile size that is fastest for the hardware

```
XQueryColor(Display* display, Colormap colormap, XColor* def_in_out);
```
Returns RGB values for a specific colormap cell

```
XQueryColors(Display* display, Colormap colormap, XColor* defs_in_out, int ncolors);
```
Returns RGB values for an array of colormap cells

```
Bool XQueryExtension(Display* display, const char* name, int* major_opcode_return, int*
first_event_return, int* first_error_return);
```
Gets information about a specific extension

```
XFontStruct *XQueryFont(Display* display, XID font_ID);
```
Returns information about a loaded font

```
XQueryKeymap(Display* display, char [32] keys_return);
```
Returns a bit vector describing status of keys

```
Bool XQueryPointer(Display* display, Window w, Window* root_return, Window* child_return,
int* root_x_return, int* root_y_return, int* win_x_return, int* win_y_return, unsigned
int* mask_return);
```
Returns the current position of the pointer

```
XQueryTextExtents(Display* display, XID font_ID, const char* string, int nchars, int*
direction_return, int* font_ascent_return, int* font_descent_return, XCharStruct*
overall_return);
```
Determines the bounding rectangle for a text string

```
XQueryTextExtents16(Display* display, XID font_ID, const XChar2b* string, int nchars,
int* direction_return, int* font_ascent_return, int* font_descent_return, XCharStruct*
overall_return);
```
Determines the bounding rectangle for a 16-bit string

```
Status XQueryTree(Display* display, Window w, Window* root_return, Window* parent_return,
Window** children_return, unsigned int* nchildren_return);
```
Gets the parent, root, and a list of children of a window

```
XRaiseWindow(Display* display, Window w);
```
Raises a window to the top

```
int XReadBitmapFile(Display* display, Drawable d, const char* filename, unsigned int*
width_return, unsigned int* height_return, Pixmap* bitmap_return, int* x_hot_return, int*
y_hot_return);
```
Reads the bitmap from a file and creates a pixmap

```
int XReadBitmapFileData(const char* filename, unsigned int* width_return, unsigned int*
height_return, unsigned char** data, int* x_hot_return, int* y_hot_return);
```
Reads bitmap data from a file and returns the data

```
XRebindKeysym(Display* display, KeySym keysym, KeySym* list, int mod_count, const
unsigned char* string, int bytes_string);
```
Binds a string to a keysym

```
XRecolorCursor(Display* display, Cursor cursor, XColor* foreground_color, XColor*
background_color);
```
Changes the color of a cursor

```
Status XReconfigureWMWindow(Display* display, Window w, int screen_number, unsigned int
mask, XWindowChanges* changes);
```
Changes the size and stacking order of a top-level window

```
int XRectInRegion(Region r, int x, int y, unsigned int width, unsigned int height);
```
Determines whether a rectangle is inside a region

```
XRefreshKeyboardMapping(XMappingEvent* event_map);
```
Updates Xlib's internal keycode-to-keysym mapping tables

```
XRemoveFromSaveSet(Display* display, Window w);
```
Removes a window from the save-set

```
XRemoveHost(Display* display, XHostAddress* host);
```
Removes a host from the server's access-control list

```
XRemoveHosts(Display* display, XHostAddress* hosts, int num_hosts);
```
Removes several hosts from the server's access-control list

```
XReparentWindow(Display* display, Window w, Window parent, int x, int y);
```
Changes the parent of a window

```
XResetScreenSaver(Display* display);
```
Redisplays the screen if it was blanked

```
XResizeWindow(Display* display, Window w, unsigned int width, unsigned int height);
```
Changes a window's size

```
XRestackWindows(Display* display, Window* windows, int nwindows);
```
Alters the stacking order in a specified manner

```
void XrmDestroyDatabase(XrmDatabase database);
```
Destroys a resource database

```
XrmDatabase XrmGetFileDatabase(const char* filename);
```
Creates a new resource database from a file

```
Bool XrmGetResource(XrmDatabase database, const char* str_name, const char* str_class,
char** str_type_return, XrmValue* value_return);
```
Gets a resource value

```
XrmDatabase XrmGetStringDatabase(const char* data null terminated string);
```
Creates a resource database from a string

```
void XrmInitialize(void);
```
Initializes the X resource manager

```
void XrmMergeDatabases(XrmDatabase source_db, XrmDatabase* target_db);
```
Merges the contents of two resource databases

```
void XrmParseCommand(XrmDatabase* database, XrmOptionDescList table, int table_count,
const char* name, int* argc_in_out, char** argv_in_out);
```
Loads a resource database from command-line options

```
void XrmPutFileDatabase(XrmDatabase database, const char* filename);
```
Saves a resource database to a file

```
void XrmPutLineResource(XrmDatabase* database, const char* line);
```
Adds a single line of resource

```
void XrmPutResource(XrmDatabase* database, const char* specifier, const char* type,
XrmValue* value);
```
Stores a new value in a resource database

```
void XrmPutStringResource(XrmDatabase* database, const char* specifier, const char*
value);
```
Adds to the database a resource specified by name and value

```
XrmQGetResource(XrmDatabase database, XrmNameList quark_name, XrmClassList quark_class,
XrmRepresentation* quark_type_return, XrmValue* value_return);
```

Gets the value of a resource identified by name and class quark

```
Bool XrmQGetSearchList(XrmDatabase database, XrmNameList names, XrmClassList classes,
XrmSearchList list_return, int list_length);
```

Prepares the search list used by `XrmQGetSearchResource`

```
Bool XrmQGetSearchResource(XrmSearchList list, XrmName name, XrmClass class,
XrmRepresentation* type_return, XrmValue* value_return);
```

Searches for a resource using a search list

```
void XrmQPutResource(XrmDatabase* database, XrmBindingList bindings, XrmQuarkList quarks,
XrmRepresentation type, XrmValue* value);
```

Stores the value of a resource identified by name and class quark

```
void XrmQPutStringResource(XrmDatabase* database, XrmBindingList bindings, XrmQuarkList
quarks, const char* value);
```

Adds to a database a resource specified by a quark

```
XrmString XrmQuarkToString(XrmQuark quark);
```

Converts a quark to a string

```
void XrmStringToBindingQuarkList(const char* string, XrmBindingList bindings_return,
XrmQuarkList quarks_return);
```

Converts a resource specification into names and bindings

```
XrmQuark XrmStringToQuark(const char* string); find quark for string, create new quark if
none already exists
```

Converts a string to a quark, an integer identifier

```
void XrmStringToQuarkList(const char* string, XrmQuarkList quarks_return);
```

Converts a resource name string to quarks

```
XrmQuark XrmUniqueQuark(void);
```

Creates a new quark

```
XRotateBuffers(Display* display, int rotate);
```

Rotates the contents of the cut buffers

```
XRotateWindowProperties(Display* display, Window w, Atom* properties, int num_prop, int
npositions);
```

Rotates the contents of an array of properties on a window

```
int XSaveContext(Display* display, XID resource_id, XContext context, const char* data);
```

Saves data using a context

```
XSelectInput(Display* display, Window w, long event_mask);
```
Selects types of events to be reported for a window

```
Status XSendEvent(Display* display, Window w, Bool propagate, long event_mask, XEvent*
event_send);
```
Sends an event to a window

```
XSetAccessControl(Display* display, int mode);
```
Enables or disables access control

```
int (*XSetAfterFunction(Display* display, int (*) (Display* display) procedure))();
```
Sets a function to be called after every protocol request

```
XSetArcMode(Display* display, GC gc, int arc_mode);
```
Sets the arc-drawing mode in a GC

```
XSetBackground(Display* display, GC gc, unsigned long background);
```
Sets the background pixel value in a GC

```
XSetClassHint(Display* display, Window w, XClassHint* class_hints);
```
Sets the XA_WM_CLASS property of a window

```
XSetClipMask(Display* display, GC gc, Pixmap pixmap);
```
Sets the clip mask in a GC

```
XSetClipOrigin(Display* display, GC gc, int clip_x_origin, int clip_y_origin);
```
Sets the origin of the clip mask in a GC

```
XSetClipRectangles(Display* display, GC gc, int clip_x_origin, int clip_y_origin,
XRectangle* rectangles, int n, int ordering);
```
Sets the clip mask in a GC to a list of rectangles

```
XSetCloseDownMode(Display* display, int close_mode);
```
Defines what happens to a client's resources after it exits

```
XSetCommand(Display* display, Window w, char** argv, int argc);
```
Stores the command-line arguments in the XA_WM_COMMAND property

```
XSetDashes(Display* display, GC gc, int dash_offset, const char* dash_list, int n);
```
Sets the style of dashes (for dashed lines) in a GC

```
XErrorHandler XSetErrorHandler(XErrorHandlerhandler);
typedef int (*XErrorHandler) (Display* display, XErrorEvent* error_event);
```
Specifies a function called when nonfatal errors occur

```
XSetFillRule(Display* display, GC gc, int fill_rule);
```
Sets the fill rule in a GC

```
XSetFillStyle(Display* display, GC gc, int fill_style);
```
Sets the fill style in a GC

```
XSetFont(Display* display, GC gc, Font font);
```
Sets the font in a GC

```
XSetFontPath(Display* display, char** directories, int ndirs);
```
Sets the list of directories to search for a font

```
XSetForeground(Display* display, GC gc, unsigned long foreground);
```
Sets the foreground pixel value in a GC

```
XSetFunction(Display* display, GC gc, int function);
```
Specifies in a GC how pixel values are combined

```
XSetGraphicsExposures(Display* display, GC gc, Bool graphics_exposures);
```
Enables or disables the generation of GraphicsExpose events

```
XIOErrorHandler XSetIOErrorHandler (XIOErrorHandler handler);
typedef int (*XIOErrorHandler)(Display*display);
```
Specifies a function to be called when a fatal I/O error occurs

```
XSetIconName(Display* display, Window w, const char* icon_name);
```
Sets the name to be displayed in a window's icon

```
XSetIconSizes(Display* display, Window w, XIconSize* size_list, int count);
```
Sets the XA_WM_ICON_SIZE property

```
XSetInputFocus(Display* display, Window focus, int revert_to, Time time);
```
Sets the keyboard focus to a window

```
XSetLineAttributes(Display* display, GC gc, unsigned int line_width, int line_style, int
cap_style, int join_style);
```
Sets the line-drawing attributes in a GC

```
int XSetModifierMapping(Display* display, XModifierKeymap* modmap);
```
Sets the keycodes used for the modifier keys

```
XSetNormalHints(Display* display, Window w, XSizeHints* hints);
```
Sets the XA_WM_NORMAL_HINTS property

```
XSetPlaneMask(Display* display, GC gc, unsigned long plane_mask);
```
Sets the plane_mask field of a GC

```
int XSetPointerMapping(Display* display, const unsigned char* map, int nmap);
```
Defines mapping from physical mouse buttons to logical ones

```
void XSetRGBColormaps(Display* display, Window w, XStandardColormap* stdcmaps, int count,
Atom property);
```
Stores colormaps in a property of type RGB_COLOR_MAP

```
XSetRegion(Display* display, GC gc, Region r);
```
Sets the clip_mask in a GC to a region

```
XSetScreenSaver(Display* display, int timeout, int interval, int prefer_blanking, int
allow_exposures);
```
Sets parameters of the screen-saver

```
XSetSelectionOwner(Display* display, Atom selection, Window owner, Time time);
```
Sets the owner of a selection

```
XSetSizeHints(Display* display, Window w, XSizeHints* hints, Atom property);
```
Sets the value of a property of type XA_SIZE_HINTS

```
void XSetStandardColormap(Display* display, Window w, XStandardColormap* colormap, Atom
property);
```
Sets the value of a standard colormap property

```
XSetStandardProperties(Display* display, Window w, const char* window_name, const char*
icon_name, Pixmap icon_pixmap, char** argv, int argc, XSizeHints* hints);
```
Sets a set of properties for the window manager

```
XSetState(Display* display, GC gc, unsigned long foreground, unsigned long background,
int function, unsigned long plane_mask);
```
Sets the several drawing attributes in a GC

```
XSetStipple(Display* display, GC gc, Pixmap stipple);
```
Specifies a bitmap to be used as a stipple pattern

```
XSetSubwindowMode(Display* display, GC gc, int subwindow_mode);
```
Indicates how graphics output affects subwindows

```
void XSetTextProperty(Display* display, Window w, XTextProperty* text_prop, Atom
property);
```
Sets a window's text property

```
XSetTile(Display* display, GC gc, Pixmap tile);
```
Sets the tile (a pixmap) in a GC

```
XSetTransientForHint(Display* display, Window w, Window prop_window); The following are
given in alphabetical order
```
Sets the XA_WM_TRANSIENT_FOR property

```
XSetTSOrigin(Display* display, GC gc, int ts_x_origin, int ts_y_origin);
```
Sets the origin of tiles and stipples

```
void XSetWMClientMachine(Display* display, Window w, XTextProperty* text_prop);
```
Sets the XA_WM_CLIENT_MACHINE property

```
Status XSetWMColormapWindows(Display* display, Window w, Window* colormap_windows, int
count);
```
Sets a window's XA_WM_COLORMAP_WINDOWS property

```
XSetWMHints(Display* display, Window w, XWMHints* wm_hints);
```
Sets a window's XA_WM_HINTS property

```
void XSetWMIconName(Display* display, Window w, XTextProperty* text_prop);
```
Sets the name to be displayed in a window's icon

```
void XSetWMName(Display* display, Window w, XTextProperty* text_prop);
```
Sets a window's XA_WM_NAME property

```
void XSetWMNormalHints(Display* display, Window w, XSizeHints* hints);
```
Provides hints to the window manager for a window

```
void XSetWMProperties(Display* display, Window w, XTextProperty* window_name,
XTextProperty* icon_name, char** argv, int argc, XSizeHints* normal_hints, XWMHints*
wm_hints, XClassHint* class_hints);
```
Sets a number of standard properties for the window manager

```
Status XSetWMProtocols(Display* display, Window w, Atom* protocols, int count);
```
Sets the XA_WM_PROTOCOLS property

```
void XSetWMSizeHints(Display* display, Window w, XSizeHints* hints, Atom property);
```
Sets a property of type XA_WM_SIZE_HINTS on a window

```
XSetWindowBackground(Display* display, Window w, unsigned long background_pixel);
```
Sets the background pixel value of a window

```
XSetWindowBackgroundPixmap(Display* display, Window w, Pixmap background_pixmap);
```
Specifies a pixmap for tiling a window's background

```
XSetWindowBorder(Display* display, Window w, unsigned long border_pixel);
```
Changes the color of a window's border

```
XSetWindowBorderPixmap(Display* display, Window w, Pixmap border_pixmap);
```
Specifies a pixmap used for tiling a window's border

```
XSetWindowBorderWidth(Display* display, Window w, unsigned int width);
```
Sets a window's border width

```
XSetWindowColormap(Display* display, Window w, Colormap colormap);
```
Sets the colormap attribute of a window

```
XSetZoomHints(Display* display, Window w, XSizeHints* zhints);
```
Sets a window's **XA_WM_ZOOM_HINTS** property

```
XShrinkRegion(Region r, int dx, int dy);
```
Expands or shrinks a region

```
XStoreBuffer(Display* display, const char* bytes, int nbytes, int buffer);
```
Stores text in a cut buffer

```
XStoreBytes(Display* display, const char* bytes, int nbytes);
```
Stores text in cut buffer 0

```
XStoreColor(Display* display, Colormap colormap, XColor* color);
```
Sets the RGB value of a read-write colormap cell

```
XStoreColors(Display* display, Colormap colormap, XColor* color, int ncolors);
```
Sets the RGB values of several read-write colormap cells

```
XStoreName(Display* display, Window w, const char* window_name);
```
Sets the name of a window

```
XStoreNamedColor(Display* display, Colormap colormap, const char* color, unsigned long
pixel, int flags);
```
Sets the RGB values of a read-write colormap cell for a named color

```
Status XStringListToTextProperty(char** list, int count, XTextProperty*
text_prop_return);
```
Sets up an **XTextProperty** structure from strings

```
KeySym XStringToKeysym(const char* string);
```
Converts a keysym name to a **KeySym**

```
XImage *XSubImage(XImage *ximage, int x, int y, unsigned int width, unsigned int height);
```
Creates a new image from a part of another

```
XSubtractRegion(Region sra, Region srb, Region dr_return);
```
Subtracts one region from another

```
XSync(Display* display, Bool discard);
```
Waits until all requests are processed by the server

```
int (*XSynchronize(Display* display, Bool onoff))();
```
Enables or disables synchronized operation

```
XTextExtents(XFontStruct* font_struct, const char* string, int nchars, int*
direction_return, int* font_ascent_return, int* font_descent_return, XCharStruct*
overall_return);
```

Gets the displayed dimensions of a text string

```
XTextExtents16(XFontStruct* font_struct, const XChar2b* string, int nchars, int*
direction_return, int* font_ascent_return, int* font_descent_return, XCharStruct*
overall_return);
```

Gets the displayed dimensions of a 16-bit text string

```
Status XTextPropertyToStringList(XTextProperty* text_prop, char*** list_return, int*
count_return);
```

Gets a list of strings from an XTextProperty

```
int XTextWidth(XFontStruct* font_struct, const char* string, int count);
```

Gets the width (in pixels) of a text string

```
int XTextWidth16(XFontStruct* font_struct, const XChar2b* string, int count);
```

Gets the width (in pixels) of a 16-bit text string

```
Bool XTranslateCoordinates(Display* display, Window src_w, Window dest_w, int src_x, int
src_y, int* dest_x_return, int* dest_y_return, Window* child_return);
```

Converts coordinates from one window to another

```
XUndefineCursor(Display* display, Window w);
```

Dissociates a cursor from a window

```
XUngrabButton(Display* display, unsigned int button, unsigned int modifiers, Window
grab_window);
```

Cancels a passive grab of a button

```
XUngrabKey(Display* display, int keycode, unsigned int modifiers, Window grab_window);
```

Releases a key from a passive grab

```
XUngrabKeyboard(Display* display, Time time);
```

Releases the keyboard from an active grab

```
XUngrabPointer(Display* display, Time time);
```

Releases the pointer from an active grab

```
XUngrabServer(Display* display);
```

Ends a server grab

```
XUninstallColormap(Display* display, Colormap colormap);
```

Reverses the effects of an XInstallColormap call

```
XUnionRectWithRegion(XRectangle* rectangle, Region src_region, Region
dest_region_return);
```
Adds a rectangle to a region

```
XUnionRegion(Region sra, Region srb, Region dr_return);
```
Computes the union of two regions

```
XUniqueContext() ((XContext) XrmUniqueQuark())
```
Creates a unique context ID

```
XUnloadFont(Display* display, Font font);
```
Requests the server to unload a font

```
void XUnlockDisplay(Display* display);
```
Enables other threads to use the specified display again (a thread is a stream of execution within a process)

```
XUnmapSubwindows(Display* display, Window w);
```
Unmaps all subwindows of a window

```
XUnmapWindow(Display* display, Window w);
```
Unmaps a window

```
int XVendorRelease(Display* display);
```
Returns the vendor's release number for the X Window System

```
VisualID XVisualIDFromVisual(Visual* visual); routines for dealing with extensions
```
Returns a visual ID from the pointer to a `Visual` structure

```
XWarpPointer(Display* display, Window src_w, Window dest_w, int src_x, int src_y,
unsigned int src_width, unsigned int src_height, int dest_x, int dest_y);
```
Forcibly moves the mouse pointer to a new location

```
XWindowEvent(Display* display, Window w, long event_mask, XEvent* event_return);
```
Retrieves the next event matching an event mask and a window

```
Status XWithdrawWindow(Display* display, Window w, int screen_number);
```
Requests the window manager to unmap a top-level window and its icon

```
int XWMGeometry(Display* display, int screen_number, const char* user_geometry, const
char* default_geometry, unsigned int border_width, XSizeHints* hints, int* x_return, int*
y_return, int* width_return, int* height_return, int* gravity_return);
```
Gets a window's geometry from a geometry specification

```
int XWriteBitmapFile(Display* display, const char* filename, Pixmap bitmap, unsigned int
width, unsigned int height, int x_hot, int y_hot);
```
Writes a bitmap to a file using the X11 bitmap file format

```
XXorRegion(Region sra, Region srb, Region dr_return);
```
Computes the exclusive-OR of two regions

Xlib Macros (X11R6)

Legend: (dpy)=*Display* * argument
            (scr)=Integer denoting screen number
            (s) = *Screen* *

```
AllPlanes
```
Constant identifying all planes

```
BitmapBitOrder(dpy)
```
`LSBFirst` or `MSBFirst`

```
BitmapPad(dpy)
```
Bitmap padding

```
BitmapUnit(dpy)
```
Size of bitmap unit

```
BlackPixel(dpy, scr)
```
Black pixel value

```
BlackPixelOfScreen(s)
```
Black pixel value for a screen

```
CellsOfScreen(s)
```
Number of cells in default colormap

```
ConnectionNumber(dpy)
```
Connection number for the display

```
DefaultColormap(dpy, scr)
```
Default colormap's ID

```
DefaultColormapOfScreen(s)
```
Default colormap for a specific screen

```
DefaultDepth(dpy, scr)
```
Depth of a screen

```
DefaultDepthOfScreen(s)
```
Depth of a screen (`Screen *`)

```
DefaultGC(dpy, scr)
```
Default `GC`

`DefaultGCOfScreen(s)`

Default GC of a specific screen

`DefaultRootWindow(dpy)`

Root window's ID

`DefaultScreen(dpy)`

Default screen's number

`DefaultScreenOfDisplay(dpy)`

Screen * for default screen

`DefaultVisual(dpy, scr)`

Pointer to default Visual structure

`DefaultVisualOfScreen(s)`

Pointer to default visual

`DisplayCells(dpy, scr)`

Number of colormap entries in default colormap

`DisplayHeight(dpy, scr)`

Display height in pixels

`DisplayHeightMM(dpy, scr)`

Display height in millimeters

`DisplayOfScreen(s)`

Display pointer from a Screen *

`DisplayPlanes(dpy, scr)`

Depth of root window

`DisplayString(dpy)`

String passed to XOpenDisplay

`DisplayWidth(dpy, scr)`

Display width in pixels

`DisplayWidthMM(dpy, scr)`

Display width in millimeters

`DoesBackingStore(s)`

Whether screen supports backing store (WhenMapped, NotUseful, or Always)

`DoesSaveUnders(s)`

Whether screen supports "save under" (True or False returned)

`EventMaskOfScreen(`*s*`)`

Event mask of root window of screen

`HeightMMOfScreen(`*s*`)`

Height of screen in millimeters

`HeightOfScreen(`*s*`)`

Height of screen in pixels

`ImageByteOrder(`*dpy*`)`

Byte order for images (`LSBFirst` or `MSBFirst`)

`IsCursorKey(`keysym`)`

`True` if it's a cursor key

`IsFunctionKey(`*keysym*`)`

`True` if it's a function key

`IsKeypadKey(`*keysym*`)`

`True` if it's a keypad key

`IsMiscFunctionKey(`*keysym*`)`

`True` if it's a miscellaneous function key

`IsModifierKey(`*keysym*`)`

`True` if it's a modifier key

`IsPFKey(`*keysym*`)`

`True` if it's a programmable function (PF) key

`LastKnownRequestProcessed(`*dpy*`)`

Serial number of last request processed by the server

`MaxCmapsOfScreen(`s`)`

Maximum number of installed colormaps supported by screen

`MinCmapsOfScreen(`s`)`

Minimum number of installed colormaps supported by screen

`NextRequest(`*dpy*`)`

Serial number to be used for next protocol request

`PlanesOfScreen(`s`)`

Depth of the root window of screen

`ProtocolRevision(`*dpy*`)`

Minor revision number of X protocol

`ProtocolVersion(`*dpy*`)`

Major version number of X protocol (11 for X11)

`QLength(`*dpy*`)`

Length of event queue for a display

`RootWindow(`*dpy, scr*`)`

Root window ID

`RootWindowOfScreen(`*s*`)`

Root window for a specified `Screen`

`ScreenCount(`*dpy*`)`

Number of screens in a display

`ScreenOfDisplay(`*dpy, scr*`)`

Returns pointer to `Screen` structure

`ServerVendor(`*dpy*`)`

Returns null-terminated string identifying vendor (for example, `X Consortium`)

`VendorRelease(`*dpy*`)`

Integer representing vendor's release number of X (`6000` for X11R6 from the X Consortium)

`WhitePixel(`*dpy, scr*`)`

White pixel value for a screen

`WhitePixelOfScreen(`*s*`)`

White pixel value for a screen

`WidthMMOfScreen(`*s*`)`

Width of a screen in millimeters

`WidthOfScreen(`*s*`)`

Width of a screen in pixels

`XAllocID(`*dpy*`)`

Returns a new resource ID

`XResourceManagerString(`*dpy*`)`

Returns a pointer to the resource database string stored in the `XA_RESOURCE_MANAGER` property

`XrmClassToString(`*class*`)`

Maps to `XrmQuarkToString(`*class*`)`

`XrmNameToString(`*name*`)`

Maps to `XrmQuarkToString(`*name*`)`

XrmRepresentationToString(*type*)

Maps to XrmQuarkToString(*type*)

XrmStringsEqual(*a1*, *a2*)

Defined as (strcmp(*a1*, *a2*) == 0)

XrmStringToClass(*class*)

Defined as XrmStringToQuark(*class*)

XrmStringToClassList(*str*,*class*)

Calls XrmStringToQuarkList(*str*, *class*)

XrmStringToName(*string*)

Calls XrmStringToQuark(*string*)

XrmStringToNameList(*str*, *name*)

Calls XrmStringToQuarkList(*str*, *name*)

XrmStringToRepresentation(*string*)

Maps to XrmStringToQuark(*string*)

XStringToContext(*string*)

Returns a context for a string

X Event Reference

Summary of X Events

X provides for a large number of events to handle everything from mouse and keyboard to messages from other X clients (see Table J.1). The types of events, shown in the first column of Table J.1, are defined in the include file <X11/X.h>. You do not have to include this file explicitly; toolkit header files already include it.

The X server never sends unsolicited events to an application. Table J.1 shows 33 events, but X applications are not required to process all of them, incurring the overhead of unnecessary event handling code. Xlib-based applications usually call the function XSelectInput to indicate the events that it wants to receive. (In Motif programs, you use XtAddEventHandler to specify a function to be called in response to an event.) This approach of selective reporting of events is good for the server because it relieves the server from keeping track of all events for all clients.

One exception to the rule of selective reporting: the MappingNotify event, generated when the meanings of keys are changed, is automatically sent to all X clients.

The 33 X events shown in Table J.1 can be broadly grouped into seven categories:

> *Mouse events.* The server generates these events when the user presses a mouse button or moves the mouse. X applications trying to provide a point-and-click graphical interface usually accept and handle these events.

Keyboard events. These events are generated when the user presses or releases any key on the keyboard. They are delivered to an application only if a window owned by the application has the input focus. Usually, the window manager decides how the focus is transferred from one window to another. There are two common models: clicking on a window to type in it (used by the Macintosh and Microsoft Windows), and giving the focus to the window containing the mouse pointer. In Motif, the `keyboardFocusPolicy` resource of the Motif window manager determines how the focus is determined.

Expose events. Of all X events, the `Expose` event is the most crucial—applications draw in their windows in response to this event. Almost all X applications request and process this event. The `GraphicsExpose` and `NoExpose` events have to do with copying from one part of a window or a pixmap to another. They enable applications to handle the case where the source of the copy operation is obscured by another window and the contents of the obscured area are unavailable for copying.

Colormap notification events. The server generates the `ColorMapNotify` event when an application changes the colormap associated with a window or installs a new colormap.

Interclient communication events. These events send information from one X application to another. The concepts of property and selection are used for this purpose.

Window state notification events. The server generates these events when a window is moved or resized, or its place in the stacking order is altered. These events are useful for keeping track of changes in the layout of windows on the screen. Typically, window managers use these events for this purpose. Your application can use them too, if you want to alter the size and position of the subwindows when the user resizes the topmost window.

Window structure control events. These events are almost exclusively used by window managers to intercept an application's attempt to change the layout of its windows. For example, by monitoring the `MapRequest` event, the window manager can tell when an application maps its top window. When this happens, the window manager can add its own frame to the window and place it at an appropriate location on the screen.

Table J.1. X Events

Event Type	When Generated
Mouse Events	
ButtonPress	Mouse button is pressed with pointer in the window
ButtonRelease	Mouse button is released with pointer in the window
EnterNotify	Mouse pointer enters the window
LeaveNotify	Mouse pointer leaves the window
MotionNotify	Mouse is moved
Keyboard Events	
FocusIn	Window receives input focus (all subsequent keyboard events come to window)
FocusOut	Window loses input focus

Event Type	When Generated
Keyboard Events	
KeyMapNotify	Used after `EnterNotify` or `FocusIn` event occurs (to inform application of the state of the keys after these events)
KeyPress	Key pressed (when window has focus)
KeyRelease	Key released (when window has focus)
MappingNotify	Keyboard reconfigured (the mapping of a key to a string is changed)
Expose Events	
Expose	Previously obscured window or part of window becomes visible
GraphicsExpose	During graphics copy operations, parts of source image are obscured (copied image not complete)
NoExpose	Graphics copy successfully completed
Colormap Notification Event	
ColorMapNotify	Window's colormap changed
Interclient Communication Events	
ClientMessage	Another client sends message using `XSendEvent` function
PropertyNotify	Property associated with window changed
SelectionClear	Window loses ownership of selection
SelectionNotify	Selection successfully converted
SelectionRequest	Selection needs conversion
Window State Notification Events	
CirculateNotify	Window raised or lowered in stacking order
ConfigureNotify	Window moved or resized, or its position in stacking order has changed
CreateNotify	Window created
DestroyNotify	Window destroyed
GravityNotify	Window moved because its parent's size changed
MapNotify	Window mapped
ReparentNotify	Window's parent changed
UnmapNotify	Window unmapped
VisibilityNotify	Window's visibility changed (became visible or invisible)

continues

Table J.1. continued

Event Type	When Generated
Window Structure Control Events	
CirculateRequest	Request received to raise or lower window in stacking order (used by window managers)
ConfigureRequest	Request received to move, resize, or restack window (used by window managers)
MapRequest	Window about to be mapped (used by window managers)
ResizeRequest	Request received to resize window (used by window managers)

Event Masks

Table J.2 shows the event masks for selecting specific X events. If you program with the Motif toolkit, you have to use the event mask when registering an event handler by calling XtAddEventHandler. (See Chapter 13, "X Toolkits," for a description of this function.)

Table J.2. Event Masks Corresponding to X Events

Event Type	Name of Event Mask in X.h
ButtonPress	ButtonPressMask
ButtonRelease	ButtonReleaseMask
CirculateNotify	StructureNotifyMask, SubstructureNotifyMask
CirculateRequest	SubstructureRedirectMask
ClientMessage*	—
ColormapNotify	ColormapChangeMask
ConfigureNotify	StructureNotifyMask, SubstructureNotifyMask
ConfigureRequest	SubstructureRedirectMask
CreateNotify	SubstructureNotifyMask
DestroyNotify	StructureNotifyMask, SubstructureNotifyMask
EnterNotify	EnterWindowMask
Expose	ExposureMask
FocusIn	FocusChangeMask
FocusOut	FocusChangeMask
GraphicsExpose	ExposureMask
GravityNotify	StructureNotifyMask, SubstructureNotifyMask

Event Type	*Name of Event Mask in X.h*
KeyMapNotify	KeymapStateMask
KeyPress	KeyPressMask
KeyRelease	KeyReleaseMask
LeaveNotify	LeaveWindowMask
MapNotify	StructureNotifyMask, SubstructureNotifyMask
MappingNotify*	—
MapRequest	SubstructureRedirectMask
MotionNotify	ButtonMotionMask, Button1MotionMask,
	Button2MotionMask, Button3MotionMask,
	Button4MotionMask, Button5MotionMask,
	PointerMotionMask, PointerMotionHintMask
NoExpose	ExposureMask
PropertyNotify	PropertyChangeMask
ReparentNotify	StructureNotifyMask, SubstructureNotifyMask
ResizeRequest	ResizeRedirectMask
SelectionClear*	—
SelectionNotify*	—
SelectionRequest*	—
UnmapNotify	StructureNotifyMask, SubstructureNotifyMask
VisibilityNotify	VisibilityChangeMask

*No event mask is available to control selection of this event.

The *XEvent* Union

When an event is reported by the X server, the program must be able to find out the type of the event and, depending on the type, other relevant information describing the event. For example, if the event reports a mouse buttonpress, you may want to know which button and the location of the mouse pointer at the time of the buttonpress. Because of the diversity of events in X, the information necessary to describe one class of events (for example, mouse events) differs significantly from that needed by another (for example, keyboard events). Thus, many different data structures are used to describe the events. Because a common format is needed to report all events, a C union of these data structures is used to hold the information. The header file <X11/Xlib.h> defines this union named XEvent:

```
typedef union _XEvent
{
    int                     type;   /* Event's type comes first */
    XAnyEvent               xany;
    XKeyEvent               xkey;
    XButtonEvent            xbutton;
    XMotionEvent            xmotion;
    XCrossingEvent          xcrossing;
    XFocusChangeEvent       xfocus;
    XExposeEvent            xexpose;
    XGraphicsExposeEvent    xgraphicsexpose;
    XNoExposeEvent          xnoexpose;
    XVisibilityEvent        xvisibility;
    XCreateWindowEvent      xcreatewindow;
    XDestroyWindowEvent     xdestroywindow;
    XUnmapEvent             xunmap;
    XMapEvent               xmap;
    XMapRequestEvent        xmaprequest;
    XReparentEvent          xreparent;
    XConfigureEvent         xconfigure;
    XGravityEvent           xgravity;
    XResizeRequestEvent     xresizerequest;
    XConfigureRequestEvent  xconfigurerequest;
    XCirculateEvent         xcirculate;
    XCirculateRequestEvent  xcirculaterequest;
    XPropertyEvent          xproperty;
    XSelectionClearEvent    xselectionclear;
    XSelectionRequestEvent  xselectionrequest;
    XSelectionEvent         xselection;
    XColormapEvent          xcolormap;
    XClientMessageEvent     xclient;
    XMappingEvent           xmapping;
    XErrorEvent             xerror;
    XKeymapEvent            xkeymap;
    long                    pad[24];
} XEvent;
```

As you can see, the data type XEvent is defined as the union of a large number of different data structures. You will encounter the structures for the common events later in this chapter.

The *XAnyEvent* Structure

The simplest event data structure is XAnyEvent, which is defined as follows:

```
typedef struct
{
    int            type;       /* The event type                */
    unsigned long  serial;     /* Number of last processed event */
    Bool           send_event; /* True = event is from SendEvent */
    Display        *display;   /* Identifies the reporting server*/
    Window         window;     /* Window requesting this event   */
} XAnyEvent;
```

The fields appearing in the XAnyEvent structure are the first five entries in every event's data structure. The type field tells you the kind of event being reported. The X server keeps track of the sequence of protocol requests it has processed so far and reports the sequence number of the last processed request in the serial field.

The next field, send_event, describes how the event originated. In X, you can send a simulated event to a window. For example, even when there is no keypress, you can prepare an event structure for a keypress event and send it to a window using the XSendEvent function. The server indicates such events by setting the send_event flag in the event structure to True. If the event was generated by the server, send_event is 0 (False).

The display field identifies the server from which the event arrived. The next field is the window that requested this type of event. The window hierarchy determines which window receives an event.

ButtonPress and *ButtonRelease* Events

ButtonPress and ButtonRelease events are generated when the user presses or releases a mouse button. You can define them as follows:

```
typedef struct
{
    int           type;          /* Type of event            */
    unsigned long serial;        /* Last processed request no. */
    Bool          send_event;    /* True if from SendEvent   */
    Display       *display;      /* This display sent event  */
    Window        window;        /* Reported to this window  */
    Window        root;          /* Root window              */
    Window        subwindow;     /* Pointer is in this child */
    Time          time;          /* Timestamp in milliseconds */
    int           x, y;          /* Position in event window */
    int           x_root, y_root; /* Position relative to root */
    unsigned int  state;         /* State of key and buttons */
    unsigned int  button;        /* Which button is involved? */
    Bool          same_screen;   /* True = grab on same screen */
} XButtonEvent;
```

CirculateNotify and *CirculateRequest* Events

CirculateNotify and CirculateRequest events are generated when the stacking order of the windows is changed. The CirculateRequest event is generated when the X server receives a request to rearrange the windows. The server sends the CirculateNotify event after the windows are restacked. The information for these events is in the xcirculate and xcirculaterequest members of the XEvent union. These members are structures of type XCirculateEvent and XCirculateRequestEvent, respectively, and are defined in <X11/Xlib.h> as follows:

```
typedef struct
{
    int           type;          /* Type of event = CirculateNotify*/
    unsigned long serial;        /* Last processed request number */
    Bool          send_event;    /* True = if from a SendEvent */
    Display       *display;      /* This display sent the event */
    Window        event;         /* Window to receive the event */
    Window        window;        /* Window that was restacked */
    int           place;         /* One of: PlaceOnTop,        */
                                 /*         PlaceOnBottom      */
```

```
} XCirculateEvent;

typedef struct
{
    int          type;        /* CirculateRequest             */
    unsigned long serial;     /* Last processed request number */
    Bool         send_event;  /* True = if from a SendEvent    */
    Display      *display;     /* This display sent the event   */
    Window       parent;      /* Parent of window restacked    */
    Window       window;      /* Window that was restacked     */
    int          place;       /* One of: PlaceOnTop,           */
                              /*         PlaceOnBottom         */
} XCirculateRequestEvent;
```

ClientMessage Event

If you write two cooperating applications that need to coordinate their actions, you can do so by sending ClientMessage events. Because X applications do their work in response to events, it is convenient to communicate with other clients through an event. You send ClientMessage events by calling the XSendEvent function.

In Xt Intrinsics, you can add event handlers for ClientMessage events by specifying the constant NoEventMask as the second argument to the XtAddEventHandler function:

```
Widget w;
void  msg_handler();

XtAddEventHandler(w, NoEventMask, TRUE, msg_handler, NULL);
```

where msg_handler is the function called when any nonmaskable event is received for the widget w. Because there are other nonmaskable events, such as SelectionClear, SelectionNotify, and SelectionRequest, the msg_handler function should first make sure that the event type is ClientMessage before processing the event. (See Chapter 6, "Xlib Programming Model," for more information about event handlers.)

Unlike other X events, which deal with user inputs and repainting of windows, the ClientMessage event is meant to transmit a small amount of information from one client to another. All the data for the ClientMessage event is in the xclient field of the XEvent union. This field is an XClientMessageEvent structure, defined in <X11/Xlib.h> as follows:

```
typedef struct
{
    int          type;        /* Type of event = ClientMessage*/
    unsigned long serial;     /* Last processed request number*/
    Bool         send_event;  /* Always True for ClientMessage*/
    Display      *display;     /* This display sent event       */
    Window       window;      /* Window to receive the event   */
    Atom         message_type;/* Atom for message type         */
    int          format;      /* Data format: 8, 16, or 32     */
    union                     /* You can pass up to 20 bytes   */
    {                         /* using ClientMessage events    */
```

```
        char b[20];        /* Data when format is  8    */
        short s[10];       /* Data when format is 16    */
        long l[5];         /* Data when format is 32    */
    } data;
} XClientMessageEvent;
```

ColormapNotify Event

The X server generates a ColormapNotify event when the colormap attribute of a window changes or when a new colormap is installed. The information for this event is in the xcolormap member of the XEvent union. The xcolormap member is a structure of type XColormapEvent, declared in <X11/Xlib.h>:

```
typedef struct
{
    int             type;       /* EnterNotify or LeaveNotify   */
    unsigned long   serial;     /* Last processed request number */
    Bool            send_event; /* True = if from a SendEvent    */
    Display         *display;    /* Display where event occurred  */
    Window          window;     /* Window whose colormap changed */
    Colormap        colormap;   /* Colormap ID or None           */
#if defined(__cplusplus) || defined(c_plusplus)
    Bool c_new;                 /* Cannot use "new" in C++       */
#else
    Bool new;                   /* True means colormap changed   */
#endif
    int state;                  /* One of: ColormapInstalled,    */
                                /*         ColormapUninstalled   */
} XColormapEvent;
```

The conditional declaration accommodates the needs of C++ programmers—in C++, new is a reserved keyword.

ConfigureNotify and *ConfigureRequest* Events

The X server sends ConfigureNotify and ConfigureRequest events when a window is reconfigured—when its size, position, border width, or stacking order changes (ConfigureNotify) or is about to be changed (ConfigureRequest). The relevant information is in the xconfigure and xconfigurerequest members of the XEvent union. These members are structures of type XConfigureEvent and XConfigureRequestEvent, which are declared as follows:

```
typedef struct
{
    int             type;       /* ConfigureNotify               */
    unsigned long   serial;     /* Last processed request number */
    Bool            send_event; /* True = if from a SendEvent    */
    Display         *display;    /* Display where event occurred  */
    Window          event;      /* Window to which event reported*/
    Window          window;     /* Window that was reconfigured  */
    int             x, y;       /* New position in parent's frame*/
    int             width,      /* New width of window           */
                    height;     /* New height of window          */
```

```
    int             border_width;/* New border width of window    */
    Window          above;       /* Set to: Sibling or None        */
    Bool            override redirect; /* If True, window manager
                                 will not intervene with the
                                 reconfiguration of this window*/
} XConfigureEvent;


typedef struct
{
    int             type;       /* ConfigureNotify                 */
    unsigned long   serial;     /* Last processed request number */
    Bool            send_event; /* True = if from a SendEvent      */
    Display         *display;    /* Display where event occurred   */
    Window          parent;     /* Parent of "window"              */
    Window          window;     /* Window to be reconfigured       */
    int             x, y;       /* New position in parent's frame*/
    int             width,      /* New width of window             */
                    height;     /* New height of window            */
    int             border_width;/* New border width of window     */
    Window          above;      /* Set to: Sibling or None         */
    int             detail;     /* One of: Above, Below, TopIf,    */
                                /*         BottomIf, Opposite      */
    unsigned long   value_mask; /* Indicates the type of changes  */
} XConfigureRequestEvent;
```

CreateNotify Event

The X server reports the CreateNotify event when a window is created. The relevant information of this event is in an XCreateWindowEvent structure:

```
typedef struct
{
    int             type;       /* CreateNotify                    */
    unsigned long   serial;     /* Last processed request number */
    Bool            send_event; /* True = if from a SendEvent      */
    Display         *display;    /* Display where event occurred   */
    Window          parent;     /* Parent of "window"              */
    Window          window;     /* ID of window that was created */
    int             x, y;       /* Location in parent's frame      */
    int             width, height; /* Size of window               */
    int             border_width; /* Border width in pixels        */
    Bool            override_redirect; /* If True, window manager
                                 will not intervene with the
                                 creation of this window          */
} XCreateWindowEvent;
```

DestroyNotify Event

The X server can send a DestroyNotify event to any client that requests information about windows being destroyed. The information for this event is in the xdestroywindow member of the XEvent union. The xdestroywindow member is an XDestroyWindowEvent structure, which is declared in <X11/Xlib.h> as follows:

```
typedef struct
{
    int         type;       /* DestroyNotify                */
    unsigned long serial;   /* Last processed request number */
    Bool        send_event; /* True = if from a SendEvent   */
    Display     *display;   /* Display where event occurred */
    Window      event;      /* Window to which event reported*/
    Window      window;     /* ID of window being destroyed */
} XDestroyWindowEvent;
```

EnterNotify and *LeaveNotify* Events

The X server reports the information for EnterNotify and LeaveNotify events in the field named xcrossing in the XEvent union. This is an XCrossingEvent data structure, defined in <X11/Xlib.h> as the following:

```
typedef struct
{
    int         type;       /* EnterNotify or LeaveNotify   */
    unsigned long serial;   /* Last processed request number */
    Bool        send_event; /* True = if from a SendEvent   */
    Display     *display;   /* Display where event occurred */
    Window      window;     /* Window to which event reported*/
    Window      root;       /* Root window in that screen   */
    Window      subwindow;  /* Child window involved in event*/
    Time        time;       /* Time in milliseconds         */
    int         x, y;       /* Final position in event window*/
    int         x_root,     /* Pointer's final position in  */
                y_root;     /* root window's coordinate frame*/
    int         mode;       /* One of the three constants:
                               NotifyNormal, NotifyGrab,
                               NotifyUngrab                 */
    int         detail;     /* One of the five constants:
                               NotifyAncestor, NotifyVirtual,
                               NotifyInferior, NotifyNonLinear,
                               NotifyNonLinearVirtual       */
    Bool        same_screen;/* Pointer/window in same screen?*/
    Bool        focus;      /* Input focus on this window?  */
    unsigned int state;     /* State of key and buttons     */
} XCrossingEvent;
```

Expose Events

Expose events are generated by the server when any of your application's windows need redrawing. This can happen when the window is first mapped, when an obscuring window is moved, or when you clear an area of a window by calling XClearArea.

In most applications, all drawing occurs in response to Expose events, because you cannot draw in a window until it is ready, and there is no good way of knowing when it is ready. However, when you receive an Expose event for a window, you can be sure that it is ready for use.

When parts of a window need redrawing, the X server generates Expose events for every rectangular region that is exposed. When you retrieve an Expose event, the relevant information is in an XExposeEvent data structure (accessed as the member xexpose of the XEvent union):

```
typedef struct
{
    int            type;        /* Event's type              */
    unsigned long  serial;      /* Last processed request number */
    Bool           send_event;  /* True means from a SendEvent */
    Display        *display;     /* Display where event occurred */
    Window         window;      /* Window that needs redrawing */
    int            x, y;        /* Origin and dimensions of the */
    int            width,       /* rectangle that has been     */
                   height;      /* "exposed"                   */
    int            count;       /*Number of expose events to come*/
} XExposeEvent;
```

The members x, y, width, and height identify the rectangle whose contents are lost and have to be redrawn. The last member of the structure count tells you how many more Expose events for the same window are yet to arrive. Knowing this, you can devise a simple strategy of handling Expose events.

Wait for the Expose event with count equal to 0. Then clear the window and redraw everything in it. In other words, ignore the information about the specific parts that need refreshing and update the whole window.

Handling Expose events on count 0 works well for simple drawings, but for complex drawings, it is better to make use of the information on the rectangle that needs redrawing. One method is to use a region. You can use XUnionRectWithRegion to add all the rectangles in a region. Set the clipping mask of the drawing GC with XSetRegion. Then redraw when the Expose event with count 0 arrives. For maximum efficiency, your application's drawing function must be smart enough to draw only within the regions. Because the server clips against the region, there is no harm in drawing everything, but that sends unnecessary graphics requests and wastes time.

FocusIn and *FocusOut* Events

FocusIn and FocusOut events are generated when the keyboard input focus changes. The structure for this event type is declared as follows:

```
typedef struct
{
    int            type;        /* FocusIn or FocusOut       */
    unsigned long  serial;      /* Last processed request number */
    Bool           send_event;  /* True = if from a SendEvent */
    Display        *display;     /* Display where event occurred */
    Window         window;      /* Window to which event reported*/
    int            mode;        /* One of the three constants: */
                                   NotifyNormal, NotifyGrab,
                                   NotifyUngrab               */
    int            detail;      /* One of the five constants:  */
                                   NotifyAncestor, NotifyVirtual,
                                   NotifyInferior, NotifyNonLinear,
                                   NotifyNonLinearVirtual      */
} XFocusChangeEvent;
```

GraphicsExpose and *NoExpose* Events

GraphicsExpose and NoExpose events are sent if a source area is obscured during copy operations initiated with calls to the Xlib functions XCopyArea or XCopyPlane. These events are sent only if the graphics_exposures member of the graphics context (GC) is set to True. When this flag is set, the X server generates a NoExpose event when a graphics operation that might have produced a GraphicsExpose event does not produce any. The structures for this event are XGraphicsExposeEvent and XNoExposeEvent, which are declared as follows:

```
typedef struct
{
    int            type;        /* Event's type = GraphicsExpose */
    unsigned long serial;       /* Last processed request number */
    Bool           send_event;  /* True means from a SendEvent   */
    Display        *display;     /* Display where event occurred  */
    Drawable       drawable;    /* Destination of copy operation */
    int            x, y;        /* Origin and dimensions of the  */
    int            width,       /* rectangle that has been       */
                   height;      /* "exposed" (in pixels)         */
    int            count;       /*Number of expose events to come*/
    int major_code;             /* One of: CopyArea or CopyPlane */
    int minor_code;             /* Reserved for extensions       */
} XGraphicsExposeEvent;

typedef struct
{
    int            type;        /* Event's type = GraphicsExpose */
    unsigned long serial;       /* Last processed request number */
    Bool           send_event;  /* True means from a SendEvent   */
    Display        *display;     /* Display where event occurred  */
    Drawable       drawable;    /* Destination of copy operation */
    int major_code;             /* One of: CopyArea or CopyPlane */
    int minor_code;             /* Reserved for extensions       */
} XNoExposeEvent;
```

GravityNotify Event

The X server generates the GravityNotify event when a window is moved because of a change in the size of its parent. The XGravityEvent contains information for this event:

```
typedef struct
{
    int            type;        /* GravityNotify                 */
    unsigned long serial;       /* Last processed request number */
    Bool           send_event;  /* True = if from a SendEvent    */
    Display        *display;     /* Display where event occurred  */
    Window         event;       /* Window to which event reported*/
    Window         window;      /* ID of window that was moved   */
    int            x, y;        /* New coordinates of window     */
} XGravityEvent;
```

KeymapNotify Event

The X server generates a KeymapNotify event (during an EnterWindow or FocusIn event) when there is a change in the state of the keyboard—the condition of each key in the keyboard. The structure for this event is defined as the following:

```
typedef struct
{
    int           type;       /* KeymapNotify                */
    unsigned long serial;     /* Last processed request number */
    Bool          send_event; /* True = if from a SendEvent   */
    Display       *display;   /* Display where event occurred  */
    Window        window;     /* "window" member of latest
                                 FocusIn or EnterNotify event  */
    char          key_vector[32]; /* A 256-bit mask, each
                                 representing status of a key  */
} XKeymapEvent;
```

KeyPress and *KeyRelease* Events

KeyPress and KeyRelease events are generated when any key is pressed or released. You find information about these events in the xkey member of the XEvent union. xkey is an XKeyEvent structure, which is declared in <X11/Xlib.h> as follows:

```
typedef struct
{
    int           type;       /* Event's type                */
    unsigned long serial;     /* Last processed request number */
    Bool          send_event; /* True = if from a SendEvent   */
    Display       *display;   /* Display where event occurred  */
    Window        window;     /* Window to which event reported*/
    Window        root;       /* Root window in that screen    */
    Window        subwindow;  /* Child window involved in event*/
    Time          time;       /* Time in milliseconds          */
    int           x, y;       /* Position in event window      */
    int           x_root,     /* Pointer's position in the     */
                  y_root;     /* root window's coordinate frame*/
    unsigned int  state;      /* State of key and buttons      */
    unsigned int  keycode;    /* detail */
    Bool          same_screen;/* Pointer/window in same screen?*/
} XKeyEvent;
```

MapNotify and *UnmapNotify* Events

The X server sends MapNotify and UnmapNotify events to an interested client when a window is mapped (made visible) or unmapped. The structures for the events are as follows:

```
typedef struct
{
    int           type;       /* Event's type = MapNotify     */
    unsigned long serial;     /* Last processed request number */
    Bool          send_event; /* True = if from a SendEvent   */
    Display       *display;   /* Display where event occurred  */
    Window        event;      /* Window to which event reported*/
```

```
    Window          window;      /* ID of window that was mapped  */
    Bool            override_redirect; /* If True, window manager
                                 will not intervene with the
                                 creation of this window        */
} XMapEvent;

typedef struct
{
    int             type;        /* Event's type = UnmapNotify    */
    unsigned long   serial;      /* Last processed request number */
    Bool            send_event;  /* True = if from a SendEvent    */
    Display         *display;     /* Display where event occurred  */
    Window          event;       /* Window to which event reported*/
    Window          window;      /* Window that was unmapped      */
    Bool            from_configure; /* True if event was generated
                                 because parent's win_gravity
                                 was set to UnmapGravity        */
} XUnmapEvent;
```

MappingNotify Event

The X server manages the translation of keycodes to keysym (a symbolic name for a key). Applications can change this mapping by calling the function XChangeKeyboardMapping. An application should not do this on its own, but the user may run a utility program such as xmodmap to alter the mapping of one or more keys. When this happens, all X client applications receive a MappingNotify event (you cannot mask this event). Future mappings of keycodes to keysyms will work properly as long as your application calls XRefreshKeyboardMapping each time it receives a MappingNotify event. The event itself is reported in the following structure:

```
typedef struct
{
    int             type;        /* Event's type                  */
    unsigned long   serial;      /* Last processed request number */
    Bool            send_event;  /* True = if from a SendEvent    */
    Display         *display;     /* Display where event occurred  */
    Window          window;      /* Unused                        */
    int             request;     /* One of: MappingModifier,
                                    MappingKeyboard, MappingPointer */
    int             first_keycode;/* First keycode altered        */
    int             count;       /* Number of keycodes changed    */
} XMappingEvent;
```

MapRequest Event

The MapRequest event is generated just before a window is mapped. Window managers can use this to detect when a new window is made visible on the display. Information for this event appears in a structure as follows:

```
typedef struct
{
    int             type;        /* MapRequest                    */
    unsigned long   serial;      /* Last processed request number */
    Bool            send_event;  /* True = if from a SendEvent    */
    Display         *display;     /* Display where event occurred  */
```

```
    Window        parent;    /* Parent of "window"        */
    Window        window;    /* Window to be mapped       */
} XMapRequestEvent;
```

MotionNotify Event

The X server generates a `MotionNotify` event when the user moves the mouse pointer. The `XMotionEvent` contains information for this event:

```
typedef struct
{
    int           type;        /* Event's type              */
    unsigned long serial;      /* Last processed request number */
    Bool          send_event;  /* True = if from a SendEvent */
    Display       *display;    /* Display where event occurred */
    Window        window;      /* Window to which event reported*/
    Window        root;        /* Root window in that screen */
    Window        subwindow;   /* Child window involved in event*/
    Time          time;        /* Time in milliseconds      */
    int           x, y;        /* Position in event window  */
    int           x_root,      /* Pointer's position in the */
                  y_root;      /* root window's coordinate frame*/
    unsigned int  state;       /* State of key and buttons  */
    char          is_hint;     /* NotifyNormal or NotifyHint */
    Bool          same_screen; /* Pointer/window in same screen?*/
} XMotionEvent;
```

PropertyNotify Event

The X server generates a `PropertyNotify` event when a property of a window is changed (a property is a value with a name associated with a window). You can request this event by using the `PropertyChangeMask` event mask. The data associated with the `PropertyNotify` event is in the xproperty field of the `XEvent` union. This field is an `XPropertyEvent` structure, defined in `<X11/Xlib.h>` as follows:

```
typedef struct
{
    int           type;        /* Type of event = PropertyNotify */
    unsigned long serial;      /* Last processed request number */
    Bool          send_event;  /* True if from SendEvent    */
    Display       *display;    /* This display sent event   */
    Window        window;      /* Window whose property changed */
    Atom          atom;        /* Name of property involved */
    Time          time;        /* Time when property changed */
    int           state;       /* One of: PropertyNewValue or */
                               /*         PropertyDelete    */
} XPropertyEvent;
```

ReparentNotify Event

The `ReparentNotify` event is generated when a window's parent is changed. The information is reported in an `XReparentEvent` structure, declared as follows:

```
typedef struct
{
    int            type;        /* ReparentNotify               */
    unsigned long serial;       /* Last processed request number */
    Bool           send_event;  /* True = if from a SendEvent   */
    Display        *display;     /* Display where event occurred */
    Window         event;        /* Event sent to this window    */
    Window         window;       /* Window that was reparented   */
    Window         parent;       /* New parent of "window"       */
    int            x, y;         /* Location in new parent       */
    Bool           override_redirect; /* If True, window manager
                                  will not intervene with the
                                  reparenting                   */
} XReparentEvent;
```

ResizeRequest Event

The server generates a `ResizeRequest` event when a window's size is about to be changed. The information for this event is reported in an `XResizeRequestEvent` structure, declared as follows:

```
typedef struct
{
    int            type;        /* ResizeRequest                */
    unsigned long serial;       /* Last processed request number */
    Bool           send_event;  /* True = if from a SendEvent   */
    Display        *display;     /* Display where event occurred */
    Window         window;       /* Window to be resized         */
    int            width, height; /* New size of window          */
} XResizeRequestEvent;
```

Selection Events

There are three events for coordinating the exchange of data through selections: `SelectionClear`, `SelectionRequest`, and `SelectionNotify`. Applications do not have to solicit these events—they are sent automatically.

The X server sends a `SelectionClear` event to the current owner of a selection when the owner of the selection changes. The information for this event is in the `xselectionclear` field of the `XEvent` union. The `xselectionclear` field in this union is an `XSelectionClearEvent` structure, defined in `<X11/Xlib.h>` as follows:

```
typedef struct
{
    int            type;        /* Type of event = SelectionClear */
    unsigned long serial;       /* Last processed request number */
    Bool           send_event;  /* True if from SendEvent        */
    Display        *display;     /* This display sent event       */
    Window         window;       /* Window losing ownership       */
    Atom           selection;    /* Name of selection involved    */
    Time           time;         /* Time when ownership was lost  */
} XSelectionClearEvent;
```

When an application wants to receive the data corresponding to a selection, it calls the `XConvertSelection` function, which causes a `SelectionRequest` event to be sent to the current owner of the selection. The `xselectionrequest` field in the XEvent union contains information on this event. The event data structure is defined in <X11/Xlib.h> as follows:

```
typedef struct
{
    int            type;        /* Type of event = SelectionRequest*/
    unsigned long  serial;      /* Last processed request number  */
    Bool           send_event;  /* True if from SendEvent          */
    Display        *display;     /* This display sent event         */
    Window         owner;       /* Window that owns the selection */
    Window         requestor;   /* Window requesting data          */
    Atom           selection;   /* Name of selection involved      */
    Atom           target;      /* Data should be converted to     */
                                /* this type by the owner          */
    Atom           property;    /* Selection's owner should copy   */
                                /* data to this property           */
    Time           time;        /* Time when selection requested   */
} XSelectionRequestEvent;
```

When a selection's owner receives the `SelectionRequest` event, it should convert the data to the type specified by the `target` atom in the event and copy the converted data to the specified property on the requesting window. After that, the owner sends a `SelectionNotify` event to the requesting window to indicate the result of the request. The information for the `SelectionNotify` event is in the `xselection` field of the XEvent union. This field is a structure of type XSelectionEvent, defined in <X11/Xlib.h> as follows:

```
typedef struct
{
    int            type;        /* Type of event = SelectionNotify*/
    unsigned long  serial;      /* Last processed request number  */
    Bool           send_event;  /* True if from SendEvent          */
    Display        *display;     /* This display sent event         */
    Window         requestor;   /* Window that had requested data */
    Atom           selection;   /* Name of selection involved      */
    Atom           target;      /* Data type of value in property */
    Atom           property;    /* Property where data has been    */
                                /* placed. "None" means failure    */
    Time           time;        /* Time when data stored           */
} XSelectionEvent;
```

VisibilityNotify Event

The X server generates a `VisibilityNotify` event when there is a change in the visibility of a window. You can select this event using the mask named `VisibilityChangeMask`. The event is reported in the following structure:

```
typedef struct
{
    int            type;        /* VisibilityNotify                */
    unsigned long  serial;      /* Last processed request number  */
    Bool           send_event;  /* True = if from a SendEvent      */
    Display        *display;     /* Display where event occurred   */
    Window         window;      /* Window whose visibility changed*/
    int            state;       /* One of: VisibilityUnobscured,   */
                                    VisibilityPartiallyObscured,
                                    VisibilityFullyObscured        */
} XVisibilityEvent;
```

Appendix K

Xt Intrinsics Quick Reference

This appendix is designed to serve as a quick reference guide to the Xt Intrinsics—the foundation on which the Motif toolkit is built. It provides a summary description of the Xt Intrinsics functions, and lists the form of callbacks, event handlers, and other functions that you have to define when programming with the Xt Intrinsics. You will also find the definitions of some commonly used Xt Intrinsic data types. The material in this quick reference guide conforms to the Xt Intrinsics that accompany X Window System, Version 11, Release 6 (X11R6).

The function prototypes shown in this appendix will help you recall the calling syntax of a function, but the short description does not fully tell you how to use that function. For detailed information on the Xt Intrinsics functions, please consult the following book: Paul J. Asente and Ralph R. Swick, *X Window System Toolkit,* Digital Press, 1990.

Xt Intrinsics Functions

The Xt Intrinsics functions are shown in ANSI standard prototype format. Each argument is explained through a comment next to the argument. A brief description of the function follows each prototype declaration. Some functions from the earlier versions of Xt Intrinsics are superseded by others in later versions of the Intrinsics. A comment on the first line of the function's declaration (see `XtAppInitialize`, for instance) tells you which function to use in X11R6.

XtAddActions

```
void XtAddActions(          /* Superseded by XtAppAddActions */
    XtActionList actions,      /* Action name and procedure */
    Cardinal    num_actions); /* Number of actions in list */
```

Registers an action table with the translation manager. An action table binds a name to a function to be called when that action's name appears in the translation resource of the application.

XtAddCallback

```
void XtAddCallback(
    Widget        widget,        /* Callback for this widget */
    const String  callback_name, /* Name of callback list    */
    XtCallbackProc callback,      /* The callback function    */
    XtPointer     client_data);  /* 2nd argument to callback */
```

Adds a callback function to the named callback list of a widget.

XtAddCallbacks

```
void XtAddCallbacks(
    Widget         widget,        /* Callbacks for this widget */
    const String   callback_name, /* Name of callback list     */
    XtCallbackList callbacks);    /* List of callback functions*/
                                  /* A NULL marks list's end   */
```

Adds several callback functions to the named callback list of a widget.

XtAddConverter

```
void XtAddConverter(      /* Superseded by XtSetTypeConverter */
    const String     from_type,    /* Convert from this type */
    const String     to_type,      /* to this data type      */
    XtConverter      converter,    /* Function that converts */
    XtConvertArgList convert_args, /* Arguments to function  */
    Cardinal         nargs);       /* Number of arguments    */
```

Registers a function that can convert values from `from_type` to `to_type`.

XtAddEventHandler

```
void XtAddEventHandler(
    Widget          widget,        /* Register for this widget */
```

```
EventMask       eventMask,   /* To handle these events   */
Boolean         nonmaskable, /* For nonmaskable events? */
XtEventHandler proc,         /* The event handler        */
XtPointer       client_data);/* Data for the handler     */
```

Registers an event handler that is called when events matching `eventMask` occur in the widget.

XtAddExposureToRegion

```
void XtAddExposureToRegion(
    XEvent* event,    /* Expose or GraphicsExpose event   */
    Region  region); /* Region to which rectangle is added */
```

Adds the "exposed" rectangle from the specified `Expose` or `GraphicsExpose` event to the specified region.

XtAddGrab

```
void XtAddGrab(
    Widget  widget,         /* Widget to be made modal       */
    Boolean exclusive,      /* True=send all events to widget */
    Boolean spring_loaded); /* True=popped up by buttonpress  */
```

Redirects user's inputs to a specified widget.

XtAddInput

```
XtInputId XtAddInput(           /* Superseded by XtAppAddInput */
    int                 source,     /* File descriptor        */
    XtPointer           condition,  /* When event generated */
    XtInputCallbackProc proc,       /* Callback function     */
    XtPointer           client_data); /* Data for callback    */
```

Adds a file as a source of input events for the default application context. Returns the descriptor for the new input source.

XtAddRawEventHandler

```
void XtAddRawEventHandler(
    Widget         widget,      /* Handler for this widget */
    EventMask      eventMask,   /* Handler for this event  */
    Boolean        nonmaskable, /* For nonmaskable event   */
    XtEventHandler proc,        /* Function to handle event */
    XtPointer      client_data); /* Data for event handler  */
```

Registers an event handler for the widget without selecting the specified event.

XtAddTimeOut

```
XtIntervalId XtAddTimeOut(  /* Superseded by XtAppAddTimeOut */
    unsigned long       interval,   /* Milliseconds          */
    XtTimerCallbackProc proc,       /* Callback function     */
    XtPointer           client_data); /* Data for callback    */
```

Sets up a function that is called when the specified time interval has elapsed. The function is called only once. You can activate the callback function repeatedly by setting up a new timeout in the timeout callback function (calling XtAddTimeOut again).

XtAddWorkProc

```
XtWorkProcId XtAddWorkProc(/* Superseded by XtAppAddWorkProc */
    XtWorkProc  proc,       /* The "work procedure"       */
    XtPointer   client_data); /* Pointer passed to WorkProc  */
```

Sets up a WorkProc—a function to be called when the application is waiting for input.

XtAllocateGC

```
GC XtAllocateGC(
    Widget      widget,/* Widget to identify the screen    */
    Cardinal    depth, /* Depth for which GC will be valid */
    XtGCMask    valueMask, /* Specifies fields that must    */
                           /* be fixed values              */
    XGCValues*  values, /* Values for fields in valueMask   */
    XtGCMask    dynamicMask, /* Fields that may be changed */
    XtGCMask    unusedMask); /* Fields that are not used    */
```

Returns a shared GC that may be modified by client applications. The GC is valid for the screen of the specified widget.

XtAppAddActionHook

```
XtActionHookId XtAppAddActionHook(
    XtAppContext    app,       /* Use hook in this context */
    XtActionHookProc proc,     /* The hook function        */
    XtPointer       client_data);/* Data passed to "proc"  */
```

Sets up a function to be called just before an action is about to be performed by the translation manager. Returns an identifier for the registered "action hook." You can use this identifier as an argument to XtRemoveActionHook to remove the function.

XtAppAddActions

```
void XtAppAddActions(
    XtAppContext app,          /* Use in this context */
    XtActionList actions,      /* List of actions     */
    Cardinal     num_actions); /* Number of actions   */
```

Registers a list of actions with the translation manager for use in the specified application context.

XtAppAddBlockHook

```
XtBlockHookId XtAppAddBlockHook(
    XtAppContext app,    /* For this application context */
    XtBlockHookProc proc, /* The hook function          */
    XtPointer client_data);/* Data passed to "proc"     */
```

Sets up a function to be called when the Intrinsics is about to block pending some input. Returns an identifier for the registered "block hook." You can use this identifier as an argument to `XtRemoveBlockHook` to remove the function.

XtAppAddConverter

```
void XtAppAddConverter(/* Superseded by XtAppSetTypeConverter */
    XtAppContext      app,          /* Use in this context    */
    const String      from_type,    /* Convert from this type */
    const String      to_type,      /* to this type           */
    XtConverter       converter,    /* Function that converts */
    XtConvertArgList  convert_args, /* Arguments to function  */
    Cardinal          nargs);       /* Number of arguments    */
```

Registers a function for converting between two data types. The function is used in the specified application context.

XtAppAddSignal

```
XtInputId XtAppAddSignal(
    XtAppContext        app,           /* Use in this context  */
    XtSignalCallbackProc proc,         /* Function to call when */
                                       /* a signal is raised   */
    XtPointer           client_data);  /* Argument to callback */
```

Provides a mechanism for handling signals in Xt-based applications. Call `XtAppAddSignal` with a callback function as argument before setting up an operating system-dependent signal handler. Store the ID returned by `XtAppAddSignal` in a place accessible to the signal handler. Then, from within the signal handler, call `XtNoticeSignal` with the ID as argument. Xt Intrinsics will then call your registered callback function, in which you can safely handle the signal.

XtAppAddInput

```
XtInputId XtAppAddInput(
    XtAppContext        app,           /* Use in this context    */
    int                 source,        /* File descriptor        */
    XtPointer           condition,     /* What types of inputs?  */
    XtInputCallbackProc proc,          /* The callback function  */
    XtPointer           client_data);  /* Argument to callback   */
```

Adds a callback function that will be called whenever there is input from the specified input source.

XtAppAddTimeOut

```
XtIntervalId XtAppAddTimeOut(
    XtAppContext        app,           /* For this application */
    unsigned long       interval,      /* In milliseconds      */
    XtTimerCallbackProc proc,          /* Call this function   */
    XtPointer           client_data);  /* Pass this to proc    */
```

Sets up a function to be called after a specified number of milliseconds. After the function is called, the timeout is removed.

XtAppAddWorkProc

```
XtWorkProcId XtAppAddWorkProc(
    XtAppContext app,          /* For this context  */
    XtWorkProc   proc,         /* "work" function   */
    XtPointer    client_data); /* Pass this to proc */
```

Sets up a work procedure—a function to be called when the application would otherwise wait for input.

XtAppCreateShell

```
Widget XtAppCreateShell(
    const String name,         /* Name of application     */
    const String class,        /* Class name of application*/
    WidgetClass  widget_class, /* Class of top-level shell */
    Display*     display,      /* Connect to this X server */
    ArgList      args,         /* List of arguments       */
    Cardinal     nargs);       /* Number of arguments     */
```

Creates the top-level shell for an application and returns its widget ID.

XtAppError

```
void XtAppError(
    XtAppContext app,          /* For this application context */
    const String message);     /* Report this error message    */
```

Calls the error-handling function of the specified application context and passes it the error message.

XtAppErrorMsg

```
void XtAppErrorMsg(
    XtAppContext app,          /* Application context         */
    const String name,         /* Error name                  */
    const String type,         /* Error type                  */
    const String class,        /* Resource class              */
    const String default,      /* Default error message       */
    String*      params,       /* Values for error message    */
    Cardinal*    nparams);     /* Number of values in "params" */
```

Calls an error handler with arguments to help locate an error message and display the message.

XtAppGetErrorDatabase

```
XrmDatabase *XtAppGetErrorDatabase(
    XtAppContext app);         /* Application context */
```

Returns the current error database.

XtAppGetErrorDatabaseText

```
void XtAppGetErrorDatabaseText(
    XtAppContext app,        /* Application context          */
    const String name,       /* Descriptive name of error    */
    const String type,       /* Error type                   */
    const String class,      /* Resource class               */
    const String default,    /* Default error message        */
    String       buffer,     /* Buffer for returned message  */
    int          nbytes,     /* Buffer size                  */
    XrmDatabase  database);  /* Use this error database      */
```

In the buffer, this function returns the error message corresponding to the specified error.

XtAppGetExitFlag

```
Boolean XtAppGetExitFlag(
    XtAppContext app_context); /* For this application context */
```

Returns the exit flag of the specified application context.

XtAppGetSelectionTimeout

```
unsigned int XtAppGetSelectionTimeout(
    XtAppContext    app);     /* Application context          */
```

Returns the selection timeout value (in milliseconds).

XtAppInitialize

```
Widget XtAppInitialize( /* Superseded by XtOpenApplication   */
    XtAppContext*    app_context_return,/* Returned context */
    const String     application_class, /* Appl. class name */
    XrmOptionDescList options,           /* Command-line opt.*/
    Cardinal         noptions,           /* Number of options*/
    Cardinal*        argc_in_out,
    String*          argv_in_out,
    const String*    fallback_resources,/* Resources         */
    ArgList          args,               /* Arguments         */
    Cardinal         nargs);             /* Num. of arguments*/
```

Initializes the Xt Intrinsics, creates an application context, opens a connection to the X server identified by the DISPLAY environment variable, and creates a top-level shell. When the function returns, the app_context_return argument will have the application context. This function returns the ID of the newly created application shell widget.

XtAppLock

```
void XtAppLock(XtAppContext app_context);
```

Locks an application context, including all its displays and widgets.

XtAppMainLoop

```
void XtAppMainLoop(
    XtAppContext app);
```

Starts processing events for the specified application context. This is equivalent to calling XtAppNextEvent followed by a call to XtDispatchEvent.

XtAppNextEvent

```
void XtAppNextEvent(
    XtAppContext app,
    XEvent*      event); /* Event info. returned here */
```

Provides the next event for the specified application context. The information is returned in the XEvent structure whose address is in the event argument.

XtAppPeekEvent

```
Boolean XtAppPeekEvent(
    XtAppContext app,
    XEvent*      event); /* Event info. returned here */
```

Returns True if there is an event for the specified application context and provides information for the event in the XEvent structure whose address you pass in the event argument.

XtAppPending

```
XtInputMask XtAppPending(
    XtAppContext app);
```

Returns a bit mask indicating the type of pending events for the specified application context. A zero return value indicates that there are no pending events. The returned bit mask will be a bitwise-OR of the following constants: XtIMXEvent (the XtIM prefix stands for *Xt Input Mask*), XtIMTime, and XtIMAlternateInput.

XtAppProcessEvent

```
void XtAppProcessEvent(
    XtAppContext app,
    XtInputMask  mask); /* Identifies event to process */
```

Processes an event from the source specified by the mask which can be one of the following:

XtAlternateInput	Refers to an alternate input (set up by XtAppAddInput)
XtIMTime	Refers to a timeout event (set up by XtAppAddTimeOut)
XtImXEvent	Refers to a normal X event

XtAppReleaseCacheRefs

```
void XtAppReleaseCacheRefs(
    XtAppContext app,
    XtICacheRef  *refs); /* Release these cache entries */
```

Decrements the reference count for the cache entries listed in the array `refs`. The cache IDs in `refs` are values previously returned by `XtAppAddConverter`.

XtAppSetErrorHandler

```
XtErrorHandler XtAppSetErrorHandler(
    XtAppContext   app,
    XtErrorHandler eproc); /* New handler for fatal errors */
```

Sets up `eproc` as the function to be called when a fatal error occurs for the specified application context. This function returns the previously installed error handler which, in most cases, is the default error handler called `_XtDefaultError`. On UNIX systems, the default error handler prints a message on `stderr` and terminates the application.

XtAppSetErrorMsgHandler

```
XtErrorMsgHandler XtAppSetErrorMsgHandler(
    XtAppContext      app,
    XtErrorMsgHandler eproc);/* New handler for fatal errors */
```

Installs `eproc` as the handler for fatal errors and returns the previously installed handler. The default handler is `_XtDefaultErrorMsg`, which calls `XtGetErrorDatabaseText` to construct an error message and passes that message to `XtAppError`.

XtAppSetExitFlag

```
void XtAppSetExitFlag(
    XtAppContext app_context); /* Exit this application context */
```

Sets a flag to indicate that the application context should exit.

XtAppSetFallbackResources

```
void XtAppSetFallbackResources(
    XtAppContext app,
    const String* defaults);/* Default values of resources */
```

Sets up the resource specifications in the defaults array as the default values for the resources applicable to that application context.

XtAppSetSelectionTimeout

```
void XtAppSetSelectionTimeout(
    XtAppContext   app,
    unsigned long  timeout); /* Time in milliseconds */
```

Sets the selection timeout value (in milliseconds) for the specified application context. This is the time within which an application must respond to a selection event from another application. The default value comes from the application's `selectionTimeout` resource. If this resource is undefined, the selection timeout is set to 5000 milliseconds (5 seconds).

XtAppSetTypeConverter

```
void XtAppSetTypeConverter(
    XtAppContext      app,
    const String      from_type,    /* Convert from this type */
    const String      to_type,      /* this type              */
    XtTypeConverter   converter,    /* Function that converts  */
    XtConvertArgList  convert_args, /* Arguments for function  */
    Cardinal          nargs,        /* Number of arguments     */
    XtCacheType       cache_type,   /* Indicates how to share  */
                                    /*    this resource        */
    XtDestructor      destructor);  /* Function to be called   */
                                    /* before freeing resource */
```

Sets up a function to be called when a resource has to be converted from `from_type` to `to_type`. These types are identified by constants such as `XtRColor`, `XtRPixel`, and `XtRString`, which are defined in the file `<X11/StringDefs.h>`. The `cache_type` argument can take one of the following values:

XtCacheAll	Share among all applications displaying at an X server
XtCacheByDisplay	Like `XtCacheAll`, but destructor is called when the display is closed by calling `XtCloseDisplay`
XtCacheNone	Do not share (in other words, no need to save in cache)
XtCacheRefCount	Share, but destroy when no application uses resource

XtAppSetWarningHandler

```
XtErrorHandler XtAppSetWarningHandler(
    XtAppContext    app,
    XtErrorHandler  wproc);/* New handler for warnings */
```

Sets up `wproc` as the function to be called to handle warnings (nonfatal errors) and returns the previously installed warning handler.

XtAppSetWarningMsgHandler

```
XtErrorMsgHandler XtAppSetWarningMsgHandler(
    XtAppContext       app,
    XtErrorMsgHandler wproc);/* Handler for warnings */
```

Installs `wproc` as the function to be called to handle warnings (nonfatal errors) and returns the previously installed warning handler.

XtAppUnlock

```
void XtAppUnlock(XtAppContext app_context);
```

Unlocks the specified application context.

XtAppWarning

```
void XtAppWarning(
    XtAppContext app,
    const String message); /* Report this warning message */
```

Calls the default warning handler with a message to be reported.

XtAppWarningMsg

```
void XtAppWarningMsg(
    XtAppContext app,      /* Application context        */
    const String name,     /* Descriptive name of warning */
    const String type,     /* Error type                 */
    const String class,    /* Resource class             */
    const String default,  /* Default warning message    */
    String*      params,   /* Values for warning message */
    Cardinal*    nparams); /* Number of values in "params"*/
```

Calls the nonfatal error handler with arguments to help locate a warning message and display the message.

XtAugmentTranslations

```
void XtAugmentTranslations(
    Widget          w,   /* Alter this widget's translations*/
    XtTranslations new);/* Merge in this translation table */
```

Merges a set of new translations into the existing translation table of the specified widget. A *translation table* specifies what function should be called when an event or a sequence of events occurs in a widget.

XtBuildEventMask

```
EventMask XtBuildEventMask(
    Widget w); /* Return event mask for this widget */
```

Returns the event mask for the specified widget. The event mask indicates what type of events the widget accepts.

XtCallAcceptFocus

```
Boolean XtCallAcceptFocus(
    Widget w,  /* Call widget's "accept_focus" function */
    Time* t); /* Timestamp of the triggering event    */
```

Calls the accept_focus procedure of the specified widget. This function returns False if the widget's accept_focus function is NULL. Otherwise, XtCallAcceptFocus returns the value returned by the widget's accept_focus function.

XtCallActionProc

```
void XtCallActionProc(
    Widget       widget,  /* Call this widget's action func */
    const String action,  /* Invoke action with this name   */
    XEvent*      event,   /* Event passed to action routine */
    String*      params,  /* Parameters passed to action    */
    Cardinal     nparams);/* Number of parameters in params */
```

Calls the action procedure bound to an action of specified name.

XtCallbackExclusive

```
void XtCallbackExclusive(
    Widget    widget,      /* Use this widget's callbacks  */
    XtPointer client_data, /* Map this pop-up shell        */
    XtPointer call_data);  /* Not used, ok to specify NULL */
```

Maps a pop-up shell from a widget's callback list. The client_data argument specifies the shell to be mapped. This function does its job by calling XtPopup with the grab_kind argument set to XtGrabExclusive. This is a modal pop-up; all inputs go the specified shell's widgets only.

XtCallbackNone

```
void XtCallbackNone(
    Widget    widget,      /* Use this widget's callbacks  */
    XtPointer client_data, /* Map this pop-up shell        */
    XtPointer call_data);  /* Not used, ok to specify NULL */
```

Maps a pop-up shell from a widget's callback list. The client_data argument specifies the shell to be mapped. This function does its job by calling XtPopup with the grab_kind argument set to XtGrabNone. In this case, user input is not restricted (a nonmodal pop-up).

XtCallbackNonexclusive

```
void XtCallbackNonexclusive(
    Widget    widget,      /* Use this widget's callbacks  */
    XtPointer client_data, /* Map this pop-up shell        */
    XtPointer call_data);  /* Not used, ok to specify NULL */
```

Pops up a shell widget from a widget's callback list. The `client_data` argument specifies the shell to be mapped. This function does its job by calling `XtPopup` with the `grab_kind` argument set to `XtGrabNonexclusive`.

XtCallbackPopdown

```
void XtCallbackPopdown(
    Widget     widget,      /* Widget activating pop-down  */
    XtPointer client_data, /* Pointer to an XtPopdownID    */
    XtPointer call_data);  /* Not used, ok to specify NULL */
```

Pops down the shell identified by the `shell_widget` field of the `XtPopdownID` structure whose address is in the `client_data` argument of the function.

XtCallbackReleaseCacheRef

```
void XtCallbackReleaseCacheRef(
    Widget     widget,      /* Affects this widget's cache  */
    XtPointer client_data, /* Pointer to an XtCacheRef      */
    XtPointer call_data);  /* Not used, ok to specify NULL */
```

Decrements the reference count for the cache entry identified by the `XtCacheRef` structure whose address is in the `client_data` argument.

XtCallbackReleaseCacheRefList

```
void XtCallbackReleaseCacheRefList(
    Widget     widget,      /* Affects this widget's cache  */
    XtPointer client_data, /* Pointer to an XtCacheRef*     */
    XtPointer call_data);  /* Not used, ok to specify NULL */
```

Decrements the reference count for the cache entries by the null-terminated list of `XtCacheRef` structure whose address is in the `client_data` argument.

XtCallCallbackList

```
void XtCallCallbackList(
    Widget     widget,      /* Call this widget's callbacks */
    XtCallbackList cblist,  /* Call this list of callbacks  */
    XtPointer      cbdata); /* Data passed to each callback */
```

Calls the callback functions listed in the argument `cblist`.

XtCallbackPopdown

```
void XtCallbackPopdown(
    Widget     widget,      /* Widget to "pop down"             */
    XtPointer client_data,/* Pointer to XtPopdownID structure */
    XtPointer call_data);  /* This argument is ignored         */
```

Unmaps a pop-up shell identified by the widget ID in the `XtPopdownID` structure whose address is passed in the second argument. This function is designed to be installed as a callback that automatically pops down a pop-up shell widget in response to some event such as pressing a button. This is why the function takes a third, unused, argument.

XtCallCallbacks

```
void XtCallCallbacks(
    Widget    widget,      /* Call this widget's callbacks */
    const String cbname,   /* Name of callback list        */
    XtPointer    cbdata);  /* Data passed to each callback */
```

Calls the callbacks in the named list of callbacks for the specified widget.

XtCallConverter

```
Boolean XtCallConverter(
    Display*       display,      /* Identifies X server*/
    XtTypeConverter converter,   /* Conversion function*/
    XrmValuePtr    args,         /* Arguments for func */
    Cardinal       nargs,        /* Number of arguments*/
    XrmValuePtr    from,         /* Convert this value */
    XrmValuePtr    to_return,    /* Returned value     */
    XtCacheRef*    cache_ref_return);/* Returned cache ID  */
```

Explicitly calls a conversion function to convert a resource from one type to another and return a cache ID for the converted resource.

XtCalloc

```
char *XtCalloc(
    Cardinal nelements,  /* Storage for these many elements */
    Cardinal elem_size); /* each of this size (bytes)       */
```

Allocates storage for an array of elements and initializes the storage to zero. Returns a pointer to the newly allocated storage. Calls `XtAppErrorMsg` if memory allocation fails.

XtCancelSelectionRequest

```
void XtCancelSelectionRequest(
    Widget requestor, /* Widget that had requested selection */
    Atom   selection);/* Identifies the selection            */
```

Cancels all selection requests queued up since the last call to `XtCreateSelectionRequest`.

XtClass

```
WidgetClass XtClass(
    Widget w); /* Return this widget's "widget class" */
```

Returns a pointer to a widget's class structure.

XtCloseDisplay

```
void XtCloseDisplay(
    Display* display); /* Connection to be closed */
```

Closes the connection to the X server identified by display.

XtConfigureWidget

```
void XtConfigureWidget(
    Widget    w,         /* Configure this widget    */
    Position  x,         /* New position of widget   */
    Position  y,
    Dimension width,     /* New width of widget      */
    Dimension height,    /* New height of widget     */
    Dimension bdwidth);  /* New border width (pixels) */
```

Moves and resizes the specified widget.

XtConvert

```
void XtConvert(         /* Superseded by XtConvertAndStore */
    Widget          widget,    /* Resource for this widget */
    const String from_type,  /* Convert from this type   */
    XrmValue*     from,       /* Convert this value       */
    const String to_type,    /* Convert to this type     */
    XrmValue*     to_return); /* Returned value           */
```

Converts a resource from one type to another.

XtConvertAndStore

```
Boolean XtConvertAndStore(
    Widget          widget,    /* Resource for this widget */
    const String from_type,  /* Convert from this type   */
    XrmValue*     from,       /* Convert this value       */
    const String to_type,    /* Convert to this type     */
    XrmValue*     to_return); /* Returned value           */
```

Converts a resource from one type to another. Returns True if conversion is successful and False otherwise.

XtConvertCase

```
void XtConvertCase(
    Display* display,       /* Identifies the X server   */
    KeySym   keysym,        /* Convert this keysym       */
    KeySym*  lower_return,  /* Returns lowercase version */
    KeySym*  upper_return); /* Returns uppercase version */
```

Converts the specified keysym into lowercase and uppercase and returns these values in the arguments lower_return and upper_return.

XtCreateApplicationContext

```
XtAppContext XtCreateApplicationContext(void);
```

Creates and returns an application context.

XtCreateApplicationShell

```
Widget XtCreateApplicationShell(
                          /* Superseded by XtAppCreateShell */
    const String name,    /* Not used (call with NULL)      */
    WidgetClass  wclass,  /* Widget's class                 */
    ArgList      args,    /* Arguments with resource values */
    Cardinal     nargs);  /* Number of arguments in args    */
```

Creates a top-level shell widget and returns its ID. This function has been superseded by XtAppCreateShell in X11R4.

XtCreateManagedWidget

```
Widget XtCreateManagedWidget(
    const String name,    /* Name of the new widget         */
    WidgetClass  wclass,  /* Widget's class                 */
    Widget       parent,  /* Create as child of this widget */
    ArgList      args,    /* Arguments with resource values */
    Cardinal     nargs);  /* Number of arguments in args    */
```

Creates and manages a widget and returns the ID of the newly created widget.

XtCreatePopupShell

```
Widget XtCreatePopupShell(
    const String name,    /* Name of the new widget         */
    WidgetClass  wclass,  /* Widget's class                 */
    Widget       parent,  /* Create as child of this widget */
    ArgList      args,    /* Arguments with resource values */
    Cardinal     nargs);  /* Number of arguments in args    */
```

Creates a pop-up shell widget as a child of a specified widget and returns the ID of the newly created widget.

XtCreateSelectionRequest

```
void XtCreateSelectionRequest(
    Widget requestor,  /* Widget requesting the selection */
    Atom   selection); /* Identifies the selection        */
```

Prepares a selection request. After you call XtCreateSelectionRequest, subsequent calls to XtGetSelectionValue and XtGetSelectionValueIncremental with the same requestor and selection as specified for XtCreateSelectionRequest are bundled into a single request that can be initiated by calling XtSendSelectionRequest.

XtCreateWidget

```
Widget XtCreateWidget(
    const String name,   /* Name of the new widget       */
    WidgetClass wclass, /* Widget's class               */
    Widget      parent, /* Create as child of this widget */
    ArgList     args,   /* Arguments with resource values */
    Cardinal    nargs); /* Number of arguments in args  */
```

Creates a widget and returns the ID of the newly created widget.

XtCreateWindow

```
void XtCreateWindow(
    Widget   widget, /* Create window for this widget  */
    unsigned class,  /* Class of window: InputOutput,  */
                     /* InputOnly, CopyFromParent      */
    Visual   visual, /* Visual type of window          */
    XtValueMask vm,  /* Indicates attributes to use    */
    XSetWindowAttributes xswa); /* Window attributes   */
```

Creates a widget's window. You normally need not call call this function directly. The `realize` procedure of a widget calls this function to create the widget's window.

XtDatabase

```
XrmDatabase XtDatabase(
    Display* d);/* Return resource database for this server */
```

Returns the resource manager database associated with a particular X server.

XtDestroyApplicationContext

```
void XtDestroyApplicationContext(
    XtAppContext app);
```

Destroys the specified application context and closes its connection to the X server.

XtDestroyGC

```
void XtDestroyGC( /* Superseded by XtReleaseGC     */
    GC gc);       /* Graphics context to be destroyed */
```

Destroys a graphics context when it is no longer needed.

XtDestroyWidget

```
void XtDestroyWidget(
    Widget w); /* Destroy this widget */
```

Destroys the specified widget.

XtDirectConvert

```
void XtDirectConvert(  /* Superseded by XtCallConverter */
    XtConverter converter,  /* Function that converts   */
    XrmValuePtr args,       /* Arguments to converter   */
    Cardinal    nargs,      /* Number of arguments      */
    XrmValuePtr from,       /* Convert from this value  */
    XrmValue*   to_return); /* Returns converted value  */
```

Converts a resource from one type to another. Starting with X11R4, you should call XtCallConverter to do this conversion.

XtDisownSelection

```
void XtDisownSelection(
    Widget widget,    /* Widget that is giving up ownership */
    Atom   selection, /* Selection being disowned           */
    Time   time);     /* Time when selection is given up    */
```

Indicates that the specified widget is giving up ownership of a selection.

XtDispatchEvent

```
Boolean XtDispatchEvent(
    XEvent* event); /* Event being dispatched */
```

Sends the event to the appropriate event handler. Returns True if an event handler is called.

XtDispatchEventToWidget

```
Boolean XtDispatchEventToWidget(
    Widget  widget, /* Send event to this widget */
    XEvent* event); /* Event being dispatched    */
```

Sends the event to the appropriate event handler in the specified widget. Returns True if an event handler is called.

XtDisplay

```
Display *XtDisplay(
    Widget w);  /* Return display for this widget */
```

Returns the X server connection ID for the specified widget.

XtDisplayInitialize

```
void XtDisplayInitialize(
    XtAppContext     app,     /* Application context    */
    Display*         display, /* Connect to this server */
    const String     name,    /* Name of application    */
    const String     class,   /* Class name of appl.    */
    XrmOptionDescRec* options, /* Acceptable options     */
```

```
    Cardinal          noptions, /* Elements in "options"   */
    Cardinal*         argc,     /* Number of cmd line args*/
    char**            argv);    /* Command-line options    */
```

Initializes the connection to an X server and adds the connection to the specified application context.

XtDisplayOfObject

```
Display *XtDisplayOfObject(
    Widget w); /* Return display for this widget */
```

Returns the display pointer for a widget.

XtDisplayStringConversionWarning

```
void XtDisplayStringConversionWarning(
    Display*    dpy,      /* Display pointer                 */
    const String from,    /* Attempted to convert this       */
    const String to_type);/* Tried conversion to this type */
```

Calls `XtAppWarningMsg` to issue a warning message when an attempted conversion fails.

XtDisplayToApplicationContext

```
XtAppContext XtDisplayToApplicationContext(Display* dpy);
```

Returns the application context in which the display is initialized.

XtError

```
void XtError(           /* Superseded by XtAppError       */
    const String msg); /* Error message passed to handler */
```

Calls the current fatal error handler with the specified error message.

XtErrorMsg

```
void XtErrorMsg(  /* Superseded by XtAppErrorMsg */
    const String name,     /* Error name                 */
    const String type,     /* Error type                 */
    const String class,    /* Resource class             */
    const String default,  /* Default error message      */
    String*      params,   /* Values for error message   */
    Cardinal*    nparams); /* Number of values in "params" */
```

Calls an error handler with arguments to help locate an error message and display the message.

XtFindFile

```
String XtFindFile(
    const String   path,  /* List of pathnames               */
```

```
Substitution    subst, /* List of substitutions    */
Cardinal        nsubst,/* Number of substitutions   */
XtFilePredicate pfunc);/* Function to evaluate names */
```

Searches for a file using substitutions in a path list. Returns a filename, if the function `pfunc` declares one to be suitable. Please consult the book on *X Window System Toolkit* by Paul Asente and Ralph Swick (see beginning of this appendix for details).

XtFree

```
void XtFree(
    char* ptr); /* Deallocate this memory */
```

Frees a block of memory allocated by a toolkit function.

XtGetActionKeysym

```
KeySym XtGetActionKeysym(
    XEvent*    ev,          /* Event passed to action proc */
    Modifiers* mod_return); /* Modifiers returned here      */
```

Returns the keysym and modifiers of an event in the translation table that match the keyboard event specified by the ev argument.

XtGetActionList

```
void XtGetActionList(
    WidgetClass  widget_class,     /* Widget class         */
    XtActionList* actions_return,  /* Actions returned here */
    Cardinal*    num_actions_return); /* Number of actions */
```

Provides information about the action table defined by the specified widget class.

XtGetApplicationNameAndClass

```
void XtGetApplicationNameAndClass(
    Display* display,      /* Identifies the X server     */
    String* name_return,   /* Instance name returned here */
    String* class_return);/* Class name returned here     */
```

Returns the instance name and the class name of the application. These are the same values that were passed to `XtDisplayInitialize`. You should not free the strings that are returned.

XtGetApplicationResources

```
void XtGetApplicationResources(
    Widget       widget,    /* Get resources for this    */
    XtPointer    base,      /* Where to write resources */
    XtResourceList resources, /* Resources to get        */
    Cardinal     nresource, /* Number of resources      */
    ArgList      args,      /* Command-line arguments    */
    Cardinal     nargs);    /* Number of arguments       */
```

Loads resources from the resource database associated with the specified widget's display.

XtGetClassExtension

```
XtPointer XtGetClassExtension(
    WidgetClass wclass,     /* Widget class with extension */
    Cardinal    byte_offset,/* Offset from base of widget  */
                            /* class extension field       */
    XrmQuark    type,       /* Name of class extension     */
    long        version,    /* Acceptable version number   */
    Cardinal    record_size);/* Minimum size of extension  */
                            /* record (you can use 0)      */
```

Returns a pointer to a class extension record.

XtGetConstraintResourceList

```
void XtGetConstraintResourceList(
    WidgetClass     wclass,     /* Resources for this class */
    XtResourceList* res_return, /* Returned resource list   */
    Cardinal*       numres_return);/* Number of resources   */
```

Returns the resources for a particular widget class. The resource list is returned in res_return.

XtGetDisplays

```
void XtGetDisplays(
    XtAppContext app_context, /* For this application context */
    Display***   dpy_return,  /* Returned list of displays    */
    Cardinal*    num_dpy_return); /* Number of displays        */
```

Provides a list of open X display connections associated with the specified application context.

XtGetErrorDatabase

```
XrmDatabase *XtGetErrorDatabase(void);
                /* Superseded by XtAppGetErrorDatabase */
```

Returns the error database.

XtGetErrorDatabaseText

```
void XtGetErrorDatabaseText(
        /* Superseded by XtAppGetErrorDatabaseText */
    const String name,    /* Name of error          */
    const String type,    /* Type of error          */
    const String class,   /* Resource class of error */
    const String default, /* Default error message   */
    String       buffer,  /* Returned error message  */
    int          nbytes); /* Size of buffer in bytes */
```

Retrieves an error message from the error database.

XtGetGC

```
GC XtGetGC(
    Widget     widget,  /* Widget used to locate GC       */
    XtGCMask   gcvmask, /* Bitmask indicates desired values */
    XGCValues* values); /* GC values returned here        */
```

Returns selected graphics attributes in the values structure. The bitmask gcvmask indicates which attributes of the graphics context should be returned.

XtGetKeyboardFocusWidget

```
Widget XtGetKeyboardFocusWidget(
    Widget widget);
```

Returns the widget that would eventually receive a keyboard event if it were sent to the specified widget.

XtGetKeysymTable

```
KeySym* XtGetKeysymTable(
    Display* dpy,      /* Get table for this X server whose */
    KeyCode* min_keycode_return,  /* Minimum valid keycode */
    int*     keysyms_per_keycode_return);/* A return value */
```

Returns a pointer to the X server's keycode-to-keysym mapping table.

XtGetMultiClickTime

```
int XtGetMultiClickTime(
    Display* dpy);
```

Returns the multiclick time in milliseconds for the specified X server.

XtGetResourceList

```
void XtGetResourceList(
    WidgetClass     wclass,     /* Resources for this class */
    XtResourceList* res_return, /* Returned resource list   */
    Cardinal*    numres_return);/* Number of resources      */
```

Returns the resources for a particular widget class. The resource list is returned in res_return. When you are finished with this list, call XtFree to deallocate it.

XtGetSelectionParameters

```
void XtGetSelectionParameters(
    Widget      owner,     /* Widget owning selection       */
    Atom        selection, /* Identifies the selection      */
    XtRequestId request_id,/* Requestor's ID for incremental */
                           /* selections                    */
```

```
Atom*        type_return, /* Property type of parameters */
XtPointer*   value_return,/* Pointer to parameters       */
unsigned long*  length_return,/* Number of elements in   */
                                  /* returned value       */
int*         format_return); /* Size in bits of element  */
```

Retrieves target parameters for a selection request.

XtGetSelectionRequest

```
XSelectionRequestEvent *XtGetSelectionRequest(
    Widget     widget,   /* Widget owning selection      */
    Atom       selection,/* Selection being processed    */
    XtRequestId req_id); /* ID for incremental conversion */
```

Returns the SelectionRequest event that triggered a call to the convert selection procedure of the widget. You generally need not call this function directly.

XtGetSelectionTimeout

```
unsigned int XtGetSelectionTimeout(void);
        /* Superseded by XtAppGetSelectionTimeout */
```

Returns the selection timeout value (in milliseconds).

XtGetSelectionValue

```
void XtGetSelectionValue(
    Widget    widget,      /* Widget requesting selection  */
    Atom      selection,   /* Get this selection           */
    Atom      target,      /* Convert to this type         */
    XtSelectionCallbackProc callback,/* Procedure to be    */
                           /* called after getting selection */
    XtPointer client_data, /* Data passed to callback      */
    Time      time);       /* Timestamp of triggering event*/
```

Retrieves the specified selection in a single transfer.

XtGetSelectionValueIncremental

```
void XtGetSelectionValueIncremental(
    Widget    widget,      /* Widget requesting selection  */
    Atom      selection,   /* Get this selection           */
    Atom      target,      /* Convert to this type         */
    XtSelectionCallbackProc callback,/* Procedure to be    */
                           /* called after getting selection */
    XtPointer client_data, /* Data passed to callback      */
    Time      time);       /* Timestamp of triggering event*/
```

Retrieves the specified selection, using incremental transfer.

XtGetSelectionValues

```
void XtGetSelectionValues(
    Widget    widget,       /* Widget requesting selection  */
    Atom      selection,    /* Get from this selection      */
    Atom      *targets,     /* Convert to these types       */
    int       count,        /* Number of atoms in targets   */
    XtSelectionCallbackProc callback,/* Procedure to be
                            called after getting selection */
    XtPointer *client_data,/* List of data for the callback*/
    Time      time);        /* Timestamp of triggering event*/
```

The effect of calling XtGetSelectionValues is identical to calling XtGetSelectionValue once for each target type in the targets array.

XtGetSelectionValuesIncremental

```
void XtGetSelectionValuesIncremental(
    Widget    widget,       /* Widget requesting selection  */
    Atom      selection,    /* Get from this selection      */
    Atom      *targets,     /* Convert to these types       */
    int       count,        /* Number of atoms in targets   */
    XtSelectionCallbackProc callback,/* Procedure to be
                            called after getting selection */
    XtPointer *client_data,/* List of data for the callback*/
    Time      time);        /* Timestamp of triggering event*/
```

The effect of calling XtGetSelectionValueIncremental is identical to calling XtGetSelectionValueIncremental once for each target type in the targets array.

XtGetSubresources

```
void XtGetSubresources(
    Widget        widget,/* Subpart of this widget     */
    XtPointer     base,  /* Write resources here       */
    const String  name,  /* Name of subpart            */
    const String  class, /* Class of subpart           */
    XtResourceList res,  /* Resource list of subpart   */
    Cardinal      nres,  /* Number of resources        */
    ArgList       args,  /* Resource specifications     */
    Cardinal      nargs);/* Number of entries in args  */
```

Gets the resources for the subpart of a widget.

XtGetSubvalues

```
void XtGetSubvalues(
    XtPointer     base,  /* Write resources here       */
    XtResourceList res,  /* Resource list of subpart   */
    Cardinal      nres,  /* Number of resources        */
    ArgList       args,  /* Resource specifications     */
    Cardinal      nargs);/* Number of entries in args  */
```

Gets values of resources that are not associated with a widget (that is why there is no widget ID in the argument list).

XtGetValues

```
void XtGetValues(
    Widget    widget, /* Get this widget's resources */
    ArgList   args,   /* Resource specifications    */
    Cardinal nargs); /* Number of entries in args  */
```

Retrieves a widget's resources. You specify the resources to be retrieved in the argument list `args`.

XtGrabButton

```
void XtGrabButton(
    Widget       widget,    /* Widget where grab occurs   */
    int          button,    /* Button to grab             */
    Modifiers    modifiers, /* Allowable modifier keys    */
    Boolean      own_events,/* True=report events normally */
    unsigned int event_mask,/* Report these events        */
    int          ptr_mode,/* GrabModeSync or GrabModeAsync */
    int          kbd_mode,/* GrabModeSync or GrabModeAsync */
    Window       cwin,      /* Confining window for pointer*/
    Cursor       cursor);   /* Cursor shown during grab   */
```

Passively grabs a specified pointer button. Grabbing means that all subsequent events are dispatched to the client that initiated the grab. A passive grab becomes active only when the user presses the button and key combination specified in the call to `XtGrabButton`.

XtGrabKey

```
void XtGrabKey(
    Widget    widget,    /* Widget where grab occurs    */
    KeyCode   keycode,   /* Key being grabbed           */
    Modifiers modifiers, /* Allowable modifier keys     */
    Boolean   own_events,/* True=report events normally */
    int       ptr_mode, /* GrabModeSync or GrabModeAsync */
    int       kbd_mode); /* GrabModeSync or GrabModeAsync */
```

Passively grabs a single key on the keyboard.

XtGrabKeyboard

```
int XtGrabKeyboard(
    Widget    widget,    /* Widget where grab occurs    */
    Boolean   own_events,/* True=report events normally */
    int       ptr_mode, /* GrabModeSync or GrabModeAsync */
    int       kbd_mode, /* GrabModeSync or GrabModeAsync */
    Time      time);     /* Timestamp or CurrentTime    */
```

Actively grabs the keyboard. Returns `GrabNotViewable` if the widget is not realized. An active grab starts as soon as the client calls one of the functions `XtGrabKeyboard` or `XtGrabPointer`.

XtGrabPointer

```
int XtGrabPointer(
    Widget      widget,    /* Widget where grab occurs       */
    Boolean     own_events,/* True=report events normally    */
    unsigned int event_mask,/* Report these events           */
    int         ptr_mode,  /* GrabModeSync or GrabModeAsync  */
    int         kbd_mode,  /* GrabModeSync or GrabModeAsync  */
    Window      cwin,      /* Confining window for pointer   */
    Cursor      cursor,    /* Cursor shown during grab       */
    Time        time);     /* Timestamp or CurrentTime       */
```

Actively grabs the pointer. Returns `GrabNotViewable` if the widget is not realized.

XtHasCallbacks

```
XtCallbackStatus XtHasCallbacks(
    Widget  w,       /* Search this widget's callback list */
    const String callback_name); /* Name of list to check */
```

Checks whether a widget has the specified callback list. The function returns one of the following values:

`XtCallbackHasNoList`	No such callback list
`XtCallbackHasNone`	The callback list exists but is empty
`XtCallbackHasSome`	The callback list exists and has at least one entry

XtHooksOfDisplay

```
Widget XtHooksOfDisplay(Display* dpy);
```

Returns a "hook" object whose resources are the callback lists for hooks.

XtInitialize

```
Widget XtInitialize(  /* Superseded by XtAppInitialize */
    const String      name,    /* Name of application    */
    const String      class,   /* Class name of appl.    */
    XrmOptionDescRec* options,  /* Acceptable options     */
    Cardinal          noptions, /* Elements in "options"  */
    Cardinal*         argc,     /* Number of cmd line args*/
    char**            argv);    /* Command-line options   */
```

Initializes the Xt Intrinsics, creates a default application context, and sets up a connection to the X server identified by the `DISPLAY` environment variable. Then, `XtInitialize` calls `XtAppCreateShell` to create a top-level shell widget and returns the widget ID.

XtInitializeWidgetClass

```
void XtInitializeWidgetClass(
    WidgetClass wclass);
```

Initializes a widget class.

XtInsertEventHandler

```
void XtInsertEventHandler(
    Widget          w, /* Register handler for this widget  */
    EventMask       eventMask, /* Handler for this event     */
    Boolean         nonmaskable,/* True=for nonmaskable events*/
    XtEventHandler proc,       /* The event handler          */
    XtPointer       client_data,/* Data passed to handler     */
    XtListPosition position);   /* Position of handler in list*/
```

Inserts an event handler at a specified position in the list of handlers for the widget.

XtInsertEventTypeHandler

```
void XtInsertEventHandler(
void XtInsertEventTypeHandler(
    Widget          w, /* Register handler for this widget  */
    int             type, /* Register for this event type    */
    XtPointer       select_data,/* Data used to select or     */
                               /*deselect events from server */
    XtEventHandler proc,       /* The event handler          */
    XtPointer       client_data,/* Data passed to handler     */
    XtListPosition position);   /* Position of handler in list*/
```

Inserts an event handler at a specified position in the list of handlers for the widget.

XtInsertRawEventHandler

```
void XtInsertRawEventHandler(
    Widget          w, /* Register handler for this widget  */
    EventMask       eventMask, /* Handler for this event     */
    Boolean         nonmaskable,/* True=for nonmaskable events*/
    XtEventHandler proc,       /* The event handler          */
    XtPointer       client_data,/* Data passed to handler     */
    XtListPosition position);   /* Position of handler in list*/
```

Inserts an event handler at a specified position in the list of handlers for the widget. Unlike `XtInsertEventHandler`, `XtInsertRawEventHandler` does not modify the widget's event mask and does not solicit events from the X server by calling the Xlib function `XSelectInput`.

XtInstallAccelerators

```
void XtInstallAccelerators(
    Widget destination,/* Install on this widget by */
    Widget source);    /* copying from this one     */
```

Augments the accelerators in the destination widget with those from the source widget.

XtInstallAllAccelerators

```
void XtInstallAllAccelerators(
    Widget destination,/* Install on this widget by */
    Widget source);    /* copying from this one    */
```

Augments the accelerators in the destination widget with those from the source widget and all the descendants of source.

XtIsApplicationShell

```
Boolean XtIsApplicationShell(widget);
```

Returns True if widget is of class ApplicationShell or is derived from an ApplicationShell.

XtIsComposite

```
Boolean XtIsComposite(Widget w);
```

Returns True if widget is of class Composite or is derived from a Composite.

XtIsConstraint

```
Boolean XtIsConstraint(Widget w);
```

Returns True if widget is of class Constraint or is derived from a Constraint.

XtIsManaged

```
c1Boolean XtIsManaged(Widget rectobj);
```

Returns True if widget is currently managed.

XtIsObject

```
Boolean XtIsObject(Widget object);
```

Returns True if widget is of class Object or is derived from an Object.

XtIsOverrideShell

```
Boolean XtIsOverrideShell(Widget w);
```

Returns True if widget is of class OverrideShell or is derived from an OverrideShell.

XtIsRealized

```
Boolean XtIsRealized(Widget widget);
```

Returns True if widget is currently realized.

XtIsRectObj

```
Boolean XtIsRectObj(Widget object);
```

Returns True if widget is of class RectObj or is derived from a RectObj.

XtIsSensitive

```
Boolean XtIsSensitive(Widget widget);
```

Returns True if widget is currently sensitive. When a widget is *sensitive*, user input events are dispatched to it.

XtIsSessionShell

```
Boolean XtIsSessionShell(Widget w);
```

Returns True if widget is of class SessionShell or is derived from a SessionShell.

XtIsShell

```
Boolean XtIsShell(Widget w);
```

Returns True if widget is of class Shell or is derived from a Shell.

XtIsSubclass

```
Boolean XtIsSubclass(
    Widget      widget, /* Is this widget  */
    WidgetClass wclass);/* of this class?  */
```

Returns True if the specified widget is of class wclass or if the widget is an instance of a subclass of wclass.

XtIsTopLevelShell

```
Boolean XtIsTopLevelShell(Widget widget);
```

Returns True if widget is of class TopLevelShell or is an instance of a subclass of TopLevelShell.

XtIsTransientShell

```
Boolean XtIsTransientShell(Widget widget);
```

Returns True if widget is of class TransientShell or is an instance of a subclass of TransientShell.

XtIsVendorShell

```
Boolean XtIsVendorShell(Widget widget);
```

Returns `True` if widget is of class `VendorShell` or is an instance of a subclass of `VendorShell`.

XtIsWidget

```
Boolean XtIsWidget(Widget object);
```

Returns `True` if widget is of class `Core` or is an instance of a subclass of `Core`.

XtIsWMShell

```
Boolean XtIsWMShell(Widget widget);
```

Returns `True` if widget is of class `WMShell` or is an instance of a subclass of `WMShell`.

XtKeysymToKeycodeList

```
void XtKeysymToKeycodeList(
    Display*  display,  /* Search key mapping of this server */
    KeySym    keysym,            /* Look for this keysym      */
    KeyCode** keycodes_return, /* Returned keycode list       */
    Cardinal* keycount_return);/* Number of keycodes in list*/
```

In `keycode_return`, this function returns all the keycodes that have the specified `keysym` in the keyboard mapping table. You have to free the memory allocated for the keycode list by calling `XtFree`.

XtLastTimestampProcessed

```
Time XtLastTimestampProcessed(
    Display* dpy); /* Identifies the X server */
```

Returns the timestamp for the most recent event (with a timestamp) received from the specified X server. The return value is zero if no event containing a timestamp has arrived from the server.

XtLastEventProcessed

```
XEvent* XtLastEventProcessed(
    Display* dpy); /* Identifies the X server */
```

Returns a pointer to an `XEvent` structure containing the last event provided to the `XtDispatchEvent` function for the specified display. The return value is `NULL` if there have been no events.

XtMainLoop

```
void XtMainLoop(void);   /* Superseded by XtAppMainLoop */
```

Starts the main event processing loop of the application. You must call `XtInitialize` before calling `XtMainLoop`. Starting with X11R4, you should use `XtAppMainLoop` in place of `XtMainLoop`.

XtMakeGeometryRequest

```
XtGeometryResult XtMakeGeometryRequest(
    Widget          widget,       /* Change this widget */
    XtWidgetGeometry* request,    /* Requested geometry */
    XtWidgetGeometry* reply_return);/* Final geometry      */
```

Requests the parent of `widget` to change `widget`'s geometry.

XtMakeResizeRequest

```
XtGeometryResult XtMakeResizeRequest(
    Widget     widget,       /* Resize this widget     */
    Dimension  width,        /* Desired width          */
    Dimension  height,       /* Desired height         */
    Dimension* replyWidth,   /* Width after resizing   */
    Dimension* replyHeight);/* Height after  resizing */
```

Requests the parent of `widget` to resize `widget`.

XtMalloc

```
char *XtMalloc(
    Cardinal numbytes); /* Number of bytes to allocate */
```

Allocates a specified number of bytes of storage and returns a pointer to the newly allocated storage. Calls the error handler if the memory allocation fails.

XtManageChild

```
void XtManageChild(Widget child);
```

Manages (resizes and positions) the specified child widget.

XtMapWidget

```
void XtMapWidget(Widget widget);
```

Maps the specified widget's window.

XtMergeArgLists

```
ArgList XtMergeArgLists(
    ArgList  args1,  /* First argument list        */
    Cardinal nargs1, /* Number of entries in args1 */
    ArgList  args2,  /* Second argument list       */
    Cardinal nargs2);/* Number of entries in args2 */
```

Appends the argument lists `args1` and `args2` and returns a pointer to the combined list. Does not check for duplicates. When you no longer need the merged list, you should free its storage by calling `XtFree`.

XtName

```
String XtName(Widget object);
```

Returns the name of `object`.

XtNameToWidget

```
Widget XtNameToWidget(
    Widget       root, /* Start of search hierarchy      */
    const String name);/* Look for a widget of this name */
```

Searches for a widget with a specific name in a hierarchy and returns the widget's ID if it finds one. If there is no such widget in the hierarchy, `XtNameToWidget` returns `NULL`.

XtNew

```
#define XtNew(type) \
    ((type *) XtMalloc((unsigned) sizeof(type)))
```

Allocates storage of a specific type by calling `XtMalloc`.

XtNewString

```
String XtNewString(String str);
```

Allocates enough storage to hold `str` and then copies `str` into that storage.

XtNextEvent

```
void XtNextEvent(       /* Superseded by XtAppNextEvent */
    XEvent* event);
```

Returns the next event from the queue of the default application context.

XtNoticeSignal

```
void XtNoticeSignal(
    XtSignalId id); /* ID returned by XtAppAddSignal */
```

Calls from an operating system-dependent signal handler to invoke an Intrinsics signal handler that was registered earlier by calling `XtAppAddSignal`.

XtNumber

```
#define XtNumber(arr) \
    ((Cardinal) (sizeof(arr)/sizeof(arr[0])))
```

Returns the size of an array.

XtOffset

```
Cardinal XtOffset(p_type,field);
```

Returns the byte offset of a field within a structure. The p_type argument is a pointer to the structure and field is the name of a field in that structure.

XtOffsetOf

```
Cardinal XtOffset(p_type,field);
```

Similar to XtOffset, but more portable. It also returns the byte offset of a field within a structure. The p_type argument is a pointer to the structure and field is the name of a field in that structure.

XtOpenApplication

```
Widget XtOpenApplication( /* Replaces XtAppInitialize in X11R6 */
    XtAppContext*    app_context_return,/* Returned context    */
    const String     application_class, /* Appl. class name    */
    XrmOptionDescList options,           /* Command-line opt.   */
    Cardinal         noptions,           /* Number of options   */
    Cardinal*        argc_in_out,        /* Command-line arg    */
    String*          argv_in_out,        /* count and args      */
    const String*    fallback_resources,/* Fallback resources */
    ArgList          args,               /* Arguments          */
    Cardinal         nargs);             /* Num. of arguments*/
```

Initializes the Xt Intrinsics, creates an application context, opens a connection to the X server identified by the DISPLAY environment variable, and creates a top-level shell. When the function returns, the app_context_return argument has the application context. This function returns the ID of the newly created application shell widget.

XtOpenDisplay

```
Display *XtOpenDisplay(
    XtAppContext     app,       /* Application context      */
    const String     dname,     /* Name of X server or NULL */
    const String     name,      /* Name of application      */
    const String     class,     /* Class name of appl.      */
    XrmOptionDescRec* options,   /* Acceptable options       */
    Cardinal         noptions,/* Elements in "options"    */
    Cardinal*        argc,      /* Number of cmd line args  */
    String*          argv);     /* Command-line arguments   */
```

Opens a connection with an X server and adds the connection to the specified application context. Returns a pointer to the Display structure that identifies the connection to this X server.

XtOverrideTranslations

```
void XtOverrideTranslations(
    Widget          w,   /* Alter this widget's translations */
    XtTranslations new);/* Merge in these translations      */
```

Merges a set of translations with a widget's existing translations. If new has a translation that already exists in the widget, the old one is overwritten by the new version.

XtOwnSelection

```
Boolean XtOwnSelection(
    Widget  widget,  /* Widget that wants to own selection */
    Atom    selection,/* Selection it wants to own          */
    Time    time,    /* Timestamp of triggering event      */
    XtConvertSelectionProc convert,/* Function to call when */
                      /* selection is requested by others   */
    XtLoseSelectionProc lose, /* Call when ownership is lost*/
    XtSelectionDoneProc done);/* Call after a successful    */
                      /* transfer of selection      */
```

Indicates that the specified widget wants ownership of a selection. Returns True if the widget receives ownership; otherwise, returns False.

XtOwnSelectionIncremental

```
Boolean XtOwnSelectionIncremental(
    Widget  widget,  /* Widget that wants to own selection */
    Atom    selection,/* Selection it wants to own          */
    Time    time,    /* Timestamp of triggering event      */
    XtConvertSelectionIncrProc convert,/* Function to call  */
              /* when selection is requested by others   */
    XtLoseSelectionIncrProc lose, /* Function to call       */
                          /* when ownership is lost */
    XtSelectionDoneIncrProc done, /* Function to call       */
                          /* when transfer is done  */
    XtCancelConvertSelectionProc cancel,/* Function to call */
                          /* if transfer is aborted */
    XtPointer client_data); /* Data passed to each callback */
```

Indicates that the specified widget wants ownership of a selection and that the widget wants to provide the selection incrementally. Returns True if the widget receives ownership; otherwise, returns False.

XtParent

```
Widget XtParent(Widget widget);
```

Returns ID of a widget's parent.

XtParseAcceleratorTable

```
XtAccelerators XtParseAcceleratorTable(
    const String source); /* Accelerator table to be parsed */
```

Parses the specified accelerator table and returns a pointer to an internal parsed representation of the table.

XtParseTranslationTable

```
XtTranslations XtParseTranslationTable(
    const String source); /* Translation table to be parsed */
```

Parses the specified translation table and returns a pointer to an internal parsed representation of the table.

XtPeekEvent

```
Boolean XtPeekEvent( /* Superseded by XtAppPeekEvent */
    XEvent* ev);    /* Returned event            */
```

If the event queue of the default application context is not empty, this function returns True and provides information about the first event in the queue through the ev argument. If the event queue is empty, this function waits for an event.

XtPending

```
XtInputMask XtPending(void); /* Superseded by XtAppPending */
```

Returns a nonzero value if there are events (from any source such as the X server or another input) waiting for the default application context.

XtPopdown

```
void XtPopdown(Widget widget);
```

Unmaps a pop-up shell widget.

XtPopup

```
void XtPopup(
    Widget     w,       /* Maps this pop-up shell widget    */
    XtGrabKind grab);   /* Controls handling of input events */
```

Pops up a shell widget. The grab argument can be one of XtGrabNone, XtGrabExclusive, or XtGrabNonexclusive.

XtPopupSpringLoaded

```
void XtPopupSpringLoaded(Widget widget);
```

Maps a spring-loaded pop-up shell widget.

XtProcessEvent

```
void XtProcessEvent(     /* Superseded by XtAppProcessEvent */
    XtInputMask  mask); /* Identifies event to process     */
```

Processes an event from the source specified by the mask, which can be one of the following:

`XtAlternateInput`	Refers to an alternate input (set up by `XtAddInput`)
`XtIMTime`	Refers to a timeout event (set up by `XtAddTimeOut`)
`XtImXEvent`	Refers to a normal X event

XtQueryGeometry

```
XtGeometryResult XtQueryGeometry(
    Widget            widget, /* Query this widget        */
    XtWidgetGeometry* intended,/* Planned geometry changes */
    XtWidgetGeometry* reply_return); /* Preferred geometry */
```

Retrieves a widget's preferred geometry. Usually called by a parent widget to determine the preferred geometry of a child.

XtRealizeWidget

```
void XtRealizeWidget(Widget widget);
```

Creates a window for the widget.

```
char *XtRealloc(
    char*   ptr, /* Resize this block of memory */
    Cardinal num);/* New size of the block      */
```

Resizes a block of memory whose address is in ptr to hold at least num bytes. The block of memory may be moved if necessary. If ptr is NULL, XtRealloc allocates a new block.

XtRegisterCaseConverter

```
void XtRegisterCaseConverter(
    Display*  dpy,  /* Identifies X server          */
    XtCaseProc proc, /* This is the converter function */
    KeySym     start,/* Handle keysyms between start  */
    KeySym     stop);/* and stop                      */
```

Registers a converter for translating keysyms to upper- and lowercase.

XtRegisterDrawable

```
void XtRegisterDrawable(
    Display* dpy,          /* Identifies drawable's display */
    Drawable drawable,  /* Register this drawable        */
    Widget    widget); /* Register for this widget     */
```

Registers a drawable (a window or a pixmap) for the specified widget so that future calls to XtWindowToWidget with that drawable as argument will return the widget.

XtRegisterExtensionSelector

```
void XtRegisterExtensionSelector(
    Display*         dpy,               /* Identifies X server  */
    int              min_event_type, /* Range of event types */
    int              max_event_type, /* for this extension   */
    XtExtensionSelectProc proc,     /* Function registered  */
    XtPointer        client_data); /* Data for the function */
```

Registers a function for delivery of extension events (events used by extensions to X protocol) to widgets.

XtRegisterGrabAction

```
void XtRegisterGrabAction(
    XtActionProc action_proc,/* Function for grab processing*/
    Boolean      own_events, /* True=report events normally */
    unsigned int event_mask, /* Report these events         */
    int          ptr_mode, /* GrabModeSync or GrabModeAsync */
    int          kbd_mode);/* GrabModeSync or GrabModeAsync */
```

Sets up a function to be called when a specified grab occurs in a widget.

XtReleaseGC

```
void XtReleaseGC(
    Widget w,   /* Determines GC's display */
    GC     gc); /* GC to be released       */
```

Frees up a shared graphics context (GC) when it is no longer needed.

XtReleasePropertyAtom

```
void XtReleasePropertyAtom(
    Widget widget, /* Widget used to reserve atom   */
    Atom   atom); /* Identifies atom to be released */
```

Releases the atom reserved by an earlier call to XtReservePropertyAtom.

XtRemoveActionHook

```
void XtRemoveActionHook(
    XtActionHookId id); /* Hook procedure to be removed */
```

Removes the specified action hook procedure.

XtRemoveBlockHook

```
void XtRemoveBlockHook(
    XtBlockHookId id); /* ID of hook procedure to remove */
```

Removes the specified block hook procedure.

XtRemoveAllCallbacks

```
void XtRemoveAllCallbacks(
    Widget       widget,         /* Affected widget      */
    const String callback_name);/* Name of callback list */
```

Removes all callback functions from the specified callback list of the widget.

XtRemoveCallback

```
void XtRemoveCallback(
    Widget         widget,        /* Affected widget       */
    const String   callback_name, /* Name of callback list */
    XtCallbackProc callback,      /* Remove this callback  */
    XtPointer      client_data);  /* Data for that callback */
```

Removes a specific callback from a widget's callback list.

XtRemoveCallbacks

```
void XtRemoveCallbacks(
    Widget         widget,        /* Affected widget       */
    const String   callback_name,/* Name of callback list */
    XtCallbackList callbacks);/* List of callbacks to remove*/
```

Removes a number of callbacks registered for the callback named `callback_name`.

XtRemoveEventHandler

```
void XtRemoveEventHandler(
    Widget         widget,      /* Remove from this widget */
    EventMask      eventMask,   /* To handle these events  */
    Boolean        nonmaskable, /* For nonmaskable events? */
    XtEventHandler proc,        /* The event handler       */
    XtPointer      client_data);/* Data for the handler    */
```

Removes an event handler meant for processing events matching `eventMask`. Use the constant `XtAllEvents` as the `eventMask` to remove event handlers for all events.

XtRemoveEventTypeHandler

```
void XtRemoveEventTypeHandler(
    Widget          widget,      /* Remove from this widget */
    int             type,        /* Event type              */
    XtPointer       select_data, /* Data used to select     */
                                 /* or deselect events      */
    XtEventHandler  proc,        /* The event handler       */
    XtPointer       client_data);/* Data for the handler    */
```

Removes an event handler registered by `XtInsertEventTypeHandler`.

XtRemoveGrab

```
void XtRemoveGrab(Widget widget);
```

Removes a grab (exclusive input redirection to a widget) for the specified widget.

XtRemoveInput

```
void XtRemoveInput(
    XtInputId id);/* ID of input source from XtAppAddInput */
```

Stops accepting input from an alternate input source identified by `id`.

XtRemoveRawEventHandler

```
void XtRemoveRawEventHandler(
    Widget          widget,      /* Remove from this widget  */
    EventMask       eventMask,   /* To handle these events   */
    Boolean         nonmaskable, /* For non-maskable events? */
    XtEventHandler  proc,        /* The event handler        */
    XtPointer       client_data);/* Data for the handler     */
```

Removes an event handler that was set up for events matching `eventMask`. This function is like `XtRemoveEventHandler` except that it does not affect the widget's event mask and it does not call the Xlib function `XSelectInput`.

XtRemoveSignal

```
void XtRemoveSignal(
    XtSignalId id); /* ID returned by XtAppAddSignal */
```

Removes the specified Intrinsics signal handler. You should disable signals before removing the signal handler.

XtRemoveTimeOut

```
void XtRemoveTimeOut(
    XtIntervalId timer);/* ID returned by XtAppAddTimeOut */
```

Removes a timeout before it has occurred.

XtRemoveWorkProc

```
void  XtRemoveWorkProc(
    XtWorkProcId id);/* ID returned when WorkProc was added */
```

Removes a "work procedure" registered earlier by calling XtAppAddWorkProc.

XtReservePropertyAtom

```
Atom XtReservePropertyAtom(
    Widget widget); /* Widget reserving the atom */
```

Returns a unique atom that may be used to store properties when handling conversion requests from the specified widget.

XtResolvePathname

```
String XtResolvePathname(
    Display*       dpy,    /* Identifies the X server    */
    const String   type,   /* Type substituted into path */
    const String   fname,  /* Filename part of path      */
    const String   suffix, /* Suffix part of path        */
    const String   path,   /* List of pathnames          */
    Substitution   subst,  /* List of substitutions      */
    Cardinal       nsubst, /* Number of substitutions    */
    XtFilePredicate pfunc); /* Function to evaluate names */
```

Searches for a file using substitutions in a path list. Returns a filename, if the function pfunc declares one to be suitable. Please consult *X Window System Toolkit* by Paul Asente and Ralph Swick (see beginning of this appendix for details). This function calls XtFindFile with the following substitutions:

%L Refers to the language specification of the X server

%N Refers to the fname argument (application's class if fname is NULL)

%S Refers to the suffix argument

%T Refers to the type argument

%c Refers to the "codeset" portion of the xnlLanguage resource

%l refers to the language portion of the xnlLanguage resource

%t refers to the territory portion of the xnlLanguage resource

XtScreen

```
Screen *XtScreen(Widget widget);
```

Returns the Screen pointer of a widget.

XtScreenDatabase

```
XrmDatabase XtScreenDatabase(Screen* screen);
```

Returns the resource database for a specified screen.

XtScreenOfObject

```
Screen *XtScreenOfObject(Widget object);
```

Same as XtScreen when object is a descendant of the Core class. However, if object is of class Object, this function returns the Screen pointer for the nearest ancestor of object that is a widget.

XtSendSelectionRequest

```
void XtSendSelectionRequest(
    Widget  requestor, /* Widget requesting selection      */
    Atom    selection, /* Identifies selection            */
    Time    time);     /* Time of event triggering request */
```

Sends a selection conversion request to the owner of the specified selection.

XtSessionGetToken

```
XtCheckpointToken XtSessionGetToken(
    Widget  widget); /* The session widget */
```

Returns a checkpoint token if the session manager has started a checkpoint operation (or NULL if no checkpoint operation is in progress). To indicate completion of the checkpoint operation, call XtSessionReturnToken with the checkpoint token.

XtSessionReturnToken

```
void XtSessionReturnToken(
    XtCheckpointToken token);/* Checkpoint token to be returned */
```

Indicates completion of a checkpoint operation by returning a token obtained by a previous call to XtSessionReturnToken.

XtSetArg

```
#define XtSetArg(arg, n, d) \
    ((void)((arg).name = (n), (arg).value = (XtArgVal)(d) ))
```

Sets up the name-value pair in a Arg structure. XtSetArg is commonly used to set up the argument list for widgets.

XtSetErrorHandler

```
void XtSetErrorHandler(/* Superseded by XtAppSetErrorHandler*/
    XtErrorHandler handler)/* New handler for fatal errors   */
```

Registers function to be called when fatal errors occur in the Xt Intrinsics library.

XtSetEventDispatcher

```
XtEventDispatchProc XtSetEventDispatcher(
    Display*              dpy,        /* Identifies X server  */
    int                   event_type, /* Specifies event type */
    XtEventDispatchProc proc);  /* Install this dispatcher  */
```

Registers function to be called when the specified type of event occurs. Returns the previous event handling function. If proc is NULL, installs the default event dispatcher.

XtSetErrorMsgHandler

```
void XtSetErrorMsgHandler(
            /* Superseded by XtAppSetErrorMsgHandler */
    XtErrorMsgHandler handler);/* New error handler  */
```

Registers a handler for fatal errors.

XtSetKeyboardFocus

```
void XtSetKeyboardFocus(
    Widget subtree,/* Set keyboard focus for this hierarchy */
    Widget descendant);/* Widget to receive keyboard events */
```

Redirects keyboard input to the descendant widget.

XtSetKeyTranslator

```
void XtSetKeyTranslator(
    Display* dpy,   /* Register for this X server      */
    XtKeyProc proc); /* Function that will translate keys */
```

Registers a function that will translate keystrokes for the specified X server.

XtSetLanguageProc

```
XtLanguageProc XtSetLanguageProc(
    XtAppContext   app, /* Use in this application context */
    XtLanguageProc proc,/* Set this "language procedure"   */
    XtPointer      client_data); /* Data for "proc"        */
```

Registers a function as the "language procedure" for an application context. The language procedure is called by XtDisplayInitialize to perform any localization required by an application. Returns the previously registered language procedure.

XtSetMappedWhenManaged

```
void XtSetMappedWhenManaged(
    Widget  widget,               /* Affects this widget    */
    Boolean mappedWhenManaged); /* New mapped_when_managed */
```

Sets the mapped_when_managed attribute of the widget. If mapped_when_managed is True, the widget is mapped as soon as it is realized and managed.

XtSetMultiClickTime

```
void XtSetMultiClickTime(
    Display* dpy,            /* Set for this X server */
    int      milliseconds); /* New multiclick time   */
```

Sets the time interval that controls the interpretation of consecutive events. For example, the Xt Intrinsics will consider two successive buttonpress events as a double-click only if the time interval between their occurrences is less than the multiclick time.

XtSetSelectionParameters

```
void XtSetSelectionParameters(
    Widget requestor,/* Widget requesting selection    */
    Atom   selection,/* Name of the selection          */
    Atom   type,     /* Type of property where parameters */
                     /* will be passed                 */
    XtPointer  value,/* Pointer to the parameters      */
    unsigned long length, /* Number of elements in value */
    int             format);/* Size of each element in bits */
```

Sets target parameters for a selection request.

XtSetSelectionTimeout

```
void XtSetSelectionTimeout(
                /* Superseded by XtAppSetSelectionTimeout */
    unsigned long timeout); /* New timeout in milliseconds */
```

Sets the selection timeout value for the default application context.

XtSetSensitive

```
void XtSetSensitive(
    Widget  widget,    /* Set sensitivity of this widget */
    Boolean sensitive);/* New value for the sensitivity  */
```

Sets the sensitivity of a widget. Only sensitive widgets receive input events.

XtSetSubvalues

```
void XtSetSubvalues(
    XtPointer     base,  /* Retrieve resources from this */
    XtResourceList res,  /* Resource list of subpart     */
    Cardinal      nres,  /* Number of resources          */
    ArgList       args,  /* Resource specifications       */
    Cardinal      nargs);/* Number of entries in args     */
```

Sets values of resources that are not associated with a widget.

XtSetTypeConverter

```
void XtSetTypeConverter(
    const String      from_type,    /* Convert from this type  */
    const String      to_type,      /* to this type            */
    XtTypeConverter   converter,    /* Function that converts  */
    XtConvertArgList  convert_args, /* Arguments for function  */
    Cardinal          nargs,        /* Number of arguments     */
    XtCacheType       cache_type,   /* Indicates how to share  */
                                    /*    this resource        */
    XtDestructor      destructor);  /* Function to be called   */
                                    /* before freeing resource */
```

Sets up a function to be called when a resource has to be converted from `from_type` to `to_type`. These types are identified by constants such as `XtRColor`, `XtRPixel`, and `XtRString` which are defined in the file `<X11/StringDefs.h>`. The `cache_type` argument can take one of the following values:

XtCacheAll	Share among all applications displaying at an X server
XtCacheByDisplay	Like `XtCacheAll`, but destructor is called when the display is closed by calling `XtCloseDisplay`
XtCacheNone	Do not share (in other words, no need to save in cache)
XtCacheRefCount	Share, but destroy when no application uses resource

XtSetValues

```
void XtSetValues(
    Widget   widget, /* Get this widget's resources */
    ArgList  args,   /* Resource specifications     */
    Cardinal nargs); /* Number of entries in args   */
```

Sets a widget's resources. You specify the resources to be modified in the argument list `args`.

XtSetWarningHandler

```
void XtSetWarningHandler(
                   /* Superseded by XtAppSetWarningHandler */
 XtErrorMsgHandler handler);/* New nonfatal error handler  */
```

Registers a function to be called when nonfatal errors occur in the Xt Intrinsics library.

XtSetWarningMsgHandler

```
void XtSetWarningMsgHandler(
                /* Superseded by XtAppSetWarningMsgHandler */
    XtErrorHandler handler);/* New nonfatal error handler  */
```

Registers a function to be called when nonfatal errors occur in the Xt Intrinsics library.

XtSetWMColormapWindows

```
void XtSetWMColormapWindows(
    Widget   widget, /* Store WM_COLORMAP_WINDOWS property */
```

```
                    /* on this window                  */
    Widget*  list,  /* List of widgets whose windows will */
                    /* be listed in the property       */
    Cardinal count); /* Number of widgets in list      */
```

Stores a list of windows in the WM_COLORMAP_WINDOWS property of widget. ICCCM standard-conforming window managers should install the colormap for a window in the list when that window receives the colormap focus.

XtStringConversionWarning

```
void XtStringConversionWarning(
    const String from,     /* Attempted to convert this   */
    const String to_type);/* Tried conversion to this type */
```

Issues a warning message when an attempted conversion fails.

XtSuperclass

```
WidgetClass XtSuperclass(Widget object);
```

Returns ID of widget's super class (the class from which widget's class is derived).

XtToolkitInitialize

```
void XtToolkitInitialize(void);
```

Initializes the Xt Intrinsics library.

XtToolkitThreadInitialize

```
Boolean XtToolkitThreadInitialize(void);
```

Initializes the toolkit for multiple threads. Returns True if the operating system supports multiple threads and the toolkit is thread-safe.

XtTranslateCoords

```
void XtTranslateCoords(
    Widget     widget, /* Coordinates in this widget      */
    Position   x,      /* Coordinates to be translated from*/
    Position   y,      /* widget frame to root window     */
    Position*  rootx,  /* x-y coordinates in root window's */
    Position*  rooty); /* coordinates frame               */
```

Translates the point (x,y) from the widget's coordinate frame to the root window's coordinates and returns the converted coordinates in rootx and rooty.

XtTranslateKey

```
void XtTranslateKey(
    Display*   dpy,                /* Identifies X server    */
    KeyCode    keycode,           /* Translate this keycode */
    Modifiers  modifiers,         /* Value of modifiers     */
    Modifiers* modifiers_return,/* Modifiers examined       */
    KeySym*    keysym_return);   /* Returned keysym         */
```

This is the default keycode-to-keysym translator.

XtTranslateKeycode

```
void XtTranslateKeycode(
    Display*   dpy,                /* Identifies X server    */
    KeyCode    keycode,           /* Translate this keycode */
    Modifiers  modifiers,         /* Value of modifiers     */
    Modifiers* modifiers_return,/* Modifiers examined       */
    KeySym*    keysym_return);   /* Returned keysym         */
```

Translates a keycode to a keysym by calling the currently registered key translator.

XtUngrabButton

```
void XtUngrabButton(
    Widget       widget,      /* Grab is on this widget */
    unsigned int button,      /* For this mouse button  */
    Modifiers    modifiers);  /* With these modifiers   */
```

Ends a passive button grab.

XtUngrabKey

```
void XtUngrabKey(
    Widget    widget,      /* Grab is on this widget */
    KeyCode   keycode,     /* For this key           */
    Modifiers modifiers);  /* With these modifiers   */
```

Ends a passsive key grab.

XtUngrabKeyboard

```
void XtUngrabKeyboard(
    Widget widget,/* Grab is on this widget   */
    Time   time); /* Timestamp or CurrentTime */
```

Ends an active keyboard grab.

XtUngrabPointer

```
void XtUngrabPointer(
    Widget widget,/* Grab is on this widget   */
    Time   time); /* Timestamp or CurrentTime */
```

Ends an active button grab.

XtUninstallTranslations

```
void XtUninstallTranslations(Widget widget);
```

Removes the translations for the specified widget.

XtUnmanageChild

```
void XtUnmanageChild(Widget widget);
```

Removes the specified child widget from its parent's list of managed children.

XtUnmanageChildren

```
void XtUnmanageChildren(
    WidgetList widget,     /* Widgets to unmanage */
    Cardinal   nwidgets); /* Number of widgets   */
```

Removes the specified child widgets from the parent's list of managed children.

XtUnmapWidget

```
void XtUnmapWidget(Widget widget);
```

Unmaps a widget's window.

XtUnrealizeWidget

```
void XtUnrealizeWidget(Widget widget);
```

Destroys the windows of the specified widget and its children.

XtUnregisterDrawable

```
void XtUnregisterDrawablo(
    Display* dpy,           /* Drawable's display      */
    Drawable  drawable); /* Unregister this drawable */
```

Removes the association between a drawable and a widget created by an earlier call to XtRegisterDrawable.

XtVaAppCreateShell

```
Widget XtVaAppCreateShell(
    const String   name ,
    const String   class ,
    WidgetClass    widget_class ,
    Display*       display ,
    ...);
```

Same as XtAppCreateShell except that the resource arguments are replaced with a variable-length argument list whose end is indicated by a NULL.

XtVaAppInitialize

```
Widget XtVaAppInitialize( /* Superseded by XtVaOpenApplication */
    XtAppContext*       app_context_return,
    const String        application_class,
    XrmOptionDescList   options,
    Cardinal            num_options,
    Cardinal*           argc_in_out,
    String*             argv_in_out,
    const String*       fallback_resources,
    ...);
```

Same as XtAppInitialize except that the resource arguments are replaced with a variable-length argument list whose end is indicated by a NULL.

XtVaCreateArgsList

```
XtVarArgsList XtVaCreateArgsList(
    XtPointer   unused, ...);
```

Creates a variable-length argument list and returns a pointer to the newly created structure.

XtVaCreateManagedWidget

```
Widget XtVaCreateManagedWidget(
    const String name,
    WidgetClass  widget_class,
    Widget       parent,
    ...);
```

Same as XtCreateManagedWidget except that the resource arguments are replaced with a variable-length argument list whose end is indicated by a NULL.

XtVaCreatePopupShell

```
Widget XtVaCreatePopupShell(
    const String   name ,
    WidgetClass    widgetClass,
    Widget         parent,
    ...);
```

Same as XtCreatePopupShell except that the resource arguments are replaced with a variable-length argument list whose end is indicated by a NULL.

XtVaCreateWidget

```
Widget XtVaCreateWidget(
    const String   name ,
    WidgetClass    widget,
    Widget         parent,
    ...);
```

Same as XtCreateWidget except that the resource arguments are replaced with a variable-length argument list whose end is indicated by a NULL.

XtVaGetApplicationResources

```
void XtVaGetApplicationResources(
    Widget        widget,
    XtPointer     base,
    XtResourceList resources,
    Cardinal      num_resources,
    ...);
```

Same as `XtGetApplicationResources` except that the resource arguments are replaced with a variable-length argument list whose end is indicated by a `NULL`.

XtVaGetSubresources

```
void XtVaGetSubresources(
    Widget        widget,
    XtPointer     base,
    const String  name,
    const String  class,
    XtResourceList resources,
    Cardinal      num_resources,
    ...);
```

Same as `XtGetSubresources` except that the resource arguments are replaced with a variable-length argument list whose end is indicated by a `NULL`.

XtVaGetSubvalues

```
void XtVaGetSubvalues(
    XtPointer      base,
    XtResourceList resources,
    Cardinal       num_resources,
    ...);
```

Same as `XtGetSubvalues` except that the resource arguments are replaced with a variable-length argument list whose end is indicated by a `NULL`.

XtVaGetValues

```
void XtVaGetValues(
    Widget    widget,
    ...);
```

Same as `XtGetValues` except that the resource arguments are replaced with a variable-length argument list whose end is indicated by a `NULL`.

XtVaOpenApplication

```
Widget XtVaOpenApplication( /* Replaces XtVaAppInitialize
                                         in X11R6 */
    XtAppContext*     app_context_return,
    const String      application_class,
    XrmOptionDescList options,
```

```
Cardinal          num_options,
Cardinal*         argc_in_out,
String*           argv_in_out,
const String*     fallback_resources,
...);
```

Same as XtOpenApplication except that the resource arguments are replaced with a variable-length argument list whose end is indicated by a NULL.

XtVaSetSubvalues

```
void XtVaSetSubvalues(
   XtPointer      base,
   XtResourceList resources,
   Cardinal       num_resources,
   ...);
```

Same as XtSetSubvalues except that the resource arguments are replaced with a variable-length argument list whose end is indicated by a NULL.

XtVaSetValues

```
void XtVaSetValues(
   Widget     widget,
   ...);
```

Same as XtSetValues except that the resource arguments are replaced with a variable-length argument list whose end is indicated by a NULL.

XtWarning

```
void XtWarning(  /* Superseded by XtAppWarning */
   const String message); /* Warning message  */
```

Calls the current nonfatal error handler and passes a message to it.

XtWarningMsg

```
void XtWarningMsg( /* Superseded by XtAppWarningMsg */
   const String name,     /* Descriptive name of warning */
   const String type,     /* Error type                  */
   const String class,    /* Resource class              */
   const String default,  /* Default warning message     */
   String*      params,   /* Values for warning message  */
   Cardinal*    nparams); /* Number of values in "params"*/
```

Calls the nonfatal error handler with arguments to help locate a warning message and display the message.

XtWidgetToApplicationContext

```
XtAppContext XtWidgetToApplicationContext(Widget widget);
```

Returns the application context for a widget.

XtWindow

```
Window XtWindow(Widget widget);
```

Returns the window ID of a widget.

XtWindowOfObject

```
Window XtWindowOfObject(Widget object);
```

Returns the window ID if object is a widget. If it is not, this function returns the window ID of the nearest ancestor of object that is a widget.

XtWindowToWidget

```
Widget XtWindowToWidget(
    Display* display,/* X server that displays this window */
    Window   window);/* Return widget for this window     */
```

Returns the widget ID for a window.

Xt Intrinsics Data Types

This section provides an alphabetic listing of some data types used in the Xt Intrinsics. In some cases, the exact definition of the data type is not shown because those details are supposed to be hidden from the programmers. However, you can always look at the header file for the definition of these types.

Arg   Defined in: <X11/Intrinsic.h>

ArgList

```
typedef struct
{
    String    name;
    XtArgVal  value;
} Arg, *ArgList;
```

Boolean   Defined in: <X11/Intrinsic.h>

An integer data type that takes the values TRUE or FALSE.

Cardinal   Defined in: <X11/Intrinsic.h>

An unsigned integer data type that, at a minimum, takes the values in the range 0 to 65,536. This data type is used for counting.

Dimension   Defined in: `<X11/Intrinsic.h>`

A data type whose inner details are supposed to be hidden from the programmer.

EventMask   Defined in: `<X11/Intrinsic.h>`

```
typedef unsigned long EventMask;
```

Modifiers   Defined in: `<X11/Intrinsic.h>`

```
typedef unsigned int Modifiers;
```

Opaque   Defined in: `<X11/Intrinsic.h>`

An unsigned integer data type that, at a minimum, takes the values in the range 0 to 65,536. It is used to specify width and height of windows.

Pixel   Defined in: `<X11/Intrinsic.h>`

```
typedef unsigned long Pixel;
```

Position   Defined in: `<X11/Intrinsic.h>`

A signed integer data type that, at a minimum, takes the values in the range -32,767 to 32,767. It is used to specify the position of windows.

String   Defined in: `<X11/Intrinsic.h>`

```
typedef char* String;
```

Substitution   Defined in: `<X11/Intrinsic.h>`

SubstitutionRec

```
typedef struct
{
    char    match;
    String substitution;
} SubstitutionRec, *Substitution;
```

Widget   Defined in: `<X11/Intrinsic.h>`

A data type that is used as a "handle" to a widget. It is a pointer to a data structure that represents a widget.

WidgetClass   Defined in: `<X11/Intrinsic.h>`

A pointer to a widget's class data structure.

WidgetList   Defined in: `<X11/Intrinsic.h>`

```
typedef Widget *WidgetList;
```

XtAccelerators   Defined in: `<X11/Intrinsic.h>`

A pointer to an internal accelerator table.

XtActionHookId   Defined in: <X11/Intrinsic.h>

```
typedef Opaque XtActionHookId;
```

XtActionHookProc   Defined in: <X11/Intrinsic.h>

```
typedef void (*XtActionHookProc)(
    Widget     w,
    XtPointer  client_data,
    String     action_name,
    XEvent*    event,
    String*    params,
    Cardinal*  num_params);
```

XtActionList   Defined in: <X11/Intrinsic.h>

```
typedef struct _XtActionsRec *XtActionList;
```

XtActionProc   Defined in: <X11/Intrinsic.h>

```
typedef void (*XtActionProc)(
    Widget     widget,
    XEvent*    event,
    String*    params,
    Cardinal* num_params);
```

XtActionsRec   Defined in: <X11/Intrinsic.h>

```
typedef struct _XtActionsRec
{
    String             string;
    XtActionProc proc;
} XtActionsRec;
```

XtAddressMode   Defined in: <X11/Intrinsic.h>

```
typedef enum
{
/* address mode         parameter representation */
/* -----------          ----------------------- */
    XtAddress,          /* Address               */
    XtBaseOffset,       /* Offset                */
    XtImmediate,        /* Constant              */
    XtResourceString,   /* Resource name string  */
    XtResourceQuark,    /* Resource name quark   */
    XtWidgetBaseOffset,/* Offset from ancestor   */
    XtProcedureArg      /* Procedure to invoke   */
} XtAddressMode;
```

XtAppContext   Defined in: `<X11/Intrinsic.h>`

A pointer to an internal data structure representing an application context.

XtArgVal   Defined in: `<X11/Intrinsic.h>`

A system-dependent data type large enough to hold a Cardinal, Dimension, Position, or XtPointer.

XtBlockHookId   Defined in: `<X11/Intrinsic.h>`

```
typedef unsigned long XtBlockHookId;
```

XtBlockHookProc   Defined in: `<X11/Intrinsic.h>`

```
typedef void (*XtBlockHookProc)(
    XtPointer  client_data
);
```

XtBoundActions   Defined in: `<X11/Intrinsic.h>`

```
typedef XtActionProc* XtBoundActions;
```

XtCacheRef   Defined in: `<X11/Intrinsic.h>`

```
typedef Opaque XtCacheRef;
```

XtCacheType   Defined in: `<X11/Intrinsic.h>`

```
typedef int XtCacheType;
```

XtCallbackList   Defined in: `<X11/Intrinsic.h>`

```
typedef struct _XtCallbackRec
{
    XtCallbackProc callback;
    XtPointer      client_data;
} XtCallbackRec,    *XtCallbackList;
```

XtCallbackProc   Defined in: `<X11/Intrinsic.h>`

```
typedef void (*XtCallbackProc)(
    Widget    widget,
    XtPointer client_data,  /* Data registered by client */
    XtPointer call_data);   /* Callback-specific data     */
```

XtCallbackStatus   Defined in: `<X11/Intrinsic.h>`

```
typedef enum
{
    XtCallbackNoList,
    XtCallbackHasNone,
    XtCallbackHasSome
} XtCallbackStatus;
```

XtCancelConvertSelectionProc

Defined in: <X11/Intrinsic.h>

```
typedef void (*XtCancelConvertSelectionProc)(
    Widget      widget,
    Atom*       selection,
    Atom*       target,
    XtRequestId*  receiver_id,
    XtPointer    client_data);
```

XtChangeHookData

Defined in: <X11/Intrinsic.h>

```
typedef struct
{
    String     type;
    Widget     widget;
    XtPointer event_data;
    Cardinal   num_event_data;
} XtChangeHookDataRec, *XtChangeHookData;
```

XtChangeHookSetValuesData

Defined in: <X11/Intrinsic.h>

```
typedef struct
{
    Widget    old, req;
    ArgList   args;
    Cardinal num_args;
} XtChangeHookSetValuesDataRec, *XtChangeHookSetValuesData;
```

XtCheckpointToken

Defined in: <X11/Intrinsic.h>

```
typedef struct _XtCheckpointTokenRec {
    int         save_type;
    int         interact_style;
    Boolean     shutdown;
    Boolean     fast;
    Boolean     cancel_shutdown;
    int         phase;
    int         interact_dialog_type;   /* return value */
    Boolean     request_cancel;         /* return value */
    Boolean     request_next_phase;     /* return value */
    Boolean     save_success;           /* return value */
    int         type;          /* implementation private */
    Widget      widget;        /* implementation private */
} XtCheckpointTokenRec, *XtCheckpointToken;
```

XtConfigureHookData

```
typedef struct
{
    String          type;
    Widget          widget;
    XtGeometryMask  changeMask;
    XWindowChanges  changes;
} XtConfigureHookDataRec, *XtConfigureHookData;
```

XtConvertSelectionProc

```
typedef Boolean (*XtConvertSelectionProc)(
    Widget          widget,
    Atom*           selection,
    Atom*           target,
    Atom*           type_return,
    XtPointer*      value_return,
    unsigned long*  length_return,
    int*            format_return);
```

XtCaseProc

```
typedef void (*XtCaseProc)(
    Display* display,
    KeySym   keysym,
    KeySym*  lower_return,
    KeySym*  upper_return);
```

XtConvertArgList

```
typedef struct
{
    XtAddressMode   address_mode;
    XtPointer       address_id;
    Cardinal        size;
} XtConvertArgRec, *XtConvertArgList;
```

XtConvertArgProc

```
typedef void (*XtConvertArgProc)(
    Widget      widget,
    Cardinal*   size,
    XrmValue*   value);
```

XtConvertArgRec

```
typedef struct
{
    XtAddressMode   address_mode;
```

```
    XtPointer      address_id;
    Cardinal       size;
} XtConvertArgRec, *XtConvertArgList;
```

XtConverter
Defined in: <X11/Intrinsic.h>

```
typedef void (*XtConverter)(
    XrmValue*    args,
    Cardinal*    num_args,
    XrmValue*    from,
    XrmValue*    to);
```

XtConvertSelectionIncrProc
Defined in: <X11/Intrinsic.h>

```
typedef Boolean (*XtConvertSelectionIncrProc)(
    Widget        widget,
    Atom*         selection,
    Atom*         target,
    Atom*         type,
    XtPointer*    value,
    unsigned      long*   length,
    int*          format,
    unsigned long* max_length,
    XtPointer     client_data,
    XtRequestId*  receiver_id);
```

XtConvertSelectionProc
Defined in: <X11/Intrinsic.h>

```
typedef Boolean (*XtConvertSelectionProc)(
    Widget        widget,
    Atom*         selection,
    Atom*         target,
    Atom*         type_return,
    XtPointer*    value return,
    unsigned long* length_return,
    int*          format_return);
```

XtCreateHookData
Defined in: <X11/Intrinsic.h>

```
typedef struct
{
    String   type;
    Widget   widget;
    ArgList  args;
    Cardinal num_args;
} XtCreateHookDataRec, *XtCreateHookData;
```

XtCreatePopupChildProc   Defined in: <X11/Intrinsic.h>

```
typedef void (*XtCreatePopupChildProc)(Widget  shell );
```

XtDestroyHookData   Defined in: <X11/Intrinsic.h>

```
typedef struct
{
    String type;
    Widget widget;
} XtDestroyHookDataRec, *XtDestroyHookData;
```

XtDestructor   Defined in: <X11/Intrinsic.h>

```
typedef void (*XtDestructor)(
    XtAppContext app,
    XrmValue*    to,
    XtPointer    converter_data,
    XrmValue*    args,
    Cardinal*    num_args);
```

XtErrorHandler   Defined in: <X11/Intrinsic.h>

```
typedef void (*XtErrorHandler)(String msg);
```

XtErrorMsgHandler   Defined in: <X11/Intrinsic.h>

```
typedef void (*XtErrorMsgHandler)(
    String     name,
    String     type,
    String     class,
    String     default,
    String*    params,
    Cardinal*  num_params);
```

XtEventDispatchProc   Defined in: <X11/Intrinsic.h>

```
typedef Boolean (*XtEventDispatchProc)(XEvent* event );
```

XtEventHandler   Defined in: <X11/Intrinsic.h>

```
typedef void (*XtEventHandler)(
    Widget     widget,
    XtPointer  client_data,
    XEvent*    event,
    Boolean*   continue_to_dispatch);
```

XtExtensionSelectProc   Defined in: <X11/Intrinsic.h>

```
typedef void (*XtExtensionSelectProc)(
    Widget       widget,
```

```
    int*         event_types,
    XtPointer*   select_data,
    int          count,
    XtPointer    client_data);
```

XtFilePredicate

Defined in: <X11/Intrinsic.h>

```
typedef Boolean (*XtFilePredicate)(String filename);
```

XtGCMask

Defined in: <X11/Intrinsic.h>

```
typedef unsigned long XtGCMask;
```

XtGeometryHookData

Defined in: <X11/Intrinsic.h>

```
typedef struct
{
    String            type;
    Widget            widget;
    XtWidgetGeometry* request;
    XtWidgetGeometry* reply;
    XtGeometryResult  result;
} XtGeometryHookDataRec, *XtGeometryHookData;
```

XtGeometryMask

Defined in: <X11/Intrinsic.h>

```
typedef unsigned int  XtGeometryMask;
```

XtGeometryResult

Defined in: <X11/Intrinsic.h>

```
typedef enum  {
    XtGeometryYes,    /* Geometry request accepted  */
    XtGeometryNo,     /* Geometry request denied    */
    XtGeometryAlmost, /* Request denied, but willing*/
                      /*    to accept next try      */
    XtGeometryDone    /* Request accepted and done  */
} XtGeometryResult;
```

XtGrabKind

Defined in: <X11/Intrinsic.h>

```
typedef enum
{
    XtGrabNone,
    XtGrabNonexclusive,
    XtGrabExclusive
} XtGrabKind;
```

XtInputCallbackProc   Defined in: <X11/Intrinsic.h>

```
typedef void (*XtInputCallbackProc)(
    XtPointer    client_data,
    int*         source,
    XtInputId*   id);
```

XtInputId   Defined in: <X11/Intrinsic.h>

```
typedef unsigned long XtInputId;
```

XtIntervalId   Defined in: <X11/Intrinsic.h>

```
typedef unsigned long XtIntervalId;
```

XtInputMask   Defined in: <X11/Intrinsic.h>

```
typedef unsigned long XtInputMask;
```

XtKeyProc   Defined in: <X11/Intrinsic.h>

```
typedef void (*XtKeyProc)(
    Display*    dpy,
    int         keycode,
    Modifiers   modifiers,
    Modifiers*  modifiers_return ,
    KeySym*     keysym_return);
```

XtLanguageProc   Defined in: <X11/Intrinsic.h>

```
typedef String (*XtLanguageProc)(
    Display*    dpy,
    String          xnl,
    XtPointer   client_data);
```

XtListPosition   Defined in: <X11/Intrinsic.h>

```
typedef enum {XtListHead, XtListTail} XtListPosition;
```

XtLoseSelectionProc   Defined in: <X11/Intrinsic.h>

```
typedef void (*XtLoseSelectionProc)(
    Widget    widget,
    Atom*     selection);
```

XtLoseSelectionIncrProc   Defined in: <X11/Intrinsic.h>

```
typedef void (*XtLoseSelectionIncrProc)(
    Widget      widget,
    Atom*       selection,
    XtPointer   client_data);
```

XtPointer   Defined in: `<X11/Intrinsic.h>`

A data type large enough to contain a pointer to any one of the following data types: `char`, `int`, `long`, any `struct`, or function.

XtPopdownID   Defined in: `<X11/Intrinsic.h>`

```
typedef struct
{
    Widget  shell_widget;
    Widget  enable_widget;
} XtPopdownIDRec, *XtPopdownID;
```

XtRequestID   Defined in: `<X11/Intrinsic.h>`

```
typedef XtPointer XtRequestId;
```

XtResource   Defined in: `<X11/Intrinsic.h>`

XtResourceList

```
typedef struct _XtResource {
    String    resource_name;  /* Resource name                */
    String    resource_class; /* Resource class               */
    String    resource_type;  /* Desired representation type */
    Cardinal  resource_size;  /* Bytes in that representation*/
    Cardinal  resource_offset;/* Store resource value at this*/
                              /* offset from base of struct  */
    String    default_type;   /* Default representation type */
    XtPointer default_addr;   /* Address of default resource */
} XtResource, *XtResourceList;
```

XtResourceDefaultProc   Defined in: `<X11/Intrinsic.h>`

```
typedef void (*XtResourceDefaultProc)(
    Widget     widget,
    int        offset,
    XrmValue*  value);
```

XtSelectionCallbackProc   Defined in: `<X11/Intrinsic.h>`

```
typedef void (*XtSelectionCallbackProc)(
    Widget          widget,
    XtPointer       client_data,
    Atom*           selection,
    Atom*           type,
    XtPointer       value,
    unsigned long*  length,
    int*            format);
```

XtSelectionDoneIncrProc   Defined in: <X11/Intrinsic.h>

```
typedef void (*XtSelectionDoneIncrProc)(
    Widget      widget,
    Atom*       selection,
    Atom*       target,
    XtRequestId* receiver_id,
    XtPointer   client_data);
```

XtSelectionDoneProc   Defined in: <X11/Intrinsic.h>

```
typedef void (*XtSelectionDoneProc)(
    Widget    widget,
    Atom*     selection,
    Atom*     target);
```

XtSignalCallbackProc   Defined in: <X11/Intrinsic.h>

```
typedef void (*XtSignalCallbackProc)(
    XtPointer    client_data,
    XtSignalId*  id
);
```

XtSignalId   Defined in: <X11/Intrinsic.h>

```
typedef unsigned long      XtSignalId;
```

XtTimerCallbackProc   Defined in: <X11/Intrinsic.h>

```
typedef void (*XtTimerCallbackProc)(
    XtPointer     client_data,
    XtIntervalId*  id);
```

XtTranslations   Defined in: <X11/Intrinsic.h>

A pointer to an internal translation table.

XtTypeConverter   Defined in: <X11/Intrinsic.h>

```
typedef Boolean (*XtTypeConverter)(
    Display*    dpy,
    XrmValue*   args,
    Cardinal*   num_args,
    XrmValue*   from,
    XrmValue*   to,
    XtPointer*  converter_data);
```

XtValueMask   Defined in: <X11/Intrinsic.h>

```
typedef unsigned long XtValueMask;
```

XtVarArgsList   Defined in: <X11/Intrinsic.h>

```
typedef XtPointerXtVarArgsList;
```

XtWidgetGeometry   Defined in: <X11/Intrinsic.h>

```
typedef struct
{
    XtGeometryMask request_mode;
    Position    x, y;
    Dimension   width, height, border_width;
    Widget      sibling;
    int         stack_mode;/* One of: Above, Below, TopIf,   */
                        /* BottomIf, Opposite, DontChange */
} XtWidgetGeometry;
```

XtWorkProc   Defined in: <X11/Intrinsic.h>

```
typedef Boolean (*XtWorkProc)(
    XtPointer client_data);/* Application registered data */
```

XtWorkProcId   Defined in: <X11/Intrinsic.h>

```
typedef unsigned long XtWorkProcId;
```

Motif Quick Reference

This appendix starts with a summary of the command-line options and resources for mwm, the Motif Window Manager. The remainder of the appendix contains reference entries for individual Motif functions and widgets. They are organized into two sections: the Motif functions and the widgets. In each section, the entries appear in alphabetic order, showing the syntax, any return value, and a short description of how each function or widget is used.

mwm Command-Line Options

You can specify the following options when starting mwm:

`-display sys_name:m.n`

This causes mwm to manage screen *n* of display *m* on the system named *sys_name*. Consult Chapter 2 for more information on naming X displays. For example, to run mwm on screen 1 of display 0 on the system named lnbsun, you enter the following:

`mwm -display lnbsun:0.1&`

> `-multiscreen`
> If you use this option, mwm will manage the clients displaying output on all screens of a display. Another way to specify this option is through the resource named `multiscreen`.

> `-name application_name`
> This gives a name under which resources for mwm will be found.

> `-screens screen_name1 screen_name2 ...`
> This assigns names to the screens that mwm is managing. You can use these names to specify resources for specific screens.

`-xrm` *resource_specification_string*

This enables you to specify a resource through the command line. For example, you can specify that you want the keyboard focus to follow the pointer by running mwm as follows:

```
mwm -xrm "keyboardFocusPolicy: pointer"&
```

mwm Resources

The Motif Window Manager uses three types of resources:

✦ *Component-specific resource.* This resource affects the appearance of the window frames, window manager menus, and icons. The color of the window frame is a resource of this type.

✦ *mwm-specific resource.* This resource affects the window manager, but is not set separately for each component. The key and button bindings for mwm fall in this category.

✦ *Client-specific resources.* This resource affects one or more of the clients managed by mwm. For instance, the amount of decoration around the top-level window of a client can be controlled by setting the client-specific resource named `clientDecoration`.

Component-Specific Resources

This section lists the resources that affect all components of the Motif window manager. You can specify these resources with the following syntax:

Mwm*resource_name: resource_value

background   **Class name: `Background`**
Specifies the background color used in all components of mwm. You specify the color using any valid color name in the X color database (the file `/usr/lib/X11/rgb.txt`). The default color depends on the visual (the X color models supported by a server) of the screen.

backgroundPixmap   **Class name: `BackgroundPixmap`**
Specifies the background pixmap used to decorate the window frame of an *inactive* window (this refers to windows that do not have the input focus). The default pixmap depends on the visual supported by the display.

bottomShadowColor   **Class name: Foreground**
Used in the lower and the right bevels of all window manager decorations. You can use any color name from the X color database (the file `/usr/lib/X11/rgb.txt`).

bottomShadowPixmap   **Class name: `BottomShadowPixmap`**
Specifies the pixmap to be used in the lower and the right bevels of all window manager decorations.

fontList   **Class name: Font**
Specifies the font to be used in all window manager decorations. The default is the `fixed` font.

foreground   **Class name: Foreground**
This is the foreground color. The default value depends on the visual supported by the display.

saveUnder   Class name: `SaveUnder`

If this resource is set to `True`, the window manager will use the "save-under" feature (the ability to save the contents of a window and redraw the contents later) of the X server when displaying the window decorations. This resource takes effect only if the "save-under" feature is available in the X server. The default value of this resource is `False`.

topShadowColor   Class name: `Background`

This is the color used in the top and left bevels of the window decorations. The default value depends on the visual supported by the display.

topShadowPixmap   Class name: `TopShadowPixmap`

Specifies the pixmap to be used in the top and left bevels of the window decorations.

Window Frame and Icons

The resources listed in this section affect the window frame and icons. You can specify the resource for a specific component by using the following syntax:

```
Mwm*component*resource_name: resource_value
```

where *component* can take one of the following values:

> `client` indicates the window frames of all X clients.
> `feedback` indicates the dialog boxes displayed by `mwm`.
> `icon` refers to the icon box.
> `menu` refers to the menus displayed by `mwm`.

You can separately configure the title area of a client window. Use the following syntax:

```
Mwm*client*title*resource_name: resource_value
```

activeBackground   Class name: `Background`

This resource specifies the background color used in the `mwm` decorations when a window is active (that means the window has input focus—all keystrokes go to the window). The default color depends on the type of visual supported by the X server.

activeBackgroundPixmap   Class name: `ActiveBackgroundPixmap`

Specifies the pixmap used as the background in the `mwm` decorations of an active window (that means the window has input focus—all keystrokes go to the window).

activeBottomShadowColor   Class name: `Foreground`

This is the color of the lower and right bevels of the window decorations of an active window. The visual supported by the display determines the default color.

activeBottomShadowPixmap   Class name: `BottomShadowPixmap`

Pixmap used for the "bottom shadow" (the lower and right bevels of the decorations) of the active window.

activeForeground   Class name: `Foreground`

Specifies the foreground color used for the decorations on an active window—a window that has the input focus.

activeTopShadowColor   Class name: `Background`

This color is used in the active window's "top shadow" (the upper and left bevels of the decorations).

activeTopShadowPixmap   **Class name: TopShadowPixmap**

Pixmap used for the "top shadow" (the upper and left bevels of the decorations) of the active window.

mwm-Specific Resources

The resources listed in this section apply to the mwm application itself. The syntax for resource specification is the following:

```
Mwm*resource_name: resource_value
```

autoKeyFocus   **Class name: AutoKeyFocus**

This resource applies only when the keyboardFocusPolicy resource is set to Explicit. This resource controls what happens to the focus when the current active window is iconified. If the autoKeyFocus resource is True, the focus automatically goes to the window that previously had the focus.

autoRaiseDelay   **Class name: AutoRaiseDelay**

If the focusAutoRaise resource is True and the keyboardFocusPolicy is set to pointer, the autoRaiseDelay resource comes into play. It specifies the number of milliseconds mwm should wait before raising a window once the window has received the input focus. The default value is 500 milliseconds.

bitmapDirectory   **Class name: BitmapDirectory**

This resource specifies a directory to be searched by mwm to locate any bitmap needed by other mwm resources. The default setting of this resource is "/usr/include/X11/ bitmaps".

buttonBindings   **Class name: ButtonBindings**

This resource specifies a set of button bindings (a table that assigns an action to a buttonpress) that augments the built-in button bindings of mwm. The value should be the name of a button binding from the mwm configuration file. The default value of the buttonBindings resource is NULL, which means the built-in bindings are the only ones available.

cleanText   **Class name: CleanText**

If this resource is set to True, text appearing in a window's title and in mwm's dialogs is displayed with a clear background. The default value is False.

clientAutoPlace   **Class name: ClientAutoPlace**

This resource affects how mwm tries to place a client's window on the screen. If clientAutoPlace is True, mwm positions each window with the upper-left corner of the frame, offset horizontally and vertically so that no two windows completely overlap. The default for clientAutoPlace is True.

colormapFocusPolicy   **Class name: ColormapFocusPolicy**

This resource controls the colormap focus—the window whose colormap is currently installed and used for displaying everything in a server. The colormapFocusPolicy resource can be one of the following three values:

     keyboard means the window with input focus has colormap focus.

     pointer means the window with the pointer has the colormap focus.

     explicit means that the colormap has to be explicitly selected for a window.

To enable explicit selection of the colormap, assign a button or key to the function named f.focus_color. The default value of the colormapFocusPolicy is keyboard.

configFile   **Class name: ConfigFile**

This resource specifies the pathname of the mwm configuration file, which is a file with mwm resource settings, menu definitions, and button and key bindings. If the pathname specified by the configFile resource begins with a "~/", mwm considers that pathname to be relative to the user's HOME directory (as indicated by the HOME environment variable); otherwise, the path is assumed to be relative to the current directory. Here is how mwm uses this resource setting:

1. If the environment variable named LANG is set, mwm looks for the specified configuration file in the directory $HOME/$LANG (which means in a subdirectory of your login directory where the name of the subdirectory is specified by the LANG environment variable).

2. If the specified configuration file does not exist in $HOME/$LANG or if the LANG environment variable is not defined, mwm looks for that file in $HOME.

3. If you do not specify a configFile resource or if the specified file does not exist in one of the places listed in steps 1 or 2, mwm looks for a configuration file named .mwmrc. If the LANG environment variable is set, it looks for $HOME/$LANG/.mwmrc; otherwise, it looks for $HOME/.mwmrc.

4. If the .mwmrc file does not exist, mwm looks for a file named system.mwmrc—first in the directory /us/lib/X11/$LANG (provided the LANG environment variable is defined), then in /usr/lib/X11.

   Typically, the workstation vendor provides a file /usr/lib/X11/system.mwmrc with the default configuration for mwm. You can copy this file to your home directory under the name .mwmrc and modify it to suit your needs.

deiconifyKeyFocus   **Class name: DeiconifyKeyFocus**

If this resource is set to True and keyboardFocusPolicy is explicit, a window receives input focus when it is *deiconified*—converted to normal size from an icon. The default value is True.

doubleClickTime   **Class name: DoubleClickTime**

This resource specifies the maximum time in milliseconds that can elapse between two clicks that are to be interpreted by mwm as a double-click. The default value is 500 milliseconds.

enableWarp   **Class name: EnableWarp**

If this resource is True, mwm will move the mouse pointer (*warp it*) to the center of the window being resized and moved through keyboard accelerators. If enableWarp is False, the pointer is left at its previous position. The default setting is True.

enforceKeyFocus   **Class name: EnforceKeyFocus**

If this resource is True, mwm will set the input focus to a selected window even if it is a *globally active window* (a window that can be operated without setting focus to it). If the resource is False, input focus is not set to any globally active window (such as a scrollbar). This resource is True by default.

fadeNormalIcon   **Class name: FadeNormalIcon**

If this resource is True, mwm will grey out an icon that has been normalized. The default setting is False.

feedbackGeometry   **Class name: FeedbackGeometry**

This resource specifies the size and position (the *geometry*) of the feedback window that mwm displays during resize and move operations. If you do not specify this resource, mwm displays the feedback window at the center of the screen.

frameBorderWidth   **Class name: FrameBorderWidth**

This resource specifies the border width (in pixels) of the border of the window frame. This border width includes the three dimensional shadows. The default value is 5 pixels.

iconAutoPlace   **Class name: IconAutoPlace**

This resource controls where mwm places the icon for a window. If True (the default), mwm places all icons in a specific area of the screen determined by the iconPlacement resource. If this resource is False, the user can place the icons anywhere on the screen.

iconBoxGeometry   **Class name: IconBoxGeometry**

This resource is a geometry specification for the icon box. For example, if you specify the following value for this resource:

        4x3+0-0

mwm will create a box large enough to hold three rows of four icons across and position the box at the lower-left corner of the screen. The default value for this resource is 6x1+0-0.

iconBoxName   **Class name: IconBoxName**

This resource is the name under which the resources for the icon box can be found. The default name is iconbox.

iconBoxSBDisplayPolicy   **Class name: IconBoxSBDisplayPolicy**

This resource controls which scrollbars are displayed for the icon box. It can take three values:

        horizontal indicates that you want a single horizontal scrollbar.

        vertical indicates a vertical scrollbar only.

        all means both horizontal and vertical scrollbars should be displayed.

The default is all.

iconBoxTitle   **Class name: IconBoxTitle**

This is a string to be displayed in the title of the icon box. The default name is Icons.

iconClick   **Class name: IconClick**

If this resource is True, the Window Menu of an icon is displayed and left visible when you click on the icon. The default setting is True.

iconDecoration   **Class name: IconDecoration**

This resource affects the amount of decoration on the icon box. The value of the resource can be a combination of the following values:

        label indicates that only the label (truncated to the width of the icon) is displayed.

        image means that only the image of the icon should be displayed.

        activelabel specifies that the complete label (not truncated) is shown when the icon is active.

For icons appearing in the icon box, the default value of `iconDecoration` is `image label`. For icons displayed on the screen, the setting is `image label activelabel`.

`iconImageMaximum`   **Class name: `IconImageMaximum`**

This resource takes a value of the form *mxn* where *m* and *n* specify the maximum width and height of an icon's image. The default is 50x50 (in pixels). The maximum allowed is 128x128.

`iconImageMinimum`   **Class name: `IconImageMinimum`**

This resource takes a value of the form *mxn* where *m* and *n* specify the minimum width and height of an icon's image. The default value for this resource is 16x16 (in pixels), which is also the minimum size supported by mwm.

`iconPlacement`   **Class name: `IconPlacement`**

This resource specifies where mwm should place the icons. The value is a sequence of two keywords of the following form:

> *primary   secondary*

where *primary* and *secondary* can take one of the following values:

> `top` means top-to-bottom placement.
> `bottom` implies bottom-to-top layout.
> `left` means left-to-right arrangement.
> `right` is for right-to-left placement.

The `primary` layout specifies where an icon is placed (in a row or a column) and in which direction. The `secondary` layout specifies where to place new rows or columns. The default value for `iconPlacement` is `left bottom` which means that the icons are placed from left to right on the screen with the first row at the bottom, and the new rows are added in the bottom-to-top direction.

`iconPlacementMargin`   **Class name: `IconPlacementMargin`**

This resource (a positive value) specifies the margin (in pixels) between the edge of the screen and the icons appearing at that edge of the screen. The default value is the same as the separation between the icons on the screen (this is determined by mwm to maximize the number of icons appearing in each row and column).

`interactivePlacement`   **Class name: `InteractivePlacement`**

If this resource is `True`, mwm will prompt the user for the position of each new window. The user has to press the mouse button to indicate where the window should be placed. By default, this resource is `False`; thus, by default, mwm does not prompt the user for the window position.

`keyBindings`   **Class name: `KeyBindings`**

This resource specifies a set of key bindings (a table that assigns an action to one or more keypresses) that replaces the built-in key bindings of mwm. The value should be the name of a key binding from the mwm configuration file. The default value of the `keyBindings` resource is `DefaultKeyBindings`.

`keyboardFocusPolicy`   **Class name: `KeyboardFocusPolicy`**

This resource specifies how mwm should assign the input focus to a window (the window with the input focus receives the keystrokes entered by the user). This resource can take one of two values:

`explicit` means the user indicates the focus window by pressing the first mouse button with the pointer in the window.

`pointer` means the keyboard focus follows the mouse pointer.

The default setting for `keyboardFocusPolicy` is `explicit`.

limitResize   **Class name: LimitResize**

If this resource is `True`, the user cannot resize a window to have a size greater than the maximum size. This resource is `True` by default.

lowerOnIconify   **Class name: LowerOnIconify**

If this resource is `True`, mwm places a window's icon at the bottom of the stack when the window is reduced to an icon. This resource is `False` by default.

maximumMaximumSize   **Class name: MaximumMaximumSize**

This resource sets the upper limit on the maximum size that you can specify for a client window. For instance, if you set this resource to the following:

        800x600

the client windows cannot be bigger than `800` by `600` pixels. The default value is twice the size of the screen.

moveOpaque   **Class name: MoveOpaque**

If this resource is `True`, the actual window (with all its contents) is moved when you move a window. The default value is `False`, which means a rectangular outline of the window is moved instead of the actual window.

moveThreshold   **Class name: MoveThreshold**

This resource controls how sensitive mwm is to *mouse drag* operations (moving the mouse with a button pressed down). The value is interpreted as the number of pixels by which the mouse must move before mwm reacts to it. The default value is 4 pixels.

multiScreen   **Class name: MultiScreen**

If this resource is `True`, mwm controls windows displayed in all screens of a display. The default value is `False`, which means mwm manages only one screen by default.

passButtons   **Class name: PassButtons**

If this resource is `True`, mwm passes buttonpress events to the client even after the events are used for some window manager functions. The default value is `False`—mwm does not forward buttonpress events that it uses for window management functions.

passSelectButtons   **Class name: PassSelectButtons**

This resource indicates whether a buttonpress that assigns input focus to a window is passed as an event to that window. By default, this resource is `True`, which means that mwm passes the buttonpress event to the window after giving the keyboard focus to that window. This resource applies only when `keyboardFocusPolicy` is `explicit` because this is the only case that requires you to transfer input focus by clicking on a window.

positionIsFrame   **Class name: PositionIsFrame**

This resource specifies how mwm interprets the information about a client window's position as it appears in the WM_NORMALHINTS property or in geometry specifications. If this resource is `True`, the position is taken to be that of the frame placed around the client window by mwm; otherwise, the position is that of the client window alone. The default value is `True`.

positionOnScreen   **Class name: PositionOnScreen**

If this resource is `True`, mwm will place a client window entirely inside the screen. If the window's size exceeds the screen size, mwm places the upper-left corner of the window within the boundaries of the screen. The default value is `True`.

quitTimeOut   **Class name: QuitTimeOut**

This is the amount of time in milliseconds that mwm will wait for a client to respond to a `WM_SAVE_YOURSELF` message. The client is supposed to reply by updating the `WM_COMMAND` property. The default value is 1,000 milliseconds (1 second). This resource applies only to those clients that have a `WM_SAVE_YOURSELF` atom but do not have a `WM_DELETE_WINDOW` atom in the `WM_PROTOCOLS` property of their top-level windows.

raiseKeyFocus   **Class name: RaiseKeyFocus**

If this resource is `True` and `keyboardFocusPolicy` is `explicit`, mwm transfers the input focus to a window that has been raised by the `f.normalize_and_raise` function. This resource is `False` by default.

resizeBorderWidth   **Class name: ResizeBorderWidth**

This is the width (in pixels) of a window frame that enables the user to resize the window by dragging the border. The default value is 10 pixels.

resizeCursors   **Class name: ResizeCursors**

If this resource is `True`, the cursor changes shape (to indicate that the resize operation is available) whenever the mouse pointer enters the window frame.

screens   **Class name: Screens**

This resource is for assigning names to the screens that mwm will be managing.

showFeedback   **Class name: ShowFeedback**

This resource specifies when mwm displays feedback information, which includes dialog boxes and boxes displaying window size and position during `move` and `resize` operations. The value of this resource is a combination of one or more of the following names:

    `all` shows all feedback information.

    `behavior` feedback is used to confirm any changes in the behavior of mwm.

    `kill` shows a dialog box when a `SIGKILL` signal is received.

    `move` shows the position during moves.

    `none` suppresses all feedback.

    `placement` shows position and size during initial placement of the window.

    `quit` shows a dialog box to confirm a request to quit mwm.

    `resize` shows the size when the window is being resized.

    `restart` shows a dialog to confirm any attempt to restart mwm.

The default for the `showFeedback` resource is `all`. You specify new values for this resource in two ways:

1. Enable selected feedbacks. For instance, if you want feedback during `move` and `resize` operations only, you can set this resource as follows:

   `Mwm*showFeedback: move resize`

2. Disable selected feedbacks. In this case, all but the specified feedbacks are shown. The syntax requires a minus sign to precede the first keyword. For example, if you want feedback in all cases except during `move`, `resize`, and `placement`, you write the following:

   `Mwm*showFeedback: -move placement resize`

startupKeyFocus   **Class name: StartupKeyFocus**

If this resource is True and keyboardFocusPolicy is set to explicit, mwm transfers input focus to a window when it is mapped. This resource is True by default.

transientDecoration   **Class name: TransientDecoration**

This resource controls the amount of decoration that mwm places around a transient (temporary) window (identified by the WM_TRANSIENT_FOR property on the window). The syntax for specification is similar to that for the clientDecoration resource (shown under client-specific resources). The default value for this resource is menu title, which means that transient windows appear with a resizable window border and a titlebar with the Window Menu button.

transientFunctions   **Class name: TransientFunctions**

This resource specifies the window management functions that mwm allows for a transient (temporary) window (identified by the WM_TRANSIENT_FOR property on the window). The syntax for specification is similar to that for the clientFunctions resource (shown under client-specific resources). The default value for this resource is -maximize minimize, which means that mwm will apply the functions f.maximize and f.minimize to transient windows.

useIconBox   **Class name: UseIconBox**

If this resource is True, mwm places all icons in an icon box. If this resource is False, mwm places the icons on the root window. The default value is False.

wMenuButtonClick   **Class name: WMenuButtonClick**

If this resource is True, mwm will display the Window Menu in response to a button click on the Window Menu button, and leave it displayed until another button click elsewhere. This resource is True by default.

wMenuButtonClick2   **Class name: WMenuButtonClick2**

If this resource is True, and the user double-clicks (clicks twice in rapid succession) on the Window Menu button, mwm will invoke the f.kill function to remove the client window.

Client-Specific Resources

The resources listed in this section apply to a specified client application. You specify these resources using the following syntax:

Mwm*client_name_or_class*resource_name: resource_value

where client_name_or_class identifies the client to which the resource applies. The client-specific resources enable you to customize the behavior of mwm for individual clients. For example, you can make mwm display the bitmap /usr/include/X11/bitmaps/terminal as the icon for the xterm application by setting the client-specific resource iconImage as follows:

Mwm*xterm*iconImage: /usr/include/X11/bitmaps/terminal

clientDecoration   **Class name: ClientDecoration**

This resource specifies the amount of decoration (buttons and frames) mwm applies to a client's top-level window. The value of this resource is a combination of one or more of the following names:

`all` includes all decorations listed:

`border` displays the window border.

`maximize` adds the titlebar with the maximize button.

`menu` displays the titlebar with the Window Menu button.

`minimize` adds the titlebar with the minimize button.

`resizeh` shows the border with resize handles.

`none` suppresses all decorations.

`title` adds the titlebar and a border to the window.

The default for the `clientDecorations` resource is `all`. You specify new values for this resource in two ways:

1. Enable selected decorations. For instance, if you want the `xclock` window to have a titlebar with a Window Menu and a resizable border only, you can set this resource as follows:

   `Mwm*xclock*clientDecorations: menu resizeh`

2. Disable selected decorations. In this case, all but the specified decorations will appear. The syntax requires a minus sign to precede the first keyword. For example, if you want all the decorations except the maximize and minimize buttons, you write the following:

   `Mwm*xclock*clientDecorations: -maximize minimize`

clientFunctions   **Class name: ClientDecoration**

This resource specifies which of the window management functions `mwm` applies to a client's window. The value of this resource is a combination of one or more of the following names:

`all` includes all functions listed:

`close` refers to the `f.kill` function.

`maximize` refers to the `f.maximize` function.

`minimize` refers to the `f.minimize` function.

`move` refers to the `f.move` function.

`none` suppresses invocation of all functions.

`resize` refers to the `f.resize` function.

The default for the `clientFunctions` resource is `all`. You specify new values for this resource in two ways:

1. Enable selected functions. For instance, if you want to invoke only the `f.move` and `f.resize` functions on the `xclock` window, you can set this resource as follows:

   `Mwm*xclock*clientFunctions: move resize`

2. Disable selected functions. In this case, all but the specified functions can be applied to a client's window. The syntax requires a minus sign to precede the first keyword. For example, if you want to apply all functions except `f.maximize` and `f.minimize`, you write the following:

   `Mwm*xclock*clientFunctions: -maximize minimize`

focusAutoRaise   **Class name: FocusAutoRaise**

If this resource is `True`, `mwm` raises a window to the top of the stacking order when the window receives the input focus. The default value depends on the `keyboardFocusPolicy`. If `keyboardFocusPolicy` is `explicit`, `focusAutoRaise` is `True`; otherwise, `focusAutoRaise` is `False`.

iconImage   Class name: `IconImage`

This is the pathname of an X bitmap file that mwm will use as the icon for a client when the client's window is minimized. By default, mwm displays a standard icon image for all applications. Note that the `useClientIcon` resource affects this resource. If `useClientIcon` is True, an image supplied by the client application (something that the programmer had set in that application) takes precedence over an icon specified by the user.

iconImageBackground   Class name: `Background`

This is the background color for the icon image. The default value is the color specified by the resource `Mwm*background` or `Mwm*icon*background`.

iconImageBottomShadowColor   Class name: `Foreground`

This is the color used to create the bottom shadow of the icon image. The default value is the color specified by the resource `Mwm*icon*bottomShadowColor`.

iconImageBottomShadowPixmap Class name: `BottomShadowPixmap`

This is the pixmap used for the bottom shadow of the icon image. The default value is the pixmap specified by the resource `Mwm*icon*bottomShadowPixmap`.

iconImageForeground   Class name: `Foreground`

This is the foreground color for the icon image. The default value is the color specified by the resource `Mwm*foreground` or `Mwm*icon*foreground`.

iconImageTopShadowColor   Class name: `Background`

This is the color used to create the top shadow of the icon image. The default value is the color specified by the resource `Mwm*icon*topShadowColor`.

iconImageTopShadowPixmap   Class name: `TopShadowPixmap`

This is the pixmap used for the top shadow of the icon image. The default value is the pixmap specified by the resource `Mwm*icon*topShadowPixmap`.

matteBackground   Class name: `Background`

This is the background color of the matte (a three-dimensional border between the client's window and the window frame added by mwm). This resource is used only if `matteWidth` is greater than zero. The default value is the color specified by the resource `Mwm*background` or `Mwm*client*background`.

matteBottomShadowColor   Class name: `Foreground`

This is the color used to create the bottom shadow of the matte (a three-dimensional border between the client's window and the window frame added by mwm). This resource is used only if `matteWidth` is greater than zero. The default value is the color specified by the resource `Mwm*bottomShadowColor` or `Mwm*client*bottomShadowColor`.

matteBottomShadowPixmap   Class name: `BottomShadowPixmap`

This is the pixmap used for the bottom shadow of the matte (a three-dimensional border between the client's window and the window frame added by mwm). This resource is used only if `matteWidth` is greater than zero. The default value is the color specified by the resource `Mwm*bottomShadowPixmap` or `Mwm*client*bottomShadowPixmap`.

matteForeground   Class name: `Foreground`

This is the foreground color of the matte (a three-dimensional border between the client's window and the window frame added by mwm). This resource is used only if `matteWidth` is greater than zero. The default value is the color specified by the resource `Mwm*foreground` or `Mwm*client*foreground`.

matteTopShadowColor   Class name: **Background**

This is the color used to create the bottom shadow of the matte (a three-dimensional border between the client's window and the window frame added by mwm). This resource is used only if `matteWidth` is greater than zero. The default value is the color specified by the resource Mwm*topShadowColor or Mwm*client*topShadowColor.

matteTopShadowPixmap   Class name: **TopShadowPixmap**

This is the pixmap used for the top shadow of the matte (a three-dimensional border between the client's window and the window frame added by mwm). This resource is used only if `matteWidth` is greater than zero. The default value is the color specified by the resource Mwm*topShadowPixmap or Mwm*client*topShadowPixmap.

matteWidth   Class name: **MatteWidth**

This is the width of the matte (a three-dimensional border between the client's window and the window frame added by mwm) in pixels. The default value is zero; thus, no matte appears by default.

maximumClientSize   Class name: **MaximumClientSize**

This resource sets the size of the client's window when it is maximized. The window manager gets the default value for this resource from the WM_NORMAL_HINTS property. If this property is not present, the maximized size is such that the window fills the screen. If you do not specify the `maximumClientSize` resource, mwm uses the value supplied in the `maximumMaximumSize` resource.

useClientIcon   Class name: **UseClientIcon**

If the `useClientIcon` resource is True, an image supplied by the client application (something that the programmer had set in that application) takes precedence over an icon specified by the user through the `imageIcon` resource.

usePPosition   Class name: **UsePPosition**

If this resource is True, mwm honors the program-specified position PPosition specified in the WM_NORMAL_HINTS property. The default is to honor program-specified positions other than (0,0).

windowMenu   Class name: **WindowMenu**

This resource specifies the name of the menu to be displayed when the Window Menu button is pressed. The value of the resource must be the name of a menu defined in the mwm configuration file (the file specified by the resource `configFile`). The default for `windowMenu` is DefaultWindowMenu.

Motif Functions

The syntax of each entry in this section appears as an ANSI standard C prototype declaration of the function, followed by a brief description of the function. Each argument is explained through a comment next to the argument.

```
XmActivateProtocol
#include <Xm/Protocols.h>
void XmActivateProtocol(
    Widget shell,      /* Protocol is for this widget */
    Atom   property,   /* Property containing protocol */
    Atom   protocol ); /* Protocol to be activated     */
```

Stores protocol in the specified property of the shell. Used for interclient communications. (Please consult a book on X Window System programming for more information on properties and atoms.)

XmActivateWMProtocol
```
#include <Xm/Protocols.h>
void XmActivateWMProtocol(
    Widget shell,      /* Protocol is for this widget  */
    Atom   protocol); /* Protocol to be activated     */
```

Calls XmActivateProtocol with property set to the atom returned by interning WM_PROTOCOLS.

XmAddProtocolCallback
```
#include <Xm/Protocols.h>
void XmAddProtocolCallback(
    Widget shell,      /* Protocol is for this widget       */
    Atom   property,   /* Property containing protocol      */
    Atom   protocol, /* Register callback for this protocol */
    XtCallbackProc callback,  /* The callback function       */
    XtPointer      client_data); /* Data passed to callback */
```

Calls XmAddProtocols to add the specified protocol to the WM_PROTOCOLS property and register callback as the function to be called when a message is received with that protocol.

XmAddProtocols
```
#include <Xm/Protocols.h>
void XmAddProtocols(
    Widget   shell,      /* Protocols are for this widget */
    Atom     property,   /* Property containing protocols */
    Atom     *protocols, /* Protocols to be registered    */
    Cardinal num_protocols); /* Number of protocols       */
```

Adds a set of protocols to the specified shell. You can activate any of these protocols by calling XmActivateProtocol.

XmAddTabGroup
```
#include <Xm/Xm.h>
void XmAddTabGroup(
    Widget widget); /* Widget to be added to tab group */
```

Adds the specified widget to the list of tab groups associated with a hierarchy of widgets. A *tab group* is a collection of widgets, within which you can move the input focus from one widget to another by using the arrow keys. You can go from one tab group to another by pressing the Tab key.

XmAddToPostFromList
```
#include <Xm/RowColumn.h>
void XmAddToPostFromList(
    Widget menu_pane, /* An XmRowColumn widget (menu pane)   */
    Widget widget);   /* Add this to pane's "post from" list */
```

Adds a widget to the XmNpostFromList resource of the XmRowColumn widget menu.

XmAddWMProtocolCallback
```
#include <Xm/Protocols.h>
void XmAddWMProtocolCallback(
    Widget shell,      /* Protocol is for this widget       */
    Atom   protocol, /* Register callback for this protocol */
    XtCallbackProc callback,  /* The callback function       */
    XtPointer      client_data); /* Data passed to callback */
```

Calls `XmAddProtocolCallback` to add `callback` for the specified `protocol` stored in the
`WM_PROTOCOLS` property.

XmAddWMProtocols
```
#include <Xm/Protocols.h>
void XmAddWMProtocols(
    Widget   shell,      /* Protocols are for this widget */
    Atom     *protocols, /* Protocols to be registered    */
    Cardinal num_protocols); /* Number of protocols       */
```

Adds a set of protocols to the specified shell's `WM_PROTOCOLS` property. You can activate any of these
protocols by calling `XmActivateProtocol`.

XmCascadeButtonGadgetHighlight
```
#include <Xm/CascadeBG.h>
void XmCascadeButtonGadgetHighlight(
    Widget   button,      /* Cascade button gadget to highlight */
    Boolean highlight);/* True (to highlight) or False        */
```

Changes the highlight attribute of the specified cascade button gadget. If the highlight argument is
`True`, a shadow is drawn around the gadget to highlight it.

XmCascadeButtonHighlight
```
#include <Xm/CascadeB.h>
void XmCascadeButtonHighlight(
    Widget   button,      /* Cascade button widget to highlight */
    Boolean highlight);/* True (to highlight) or False        */
```

Changes the highlight attribute of the specified cascade button widget. If the highlight argument is
`True`, the shadow highlight around the button's window is drawn.

XmChangeColor
```
#include <Xm/Xm.h>
void XmChangeColor(
    Widget widget,        /* ID of widget whose colors are updated */
    Pixel  background); /* New background color pixel value        */
```

Recalculates the foreground, select, and shadow colors of a widget for a specified background color.

XmClipboardBeginCopy
```
#include <Xm/CutPaste.h>
int XmClipboardBeginCopy(
    Display *display,  /* This identifies the X server  */
    Window   window,   /* This application's window ID  */
    XmString clip_label,/* A label to describe the data */
    Widget   widget,   /* Widget with callback to       */
                       /* handle data passed by name    */
    VoidProc callback, /* Function to call when          */
                       /* clipboard needs data           */
    long     *item_id); /* On return, ID of data item    */
```

`XmClipboardBeginCopy` is similar to `XmClipboardStartCopy` except that `XmClipboardBeginCopy`
uses the `CurrentTime` as the timestamp to begin a copy operation.

XmClipboardCancelCopy
```
#include <Xm/CutPaste.h>
void XmClipboardCancelCopy(
    Display *display, /* Identifies the X server          */
    Window  window,   /* Client application's window ID   */
    long    item_id); /* ID of data being copied          */
```

Cancels an ongoing copy (identified by `item_id`) to the clipboard and releases any temporary storage.

XmClipboardCopy
```
#include <Xm/CutPaste.h>
int XmClipboardCopy(
    Display *display, /* Identifies the X server          */
    Window  window,   /* Client application's window ID   */
    long    item_id,  /* ID of data being copied          */
    char    *format name, /* Format of data in buffer     */
    char    *buffer,  /* Data to be copied to the clipboard */
    unsigned long length, /* Number of bytes in buffer    */
    int     private_id, /* Private data stored with item_id */
    int     *data_id ); /* Returned ID when buffer is NULL  */
```

Copies data in `buffer` to a temporary storage for later transfer to the clipboard. Returns `ClipboardSuccess` if all goes well, or `ClipboardLocked` if the clipboard is in use by another application. You must call `XmClipboardStartCopy` before calling `XmClipboardCopy`.

XmClipboardCopyByName
```
#include <Xm/CutPaste.h>
int XmClipboardCopyByName(
    Display *display, /* Identifies the X server          */
    Window  window,   /* Client application's window ID   */
    int     data_id   /* ID of data item passed by name   */
    char    *buffer,  /* Data copied from this buffer     */
    unsigned long length,/* Number of bytes in buffer     */
    int     private_id); /* Private data stored with data_id*/
```

Copies a data item passed by name. Returns `ClipboardSuccess` if all goes well, or `ClipboardLocked` if the clipboard is being used by another application.

XmClipboardEndCopy
```
#include <Xm/CutPaste.h>
int XmClipboardEndCopy(
    Display *display, /* Identifies the X server          */
    Window  window,   /* Client application's window ID   */
    long    item_id); /* ID of data being copied          */
```

Ends a copy to the clipboard by transferring data from temporary storage into the clipboard. Returns `ClipboardSuccess` if the operation succeeds, or `ClipboardLocked` if the clipboard is being used by another application.

XmClipboardEndRetrieve
```
#include <Xm/CutPaste.h>
int XmClipboardEndRetrieve(
    Display *display, /* Identifies the X server          */
    Window  window);  /* Client application's window ID   */
```

Ends an incremental copy operation started by `XmClipboardStartRetrieve`. Returns `ClipboardSuccess` if all goes well, or `ClipboardLocked` if the clipboard is being used by another application.

XmClipboardInquireCount
```
#include <Xm/CutPaste.h>
int XmClipboardInquireCount(
    Display *display, /* Identifies the X server          */
```

```
    Window  window,   /* Client application's window ID   */
    int     *num_format,/* Returns number of formats       */
    int     *max_length );/* Returns maximum length of all */
                        /* format names in current item    */
```

On return, the number of formats for the current clipboard item will be in num_format and the maximum length of the format names in max_length. The function itself returns ClipboardSuccess if all goes well, or ClipboardLocked if the clipboard is in use by some other application.

XmClipboardInquireFormat
```
#include <Xm/CutPaste.h>
int XmClipboardInquireFormat(
    Display *display,/* Identifies the X server            */
    Window  window,  /* Client application's window ID     */
    int     index,   /* Return format name with this index */
    char    *format_name,/* Format name is returned here   */
    unsigned long format_length, /* Bytes in format_name   */
    unsigned long *copied_length ); /* Bytes returned       */
```

Copies the format name specified by index to the buffer format_name, which has room for format_length bytes. On return, *copied_length is the number of bytes copied into format_name. Returns one of the following:

> ClipboardLocked if the clipboard is locked by another application
>
> ClipboardNoData if the clipboard is empty
>
> ClipboardSuccess if the function succeeds
>
> ClipboardTruncate if format_name is not large enough for requested name

XmClipboardInquireLength
```
#include <Xm/CutPaste.h>
int XmClipboardInquireLength(
    Display *display,/* Identifies the X server            */
    Window  window,  /* Client application's window ID     */
    char    *format_name, /* Name of data format           */
    unsigned long *length); /* Returns length of clipboard */
                          /* data item in bytes            */
```

On return, *length will be the length of data in the clipboard whose format is specified by format_name. This function returns one of the following:

> ClipboardLocked if the clipboard is locked by another application
>
> ClipboardNoData if the clipboard is empty
>
> ClipboardSuccess if the function succeeds

XmClipboardInquirePendingItems
```
#include <Xm/CutPaste.h>
int XmClipboardInquirePendingItems(
    Display *display,/* Identifies the X server            */
    Window  window,  /* Client application's window ID     */
    int     index,   /* Return format name with this index */
    char    *format_name,/* Format name is returned here   */
    XmClipboardPendingList *item_list, /* Array where ID of*/
                    /* pending data items is returned      */
    unsigned long   *num_item /* On return, this holds the*/
                    /* number of entries in item_list      */
```

Gets a list of pending items (data items passed to the clipboard by name, but not requested by any application). This function returns `ClipboardSuccess` if the function succeeds, or `ClipboardLocked` to indicate that the clipboard is reserved for exclusive use by an application.

XmClipboardLock
```
#include <Xm/CutPaste.h>
int XmClipboardLock(
    Display *display, /* This identifies the X server   */
    Window  window); /* This application's window ID   */
```

Locks the clipboard to prevent access by other applications. Use `XmClipboardUnlock` to release the clipboard. The clipboard is automatically locked between calls to `XmClipboardStartCopy` and `XmClipboardEndCopy`, as well as to `XmClipboardStartRetrieve` and `XmClipboardEndRetrieve`. `XmClipboardLock` returns `ClipboardSuccess` if the clipboard is successfully locked. If the clipboard is already locked by another application, this function returns `ClipboardLocked`.

XmClipboardRegisterFormat
```
#include <Xm/CutPaste.h>
int XmClipboardRegisterFormat(
    Display *display, /* This identifies the X server        */
    char    *format_name  /* Name assigned to the new format */
    unsigned long format_length);/* Length in bits 8,16,or 32*/
```

Registers a new data format with the X server and assigns it a name. This function returns one of the following:

> `ClipboardBadFormat` if the name is `NULL` or length is not one of 8, 16, or 32
>
> `ClipboardLocked` if the clipboard is locked by another application
>
> `ClipboardSuccess` if the function succeeds

XmClipboardRetrieve
```
#include <Xm/CutPaste.h>
int XmClipboardRetrieve(
    Display *display, /* This identifies the X server   */
    Window  window,   /* This application's window ID    */
    char    *format_name, /* Format of clipboard data    */
    char    *buffer,  /* Clipboard data returned here   */
    unsigned long  length,  /* Size of buffer in bytes   */
    unsigned long  *num_bytes,/* On return, bytes copied*/
    int     *private_id );/* Returns private data if any*/
```

Retrieves the current data item from the clipboard into `buffer`. Returns one of the following:

> `ClipboardLocked` if the clipboard is locked by another application
>
> `ClipboardNoData` if the clipboard is empty
>
> `ClipboardSuccess` if the function succeeds
>
> `ClipboardTruncate` if `buffer` is not large enough for requested data

XmClipboardStartCopy
```
#include <Xm/CutPaste.h>
int XmClipboardStartCopy(
    Display *display, /* This identifies the X server   */
    Window  window,   /* This application's window ID    */
    XmString clip_label,/* A label to describe the data */
    Time    timestamp, /* Time of the initiating event */
```

```
    Widget  widget,      /* Widget with callback to      */
                         /* handle data passed by name   */
    VoidProc callback,   /* Function to call when        */
                         /* clipboard needs data         */
    long  *item_id);     /* On return, ID of data item   */
```

Sets up temporary storage areas and initializes the data structures to receive clipboard data. You must call this function before copying data to and from the clipboard. On return, item_id will be an identifier for the copy operation. You should use this item_id as argument in calls to functions such as XmClipboardCopy and XmClipboardEndCopy. XmClipboardStartCopy returns ClipboardSuccess if it succeeds, or ClipboardLocked to indicate that the clipboard is already in use by another application.

XmClipboardStartRetrieve
```
#include <Xm/CutPaste.h>
int XmClipboardStartRetrieve(
    Display *display, /* This identifies the X server    */
    Window  window,   /* This application's window ID    */
    Time    timestamp); /* Time of the initiating event */
```

Locks the clipboard in preparation for data retrieval from the clipboard with a call to XmClipboardRetrieve. Returns ClipboardSuccess if all goes well, or ClipboardLocked if the clipboard is already locked by another application.

XmClipboardUndoCopy
```
#include <Xm/CutPaste.h>
int XmClipboardUndoCopy(
    Display *display, /* This identifies the X server    */
    Window  window);  /* This application's window ID    */
```

Deletes the last item placed in the clipboard. The item must have been placed by an application with the same display and window IDs. This function returns ClipboardSuccess if the undo operation is successful, or ClipboardLocked if the clipboard is already in use.

XmClipboardUnlock
```
#include <Xm/CutPaste.h>
int XmClipboardUnlock(
    Display *display, /* This identifies the X server     */
    Window  window,   /* This application's window ID     */
    Boolean unlock_all); /* If True, all locks are removed */
```

Unlocks the clipboard. Normally, each call to XmClipboardLock must be undone with a corresponding call to XmClipboardUnlock. However, a single call to XmClipboardUnlock suffices, provided you set the unlock_all argument to True.

XmClipboardWithdrawFormat
```
#include <Xm/CutPaste.h>
int XmClipboardWithdrawFormat(
    Display *display, /* This identifies the X server     */
    Window  window,   /* This application's window ID     */
    int     data_id); /* Identifies data item and format  */
```

Sets the internal state of the clipboard to indicate that the application will no longer honor requests for the data identified by data_id. This function returns ClipboardSuccess if all goes well, or ClipboardLocked if the clipboard is already in use.

XmCommandAppendValue
```
#include <Xm/Command.h>
void XmCommandAppendValue(
    Widget   widget,    /* XmCommand widget affected by this  */
    XmString command); /* Append this string to command line */
```

Appends a string to the string being displayed in the command area of the XmCommand widget.

XmCommandError
```
#include <Xm/Command.h>
void XmCommandError(
    Widget   widget, /* XmCommand widget affected by this  */
    XmString error); /* Error message to be displayed      */
```

Displays the specified error message in the history area of the XmCommand widget.

XmCommandGetChild
```
#include <Xm/Command.h>
Widget XmCommandGetChild(
    Widget           widget, /* XmCommand widget being queried */
    unsigned char child); /* Child widget ID to be returned */
```

Returns the widget ID of a child of the XmCommand widget. The child argument specifies the child whose ID is returned. It can take one of the following values: XmDIALOG_COMMAND_TEXT, XmDIALOG_PROMPT_LABEL, or Xm_DIALOG_HISTORY_LIST.

XmCommandSetValue
```
#include <Xm/Command.h>
void XmCommandSetValue(
    Widget   widget,    /* Applies to this XmCommand widget */
    XmString command); /* This is the new command string   */
```

Displays the command as the new string in the command area of the XmCommand widget.

XmConvertUnits
```
#include <Xm/Xm.h>
int XmConvertUnits(
    Widget widget,       /* Convert data for this widget */
    int    orientation,/* XmHORIZONTAL or XmVERTICAL   */
    int    from_unit,  /* Unit of from_value           */
    int    from_value, /* Data to be converted         */
    int    to_unit);   /* Convert to convert this unit */
```

Converts a value from one unit to another. The from_unit and to_unit arguments can be one of: XmPIXELS, Xm100TH_MILLIMETERS, Xm1000TH_INCHES, Xm100TH_POINTS, or Xm100TH_FONT_UNITS. If successful, this function returns the converted value; otherwise, it returns zero.

XmCreateArrowButton
```
#include <Xm/ArrowB.h>
Widget XmCreateArrowButton(
    Widget   parent,   /* ID of parent widget            */
    String   name,     /* Name of new widget             */
    ArgList  arglist,  /* Array of resource values       */
    Cardinal nargs);   /* Number of arguments in arglist */
```

Creates an XmArrowButton widget as a child of the widget parent and returns the ID of the newly created widget. Consult the reference entry of the XmArrowButton widget for a list of its resources.

XmCreateArrowButtonGadget
```
#include <Xm/ArrowBG.h>
Widget XmCreateArrowButtonGadget(
    Widget    parent,   /* ID of parent widget        */
    String    name,     /* Name of new widget         */
    ArgList   arglist,  /* Array of resource values   */
    Cardinal  nargs);   /* Number of arguments in arglist */
```

Creates an XmArrowButtonGadget as a child of the widget parent and returns the ID of the newly created widget. Consult the reference entry of XmArrowButtonGadget for a list of its resources.

XmCreateBulletinBoard
```
#include <Xm/BulletinB.h>
Widget XmCreateBulletinBoard(
    Widget    parent,   /* ID of parent widget        */
    String    name,     /* Name of new widget         */
    ArgList   arglist,  /* Array of resource values   */
    Cardinal  nargs);   /* Number of arguments in arglist */
```

Creates an XmBulletinBoard widget as a child of the widget parent and returns the ID of the newly created widget. Consult the reference entry of the XmBulletinBoard widget for a list of its resources.

XmCreateBulletinBoardDialog
```
#include <Xm/BulletinB.h>
Widget XmCreateBulletinBoardDialog(
    Widget    parent,   /* ID of parent widget        */
    String    name,     /* Name of new widget         */
    ArgList   arglist,  /* Array of resource values   */
    Cardinal  nargs);   /* Number of arguments in arglist */
```

Creates an XmDialogShell (as a child of parent) and an XmBulletinBoard widget as an unmanaged child of the XmDialogShell widget. This function returns the ID of the XmBulletinBoard widget. You can pop up the dialog by calling XtManage with the XmBulletinBoard's ID as argument. Consult the reference entries of the XmDialogShell and XmBulletinBoard widgets for a list of their resources.

XmCreateCascadeButton
```
#include <Xm/CascadeB.h>
Widget XmCreateCascadeButton(
    Widget    parent,   /* ID of parent widget        */
    String    name,     /* Name of new widget         */
    ArgList   arglist,  /* Array of resource values   */
    Cardinal  nargs);   /* Number of arguments in arglist */
```

Creates an XmCascadeButton widget as a child of the widget parent and returns the ID of the newly created widget. Consult the reference entry of the XmCascadeButton widget for a list of its resources.

XmCreateCascadeButtonGadget
```
#include <Xm/CascadeBG.h>
Widget XmCreateCascadeButtonGadget(
    Widget    parent,   /* ID of parent widget        */
    String    name,     /* Name of new widget         */
    ArgList   arglist,  /* Array of resource values   */
    Cardinal  nargs);   /* Number of arguments in arglist */
```

Creates an `XmCascadeButtonGadget` widget as a child of the widget `parent` and returns the ID of the newly created widget. Consult the reference entry of `XmCascadeButtonGadget` for a list of its resources.

XmCreateCommand
```
#include <Xm/Command.h>
Widget XmCreateCommand(
    Widget   parent,    /* ID of parent widget          */
    String   name,      /* Name of new widget           */
    ArgList  arglist,   /* Array of resource values      */
    Cardinal nargs);    /* Number of arguments in arglist */
```

Creates an `XmCommand` widget as a child of the widget `parent` and returns the ID of the newly created widget. Consult the reference entry of the `XmCommand` widget for a list of its resources.

XmCreateDialogShell
```
#include <Xm/DialogS.h>
Widget XmCreateDialogShell(
    Widget   parent,    /* ID of parent widget          */
    String   name,      /* Name of new widget           */
    ArgList  arglist,   /* Array of resource values      */
    Cardinal nargs);    /* Number of arguments in arglist */
```

Creates an `XmDialogShell` widget as a child of the widget `parent` and returns the ID of the newly created widget. Consult the reference entry of the `XmDialogShell` widget for a list of its resources.

XmCreateDragIcon
```
#include <Xm/DragIcon.h>
Widget XmCreateDragIcon(
    Widget   parent,    /* ID of parent widget          */
    String   name,      /* Name of new widget           */
    ArgList  arglist,   /* Array of resource values      */
    Cardinal nargs);    /* Number of arguments in arglist */
```

Creates an `XmDragIcon` widget as a child of the widget `parent` and returns the ID of the newly created widget. Consult the reference entry of the `XmDragIcon` widget for a list of its resources.

XmCreateDrawingArea
```
#include <Xm/DrawingA.h>
Widget XmCreateDrawingArea(
    Widget   parent,    /* ID of parent widget          */
    String   name,      /* Name of new widget           */
    ArgList  arglist,   /* Array of resource values      */
    Cardinal nargs);    /* Number of arguments in arglist */
```

Creates an `XmDrawingArea` widget as a child of the widget `parent` and returns the ID of the newly created widget. Consult the reference entry of the `XmDrawingArea` widget for a list of its resources.

XmCreateDrawButton
```
#include <Xm/DrawnB.h>
Widget XmCreateDrawButton(
    Widget   parent,    /* ID of parent widget          */
    String   name,      /* Name of new widget           */
    ArgList  arglist,   /* Array of resource values      */
    Cardinal nargs);    /* Number of arguments in arglist */
```

Creates an `XmDrawnButton` widget as a child of the widget `parent` and returns the ID of the newly created widget. Consult the reference entry of the `XmDrawnButton` widget for a list of its resources.

XmCreateErrorDialog
```
#include <Xm/MessageB.h>
Widget XmCreateErrorDialog(
    Widget   parent,    /* ID of parent widget        */
    String   name,      /* Name of new widget         */
    ArgList  arglist,   /* Array of resource values   */
    Cardinal nargs);    /* Number of arguments in arglist */
```

Creates an XmDialogShell widget (as a child of parent) and an XmMessageBox widget as an unmanaged child of the XmDialogShell widget. This function returns the ID of the XmMessageBox widget. You can pop up the dialog by calling XtManage with the XmMessageBox's ID as argument. The error dialog includes a symbol, a message, and three buttons labeled OK, Cancel, and Help. The default symbol is an octagon with a diagonal slash across it. Consult the reference entries of the XmDialogShell and XmMessageBox widgets for a list of their resources.

XmCreateFileSelectionBox
```
#include <Xm/FileSB.h>
Widget XmCreateFileSelectionBox(
    Widget   parent,    /* ID of parent widget        */
    String   name,      /* Name of new widget         */
    ArgList  arglist,   /* Array of resource values   */
    Cardinal nargs);    /* Number of arguments in arglist */
```

Creates an XmFileSelectionBox widget as a child of the widget parent and returns the ID of the newly created widget. Consult the reference entry of the XmFileSelectionBox widget for a list of its resources.

XmCreateFileSelectionDialog
```
#include <Xm/FileSB.h>
Widget XmCreateFileSelectionDialog(
    Widget   parent,    /* ID of parent widget        */
    String   name,      /* Name of new widget         */
    ArgList  arglist,   /* Array of resource values   */
    Cardinal nargs);    /* Number of arguments in arglist */
```

Creates an XmDialogShell widget (as a child of parent) and an XmFileSelectionBox widget as an unmanaged child of the XmDialogShell widget. This function returns the ID of the XmFileSelectionBox widget. You can pop up the dialog by calling XtManage with the XmFileSelectionBox's ID as argument. Consult the reference entries of the XmDialogShell and XmFileSelectionBox widgets for a list of their resources.

XmCreateForm
```
#include <Xm/Form.h>
Widget XmCreateForm(
    Widget   parent,    /* ID of parent widget        */
    String   name,      /* Name of new widget         */
    ArgList  arglist,   /* Array of resource values   */
    Cardinal nargs);    /* Number of arguments in arglist */
```

Creates an XmForm widget as a child of the widget parent and returns the ID of the newly created widget. Consult the reference entry of the XmForm widget for a list of its resources.

XmCreateFormDialog
```
#include <Xm/Form.h>
Widget XmCreateFormDialog(
    Widget   parent,    /* ID of parent widget        */
    String   name,      /* Name of new widget         */
```

```
     ArgList  arglist,  /* Array of resource values      */
     Cardinal nargs);   /* Number of arguments in arglist */
```

Creates an XmDialogShell widget (as a child of parent) and an XmForm widget as an unmanaged child of the XmDialogShell widget. This function returns the ID of the XmForm widget. You can pop up the dialog by calling XtManage with the XmForm's ID as argument. Consult the reference entries of the XmDialogShell and XmForm widgets for a list of their resources.

XmCreateFrame
```
#include <Xm/Frame.h>
Widget XmCreateFrame(
     Widget   parent,   /* ID of parent widget            */
     String   name,     /* Name of new widget             */
     ArgList  arglist,  /* Array of resource values       */
     Cardinal nargs);   /* Number of arguments in arglist */
```

Creates an XmFrame widget as a child of the widget parent and returns the ID of the newly created widget. Consult the reference entry of the XmFrame widget for a list of its resources.

XmCreateInformationDialog
```
#include <Xm/MessageB.h>
Widget XmCreateInformationDialog(
     Widget   parent,   /* ID of parent widget            */
     String   name,     /* Name of new widget             */
     ArgList  arglist,  /* Array of resource values       */
     Cardinal nargs);   /* Number of arguments in arglist */
```

Creates an XmDialogShell widget (as a child of parent) and an XmMessageBox widget as an unmanaged child of the XmDialogShell widget. This function returns the ID of the XmMessageBox widget. You can pop up the dialog by calling XtManage with the XmMessageBox's ID as argument. The information dialog includes a symbol, a message, and three buttons labeled OK, Cancel, and Help. The default symbol is i. Consult the reference entries of the XmDialogShell and XmMessageBox widgets for a list of their resources.

XmCreateLabel
```
#include <Xm/Label.h>
Widget XmCreateLabel(
     Widget   parent,   /* ID of parent widget            */
     String   name,     /* Name of new widget             */
     ArgList  arglist,  /* Array of resource values       */
     Cardinal nargs);   /* Number of arguments in arglist */
```

Creates an XmLabel widget as a child of parent and returns the ID of the newly created widget. Consult the reference entry of the XmLabel widget for a list of its resources.

XmCreateLabelGadget
```
#include <Xm/LabelG.h>
Widget XmCreateLabelGadget(
     Widget   parent,   /* ID of parent widget            */
     String   name,     /* Name of new widget             */
     ArgList  arglist,  /* Array of resource values       */
     Cardinal nargs);   /* Number of arguments in arglist */
```

Creates an XmLabelGadget widget as a child of parent and returns the ID of the newly created widget. Consult the reference entry of XmLabelGadget for a list of its resources.

XmCreateList
```
#include <Xm/List.h>
Widget XmCreateList(
    Widget   parent,    /* ID of parent widget         */
    String   name,      /* Name of new widget          */
    ArgList  arglist,   /* Array of resource values    */
    Cardinal nargs);    /* Number of arguments in arglist */
```

Creates an XmList widget as a child of parent and returns the ID of the newly created widget. Consult the reference entry of the XmList widget for a list of its resources.

XmCreateMainWindow
```
#include <Xm/MainW.h>
Widget XmCreateMainWindow(
    Widget   parent,    /* ID of parent widget         */
    String   name,      /* Name of new widget          */
    ArgList  arglist,   /* Array of resource values    */
    Cardinal nargs);    /* Number of arguments in arglist */
```

Creates an XmMainWindow widget as a child of parent and returns the ID of the newly created widget. Consult the reference entry of the XmMainWindow widget for a list of its resources.

XmCreateMenuBar
```
#include <Xm/RowColumn.h>
Widget XmCreateMenuBar(
    Widget   parent,    /* ID of parent widget         */
    String   name,      /* Name of new widget          */
    ArgList  arglist,   /* Array of resource values    */
    CARDINAL NARGS);    /* NUMBER OF ARGUMENTS IN ARGLIST */
```

Creates an XmRowColumn widget of type XmMENUBAR as a child of parent and returns the ID of the newly created widget. The newly created widget will only accept child widgets of type XmCascadeButton (or a subclass of XmCascadeButton). You can construct pull-down menus by inserting XmCascadeButtons as children of the menubar. Consult the reference entry of the XmRowColumn widget for a list of its resources.

XmCreateMenuShell
```
#include <Xm/MenuShell.h>
Widget XmCreateMenuShell(
    Widget   parent,    /* ID of parent widget         */
    String   name,      /* Name of new widget          */
    ArgList  arglist,   /* Array of resource values    */
    Cardinal nargs);    /* Number of arguments in arglist */
```

Creates an XmMenuShell widget as a child of parent and returns the ID of the newly created widget. Consult the reference entry of the XmMenuShell widget for a list of its resources.

XmCreateMessageBox
```
#include <Xm/MessageB.h>
Widget XmCreateMessageBox(
    Widget   parent,    /* ID of parent widget         */
    String   name,      /* Name of new widget          */
    ArgList  arglist,   /* Array of resource values    */
    Cardinal nargs);    /* Number of arguments in arglist */
```

Creates an XmMessageBox widget as a child of parent and returns the ID of the newly created widget. The XmMessageBox widget includes a symbol, a message, and three pushbuttons whose default labels are OK, Cancel, and Help. By default, the message box does not have any symbol. Consult the reference entry of the XmMessageBox widget for a complete list of its resources.

XmCreateMessageDialog
```
#include <Xm/MessageB.h>
Widget XmCreateMessageDialog(
    Widget    parent,    /* ID of parent widget            */
    String    name,      /* Name of new widget             */
    ArgList   arglist,   /* Array of resource values       */
    Cardinal nargs);     /* Number of arguments in arglist */
```

Creates an XmDialogShell widget (as a child of parent) and an XmMessageBox widget as an unmanaged child of the XmDialogShell widget. This function returns the ID of the XmMessageBox widget. You can pop up the dialog by calling XtManage with the XmMessageBox's ID as argument. Consult the reference entries of the XmDialogShell and XmMessageBox widgets for a list of their resources.

XmCreateOptionMenu
```
#include <Xm/RowColumn.h>
Widget XmCreateOptionMenu(
    Widget    parent,    /* ID of parent widget            */
    String    name,      /* Name of new widget             */
    ArgList   arglist,   /* Array of resource values       */
    Cardinal nargs);     /* Number of arguments in arglist */
```

Creates an XmRowColumn widget of type XmMENU_OPTION as a child of parent and returns the ID of the newly created widget. Consult the reference entry of the XmRowColumn widget for a list of its resources.

XmCreatePanedWindow
```
#include <Xm/PanedW.h>
Widget XmCreatePanedWindow(
    Widget    parent,    /* ID of parent widget            */
    String    name,      /* Name of new widget             */
    ArgList   arglist,   /* Array of resource values       */
    Cardinal nargs);     /* Number of arguments in arglist */
```

Creates an XmPanedWindow widget as a child of parent and returns the ID of the newly created widget. Consult the reference entry of the XmPanedWindow widget for a list of its resources.

XmCreatePopupMenu
```
#include <Xm/RowColumn.h>
Widget XmCreatePopupMenu(
    Widget    parent,    /* ID of parent widget            */
    String    name,      /* Name of new widget             */
    ArgList   arglist,   /* Array of resource values       */
    Cardinal nargs);     /* Number of arguments in arglist */
```

Creates an XmMenuShell widget (as a child of parent) and an XmRowColumn widget of type XmMENU_POPUP as an unmanaged child of the XmMenuShell widget. This function returns the ID of the XmRowColumn widget. You can use the pop-up menu by first positioning it with the XmMenuPosition function and then managing the menu by calling XtManage with the XmRowColumn's ID as argument. Consult the reference entry of the XmRowColumn widget for a list of its resources.

XmCreatePromptDialog
```
#include <Xm/SelectioB.h>
```

```
Widget XmCreatePromptDialog(
    Widget   parent,   /* ID of parent widget             */
    String   name,     /* Name of new widget              */
    ArgList  arglist,  /* Array of resource values        */
    Cardinal nargs);   /* Number of arguments in arglist  */
```

Creates an XmDialogShell widget (as a child of parent) and an XmSelectionBox widget as an unmanaged child of the XmDialogShell widget. This function returns the ID of the XmSelectionBox widget. You can pop up the dialog by calling XtManage with the XmSelectionBox's ID as argument. Consult the reference entries of the XmDialogShell and XmSelectionBox widgets for a list of their resources.

XmCreatePulldownMenu
```
#include <Xm/RowColumn.h>
Widget XmCreatePulldownMenu(
    Widget   parent,   /* ID of parent widget             */
    String   name,     /* Name of new widget              */
    ArgList  arglist,  /* Array of resource values        */
    Cardinal nargs);   /* Number of arguments in arglist  */
```

Creates an XmMenuShell widget (as a child of parent) and an XmRowColumn widget of type XmMENU_PULLDOWN as an unmanaged child of the XmMenuShell widget. This function returns the ID of the XmRowColumn widget. Consult the reference entry of the XmRowColumn widget for a list of its resources.

XmCreatePushButton
```
#include <Xm/PushB.h>
Widget XmCreatePushButton(
    Widget   parent,   /* ID of parent widget             */
    String   name,     /* Name of new widget              */
    ArgList  arglist,  /* Array of resource values        */
    Cardinal nargs);   /* Number of arguments in arglist  */
```

Creates an XmPushButton widget as a child of parent and returns the ID of the newly created widget. Consult the reference entry of the XmPushButton widget for a list of its resources.

XmCreatePushButtonGadget
```
#include <Xm/PushBG.h>
Widget XmCreatePushButtonGadget(
    Widget   parent,   /* ID of parent widget             */
    String   name,     /* Name of new widget              */
    ArgList  arglist,  /* Array of resource values        */
    Cardinal nargs);   /* Number of arguments in arglist  */
```

Creates an XmPushButtonGadget widget as a child of parent and returns the ID of the newly created widget. Consult the reference entry of XmPushButtonGadget for a list of its resources.

XmCreateQuestionDialog
```
#include <Xm/MessageB.h>
Widget XmCreateQuestionDialog(
    Widget   parent,   /* ID of parent widget             */
    String   name,     /* Name of new widget              */
    ArgList  arglist,  /* Array of resource values        */
    Cardinal nargs);   /* Number of arguments in arglist  */
```

Creates an XmDialogShell widget (as a child of parent) and an XmMessageBox widget as an unmanaged child of the XmDialogShell widget. This function returns the ID of the XmMessageBox widget. You can pop up the dialog by calling XtManage with the XmMessageBox's ID as argument. The question dialog includes a symbol, a message, and three buttons labeled OK, Cancel, and Help. The default symbol is a question mark. Consult the reference entries of the XmDialogShell and XmMessageBox widgets for a list of their resources.

XmCreateRadioBox
```
#include <Xm/RowColumn.h>
Widget XmCreateRadioBox(
    Widget   parent,   /* ID of parent widget         */
    String   name,     /* Name of new widget          */
    ArgList  arglist,  /* Array of resource values     */
    Cardinal nargs);   /* Number of arguments in arglist */
```

Creates an XmRowColumn widget of type XmWORK_AREA as a child of parent and returns the ID of the newly created widget. You typically place a number of toggle buttons inside this XmRowColumn widget and use it as a "radio menu" to enable selection of one out of a set of choices. Consult the reference entry of the XmRowColumn widget for a list of its resources.

XmCreateRowColumn
```
#include <Xm/RowColumn.h>
Widget XmCreateRowColumn(
    Widget   parent,   /* ID of parent widget         */
    String   name,     /* Name of new widget          */
    ArgList  arglist,  /* Array of resource values     */
    Cardinal nargs);   /* Number of arguments in arglist */
```

Creates an XmRowColumn widget as a child of parent and returns the ID of the newly created widget. The XmNrowColumnType resource specifies the type of XmRowColumn widget you want to create. If the XmNrowColumnType resource is unspecified, it will be of type XmWORK_AREA by default. Consult the reference entry of the XmRowColumn widget for a complete list of its resources.

XmCreateScale
```
#include <Xm/Scale.h>
Widget XmCreateScale(
    Widget   parent,   /* ID of parent widget         */
    String   name,     /* Name of new widget          */
    ArgList  arglist,  /* Array of resource values     */
    Cardinal nargs);   /* Number of arguments in arglist */
```

Creates an XmScale widget as a child of parent and returns the ID of the newly created widget. Consult the reference entry of the XmScale widget for a list of its resources.

XmCreateScrollBar
```
#include <Xm/ScrollBar.h>
Widget XmCreateScrollBar(
    Widget   parent,   /* ID of parent widget         */
    String   name,     /* Name of new widget          */
    ArgList  arglist,  /* Array of resource values     */
    Cardinal nargs);   /* Number of arguments in arglist */
```

Creates an XmScrollBar widget as a child of parent and returns the ID of the newly created widget. Consult the reference entry of the XmScrollBar widget for a list of its resources.

XmCreateScrolledList
```
#include <Xm/List.h>
Widget XmCreateScrolledList(
```

```
Widget   parent,     /* ID of parent widget            */
String   name,       /* Name of new widget             */
ArgList  arglist,    /* Array of resource values       */
Cardinal nargs);     /* Number of arguments in arglist */
```

Creates an XmScrolledWindow widget (as a child of parent) and an XmList widget as an unmanaged child of the XmScrolledWindow widget. This function returns the ID of the XmList widget. You can get the ID of the XmScrolledWindow by using the XtParent function with the XmList widget's ID as argument. Consult the reference entries of the XmScrolledWindow and XmList widgets for a list of their resources.

XmCreateScrolledText
```
#include <Xm/Text.h>
Widget XmCreateScrolledText(
     Widget   parent,     /* ID of parent widget            */
     String   name,       /* Name of new widget             */
     ArgList  arglist,    /* Array of resource values       */
     Cardinal nargs);     /* Number of arguments in arglist */
```

Creates an XmScrolledWindow widget (as a child of parent) and an XmText widget as an unmanaged child of the XmScrolledWindow widget. This function returns the ID of the XmText widget. You can get the ID of the XmScrolledWindow by using the XtParent function with the XmText widget's ID as argument. Consult the reference entries of the XmScrolledWindow and XmText widgets for a list of their resources.

XmCreateScrolledWindow
```
#include <Xm/ScrolledW.h>
Widget XmCreateScrolledWindow(
     Widget   parent,     /* ID of parent widget            */
     String   name,       /* Name of new widget             */
     ArgList  arglist,    /* Array of resource values       */
     Cardinal nargs);     /* Number of arguments in arglist */
```

Creates an XmScrolledWindow widget as a child of parent and returns the ID of the newly created widget. Consult the reference entry of the XmScrolledWindow widget for a list of its resources.

XmCreateSelectionBox
```
#include <Xm/SelectioB.h>
Widget XmCreateSelectionBox(
     Widget   parent,     /* ID of parent widget            */
     String   name,       /* Name of new widget             */
     ArgList  arglist,    /* Array of resource values       */
     Cardinal nargs);     /* Number of arguments in arglist */
```

Creates an XmSelectionBox widget as a child of parent and returns the ID of the newly created widget. Consult the reference entry of the XmSelectionBox widget for a list of its resources.

XmCreateSelectionDialog
```
#include <Xm/SelectioB.h>
Widget XmCreateSelectionDialog(
     Widget   parent,     /* ID of parent widget            */
     String   name,       /* Name of new widget             */
     ArgList  arglist,    /* Array of resource values       */
     Cardinal nargs);     /* Number of arguments in arglist */
```

Creates an `XmDialogShell` widget (as a child of `parent`) and an `XmSelectionBox` widget as an unmanaged child of the `XmDialogShell` widget. This function returns the ID of the `XmSelectionBox` widget. You can pop up the dialog by calling `XtManage` with the `XmSelectionBox`'s ID as argument. Consult the reference entries of the `XmDialogShell` and `XmSelectionBox` widgets for a list of their resources.

XmCreateSeparator
```
#include <Xm/Separator.h>
Widget XmCreateSeparator(
    Widget   parent,   /* ID of parent widget         */
    String   name,     /* Name of new widget          */
    ArgList  arglist,  /* Array of resource values     */
    Cardinal nargs);   /* Number of arguments in arglist */
```

Creates an `XmSeparator` widget as a child of `parent` and returns the ID of the newly created widget. Consult the reference entry of the `XmSeparator` widget for a list of its resources.

XmCreateSeparatorGadget
```
#include <Xm/SeparatoG.h>
Widget XmCreateSeparatorGadget(
    Widget   parent,   /* ID of parent widget         */
    String   name,     /* Name of new widget          */
    ArgList  arglist,  /* Array of resource values     */
    Cardinal nargs);   /* Number of arguments in arglist */
```

Creates an `XmSeparatorGadget` widget as a child of `parent` and returns the ID of the newly created widget. Consult the reference entry of `XmSeparatorGadget` for a list of its resources.

XmCreateSimpleCheckBox
```
#include <Xm/Xm.h>
Widget XmCreateSimpleCheckBox(
    Widget   parent,   /* ID of parent widget         */
    String   name,     /* Name of new widget          */
    ArgList  arglist,  /* Array of resource values     */
    Cardinal nargs);   /* Number of arguments in arglist */
```

Creates an `XmRowColumn` widget of type `XmWORK_AREA` as a child of `parent` and returns the ID of the newly created widget. This function also creates a number of `XmToggleButtonGadgets` that you specify through the list of resources `arglist`. You have to specify the following resources of the `XmRowColumn` widget: `XmNbuttons`, `XmNbuttonCount`, `XmNbuttonSet`, and `XmNsimpleCallback`. Additionally, this function sets the `XmNradioAlwaysOne` resource to `False`.

XmCreateSimpleMenuBar
```
#include <Xm/Xm.h>
Widget XmCreateSimpleMenuBar(
    Widget   parent,   /* ID of parent widget         */
    String   name,     /* Name of new widget          */
    ArgList  arglist,  /* Array of resource values     */
    Cardinal nargs);   /* Number of arguments in arglist */
```

Creates an `XmRowColumn` widget of type `XmMENU_BAR` as a child of `parent` and returns the ID of the newly created widget. This function also creates a number of buttons whose style and callbacks you specify through the list of resources in `arglist`. You have to specify the following resources of the `XmRowColumn` widget: `XmNbuttonAccelerators`, `XmNbuttonAcceleratorText`, `XmNbuttonMnemonics`, `XmNbuttonMnemonicCharSets`, `XmNbuttons`, `XmNbuttonType`, `XmNbuttonCount`, `XmNbuttonSet`, and `XmNsimpleCallback`.

XmCreateSimpleOptionMenu
```
#include <Xm/Xm.h>
Widget XmCreateSimpleOptionMenu(
    Widget   parent,    /* ID of parent widget           */
    String   name,      /* Name of new widget            */
    ArgList  arglist,   /* Array of resource values      */
    Cardinal nargs);    /* Number of arguments in arglist */
```

Creates an XmRowColumn widget of type XmMENU_OPTION as a child of parent and returns the ID of the newly created widget. This function also creates a submenu with a number of XmPushButtonGadget children. To create the option menu, you have to specify the following resources of the XmRowColumn widget: XmNbuttonAccelerators, XmNbuttonAcceleratorText, XmNbuttonMnemonics, XmNbuttonMnemonicCharSets, XmNbuttons, XmNbuttonType, XmNbuttonCount, XmNbuttonSet, and XmNsimpleCallback. Additionally, you can use the XmNoptionLabel to set the label to be displayed to the left of the option menu.

XmCreateSimplePopupMenu
```
#include <Xm/Xm.h>
Widget XmCreateSimplePopupMenu(
    Widget   parent,    /* ID of parent widget           */
    String   name,      /* Name of new widget            */
    ArgList  arglist,   /* Array of resource values      */
    Cardinal nargs);    /* Number of arguments in arglist */
```

Creates an XmRowColumn widget of type XmMENU_POPUP as a child of parent and returns the ID of the newly created widget. This function also creates a number of buttons as children. You have to specify the button's parameters through the resources in arglist.

XmCreateSimplePulldownMenu
```
#include <Xm/Xm.h>
Widget XmCreateSimplePulldownMenu(
    Widget   parent,    /* ID of parent widget           */
    String   name,      /* Name of new widget            */
    ArgList  arglist,   /* Array of resource values      */
    Cardinal nargs);    /* Number of arguments in arglist */
```

Creates an XmRowColumn widget of type XmMENU_PULLDOWN as a child of parent and returns the ID of the newly created widget. This function also creates a number of buttons as children. You have to specify the button's parameters through the resources in arglist. Additionally, you can attach the newly created pull-down menu to an XmCascadeButton or an XmCascadeButtonGadget whose ID you provide in the XmNpostFromButton resource of the XmRowColumn widget.

XmCreateSimpleRadioBox
```
#include <Xm/Xm.h>
Widget XmCreateSimpleRadioBox(
    Widget   parent,    /* ID of parent widget           */
    String   name,      /* Name of new widget            */
    ArgList  arglist,   /* Array of resource values      */
    Cardinal nargs);    /* Number of arguments in arglist */
```

Creates an XmRowColumn widget of type XmWORK_AREA as a child of parent and returns the ID of the newly created widget. This function also creates a number of XmToggleButtonGadgets as children. You have to specify the toggle buttons through the resources in arglist.

XmCreateTemplateDialog
```
#include <Xm/MessageB.h>
```

```
Widget XmCreateTemplateDialog(
    Widget    parent,    /* ID of parent widget            */
    String    name,      /* Name of new widget             */
    ArgList   arglist,   /* Array of resource values       */
    Cardinal nargs);     /* Number of arguments in arglist */
```

Creates a `DialogShell` widget and an unmanaged `MessageBox` child of the `DialogShell`. This function returns the widget ID of the `MessageBox`. You can build a custom dialog by adding other children to the `MessageBox`.

XmCreateText
```
#include <Xm/Text.h>
Widget XmCreateText(
    Widget    parent,    /* ID of parent widget            */
    String    name,      /* Name of new widget             */
    ArgList   arglist,   /* Array of resource values       */
    Cardinal nargs);     /* Number of arguments in arglist */
```

Creates an `XmText` widget as a child of `parent` and returns the ID of the newly created widget. Consult the reference entry of the `XmText` widget for a list of its resources.

XmCreateTextField
```
#include <Xm/TextF.h>
Widget XmCreateTextField(
    Widget    parent,    /* ID of parent widget            */
    String    name,      /* Name of new widget             */
    ArgList   arglist,   /* Array of resource values       */
    Cardinal nargs);     /* Number of arguments in arglist */
```

Creates an `XmTextField` widget as a child of `parent` and returns the ID of the newly created widget. Consult the reference entry of the `XmTextField` widget for a list of its resources.

XmCreateToggleButton
```
#include <Xm/ToggleB.h>
Widget XmCreateToggleButton(
    Widget    parent,    /* ID of parent widget            */
    String    name,      /* Name of new widget             */
    ArgList   arglist,   /* Array of resource values       */
    Cardinal nargs);     /* Number of arguments in arglist */
```

Creates an `XmToggleButton` widget as a child of `parent` and returns the ID of the newly created widget. Consult the reference entry of the `XmToggleButton` widget for a list of its resources.

XmCreateToggleButtonGadget
```
#include <Xm/ToggleBG.h>
Widget XmCreateToggleButtonGadget(
    Widget    parent,    /* ID of parent widget            */
    String    name,      /* Name of new widget             */
    ArgList   arglist,   /* Array of resource values       */
    Cardinal nargs);     /* Number of arguments in arglist */
```

Creates an `XmToggleButtonGadget` widget as a child of `parent` and returns the ID of the newly created widget. Consult the reference entry of `XmToggleButtonGadget` for a list of its resources.

XmCreateWarningDialog
```
#include <Xm/MessageB.h>
Widget XmCreateWarningDialog(
    Widget    parent,    /* ID of parent widget            */
```

```
String    name,     /* Name of new widget            */
ArgList   arglist,  /* Array of resource values      */
Cardinal  nargs);   /* Number of arguments in arglist */
```

Creates an XmDialogShell widget (as a child of parent) and an XmMessageBox widget as an unmanaged child of the XmDialogShell widget. This function returns the ID of the XmMessageBox widget. You can pop up the dialog by calling XtManage with the XmMessageBox's ID as argument. The warning dialog includes a symbol, a message, and three buttons labeled OK, Cancel, and Help. The default symbol is an exclamation mark. Consult the reference entries of the XmDialogShell and XmMessageBox widgets for a list of their resources.

XmCreateWorkArea
```
#include <Xm/RowColumn.h>
Widget XmCreateWorkArea(
    Widget    parent,   /* ID of parent widget          */
    String    name,     /* Name of new widget           */
    ArgList   arglist,  /* Array of resource values     */
    Cardinal  nargs);   /* Number of arguments in arglist */
```

Creates an XmRowColumn widget of type XmWORK_AREA as a child of parent and returns the ID of the newly created widget. You can have the same effect by calling XmCreateRowColumn with the XmNrowColumnType resource set to XmWORK_AREA.

XmCreateWorkingDialog
```
#include <Xm/MessageB.h>
Widget XmCreateWorkingDialog(
    Widget    parent,   /* ID of parent widget          */
    String    name,     /* Name of new widget           */
    ArgList   arglist,  /* Array of resource values     */
    Cardinal  nargs);   /* Number of arguments in arglist */
```

Creates an XmDialogShell widget (as a child of parent) and an XmMessageBox widget as an unmanaged child of the XmDialogShell widget. This function returns the ID of the XmMessageBox widget. You can pop up the dialog by calling XtManage with the XmMessageBox's ID as argument. The working dialog includes a symbol, a message, and three buttons labeled OK, Cancel, and Help. The default symbol is an hourglass. Consult the reference entries of the XmDialogShell and XmMessageBox widgets for a list of their resources.

XmCvtCTToXmString
```
#include <Xm/Xm.h>
XmString XmCvtCTToXmString(
    char *text);    /* Convert this compound text */
```

Converts the specified compound text to an XmString type and returns the converted XmString.

XmCvtStringToUnitType
```
#include <Xm/Xm.h>
void XmCvtStringToUnitType(
    XmValuePtr args,   /* Arguments to the converter   */
    Cardinal   nargs), /* Number of arguments in args */
    XrmValue   *from,  /* Convert from this value and */
    XrmValue   *to);   /* return converted value here */
```

Converts a string to a unit type. You do not call this function directly; instead, install XmCvtStringToUnitType as a converter by calling the Xt Intrinsics function XtAddConverter.

XmCvtXmStringToCT
```
#include <Xm/Xm.h>
char* XmCvtXmStringToCT(
    XmString string); /* Convert this to compound text */
```

Converts an XmString to a compound text and returns the resulting compound text.

XmDeactivateProtocol
```
#include <Xm/Protocols.h>
void XmDeactivateProtocol(
    Widget shell,      /* Protocol is for this widget  */
    Atom   property,   /* Property containing protocol */
    Atom   protocol ); /* Protocol to be deactivated   */
```

Removes protocol from the specified property of the shell. Used for interclient communications. (Please consult a book on X Window System programming for more information on properties and atoms.)

XmDeactivateWMPProtocol
```
#include <Xm/Protocols.h>
void XmDeactivateWMPProtocol(
    Widget shell,      /* Protocol is for this widget  */
    Atom   protocol);  /* Protocol to be activated     */
```

Calls XmDeactivateProtocol with property set to the atom returned by interning WM_PROTOCOLS.

XmDestroyPixmap
```
#include <Xm/Xm.h>
Boolean XmDestroyPixmap(
    Screen *screen, /* Screen for which pixmap was cached */
    Pixmap pixmap); /* Pixmap to be removed from cache    */
```

Removes the specified pixmap from Motif's pixmap cache. Returns True if all goes well, or False if no such pixmap exists for the specified Screen.

XmDragCancel
```
#include <Xm/DragDrop.h>
void XmDragCancel(
    Widget drag_context); /* ID of DragContext with information
                             about the drag-and-drop operation */
```

Cancels a drag operation in progress.

XmDragStart
```
#include <Xm/DragDrop.h>
Widget XmDragStart(
    Widget   w,      /* ID of smallest widget that
                        encloses items being dragged */
    XEvent  *event, /* XEvent that triggered drag    */
    ArgList  args,   /* Argument list with resources  */
    Cardinal nargs); /* Number of arguments in args   */
```

Starts a drag operation by creating a DragContext widget, initializing it, and returning that widget's ID.

XmDropSiteConfigureStackingOrder
```
#include <Xm/DragDrop.h>
void XmDropSiteConfigureStackingOrder(
```

```
    Widget    widget,      /* Drop site to be restacked   */
    Widget    sibling,     /* A sibling drop site         */
    Cardinal stack_mode); /* One of: XmABOVE or XmBELOW */
```

Changes the stacking order of the drop site specified by the widget argument.

XmDropSiteEndUpdate
```
#include <Xm/DragDrop.h>
void XmDropSiteEndUpdate(
    Widget anyWidget); /* Widget used to identify the shell
                          that contains the drop sites    */
```

Ends the update process initiated by XmDropSiteStartUpdate.

XmDropSiteGetActiveVisuals
```
#include <Xm/DragDrop.h>
XmDropSiteVisuals XmDropSiteGetActiveVisuals(
    Widget widget); /* Drop site ID */
```

Returns information about the currently active visual appearance of a drop site.

XmDropSiteQueryStackingOrder
```
#include <Xm/DragDrop.h>
void XmDropSiteQueryStackingOrder(
    Widget    widget,      /* Return info for this widget     */
    Widget    *parent,     /* ID of parent                    */
    Widget    **children,  /* List of children drop sites     */
    Cardinal *nchildren); /* Number of children returned here */
```

Returns the parent and the list of children registered as drop sites for a specified widget. You are responsible for calling XtFree to release the memory allocated for the list of children.

XmDropSiteRegister
```
#include <Xm/DragDrop.h>
void XmDropSiteRegister(
    Widget    widget, /* Widget being registered as a drop site */
    ArgList   args,   /* List of resources for the drop site    */
    Cardinal nargs); /* Number of entries in args               */
```

Registers the specified widget as a drop site and sets the resources that define the behavior of the drop site.

XmDropSiteRetrieve
```
#include <Xm/DragDrop.h>
void XmDropSiteRetrieve(
    Widget    widget, /* Drop site whose resources are retrieved*/
    ArgList   args,   /* List of resources for the drop site    */
    Cardinal nargs); /* Number of entries in args               */
```

Retrieves the resources from a specified drop site.

XmDropSiteStartUpdate
```
#include <Xm/DragDrop.h>
void XmDropSiteStartUpdate(
    Widget anyWidget); /* Widget used to identify the shell
                          that contains the drop sites    */
```

Starts the process of updating all drop sites within the same shell widget.

XmDropSiteUnregister
```
#include <Xm/DragDrop.h>
void XmDropSiteUnregister(
    Widget widget); /* Unregister this drop site */
```

Frees the drop site information associated with the specified widget.

XmDropSiteUpdate
```
#include <Xm/DragDrop.h>
void XmDropSiteUpdate(
    Widget   widget, /* Drop site whose resources are altered */
    ArgList  args,   /* List of resources for the drop site   */
    Cardinal nargs); /* Number of entries in args             */
```

Modifies the resources of a specified drop site.

XmDropTransferAdd
```
#include <Xm/DragDrop.h>
void XmDropTransferAdd(
    Widget widget,                 /* ID of XmDropTransfer widget */
    XmDropTransferEntry transfers, /* Entries that receiver     */
                                   wants processed            */
    Cardinal num_trans); /* Number of entries to be processed */
```

Called by the receiver of a drop to add a list of drop transfer entries to be processed after a drop transfer is started.

XmDropTransferStart
```
#include <Xm/DragDrop.h>
Widget XmDropTransferStart(
    Widget   widget, /* Start drop for this DragContext widget */
    ArgList  args,   /* List of resources for the DropTransfer */
    Cardinal nargs); /* Number of entries in args             */
```

Initiates a drop transfer by creating an XmDropTransfer object and initializing its resources with the contents of the ArgList. Returns the ID of the newly created XmDropTransfer widget.

XmFileSelectionBoxGetChild
```
#include <Xm/FileSB.h>
Widget XmFileSelectionBoxGetChild(
    Widget widget, /* Query this FileSelectionBox widget */
    unsigned char child); /* Identifies the child whose  */
                          /* widget ID will be returned  */
```

Returns the ID of a child widget of an XmFileSelectionBox widget. You specify the child widget by setting the child argument to one of the following: XmDIALOG_APPLY_BUTTON, XmDIALOG_CANCEL_BUTTON, XmDIALOG_DEFAULT_BUTTON, XmDIALOG_FILTER_LABEL, XmDIALOG_FILTER_TEXT, XmDIALOG_HELP_BUTTON, XmDIALOG_LIST, XmDIALOG_LIST_LABEL, XmDIALOG_OK_BUTTON, XmDIALOG_SELECTION_LABEL, or XmDIALOG_TEXT.

XmFileSelectionDoSearch
```
#include <Xm/FileSB.h>
void XmFileSelectionDoSearch(
    Widget   widget, /* Affects this FileSelectionBox widget */
    XmString dirmask); /* New directory mask                 */
```

Copies the XmString dirmask into the XmNdirMask resource of the specified XmFileSelectionBox widget and updates the list of files to reflect the new directory search attribute. Nothing happens if dirmask is NULL.

XmFontListAdd
```
#include <Xm/Xm.h>
XmFontList XmFontListAdd(
    XmFontList      flist,   /* Add font to this list    */
    XFontStruct     *font,   /* Font being added to list */
    XmStringCharSet charset);/* Character set of the font */
```

Creates and returns a new font list by adding the specified font to an existing font list (flist). You can use the constant XmSTRING_DEFAULT_CHARSET for the charset argument.

XmFontListAppendEntry
```
#include <Xm/Xm.h>
XmFontList XmFontListAppendEntry(
    XmFontList      flist,   /* Append entry to this list */
    XmFontListEntry entry);  /* Add this font list entry   */
```

Creates a new XmFontList by appending a font list entry to an existing font list and returns the new font list. Remember to free the font list entry by calling XmFontListEntryFree.

XmFontListCopy
```
#include <Xm/Xm.h>
XmFontList XmFontListCopy(
    XmFontList      flist);  /* Make a copy of this list  */
```

Returns a copy of a specified font list.

XmFontListCreate
```
#include <Xm/Xm.h>
XmFontList XmFontListCreate(
    XFontStruct     *font,   /* Font used to create new list*/
    XmStringCharSet charset);/* Character set of the font   */
```

Creates a new font list that contains the specified font. Returns the resulting XmFontList.

XmFontListEntryCreate
```
#include <Xm/Xm.h>
XmFontList XmFontListEntryCreate(
    char *tag,         /* Tag for the font list entry      */
    XmFontType type, /* One of: XmFONT_IS_FONT or
                        XMFONT_IS_FONTSET           */
    XtPointer font); /* Either an XFontSet or an XFontStruct */
```

Creates a new font list entry for a specific font. You should not free the XFontSet or the XFontStruct as long as the font lists and font list entries are in use.

XmFontListEntryFree
```
#include <Xm/Xm.h>
void XmFontListEntryFree(
    XmFontListEntry *entry); /* Entry to be freed */
```

Frees the memory used by the specified font list entry.

XmFontListEntryGetFont
```
#include <Xm/Xm.h>
XtPointer XmFontListEntryGetFont(
    XmFontListEntry *entry);  /* Return tag for this entry */
```

Returns the tag of the specified font list entry.

XmFontListEntryGetTag
```
#include <Xm/Xm.h>
char *XmFontListEntryGetTag(
    XmFontListEntry *entry,  /* Return info for this entry */
    XmFontType      *ftype); /* Font type returned here    */
```

Returns the font information for the specified font list entry. Interpret the returned pointer as a pointer to XFontStruct or XFontSet, depending on the value returned in the ftype argument.

XmFontListEntryLoad
```
#include <Xm/Xm.h>
XmFontListEntry XmFontListEntryLoad(
    Display *display, /* Display where font list will be used */
    char *font_name,  /* Font name                            */
    XmFontType type,  /* Type (XmFONT_IS_FONT or
                         XmFONT_IS_FONTSET)                   */
    char *tag) ;      /* Tag for the font list being created  */
```

Creates a font list entry after loading a specified font or font set.

XmFontListFree
```
#include <Xm/Xm.h>
void XmFontListFree(
    XmFontList  flist); /* Font list to be freed */
```

Deallocates memory being used by the specified font list.

XmFontListFreeFontContext
```
#include <Xm/Xm.h>
void XmFontListFreeFontContext(
    XmFontContext  fc); /* Font context to be freed */
```

Indicates that the specified font context (created by XmFontListInitFontContext) is no longer needed.

XmFontListGetNextFont
```
#include <Xm/Xm.h>
Boolean XmFontListGetNextFont(
    XmFontContext context,   /* Font list context          */
    XmStringCharSet *charset,/* Character set returned here */
    XFontStruct **font) ;    /* Font returned here          */
```

Provides access to the character set and font in a font list identified by context. You have to free the memory allocated for the character set. Returns True if the returned values are valid.

XmFontListInitFontContext
```
#include <Xm/Xm.h>
Boolean XmFontListInitFontContext(
    XmFontContext *context, /* Pointer to allocated context   */
    XmFontList fontlist) ;  /* Initialize context for this list */
```

Allocates and initializes a context for a specified font list so that applications can access the contents of the font list.

XmFontListNextEntry
```
#include <Xm/Xm.h>
XmFontListEntry XmFontListNextEntry(
    XmFontContext context); /* Context of the font list */
```

Returns the next entry from a font list. Returns NULL in case of any error.

XmFontListRemoveEntry
```
#include <Xm/Xm.h>
XmFontList XmFontListAppendEntry(
    XmFontList      flist,   /* Remove entry from this list  */
    XmFontListEntry entry);  /* Remove this font list entry  */
```

Creates a new XmFontList by removing a font list entry from an existing font list and returns the new font list. Remember to free the font list entry by calling XmFontListEntryFree.

XmGetAtomName
```
#include <Xm/AtomMgr.h>
String XmGetAtomName(
    Display *display, /* Identifies the X server        */
    Atom    *atom);   /* Atom whose name will be returned */
```

Returns a string containing the name of a specified atom.

XmGetColorCalculation
```
#include <Xm/Xm.h>
XmColorProc XmGetColorCalculation(void);
```

Returns a pointer to the function used to compute the default colors (foreground, select, and shadow).

XmGetColors
```
#include <Xm/Xm.h>
void *XmGetColors(
    Screen   *screen,      /* Allocate colors for this screen */
    Colormap colormap,     /* Allocate from this colormap     */
    Pixel    background,   /* Based on this background color   */
    Pixel *foreground,     /* Foreground pixel returned here   */
    Pixel *top_shadow,     /* Top and bottom shadow pixels     */
    Pixel *bottom_shadow,/* are returned here                  */
    Pixel *select) ;       /* Select color returned here       */
```

Generates a reasonable set of foreground, select, and shadow colors for the specified screen, colormap, and background.

XmGetDestination
```
#include <Xm/Xm.h>
Widget XmGetDestination(
    Display *display); /* Identifies the X server */
```

Returns the ID of the widget to be used as the current destination for paste and other clipboard operations.

XmGetDragContext
```
#include <Xm/DragC.h>
Widget XmGetDragContext(
    Widget w,  /* Widget used to identify the Display       */
    Time   t); /* A timestamp to identify active DragContext */
```

Returns the ID of the DragContext widget that is active for the specified timestamp.

XmGetFocusWidget
```
#include <Xm/Xm.h>
Widget XmGetFocusWidget(
    Widget w); /* Widget used to identify the hierarchy */
```

Returns the ID of the widget (within the hierarchy identified by w) that has the keyboard focus.

XmGetMenuCursor
```
#include <Xm/Xm.h>
Cursor XmGetMenuCursor(
    Display *display);  /* Identifies the X server */
```

Returns the ID of the current menu cursor for the specified display. If the menu cursor is undefined, XmGetMenuCursor returns None.

XmGetPixmap
```
#include <Xm/Xm.h>
Pixmap XmGetPixmap(
    Screen *screen,     /* Locate pixmap for this screen   */
    char   *bm_name,    /* Bitmap name (cached or filename) */
    Pixel  foreground,  /* Foreground color for pixmap     */
    Pixel  background); /* Background color for pixmap     */
```

Uses bm_name as the name of a bitmap to be used as the basis of a pixmap. If the pixmap already
exists in Motif's pixmap cache, this function returns the Pixmap identifier. Otherwise, XmGetPixmap
looks for a bitmap file using bm_name as the name. It searches for this file in the directories listed in
the XBMLANGPATH environment variable. If XmGetPixmap cannot find the bitmap file and the pixmap
is not in the cache, it returns XmUNSPECIFIED_PIXMAP.

XmGetPixmapByDepth
```
#include <Xm/Xm.h>
Pixmap XmGetPixmapByDepth(
    Screen *screen,     /* Locate pixmap for this screen   */
    char   *bm_name,    /* Bitmap name (cached or filename) */
    Pixel  foreground,  /* Foreground color for pixmap     */
    Pixel  background,  /* Background color for pixmap     */
    int    depth);      /* Depth of pixmap                 */
```

Uses bm_name as the name of a bitmap to be used as the basis of a pixmap. If the pixmap already
exists in Motif's pixmap cache, this function returns the Pixmap identifier. Otherwise,
XmGetPixmapByDepth looks for a bitmap file using bm_name as the name. It searches for this file in
the directories listed in the XBMLANGPATH environment variable. If XmGetPixmapByDepth cannot
find the bitmap file and the pixmap is not in the cache, it returns XmUNSPECIFIED_PIXMAP.

XmGetPostedFromWidget
```
#include <Xm/RowColumn.h>
Widget XmGetPostedFromWidget(
    Widget menu);        /* Menu (XmRowColumn) widget's ID */
```

Returns the ID of the widget that had posted the specified menu (a menu is created out of an
XmRowColumn widget).

XmGetSecondaryResourceData
```
#include <Xm/Xm.h>
Cardinal XmGetSecondaryResourceData(
    WidgetClass wc, /* Widget class whose secondary
                                   resources are retrieved */
    XmSecondaryResourceData **data); /* Returned information */
```

Provides access to resources that are not accessible through XtGetResourceList or
XtGetConstraintResourceList. Returns resource structures associated with the specified widget
class.

XmGetTabGroup
```
#include <Xm/Xm.h>
Widget XmGetTabGroup(
    Widget w); /* Widget within a tab group */
```

Returns the widget ID of the tab group containing the specified widget.

XmGetTearOffControl
```
#include <Xm/Xm.h>
Widget XmGetTearOffControl(
    Widget w); /* Widget ID of menu */
```

Returns the widget ID of the internally created tear-off control in a tear-off menu.

XmGetVisibility
```
#include <Xm/Xm.h>
Widget XmGetVisibility(
    Widget w); /* Widget whose visibility is sought */
```

Returns the visibility of the specified widget. The returned value is one of:
XmVISIBILITY_UNOBSCURED, XmVISIBILITY_PARTIALLY_OBSCURED, or
XmVISIBILITY_FULLY_OBSCURED.

XmGetXmDisplay
```
#include <Xm/Xm.h>
Widget XmGetXmDisplay(
    Display *dpy); /* Identifies the X server */
```

Returns the ID of the XmDisplay object associated with the display. You can use the returned ID to get or set resources of the XmDisplay object.

XmGetXmScreen
```
#include <Xm/Xm.h>
Widget XmGetXmScreen(
    Screen *s); /* Identifies the screen */
```

Returns the ID of the XmScreen object associated with the screen. You can use the returned ID to get or set resources of the XmScreen object.

XmInstallImage
```
#include <Xm/Xm.h>
Boolean XmInstallImage(
    XImage *image,       /* Install this image           */
    char   *image_name); /* Assign this name to the image */
```

Stores an image in an image cache for later use in generating a pixmap. You can use image_name to refer to a pixmap based on this image. There are seven predefined images in Motif. You can refer to these images with the following names:

Background	Solid Background
25_foreground	25% foreground and 75% background
50_foreground	50% foreground and 50% background
75_foreground	75% foreground and 25% background
horizontal	Horizontal lines of alternating colors

continues

Background	*Solid Background*
vertical	Vertical lines of alternating colors
slant_left	Slanting lines of alternating colors
slant_right	Slanting lines of alternating colors

The XmInstallImage function returns True if it successfully installs the image, or False if the image argument is NULL or if an image with the same name already exists in the image cache.

XmInternAtom
```
#include <Xm/AtomMgr.h>
Atom XmInternAtom(
    Display *display,   /*Identifies the X server     */
    String name,        /* Return atom of this name  */
    Boolean if_exists); /* False = create atom if it */
                        /* does not already exist    */
```

Returns an atom corresponding to a specified name. If the atom does not exist, it is created only if the if_exists argument is False. If if_exists is True and the atom does not already exist, XmInternAtom will return None.

XmIsMotifWMRunning
```
#include <Xm/Xm.h>
Boolean XmIsMotifWMRunning(
    Widget shell);/* Is mwm running on this widget's screen? */
```

Returns True if mwm is running on the screen where the specified shell widget appears.

XmIsTraversable
```
#include <Xm/Xm.h>
Boolean XmIsTraversable(
    Widget w);     /* Can this widget receive focus through
                      keyboard traversal?                    */
```

Returns True if the specified widget is eligible to receive input focus through keyboard traversal.

XmListAddItem
```
#include <Xm/List.h>
void XmListAddItem(
    Widget    widget,    /* Add item to this XmList widget */
    XmString item,       /* Item being added to the list  */
    int      position); /* Position where item is added   */
```

Adds an item to a specified XmList widget. The position indicates where the item is added. The position numbers start at 1 (for the first position). If position is zero, the item is added at the end of the list. If item matches an entry in the XmNselectedItems resource, item will appear as selected (in "reverse video" with the foreground and background colors swapped).

XmListAddItems
```
#include <Xm/List.h>
void XmListAddItems(
    Widget    widget,    /* Add items to this XmList widget*/
    XmString *item_list,/* Items being added to the list  */
    int      nitems,     /* Number of items in item_list   */
    int      position); /* Position where items are added */
```

Adds an array of items to a specified XmList widget. The position indicates where the items are added. The position starts at 1 (for the first position). If position is zero, the item is added at the end of the list.

XmListAddItemsUnselected
```
#include <Xm/List.h>
void XmListAddItemsUnselected(
    Widget    widget,    /* Add items to this XmList widget*/
    XmString *item_list,/* Items being added to the list  */
    int       nitems,    /* Number of items in item_list   */
    int       position); /* Position where items are added */
```

Works the way XmListAddItems does except that the inserted items remain unselected even if they appear in the XmNselectedItems list.

XmListAddItemUnselected
```
#include <Xm/List.h>
void XmListAddItemUnselected(
    Widget    widget,    /* Add item to this XmList widget */
    XmString  item,      /* Item being added to the list   */
    int       position); /* Position where item is added   */
```

Works the way XmListAddItem does except that item does not appear selected.

XmListDeleteAllItems
```
#include <Xm/List.h>
void XmListDeleteAllItems(
    Widget    widget);/* Delete items from this XmList widget */
```

Deletes all items from the specified XmList widget.

XmListDeleteItem
```
#include <Xm/List.h>
void XmListDeleteItem(
    Widget    widget,/* Delete item from this XmList widget */
    XmString item); /* Item being deleted from the list    */
```

Deletes an item from the specified XmList widget.

XmListDeleteItems
```
#include <Xm/List.h>
void XmListDeleteItems(
    Widget    widget, /* Delete items from this XmList widget*/
    XmString *items, /* Items being deleted from the list   */
    int       nitems);/* Number of items in items array      */
```

Deletes an array of items from the specified XmList widget.

XmListDeleteItemsPos
```
#include <Xm/List.h>
void XmListDeleteItemsPos(
    Widget    widget, /* Delete items from this XmList widget*/
    int       nitems, /* Number of items to delete          */
    int       pos);   /* Delete starting at this position   */
```

Deletes nitems items from the specified XmList widget starting with the item at position pos. Deletes only up to the end of the list.

XmListDeletePos
```
#include <Xm/List.h>
void XmListDeletePos(
    Widget   widget, /* Delete item from this XmList widget*/
    int      pos);   /* Delete item at this position       */
```

Deletes the item at position pos from the specified XmList widget. If pos is zero, XmListDeletePos removes the last item in the list.

XmListDeletePositions
```
#include <Xm/List.h>
void XmListDeletePositions(
    Widget   widget, /* Delete items from this XmList widget */
    int      *poslist, /* Delete items at these positions    */
    int      count); /* Number of entries in poslist array   */
```

Deletes the items whose positions appear in the array poslist from the specified XmList widget.

XmListDeselectAllItems
```
#include <Xm/List.h>
void XmListDeselectAllItems(
    Widget widget); /* Deselect all items from this widget */
```

Unhighlights all items in the specified XmList widget and removes them from the widget's list of selected items.

XmListDeselectItem
```
#include <Xm/List.h>
void XmListDeselectItem(
    Widget   widget, /* Deselect an item from this widget */
    XmString item);  /* Item being deselected             */
```

Unhighlights an item from an XmList widget and removes the item from the widget's list of selected items.

XmListDeselectPos
```
#include <Xm/List.h>
void XmListDeselectPos(
    Widget   widget, /* Deselect item from this widget  */
    int      pos);   /* Deselect item at this position  */
```

Unhighlights the item at position pos from the specified XmList widget. If pos is zero, XmListDeletePos unhighlights the last item in the list. The deselected item is also removed from the XmList widget's list of selected items.

XmListGetKbdItemPos
```
#include <Xm/List.h>
int XmListGetKbdItemPos(
    Widget   widget); /* Identifies the List widget  */
```

Returns the position of the item at the location cursor in the specified List widget. A return value of 0 indicates that the list is empty, a 1 indicates that the location cursor is at the first element of the list, a value of 2 means the cursor on the second item, and so on.

XmListGetMatchPos
```
#include <Xm/List.h>
Boolean XmListGetMatchPos(
    Widget   widget, /* Search this XmList widget       */
```

```
    XmString item,   /* Look for this item            */
    int      **pos,  /* Array of positions returned   */
    int      *count);/* Number of values in pos array */
```

On return, the array pos will contain the positions where item was found in the currently selected items in the XmList widget. The number of matching items is returned in the variable whose address is in the last argument (count). The function returns True if the XmList has one or more selected items; otherwise, it returns False.

XmListGetSelectedPos

```
#include <Xm/List.h>
Boolean XmListGetSelectedPos(
    Widget   widget, /* Query this XmList widget       */
    int      **pos,  /* Array of positions returned    */
    int      *count);/* Number of values in pos array  */
```

On return, the array pos will have the positions of all currently selected items in the specified XmList widget. The variable count will contain the number of selected items. The function returns True if the XmList has one or more selected items; otherwise, it returns False.

XmListItemExists

```
#include <Xm/List.h>
Boolean XmListItemExists(
    Widget   widget, /* Check for item in this XmList widget */
    XmString item);  /* Check whether this item exists       */
```

Returns True if item exists in the specified XmList widget and False if it does not.

XmListItemPos

```
#include <Xm/List.h>
int XmListItemPos(
    Widget   widget, /* Find position of item in this widget */
    XmString item);  /* Return position of this item         */
```

Returns the position of item in the XmList widget.

XmListPosSelected

```
#include <Xm/List.h>
Boolean XmListPosSelected(
    Widget   widget, /* ID of the List widget             */
    int      pos);   /* Position of item (1 = first item,
                        2 = second item, ..., 0 = last item */
```

Returns True if the item at the specified position is selected. Returns False if the item is not selected or if the specified position is invalid.

XmListPosToBounds

```
#include <Xm/List.h>
Boolean XmListPosToBounds(
    Widget    widget, /* ID of the List widget             */
    int       pos,    /* Position of item (1 = first item,
                         2 = second item, ..., 0 = last item */
    Position  *x,     /* x and y coords of the upper-left   */
    Position  *y,     /* corner of bounding box returned    */
    Dimension *width, /* Width and height of bounding box */
    Dimension *height); /* returned in these variables     */
```

Provides information about the bounding box of an item at a specified position in a `List` widget. The values are valid only if the specified item is visible—the function returns `True` if the item is visible; otherwise, it returns `False` (in which case the bounding box information is not valid).

XmListReplaceItems
```
#include <Xm/List.h>
void XmListReplaceItems(
    Widget   widget,   /* Replace items in this widget   */
    XmString *oitems,  /* List of items to be replaced   */
    int      numitems, /* Number of items to be replaced */
    XmString *nitems); /* List of replacement items      */
```

Replaces each item in `oitems` with a corresponding item in `nitems`. After replacement, items in the `XmNselectedItems` list will appear selected.

XmListReplaceItemsPos
```
#include <Xm/List.h>
void XmListReplaceItemsPos(
    Widget   widget,  /* Replace items in this widget   */
    XmString *items,  /* List of replacement items      */
    int      nitems,  /* Number of items to be replaced */
    int      pos);    /* Start replacing at this position */
```

Replaces items in the `XmList` widget starting at the position `pos` with items from the `items` array. After replacement, items in the `XmNselectedItems` list will appear selected.

XmListReplaceItemsPosUnselected
```
#include <Xm/List.h>
void XmListReplaceItemsPosUnselected(
    Widget   widget,  /* Replace items in this widget   */
    XmString *items,  /* List of replacement items      */
    int      nitems,  /* Number of items to be replaced */
    int      pos);    /* Start replacing at this position */
```

Works the way `XmListReplaceItemsPos` does except that the replacement items are not selected even if they appear in the `XmNselectedItems` list.

XmListReplaceItemsUnselected
```
#include <Xm/List.h>
void XmListReplaceItemsUnselected(
    Widget   widget,   /* Replace items in this widget   */
    XmString *oitems,  /* List of items to be replaced   */
    int      numitems, /* Number of items to be replaced */
    XmString *nitems); /* List of replacement items      */
```

Works the way `XmListReplaceItems` does except that the replacement items are not selected even if they appear in the `XmNselectedItems` list.

XmListReplacePositions
```
#include <Xm/List.h>
void XmListReplacePositions(
    Widget   widget,  /* Replace items in this widget   */
    int      poslist, /* Positions of items to be replaced */
    XmString *items,  /* List of replacement items      */
    int      nitems); /* Number of items to be replaced */
```

Replaces items at the position specified in the array `poslist` with items from the `items` array. After replacement, items in the `XmNselectedItems` list will appear selected.

XmListSelectItem
```
#include <Xm/List.h>
void XmListSelectItem(
    Widget    widget,  /* Select item from this widget */
    XmString item,     /* Highlight this item          */
    Boolean   notify); /* True = selection callback    */
```

Highlights item in the specified XmList widget and adds it to the widget's list of selected items. If notify is True, a selection callback is generated.

XmListSelectPos
```
#include <Xm/List.h>
void XmListSelectPos(
    Widget    widget,  /* Select item from this widget   */
    int       pos,     /* Highlight item at this position */
    Boolean   notify); /* True = selection callback       */
```

Highlights item at position pos in the specified XmList widget and adds it to the widget's list of selected items. If notify is True, a selection callback is generated.

XmListSetAddMode
```
#include <Xm/List.h>
void XmListSetAddMode(
    Widget    widget,    /* Affects this XmList widget */
    Boolean   add_mode); /* True = Turn on AddMode     */
```

Sets the add mode for the specified XmList widget. If the add mode is True, the user can move the location cursor without deselecting any other selected items.

XmListSetBottomItem
```
#include <Xm/List.h>
void XmListSetBottomItem(
    Widget    widget, /* Affects this XmList widget    */
    XmString item);  /* Make this the last visible item */
```

Makes item the last visible item in the specified XmList widget.

XmListSetBottomPos
```
#include <Xm/List.h>
void XmListSetBottomItem(
    Widget widget, /* Affects this XmList widget    */
    int    pos);   /* Make this the last visible itom */
```

Makes the item at position pos the last visible item in the specified XmList widget.

XmListSetHorizPos
```
#include <Xm/List.h>
void XmListSetHorizPos(
    Widget widget, /* Affects this XmList widget    */
    int    pos);   /* Set horizontal scrollbar to this */
```

Sets the horizontal scrollbar of the XmList widget to the position specified by pos.

XmListSetItem
```
#include <Xm/List.h>
void XmListSetItem(
    Widget widget, /* Affects this XmList widget    */
    XmString item);/* Make this the first visible item */
```

Makes item the first visible item in the specified XmList widget.

XmListSetKbdItemPos
```
#include <Xm/List.h>
Boolean XmListSetKbdItemPos(
    Widget widget, /* Affects this XmList widget        */
    int    pos);   /* Set cursor to this position. 1=first, */
                   /* 2=second, ..., 0=last item in list    */
```

Sets the location cursor at a specified position. Returns True if the operation succeeds; returns False if the list is empty or if the specified position is invalid.

XmListSetPos
```
#include <Xm/List.h>
void XmListSetPos(
    Widget widget, /* Affects this XmList widget        */
    int    pos);   /* Make this the first visible item  */
```

Makes the item at position pos the first visible item in the specified XmList widget.

XmListUpdateSelectedList
```
#include <Xm/List.h>
void XmListUpdateSelectedList(
    Widget w); /* Update this list's XmNselectedItems list */
```

Updates the XmNselectedItems list of the specified List widget.

XmListYToPos
```
#include <Xm/List.h>
int XmListYToPos(
    Widget  w,  /* Identifies the List widget          */
    Position y); /* Find position of item at this y-coord */
```

Returns the position of the item at a specified y-coordinate in a List widget. A return value of 1 indicates the first item, 2 means the second item, and so on. A return value of 0 means that there are no items at the specified y-coordinate.

XmMainWindowSep1
```
#include <Xm/MainW.h>
Widget XmMainWindowSep1(
    Widget widget); /* Query this XmMainWindow widget */
```

Returns the widget ID of the first XmSeparator widget in the specified XmMainWindow widget. This XmSeparator widget is located between the XmMenuBar and the XmCommand widget in the XmMainWindow widget.

XmMainWindowSep2
```
#include <Xm/MainW.h>
Widget XmMainWindowSep2(
    Widget widget); /* Query this XmMainWindow widget */
```

Returns the widget ID of the second XmSeparator widget in the specified XmMainWindow widget. This XmSeparator widget is located between the XmCommand widget and the XmScrolledWindow widget in the XmMainWindow widget.

XmMainWindowSep3
```
#include <Xm/MainW.h>
Widget XmMainWindowSep3(
    Widget widget); /* Query this XmMainWindow widget */
```

Returns the widget ID of the third XmSeparator widget in the specified XmMainWindow widget. This XmSeparator widget is located between the message window and the widget above it.

XmMainWindowSetAreas
```
#include <Xm/MainW.h>
void XmMainWindowSetAreas(
    Widget widget,  /* These are for this MainWindow widget */
    Widget menubar, /* The menubar's widget ID             */
    Widget command, /* The command window's widget ID       */
    Widget hscroll, /* The horizontal scrollbar's widget ID */
    Widget vscroll, /* The vertical scrollbar's widget ID   */
    Widget work);   /* Widget ID of the work area           */
```

Sets the child widgets for a main window widget. Use NULL for components that you do not want to include in the main window.

XmMapSegmentEncoding
```
#include <Xm/Xm.h>
char *XmMapSegmentEncoding(
    char *fontlist_tag); /* Identifies the font list */
```

Returns the compound text encoding format for a specified font list. The toolkit allocates memory and copies the encoding format; you have to free the memory by calling XtFree when you no longer need the returned information.

XmMenuPosition
```
#include <Xm/RowColumn.h>
void XmMenuPosition(
    Widget                 widget, /* Position this pop-up Menu */
    XButtonPressedEvent *event);/* Event passed to action     */
                            /* procedure of the pop-up menu */
```

Positions a pop-up menu (an XmRowColumn widget of type XmMENU_POPUP) using the x_root and y_root values from a buttonpress event (see Chapter 11 for the definition of the XButtonPressedEvent structure).

XmMessageBoxGetChild
```
#include <Xm/MessageB.h>
Widget XmMessageBoxGetChild(
    Widget        widget, /* XmMessageBox being queried    */
    unsigned char child), /* Child widget ID to be returned */
```

Returns the widget ID of a child of the XmMessageBox widget. The child argument specifies the child whose ID is returned. It can take one of the following values: XmDIALOG_CANCEL_BUTTON, XmDIALOG_DEFAULT_BUTTON, XmDIALOG_HELP_BUTTON, XmDIALOG_MESSAGE_LABEL, XmDIALOG_OK_BUTTON, XmDIALOG_SEPARATOR, or Xm_DIALOG_SYMBOL_LABEL.

XmOptionButtonGadget
```
#include <Xm/RowColumn.h>
Widget XmOptionButtonGadget(
    Widget option_menu); /* Query this Option menu widget */
```

Returns the ID of the XmCascadeButtonGadget created by the XmCreateOptionMenu function.

XmOptionLabelGadget
```
#include <Xm/RowColumn.h>
```

```
Widget XmOptionLabelGadget(
    Widget option_menu); /* Query this Option menu widget */
```

Returns the ID of the XmLabelGadget created by the XmCreateOptionMenu function.

XmProcessTraversal
```
#include <Xm/Xm.h>
Widget XmProcessTraversal(
    Widget  w,    /* Widget whose hierarchy is traversed */
    XmTraversalDirection dir); /* Direction of traversal */
```

Changes the input focus to a widget in the specified hierarchy. The traversal direction dir determines which widget gets the input focus. The direction can be one of the following:

XmTRAVERSE_CURRENT	Activate tab group; if tab group is already active, activate first item.
XmTRAVERSE_NEXT	Activate next item in currently active tab group.
XmTRAVERSE_PREV	Activate previous item in currently active tab group.
XmTRAVERSE_HOME	Activate first item in currently active tab group.
XmTRAVERSE_NEXT_TAB_GROUP	Activate next tab group.
XmTRAVERSE_PREV_TAB_GROUP	Activate previous tab group.
XmTRAVERSE_UP	Activate the item above.
XmTRAVERSE_DOWN	Activate the item below.
XmTRAVERSE_LEFT	Activate the item to the left.
XmTRAVERSE_RIGHT	Activate the item to the right.

[cm]RegisterSegmentEncoding
```
#include <Xm/Xm.h>
char *XmRegisterSegmentEncoding(
    char *flist_tag,    /* Register encoding for this font list*/
    char *ct_encoding);/* Character set to be used for segments
                        with the specified font list tags  */
```

Registers a compound text encoding format for a specified font list. Returns the previous encoding for an already registered font list; otherwise, returns NULL. When the return value is not NULL, you are responsible for calling XtFree to release the storage allocated for the returned information.

XmRemoveFromPostFromList
```
#include <Xm/RowColumn.h>
void XmRemoveFromPostFromList(
    Widget menu,/* Modify this widget's "post from" list    */
    Widget w);  /* Remove this widget from "post from" list */
```

Removes the widget w from the XmNpostFromList of the specified pull-down menu (an XmRowColumn widget of type XmMENU_PULLDOWN).

XmRemoveProtocolCallback
```
#include <Xm/Protocols.h>
void XmRemoveProtocolCallback(
    Widget shell,     /* Protocol is in this widget       */
    Atom   property,   /* Property containing protocol     */
    Atom   protocol, /* Remove callback for this protocol  */
    XtCallbackProc callback,  /* The callback function     */
    XtPointer      client_data); /* Data passed to callback */
```

Removes `callback` from the list of callbacks of the specified protocol.

XmRemoveProtocols
```
#include <Xm/Protocols.h>
void XmRemoveProtocols(
    Widget   shell,      /* Remove protocols from widget  */
    Atom     property,   /* Property containing protocols */
    Atom     *protocols, /* Protocols to be removed       */
    Cardinal num_protocols); /* Number of protocols       */
```

Removes a set of protocols from the specified `shell`.

XmRemoveTabGroup
```
#include <Xm/Xm.h>
void XmRemoveTabGroup(
    Widget widget); /* Widget to be removed from tab group */
```

Removes the specified widget from the list of tab groups associated with a hierarchy of widgets. A *tab group* is a collection of widgets, within which you can move the input focus from one widget to another by using the arrow keys. You can go from one tab group to another by pressing the Tab key.

XmRemoveWMProtocolCallback
```
#include <Xm/Protocols.h>
void XmRemoveWMProtocolCallback(
    Widget shell,      /* Remove protocol from this widget */
    Atom   protocol,   /* Remove callback for this protocol */
    XtCallbackProc callback,  /* The callback function      */
    XtPointer      client_data); /* Data passed to callback */
```

Calls XmRemoveProtocolCallback to remove `callback` for the specified `protocol` stored in the WM_PROTOCOLS property.

XmRemoveWMProtocols
```
#include <Xm/Protocols.h>
void XmRemoveWMProtocols(
    Widget   shell,      /* Protocols are in this widget */
    Atom     *protocols, /* Protocols to be removed       */
    Cardinal num_protocols); /* Number of protocols       */
```

Removes a set of protocols from the specified shell's WM_PROTOCOLS property. This function calls XmRemoveProtocols with the property argument set to WM_PROTOCOLS.

XmRepTypeAddReverse
```
#include <Xm/RepType.h>
void XmRepTypeAddReverse(
    XmRepTypeId rid); /* Identifies the representation type */
```

Installs a reverse converter (from value to string) for a previously registered representation type.

XmRepTypeGetId
```
#include <Xm/RepType.h>
XmRepTypeId XmRepTypeGetId(
    String rtype); /* Name of the representation type */
```

Returns the ID of a representation type identified by name. Returns XmREP_TYPE_INVALID if the representation type is not registered.

XmRepTypeGetNameList
```
#include <Xm/reptype.h>
String *XmRepTypeGetNameList(
    XmRepTypeId rid,    /* Identifies the representation type */
    Boolean use_ucase);/* True = Return values in uppercase  */
```

Returns an array of value names associated with the specified representation type. You are responsible for calling XtFree to free the memory allocated for the returned list.

XmRepTypeGetRecord
```
#include <Xm/RepType.h>
XmRepTypeEntry XmRepTypeGetRecord(
    XmRepTypeId rid); /* Identifies the representation type */
```

Returns an XmRepTypeId structure with information about the specified representation type. You are responsible for calling XtFree to free the memory allocated for the returned structure. The XmRepTypeId structure is declared in <Xm/RepType.h> as follows:

```
typedef struct
{
    String        rep_type_name ; /* Name of representation type*/
    String        *value_names ;  /* Array of value names       */
    unsigned char *values ;       /* Array of numerical values  */
    unsigned char num_values ;    /* Number of values           */
    Boolean       reverse_installed ; /* True = reverse converter
                                                   installed      */
    XmRepTypeId   rep_type_id ;   /* ID of representation type  */
}XmRepTypeEntryRec, *XmRepTypeEntry, XmRepTypeListRec, *XmRepTypeList ;
```

XmRepTypeGetRegistered
```
#include <Xm/RepType.h>
XmRepTypeList XmRepTypeGetRegistered(void);
```

Returns an array of registered representation types (see entry for XmRepTypeGetRecord for declaration of XmRepTypeList).

XmRepTypeInstallTearOffModelConverter
```
#include <Xm/RepType.h>
void XmRepTypeInstallTearOffModelConverter(void);
```

Installs a resource converter that enables the XmNtearOffModel resource to be specified in resource files.

XmRepTypeRegister
```
#include <Xm/RepType.h>
XmRepTypeId XmRepTypeRegister(
    String        rep_type,    /* Name of representation type */
    String        *value_names, /* Array of value names        */
    unsigned char *values,     /* Array of numerical values    */
    unsigned int num_values) ; /* Number of values             */
```

Registers a representation type and returns an identification number.

XmRepTypeValidValue
```
#include <Xm/RepType.h>
Boolean XmRepTypeValidValue(
    XmRepTypeId rep_type_id,  /* ID of representation type */
    unsigned char test_value, /* Numerical value to test   */
    Widget  w_msg); /* ID of widget with warning message */
```

Returns True if a numerical value is valid for the specified representation type.

XmResolveAllPartOffsets
```
#include <Xm/Xm.h>
void XmResolveAllPartOffsets(
    WidgetClass  wclass, /* Offset records for this class     */
    XmOffsetPtr *offset, /* Array of widget record offsets     */
    XmOffsetPtr *c_off); /* Array of constraint record offsets */
```

This function is meant for writing new widgets compatible with existing Motif widgets. A widget writer calls XmResolveAllPartOffsets during class initialization to enable the Motif toolkit to allocate arrays of offset values for the widget and constraint records of the widget class wclass.

XmResolvePartOffsets
```
#include <Xm/Xm.h>
void XmResolvePartOffsets(
    WidgetClass  wclass,  /* Offset records for this class */
    XmOffsetPtr *offset); /* Array of offsets on return    */
```

This function is meant for writing new widgets compatible with existing Motif widgets. A widget writer calls XmResolvePartOffsets during class initialization to enable the Motif toolkit to compute an array of offsets for the widget class wclass.

XmScaleGetValue
```
#include <Xm/Scale.h>
void XmScaleGetValue(
    Widget widget,  /* Get slider pos. of this scale widget */
    int    *value); /* Current slider pos. returned here    */
```

On return, value will contain the current position of the slider of the specified XmScale widget.

XmScaleSetValue
```
#include <Xm/Scale.h>
void XmScaleSetValue(
    Widget widget,  /* Set slider pos. of this scale widget */
    int    value);  /* This is the new slider position      */
```

Sets the current position of the slider of the specified XmScale widget to value.

XmScrollBarGetValue
```
#include <Xm/ScrollBar.h>
void XmScrollBarGetValue(
    Widget widget, /* Get values for this ScrollBar widget */
    int    *spos,  /* Current position of slider returned  */
    int    *ssize, /* Current size of slider returned      */
    int    *bincr, /* Button increment/decrement returned  */
    int    *pincr);/* Page increment/decrement returned    */
```

Accepts pointers to four int variables in which the function returns the current slider position, the slider's size, the amount of button increment, and the amount of page increment.

XmScrollBarSetValue
```
#include <Xm/ScrollBar.h>
void XmScrollBarSetValue(
    Widget widget, /* Get values for this ScrollBar widget */
    int    spos,   /* New position of slider               */
    int    ssize,  /* New size of slider                   */
    int    bincr,  /* New button increment/decrement       */
    int    pincr); /* New page increment/decrement         */
```

Sets four attributes of the specified XmScrollBar widget: slider's position, slider's size, amount of button increment, and amount of page increment.

XmScrollVisible
```
#include <Xm/ScrolledW.h>
void XmScrollVisible(
    Widget widget, /* ID of the XmScrolledWindow windows */
    Widget w,      /* Widget to be made visible          */
    Dimension lr_margin,
    Dimension tb_margin);
```

Makes an invisible descendant of an XmScrolledWindow widget visible. You can use a NULL for any child that you do not want to use.

XmScrolledWindowSetAreas
```
#include <Xm/ScrolledW.h>
void XmScrolledWindowSetAreas(
    Widget widget, /* Set children of this XmScrolledWindow */
    Widget hsbar,  /* The horizontal scrollbar's widget ID */
    Widget vsbar,  /* The vertical scrollbar's widget ID   */
    Widget warea); /* Widget ID of the work window         */
```

Sets up the standard children of an XmScrolledWindow widget. You can use a NULL for any child that you do not want to use.

XmSelectionBoxGetChild
```
#include <Xm/SelectioB.h>
Widget XmSelectionBoxGetChild(
    Widget widget, /* Query this XmSelectionBox widget */
    unsigned char child); /* Identifies the child whose   */
                          /* widget ID will be returned   */
```

Returns the ID of a child widget of an XmSelectionBox widget. You have to indicate the child widget whose ID you want by setting the child argument to one of the following: XmDIALOG_APPLY_BUTTON, XmDIALOG_CANCEL_BUTTON, XmDIALOG_DEFAULT_BUTTON, XmDIALOG_HELP_BUTTON, XmDIALOG_LIST, XmDIALOG_LIST_LABEL, XmDIALOG_OK_BUTTON, XmDIALOG_SELECTION_LABEL, XmDIALOG_SEPARATOR, XmDIALOG_TEXT, or XmDIALOG_WORK_AREA.

XmSetColorCalculation
```
#include <Xm/Xm.h>
XmColorProc XmSetColorCalculation(
    XmColorProc cproc); /* Function to use for color calculation */
```

Sets the routine to be used for color calculation. This is the function that computes the foreground, shadow, and select (highlight) colors for a given background color. The cproc function should have the following prototype:

```
typedef void (*XmColorProc) (
    XColor *bg_color,  /* Background color (input)        */
    XColor *fg_color,  /* Foreground color returned here  */
    XColor *sel_color, /* Select color returned here      */
    XColor *ts_color,  /* Top Shadow color returned here  */
    XColor *bs_color); /* Bottom Shadow color returned here */
```

This function returns the previous color calculation routine. If you call XmSetColorCalculation with a NULL argument, it restores the default procedure used to calculate colors.

XmSetFontUnit
```
#include <Xm/Xm.h>
```

```
void XmSetFontUnit(    /* Superseded by XmSetFontUnits */
    Display *display, /* Identifies the X server     */
    int      fvalue); /* font unit value to be used  */
```

Sets the font unit value for an X server. This value is used in computing screen positions when a widget uses a resolution-independent, font-based unit to position text. By default, the font unit is the `QUAD_WIDTH` property of the font.

XmSetFontUnits
```
#include <Xm/Xm.h>
void XmSetFontUnits(  /* Obsolete (see description) */
    Display *display, /* Identifies the X server    */
    int      h_value, /* Horizontal font unit value */
    int      v_value); /* Vertical font unit value  */
```

Sets the horizontal and vertical font unit values for an X server. These values are used in computing screen positions when a widget uses a resolution-independent, font-based unit to position text. This function is obsolete now; instead, call `XmGetXmScreen` to obtain the `XmScreen` widget's ID, and then call `XtSetValues` to set the values of the `XmNhorizontalFontUnit` and `XmNverticalFontUnit` resources.

XmSetMenuCursor
```
#include <Xm/Xm.h>
void XmSetMenuCursor(
    Display *display, /* Identifies the X server    */
    Cursor   cursor); /* ID of cursor for Motif menus */
```

Sets the cursor to be displayed whenever the client application displays a Motif menu on the specified X server.

XmSetProtocolHooks
```
#include <Xm/Protocols.hL
void XmSetProtocolHooks(
    Widget shell,      /* Protocol is in this widget        */
    Atom    property,  /* Property containing protocol      */
    Atom    protocol, /* Set hook callbacks for this protocol */
    XtCallbackProc pre, /* The prehook callback function    */
    caddr_t predata,    /* Data passed to prehook callback  */
    XtCallbackProc post, /* The posthook callback function  */
    caddr_t postdata);  /* Data passed to posthook callback */
```

Sets up callbacks to be called before (*prehook*) and after (*posthook*) a specified protocol message is received from the window manager.

XmSetWMProtocolHooks
```
#include <Xm/Protocols.h>
void XmSetProtocolHooks(
    Widget shell,      /* Protocol is in this widget        */
    Atom    protocol, /* Set hook callbacks for this protocol */
    XtCallbackProc pre, /* The prehook callback function    */
    caddr_t predata,    /* Data passed to prehook callback  */
    XtCallbackProc post, /* The posthook callback function  */
    caddr_t postdata);  /* Data passed to posthook callback */
```

Calls `XmSetProtocolHooks` with the property argument set to the `WM_PROTOCOL` atom.

XmStringBaseline
```
#include <Xm/Xm.h>
Dimension XmStringBaseline(
    XmFontList fontlist, /* Use the fonts in this list      */
    XmString   string);  /* Return "baseline" for this string */
```

Returns the number of pixels between the top of the character box and the baseline of the first line of text in `string`.

XmStringByteCompare
```
#include <Xm/Xm.h>
Boolean XmStringByteCompare(
    XmString s1,  /* Compare this compound string */
    XmString s2); /* with this one               */
```

Returns `True` if `s1` and `s2` are identical byte-for-byte, or `False` if the two strings differ in any byte.

XmStringCompare
```
#include <Xm/Xm.h>
Boolean XmStringCompare(
    XmString s1,  /* Compare this compound string */
    XmString s2); /* with this one               */
```

Returns `True` if `s1` and `s2` have the same components (compound strings represented by the `XmString` data type include components such as text, direction, separators, and character set), or `False` if the two strings differ in any component.

XmStringConcat
```
#include <Xm/Xm.h>
XmString XmStringConcat(
    XmString s1,  /* Concatenate this compound string  */
    XmString s2); /* with this one (s2 comes after s1) */
```

Concatenates `s1` and `s2` and returns the resulting compound string.

XmStringCopy
```
#include <Xm/Xm.h>
XmString XmStringCopy(
    XmString s); /* Return a copy of this compound string */
```

Returns a copy of the compound string `s`.

XmStringCreate
```
#include <Xm/Xm.h>
XmString XmStringCreate(
    char            *text,/* Null-terminated C-style string */
    XmStringCharSet charset);     /* Character set to use */
```

Allocates storage for a compound string and initializes it with a specified null-terminated string `text` using the character set `charset`. Returns the newly created compound string. When you no longer need the compound string, you should free the storage used by that string by calling `XmStringFree`.

XmStringCreateLocalized
```
#include <Xm/Xm.h>
XmString XmStringCreateLocalized(
    char *text); /* Null-terminated string in current locale */
```

Creates a compound string in the current locale and returns the newly created compound string. When you no longer need the compound string, you should free the storage used by that string by calling `XmStringFree`.

XmStringCreateLtoR
```
#include <Xm/Xm.h>
XmString XmStringCreateLtoR(
    char            *text,/* Null-terminated C-style string */
    XmStringCharSet charset);      /* Character set to use */
```

Allocates storage for a compound string and initializes it with a specified null-terminated string `text` using the character set `charset`. Replaces newline (`\n`) characters in text with separators in the compound string. Returns the newly created compound string. When you no longer need the compound string, you should free the storage used by that string by calling `XmStringFree`.

XmStringCreateSimple
```
#include <Xm/Xm.h>
XmString XmStringCreateSimple(
    Widget widget, /* Use language environment of this widget */
    char   *text); /* Null-terminated C-style string        */
```

Returns a compound string initialized with the specified text and based on the character set specified by resources of the widget. Use `XmStringFree` to deallocate the compound string when you no longer need it.

XmStringDirectionCreate
```
#include <Xm/Xm.h>
XmString XmStringDirectionCreate(
    XmStringDirection direction);
```

Creates a compound string with a direction component only and initializes that direction with the value provided in the function's argument. Two common values for the direction argument are `XmSTRING_DIRECTION_L_TO_R` and `XmSTRING_DIRECTION_R_TO_L`. Use `XmStringFree` to deallocate the compound string when you no longer need it.

XmStringDraw
```
#include <Xm/Xm.h>
void XmStringDraw(
    Display *display,     /* X server where string is drawn */
    Window  w,            /* Window where string is drawn   */
    XmFontList flist,     /* Use this font to draw string   */
    XmString   string,    /* Compound string being drawn    */
    GC         gc,        /* Graphics context used to draw  */
                          /*     the compound string        */
    Position   x,y,       /* Position of rectangle where    */
                          /*     text will appear           */
    Dimension  width,     /* Width (pixels) of rectangle    */
                          /* where text will be displayed   */
    unsigned char align,  /* one of: XmALIGNMENT_BEGINNING, */
                          /*         XmALIGNMENT_CENTER, or */
                          /*         XmALIGNMENT_END        */
    unsigned char dir,    /* Direction of text display      */
    XRectangle    *clip); /* Clip against this rectangle or */
                          /*     NULL if no clipping        */
```

Draws the compound string in a rectangle within a window, using a specified graphics context.

XmStringDrawImage
```
#include <Xm/Xm.h>
void XmStringDrawImage(
    Display *display,     /* X server where string is drawn */
    Window  w,            /* Window where string is drawn   */
```

```
    XmFontList flist,     /* Use this font to draw string    */
    XmString   string,    /* Compound string being drawn     */
    GC         gc,        /* Graphics context used to draw   */
                          /*     the compound string         */
    Position   x,y,       /* Position of rectangle where     */
                          /*     text will appear            */
    Dimension  width,     /* Width (pixels) of rectangle     */
                          /* where text will be displayed    */
    unsigned char align,  /* one of: XmALIGNMENT_BEGINNING,  */
                          /*         XmALIGNMENT_CENTER, or  */
                          /*         XmALIGNMENT_END          */
    unsigned char dir,    /* Direction of text display       */
    XRectangle    *clip); /* Clip against this rectangle or  */
                          /*     NULL if no clipping          */
```

Draws the compound string in a rectangle within a window, using a specified graphics context. Each character is drawn in the foreground, and then the background of the character cell is painted with the background color specified in the graphics context.

XmStringDrawUnderline
```
#include <Xm/Xm.h>
void XmStringDrawUnderline(
    Display *display,     /* X server where string is drawn */
    Window  w,            /* Window where string is drawn    */
    XmFontList flist,     /* Use this font to draw string    */
    XmString   string,    /* Compound string being drawn     */
    GC         gc,        /* Graphics context used to draw   */
                          /*     the compound string         */
    Position   x,y,       /* Position of rectangle where     */
                          /*     text will appear            */
    Dimension  width,     /* Width (pixels) of rectangle     */
                          /* where text will be displayed    */
    unsigned char align,  /* one of: XmALIGNMENT_BEGINNING,  */
                          /*         XmALIGNMENT_CENTER, or  */
                          /*         XmALIGNMENT_END          */
    unsigned char dir,    /* Direction of text display       */
    XRectangle    *clip,  /* Clip against this rectangle or  */
                          /*     NULL if no clipping          */
    XmString      uline); /* Portion to be underlined         */
```

Draws the compound string in a rectangle within a window using a specified graphics context. Also underlines the substring indicated by the argument `uline`.

XmStringEmpty
```
#include <Xm/Xm.h>
Boolean XmStringEmpty(
    XmString s); /* Is this compound string empty? */
```

Returns `True` if the text segments in the compound string `s` are all empty and `False` if they are not empty.

XmStringExtent
```
#include <Xm/Xm.h>
void XmStringExtent(
    XmFontList fontlist, /* Use this font and char. set    */
    XmString   string,   /* Get extent of this string      */
    Dimension  *width,   /* Width of text extent returned  */
    Dimension  *height); /* Height of text extent returned */
```

On return, the arguments `width` and `height` will hold the dimensions of the smallest rectangle capable of displaying the specified compound string in a particular font.

XmStringFree
```
#include <Xm/Xm.h>
void XmStringFree(
    XmString s);        /* Deallocate this compound string */
```

Releases the storage allocated for the compound string s.

XmStringFreeContext
```
#include <Xm/Xm.h>
void XmStringFreeContext(
    XmStringContext sc); /* Deallocate this string context */
```

Frees storage used for the string context sc.

XmStringGetLtoR
```
#include <Xm/Xm.h>
Boolean XmStringGetLtoR(
    XmString        s,      /* Search this compound string */
    XmStringCharset cset,   /* Use this character set      */
    char            **text); /* Look for this text in string*/
```

Searches for any occurrence of `text` in the compound string s. If found, the function returns True and sets `text` to point to the matching text segment in s. Otherwise, the return value is `False`.

XmStringGetComponent
```
#include <Xm/Xm.h>
XmStringComponentType XmStringGetComponent(
    XmStringContext context, /* Use this string context    */
    char            **text,  /* Returned pointer to text    */
    XmStringCharset *charset,/* Returned character set       */
    XmStringDirection *direction,/* Returned direction         */
    XmStringComponentType *tag,/* Tag for unknown component */
    Short *length, /* Returned length of unknown component  */
    char **value); /* Returned value of unknown component   */
```

Returns information about the next component of a compound string identified by a context (see `XmStringInitContext`). The function returns the type of the next component and information about that component in an appropriate argument. The return value is one of the following:

XmSTRING_COMPONENT_CHARSET	Value returned in charset
XmSTRING_COMPONENT_DIRECTION	Value returned in direction
XmSTRING_COMPONENT_END	No more components in string
XmSTRING_COMPONENT_SEPARATOR	Next component is a separator
XmSTRING_COMPONENT_TEXT	Value returned in text (you have to `free this string`)
XmSTRING_COMPONENT_UNKNOWN	Type, length, and value returned

XmStringGetNextSegment
```
#include <Xm/Xm.h>
Boolean XmStringGetNextSegment(
    XmStringContext context, /* Use this string context    */
    char            **text,  /* Returned pointer to text    */
    XmStringCharset *charset,/* Returned character set       */
    XmStringDirection *direction,/* Returned direction         */
    Boolean *separator);     /* Returns True if separator    */
```

Returns the text string, character set, and direction of the next segment of the compound string specified by context (see XmStringInitContext).

XmStringHasSubstring
```
#include <Xm/Xm.h>
Boolean XmStringHasSubstring(
    XmString string,      /* Search this compound string */
    XmString substring); /* for occurrences of this one */
```

Returns True if substring has one text segment and that segment is completely contained in one of the text segments of string. Otherwise, the function returns False.

XmStringHeight
```
#include <Xm/Xm.h>
Dimension XmStringHeight(
    XmFontList flist, /* Use this font and character set */
    XmString     s);   /* and find height of this string  */
```

Returns the combined height (in pixels) of all the lines contained in the compound string s.

XmStringInitContext
```
#include <Xm/Xm.h>
Boolean XmStringInitContext(
    XmStringContext  *sc, /* Return a string context for    */
    XmString  s);         /* accessing this compound string */
```

Sets up a context for accessing the specified compound string. If all goes well, the function returns True and returns the context in sc. Otherwise, the function returns False to indicate failure.

XmStringLength
```
#include <Xm/Xm.h>
int XmStringLength(
     XmString s); /* Return length of this compound string */
```

Returns the length (in bytes) of the compound string s. A return value of zero indicates that the compound string s has an invalid structure.

XmStringLineCount
```
#include <Xm/Xm.h>
int XmStringLineCount(
    XmString s); /* Return no. of lines in s */
```

Returns the number of lines (one more than the number of separators) in the compound string s.

XmStringNConcat
```
#include <Xm/Xm.h>
XmString XmStringNConcat(
    XmString s1, /* Concatenate this compound string */
    XmString s2, /* with this one                    */
    int      n); /* Number of bytes to concatenate   */
```

Returns a new compound that is formed by concatenating *n* bytes of s2 to s1. You are responsible for deallocating the newly created XmString (by calling XmStringFree) when you no longer need it.

XmStringNCopy
```
#include <Xm/Xm.h>
XmString XmStringNCopy(
    XmString s,  /* Make a copy of this compound string */
    int      n); /* Number of bytes to copy             */
```

Returns a new compound string which is formed by copying *n* bytes (includes tags, separators, and direction indicators) of s. Use XmStringFree to deallocate the newly created compound string when you no longer need it.

XmStringPeekNextComponent
```
#include <Xm/Xm.h>
XmStringComponentType XmStringPeekNextComponent(
    XmStringContext sc); /* Use this string context */
```

Returns the type of the next component of the compound string identified by the context sc (see XmStringInitContext). See the description of XmStringGetNextComponent for a list of the possible return values.

XmStringSegmentCreate
```
#include <Xm/Xm.h>
XmString XmStringSegmentCreate(
    char             *text, /* This is the text       */
    XmString         cset,  /* Use this character set  */
    XmStringDirection dir,  /* and this direction      */
    Boolean          sep);  /* True=add separator at end */
```

Assembles a compound string from a given set of components. Use XmStringFree to deallocate the newly created compound string when you no longer need it.

XmStringSeparatorCreate
```
#include <Xm/Xm.h>
XmString XmStringSeparatorCreate();
```

Returns a new compound string containing a single separator component.

XmStringwidth
```
#include <Xm/Xm.h>
Dimension XmStringwidth(
    XmFontList flist, /* Use this font and character set   */
    XmString   s);    /* Need width of this compound string */
```

Returns the width (in pixels) of the longest line in the compound string s.

XmTargetsAreCompatible
```
#include <Xm/DragDrop.h>
Boolean XmTargetsAreCompatible(
    Display *dpy,                    /* Identifies the X server  */
    Atom *export_targets,           /* List of export targets   */
    Cardinal num_export_targets,    /* Number of export targets */
    Atom *import_targets,           /* List of import targets   */
    Cardinal num_import_targets);   /* Number of import targets */
```

Returns True if there is at least one match between the import targets of a destination and the export targets of a source.

XmTextClearSelection
```
#include <Xm/Text.h>
void XmTextClearSelection(
    Widget widget,/* Clear selection on this XmText widget */
    Time   time); /* Time of event that triggered this     */
```

Clears the primary selection in the specified XmText widget.

XmTextCopy
```
#include <Xm/Text.h>
Boolean XmTextCopy(
    Widget w,  /* Copy selection from this XmText widget */
    Time   t); /* Time of event triggering this request  */
```

Copies the primary selection from the specified XmText widget to the clipboard. Returns True if successful, False if operation cannot be completed (because the selection is NULL or the widget does not own the selection).

XmTextCut
```
#include <Xm/Text.h>
Boolean XmTextCut(
    Widget w,  /* Cut selection from this XmText widget */
    Time   t); /* Time of event triggering this request */
```

Copies the primary selection from the specified XmText widget to the clipboard and then clears the selected text. Returns True if successful, False if operation cannot be completed (because the selection is NULL or the widget does not own the selection).

XmTextDisableRedisplay
```
#include <Xm/Text.h>
void XmTextDisableRedisplay(
    Widget w); /* Disable visual update of this Text widget */
```

Disables visual update of the Text widget's window. Use this function together with XmTextEnableRedisplay to make multiple changes to the Text widget without intermediate redrawing of the window.

XmTextEnableRedisplay
```
#include <Xm/Text.h>
void XmTextEnableRedisplay(
    Widget w); /* Enable visual update of this Text widget */
```

Forces visual update of the Text widget's window. Use this function together with XmTextDisableRedisplay to make multiple changes to the Text widget without intermediate redrawing of the window.

XmTextFieldClearSelection
```
#include <Xm/TextF.h>
void XmTextFieldClearSelection(
    Widget widget,/* Clear selection on this XmTextField */
    Time   time); /* Time of event that triggered this   */
```

Clears the primary selection in the specified XmTextField widget.

XmTextFieldCopy
```
#include <Xm/TextF.h>
Boolean XmTextFieldCopy(
    Widget w,  /* Copy selection from this XmTextField   */
    Time   t); /* Time of event triggering this request */
```

Copies the primary selection from the specified XmTextField widget to the clipboard. Returns True if successful, False if operation cannot be completed (because the selection is NULL or the widget does not own the selection).

XmTextFieldCut
```
#include <Xm/TextF.h>
Boolean XmTextFieldCut(
    Widget w,   /* Cut selection from this XmTextField   */
    Time    t); /* Time of event triggering this request */
```

Copies the primary selection from the specified XmTextField widget to the clipboard and then clears the selected text. Returns True if successful, False if operation cannot be completed (because the selection is NULL or the widget does not own the selection).

XmTextFieldGetAddMode
```
#include <Xm/TextF.h>
Boolean XmTextFieldGetAddMode(
    Widget  w); /* Get add mode of this TextField widget */
```

Returns the current setting of the XmTextField widget's add mode. If the add mode is True, you can move the cursor within the XmTextField without altering the primary selection.

XmTextFieldGetBaseline
```
#include <Xm/TextF.h>
int XmTextFieldGetBaseline(
    Widget w); /* Return baseline of this XmTextField */
```

Returns the position of the baseline for the specified XmTextField widget (based on the first font in the font list).

XmTextFieldGetCursorPosition
```
#include <Xm/TextF.h>
XmTextPosition XmTextFieldGetCursorPosition(
    Widget w); /* Return cursor pos. of this XmTextField */
```

Returns the cursor position (where text will be inserted) for the specified XmTextField widget. The positions are numbered from zero onward, with zero denoting the first character.

XmTextFieldGetEditable
```
#include <Xm/TextF.h>
Boolean XmTextFieldGetEditable(
    Widget w); /* Is this XmTextField editable? */
```

Returns the XmNeditable resource of the specified XmTextField widget. If this resource is True, the contents of the XmTextField can be edited.

XmTextFieldGetInsertionPosition
```
#include <Xm/TextF.h>
XmTextPosition XmTextFieldGetInsertionPosition(
    Widget w);/* Return insertion pos of this XmTextField */
```

Returns the position of the insertion cursor in the specified XmTextField widget. The character positions are numbered from zero onward, with zero denoting the first character.

XmTextFieldGetLastPosition
```
#include <Xm/TextF.h>
XmTextPosition XmTextFieldGetLastPosition(
    Widget w);/* Return last char. pos of this XmTextField */
```

Returns the position of the last character in the specified XmTextField widget. The character positions are numbered from zero onward, with zero denoting the first character.

XmTextFieldGetMaxLength
```
#include <Xm/TextF.h>
int XmTextFieldGetMaxLength(
    Widget w);/* Return max length of this XmTextField */
```

Returns the maximum number of characters that the specified XmTextField can store. This is the XmTextField widget's XmNmaxLength resource.

XmTextFieldGetSelection
```
#include <Xm/TextF.h>
char* XmTextFieldGetSelection(
    Widget w);/* Return selection of this XmTextField */
```

Returns a pointer to a buffer containing the primary selection of the specified XmTextField widget or NULL if there is no selection in the widget. You are responsible for deallocating the storage to which the returned pointer points. Use XtFree to deallocate this buffer when you no longer need it.

XmTextFieldGetSelectionPosition
```
#include <Xm/TextF.h>
Boolean XmTextFieldGetSelectionPosition(
    Widget w,     /* Need selection of this XmTextField    */
    XmTextPosition *l, /* Returns start of selection */
    XmTextPosition *r);/* Returns end of selection    */
```

Returns True if the specified XmTextField widget owns the primary collection. If it does, the arguments l and r contain the starting and ending positions of the primary selection in the XmTextField widget. A False return value indicates that the XmTextField widget does not have the primary selection.

XmTextFieldGetSelectionWcs
```
#include <Xm/TextF.h>
wchar_t *XmTextFieldGetSelectionWcs(
    Widget w);/* Return selection of this XmTextField */
```

Returns a pointer to a wide-character buffer containing the primary selection of the specified XmTextField widget, or NULL if there is no selection in the widget. You are responsible for deallocating the storage to which the returned pointer points. Use XtFree to deallocate this buffer when you no longer need it.

XmTextFieldGetString
```
#include <Xm/TextF.h>
char *XmTextFieldGetString(
    Widget w); /* Return string from this XmTextField */
```

Returns the string displayed in the specified XmTextField widget. You are responsible for releasing the storage allocated for the returned string. Use XtFree to free this storage when you no longer need the returned string.

XmTextFieldGetStringWcs
```
#include <Xm/TextF.h>
char *XmTextFieldGetStringWcs(
    Widget w); /* Return string from this XmTextField */
```

Returns the wide-character string value of the specified XmTextField widget. You are responsible for releasing the storage allocated for the returned string. Use XtFree to free this storage when you no longer need the returned string.

XmTextFieldGetSubstring
```
#include <Xm/TextF.h>
int XmTextFieldGetSubstring(
    Widget        widget,  /* Get substring from this TextField */
    XmTextPosition start,  /* Beginning character position      */
    int           num_chars,/* Number of characters to get      */
    int           buf_size, /* Size of buffer in bytes (provide */
                            /* room for a terminating null char)*/
    char          *buffer); /* Buffer to hold the substring     */
```

Gets a substring from the string displayed in the specified XmTextField widget. You are responsible for allocating a buffer that holds the returned substring. This function returns the constant XmCOPY_SUCCEEDED if the operation succeeds.

XmTextFieldGetSubstringWcs
```
#include <Xm/TextF.h>
int XmTextFieldGetSubstringWcs(
    Widget        widget,  /* Get substring from this TextField */
    XmTextPosition start,  /* Beginning character position      */
    int           num_chars,/* Number of characters to get      */
    int           buf_size, /* Size of buffer as a number of    */
                            /* wchar_t locations                */
    wchar_t       *buffer); /* Buffer to hold the substring      */
```

Gets a wide-character substring from the string displayed in the specified XmTextField widget. You are responsible for allocating a buffer that holds the returned wide-character string. This function returns the constant XmCOPY_SUCCEEDED if the operation succeeds.

XmTextFieldInsert
```
#include <Xm/TextF.h>
void XmTextFieldInsert(
    Widget widget,        /* Insert into this XmTextField */
    XmTextPosition pos, /* Insert at this char. pos. */
    char *string);  /* Insert this null-terminated string */
```

Inserts a null-terminated string starting at a specified position in an XmTextField widget.

XmTextFieldInsertWcs
```
#include <Xm/TextF.h>
void XmTextFieldInsertWcs(
    Widget widget,        /* Insert into this XmTextField     */
    XmTextPosition pos, /* Insert at this char. position    */
    wchar_t *wstring); /* Insert this wide-character string */
```

Inserts a wide-character string starting at a specified position in an XmTextField widget.

XmTextFieldPaste
```
#include <Xm/TextF.h>
Boolean XmTextFieldPaste(
    Widget w); /* Paste selection into this XmTextField */
```

Pastes the current selection from the clipboard into the specified XmTextField widget at the current position of the insertion cursor. Returns True if the paste operation is successful and False if the widget does not own the primary selection.

XmTextFieldPosToXY
```
#include <Xm/TextF.h>
Boolean XmTextFieldPosToXY(
    Widget widget,        /* Query this XmTextField */
    XmTextPosition pos,/* Character position    */
    Position *x, *y);     /* Returned x-y position */
```

Converts the character position pos into x-y coordinates (with respect to the widget's upper-left corner) and returns the values in the arguments x and y.

XmTextFieldRemove
```
#include <Xm/TextF.h>
Boolean XmTextFieldRemove(
    Widget w);/* Delete selected text from this XmTextField */
```

Deletes the selected text (which constitutes the primary selection) from the specified XmTextField widget. This function returns True if the operation succeeds or False if the widget does not own the primary selection.

XmTextFieldReplace
```
#include <Xm/TextF.h>
void XmTextFieldReplace(
    Widget w, /* Modify contents of this XmTextField widget */
    XmTextPosition from,/* Start at this char position */
    XmTextPosition to,  /* End at this char position   */
    char *string);    /* Null-terminated replacement string  */
```

Replaces the block of characters (in the XmTextField widget) between the positions from and to with the null-terminated string. You can insert the string after a character position by setting both from and to arguments to that character position.

XmTextFieldReplaceWcs
```
#include <Xm/TextF.h>
void XmTextFieldReplaceWcs(
    Widget w, /* Modify contents of this XmTextField widget  */
    XmTextPosition from,/* Start at this char position        */
    XmTextPosition to,  /* End at this char position          */
    wchar_t *wstring); /* Replacement wide-character string */
```

Replaces the block of wide characters (in the XmTextField widget) between the positions from and to with the wide-character string. You can insert the string after a character position by setting both from and to arguments to that character position.

XmTextFieldSetAddMode
```
#include <Xm/TextF.h>
Boolean XmTextFieldSetAddMode(
    Widget  widget, /* Affects this XmTextField widget */
    Boolean mode ); /* New value for the add mode    */
```

Returns the current setting of the XmTextField widget's add mode and sets the add mode to the Boolean value in the mode argument. If the add mode is True, you can move the cursor within the XmTextField without altering the primary selection.

XmTextFieldSetCursorPosition
```
#include <Xm/TextF.h>
void XmTextFieldSetCursorPosition(
    Widget w, /* Set cursor position of this XmTextField */
    XmTextPosition pos);/* Position cursor here    */
```

Positions the insertion cursor at the character position pos in a specified XmTextField widget.

XmTextFieldSetEditable
```
#include <Xm/TextF.h>
void XmTextFieldSetEditable(
    Widget  w,    /* Alter "editability" of this XmTextField */
    Boolean edit);/* New value for the XmNeditable resource */
```

Sets the XmNeditable resource of the specified XmTextField widget with the value given in the edit argument. When the XmNeditable resource is True, the user can edit the contents of the XmTextField widget.

XmTextFieldSetHighlight
```
#include <Xm/TextF.h>
void XmTextFieldSetHighlight(
    Widget w,    /* Set highlight fo this XmTextField  */
    XmTextPosition left,       /* Starting position   */
    XmTextPosition right,      /* Ending position     */
    XmHighlightMode mode);     /* One of: XmNORMAL,
                XmSELECTED, or XmSECONDARY_SELECTED    */
```

Sets the highlighting of the block of characters between the character positions left and right. If mode is XmNORMAL, the text is not highlighted. If mode is XmSELECTED, the selected characters appear in "reverse video" (with foreground and background colors swapped). If the mode argument is XmSECONDARY_SELECTED, the characters between left and right are underlined.

XmTextFieldSetInsertionPosition
```
#include <Xm/TextF.h>
void XmTextFieldSetInsertionPosition(
    Widget w,     /* Set insertion pos of this XmTextField */
    XmTextPosition pos);   /* New insertion position       */
```

Sets the insertion cursor of the TextField widget to a specified character position. The character positions are numbered sequentially, with zero denoting the start of the text.

XmTextFieldSetMaxLength
```
#include <Xm/TextF.h>
void XmTextFieldSetMaxLength(
    Widget w,     /* Set max length for this XmTextField */
    int    nchar); /* Allow up to these many characters  */
```

Sets the XmNmaxLength resource of the specified XmTextField widget. This resource specifies the maximum number of characters that the XmTextField widget can hold.

XmTextFieldSetSelection
```
#include <Xm/TextF.h>
void XmTextFieldSetSelection(
    Widget w,    /* Set selection from this XmTextField */
    XmTextPosition start, /* Starting position     */
    XmTextPosition end,   /* Ending position       */
    Time time);       /* Timestamp of triggering event */
```

Sets the characters between positions start and end in the specified XmTextField widget as the current primary selection.

XmTextFieldSetString
```
#include <Xm/TextF.h>
void XmTextFieldSetString(
```

```
    Widget w,  /* Set the text of this XmTextField  */
    char  *s); /* to this null-terminated string    */
```

Sets the text string of the specified XmTextField widget to the null-terminated string s.

XmTextFieldSetStringWcs
```
#include <Xm/TextF.h>
void XmTextFieldSetStringWcs(
    Widget  w,       /* Set the text of this XmTextField */
    wchar_t *wcs); /* to this wide-character string     */
```

Sets the text string of the specified XmTextField widget to the wide-character string wcs.

XmTextFieldShowPosition
```
#include <Xm/TextF.h>
void XmTextFieldShowPosition(
    Widget w,              /* Affects this XmTextField  widget */
    XmTextPosition pos); /* Display text starting here  */
```

Displays the text starting at the character position pos.

XmTextFieldXYToPos
```
#include <Xm/TextF.h>
XmTextPosition XmTextFieldXYToPos(
    Widget   w,   /* For this XmTextField widget       */
    Position x,y);/* Return char pos for this x-y coord */
```

Returns the character position corresponding to the x-y coordinate (with respect to the upper-left corner of the widget).

XmTextFindString
```
#include <Xm/Text.h>
Boolean XmTextFindString(
    Widget w,             /* Search in this TextField widget   */
    XmTextPosition start,/* Start searching from this position*/
    char *search_string, /* Look for this string              */
    XmTextDirection dir, /* Direction of search:
                            XmTEXT_FORWARD or XmTEXT_BACKWARD */
    XmTextPosition *pos);/* Beginning position returned here  */
```

Searches for a string in a TextField widget. Returns True if the string is found.

XmTextFindStringWcs
```
#include <Xm/Text.h>
Boolean XmTextFindStringWcs(
    Widget w,             /* Search in this TextField widget   */
    XmTextPosition start,/* Start searching from this position*/
    wchar_t *wstring,    /* Look for this wide-char string     */
    XmTextDirection dir, /* Direction of search:
                            XmTEXT_FORWARD or XmTEXT_BACKWARD */
    XmTextPosition *pos);/* Beginning position returned here  */
```

Searches for a wide-character string in a TextField widget. Returns True if the string is found.

XmTextGetAddMode
```
#include <Xm/Text.h>
Boolean XmTextGetAddMode(
    Widget w); /* Return add mode of this XmText widget */
```

Returns the current setting of the XmText widget's add mode. If the add mode is True, you can move the cursor within the XmText without altering the primary selection.

XmTextGetBaseline
```
#include <Xm/Text.h>
int XmTextGetBaseline(
    Widget w); /* Return baseline of this XmText widget */
```

Returns the position of the baseline for the specified `XmText` widget (based on the first font in the font list).

XmTextGetCursorPosition
```
#include <Xm/Text.h>
XmTextPosition XmTextGetCursorPosition(
    Widget w); /* Return cursor position of this XmText */
```

Returns the cursor position (where text will be inserted) for the specified `XmText` widget. The positions are numbered from zero onward, with zero denoting the first character.

XmTextGetEditable
```
#include <Xm/Text.h>
Boolean XmTextGetEditable(
    Widget w); /* Return edit permission of this XmText */
```

Returns the `XmNeditable` resource of the specified `XmText` widget. If this resource is `True`, the contents of the `XmText` widget can be edited.

XmTextGetInsertionPosition
```
#include <Xm/Text.h>
XmTextPosition XmTextGetInsertionPosition(
    Widget w); /* Return insertion position of this XmText */
```

Returns the insertion position (where text will be inserted) for the specified `XmText` widget. The character positions are numbered from zero onward, with zero denoting the first character.

XmTextGetLastPosition
```
#include <Xm/Text.h>
XmTextPosition XmTextGetLastPosition(
    Widget w);/* Return last char. pos of this XmText */
```

Returns the position of the last character in the specified `XmText` widget. The character positions are numbered from zero onward, with zero denoting the first character.

XmTextGetMaxLength
```
#include <Xm/Text.h>
int XmTextGetMaxLength(
    Widget w);/* Return max length of this XmText */
```

Returns the maximum number of characters that the specified `XmText` can store. This is the `XmText` widget's `XmNmaxLength` resource.

XmTextGetSelection
```
#include <Xm/Text.h>
char* XmTextGetSelection(
    Widget w);/* Return selection of this XmText */
```

Returns a pointer to a buffer containing the primary selection of the specified `XmText` widget or `NULL` if there is no selection in the widget. You are responsible for deallocating the storage to which the returned pointer points. Use `XtFree` to deallocate this buffer when you no longer need it.

XmTextGetSelectionPosition
```
#include <Xm/Text.h>
Boolean XmTextGetSelectionPosition(
    Widget w,            /* Need selection of this XmText */
    XmTextPosition *l,   /* Returns start of selection    */
    XmTextPosition *r);  /* Returns end of selection      */
```

Returns True if the specified XmText widget owns the primary collection. If it does, the arguments l and r will contain the starting and ending positions of the primary selection in the XmText widget. A False return value indicates that the XmText widget does not have the primary selection.

XmTextGetSelectionWcs
```
#include <Xm/Text.h>
wchar_t *XmTextGetSelectionWcs(
    Widget w);/* Return selection of this XmText */
```

Returns a pointer to a wide-character buffer containing the primary selection of the specified XmText widget, or NULL if there is no selection in the widget. You are responsible for deallocating the storage to which the returned pointer points. Use XtFree to deallocate this buffer when you no longer need it.

XmTextGetSource
```
#include <Xm/Text.h>
XmTextSource XmTextGetSource(
    Widget w); /* Return text source of this XmText widget */
```

Returns the text source of this XmText widget. Two or more XmText widgets may share a text source so that when the user edits the text in one widget, the changes are reflected in the others.

XmTextGetString
```
#include <Xm/Text.h>
char  *XmTextGetString(
    Widget w); /* Return string from this XmText widget */
```

Returns the string displayed in the specified XmText widget. You are responsible for releasing the storage allocated for the returned string. Use XtFree to free this storage when you no longer need the returned string.

XmTextGetStringWcs
```
#include <Xm/Text.h>
wchar_t  *XmTextGetStringWcs(
    Widget w); /* Return string from this XmText widget */
```

Returns the wide-character string value of the specified XmText widget. You are responsible for calling XtFree to release the storage allocated for the returned string when you no longer need the string.

XmTextGetSubstring
```
#include <Xm/Text.h>
int XmTextGetSubstring(
    Widget         widget,  /* Get substring from this widget  */
    XmTextPosition start,   /* Beginning character position    */
    int            num_chars,/* Number of characters to get     */
    int            buf_size, /* Size of buffer in bytes (provide */
                             /* room for a terminating null char)*/
    char           *buffer); /* Buffer to hold the substring    */
```

Gets a substring from the string displayed in the specified XmTextField widget. You are responsible for allocating a buffer that holds the returned substring. This function returns the constant XmCOPY_SUCCEEDED if the operation succeeds.

XmTextGetSubstringWcs
```
#include <Xm/Text.h>
int XmTextGetSubstringWcs(
    Widget          widget,  /* Get substring from this widget  */
    XmTextPosition start,   /* Beginning character position    */
    int             num_chars,/* Number of characters to get   */
    int             buf_size, /* Size of buffer in terms of
                                number of wchar_t characters   */
    wchar_t         *buffer); /* Buffer to hold the substring   */
```

Gets a substring from the wide-character string value of the specified XmTextField widget. You are responsible for allocating a buffer that holds the returned substring. This function returns the constant XmCOPY_SUCCEEDED if the operation succeeds.

XmTextGetTopCharacter
```
#include <Xm/Text.h>
XmTextPosition XmTextGetTopCharacter(
    Widget w); /* Return pos of first char in XmText widget */
```

Returns the position of the first character displayed in the specified XmText widget.

XmTextInsert
```
#include <Xm/Text.h>
void XmTextInsert(
    Widget widget,      /* Insert into this XmText widget */
    XmTextPosition pos, /* Insert at this char. position  */
    char *string);  /* Insert this null-terminated string */
```

Inserts a null-terminated string starting at a specified position in an XmText widget.

XmTextInsertWcs
```
#include <Xm/Text.h>
void XmTextInsertWcs(
    Widget widget,      /* Insert into this XmText widget */
    XmTextPosition pos, /* Insert at this char. position  */
    wchar_t *wcs);   /* Insert this wide-character string */
```

Inserts a wide-character string starting at a specified position in an XmText widget.

XmTextPaste
```
#include <Xm/Text.h>
Boolean XmTextPaste(
    Widget w); /* Paste selection into this XmText widget */
```

Pastes the current selection from the clipboard into the specified XmText widget at the current position of the insertion cursor. Returns True if the paste operation is successful and False if the widget does not own the primary selection.

XmTextPosToXY
```
#include <Xm/Text.h>
Boolean XmTextPosToXY(
    Widget widget,      /* For this XmText widget         */
    XmTextPosition pos, /* Character position to convert */
    Position *x, *y);   /* Returned x-y coordinate        */
```

Converts the character position `pos` into x-y coordinates (with respect to the widget's upper-left corner) and returns the values in the arguments `x` and `y`.

XmTextRemove
```
#include <Xm/Text.h>
Boolean XmTextRemove(
    Widget w);/* Delete selected text from this XmText */
```

Deletes the selected text (which constitutes the primary selection) from the specified `XmText` widget. This function returns `True` if the operation succeeds and `False` if the primary selection is `NULL` or if the widget does not own the primary selection.

XmTextReplace
```
#include <Xm/Text.h>
void XmTextReplace(
    Widget w,        /* Modify contents of this XmText widget */
    XmTextPosition from, /* Start at this char position     */
    XmTextPosition to,   /* End at this char position       */
    char *string); /* Null-terminated replacement string   */
```

Replaces the block of characters (in the `XmText` widget) between the positions `from` and `to` with the null-terminated string. You can insert the string at a specific character position by setting both `from` and `to` arguments to that character position.

XmTextReplaceWcs
```
#include <Xm/Text.h>
void XmTextReplaceWcs(
    Widget w,        /* Modify contents of this XmText widget */
    XmTextPosition from, /* Start at this char position     */
    XmTextPosition to,   /* End at this char position       */
    wchar_t *wcs); /* Replacement wide-character string    */
```

Replaces the block of wide characters (in the `XmText` widget) between the positions `from` and `to` with the wide-character string `wcs`. You can insert the string after a specific character position by setting both `from` and `to` arguments to that character position.

XmTextScroll
```
#include <Xm/Text.h>
Boolean XmTextScroll(
    Widget w,        /* Scroll text in this XmText widget */
    int    nlines); /* Scroll by these many lines        */
```

Scrolls the text in the specified `XmText` widget by a number of lines. If `nlines` is positive, the text scrolls up. If `nlines` is negative, the text scrolls down.

XmTextSetAddMode
```
#include <Xm/Text.h>
Boolean XmTextSetAddMode(
    Widget  widget, /* Affects this XmText widget   */
    Boolean mode ); /* New value for the add mode */
```

Returns the current setting of the `XmText` widget's add mode and sets the add mode to the `Boolean` value in the mode argument. If the add mode is `True`, you can move the cursor within the `XmText` without altering the primary selection.

XmTextSetCursorPosition
```
#include <Xm/Text.h>
```

```
void XmTextSetCursorPosition(
    Widget w, /* Set cursor position of this XmText  */
    XmTextPosition pos);/* Position cursor here */
```

Positions the insertion cursor at the character position pos in a specified XmText widget.

XmTextSetEditable
```
#include <Xm/Text.h>
void XmTextSetEditable(
    Widget  w,   /* Alter "editability" of this XmText    */
    Boolean edit);/* New value for the XmNeditable resource */
```

Sets the XmNeditable resource of the specified XmText widget with the value given in the edit argument. When the XmNeditable resource is True, the user can edit the contents of the XmText widget.

XmTextSetHighlight
```
#include <Xm/Text.h>
void XmTextSetHighlight(
    Widget w,   /* Set highlight fo this XmText */
    XmTextPosition left,   /* Starting position */
    XmTextPosition right,  /* Ending position   */
    XmHighlightMode mode); /* One of: XmNORMAL,
            XmSELECTED, or XmSECONDARY_SELECTED */
```

Sets the highlighting of the block of characters between the character positions left and right. If mode is XmNORMAL, the text is not highlighted. If mode is XmSELECTED, the selected characters appear in "reverse video" (with foreground and background colors swapped). If the mode argument is XmSECONDARY_SELECTED, the characters between left and right are underlined.

XmTextSetInsertionPosition
```
#include <Xm/Text.h>
void XmTextSetInsertionPosition(
    Widget w, /* Set insertion position of this XmText  */
    XmTextPosition pos);       /* New insertion position */
```

Positions the insertion cursor at the character position pos in a specified XmText widget.

XmTextSetMaxLength
```
#include <Xm/Text.h>
void XmTextSetMaxLength(
    Widget w,      /* Set max length of this XmText widget */
    int    nchar);/* Allow up to these many characters    */
```

Sets the XmNmaxLength resource of the specified XmText widget. This resource specifies the maximum number of characters that the XmText widget can hold.

XmTextSetSelection
```
#include <Xm/Text.h>
void XmTextSetSelection(
    Widget w,    /* Set selection from this XmText */
    XmTextPosition start, /* Starting position    */
    XmTextPosition end,   /* Ending position      */
    Time time);  /* Timestamp of triggering event */
```

Sets the characters between positions start and end in the specified XmText widget as the current primary selection.

XmTextSetSource
```
#include <Xm/Text.h>
void XmTextSetSource(
    Widget w,    /* Set text source for this XmText widget */
    XmTextSource   src,    /* New text source for widget    */
    XmTextPosition top,    /* Char pos displayed at top     */
    XmTextPosition cpos); /* Insertion cursor position     */
```

Sets a text source for the specified XmText widget. Two or more XmText widgets may share a text source so that when the user edits the text in one widget, the changes are reflected in the others.

XmTextSetString
```
#include <Xm/Text.h>
void XmTextSetString(
    Widget w,  /* Set the text of this XmText widget */
    char  *s); /* to this null-terminated string     */
```

Sets the text string of the specified XmText widget to the null-terminated string s.

XmTextSetStringWcs
```
#include <Xm/Text.h>
void XmTextSetStringWcs(
    Widget  w,      /* Set the text of this XmText widget */
    wchar_t *wcs); /* to this wide-character string      */
```

Sets the text string of the specified XmText widget to the wide-character string wcs.

XmTextSetTopCharacter
```
#include <Xm/Text.h>
void XmTextSetTopCharacter(
    Widget w, /* Set the "top" char for this XmText widget */
    XmTextPosition pos); /* Display this char in widget    */
```

Displays the character at position pos as the first character in the specified XmText widget.

XmTextShowPosition
```
#include <Xm/Text.h>
void XmTextShowPosition(
    Widget w,             /* Affects this XmText widget */
    XmTextPosition pos); /* Display text starting here */
```

Displays the text starting at the character position pos.

XmTextXYToPos
```
#include <Xm/Text.h>
XmTextPosition XmTextXYToPos(
    Widget  w,    /* For this XmText widget            */
    Position x,y);/* Return char pos for this x-y coord */
```

Returns the character position corresponding to the x-y coordinate (with respect to the upper-left corner of the widget).

XmToggleButtonGadgetGetState
```
#include <Xm/ToggleBG.h>
Boolean XmToggleButtonGadgetGetState(
    Widget g); /* Return state of this toggle button gadget */
```

Returns the current state (True if "on" and False if "off") of the specified XmToggleButtonGadget.

XmToggleButtonGadgetSetState
```
#include <Xm/ToggleBG.h>
```

```
void XmToggleButtonGadgetSetState(
    Widget  g,  /* Set state of this toggle button gadget */
    Boolean state,  /* New state of toggle button gadget */
    Boolean notify); /* True=call XmNvalueChangedCallback */
```

Sets the state of the specified XmToggleButtonGadget from the value given in the state argument (True means "on" and False means "off"). If the notify argument is True, the callbacks listed in the gadget's XmNvalueChangedCallback are called.

XmToggleButtonGetState
```
#include <Xm/ToggleB.h>
Boolean XmToggleButtonGetState(
    Widget w); /* Return state of this toggle button widget */
```

Returns the current state (True if "on" and False if "off") of the specified XmToggleButton widget.

XmToggleButtonSetState
```
#include <Xm/ToggleB.h>
void XmToggleButtonSetState(
    Widget  w,  /* Set state of this toggle button widget */
    Boolean state,  /* New state of toggle button widget */
    Boolean notify); /* True=call XmNvalueChangedCallback */
```

Sets the state of the specified XmToggleButton widget from the value given in the state argument (True means "on" and False means "off"). If the notify argument is True, the callbacks listed in the gadget's XmNvalueChangedCallback are called.

XmTrackingEvent
```
#include <Xm/Xm.h>
Widget XmTrackingEvent(
    Widget  w,  /* Use this widget for a modal interaction */
    Cursor  c,  /* Use this cursor during the interaction */
    Boolean restrict, /* True = confine cursor to widget w */
    XEvent  *ev); /* On return, this would be the event
                        that caused function to return      */
```

Takes over exclusive control of the pointer (grabs) and returns ID of the widget where the user clicks button 1 of the mouse. A NULL return value signifies that the window where the user clicked the mouse is not part of the application.

XmTrackingLocate
```
#include <Xm/Xm.h>
Widget XmTrackingLocate(
    Widget  w,  /* Use this widget for a modal interaction */
    Cursor  c,  /* Use this cursor during the interaction */
    Boolean restrict);/* True = confine cursor to widget w */
```

Takes over exclusive control of the pointer (grabs) and returns ID of the widget where the user clicks button 1 of the mouse. A NULL return value signifies that the window where the user clicked the mouse is not part of the application.

XmTranslateKey
```
#include <Xm/Xm.h>
void XmTranslateKey(
    Display *dpy,        /* Keycode is from this display   */
    KeyCode keycode,     /* Keycode to translate           */
```

```
    Modifiers mod,        /* Modifiers to be applied      */
    Modifiers *mod_ret,  /* Mask of modifiers actually used */
    KeySym *keysym_ret); /* Returned keysym              */
```

Translates a keycode with modifiers into a keysym. This is the default keycode-to-keysym translator.

XmUninstallImage
```
#include <Xm/Xm.h>
Boolean XmUninstallImage(
    XImage *image); /* Remove this image from image cache */
```

Removes the specified image from the image cache. Returns True if successful and False if the image argument is NULL or if image is not present in the image cache.

XmUpdateDisplay
```
#include <Xm/Xm.h>
void XmUpdateDisplay(
    Widget w); /* Update display used by this widget*/
```

Sends all pending Expose events to the X server associated with the specified widget. You can call XmUpdateDisplay before starting a time-consuming operation. This ensures that the display appears up-to-date while the application performs the lengthy operation.

```
XmVaCreateSimpleCheckBox
#include <Xm/Xm.h>
Widget XmVaCreateSimpleCheckBox(
    Widget parent,        /* ID of parent widget          */
    String name,          /* Name of widget to be created  */
    XtCallbackProc callback, /* Function to be called when
                              value changes              */
    ...);          /* One of: XmVaCHECKBUTTON, XtVaTypedArg,
             or XtVaNestedList with appropriate aruguments */
```

Creates a CheckBox with ToggleButton gadgets the way that XmCreateSimpleCheckBox does, but accepts a variable-length argument list that ends with a NULL. Each entry in the variable-length argument list can be a resource name-value pair or start with one of the following constants:

XmVaCHECKBUTTON followed by four arguments:

```
    label       /* XmString with label            */
    mnemonic    /* KeySym denoting mnemonic key    */
    accelerator /* String with accelerator         */
    acc_text    /* XmString with accelerator text */
```

XtVaTypedArg followed by four arguments:

```
    name    /* String with resource name       */
    type    /* String with data type           */
    value   /* Resource value of type XtArgVal */
    size    /* int with bytes in value          */
```

XtVaNestedList followed by one XtVarArgsList argument, which is a list returned by XtVaCreateArgsList

This function returns the ID of the RowColumn widget that represents the CheckBox.

XmVaCreateSimpleMenuBar

```
#include <Xm/Xm.h>
Widget XmVaCreateSimpleMenuBar(
    Widget parent, /* ID of parent widget    */
    String name,   /* Name of MenuBar widget */
    ...) ;
```

Creates a MenuBar with CascadeButton gadgets the way that XmCreateSimpleMenuBar does, but accepts a variable-length argument list that ends with a NULL. Each entry in the variable-length argument list can be a resource name-value pair or start with one of the following constants:

XmVaCASCADEBUTTON followed by two arguments:

```
    label      /* XmString with label        */
    mnemonic  /* KeySym denoting mnemonic key   */
```

XtVaTypedArg (see XmVaCreateSimpleCheckBox)

XtVaNestedList (see XmVaCreateSimpleCheckBox)

This function returns the ID of the RowColumn widget that represents the MenuBar.

XmVaCreateSimpleOptionMenu

```
#include <Xm/Xm.h>
Widget XmVaCreateSimpleOptionMenu(
    Widget       parent,    /* ID of parent widget         */
    String       name,      /* Name of new widget          */
    XmString option_label,  /* Label on the left side      */
    KeySym option_mnemonic, /* Key that activated menu      */
    int         button_set, /* Button to be initially set   */
    XtCallbackProc callback,/* Function to call when button */
                            /*  is activated               */
    ...) ; /* Variable-length argument list (end with NULL) */
```

Creates an OptionMenu the way that XmCreateSimpleOptionMenu does, but accepts a variable-length argument list that ends with a NULL. Each entry in the variable-length argument list can be a resource name-value pair or start with one of the following constants:

XmVaCASCADEBUTTON followed by two arguments:

```
    label      /* XmString with label          */
    mnemonic  /* KeySym denoting mnemonic key   */
```

XmVaPUSHBUTTON followed by four arguments:

```
    label        /* XmString with label            */
    mnemonic    /* KeySym denoting mnemonic key     */
    accelerator /* String with accelerator          */
    acc_text    /* XmString with accelerator text */
```

XtVaTypedArg (see XmVaCreateSimpleCheckBox)

XtVaNestedList (see XmVaCreateSimpleCheckBox)

This function returns the ID of the RowColumn widget that represents the OptionMenu.

XmVaCreateSimplePopupMenu
```
#include <Xm/Xm.h>
Widget XmVaCreateSimplePopupMenu(
    Widget          parent,    /* Parent of MenuShell widget   */
    String          name,      /* Name of new widget           */
    XtCallbackProc callback,   /* Function to call when button */
                               /* is activated                 */
    ...);     /* Variable-length argument list (end with NULL) */
```

Creates a pop-up MenuPane the way that XmCreateSimplePopupMenu does, but accepts a variable-length argument list that ends with a NULL. Each entry in the variable-length argument list can be a resource name-value pair or start with one of the following constants:

XmVaCASCADEBUTTON followed by two arguments:

```
    label       /* XmString with label            */
    mnemonic  /* KeySym denoting mnemonic key   */
```

XmVaPUSHBUTTON followed by four arguments:

```
    label       /* XmString with label            */
    mnemonic  /* KeySym denoting mnemonic key   */
    accelerator  /* String with accelerator       */
    acc_text    /* XmString with accelerator text */
```

XmVaCHECKBUTTON followed by four arguments that have the same meaning as for XmVaPUSHBUTTON

XmVaRADIOBUTTON followed by four arguments that have the same meaning as for XmVaPUSHBUTTON

XmVaTITLE followed by an XmString argument that specifies a LabelGadget in the pop-up menu pane

XmVaSEPARATOR without argument (to display a separator in the pop-up menu pane)

XmVaDOUBLE_SEPARATOR without argument (to display a separator of type XmDOUBLE_LINE in the pop-up menu pane)

XtVaTypedArg (see XmVaCreateSimpleCheckBox)

XtVaNestedList (see XmVaCreateSimpleCheckBox)

This function returns the ID of the RowColumn widget that represents the pop-up MenuPane.

XmVaCreateSimplePulldownMenu
```
#include <Xm/Xm.h>
Widget XmVaCreateSimplePulldownMenu(
    Widget          parent,    /* Parent of MenuShell widget   */
    String          name,      /* Name of new widget           */
    int post_from_button,      /* Parent's cascade button that */
                               /* posts (displays) this menu   */
    XtCallbackProc callback,   /* Function to call when button */
                               /* is activated                 */
    ...);    /* Variable-length argument list (end with NULL) */
```

Creates a pull-down MenuPane the way that XmCreateSimplePulldownMenu does, but accepts a variable-length argument list that ends with a NULL. The entries in the variable-length argument list are similar to those allowed for XmVaCreateSimplePopupMenu. This function returns the ID of the RowColumn widget that represents the pull-down MenuPane.

XmVaCreateSimpleRadioBox

```
#include <Xm/Xm.h>
Widget XmVaCreateSimpleRadioBox(
    Widget        parent,      /* ID of parent widget         */
    String        name,        /* Name of new widget          */
    int           button_set,  /* Button to be initially set  */
    XtCallbackProc callback,   /* Function to call when        */
                               /* button's value changes      */
    ...) ; /* Variable-length argument list (end with NULL) */
```

Creates a RadioBox with ToggleButton gadgets the way that XmCreateSimpleRadioBox does, but XmVaCreateSimpleRadioBox accepts a variable-length argument list that ends with a NULL. Each entry in the variable-length argument list can be a resource name-value pair or start with one of the following constants:

XmVaRADIOBUTTON followed by four arguments:

```
    label       /* XmString with label            */
    mnemonic    /* KeySym denoting mnemonic key   */
    accelerator /* String with accelerator        */
    acc_text    /* XmString with accelerator text */
```

XtVaTypedArg   followed by four arguments:

```
    name        /* String with resource name      */
    type        /* String with data type          */
    value       /* Resource value of type XtArgVal */
    size        /* int with bytes in value        */
```

XtVaNestedList followed by one XtVarArgsList argument, which is a list returned by XtVaCreateArgsList

This function returns the ID of the RowColumn widget that represents the RadioBox.

XmWidgetGetBaselines

```
#include <Xm/Xm.h>
Boolean XmWidgetGetBaselines(
    Widget    wid,         /* Info requested for this widget */
    Dimension **baselines,/* Array of baselines for each
                             line of text in widget          */
    int       *nlines); /* Number of lines of text in widget */
```

Provides the baseline values in a widget. The baseline value of a line of text is the vertical offset in pixels from the origin of the widget's bounding box to the text's baseline. Returns True if the widget contains at least one line of text.

XmWidgetGetDisplayRect

```
#include <Xm/Xm.h>
Boolean XmWidgetGetDisplayRect(
    Widget     wid,        /* Info requested for this widget */
    XRectangle *disprect); /* Display rectangle returned here */
```

Provides information about a widget's display rectangle (the smallest rectangle that encloses a string or a pixmap). Returns True if the widget has a display rectangle.

Motif Widgets

This section includes reference entries for the Motif widgets, arranged alphabetically. For each widget, you will find the class name, the class pointer, and the class from which it inherits. Each widget's resources are listed in a tabular form. The resource table shows the name, type, and default value of each resource. The letters in the last column mean the following:

✦ A C indicates that you can set that particular resource at the time of creation through an argument list.

✦ An S means that you can use XtSetValues to set that resource.

✦ A G implies that you can retrieve a resource's value using XtGetValues.

✦ A * for a default value indicates that default is determined at run-time.

The symbols appearing in the resource table are defined in the header file <Xm/Xm.h>.

A word about the resources: A widget inherits the resources of its superclass (the class from which it inherits); the superclass, in turn, inherits the resources of its superclass; and so on. The resource table of each widget shows only the new resources for that class. To learn about all the resources that the widget can have, you have to follow the inheritance hierarchy all the way up to the Core class, which is at the root of the inheritance hierarchy. To do this, start with the class name shown in the Inherits from: field in the widget's documentation and continue following the inheritance hierarchy. For example, if you do this for the ApplicationShell class, you get the following inheritance hierarchy (read -> as "inherits from"):

```
ApplicationShell->TopLevelShell->VendorShell->WMShell->Shell
->Composite->Core
```

ApplicationShell

Class name: ApplicationShell   Class pointer: applicationShellWidgetClass
Include file: <X11/Shell.h>   Inherits from: TopLevelShell

This widget provides the main top-level window for an application.

Name	Type	Default	Set/Get
XmNargc	int	0	CSG
XmNargv	String*	NULL	CSG

Composite

Class name: Composite   Class pointer: compositeWidgetClass
Include file: <Xm/Xm.h>   Inherits from: Core

Composite widgets act as containers for other widgets. A Composite widget takes care of the overall management of its children from creation to destruction. This includes mapping and unmapping the children and the physical arrangement of the managed children.

Name	Type	Default	Set/Get
XmNchildren	WidgetList	NULL	G
XmNinsertPosition	XtOrderProc	NULL	CSG
XmNnumChildren	Cardinal	0	G

Constraint

Class name: Constraint   Class pointer: constraintWidgetClass
Include file: <Xm/Xm.h>   Inherits from: Composite

A Constraint widget attaches additional resources to its children. This class defines no new resources.

Core

Class name: Core   Class pointer: widgetClass
Include file: <Xm/Xm.h>   Inherits from: None

Xt Intrinsics defines Core as the basis of all widgets in the toolkit. The resources in the Core class are important because they are available in every widget in the toolkit.

Name	Type	Default	Set/Get
XmNaccelerators	XtAccelerators	*	CSG
XmNancestorSensitive	Boolean	*	G
XmNbackground	Pixel	*	CSG
XmNbackgroundPixmap	Pixmap	XmUNSPECIFIED_PIXMAP	CSG
XmNborderColor	Pixel	*	CSG
XmNborderPixmap	Pixmap	XmUNSPECIFIED_PIXMAP	CSG
XmNborderWidth	Dimension	1	CSG
XmNcolormap	Colormap	*	C G
XmNdepth	int	*	C G
XmNdestroyCallback	XtCallbackList	NULL	C
XmNheight	Dimension	*	CSG
XmNmappedWhenManaged	Boolean	True	CSG
XmNscreen	Screen*	*	C G
XmNsensitive	Boolean	True	CSG
XmNtranslations	XtTranslations	*	CSG
XmNwidth	Dimension	*	CSG
XmNx	Position	0	CSG
XmNy	Position	0	CSG

See Chapter 14 for a description of the Core widget's resources.

Object

Class name: Object   Class pointer: objectClass
Include file: <Xm/Xm.h>   Inherits from: None

The Object class serves as a building block for other widget classes. You never have to create an instance of the Object class.

Name	Type	Default	Set/Get
XmNdestroyCallback	XtCallbackList	NULL	C

OverrideShell

Class name: OverrideShell   Class pointer: overrideShellWidgetClass
Include file: <X11/Shell.h>   Inherits from: Shell

Widgets of this class are used to create windows (such as pop-up menu windows) that bypass the window manager. OverrideShell widgets do not define any new resource.

RectObj

Class name: RectObj   Class pointer: rectObjClass
Include file: <Xm/Xm.h>   Inherits from: Object

As with the Object class, RectObj serves as a building block for other widget classes. You never have to create an instance of the RectObj class.

Name	Type	Default	Set/Get
XmNancestorSensitive	Boolean	*	G
XmNborderWidth	Dimension	1	CSG
XmNheight	Dimension	*	CSG
XmNsensitive	Boolean	True	CSG
XmNwidth	Dimension	*	CSG
XmNx	Position	0	CSG
XmNy	Position	0	CSG

Shell

Class name: Shell   Class pointer: shellWidgetClass
Include file: <X11/Shell.h>   Inherits from: Composite

A Shell is a top-level widget with one managed child. This class takes care of interactions with the window manager.

Name	Type	Default	Set/Get
XmNallowShellResize	Boolean	False	C G
XmNcreatePopupChild	ProcXtCreatePopupChildProc	NULL	CSG
XmNgeometry	String	NULL	CSG
XmNoverrideRedirect	Boolean	False	CSG
XmNpopdownCallback	XtCallbackList	NULL	C
XmNpopupCallback	XtCallbackList	NULL	C
XmNsaveUnder	Boolean	False	CSG
XmNVisual	Visual	XtCopyFromParent	CSG

TopLevelShell

Class name: TopLevelShell   Class pointer: topLevelShellWidgetClass
Include file: <X11/Shell.h>   Inherits from: VendorShell

The `TopLevelShell` class provides the normal top-level windows for an application.

Name	Type	Default	Set/Get
XmNiconic	Boolean	False	CSG
XmNiconName	String	NULL	CSG
XmNiconNameEncoding	Atom	*	CSG

TransientShell

> Class name: `TransientShell`   Class pointer: `transientShellWidgetClass`
> Include file: `<X11/Shell.h>`   Inherits from: `VendorShell`

The `TransientShell` class provides windows that can be manipulated by the window manager but cannot be iconified.

Name	Type	Default	Set/Get
XmNtransientFor	Widget	NULL	CSG

VendorShell

> Class name: `VendorShell`   Class pointer: `vendorShellWidgetClass`
> Include file: `<X11/Shell.h>`   Inherits from: `WMShell`

The `VendorShell` class is the basis for all shell widgets that are visible to the window manager. The `XmNshellUnitType` resource is worth noting. It determines the unit to be used for interpreting the resources that specify geometry (size and position). You can specify the unit with one of the constants: `XmPIXELS`, `Xm100TH_MILLIMETERS`, `Xm1000TH_INCHES`, `Xm100TH_POINTS`, or `Xm100TH_FONT_UNIT`, defined in the header file `<Xm/Xm.h>`. The default setting of `XmPIXELS` indicates that everything is specified in pixels. To specify really device-independent units, you can use `Xm100TH_MILLIMETERS` for 1/100-millimeter, `Xm1000TH_INCHES` for 1/1000-inch, and `Xm100TH_POINTS` for 1/100-point, where a point is 1/72-inch. Use `Xm100TH_FONT_UNIT` to indicate that all dimensions are in terms of one hundredth of a font's unit, which is taken from the font's `QUAD_WIDTH` property. You can also explicitly set the font unit with the `XmSetFontUnits` function.

Name	Type	Default	Set/Get
XmNaudibleWarning	unsigned char	XmBELL	CSG
XmNbuttonFontList	XmFontList	*	CSG
XmNdefaultFontList	XmFontList	*	C G
XmNdeleteResponse	unsigned char	XmDESTROY	CSG
XmNinputMethod	String	NULL	CSG
XmNkeyboardFocusPolicy	unsigned char	XmEXPLICIT	CSG
XmNlabelFontList	XmFontList	*	CSG
XmNmwmDecorations	int	-1	CSG
XmNmwmFunctions	int	-1	CSG
XmNmwmInputMode	int	-1	CSG
XmNmwmMenu	String	NULL	CSG
XmNpreeditType	String	*	CSG
XmNshellUnitType	unsigned char	XmPIXELS	CSG
XmNtextFontList	XmFontList	*	CSG
XmNuseAsyncGeometry	Boolean	False	CSG

WMShell

Class name: WMShell   Class pointer: wmShellWidgetClass
Include file: <X11/Shell.h>   Inherits from: Shell

The WMShell class takes care of interactions with the window manager.

Name	Type	Default	Set/Get
XmNbaseHeight	int	XtUnspecifiedShellInt	CSG
XmNbaseWidth	int	XtUnspecifiedShellInt	CSG
XmNheightInc	int	XtUnspecifiedShellInt	CSG
XmNiconMask	Pixmap	NULL	CSG
XmNiconPixmap	Pixmap	NULL	CSG
XmNiconWindow	Window	NULL	CSG
XmNiconX	int	-1	CSG
XmNiconY	int	-1	CSG
XmNinitalState	int	NormalState	CSG
XmNinput	Boolean	True	CSG
XmNmaxAspectX	int	XtUnspecifiedShellInt	CSG
XmNmaxAspectY	int	XtUnspecifiedShellInt	CSG
XmNminAspectX	int	XtUnspecifiedShellInt	CSG
XmNminAspectY	int	XtUnspecifiedShellInt	CSG
XmNmaxHeight	int	XtUnspecifiedShellInt	CSG
XmNmaxWidth	int	XtUnspecifiedShellInt	CSG
XmNminHeight	int	XtUnspecifiedShellInt	CSG
XmNminWidth	int	XtUnspecifiedShellInt	CSG
XmNtitle	String	NULL	CSG
XmNtitleEncoding	Atom	*	CSG
XmNtransient	Boolean	False	CSG
XmNwaitForWm	Boolean	True	CSG
XmNwidthInc	int	XtUnspecifiedShellInt	CSG
XmNwindowGroup	Window	*	CSG
XmNwinGravity	int	*	CSG
XmNwmTimeOut	int	5000 (milliseconds)	CSG

XmArrowButton

Class name: XmArrowButton   Class pointer: xmArrowButtonWidgetClass
Include file: <Xm/ArrowB.h>   Inherits from: XmPrimitive

The XmArrowButton class displays an arrow (you specify the direction) in a window. The arrow has a shadow around it to give it a three-dimensional look.

Name	Type	Default	Set/Get
XmNactivateCallback	XtCallbackList	NULL	C
XmNarmCallback	XtCallbackList	NULL	C
XmNarrowDirection	unsigned char	XmARROW_UP	CSG
XmNdisarmCallback	XtCallbackList	NULL	C
XmNmultiClick	unsigned char	*	CSG

XmArrowButtonGadget

Class name: XmArrowButtonGadge   Class pointer: xmArrowButtonGadgetClass
Include file: <Xm/ArrowBG.h>   Inherits from: XmGadget

The `XmArrowButtonGadget` class behaves as the `XmArrowButton` class does except that it does not use a window to display the arrow.

Name	Type	Default	Set/Get
XmNactivateCallback	XtCallbackList	NULL	C
XmNarmCallback	XtCallbackList	NULL	C
XmNarrowDirection	unsigned char	XmARROW_UP	CSG
XmNdisarmCallback	XtCallbackList	NULL	C
XmNmultiClick	unsigned char	*	CSG

XmBulletinBoard

Class name: `XmBulletinBoard`
Include file: `<Xm/BulletinB.h>`

Class pointer: `xmBulletinBoardWidgetClass`
Inherits from: `XmManager`

`XmBulletinBoard` is a general-purpose container widget that serves as the base widget for most dialog widgets. The `XmNBulletinBoard` widget does not enforce any particular position or size on its children.

Name	Type	Default	Set/Get
XmNallowOverlap	Boolean	True	CSG
XmNautoUnmanage	Boolean	True	C G
XmNbuttonFontList	XmFontList	NULL	CSG
XmNcancelButton	Widget	NULL	SG
XmNdefaultButton	Widget	NULL	SG
XmNdefaultPosition	Boolean	True	CSG
XmNdialogStyle	unsigned char	*	CSG
XmNdialogTitle	XmString	NULL	CSG
XmNfocusCallback	XtCallbackList	NULL	C
XmNlabelFontList	XmFontList	NULL	CSG
XmNmapCallback	XtCallbackList	NULL	C
XmNmarginHeight	Dimension	10	CSG
XmNmarginWidth	Dimension	10	CSG
XmNnoResize	Boolean	False	CSG
XmNresizePolicy	unsigned char	XmRESIZE_ANY	CSG
XmNshadowType	unsigned char	XmSHADOW_OUT	CSG
XmNtextFontList	XmFontList	NULL	CSG
XmNtextTranslations	XtTranslations	NULL	C
XmNunmapCallback	XtCallbackList	NULL	C

XmCascadeButton

Class name: `XmCascadeButton`
Include file: `<Xm/CascadeB.h>`

Class pointer: `xmCascadeButtonWidgetClass`
Inherits from: `XmLabel`

The `XmCascadeButton` widget accepts a pull-down menu attached to it as a submenu. The pull-down menu is displayed when the `XmCascadeButton` widget is activated.

Name	Type	Default	Set/Get
XmNactivateCallback	XtCallbackList	NULL	C
XmNcascadePixmap	Pixmap	*	CSG
XmNcascadingCallback	XtCallbackList	NULL	C
XmNmappingDelay	int	180 (milliseconds)	CSG
XmNsubmenuId	Widget	NULL	CSG

XmCascadeButtonGadget

Class name: XmCascadeButton   Class pointer: xmCascadeButtonGadgetClass
Include file: <Xm/CascadeBG.h>   Inherits from: XmLabelGadget

The XmCascadeButtonGadget is a gadget (a gadget is a widget without a window) that performs the same function as the XmCascadeButton widget.

Name	Type	Default	Set/Get
XmNactivateCallback	XtCallbackList	NULL	C
XmNcascadePixmap	Pixmap	*	CSG
XmNcascadingCallback	XtCallbackList	NULL	C
XmNmappingDelay	int	180 (milliseconds)	CSG
XmNsubmenuId	Widget	NULL	CSG

XmCommand

Class name: XmCommand   Class pointer: xmCommandWidgetClass
Include file: <Xm/Command.h>   Inherits from: XmSelectionBox

The XmCommand widget accepts commands from the user. It includes a text field for entering the commands, a prompt, and a scrollable history of past commands.

Name	Type	Default	Set/Get
XmNcommand	XmString	" "	CSG
XmNcommandChangedCallback	XtCallbackLis	NULL	Ct
XmNcommandEnteredCallback	XtCallbackList	NULL	C
XmNhistoryItems	XmStringTable	NULL	CSG
XmNhistoryItemCount	int	0	CSG
XmNhistoryMaxItems	int	100	CSG
XmNhistoryVisibleItemCount	int	*	CSG
XmNpromptString	XmString	">" (in C locale)	CSG

XmDialogShell

Class name: XmDialogShell   Class pointer: xmDialogShellWidgetClass
Include file <Xm/DialogS.h>   Inherits from: TransientShell

The XmDialogShell widget is the basis for most pop-up dialogs. This class does not define any new resources.

XmDisplay

Class name: XmDisplay   Class pointer: xmDisplaytClass
Include file: <Xm/Display.h>   Inherits from: ApplicationShell

The Motif toolkit uses the XmDisplay widget to store information about a specific display. The toolkit automatically creates an XmDisplay object when your application creates the first shell on a display. You cannot specify the initial values of the XmDisplay widget's resources, but you can alter the resources after you create the first shell on a display. To change the resources of the `XmDisplay` widget, call `XmGetXmDisplay` to get the widget ID of the `XmDisplay` object, and then call `XtSetValues` or `XtVaSetValues` to set the resources.

Name	Type	Default	Set/Get
XmNdefaultVirtualBindings	String	*	C G
XmNdragInitiatorProtocolStyle	unsigned char	XmDRAG_PREFER_RECEIVER	C G
XmNdragReceiverProtocolStyle	unsigned char	XmDRAG_PREFER_PREREGISTER	C G

XmDragContext

Class name: `XmDragContext`   Class pointer: `xmDragContextClass`
Include file: `<Xm/DragDrop.h>`   Inherits from: `Core`

The `XmDragContext` widget is meant for supporting drag-and-drop operations. You call the `XmDragStart` function to create an `XmDragContext` widget.

Name	Type	Default	Set/Get
XmNblendModel	unsigned char	XmBLEND_ALL	C G
XmNclientData	XtPointer	NULL	CSG
XmNconvertProc	XtConvertSelectionIncrProc	NULL	CSG
XmNcursorBackground	Pixel	*	CSG
XmNcursorForeground	Pixel	*	CSG
XmNdragDropFinishCallback	XtCallbackList	NULL	CSG
XmNdragMotionCallback	XtCallbackList	NULL	C
XmNdragOperations	unsigned char	XmDROP_COPY ¦ XmDROP_MOVE	C
XmNdropFinishCallback	XtCallbackList	NULL	C
XmNdropSiteEnterCallback	XtCallbackList	NULL	C
XmNdropSiteLeaveCallback	XtCallbackList	NULL	C
XmNdropStartCallback	XtCallbackList	NULL	C
XmNexportTargets	Atom *	NULL	CSG
XmNincremental	Boolean	False	CSG
XmNinvalidCursorForeground	Pixel	*	CSG
XmNnoneCursorForeground	Pixel	*	CSG
XmNnumExportTargets	Cardinal	0	CSG
XmNoperationChangedCallback	XtCallbackList	NULL	C
XmNoperationCursorIcon	Widget	*	CSG
XmNsourceCursorIcon	Widget	*	CSG
XmNsourcePixmapIcon	Widget	*	CSG
XmNstateCursorIcon	Widget	*	CSG
XmNtopLevelEnterCallback	XtCallbackList	NULL	C
XmNtopLevelLeaveCallback	XtCallbackList	NULL	C
XmNvalidCursorForeground	Pixel	*	CSG

XmDragIcon

Class name: `XmDragContext`   Class pointer: `xmDragIconObjectClass`
Include file: `<Xm/DragDrop.h>`   Inherits from: `Object`

The `XmDragIcon` widget is used to provide visual feedback during drag-and-drop operations. You call the `XmCreateDragIcon` function to create an `XmDragIcon` widget.

Name	Type	Default	Set/Get
XmNattachment	unsigned char	XmATTACH_NORTH_WEST	CSG
XmNdepth	int	1	CSG
XmNheight	Dimension	0	CSG
XmNhotX	Position	0	CSG
XmNhotY	Position	0	CSG
XmNmask	Pixmap	XmUNSPECIFIED_PIXMAP	CSG
XmNoffsetX	Position	0	CSG
XmNoffsetY	Position	0	CSG
XmNpixmap	Pixmap	XmUNSPECIFIED_PIXMAP	CSG
XmNwidth	Dimension	0	CSG

XmDrawingArea

Class name: XmDrawingArea   Class pointer: xmDrawingAreaWidgetClass
Include file: <Xm/DrawingA.h>   Inherits from: XmManager

The XmDrawingArea widget provides an empty window in which you can draw graphics or text (by calling appropriate Xlib functions).

Name	Type	Default	Set/Get
XmNexposeCallback	XtCallbackList	NULL	C
XmNinputCallback	XtCallbackList	NULL	C
XmNmarginHeight	Dimension	10	CSG
XmNmarginWidth	Dimension	10	CSG
XmNresizeCallback	XtCallbackList	NULL	C
XmNresizePolicy	unsigned char	XmRESIZE_ANY	CSG

XmDrawnButton

Class name: XmDrawnButton   Class pointer: xmDrawnButtonWidgetClass
Include file: <Xm/DrawnB.h>   Inherits from: XmLabel

The XmDrawingArea widget provides an empty window in which you can draw graphics or text (by calling appropriate Xlib functions).

Name	Type	Default	Set/Get
XmNactivateCallback	XtCallbackList	NULL	C
XmNarmCallback	XtCallbackList	NULL	C
XmNdisarmCallback	XtCallbackList	NULL	C
XmNexposeCallback	XtCallbackList	NULL	C
XmNmultiClick	XmMultiClick	*	CSG
XmNpushButtonEnabled	Boolean	False	CSG
XmNresizeCallback	XtCallbackList	NULL	C
XmNshadowType	unsigned char	XmSHADOW_ETCHED_IN	CSG

XmDropSite

Class name: Not applicable   Class pointer: Not applicable
Include file: <Xm/DragDrop.h>   Inherits from: None

This is not a widget; it is a set of resources that becomes associated with a widget that you register as a drop site by calling XmDropSiteRegister.

Name	Type	Default	Set/Get
XmNanimationMask	Pixmap	XmUNSPECIFIED_PIXMAP	CSG
XmNanimationPixmap	Pixmap	XmUNSPECIFIED_PIXMAP	CSG
XmNanimationPixmapDepth	int	0	CSG
XmNanimationStyle	unsigned char	XmDRAG_UNDER_HIGHLIGHT	CSG
XmNdragProc	XtCallbackProc	NULL	CSG
XmNdropProc	XtCallbackProc	NULL	CSG
XmNdropRectangles	XRectangle *	*	CSG
XmNdropSiteActivity	unsigned char	XmDROP_SITE_ACTIVE	CSG
XmNdropSiteOperations	unsigned char	XmDROP_MOVE ¦XmDROP_COPY	CSG
XmNdropSiteType	unsigned char	XmDROP_SITE_SIMPLE	C G
XmNimportTargets	Atom *	NULL	CSG
XmNnumDropRectangles	Cardinal	1	CSG
XmNnumImportTargets	Cardinal	0	CSG

XmDropTransfer

Class name: XmDropTransfer Class pointer: xmDropTransferObjectClass

Include file: <Xm/DragDrop.h> Inherits from: Object

The XmDropTransfer widget provides the resources and the callback functions necessary to complete a drop transaction in drag-and-drop operations. You call the XmDropTransferStart function to create an XmDropTransfer widget.

Name	Type	Default	Set/Get
XmNdropTransfers	XmDropTransferEntryRec	*	NULL C G
XmNincremental	Boolean	False	CSG
XmNnumDropTransfers	Cardinal	0	CSG
XmNtransferProc	XtSelectionCallbackProc	NULL	CSG
XmNtransferStatus	unsigned char	XmTRANSFER_SUCCESS	CSG

XmFileSelectionBox

Class name: XmFileSelectionBox Class pointer: xmFileSelectionBoxWidgetClass

Include file: <Xm/FileSB.h> Inherits from: XmSelectionBox

The XmFileSelectionBox widget enables the user to browse through directories, view the files in a directory, and pick a file.

Name	Type	Default	Set/Get
XmNdirectory	XmString	*	CSG
XmNdirectoryValid	Boolean	*	SG
XmNdirListItems	XmStringTable	*	SG
XmNdirListItemCount	int	*	SG
XmNdirListLabelString	XmString	*	CSG
XmNdirMask	XmString	*	CSG
XmNdirSearchProc	XmSearchProc	default procedure	CSG
XmNdirSpec	XmString	*	CSG
XmNfileListItems	XmStringTable	*	SG
XmNfileListItemCount	int	*	SG
XmNfileListLabelString	XmString	*	CSG
XmNfileSearchProc	XmSearchProc	default procedure	CSG

continues

Name	Type	Default	Set/Get
XmNfileTypeMask	unsigned char	XmFILE_REGULAR	CSG
XmNfilterLabelString	XmString	*	CSG
XmNlistUpdated	Boolean	*	SG
XmNnoMatchString	XmString	"[ ]"	CSG
XmNpattern	XmString	*	CSG
XmNqualifySearchDataProc	XmQualifyProc	default procedure	CSG

XmForm

Class name: XmForm   Class pointer: xmFormWidgetClass
Include file: <Xm/Form.h>   Inherits from: XmBulletinBoard

The XmForm widget is a container widget that enables you to specify a layout for its children. The layout is specified by attaching child widgets to each other, to the XmForm widget, or to a relative position within the XmForm widget.

Name	Type	Default	Set/Get
XmNbottomAttachment	unsigned char	XmATTACH_NONE	CSG
XmNbottomOffset	int	0	CSG
XmNbottomPosition	int	0	CSG
XmNbottomWidget	Widget	NULL	CSG
XmNfractionBase	int	100	CSG
XmNhorizontalSpacing	Dimension	0	CSG
XmNleftAttachment	unsigned char	XmATTACH_NONE	CSG
XmNleftOffset	int	0	CSG
XmNleftPosition	int	0	CSG
XmNleftWidget	Widget	NULL	CSG
XmNresizable	Boolean	True	CSG
XmNrightAttachment	unsigned char	XmATTACH_NONE	CSG
XmNrightOffset	int	0	CSG
XmNrightPosition	int	0	CSG
XmNrightWidget	Widget	NULL	CSG
XmNrubberPositioning	Boolean	False	CSG
XmNtopAttachment	unsigned char	XmATTACH_NONE	CSG
XmNtopOffset	int	0	CSG
XmNtopPosition	int	0	CSG
XmNtopWidget	Widget	NULL	CSG
XmNverticalSpacing	Dimension	0	CSG

XmFrame

Class name: XmFrame   Class pointer: xmFrameWidgetClass
Include file: <Xm/Frame.h>   Inherits from: XmManager

The XmFrame widget provides a frame (with a three-dimensional look) around a single child widget.

Name	Type	Default	Set/Get
XmNchildHorizontalAlignment	unsigned char	XmALIGNMENT_BEGINNING	CSG
XmNchildHorizontalSpacing	unsigned char	*	CSG
XmNchildType	unsigned char	XmFRAME_WORKAREA_CHILD	CSG
XmNchildVerticalAlignment	unsigned char	XmALIGNMENT_CENTER	CSG
XmNmarginHeight	Dimension	0	CSG

Name	Type	Default	Set/Get
XmNmarginWidth	Dimension	0	CSG
XmNshadowType	unsigned char	*	CSG

XmGadget

Class name: XmGadget   Class pointer: xmGadgetClass

Include file: <Xm/Gadget.h>   Inherits from: RectObj

The XmGadget class is the basis for all gadgets (a gadget is a widget that does not have a window of its own and displays itself in its parent's window). You never have to create an instance of XmGadget class, but you should know about the resources defined for this class because all gadgets inherit them. The XmNunitType resource is similar to the XmNshellUnitType resource of the VendorShell widget. Please consult the reference entry for VendorShell widget for a description of this resource.

Name	Type	Default	Set/Get
XmNbottomShadowColor	Pixel	*	G
XmNhelpCallback	XtCallbackList	NULL	C
XmNhighlightColor	Pixel	*	G
XmNhighlightOnEnter	Boolean	False	CSG
XmNhighlightThickness	Dimension	2	CSG
XmNnavigationType	XmNavigationType	XmNONE	CSG
XmNshadowThickness	Dimension	2	CSG
XmNtraversalOn	Boolean	True	CSG
XmNunitType	unsigned char	XmPIXELS	CSG
XmNuserData	XtPointer	NULL	CSG

XmLabel

Class name: XmLabel   Class pointer: xmLabelWidgetClass

Include file: <Xm/Label.h>   Inherits from: XmPrimitive

The XmLabel widget displays text or pixmap in a window. The text is a compound string (of type XmString).

Name	Type	Default	Set/Get
XmNaccelerator	String	NULL	CSG
XmNacceleratorText	XmString	NULL	CSG
XmNalignment	unsigned char	*	CSG
XmNfontList	XmFontList	*	CSG
XmNlabelInsensitivePixmap	Pixmap	XmUNSPECIFIED_PIXMAP	CSG
XmNlabelPixmap	Pixmap	XmUNSPECIFIED_PIXMAP	CSG
XmNlabelString	XmString	*	CSG
XmNlabelType	unsigned char	XmSTRING	CSG
XmNmarginBottom	Dimension	0	CSG
XmNmarginHeight	Dimension	2	CSG
XmNmarginLeft	Dimension	0	CSG
XmNmarginRight	Dimension	0	CSG
XmNmarginTop	Dimension	0	CSG
XmNmarginWidth	Dimension	2	CSG
XmNmnemonic	KeySym	*	CSG
XmNmnemonicCharSet	String	XmFONTLIST_DEFAULT_TAG	CSG
XmNrecomputeSize	Boolean	True	CSG
XmNstringDirection	XmStringDirection	*	CSG

XmLabelGadget

Class name: XmLabelGadget   Class pointer: xmLabelGadgetClass
Include file: <Xm/LabelG.h>   Inherits from: XmGadget

The XmLabelGadget is a gadget version of the XmLabel widget. It behaves the way an XmLabel widget does except that an XmLabelGadget does not have its own window.

Name	Type	Default	Set/Get
XmNaccelerator	String	NULL	CSG
XmNacceleratorText	XmString	NULL	CSG
XmNalignment	unsigned char	*	CSG
XmNfontList	XmFontList	*	CSG
XmNlabelInsensitivePixmap	Pixmap	XmUNSPECIFIED_PIXMAP	CSG
XmNlabelPixmap	Pixmap	XmUNSPECIFIED_PIXMAP	CSG
XmNlabelString	XmString	*	CSG
XmNlabelType	unsigned char	XmSTRING	CSG
XmNmarginBottom	Dimension	0	CSG
XmNmarginHeight	Dimension	2	CSG
XmNmarginLeft	Dimension	0	CSG
XmNmarginRight	Dimension	0	CSG
XmNmarginTop	Dimension	0	CSG
XmNmarginWidth	Dimension	2	CSG
XmNmnemonic	KeySym	*	CSG
XmNmnemonicCharSet	String	XmFONTLIST_DEFAULT_TAG	CSG
XmNrecomputeSize	Boolean	True	CSG
XmNstringDirection	XmStringDirection	*	CSG

XmList

Class name: XmList   Class pointer: xmListWidgetClass
Include file: <Xm/List.h>   Inherits from: XmPrimitive

The XmList widget displays a number of items in a window and enables the user to select one or more items from the list of items.

Name	Type	Default	Set/Get
XmNautomaticSelection	Boolean	False	CSG
XmNbrowseSelectionCallback	XtCallbackList	NULL	C
XmNdefaultActionCallback	XtCallbackList	NULL	C
XmNdoubleClickInterval	int	*	
XmNextendedSelectionCallback	XtCallbackList	NULL	C
XmNfontList	XmFontList	*	CSG
XmNitemCount	int	0	CSG
XmNitems	XmStringTable	NULL	CSG
XmNlistMarginHeight	Dimension	0	CSG
XmNlistMarginWidth	Dimension	0	CSG
XmNlistSizePolicy	unsigned char	XmVARIABLE	C G
XmNlistSpacing	Dimension	0	CSG
XmNmultipleSelectionCallback	XtCallbackList	NULL	C
XmNscrollBarDisplayPolicy	unsigned char	XmAS_NEEDED	CSG
XmNselectedItemCount	int	0	CSG
XmNselectedItems	XmStringTable	NULL	CSG
XmNselectionPolicy	unsigned char	XmBROWSE_SELECT	CSG

Name	Type	Default	Set/Get
XmNsingleSelectionCallback	XtCallbackList	NULL	C
XmNstringDirection	XmStringDirection	*	CSG
XmNtopItemPosition	int	1	CSG
XmvisibleItemCount	int	*	CSG

XmMainWindow

Class name: XmMainWindow

Include file: <Xm/MainW.h>

Class pointer: xmMainWindowWidgetClass

Inherits from: XmScrolledWindow

The XmMainWindow class provides a standard layout for the main window of an application. The XmMainWindow widget can manage a combination of a menubar, an XmCommand widget, an XmDrawingArea widget, and scrollbars.

Name	Type	Default	Set/Get
XmNcommandWindow	Widget	NULL	CSG
XmNcommandWindowLocation	XmCommandWindowLocation	ABOVE_WORKSPACE	C G
XmNmainWindowMarginHeight	Dimension	0	CSG
XmNmainWindowMarginWidth	Dimension	0	CSG
XmNmenuBar	Widget	NULL	CSG
XmNmessageWindow	Widget	NULL	CSG
XmNshowSeparator	Boolean	False	CSG

XmManager

Class name: XmManager

Include file: <Xm/Xm.h>

Class pointer: xmManagerWidgetClass

Inherits from: Constraint

The XmManager widget is the basis for all widgets that manage the layout of several child widgets. You never have to create an instance of XmManager class, but you should know about the resources defined for this class because many widgets inherit them. The purpose of the XmNunitType resource is the same as that of the XmNshellUnitType resource of the VendorShell widget. Please consult the reference entry for VendorShell widget for a description of that resource.

Name	Type	Default	Set/Get
XmNbottomShadowColor	Pixel	*	CSG
XmNbottomShadowPixap	Pixmap	XmUNSPECIFIED_PIXMAP	CSG
XmNforeground	Pixel	*	CSG
XmNhelpCallback	XtCallbackList	NULL	C
XmNhighlightColor	Pixel	*	CSG
XmNhighlightPixmap	Pixmap	*	CSG
XmNinitialFocus	Widget	NULL	CSG
XmNnavigationType	XmNavigationType	XmTAB_GROUP	CSG
XmNshadowThickness	Dimension	0	CSG
XmNtopShadowColor	Pixel	*	CSG
XmNtopShadowPixmap	Pixmap	*	CSG
XmNtraversalOn	Boolean	True	CSG
mNunitType	unsigned char	*	CSG
XmNuserData	XtPointer	NULL	CSG

XmMenuShell

Class name: XmMenuShell   Class pointer: xmMenuShellWidgetClass
Include file: <Xm/MenuShell.h>   Inherits from: OverrideShell

The XmMenuShell class serves as the basis of pop-up and pull-down menus whose windows bypass the window manager. When writing Motif programs, you do not have to create instances of XmMenuShell directly. Instead, you use convenience functions, such as XmCreatePopupMenu or XmCreatePulldownMenu, that create the XmMenuShell widgets.

Name	Type	Default	Set/Get
XmNbuttonFontList	XmFontList	*	CSG
XmNdefaultFontList	XmFontList	"	C G
XmNlabelFontList	XmFontList	*	CSG

XmMessageBox

Class name: XmMessageBox   Class pointer: xmMessageBoxWidgetClass
Include file: <Xm/MessageB.h>   Inherits from: XmBulletinBoard

The XmMessageBox widget is used to display a message in a window. The widget can contain a message symbol (a pixmap), a message, and up to three standard pushbuttons labeled OK, Cancel, and Help. You can change these labels.

Name	Type	Default	Set/Get
XmNcancelCallback	XtCallbackList	NULL	C
XmNcancelLabelString	XmString	"Cancel" (in C locale)	CSG
XmNdefaultButtonType	unsigned char	XmDIALOG_OK_BUTTON	CSG
XmNdialogType	unsigned char	XmDIALOG_MESSAGE	CSG
XmNhelpLabelString	XmString	"Help" (in C locale)	CSG
XmNmessageAlignment	unsigned char	XmALIGNMENT_BEGINNING	CSG
XmNmessageString	XmString	""	CSG
XmNminimizeButton	Boolean	False	CSG
XmNokCallback	XtCallbackList	NULL	C
XmNokLabelString	XmString	"OK" (in C locale)	CSG
XmNsymbolPixmap	Pixmap	*	CSG

XmPanedWindow

Class name: XmPanedWindow   Class pointer: xmPanedWindowWidgetClass
Include file: <Xm/PanedW.h>   Inherits from: XmManager

XmPanedWindow is a manager widget that lays out its children in vertical panes. The child widgets appear in top-to-bottom order with the first child appearing at the top.

Name	Type	Default	Set/Get
XmNallowResize	Boolean	False	CSG
XmNmarginHeight	Dimension	3	CSG
XmNmarginWidth	Dimension	3	CSG
XmpaneMaximum	Dimension	1	CSG
XmNpaneMinimum	Dimension	1	CSG
XmNpositionIndex	short	XmLAST_POSITION	CSG

Name	Type	Default	Set/Get
XmNrefigureMode	Boolean	True	CSG
XmNsashHeight	Dimension	10	CSG
XmNsashIndent	Position	-10	CSG
XmNsashShadowThickness	Dimension	*	CSG
XmNsashWidth	Dimension	10	CSG
XmNseparatorOn	Boolean	True	CSG
XmNskipAdjust	Boolean	False	CSG
XmNspacing	Dimension	8	CSG

XmPrimitive

Class name: XmPrimitive   Class pointer: xmPrimitiveWidgetClass
Include file: <Xm/Xm.h>   Inherits from: Core

All stand-alone widgets (such as XmLabel, XmList, and XmPushButton) in the Motif toolkit inherit from the XmPrimitive class. This class contains the resources that are used to control the three-dimensional look of Motif widgets. You never directly create an instance of the XmPrimitive class, but you should know about the resources defined for this class because many widgets inherit them. The purpose of the XmNunitType resource is the same as that of the XmNshellUnitType resource of the VendorShell widget. Please consult the reference entry for the VendorShell widget for a description of that resource.

Name	Type	Default	Set/Get
XmNbottomShadowColor	Pixel	*	CSG
XmNbottomShadowPixap	Pixmap	XmUNSPECIFIED_PIXMAP	CSG
XmNforeground	Pixel	*	CSG
XmNhelpCallback	XtCallbackList	NULL	C
XmNhighlightColor	Pixel	*	CSG
XmNhighlightOnEnter	Boolean	False	CSG
XmNhighlightPixmap	Pixmap	*	CSG
XmNhighlightThickness	Dimension	2	CSG
XmNnavigationType	XmNavigationType	XmNONE	CSG
XmNshadowThickness	Dimension	2	CSG
XmNtopShadowColor	Pixel	*	CSG
XmNtopShadowPixmap	Pixmap	*	CSG
XmNtraversalOn	Boolean	True	CSG
XmNunitType	unsigned char	*	CSG
XmNuserData	XtPointer	NULL	CSG

XmPushButton

Class name: XmPushButton   Class pointer: xmPushButtonWidgetClass
Include file: <Xm/PushB.h>   Inherits from: XmLabel

XmPushButton widget displays a text label or a pixmap in a window. You can optionally set up callbacks that the XmPushButton widget will call when the user presses the mouse button with the pointer inside the "button" window. Thus, the user can issue a command by pushing on a button.

Name	Type	Default	Set/Get
XmNactivateCallback	XtCallbackList	NULL	C
XmNarmCallback	XtCallbackList	NULL	C
XmNarmColor	Pixel	*	CSG
XmNarmPixmap	Pixmap	XmUNSPECIFIED_PIXMAP	CSG
XmNdefaultButtonShadowThickness	Dimension	*	CSG
XmNdisarmCallback	XtCallbackList	NULL	C
XmNfillOnArm	Boolean	True	CSG
XmNmultiClick	XmMultiClick	*	CSG
XmNshowAsDefault	Dimension	0	CSG

XmPushButtonGadget

Class name: XmPushButtonGadget   Class pointer: xmPushButtonGadgetClass
Include file: <Xm/PushBG.h>   Inherits from: XmGadget

XmPushButtonGadget is similar to the XmPushButton widget except that XmPushButtonGadget
does not have its own window (because it is a gadget) and displays the button in its parent's window.

Name	Type	Default	Set/Get
XmNactivateCallback	XtCallbackList	NULL	C
XmNarmCallback	XtCallbackList	NULL	C
XmNarmColor	Pixel	*	CSG
XmNarmPixmap	Pixmap	XmUNSPECIFIED_PIXMAP	CSG
XmNdefaultButtonShadowThickness	Dimension	*	CSG
XmNdisarmCallback	XtCallbackList	NULL	C
XmNfillOnArm	Boolean	True	CSG
XmNmultiClick	XmMultiClick	*	CSG
XmNshowAsDefault	Dimension	0	CSG

XmRowColumn

Class name: XmRowColumn   Class pointer: xmRowColumnWidgetClass
Include file: <Xm/RowColumn.h>   Inherits from: XmManager

The XmRowColumn widget arranges its children in rows and columns. You can use this widget in
menubars and menu panes.

Name	Type	Default	Set/Get
XmNadjustLast	Boolean	True	CSG
XmNadjustMargin	Boolean	True	CSG
XmNbuttonAccelerators	StringTable	NULL	C
XmNbuttonAcceleratorText	XmStringTable	NULL	C
XmNbuttonCount	int	0	C
XmNbuttonMnemonicCharSets	XmStringCharSetTable	NULL	C
XmNbuttonMnemonics	XmKeySymTable	NULL	C
XmNbuttons	XmStringTable	NULL	C
XmNbuttonSet	int	-1	C
XmNbuttonType	XmButtonTypeTable	NULL	C
XmNentryAlignment	unsigned char	XmALIGNMENT_BEGINNING	CSG
XmNentryBorder	Dimension	0	CSG
XmNentryCallback	XtCallbackList	NULL	C
XmNentryClass	WidgetClass	*	CSG

Name	Type	Default	Set/Get
XmNentryVerticalAlignment	unsigned char	XmALIGNMENT_CENTER	CSG
XmNisAligned	Boolean	True	CSG
XmNisHomogeneous	Boolean	*	CSG
XmNlabelString	XmString	NULL	C
XmNmapCallback	XtCallbackList	NULL	C
XmNmarginHeight	Dimension	*	CSG
XmNmarginWidth	Dimension	*	CSG
XmNmenuAccelerator	String	*	CSG
XmNmenuHelpWidget	Widget	NULL	CSG
XmNmenuHistory	Widget	NULL	CSG
XmNmenuPost	String	NULL	CSG
XmNmnemonic	KeySym	*	CSG
XmNmnemonicCharSet	String	XmFONTLIST_DEFAULT_TAG	CSG
XmNnumColumns	short	1	CSG
XmNoptionLabel	XmString	NULL	C
XmNoptionMnemonic	KeySym	NULL	C
XmNorientation	unsigned char	*	CSG
XmNpacking	unsigned char	*	CSG
XmNpopupEnabled	Boolean	True	CSG
XmNpostFromButton	int	-1	C
XmNradioAlwaysOne	Boolean	True	CSG
XmNradioBehavior	Boolean	False	CSG
XmNresizeHeight	Boolean	True	CSG
XmNresizeWidth	Boolean	True	CSG
XmNrowColumnType	unsigned char	XmWORK_AREA	C G
XmNsimpleCallback	XtCallbackList	NULL	C
XmNspacing	Dimension	*	CSG
XmNsubmenuId	Widget	NULL	CSG
XmNtearOffMenuActivateCallback	XtCallbackList	NULL	C
XmNtearOffMenuDeactivateCallback	XtCallbackList	NULL	C
XmNtearOffModel	unsigned char	XmTEAR_OFF_DISABLED	CSG
XmNunmapCallback	XtCallbackList	NULL	C
XmNwhichButton	unsigned int	*	CSG

XmScale

Class name: XmScale　　　　Class pointer: xmScaleWidgetClass
Include file: <Xm/Scale.h>　　Inherits from: XmManager

The XmScale widget displays a scale with a range of values from which the user can specify a value by moving the slider within the scale.

Name	Type	Default	Set/Get
XmNdecimalPoint	short	0	CSG
XmNdragCallback	XtCallbackList	NULL	C
XmNfontList	XmFontList	*	CSG
XmNhighlightOnEnter	Boolean	False	CSG
XmNhighlightThickness	Dimension	2	CSG
XmNmaximum	int	100	CSG
XmNminimum	int	0	CSG
XmNorientation	unsigned char	XmVERTICAL	CSG
XmNprocessingDirection	unsigned char	*	CSG
XmNscaleHeight	Dimension	0	CSG

continues

Name	Type	Default	Set/Get
XmNscaleMultiple	int	*	CSG
XmNscaleWidth	Dimension	0	CSG
XmNshowValue	Boolean	False	CSG
XmNtitleString	XmString	NULL	CSG
XmNvalue	int	*	CSG
XmNvalueChangedCallback	XtCallbackList	NULL	C

XmScreen

Class name: XmScreen   Class pointer: xmSreenClass
Include file: <Xm/Screen.h> Inherits from: Core

The Motif toolkit uses the XmScreen widget to store information about a specific screen. The toolkit automatically creates an XmScreen object when your application creates the first shell on a screen. You cannot specify the initial values of these resources, but you can alter the resources after you create the first shell on a screen. To change the resources of the XmScreen widget, call XmGetXmScreen to get the widget ID of the XmScreen, and then call XtSetValues or XtVaSetValues to set the resources.

Name	Type	Default	Set/Get
XmNdarkThreshold	int	*	C
XmNdefaultCopyCursorIcon	Widget	NULL	CSG
XmNdefaultInvalidCursorIcon	Widget	NULL	CSG
XmNdefaultLinkCursorIcon	Widget	NULL	CSG
XmNdefaultMoveCursorIcon	Widget	NULL	CSG
XmNdefaultNoneCursorIcon	Widget	NULL	CSG
XmNdefaultSourceCursorIcon	Widget	NULL	CSG
XmNdefaultValidCursorIcon	Widget	NULL	CSG
XmNfont	XFontStruct*	NULL	CSG
XmNforegroundThreshold	int	*	C
XmNhorizontalFontUnit	int	*	CSG
XmNlightThreshold	int	*	C
XmNmenuCursor	String	arrow	C
XmNmoveOpaque	Boolean	False	CSG
XmNunpostBehavior	unsigned char	XmUNPOST_AND_REPLAY	CSG
XmNverticalFontUnit	int	*	CSG

XmScrollBar

Class name: XmScrollBar   Class pointer: xmScrollBarWidgetClass
Include file: <Xm/ScrollB.h> Inherits from: XmPrimitive

The XmScrollBar widget displays a scrollbar. You can set up callbacks to scroll the contents of the work area when the user presses on various parts of the scrollbar.

Name	Type	Default	Set/Get
XmNdecrementCallback	XtCallbackList	NULL	C
XmNdragCallback	XtCallbackList	NULL	C
XmNincrement	int	1	CSG
XmNincrementCallback	XtCallbackList	NULL	C
XmNinitialDelay	int	250 (milliseconds)	CSG
XmNmaximum	int	*	CSG

Name	Type	Default	Set/Get
XmNminimum	int	0	CSG
XmNorientation	unsigned char	XmVERTICAL	CSG
XmNpagedecrementCallback	XtCallbackList	NULL	C
XmNpageIncrement	int	10	CSG
XmNpageincrementCallback	XtCallbackList	NULL	C
XmNprocessingDirection	unsigned char	*	CSG
XmNrepeatDelay	int	50 (milliseconds)	CSG
XmNshowArrows	Boolean	True	CSG
XmNsliderSize	int	*	CSG
XmNtoBottomCallback	XtCallbackList	NULL	C
XmNtoTopCallback	XtCallbackList	NULL	C
XmNtroughColor	Pixel	*	CSG
XmNvalue	int	*	CSG
XmNvalueChangedCallback	XtCallbackList	NULL	C

XmScrolledWindow

Class name: XmScrolledWindow Class pointer: xmScrolledWindowWidgetClass
Include file: <Xm/ScrolledW.h> Inherits from: XmManager

The XmScrolledWindow widget manages a work area and two scrollbars (vertical and horizontal).

Name	Type	Default	Set/Get
XmNclipWindow	Widget	*	G
XmNhorizontalScrollBar	Widget	*	CSG
XmNscrollBarDisplayPolicy	unsigned char	*	C G
XmNscrollBarPlacement	unsigned char	XmBOTTOM_RIGHT	CSG
XmNscrolledWindowMarginHeight	Dimension	0	CSG
XmNscrolledWindowMarginWidth	Dimension	0	CSG
XmNscrollingPolicy	unsigned char	XmAPPLICATION_DEFINED	C G
XmNspacing	int	4	CSG
XmNtraverseObscuredCallback	XtCallbackList	NULL	CSG
XmNverticalScrollBar	Widget	NULL	CSG
XmNvisualPolicy	unsigned char	XmVARIABLE	C G
XmNworkWindow	Widget	NULL	CSG

XmSelectionBox

Class name: XmSelectionBox Class pointer: xmSelectionBoxWidgetClass
Include file: <Xm/SelectioB.h> Inherits from: XmBulletinBoard

The XmSelectionBox widget enables users to select one item from a list of items. This widget manages an XmList widget, an area for text entry, and three buttons labeled OK, Cancel, and Help. A button labeled Apply is also available. You can change these labels by setting appropriate resources.

Name	Type	Default	Set/Get
XmNapplyCallback	XtCallbackList	NULL	C
XmNapplyLabelString	XmString	"Apply" (in C locale)	CSG
XmNcancelCallback	XtCallbackList	NULL	C
XmNcancelLabelString	XmString	"Cancel" (in C locale)	CSG
XmNchildPacement	unsigned char	XmPLACE_ABOVE_SELECTION	CSG

continues

Name	Type	Default	Set/Get
XmNdialogType	unsigned char	*	C G
XmNhelpLabelString	XmString	"Help" (in C locale)	CSG
XmNlistItemCount	int	0	CSG
XmNListItems	XmStringTable	NULL	CSG
XmNlistLabelString	XmString	*	CSG
XmNlistVisibleItemCount	int	*	CSG
XmNminimizeButton	Boolean	False	CSG
XmNmustMatch	Boolean	False	CSG
XmNnoMatchCallback	XtCallbackList	NULL	C
XmNokCallback	XtCallbackList	NULL	C
XmNokLabelString	XmString	"OK" (in C locale)	CSG
XmNselectionLabelString	XmString	"Selection" (in C locale)	CSG
XmNtextAccelerators	XtTranslations	(predefined)	C
XmNtextColumns	int	*	CSG
XmNtextString	XmString	NULL	CSG

XmSeparator

Class name: XmSeparator   Class pointer: xmSeparatorWidgetClass
Include file: <Xm/Separator.h>   Inherits from: XmPrimitive

The XmSeparator widget can display a horizontal or vertical line with a three-dimensional look. You can use XmSeparator widgets as separators in lists and menu panes.

Name	Type	Default	Set/Get
XmNmargin	Dimension	0	CSG
XmNorientation	unsigned char	XmHORIZONTAL	CSG
XmNseparatorType	unsigned char	XmSHADOW_ETCHED_IN	CSG

XmSeparatorGadget

Class name: XmSeparatorGadget   Class pointer: xmSeparatorGadgetClass
Include file: <Xm/SeparatoG.h>   Inherits from: XmGadget

The XmSeparatorGadget is a gadget version of the XmSeparator widget.

Name	Type	Default	Set/Get
XmNmargin	Dimension	0	CSG
XmNorientation	unsigned char	XmHORIZONTAL	CSG
XmNseparatorType	unsigned char	XmSHADOW ETCHED IN	CSG

XmText

Class name: XmText   Class pointer: xmTextWidgetClass
Include file: <Xm/Text.h>   Inherits from: XmPrimitive

The XmText widget acts as a single or multiline text editor.

Name	Type	Default	Set/Get
XmNactivateCallback	XtCallbackList	NULL	C
XmNautoShowCursorPosition	Boolean	True	CSG
XmNblinkRate	int	500 (milliseconds)	CSG

Name	Type	Default	Set/Get
XmNcolumns	short	*	CSG
XmNcursorPosition	XmTextPosition	0	CSG
XmNcursorPositionVisible	Boolean	True	CSG
XmNeditable	Boolean	True	CSG
XmNeditMode	int	XmSINGLE_LINE_EDIT	CSG
XmNfocusCallback	XtCallbackList	NULL	C
XmNfontList	XmFontList	*	CSG
XmNgainPrimaryCallback	XtCallbackList	NULL	C
XmNlosePrimaryCallback	XtCallbackList	NULL	C
XmNlosingFocusCallback	XtCallbackList	NULL	C
XmNmarginHeight	Dimension	5	CSG
XmNmarginWidth	Dimension	5	CSG
XmNmaxLength	int	MAXINT	CSG
XmNmodifyVerifyCallback	XtCallbackList	NULL	C
XmNmodifyVerifyCallbackWcs	XtCallbackList	NULL	C
XmNmotionVerifyCallback	XtCallbackList	NULL	C
XmNpendingDelete	Boolean	True	CSG
XmNresizeHeight	Boolean	False	CSG
XmNresizeWidth	Boolean	False	CSG
XmNrows	int	*	CSG
XmNscrollHorizontal	Boolean	True	C G
XmNscrollLeftSide	Boolean	*	C G
XmNscrollTopSide	Boolean	False	C G
XmNscrollVertical	Boolean	True	C G
XmNselectionArray	XtPointer	default array	CSG
XmNselectionArrayCount	int	4	CSG
XmNselectThreshold	int	5	CSG
XmNsource	XmTextSource	default source	CSG
XmNtopCharacter	XmTextPosition	0	CSG
XmNvalue	String	""	CSG
XmNvalueChangedCallback	XtCallbackList	NULL	C
XmNvalueWcs	wchar_t*	(wchar_t*)""	CSG
XmNverifyBell	Boolean	*	CSG
XmNwordWrap	Boolean	False	CSG

XmTextField

 Class name: XmTextField Class pointer: xmTextFieldWidgetClass
 Include file: <Xm/TextF.h> Inherits from: XmPrimitive

The XmTextField widget provides a single-line editable text field.

Name	Type	Default	Set/Get
XmNactivateCallback	XtCallbackList	NULL	C
XmNblinkRate	int	500 (milliseconds)	CSG
XmNcolumns	short	*	CSG
XmNcursorPosition	XmTextPosition	0	CSG
XmNcursorPositionVisible	Boolean	True	CSG
XmNeditable	Boolean	True	CSG
XmNfocusCallback	XtCallbackList	NULL	C
XmNfontList	XmFontList	*	CSG
XmNgainPrimaryCallback	XtCallbackList	NULL	C
XmNlosePrimaryCallback	XtCallbackList	NULL	C

continues

Name	Type	Default	Set/Get
XmNlosingFocusCallback	XtCallbackList	NULL	C
XmNmarginHeight	Dimension	5	CSG
XmNmarginWidth	Dimension	5	CSG
XmNmaxLength	int	MAXINT	CSG
XmNmodifyVerifyCallback	XtCallbackList	NULL	C
XmNmodifyVerifyCallbackWc	XtCallbackList	NULL	C
XmNmotionVerifyCallback	XtCallbackList	NULL	C
XmNpendingDelete	Boolean	True	CSG
XmNresizeWidth	Boolean	False	CSG
XmNselectionArray	Pointer	default array	CSG
XmNselectionArrayCount	int	3	CSG
XmNselectThreshold	int	5	CSG
XmNvalue	String	""	CSG
XmNvalueChangedCallback	XtCallbackList	NULL	C
XmNvalueWcs	wchar_t*	(wchar_t*)""	CSG
XmNverifyBell	Boolean	*	CSG

XmToggleButton

Class name: XmToggleButton   Class pointer: xmToggleButtonWidgetClass
Include file: <Xm/ToggleB.h>   Inherits from: XmLabel

The XmToggleButton widget is used to select one or more of a fixed set of selections that are displayed as buttons that can be toggled on or off.

Name	Type	Default	Set/Get
XmNarmCallback	XtCallbackList	NULL	C
XmNdisarmCallback	XtCallbackList	NULL	C
XmNfillOnSelect	Boolean	*	CSG
XmNindicatorOn	Boolean	True	CSG
XmNindicatorSize	Dimension	*	CSG
XmNindicatorType	unsigned char	*	CSG
XmNselectColor	Pixel	*	CSG
XmNselectInsensitivePixmap	Pixmap	XmUNSPECIFIED_PIXMAP	CSG
XmNselectPixmap	Pixmap	XmUNSPECIFIED_PIXMAP	CSG
XmNset	Boolean	False	CSG
XmNspacing	Dimension	4	CSG
XmNvalueChangedCallback	XtCallbackList	NULL	C
XmNvisibleWhenOff	Boolean	*	CSG

XmToggleButtonGadget

Class name: XmToggleButtonGadget   Class pointer: xmToggleButtonGadgetClass
Include file: <Xm/ToggleBG.h>   Inherits from: XmGadget

The XmToggleButtonGadget is the gadget version of the XmToggleButton widget.

Name	Type	Default	Set/Get
XmNarmCallback	XtCallbackList	NULL	C
XmNdisarmCallback	XtCallbackList	NULL	C
XmNfillOnSelect	Boolean	*	CSG
XmNindicatorOn	Boolean	True	CSG
XmNindicatorSize	Dimension	*	CSG
XmNindicatorType	unsigned char	*	CSG

Name	Type	Default	Set/Get
XmNselectColor	Pixel	*	CSG
XmNselectInsensitivePixmap	Pixmap	XmUNSPECIFIED_PIXMAP	CSG
XmNselectPixmap	Pixmap	XmUNSPECIFIED_PIXMAP	CSG
XmNset	Boolean	False	CSG
XmNspacing	Dimension	4	CSG
XmNvalueChangedCallback	XtCallbackList	NULL	C
XmNvisibleWhenOff	Boolean	*	CSG

Motif Data Types

This section provides an alphabetic listing of some of the important data types in the Motif toolkit. Each entry shows the name of the header file where that data type is defined.

The callback data structures are of special significance because much of an application's work is done in the callback functions, and the toolkit uses the callback structures to pass information to the callback function. In Xt Intrinsics-based toolkits such as Motif, a callback function has three arguments:

> *First argument.* This is the ID of the widget for which the callback is registered.

> *Second argument.* In this argument, the callback receives a pointer which you have to provide when registering the callback. Through this pointer, you can pass to the callback function any information you deem necessary for your application.

> *Third argument.* This argument is a pointer to a *callback structure*—a Motif data structure that usually includes information on the event that caused the callback and any other information about the widget that will help you perform the appropriate action in the callback.

This section shows the data structures for a number of callback structures. The XmAnyCallbackStruct is the most common callback structure, but many widgets have special structures to convey information specific to those widgets.

VoidProc   Defined in: <Xm/CutPaste.h>

```
typedef void (*VoidProc)(Widget w, int * data_id, int *private_id,
                         int *reason);
```

XmAnyCallbackStruct   Defined in: <Xm/Xm.h>

```
typedef struct
{
    int     reason;
    XEvent  *event;
} XmAnyCallbackStruct;
```

XmArrowButtonCallbackStruct   Defined in: <Xm/Xm.h>

```
typedef struct
{
    int     reason;
    XEvent  *event;
    int     click_count;
} XmArrowButtonCallbackStruct;
```

XmButtonType   Defined in: <Xm/Xm.h>

```
typedef unsigned char XmButtonType;
```

XmButtonTypeTable   Defined in: <Xm/Xm.h>

```
typedef XmButtonType *XmButtonTypeTable;
```

XmClipboardPendingList Defined in: <Xm/CutPaste.h>

```
typedef struct
{
    long DataId;
    long PrivateId;
} XmClipboardPendingRec, *XmClipboardPendingList;
```

XmColorProc   Defined in: <Xm/Xm.h>

```
typedef void (*XmColorProc) (XColor *bg_color, XColor *fg_color,
                             XColor *sel_color, XColor *ts_color,
                             XColor *bs_color);
```

XmCommandCallbackStruct   Defined in: <Xm/Xm.h>

```
typedef struct
{
    int      reason;
    XEvent   *event;
    XmString value;
    int      length;
} XmCommandCallbackStruct;
```

XmCutPasteProc   Defined in: <Xm/CutPaste.h>

```
typedef void (*XmCutPasteProc)(Widget w, long *data_id,
                               long *private_id, int *reason);
```

XmDrawingAreaCallbackStruct   Defined in: <Xm/Xm.h>

```
typedef struct
{
    int     reason;
    XEvent  *event;
    Window  window;
} XmDrawingAreaCallbackStruct;
```

XmDrawnButtonCallbackStruct   Defined in: <Xm/Xm.h>

```
typedef struct
{
    int     reason;
    XEvent  *event;
    Window  window;
    int click_count;
} XmDrawnButtonCallbackStruct;
```

XmFileSelectionBoxCallbackStruct   Defined in: <Xm/Xm.h>

```
typedef struct
{
```

```
    int        reason;
    XEvent     *event;
    XmString   value;
    int        length;
    XmString   mask;
    int        mask_length;
    XmString   dir;
    int        dir_length;
    XmString   pattern;
    int        pattern_length;
} XmFileSelectionBoxCallbackStruct;
```

XmFontType   Defined in: <Xm/Xm.h>

```
typedef enum{ XmFONT_IS_FONT, XmFONT_IS_FONTSET } XmFontType;
```

XmHighlightMode   Defined in: <Xm/Xm.h>

```
typedef enum
{
    XmHIGHLIGHT_NORMAL,    XmHIGHLIGHT_SELECTED,
    XmHIGHLIGHT_SECONDARY_SELECTED
} XmHighlightMode;
```

XmID   Defined in: <Xm/DragC.h>

```
typedef unsigned int    XmID;
```

XmKeySymTable   Defined in: <Xm/Xm.h>

```
typedef KeySym *XmKeySymTable;
```

XmListCallbackStruct   Defined in: <Xm/Xm.h>

```
typedef struct
{
    int        reason;
    XEvent     *event;
    XmString   item;
    int        item_length;
    int        item_position;
    XmString   *selected_items;
    int        selected_item_count;
    int        *selected_item_positions;
    char       selection_type;
} XmListCallbackStruct;
```

XmNavigationType   Defined in: <Xm/Xm.h>

```
typedef unsigned char    XmNavigationType;
```

XmPushButtonCallbackStruct   Defined in: <Xm/Xm.h>

```
typedef struct
{
    int        reason;
    XEvent     *event;
    int        click_count;
} XmPushButtonCallbackStruct;
```

XmRowColumnCallbackStruct Defined in: <Xm/Xm.h>

```
typedef struct
{
    int     reason;
    XEvent  *event;
    Widget  widget;
    char    *data;
    char    *callbackstruct;
} XmRowColumnCallbackStruct;
```

XmScaleCallbackStruct Defined in: <Xm/Xm.h>

```
typedef struct
{
    int    reason;
    XEvent *event;
    int    value;
} XmScaleCallbackStruct;
```

XmScrollBarCallbackStruct Defined in: <Xm/Xm.h>

```
typedef struct
{
    int    reason;
    XEvent *event;
    int    value;
    int    pixel;
} XmScrollBarCallbackStruct;
```

XmSelectionBoxCallbackStruct Defined in: <Xm/Xm.h>

```
typedef struct
{
    int      reason;
    XEvent   *event;
    XmString value;
    int      length;
} XmSelectionBoxCallbackStruct;
```

XmString Defined in: <Xm/Xm.h>

```
typedef unsigned char *XmString; /* Details hidden from programmer */
```

XmStringComponentType Defined in: <Xm/Xm.h>

```
typedef unsigned char XmStringComponentType;
```

XmStringDirection Defined in: <Xm/Xm.h>

```
typedef unsigned char XmStringDirection;
```

XmStringCharSetTable Defined in: <Xm/Xm.h>

```
typedef char *XmStringCharSet;  /* Null-terminated string */
```

XmStringCharSetTable Defined in: <Xm/Xm.h>

```
typedef XmStringCharSet *XmStringCharSetTable;
```

XmStringTable   Defined in: <Xm/Xm.h>

```
typedef XmString *XmStringTable;
```

XmTextBlockRec, **XmTextBloc**   Defined in: <Xm/Xm.h>

```
typedef struct
{
    char        *ptr;         /* Pointer to data          */
    int         length;       /* Number of bytes of data */
    XmTextFormat format;      /* Data format              */
} XmTextBlockRec, *XmTextBlock;
```

XmTextBlockRecWcs, **XmTextBlocWcs**   Defined in: <Xm/Xm.h>

```
typedef struct {
    wchar_t *wcsptr;               /* Pointer to data          */
    int length;                    /* Number of bytes of data */
} XmTextBlockRecWcs, *XmTextBlockWcs;
```

XmTextDirection   Defined in: <Xm/Xm.h>

```
typedef enum
{
    XmTEXT_FORWARD,
    XmTEXT_BACKWARD
} XmTextDirection;
```

XmTextFormat   Defined in: <Xm/Xm.h>

```
typedef Atom XmTextFormat;
```

XmTextPosition   Defined in: <Xm/Xm.h>

```
Typedef long XmTextPosition;
```

XmTextScanType   Defined in: <Xm/Xm.h>

```
typedef enum
{
    XmSELECT_POSITION,   XmSELECT_WHITESPACE,   XmSELECT_WORD
    XmSELECT_LINE,       XmSELECT_ALL,          XmSELECT_PARAGRAPH
} XmTextScanType;
```

XmTextVerifyCallbackStruct   Defined in: <Xm/Xm.h>

```
typedef struct
{
    int         reason;
    XEvent      *event;
    Boolean     doit;
    long        currInsert, newInsert;
    long        startPos, endPos;
    XmTextBlock text;
} XmTextVerifyCallbackStruct, *XmTextVerifyPtr;
```

XmTextVerifyCallbackStructWcs   Defined in: <Xm/Xm.h>

```
typedef struct
{
    int            reason;
    XEvent         *event;
    Boolean        doit;
    long           currInsert, newInsert;
    long           startPos, endPos;
    XmTextBlockWcs text;
} XmTextVerifyCallbackStructWcs, *XmTextVerifyPtrWcs;
```

XmToggleButtonCallbackStruct   Defined in: <Xm/Xm.h>

```
typedef struct
{
   int    reason;
   XEvent *event;
   int    set;
} XmToggleButtonCallbackStruct;
```

XmTraversalDirection   Defined in: <Xm/Xm.h>

```
typedef enum
{
    XmTRAVERSE_CURRENT,          XmTRAVERSE_NEXT,
    XmTRAVERSE_PREV,             XmTRAVERSE_HOME,
    XmTRAVERSE_NEXT_TAB_GROUP,   XmTRAVERSE_PREV_TAB_GROUP,
    XmTRAVERSE_UP,               XmTRAVERSE_DOWN,
    XmTRAVERSE_LEFT,             XmTRAVERSE_RIGHT
} XmTraversalDirection;
```

XmTraverseObscuredCallbackStruct   Defined in: <Xm/Xm.h>

```
typedef struct _XmTraverseObscuredCallbackStruct
{
    int                  reason;
    XEvent               *event;
    Widget               traversal_destination;
    XmTraversalDirection direction;
} XmTraverseObscuredCallbackStruct;
```

XmVisibility   Defined in: <Xm/Xm.h>

```
typedef enum
{
    XmVISIBILITY_UNOBSCURED,    XmVISIBILITY_PARTIALLY_OBSCURED,
    XmVISIBILITY_FULLY_OBSCURED
} XmVisibility;
```

Index

M

Add to Your Sams Library Today with the Best Books for Programming, Operating Systems, and New Technologies

The easiest way to order is to pick up the phone and call

1-800-428-5331

between 9:00 a.m. and 5:00 p.m. EST.

For faster service please have your credit card available.

ISBN	Quantity	Description of Item	Unit Cost	Total Cost
0-672-30535-6		Teach Yourself the Internet: Around the World in 21 Days	$25.00	
0-672-30520-8		Your Internet Consultant	$25.00	
0-672-30466-X		Internet Unleashed	$44.95	
0-672-30402-3		UNIX Unleashed	$44.95	
0-672-30457-0		Learning UNIX	$39.95	
0-672-30485-6		Navigating the Internet, Deluxe Edition	$29.95	
❏ 3 ½" Disk		Shipping and Handling: See information below.		
❏ 5 ¼" Disk		TOTAL		

Shipping and Handling: $4.00 for the first book, and $1.75 for each additional book. Floppy disk: add $1.75 for shipping and handling. If you need to have it NOW, we can ship product to you in 24 hours for an additional charge of approximately $18.00, and you will receive your item overnight or in two days. Overseas shipping and handling adds $2.00 per book and $8.00 for up to three disks. Prices subject to change. Call for availability and pricing information on latest editions.

201 W. 103rd Street, Indianapolis, Indiana 46290

1-800-428-5331 — Orders   1-800-835-3202 — FAX   1-800-858-7674 — Customer Service

Book ISBN 0-672-30542-9